THE LYLE OFFICIAL

ANTIQUES REVIEW 1988

COMPILED & EDITED BY
TONY CURTIS

FRONT COVER

Royal Doulton figure, 'Sunshine Girl', HN1344, designed by L. Harradine, 5in. high, issued 1929, withdrawn 1938. *(Abridge Auctions)*

SPINE

A bronze and ivory figure, cast and carved after a model by P. Phillippe, signed on the base F. Preiss, 61.5cm. high. *(Christie's)*

BACK COVER

A fully rigged bone and horn model of a hundred and twenty-eight gun ship of the line, 19¾ x 27in. *(Christie's)*
A Lyon Istoriato deep dish, decorated in the Italian manner with Moses receiving the tablets on Mount Sinai, circa 1580, 45cm. diam. *(Christie's)*
A William and Mary stained burr elm kneehole bureau in the manner of Coxed & Woster, 39½in. wide. *(Christie's)*

While every care has been taken in the compiling of information contained in this volume the publishers cannot accept any liability for loss, financial or otherwise, incurred by reliance placed on the information herein.

All prices quoted in this book are obtained from a variety of auctions in various countries during the twelve months prior to publication and are converted to dollars at the rate of exchange prevalent at the time of sale.

The publishers wish to express their sincere thanks to the following for their involvement and assistance in the production of this volume:

KAREN DOUGLASS (Art Editor)
JANICE MONCRIEFF (Assistant Editor)
ANNETTE CURTIS
SUSAN CAMERON
NICHOLA FAIRBURN
TANYA FAIRBAIRN
SALLY DALGLIESH
FRANK BURRELL
ROBERT NISBET
EILEEN BURRELL
ISHBELL MAC PHAIL

British Library Cataloguing in Publication Data

The Lyle official antiques review. — 1988-
 1. Antiques — Prices — Periodicals
338.4'37451   NKI

ISBN 0-86248-100-7

SBN 0-86248-100-7

INTRODUCTION

This year over 100,000 Antique Dealers and Collectors will make full and profitable use of their Lyle Official Antiques Review. They know that only in this one volume will they find the widest possible variety of goods — illustrated, described and given a current market value to assist them to BUY RIGHT AND SELL RIGHT throughout the year of issue.

They know, too, that by building a collection of these immensely valuable volumes year by year, they will equip themselves with an unparalleled reference library of facts, figures and illustrations which, properly used, cannot fail to help them keep one step ahead of the market.

In its sixteen years of publication, Lyle has gone from strength to strength and has become without doubt the pre-eminent book of reference for the antique trade throughout the world. Each of its fact filled pages are packed with precisely the kind of profitable information the professional Dealer needs — including descriptions, illustrations and values of thousands and thousands of individual items carefully selected to give a representative picture of the current market in antiques and collectibles — and remember all values are prices actually paid, based on accurate sales records in the twelve months prior to publication from the best established and most highly respected auction houses and retail outlets in Europe and America.

This is THE book for the Professional Antiques Dealer. 'The Lyle Book' — we've even heard it called 'The Dealer's Bible'.

Compiled and published afresh each year, the Lyle Official Antiques Review is the most comprehensive up-to-date antiques price guide available. THIS COULD BE YOUR WISEST INVESTMENT OF THE YEAR!

Tony Curtis

Printed by A. Wheaton & Co. Ltd., Exeter, Devon.
Bound by Dorstel Press, Harlow, Essex.

CONTENTS

Acknowledgements

Abridge Auctions, *(Michael Yewman), Market Place, Abridge, Essex*
Anderson & Garland, *Anderson House, Market Street, Newcastle NE1 6XA*
Ball & Percival, *132 Lord Street, Southport*
Banks & Silvers, *66 Foregate Street, Worcester*
Barbers Fine Art Auctioneers, *(Chobham Ltd.), The Mayford Centre, Smarts Heath Rd., Mayford, Woking*
Bearnes, *Rainbow, Avenue Road, Torquay*
Bermondsey Antiques Market, *Tower Bridge Road, London*
Biddle & Webb, *Ladywood Middleway, Birmingham B16 0PP*
Bloomsbury Book Auctions, *3 & 4 Hardwick Street, London*
Boardman Fine Art Auctioneers, *Station Road Corner, Haverhill, Suffolk*
Bonham's, *Montpelier Gardens, Montpelier Street, London*
Bracketts, *27-29 High Street, Tunbridge Wells*
J. R. Bridgford & Sons, *1 Heyes Lane, Alderley Edge, Cheshire*
British Antique Exporters, *206 London Road, Burgess Hill, W. Sussex*
Wm. H. Brown, *Westgate Hall, Grantham, Lincs*
Lawrence Butler & Co., *Butler House, 86 High Street, Hythe, Kent CT21 5AJ*
Capes, Dunn & Co., *The Auction Galleries, 38 Charles Street, Manchester 1*
Chancellors Hollingsworths, *31 High Street, Ascot, Berkshire SL5 7HG*
Christie's, *8 King Street, St. James's, London*
Christie's (International) S.A., *8 Place de la Taconnerie, 1204 Geneva*
Christie's, *502 Park Avenue, New York, N.Y. 10022*
Christie's (Monaco) S.A.N., *Park Palace, 98000 Monte Carlo*
Christie's (Hong Kong) Ltd., *3607 Edinburgh Tower, 15 Queen's Rd., Hong Kong*
Christie's, *Cornelis Schuystraat 57, 1071 JG, Amsterdam*
Christie's East, *219 East 67th Street, New York, N.Y. 10021*
Christie's & Edmiston's, *164/166 Bath Street, Glasgow*
Christie's S. Kensington, *85 Old Brompton Road, London*
Coles, Knapp & Kennedy, *Georgian Rooms, Ross-on-Wye, Herefordshire*
Cooper Hirst, *Goldway House, Parkway, Chelmsford CM20 7PR*
County Group Estate Agents, *The Auction Sale Rooms, 102 High St., Tenterden, Kent*
Dacre, Son & Hartley, *1-5 The Grove, Ilkley, Yorkshire*
Dee & Atkinson, *The Exchange Saleroom, Driffield, Yorkshire*
Dickinson, Davy & Markham, *Elwes Street, Brigg, S. Humberside DN20 8LB*
Dreweatts, *Donnington Priory, Newbury, Berkshire RG13 2JE*
Hy. Duke & Son, *Weymouth Avenue, Dorchester, Dorset*
Du Mouchelles Art Galleries, *409 E. Jefferson, Detroit, Michigan 48226*
Elliott & Green, *40 High Street, Lymington, Hants*
R. H. Ellis & Sons, *44-46 High Street, Worthing, Sussex*
Frank H. Fellows & Son, *Bedford House, 88 Hagley Road, Edgbaston, Birmingham*
John D. Fleming & Co., *8 Fore Street, Dulverton, Somerset TA22 9EX*
Fox & Sons, *41 Chapel Road, Worthing*
Geering & Colyer, *22-24 High Street, Tunbridge Wells*
Goss & Crested China, *(N. J. Pine), 62 Murray Road, Horndean*
Andrew Grant, *59-60 Foregate Street, Worcester*

ANTIQUES REVIEW

Graves, Son & Pilcher, *71 Church Road, Hove, Sussex*
Giles Haywood, *The Auction House, St. John's Road, Stourbridge, W. Midlands DY8 1EW*
Heathcote Ball & Co., *The Old Rectory, Appleby Magna, Leicestershire*
Hobbs & Chambers, *'At the Sign of the Bell', Market Place, Cirencester GL7 1QQ*
John Hogbin & Son, *8 Queen Street, Deal, Kent*
Edgar Horn, *49-50 South Street, Eastbourne, Sussex*
Jacobs & Hunt, *Lavant Street, Petersfield, Hants*
Lalonde Fine Art, *The Auction Room, Oakfield Road, Bristol BS8 2BE*
W. H. Lane & Son, *64 Morrab Road, Penzance, Cornwall*
Lawrence Fine Art, *South Street, Crewkerne, Somerset TA18 8AB*
Locke & England, *Walton House, 11 The Parade, Leamington Spa*
Lots Road Chelsea Auction Galleries, *71 Lots Road, London*
Thomas Love & Son, *South St. John Street, Perth*
Mallams, *24 St. Michael's Street, Oxford*
May, Whetter & Grose, *Cornubia Hall, Par, Cornwall*
Morphets, *4-6 Albert Street, Harrogate, Yorkshire HG1 1JL*
Neales of Nottingham, *192 Mansfield Road, Nottingham*
D. M. Nesbit & Co., *7 Clarendon Road, Southsea, Hants*
Onslows, *123 Hursley, Winchester, Hants*
Outhwaite & Litherland, *Kingsway Galleries, Fontenoy Street, Liverpool L3 2BE*
Parsons, Welch & Cowell, *The Argyle Salerooms, Argyle Road, Sevenoaks, Kent*
Phillips, *Marylebone Auction Rooms, Hayes Place, London*
Phillips, *65 George Street, Edinburgh*
Phillips, *98 Sauchiehall Street, Glasgow*
Phillips, *Blenstock House, 7 Blenheim Street, New Bond St., London*
Phillips, *The Old House, Station Road, Knowle, Solihull, W. Midlands*
Phillips & Jolly's, *The Auction Rooms, 1 Old King Street, Bath*
Prudential Fine Art Auctioneers, *Millmead Auction Rooms, Guildford, Surrey*
John H. Raby & Sons, *21 St. Mary's Road, Bradford*
Reeds Rains, *Trinity House, 114 Northenden Road, Sale, Manchester M33 3HD*
Russell, Baldwin & Bright, *Ryelands Road, Leominster, Herefordshire*
Sandoe, Luce Panes, *Chipping Manor Salerooms, Wotton-under-Edge*
Robt. W. Skinner Inc., *Bolton Gallery, Route 117, Bolton, Mass.*
H. Spencer & Sons Ltd., *20 The Square, Retford, Notts.*
David Stanley Auctions, *Stordan Grange, Osgathorpe, Leics. LE12 9SR*
Street Jewellery, *10 Summerhill Terrace, Newcastle-upon-Tyne*
Stride & Son, *Southdown House, St. John's Street, Chichester, Sussex*
G. E. Sworder's & Sons, *19 North Street, Bishops Stortford, Herts*
Osmond Tricks, *Regent Street Auction Rooms, Clifton, Bristol BS8 4HG*
Vidler & Co., *Auction Offices, Cinque Ports St., Rye, Sussex*
Wallis & Wallis, *West Street Auction Galleries, Lewes, Sussex BN7 2NJ*
Ward & Partners, *16 High Street, Hythe, Kent*
Warner, Sheppard & Wade, *16-18 Halford Street, Leicester*
Peter Wilson Fine Art Auctioneers, *Victoria Gallery, Market Street, Nantwich CW5 5DG*
Woolley & Wallis, *The Castle Auction Mart, Castle Street, Salisbury*
Worsfolds Auction Galleries, *40 Station Road West, Canterbury*

PERIODS

TUDOR PERIOD	1485 - 1603
ELIZABETHAN PERIOD	1558 - 1603
INIGO JONES	1572 - 1652
JACOBEAN PERIOD	1603 - 1688
STUART PERIOD	1603 - 1714
A. C. BOULLE	1642 - 1732
LOUIS X1V PERIOD	1643 - 1715
GRINLING GIBBONS	1648 - 1726
CROMWELLIAN PERIOD	1649 - 1660
CAROLEAN PERIOD	1660 - 1685
WILLIAM KENT	1684 - 1748
WILLIAM & MARY PERIOD	1689 - 1702
QUEEN ANNE PERIOD	1702 - 1714
GEORGIAN PERIOD	1714 - 1820
T. CHIPPENDALE	1715 - 1762
LOUIS XV PERIOD	1723 - 1774
A. HEPPLEWHITE	1727 - 1788
ADAM PERIOD	1728 - 1792
ANGELICA KAUFMANN	1741 - 1807
T. SHERATON	1751 - 1806
LOUIS XV1	1774 - 1793
T. SHEARER	(circa) 1780
REGENCY PERIOD	1800 - 1830
EMPIRE PERIOD	1804 - 1815
VICTORIAN PERIOD	1837 - 1901
EDWARDIAN PERIOD	1901 - 1910

MONARCHS

HENRY 1V	1399 - 1413
HENRY V	1413 - 1422
HENRY V1	1422 - 1461
EDWARD 1V	1461 - 1483
EDWARD V	1483 - 1483
RICHARD 111	1483 - 1485
HENRY V11	1485 - 1509
HENRY V111	1509 - 1547
EDWARD V1	1547 - 1553
MARY	1553 - 1558
ELIZABETH	1558 - 1603
JAMES 1	1603 - 1625
CHARLES 1	1625 - 1649
COMMONWEALTH	1649 - 1660
CHARLES 11	1660 - 1685
JAMES 11	1685 - 1689
WILLIAM & MARY	1689 - 1695
WILLIAM 111	1695 - 1702
ANNE	1702 - 1714
GEORGE 1	1714 - 1727
GEORGE 11	1727 - 1760
GEORGE 111	1760 - 1820
GEORGE 1V	1820 - 1830
WILLIAM 1V	1830 - 1837
VICTORIA	1837 - 1901
EDWARD V11	1901 - 1910

SILVER MARKS

Birmingham	(anchor) B (head)
Chester	(crest) (shield) M (head)
Dublin	K e (crown) (head)
Edinburgh	(castle) (thistle) T (head)
Exeter	(castle) (lion) G (head)
Glasgow	(tree) (lion) F (head)
London	(head) (lion) P (head)
Newcastle	(crest) (shield) V L (head)
Sheffield	(crown) (rose) G O
York	(cross) (crest) E O (head)

Example for 1850

Year	B	C	D	Ed	Ex	G	L	N	S	Y
1700			b		U		C			A
1701	A	D	W	A	D	ff				B
1702	B	P	X	B	O	A				C
1703	C	Q	Y	C	b	B				D
1704	D	R	Z	D	P	C				
1705	E		A	E	Z	K	D			F
1706	F	S	B	F	P	E				G
1707	G		C	G	B	N	F			
1708	H	T	D	H	N	O				O
1709	I		E	I	D	O				
1710	K	U	F	K		S				
1711	L		G	L	O					w
1712	M	W	H	M	B	M				
1713	N		I	N	O					O
1714	O	X	K	O	H	D				
1715	P		L	P	H					
1716	Q	Z	M	Q	A					
1717	R	A	N	R	B	P				
1718	S	B	O	S	C	D				
1719	T	C	P	T	D	D				
1720	U	A	Q	V	E	E				
1721	V	B	R	W	F	a				
1722	W	C	S	X	G	B				
1723	X	D	T	Y	H	D				
1724	Y	E	U	Z	I	D				
1725	Z	F	V	O	K	E				
1726	A	G	W	b	L	F				
1727	B	H	X	C	M	G				
1728	C	J	Y	d	S	N	B			
1729	D	K	Z	e	O	J				
1730	E	L	A	f	P	K				

Year	B	C	D	Ed	Ex	G	L	N	S	Y
1731	F	L	B	J			Q	L		
1732	G	M	C	H			R	M		
1733	H	N	D	U			S	N		
1734	J	O	E	K	S		T	D		
1735	K	P	F	L			V	P		
1736	L	Q	G	m			a	Q		
1737	M	R	H	n			b	R		
1738	N	S	J	o			C	S		
1739	O	T	K	P			d	T		
1740	P	U	L	q			e	A		
1741	Q	W	M	r			f	B		
1742	R	W	N	s			g	C		
1743	S	X	O	t	S		h	D		
1744	T	X	P	u			i	E		
1745	U	Y	Q	w			K	F		
1746	V	Z	R	x			l	G		
1747	W	A	S	y	S		m	H		
1748	X	B	T	z			n	I		
1749	Y	C	U	A			O	K		
1750	Z	D	V	B			P	L		
1751	a	E	W	C			q	M		
1752	b	F	X	D			r	N		
1753	c	G	Y	E			s	O		
1754	d	H	Z	F			t	P		
1755	e		A	G			u	Q		
1756	f		B	H	S		A	R		
1757	G	I	C	I			B	S		
1758	h	K	D	K	S		C	T		
1759	i	L	E	L			D			A
1760	k	M	F	M			E			B
1761	l	N	G	N			F			
1762	m	O	H	O			G			
1763	n	P	J	P	E		H			
1764	O	Q	K	Q			J			
1765	P	R	L	R			K			
1766	Q	S	M	S			L			
1767	R	T	N	T			M			
1768	S	U	O	U			N			
1769	T	W	P	W			O		G	
1770	U	X	Q	X			P		D	
1771	U	Y	R	Y			R		E	
1772	V	Z	S	Z			R		F	
1773	A	W	A	A	A	S	S		G	C
1774	B	X	B	B	B		T		H	F

	B	C	D	Ed	Ex	G	L	N	S	Y
1775	C	Y	Ĉ	D	C		U		D	
1776	D	a	D	I	O	O	a	K	R	
1777	E	b	E	E			b		h	
1778	F	C	C	Z	F	C	M	S	C	
1779	G	d	G	U	G	d	N	A	D	
1780	H	e	H	A	H	e	O	E	E	
1781	I	f	I	B	U		f	P	D	F
1782	K	g	K	C			g	Q	G	G
1783	L	h	L	D	K	S	h	R	B	H
1784	M	i	E	L			i	S	I	J
1785	N	k	Ñ	F	M	S	k	T	V	K
1786	O	l	O	G	N		l	U	R	L
1787	P	m	P	P			m	W	T	A
1788	Q	n	H	P			n	X	W	B
1789	R	O	I J	J			o	Y	M	C
1790	S	P	Š	K	T	S	p	Z	L	d
1791	T	q	L	f			q	A	P	e
1792	U	r	M	t			r	B	U	f
1793	V	S	W	U			S	C	G	g
1794	W	t	X	W	W		t	D	M	h
1795	X	u	Y	P	X	S	u	E	Q	i
1796	Y	V	Z	Q	Y		A	F	Z	k
1797	Z	A	A	R	A		B	G	X	L
1798	a	B	B	S	B		C	H	V	M
1799	b	C	C	T	C		D	I	E	N
1800	C	D	D	U	D	S	E	K	N	O
1801	d	E	E	V	E		F	L	H	P
1802	e	F	F	W	F		G	M	M	Q
1803	f	G	G	X	G		H	N	O	R
1804	g	H	H	Y	H		I	O	G	S
1805	h	I	I	Z	I		K	P	B	T
1806	i	K	K	a	K		L	Q	A	U
1807	j	L	L	b	L		M	R	S	V
1808	k	M	M	C	M		N	S	P	W
1809	l	N	N	d	N		O	T	K	X
1810	m	O	O	e	O		P	U	L	Y
1811	n	P	P	f	P		Q	W	C	Z
1812	O	Q	Q	g	Q		R	X	D	a
1813	P	R	R	h	R		S	Y	R	b
1814	q	S	S	i	S		T	Z	W	C
1815	r	T	T	j	T		U	A	O	d
1816	S	U	U	k	U		a	B	T	e
1817	t	V	W	l	a		b	C	X	f
1818	u	A	X	m	b		C	D	I	g
1819	V	B	Y	n	C	A	d	E	V	h
1820	W	C	Z	O	d	B	e	F	Q	i
1821	X	D	A	P	e	C	f	G	Y	k
1822	y	D	B	q	f	g	H	Z	u	
1823	Z	E	C	r	g	E	h	I	U	m
1824	A	F	D	S	h	F	i	K	a	n
1825	B	G	E	t	i	g	K	L	b	o
1826	C	H	F	u	j	H	L	M	C	p
1827	D	I	G	v	l	m	N	d	q	
1828	E	K	H	w	m	J	n	O	e	r
1829	F	L	I	X	n	K	O	P	f	s
1830	G	M	K	y	O	L	P	Q	g	t
1831	H	N	L	Z	P	m	q	R	h	u
1832	I	O	M	A	q	N	r	S	k	v
1833	K	P	N	S	r	O	S	T	l	w
1834	L	Q	O	C	S	P	t	u	m	r
1835	M	R	P	D	t	Q	U	W	P	y
1836	A	S	Q	E	u	R	A	X	q	z
1837	D	T	R	f	A	S	B	Y	r	A
1838	P	U	S	G	B	T	C	Z	S	B
1839	Q	A	T	H	C	U	D	A	t	C
1840	R	B	U	J	D	V	E	B	u	D
1841	S	C	V	K	E	W	f	C	V	E
1842	T	D	W	L	f	X	G	D	X	F
1843	U	E	X	M	G	Y	H	E	Z	G
1844	U	F	Y	N	D	Z	J	F	A	H
1845	W	G	Z	O	J	A	K	G	B	I
1846	X	H	a	P	K	L	H	C	K	
1847	Y	J	b	Q	T	M	D	L		
1848	Z	K	C	R	M	N	J	E	M	
1849	A	L	d	S	A	O	K	F	N	
1850	B	M	e	T	G	f	P	L	G	O
1851	C	N	f	U	P	G	Q	M	H	P
1852	D	O	g	V	R	R	N	I	Q	
1853	E	P	h	W	R	S	O	K	R	
1854	F	Q	j	X	S	T	P	L	S	
1855	G	R	K	Y	R	U	Q	M	T	
1856	H	S	l	Z	a	r	N	V		
1857	I	C	m	A	A	M	b	S	O	
1858	J	T	n	B	B	C	C	T	P	
1859	K	U	O	C	C	N	U	R		
1860	L	W	P	D	D	e	W	S		
1861	M	X	Q	E	E	f	X	T		
1862	N	Y	R	F	F	R	g	U		
1863	O	Z	S	G	G	h	Z	V		
1864	P	a	t	H	H	T	i	a	w	

17

	B	C	D	Ed	Ex	G	L	N	S	Y
1865	Q	b	u	i	I	M	k	b		X
1866	R	c	v	K	K	N	l	c		Y
1867	S	d	w	L	L	M	m	d		Z
1868	T	e	x	M	M	I	n	e		A
1869	U	f	y	N	N	O	p	f		B
1870	V	g	z	O	O	Z	p	g		C
1871	W	h	C	P	P	B	r	h		D
1872	X	i	B	Q	Q	B	t	i		E
1873	Y	k	c	R	R	C	s	k		F
1874	Z	l	s	S	S	t	t	l		G
1875	a	m	E	T	T	U	m	m		H
1876	b	n	F	U	U	F	A	n		J
1877	c	o	G	V	A	G	B	o		K
1878	d	p	H	W	B	H	C	p		L
1879	e	q	U	X	C	I	D	q		M
1880	f	r	K	Y	D	J	E	r		N
1881	g	s	L	Z	E	K	F	s		O
1882	h	t	M	a	F	L	G	t		P
1883	i	u	b		M	H	H	u		Q
1884	k	A	o	c		N	I			R
1885	l	B	p	d		O	K			S
1886	m	C	Q	e		P	L			T
1887	n	D	R	f		M	M			U
1888	o	E	S	g		R	N			V
1889	p	F	T	h		S	O			W
1890	q	G	U	i		T	P			X
1891	r	H	V	k		U	Q			Y
1892	s	I	W	l		V	R			Z
1893	t	K	X	m		W	S			a
1894	u	L	Y	n		X	T			b
1895	v	M	Z	o		Y	U			c
1896	w	N	A	p		Z	a			d
1897	x	O	B	q		A	b			e
1898	y	P	C	r		B	c			f
1899	z	Q	D	s		C	d			g
1900	a	R	C	t		D	e			h
1901	b	A	f	u		E	f			i
1902	c	B	G	w		F	g			k
1903	d	C	H	r		G	h			l
1904	e	D	K	u		H	j			m
1905	f	E	K	3		I	k			n
1906	g	F	L	A		J	l			o
1907	h	G	M	B		K	m			p
1908	i	H	N	C		L	n			q
1909	k	J	O	D		M	o			r
1910	l	K	P	E		N	p			s
1911	m	L	Q	F		O	q			t
1912	n	M	R	G		P	r			u
1913	o	N	S	H		Q	s			v
1914	p	O	T	I		R	t			w
1915	q	P	U	K		S	u			x
1916	r	Q	A	L		T	v			y
1917	s	R	b	M		U	b			z
1918	t	S	C	N		W	c			a
1919	u	T	D	O		W	d			b
1920	v	U	e	P		X	e			c
1921	w	V	F	Q		Y	f			d
1922	x	W	S	R		Z	g			e
1923	y	X	h	S		a	h			f
1924	z	Y	i	T		b	i			g
1925	A	Z	K	U		C	k			h
1926	B	a	l	v		d	l			i
1927	C	b	m	w		e	m			k
1928	D	c	n	x		f	n			l
1929	E	P	O	y		g	o			m
1930	F	e	P	z		h	p			n
1931	G	ff	P	A		i	q			o
1932	H	G	Q	B		j	r			p
1933	J	H	R	C		k	s			q
1934	K	I	S	D		l	t			r
1935	L	K	T	E		m	u			s
1936	M	L	U	F		n	A			t
1937	N	m	V	G		o	B			u
1938	O	N	W	H		p	C			v
1939	P	O	X	J		q	D			w
1940	Q	P	Z	K		r	E			X
1941	R	Q	Z	L		s	F			y
1942	S	R	A	M		t	G			Z
1943	T	S	B	N		u	H			A
1944	U	T	C	O		v	I			B
1945	V	U	D	P		w	K			C
1946	W	V	E	Q		X	L			D
1947	X	W	F	R		Y	M			E
1948	Y	X	G	J		Z	N			F
1949	Z	Y	H	J		A	O			G
1950	A	Z	I	U		B	P			H
1951	B	A	J	W		C	Q			J
1952	C	B	K	W		D	R			K
1953	D	C	L	X		E	S			L
1954	E	D	M	Y		F	T			M

REGISTRY OF DESIGNS

BELOW ARE ILLUSTRATED THE TWO FORM OF 'REGISTRY OF DESIGN' MARK USED BETWEEN THE YEARS OF 1842 to 1883.

DATE AND LETTER CODE USED 1842 to 1883

EXAMPLE: An article produced between 1842 and 1867 would bear the following marks. (Example for the 12th of November 1852).

EXAMPLE: An article produced between 1868 and 1883 would bear the following marks. (Example the 22nd of October 1875).

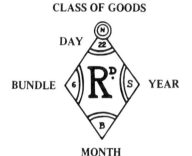

1842	X	63	G
43	H	64	N
44	C	65	W
45	A	66	Q
46	I	67	T
47	F	68	X
48	U	69	H
49	S	70	O
50	V	71	A
51	P	72	I
52	D	73	F
53	Y	74	U
54	J	75	S
55	E	76	V
56	L	77	P
57	K	78	D
58	B	79	Y
59	M	80	J
60	Z	81	E
61	R	82	L
62	O	83	K

January	C	July	I
February	G	August	R
March	W	September	D
April	H	October	B
May	E	November	K
June	M	December	A

CHINESE DYNASTIES   REIGN PERIODS

Shang	1766 – 1123BC
Zhou	1122 – 249BC
Warring States	403 – 221BC
Qin	221 – 207BC
Han	206BC – AD220
6 Dynasties	317 – 589
Sui	590 – 618
Tang	618 – 906
5 Dynasties	907 – 960
Liao	907 – 1125
Song	960 – 1279
Jin	1115 – 1234
Yuan	1260 – 1368
Ming	1368 – 1644
Qing	1644 – 1911

MING

Hongwu	1368 – 1398	Hongzhi	1488 – 1505
Jianwen	1399 – 1402	Zhengde	1506 – 1521
Yongle	1403 – 1424	Jiajing	1522 – 1566
Hongxi	1425	Longqing	1567 – 1572
Xuande	1426 – 1435	Wanli	1573 – 1620
Zhengtong	1436 – 1449	Taichang	1620
Jingtai	1450 – 1456	Tianqi	1621 – 1627
Tianshun	1457 – 1464	Chongzheng	1628 – 1644
Chenghua	1465 – 1487		

QING

Shunzhi	1644 – 1662	Daoguang	1821 – 1850
Kangxi	1662 – 1722	Xianfeng	1851 – 1861
Yongzheng	1723 – 1735	Tongzhi	1862 – 1874
Qianlong	1736 – 1795	Guangxu	1875 – 1908
Jiali	1796 – 1820	Xuantong	1908 – 1911

CHINA MARKS

BELLEEK
1857 onwards

BLOOR DERBY
1815-1840

BOW
1750-1776

1750   1760   1770

CAUGHLEY
1772-1814

imitation Worcester   in blue   in blue   SALOPIAN impressed

CHELSEA
1745-1784

Chelfea 1745
incised
1745-1749

in relief
1750-1753

red
1755

gold
1758-1770

COLEBROOK DALE
1785-1820

CDale.   Coalport
1785-1820

COPELAND
1847

1847

COPELAND & GARRETT
1833

1847-1891   1833-1847

DAVENPORT
1793-1882

Davenport

DAVENPORT LONGPORT STAFFORDSHIRE

DERBY
1745 onwards

1750   1760   1770-1780

DOULTON
1815

pre 1836   1872

FRANKENTHAL
1755-1800

blue 1756   blue 1756-1759   blue 1762-1793   blue 1771

HOCHST
1750-1798

red 1750-1762   blue 1762-1796   1765-1774   impressed 1760-1765

LEEDS
1760-1878

Hartley, Creens & Co
LEEDS POTTERY
1760-1783

LEEDS POTTERY
LEEDS POTTERY
impressed 1864

MARTIN BROS
1873-1915

Martin Bros
London & Southall
1873

R.W. MARTIN & BROS
1900

MASONS
1795-1854

MASONS
PATENT IRONSTONE CHINA

FENTON STONE WORKS

MEISSON
1713

1713-1724   1725-1750   modern

MENNECY
1734-1748

DV
incised

.D.V.
in blue

MINTON
1793 onwards

1800-1836   1851   MINTON 1860-1880

MINTON B B New Stone   MINTONS
1861 onward   20th century

NANTGARW
1811-1820

Nantgaru
1811

NANTGARW
1813

SWANSEA NANGARW
1814

NANT GARW O.W.
1816-1820

NEWHALL
1782-1835

N 332

PETIT JACOB
1796-1862

J.P.
1800

J P
XX 1820

PLYMOUTH
1768-1772

X II 21

ROCKINGHAM

ARD MELO
Rockingham
ROCKINGHAM
early 19th century

Baguley
Rockingham Works.
red 1824

CHINA MARKS

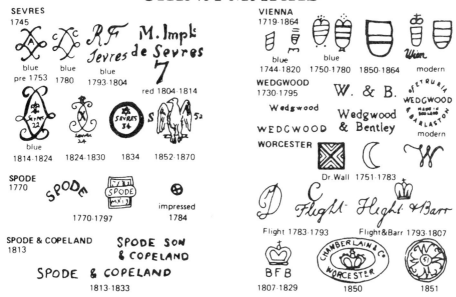

RECOGNITION & DATING

Obviously the task of committing every china mark to memory is one which will be outside the scope of most collectors and, indeed, most dealers too. For this reason, the following simple guides may prove to be of some assistance in determining the approximate date of a piece without having recourse to long, and frequently involved, lists of the marks used by various manufacturers over the years.

Any piece bearing the words 'English Bone China' or simply 'Bone China' is a product of the twentieth century and the words 'Made in England' also suggest twentieth century manufacture, though they could relate to pieces dating from 1875 onwards.

The word 'England' stamped on a piece suggests compliance with the McKinley Tariff Act of America, 1891 which required all imports to America to bear the name of the country of origin.

In 1862, the Trade Mark Act became law. Any piece bearing the words 'Trade Mark' therefore, can be assumed to date from 1862 onward.

Following the law relating to companies of limited liability, the word Limited or its abbreviations appears after 1860, though more commonly on pieces dating from 1885 onwards.

When a piece bears a pattern number or name, it can be assumed to date no earlier than about 1810.

Royal Arms incorporated into a small mark indicates a date after 1800.

During the mid 19th century the word 'Royal' was commonly added to the Manufacturer's name or trade name and, consequently, pieces bearing this word can usually be placed after 1850.

CHAIR BACKS

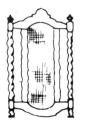

1660
Charles II.

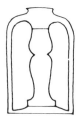

1705
Queen Anne.

1745
Chippendale.

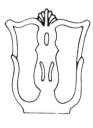

1745
Chippendale.

1750
Georgian.

1750
Hepplewhite.

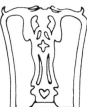

1750
Chippendale.

1760
French Rococo.

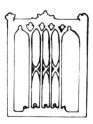

1760
Gothic.

1760
Splat back.

1770
Chippendale
ladder back.

1785
Windsor
wheel back.

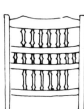

1785
Lancashire
spindle back.

1785
Lancashire
ladder back.

1790
Shield and
feathers.

1795
Shield back.

1795
Hepplewhite.

1795
Hepplewhite
camel back.

1795
Hepplewhite.

1810
Late Georgian
bar back.

CHAIR BACKS

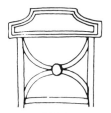

1810
Thomas Hope
'X' frame.

1810
Regency
rope back.

1815
Regency.

1815
Regency
cane back.

1820
Regency.

1820
Empire.

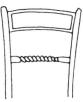

1820
Regency
bar back.

1825
Regency
bar back.

1830
Regency
bar back.

1830
Bar back.

1830
William IV
bar back.

1830
William IV.

1835
Lath back.

1840
Victorian
balloon back.

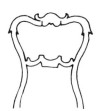

1845
Victorian.

1845
Victorian
bar back.

1850
Victorian.

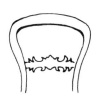

1860
Victorian.

1870
Victorian.

1875
Cane back.

LEGS

1600 Elizabethan Turned	**1605** Stuart Baluster	**1690** Spanish	**1695** William and Mary 'S' Curve	**1700** Trumpet	**1700** Portugese Bulb	**1700** Mushroom
1705 Inverted Cup	**1705** Queen Anne Cabriole	**1710** Hoof Foot	**1715** Modified Cabriole	**1715** Pad Foot	**1715** Cabriole	**1715** Hoof
1725 Ball and Claw	**1760** Cluster Column	**1780** Sheraton Tapered	**1785** Chinese Chippendale	**1790** Turned and Tapered	**1790** Tapered Scroll	**1790** Tapered Spiral
1805 Lions Paw	**1810** Regency Sabre	**1830** Windsor Baluster	**1830** Turned and Fluted	**1835** Victorian turned.	**1840** Victorian Cabriole	**1865** Victorian Reeded

FEET

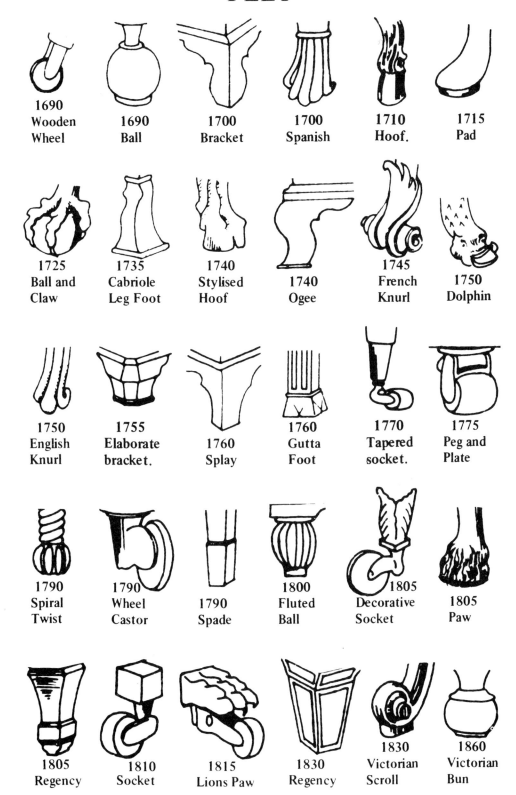

1690 Wooden Wheel

1690 Ball

1700 Bracket

1700 Spanish

1710 Hoof.

1715 Pad

1725 Ball and Claw

1735 Cabriole Leg Foot

1740 Stylised Hoof

1740 Ogee

1745 French Knurl

1750 Dolphin

1750 English Knurl

1755 Elaborate bracket.

1760 Splay

1760 Gutta Foot

1770 Tapered socket.

1775 Peg and Plate

1790 Spiral Twist

1790 Wheel Castor

1790 Spade

1800 Fluted Ball

1805 Decorative Socket

1805 Paw

1805 Regency

1810 Socket

1815 Lions Paw

1830 Regency

1830 Victorian Scroll

1860 Victorian Bun

HANDLES

1550
Tudor
drop.

1560
Early
Stuart
loop.

1570
Early
Stuart
loop.

1620
Early
Stuart
loop.

1660
Stuart
drop.

1680
Stuart
drop.

1690
William &
Mary solid
backplate.

1700
William &
Mary split
tail.

1700
Queen Anne
solid back-
plate.

1705
Queen Anne
ring.

1710
Queen Anne
loop.

1720
Early
Georgian
pierced.

1720
Early
Georgian
brass drop.

1730
Cut away
backplate.

1740
Georgian
plain brass
loop.

1750
Georgian
shield drop.

1755
French
style.

1760
Rococo
style.

1765
Chinese
style.

1770
Georgian
ring.

1780
Late Georgian
stamped.

1790
Late Georgian
stamped.

1810
Regency
knob.

1820
Regency
lions mask.

1825
Campaign.

1840
Early
Victorian
porcelain.

1850
Victorian
reeded.

1880
Porcelain or
wood knob.

1890
Late Victorian
loop.

1910
Art
Nouveau.

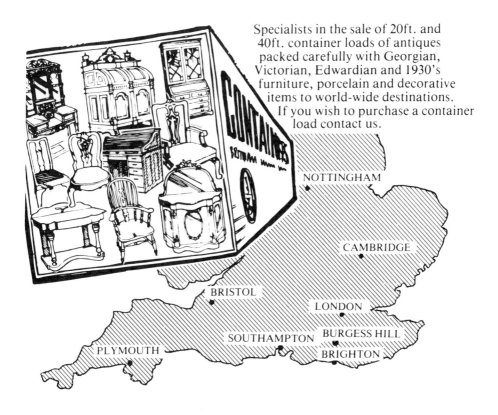

27

THERE ARE A GREAT MANY ANTIQUE SHIPPERS IN BRITAIN

but few, if any, who are as quality conscious as Norman Lefton, Chairman and Managing Director of British Antique Exporters Ltd. of Burgess Hill, Nr. Brighton, Sussex. Twenty-five years' experience of shipping goods to all parts of the globe have confirmed his original belief that the way to build clients' confidence in his services is to supply them only with goods which are in first class saleable condition. To this end, he employs a cottage industry staff of over 50, from highly skilled antique restorers, polishers and packers to representative buyers and executives. Through their knowledgeable hands passes each piece of furniture before it leaves the B.A.E. warehouses, ensuring that the overseas buyer will only receive the best and most saleable merchandise for their particular market. This attention to detail is obvious on a visit to the Burgess Hill showrooms where potential customers can view what must be the most varied assortment of Georgian, Victorian, Edwardian and 1930s furniture in the UK. One cannot fail to be impressed by, not only the varied range of merchandise, but also the fact that each piece is in showroom condition awaiting shipment.

BRITISH ANTIQUE EXPORTERS LTD

QUEEN ELIZABETH AVENUE
BURGESS HILL
WEST SUSSEX, RH15 9RX, ENGLAND
Telex 87688

Member of L.A.P.A.D.A.
Guild of Master Craftsmen

Telephone BURGESS HILL (04446) 45577

28

As one would expect, packing is considered somewhat of an art at B.A.E. and the manager in charge of the works ensures that each piece will reach its final destination in the condition a customer would wish. B.A.E. set a very high standard and, as a further means of improving each container load, their customer/container liaison dept. invites each customer to return detailed information on the saleability of each piece in the container, thereby ensuring successful future shipments. This feedback of information is the all important factor which guarantees the profitability of future containers. "By this method" Mr. Lefton explains, "we have established that an average £7500 container will immediately it is unpacked at its final destination realise in the region of £10000 to £14000 for our clients selling the goods on a quick wholesale turnover basis". When visiting the warehouses various container loads can be seen in the course of completion. The intending buyer can then judge for himself which type of container load would be best suited to his market.

In an average 20-foot container B.A.E. put approximately 75 to 150 pieces carefully selected to suit the particular destination. There are always at least 10 outstanding or unusual items in each shipment, but every piece included looks as though it has something special about it.

Based at Burgess Hill, 7 miles from Brighton and 39 miles from London on a direct rail link, (only 40 minutes journey), the Company is ideally situated to ship containers to all parts of the world. The showrooms, restoration and packing departments are open to overseas buyers and no visit to purchase antiques for re-sale in other countries is complete without a visit to their Burgess Hill premises where a welcome is always found.

OFFICE FURNITURE

DESKS, DESK CHAIRS, FILE CABINETS, BOOKCASES, BOARD ROOM TABLES.

BRITISH ANTIQUE INTERIORS LTD.
SCHOOL CLOSE, QUEEN ELIZABETH AVENUE
BURGESS HILL, WEST SUSSEX RH15 9RX
Tel: Burgess Hill (04446) 45577

ANTIQUES
REVIEW

1987 was the Year of the Collections It was the year when a variety of treasures, painstakingly amassed over the years by people of wealth – many of them women – re-emerged to tempt other would-be collectors. This must be a sign of hope for everyone connected with the antiques trade, dealers, collectors and salerooms alike, because without the impetus of collections being broken up, the supply of high quality items would eventually run out.

Perhaps the most dazzling collection of the year – in diamond sparkling mega-power at least – was the jewellery of the late Duchess of Windsor which Sotheby's auctioned off at the Beau Rivage Hotel overlooking Lake Geneva in April. The 306 lots, which Sotheby's presented to the public as symbols of a great love affair, fetched the staggering sum of over £31 million, outstripping the original estimate by more than three times. This was achieved in spite of carping from some critics who said that the lavishness of some of the jewellery showed both the Duke and the Duchess to have been people of little taste. Souvenir hungry American millionaires and millionairesses, including actress Elizabeth Taylor, bid feverishly for items like the Duchess's flamingo clip (1.2 million Swiss francs) and her cross hung charm bracelet, (570,000 Swiss francs).

The success of this sale marked the high point of a recent escalation in price of jewellery which has languished in the doldrums for some years. Other significant prices recorded over the period under review include £23,100 paid for a Cartier hat brooch set with emeralds, onyx and diamonds at Sotheby's London saleroom, a solitaire

An important solitaire diamond ring, the circular brilliant cut stone weighing 12.36ct. (Phillips) £42,000

diamond ring set with a 12.36 carat stone that Phillips of London sold for £42,000, and a 10.53 sapphire and diamond set ring they sold for £24,000 at the same sale. Phillips also sold an impressive Victorian emerald and diamond necklace with earrings, in its original fitted case, for £20,000 and an unusual pale brown agate

Victorian emerald and diamond necklace and matching earrings. (Phillips) £20,000

A Faberge pale brown agate group by Work-master Henrik Wigstrom. (Phillips) £13,000

group by Faberge carved in the design of two doves perching upon a silver tree branch for £13,000.

Like jewellery, the world of books has also recently emerged from the shadows to reclaim attention. Several valuable collections have been sold over the year, including the Marcel Jeanson Collection of Sporting Books which Sotheby's put under the hammer at Monte Carlo and achieved several world records.

First edition in three volumes of Dickens 'Great Expectations', 1861. (Phillips) £12,000

This collection was built up by a Belgian industrialist between 1920 and 1942 and contained such fine items as manuscripts by Gaston Phebus, Count of Foix, an artist and keen follower of "la chasse" in the 14th and early 15th centuries. His "La Livre De Chasse", which had once been in Tsarist hands and was bought by M. Jeanson from the Soviet government in the 1930's, was sold for £705,846, a world record for a 15th century manuscript.

Among other notable book prices through the year, was the £2,600 paid for a 1902 first edition of Kipling's "Just So" stories. This book's dust cover explained the high price for without the cover, it would only be worth around £100!

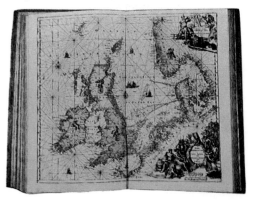

Louis Renard 'Atlas de la Navigation et du Commerce', Amsterdam, 1715. (Phillips) £4,700

A world record was notched up by Phillips in Edinburgh when they sold a three volume first edition set of "Emma" by Jane Austen for £4,100. The estimate had only been £900 so the auctioneers were agreeably surprised at the price paid. This book came from yet another collection, that of the late Dr Robert Mowbray of Penrith, whose library Phillips sold off in two parts during the year. Another of the star lots from the Mowbray Collection was William Withering's 1785 treatise on the medicinal uses of the foxglove, "An Account of the Foxglove", which sold for £6,700. Phillips also sold a battered little notebook entitled 'Historical Gossip about Golf and Golfers'

'Historical Gossip About Golf And Golfers, Edinburgh, 1863'. (Phillips)   £11,200

in their Edinburgh rooms for £11,200, while their Chester saleroom had the distinction of selling the world's most expensive golf ball for £4,500. It was a 'feathery' golf ball by William Gourlay which was reputed to contain enough compressed feathers to fill a top hat.

A third book collection which achieved star status was the library of botanical books built up by Robert de Belder. This was the most important collection of botanical colour-plate books ever offered at auction. Sotheby's sold them in London at the end of April after having mounted exhibitions of the books at both London and New York in the earlier part of the year.

Toys continue to sell well and yet another collection figured in the high spots when Mrs Kay Desmond's collection of toys and dolls, the basis of her Toy Museum, was broken up. Among the most sought after pieces were miniature items like the tiny early 20th century German sewing machines, each estimated at around £300. The world's most expensive set of toy soldiers, a rare display set of 281 figures issued by Britain's in 1905, was sold for £10,000 by Phillips in January 1987. Among the figures were cavalrymen, infantrymen, bandsmen, sailors and Camel Corps soldiers. This was the largest set ever made by Britain's and came complete with its original box and two lift-out trays. Another good price at the same sale was the £3,600 paid for a nicely made German wood and papier-mâché Royal Horse Artillery Gun Team of the Crimean War period,

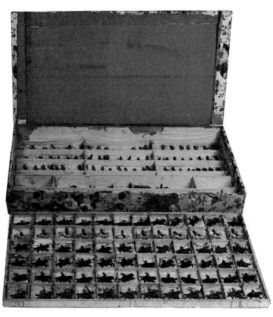

Britains extremely rare display set 131, the largest set ever made by Britains. (Phillips)
£10,000

A German, Royal Horse Artillery gun team of the Crimean War Period, 1870. (Phillips)
£3,600

comprising galloper gun with limber, seated gunner and two horse team, officer and seven mounted gunners.

Dinky toys are also holding up well. Around £300 can be expected for many 25 year old Dinky toys but if they are pre-1940's, the price can soar into four figures. Phillips sold a pre-war 'Aeroplane' set by Dinky, in its original box, for the good price of £1,700 and achieved the same price for a similar pre-war set from their French factory.

A German clockwork tinplate racing car by Guntherman, circa 1911. (Phillips) £4,000

Pre-war aeroplane sets by Dinky. (Phillips)
£1,700 each

An early hand enamelled four-seater open tourer, German, circa 1910, 8¼in. long. (Christie's) £4,200

A Constructor Car No. 2 by Meccano Ltd.,
1930's. (Phillips)   £1,200

Toy cars were particularly popular with Christie's selling a German four-seater open tourer for £4,200 and Phillips a German tinplate racing car by Guntherman, circa 1911, for £4,000.

Teddy bears continue to make big money but only if they are very early, have long snouts, long limbs, humped backs and a Steiff button in their ears. If they still have their 'growlers' so much the better. Last year a record price of £5,720 was paid for a bear at Sotheby's that still carried its original price tag. It was a fine yellow short plush bear by Steiff, circa 1904, with close together black boot button eyes, pricked wide apart ears and it answered to the name of Archibald. The record didn't last long however for it was soon surpassed by a Steiff white plush muzzled bear which sold for £8,800 to the same Californian dealer who bought Archibald.

Dolls always demand good prices too, especially if they are 'plain Janes' for it is often the unusual and less classically pretty ones that really hit the high spots. Good pretty dolls sell for around £500 each but a much plainer 1909 Kramer Reinhardt model was sold this year for over £26,000. At Phillips, a pensioner watched while her treasured German doll was sold for nearly £4,000 although one of its legs was detached, but Sotheby's took the high spot with a

world record price of £67,100, including premium, for a William and Mary wooden doll, complete with original clothes, but unfortunately minus one hand and a lower leg.

Post war toys also did well especially those popular with sci-fi collectors. Phillips sold a 1950's Japanese tinplate clockwork robot entitled Lilliput for £280.

An early Japanese tinplate clockwork robot
entitled Lilliput. (Phillips)   £280

Ceramics have been fairly slow this year and higher priced items seem to have stayed static or even fallen in price. There were hopes of a recovery when the second part of Mr T. Y. Chao's collection was sold by Sotheby's in Hong Kong in the spring but Mr Chao was one of the buyers who pushed the price of Chinese ceramics, especially blue and white Ming, to high spots in the 1970's and judging by Sotheby's estimates some of his pieces had fallen in price, when inflation is taken into account. For example a 15th century flask painted with a dragon and leaping waves was estimated at the same £300,000 that Chao had paid for it in 1981.

Rare items however always find buyers and these included Barbara Hutton's pair of jadeite pillows and an Imperial famille rose bowl of the Kangxi period (around 1700) which doubled its 1979 price of £25,000.

This time around the buyers were not Hong Kong millionaires but collectors from Taiwan.

Ceramic buyers in the more expensive bracket are also switching their interest to Japanese objects which have until now been overshadowed by Chinese items. Kakeimon porcelain is particularly favoured by Americans and by the Japanese themselves who have been able to push up prices because of the strength of the yen. For example a pair of Kakeimon seated tigers which the late Duchess of Kent sold in 1947 for just over £115 are today worth £52,800.

The lower priced ceramic market is still reeling slightly from the impact of Christie's Amsterdam sale last year of Captain Michael Hatcher's haul of blue and white china. Because Dutch museums boycotted the Hatcher sale, pieces were more easily available for the general public who have since taken to Chinese ceramics in a big way.

For example in Glasgow, Christie's can get good prices for any Chinese item that comes their way and a warped and cracked famille rose punch bowl fetched £1,300 in their rooms this year.

There is always keen competition for Art Deco and 20th century ceramics and among prices recorded was the £320 paid for a Shelley Art Deco Rising Sun tea service in fawn, ochre and black and £500 paid for an incomplete and chipped seven piece Clarice Cliff breakfast set painted in a multi coloured geometric design. Both of those prices were achieved at Christie's Glasgow rooms.

Also in the ceramic field, Phillips sold a Wemyss Ware pig 40 cm long for a record £2,500 and in their Cornwall office a Lowestoft mug painted with the name Ann Sawyer and the date 1773, sold for £2,500.

A large London delft white table salt with three double scrolled horns made £19,000 in Phillips' at London. The demand for Doulton does not decrease and in February, Phillips sold a Royal Doulton covered jug modelled on comedian George Robey for £2,400, while Abridge Auction Rooms in Essex sold a similar jug depicting Charlie Chaplin for the same price. They also negotiated the sale of an extremely rare pilot character jug 'The Maori', made in 1939, for a reputed £12,500.

A fine and rare pair of Kakiemon tigers seated on rockwork bases. (Christie's) £52,800

Royal Doulton pilot character jug, 'The Maori', circa 1939. (Abridge)   £12,500

A London white delft posset pot, circa 1650. (Phillips)   £13,000

A rare 17th century tin glazed earthenware. table salt. (Phillips)   £19,000

A Staffordshire saltglaze bear jug and cover, circa 1740. (Phillips)   £2,400

Royal Doulton 'Charlie Chaplin' Toby jug, circa 1918, 11in. high. (Abridge) £2,400

London delft royal portrait plate, 22cm., circa 1690. (Phillips)   £2,100

'Myfanwy Jones', HN39, designer E. W. Light, issued 1914-1938. £1,000

'Ermine Muff', HN54, designer C. J. Noke, issued 1916-1938.   £450

'Marianne', HN2074, designer L. Harradine, issued 1951-1953. £220

'Fruit Gathering', HN562, designer L. Harradine, issued 1923-1938.   £750

'Promenade', HN2076, designer M. Davies, issued 1951-1953.   £800

'One of the Forty', HN665, designer H. Tittensor, issued 1924-1938.   £480

'Gainsborough Hat', HN705, designer H. Tittensor, issued 1925-1938.   £350

'Madonna of the Square, HN2034, designer P. Stabler, issued 1949-1951.   £450

'Prudence', HN1883, designer L. Harradine, issued 1938-1949. £200

The Lyle Price Guide to DOULTON

ISBN 0-86248-058-2
448 Pages
Size 10 x 7in. Hardback

* More than 5000 prices together with a history of the Doulton Factory.

* Over 2500 clear illustrations, many in full colour.

* Descriptions, dates of manufacture, designers, height and colour variations listed.

* Complete listing of all figures, character jugs, Toby jugs and limited editions.

NEW EDITION

JUST £9·95

* Accurate and up-to-date prices backed by forty years of dealing.

* Special sections on Doulton marks, artists and rarities.

* Advertising Ware . . . Animal Figures . . . Art Pottery . . . Chang . . Character Jugs . . . Figures . . . Flambe . . . Kingsware . . . Loving Cups . . . Limited Editions . . . Series Ware . . . Stoneware . . .

Louis XIV marquetry bureau mazarin, 1.17m. wide. (Phillips) £12,500

In furniture, tips for best buys are still Edwardian and fine 18th century pieces. Victorian furniture has dropped in price, mainly because the American market for it has fallen off. Fine furniture always sells well because there simply is not enough of it to meet the demand. At their London rooms in the spring, Phillips sold a Regency carved mahogany table for £48,000 and a Louis XIV Bureau Mazarin for £12,500. From the collection of the late Mrs Dolly Burns, a daughter of Duveen the art dealer, Phillips also sold a pair of antique parcel giltwood side tables in the Adam style, for £6,600.

A fine carved Black Forest hall stand, 7ft.6in. high. (John D. Fleming & Co.) £2,200

A Queen Anne walnut bachelor's chest, 31½in. wide. (Christie's) £37,400

A fine Queen Anne walnut bureau, 28¾in. wide. (Coles, Knapp & Kennedy) £7,000

George II carved giltwood console table in the manner of William Jones. (Phillips)
£8,500

George III mahogany desk reputed to have been the property of Dr. Samuel Johnson. (Phillips)
£40,000

Federal mahogany and curly maple veneered square sofa, New England, circa 1805. (Phillips)
$46,000

Louis XV kingwood floral marquetry bombe commode, stamped by Nicholas Petit, 98cm. wide. (Phillips)
£13,500

A George II mahogany library armchair with cartouche shaped padded back. (Christie's)
£8,800

Cash-in on Collecting

* This book contains the stories of many fascinating and successful collectors. They are men and women of all ages and from all walks of life who have been bitten by the collecting bug. Their specialities range from old bank notes to cigarette lighters; from dolls to picture postcards.

ISBN 0-86248-055-8
448 Pages
Size 10 x 7in. Hardback
32 Pages in full colour

From their own experience they give first hand tips on collecting including how to start, where to go and, most interesting of all for the would be collector, what to start specialising in now so that your hobby can be turned into money.

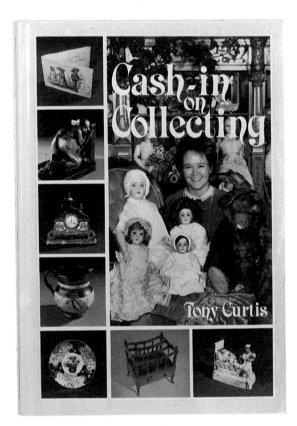

JUST £9·95

* Everything and anything can be collected from 18th century prints to today's throwaway beer cans. In this book you learn how to build up your collection and also how to add an unexpected pleasure to your life for collecting can not only be a cure for boredom and the blues but it carries with it the very real possibility of turning a modest outlay into a considerable nest egg.

An aesthetic movement ebonised and deco-
rated dresser. (Phillips) £400

A Queen Anne green and gold lacquer bureau
cabinet, 40in. wide. (Christie's) £77,000

An 18th century tallboy veneered in burr
elm. (Phillips) £2,600

One of a set of twelve Regency carved
mahogany chairs. (Phillips) £22,000

One of a pair of gentleman's Austrian satin birch upright dressing chests. (Phillips)
£3,200

Oak vitrine with sculptural decoration, by Francois Rupert Carabin, 1904, 160cm. high. (Christie's) *£23,896*

There is a strong demand on both sides of the Atlantic for Arts and Crafts and Art Deco furniture. For example, in New York, Phillips sold an Aesthetic Movement (circa 1880) carved and inlaid walnut fireplace by "Herter Brothers" for $16,000.

An Art Deco bronze and ivory figure of a flute player, by Ferdinand Preiss, 42cm. high. (Phillips) *£6,500*

The fashion for the same period is reflected in the soaring prices being paid for Art Deco Figures by sculptors like Preiss, Chiparus and Prof. Otto Poertzel. At Glasgow, Christie's sold a damaged bronze and ivory Poertzel figure of a dancer for £2,900 and in Edinburgh, during the same week in March, Phillips sold a 17 inch tall Preiss figure of a male flute player for £6,500. "Oriental Dancer" a bronze and ivory figure by Chiparus fetched £12,000 at Phillips in March 1986.

✳ one paperback worth £100
✳ an American comic worth £7,500
✳ a licence for a male servant worth £2

ONLY
£6·95

✳ The only book of its kind on the market.

The Lyle Price Guide to PRINTED COLLECTIBLES

Tony Curtis

9¾ x 6¾in. Paperback.
Over 3,000 Illustrations.
SBN 0-86248-047-7
448 Pages

This volume deals with the question — 'Just pieces of paper!' or valuable collectibles.
We throw away today's newspaper or the empty soap powder packet without a second
thought, light the fire with last week's comic and drop the used bus ticket in the waste
bin. Yet the passing of a few years gives all these items a nostalgic fascination and in
many cases a real monetary value.

✳ FASCINATING – check out over 3000 more
amazing money-making facts

An Art Deco cocktail bar trolley, the top inset
with two clear and satin glass panels, by
Lalique, 88cm. wide. (Christie's) £6,480

'Oiseau de Feu', a Lalique semi-circular
luminaire in clear and satin finished glass, 43cm.
high, including stand. (Christie's) £8,640

An Art Deco partner's desk with its two armchairs in the style of Andre Groult, sycamore,
goatskin, gilt bronze and glass. (Christie's) £10,753

A Marinot enamelled glass vase, the clear glass
enamelled with a frieze of three nude female
figures, 20.2cm. high. (Christie's) £4,540

A Gustave Serrurier Bovy three-fold screen of
mahogany and stained glass, 376 x 165cm. high.
(Christie's) £6,571

'Danseuse de Thebes', a bronze and ivory figure cast and carved from a model by Clair Jeanne Roberte Colinet, 25.8cm. high. (Christie's) £8,100

'Dancer with Lamp', a good Chiparus figural lamp, 37cm. high. (Phillips) £8,700

A Karl Maes carpet, woollen with geometric design, 120 x 60cm. (Christie's) £4,779

A Galle blowout vase with overall moulded decoration of flowering clematis, 25.5cm. high. (Christie's) £3,456

An atelier Jean Prouve double-fronted bookcase of polished pine and lacquered aluminium, 185cm. long. (Christie's) £9,797

'Fate', a green patinated bronze mask from a model by Richard Garbe, 13in. high, 1921. (Christie's) £2,000

ANTIQUE DEALERS POCKET BOOK

At last! Instant recognition and dating of thousands of antiques is possible – with this clear and comprehensive pocket manual from the world's foremost publisher of antiques reference books. There is more information to the square inch in this book than in any you can buy, whether you are a dealer, collector, or merely interested in identifying your own family heirlooms. Here are over 3,500 clear illustrations, not only of expensive objects but especially of the day-to-day items (many less than 100 years old but still of value) which make up the bulk of the antiques market. The Antique Dealers Pocket Book is a must for everyone interested in antiques – and an education in itself.

ISBN 0-86248-062-0
256 Pages
Size 8 x 5½in. Hardback
Over 3,500 clear illustrations

JUST £3·95

Monarchs, Chinese Dynasties, Periods, Registry of Designs, China Marks, Handles, Pediments, Legs, Feet, Chair Backs, Silver Marks, Barometers, Bronze, Caddies & Boxes, Cameras, Cane Handles, Carved Wood, China, Clocks, Cloisonne, Copper & Brass, Dolls, Enamel, Fans, Furniture, Glass, Gold, Horn, Inros, Instruments, Iron & Steel, Ivory, Jade, Jewellery, Lamps, Lead, Marble, Mirrors, Model Ships, Model Trains, Money Banks, Musical Boxes, Netsuke, Quilts, Rugs, Samplers, Seals, Shibayama, Tsubas.

'Les Amis De Toujours', a bronze and ivory figure by Demetre Chiparus. (Christie's) £22,000

Still in the Art Deco period, a clock designed by Charles Rennie Mackintosh as a wedding present for an Edinburgh couple sold at Phillips' saleroom in that city for a staggering £42,000. In their London rooms, the same firm sold another wedding present clock with a sad history. It had been presented to the great jockey Fred Archer in 1883. When Archer shot himself in a fit of depression three years later at the age of 29, the clock was returned to the donor whose family sent it for auction. It was a French gilt bronze carriage clock and the Archer association pushed the price up to £1,200.

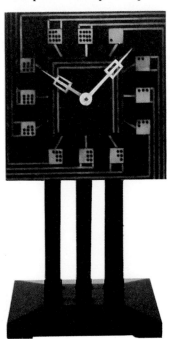

A Lalique hanging lampshade, 31 cm. diam., signed and dated 1922. (Phillips) £5,200

Clock designed by Charles Rennie Mackintosh. (Phillips) £42,000

51

A Donegal carpet designed by Charles E. Annesley Voysey. (Phillips)   £5,000

Galle artistic blowout table lamp, 46cm. high. (Christie's)   £44,000

The Archer, a figure by Ferdinand Preiss, 23½in. high. (Christie's)   £11,500

A Galle inlaid and carved mahogany etagere. (Christie's)   £8,961

Crazy quilt, New York State, inscribed 'Columbus – Gods Fair World 1492-1892'. (Robt. W. Skinner)   *$2,250*

Nostalgia for the 1920's and '30's extends to clothes and period trimmings like silk flowers and old buttons. Boxes of silk ribbons and flowers that could have been bought in junk shops for a few shillings until very recently, can now fetch up to £100 at auction and Phillips recently sold a box of 1930's 'Excelsior Make' buttons for £80 over a £20 estimate. They also achieved a good price for two silk dresses by Mariano Fortuny of £3,000 each and £1,200 for an interesting pair of child's shoes of cord quilted green silk, circa 1740.

Two 1920's silk dresses by Mariano Fortuny with Delphos pleating and stencilled belt. (Phillips)   *£3,000 each*

A pair of mid 18th century child's shoes of cord quilted green silk. (Phillips)   £1,200

53

Mid 18th century beadwork bag. (Phillips)
£420

An unusual James Dixon plated teapot,
designed by Christopher Dresser, circa 1879.
(Phillips)   £36,000

As far as silver is concerned there has been a steady decline in top quality pieces coming to the market — a good collection to sell is much needed in this field. Pieces which are available can almost double their price in a year, as for example had the Duke of Dorset's 1742 toilet set, sold by Christie's in New York for £68,750 in 1986 and on offer in this year's International Silver and Jewellery Fair at London's Dorchester Hotel for £150,000. A King Charles II tankard sold for £360 twenty five years ago is today worth £5,000 while a Queen Anne tankard with a lion's head handle which cost £600 in 1966 is now also worth £5,000. From Mrs Dolly Burns' collection came a George II oval cake basket by John Jacob, 1742, which fetched £12,000 at Phillips'.

A late 17th century lady's linen waistcoat,
circa 1680. (Phillips)   £3,600

Early 19th century needlework sampler.
(Phillips)   £500

A George III oval teapot and stand by Paul
Storr. (Phillips)   £8,200

* one light bulb worth £300
* a fire insurance mark worth £2,500
* 20th century French doll worth £24,000

* Nearly 200 types of collectibles.

The Lyle Price Guide to COLLECTIBLES

Tony Curtis

9¾ x 6¾in. Paperback.
Over 3,000 Illustrations.
SBN 0-86248-048-5
448 Pages

This down to earth publication deals with the vast range of collectible items which do not always fall into the recognised category of antiques. Compiled with the close co-operation of collectors in many specialised fields this book contains information and prices on a diverse range of subjects including electric light bulbs, Robertson's Golly Badges, keys and fishing reels.

* AMAZED — then check out over 3000 more amazing money-making facts

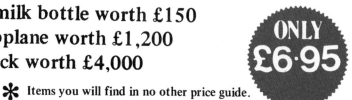

A miniature by Richard Cosway, circa 1805. (Phillips) £2,000

Record price for a silhouette by William Welling, signed and dated 1874. (Phillips) £3,200

Thomas Jefferson's mahogany lap desk. (Phillips) $55,000

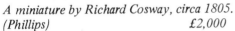

16th century leather nose spectacles, discovered in the roof of a house. (Phillips) £1,600

A 17th century brass candlestick. (Phillips) £1,500

A rare Hardy Bros. 2½in. 'Perfect' brass fly reel of 1891 pattern. (Phillips) £2,700

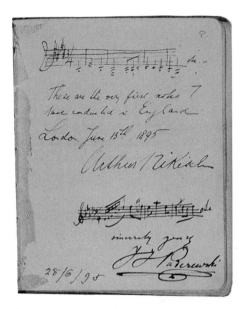

A rare autograph album containing the signatures of important late 19th and early 20th century musicians, composers and performers. (Phillips)   £1,250

Autograph letters is a field which is receiving a good deal of attention at the moment. It has been noticed that letters from famous people have been steadily climbing in price and, for example, Churchill's signature has gone up from £100 to £700 in ten years. Over the same period Byron's has risen from £500 to £3,000. In 1975, anything signed by Einstein was worth around £75, today it would fetch £750. Even an old hotel bill for £46.16s.1d and signed by Oscar Wilde can now bring in £1,760. The signature need not even be from someone who is dead for Edward Heath's is selling for around £30 at the moment.

The more interesting the document the signature is attached to, the higher the price, and of course, the older the signature, the better. Mary Queen of Scots' and Elizabeth I's signatures are now worth thousands of pounds even on the most mundane documents.

Music manuscripts which used to share in the autograph letter boom, have however dropped in price. When Sotheby's recently offered the first draft of Wagner's "Tannhauser" Overture, it failed to find a buyer. Sotheby's estimate for it was £99,000 which would not have been out of the way

Signed photograph of Sir Winston Churchill, September 1898. (Phillips)   £1,500

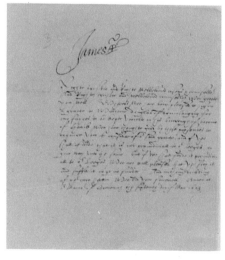

James I letter signed by the King, 1623. (Phillips)   £580

Popular ANTIQUES and their VALUES 1800-1875

The purpose of this publication, and its companion, is to make it easy for those either buying, selling, or merely interested in the value of the pieces in their own home to identify and have a knowledge of the price an Antique Dealer is likely to pay for a piece in average condition.

ISBN 0-86248-060-4
256 Pages
Size 8 x 5½in. Hardback
Over 2,000 photographs

JUST £3·95

Badges, Barometers, Bronze, Buckets, Caddies & Boxes, Card Cases, Carved Wood, Chandeliers, China, Clocks & Watches, Copper & Brass, Dolls, Enamel, Furniture, Glass, Gold, Helmets, Icons, Inros, Instruments, Iron & Steel, Ivory, Jade, Jewellery, Lacquer, Medals, Mirrors, Model Ships, Musical Instruments, Netsuke, Pewter, Photographs, Portrait Miniatures, Powder Flasks, Quilts, Samplers, Seals, Silhouettes, Silver, Snuff Bottles, Textiles, Toys,

Popular ANTIQUES and their VALUES 1875-1950

People with an eye for a bargain never move house, clear out an attic or pass a junk shop without consulting their Popular Antiques & Their Values books.

ISBN 0-86248-061-2
256 Pages
Size 8 x 5½in. Hardback
Over 2,000 photographs

JUST £3·95

Advertising Signs, Amusement Machines, Automatons, Bronze, Caddies & Boxes, Cameras, China, Clocks, Cloisonne, Copper & Brass, Dolls, Enamel, Furniture, Glass, Gold, Icons, Instruments, Ivory, Jewellery, Lamps, Model Ships, Model Trains, Money Banks, Musical Boxes, Netsuke, Pewter, Photographs, Posters, Rock 'n' Roll, Rugs, Shibayama, Silver, Textiles, Toys, Transport, Weathervanes, Wood.

One of a collection of twelve previously unpublished colour pictures of The Beatles. (Christie's) £650

a couple of years ago for such an important manuscript.

They did however achieve a world record for a musical manuscript with the sale of an autographed copy of nine symphonies by Mozart for £2,585,000.

World record auction price for a pot lid, 'Eastern Lady and Black Attendant'. (Phillips) £3,600

Among the smaller categories which would repay interest by collectors, are Staffordshire pot lids for Phillips in London recently achieved a world record when they sold a pot lid decorated with an Eastern Lady and her Black Attendant for £3,600. The previous pot lid record was £3,000 for 'The Spanish Lady' also at Phillips.

At the sale of the Eric Young Collection of Snuff bottles, a porcelain bottle in gourd form decorated with fruit vines, went for an amazing £29,700 over a £500 estimate.

There is a good market at the moment also for leather suitcases and Vuitton trunks that the rich used to take with them on steamer voyages. They are being bought by status conscious 'yuppies' as personal luggage or for room decoration and a trunk can make around £300 in auction while a suitcase costs between £50 and £100. So turn out your attic, there must be lots of them around.

Items connected with Pop Music can still arouse saleroom frenzy though it seems to be dying off slightly. Among the interesting prices notched up in this field over the year was the £2,000 paid for Paul McCartney's grey and black velvet stage suit of 1965, which was sold by Phillips in London. They also sold a suit worn by John Lennon, based on one the firm of D. A. Millings made for Gene Vincent, for £1,500.

A set of Beatles 'Bobb'n Head' figures, 1964. (Phillips) £130

Photographs are doing well at the moment, especially old ones of India and good examples of work done by 20th century photographers.

A rare find sold at Phillips' in London for £8,000 was a set of three original glass negatives taken by the Rev. Charles Lutwidge Dodgson — Lewis Carroll — in 1879. They were of 11-year old Leila Campbell Taylor and her younger sister May and they turned up in a brown paper parcel tucked away in a drawer in a country mill near Cambridge. Two of the negatives were bought by "The Sunday Times Magazine", who after publishing a special limited edition of presentation prints of Leila, donated them to The National Museum of Photography at Bradford who had bought the negative depicting May.

An album of 27 calotypes by D. O. Hill and R. Adamson. (Christie's)   £17,000

One of three glass negatives taken by the Rev. Charles Lutwidge Dodgson — Lewis Carroll — in 1879. (Phillips)   £8,000

An item of interest in the saleroom world that is not likely to have a parallel for some time is the oil rig Glomar which Phillips sold for $22 million at the end of 1986. For a short time it had the distinction of being the most expensive item ever sold at auction — that was before Christie's smash hit with Vincent Van Gogh's 'Sunflowers', however.

Close, No. 46 Saltmarket, albumen print by Thomas Annan, 11 x 8¾in., a set of 31 photographs. (Christie's)   £15,000

A mint corner block of 12 Penny Blacks. (Phillips) £80,000

Finally, a word of warning. There has been a great upsurge recently in faking which is turning into an antiques growth industry.

Great Britain 1840 Mulready 2d envelope used with 1840 2d plate 1. (Phillips) £4,200

Sicily 1859 50 grana lake-brown pair used with seven single 20 grana dark slate-grey and two grana plate 1 cobalt-blue to make a rate of 242 grana. (Phillips)   £30,000

Among the items that are being faked are old Teddy Bears, cloisonne enamel, American silver and ceramics, especially the work of Clarice Cliff. The fake Clarice Cliff's however have an unsteady outline and the interior glazing is streaky.

Preiss and Chiparus figures are being more successfully faked as are netsuke, scrimshaw and pieces of mediaeval ivory. They are often almost indistinguishable from the real thing and the only sure way to test ivories is with a heated pin.

Silver items are being recast, especially candlesticks, and there is a brisk trade in enamelled pill boxes and scent bottles. The colours of the enamel however are often harsh and new looking.

Fake Tang is being made in Taiwan and there are fake Saudi Arabian and Lebanese gold coins in circulation. Scientific instruments are being faked with the brass given false ageing – but often plastic lenses are used which is a big giveaway. Stamps of course are still one of the biggest areas for faking which is so widespread that there are some collectors who specialise in fakes.

The golden rule is to develop a good eye and never buy anything that makes you doubt it, even if you are not sure why. Salerooms will usually compensate buyers if purchases are proven to be faked.

Liz Taylor

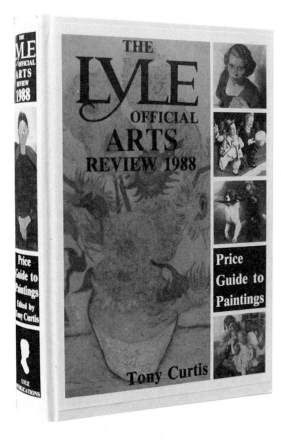

ANTIQUES
REVIEW 1988

T HE Lyle Official Antiques Review is compiled and published with completely fresh information annually, enabling you to begin each new year with an up-to-date knowledge of the current trends, together with the verified values of antiques of all descriptions.

We have endeavoured to obtain a balance between the more expensive collector's items and those which, although not in their true sense antiques, are handled daily by the antiques trade.

The illustrations and prices in the following sections have been arranged to make it easy for the reader to assess the period and value of all items with speed.

You will find illustrations for almost every category of antique and curio, together with a corresponding price collated during the last twelve months, from the auction rooms and retail outlets of the major trading countries.

When dealing with the more popular trade pieces, in some instances, a calculation of an average price has been estimated from the varying accounts researched.

As regards prices, when 'one of a pair' is given in the description the price quoted is for a pair and so that we can make maximum use of the available space it is generally considered that one illustration is sufficient.

It will be noted that in some descriptions taken directly from sales catalogues originating from many different countries, terms such as bureau, secretary and davenport are used in a broader sense than is customary, but in all cases the term used is self explanatory.

Royal Ediswan Lamps enamel advertising sign, 28 x 20in. (Onslow's) $82 £55

A painted metal figure in 18th century costume, the body shaped as a bottle bearing a Guinness lable. (Christie's) $173 £121

An advertising sign for Walbran Ltd., Leeds for High Class Fishing Tackle of every Kind, 30 x 24in. (Onslow's) $9 £6

A pictorial tinplate sign for Green's Lawn Mowers, 18 x 24in. (Onslow's) $165 £110

An enamel advertising sign for Puritan soap, 24 x 36in. (Onslow's) $33 £22

An enamel advertising sign for Fry's Pure Breakfast Cocoa, 36 x 24in. (Onslow's) $13 £9

Fry's Chocolate, pictorial Five Boys enamel sign, mounted on wood frame, 30 x 36in. (Onslow's) $150 £100

A W. D. & H. O. Wills Westward Ho! Smoking Mixture, enamel sign, 36 x 18in. (Onslow's) $52 £35

An enamel advertising sign
for Royal Ediswan The King
of Lamps, 28 x 20in.
(Onslow's) $195 £130

A painted wooden imitation
'Heinz Salad Cream' bottle,
48in. high. (Christie's)
           $282 £200

A pictorial enamel advertising
sign for Mew's, Isle of Wight,
40 x 28in. (Onslow's)
                $75 £50

A pair of advertising plaques by T. J. & J.
Mayer. (Phillips) $1,600 £1,000

A pictorial advertisement for Ransomes' Lawn
Mowers, The Best in The World, The Auto-
matons and Anglo-Paris, 16½ x 21½in.
(Onslow's) $210 £140

An enamel advertising sign
for Smilax cigarettes, 36 x
24in. (Onslow's) $45 £30

A painted metal figure of a
cockerel, plinth inscribed
'Courage, London & Country
Brewers', 12½in. high. (Christie's)
                $141 £99

An Eat Quaker Oats enamel
sign, mounted on wood frame,
42 x 24in. (Onslow's) $27 £18

After Gamy — Garros Gagne le Grand Prix de l'Aero Club, hand-coloured lithograph, 17¾ x 35¾in. (Onslow's) $75 £50

A 1:24th scale wood and metal model of the Royal Aircraft Factory SE5a, built by R. Walden, 1976. (Onslow's) $260 £170

A flying scale model of the Gloster Gladiator single seater fighter Serial No. K.8032 with external details, finished in silver with R.A.F. markings, wingspan 56in. (Christie's) $581 £380

1942 Vickers Supermarine Spitfire Mk. IX, constructor's number BR601, wingspan 36ft. 11in., length 31ft.4in. (Christie's)
$111,390 £79,000

Geoffrey Watson — Women's Royal Air Force, published by Employment Exchange, 30 x 20in. (Onslow's)
$498 £330

Blackpool Aviation Meeting, 1910, a silver cup with three reeded handles on acanthus legs, 8½in. diam. (Christie's)
$1,551 £1,100

Schneider Trophy, 1931, Official Souvenir Programme, together with two others. (Christie's) $155 £110

Studio of Roy Nockolds — Supersonic, signed, on board — 16 x 20in. (Onslow's) $83 £55

William Munro, Marine Aircraft design, 1st edition, plates, diagrams, some folding, 1933. (Onslow's) $377 £250

Studio of Roy Nockolds — Hawker Fury 1 Serial No. K2074, signed and dated 1940, watercolour, 15 x 19in. (Onslow's) $51 £34

After Gamy — Grand Prix de la Champagne, hand-coloured lithograph, 17¾ x 35¾in. (Onslow's) $83 £55

James Goulding, Vickers Vimy, airbrush drawing, signed, on board, five elevations, 21 x 15in. (Onslow's) $60 £40

Bleriot Monoplane Type XI, engine 15 h.p. 3—cylinder air cooled 'Fan' type Anzani, wingspan 25ft., length 26ft. (Christie's) $18,330 £13,000

W. G. Barrett — The Schneider Trophy, published by Pools Advertising Service Ltd., 30 x 20in. (Onslow's) $75 £50

Geoffrey Watson — Special Shell Aviation Petrol, No. 356, published by Vincent Brooks Day & Son, 30 x 45in. (Onslow's) $166 £110

The Aerial Derby, published by The Dangerfield Printing Co., London, '15, on linen, 29¾ x 20in. (Onslow's) $270 £180

Peter Endsleigh Castle — Supermarine Spitfire Mk 1 AZH — N3277 over countryside, watercolour and gouache, 6 x 12in. (Onslow's) $90 £60

Studio of Roy Nockolds — Sopwith Transport Ditched in the Sea near Shipping, signed, on board — 20 x 30in. (Onslow's) $30 £20

Northwest coast polychrome wood face mask, carved and incised cedar, 9½in. high. (Robt. W. Skinner Inc.) $2,500 £1,748

Southwestern coiled basketry bowl, Apache, woven in willow and devil's claw, 10¾in. diam. (Robt. W. Skinner Inc.) $450 £314

Woodlands wood face mask, Seneca False Face Soc., 14in. high. (Robt. W. Skinner Inc.) $475 £332

Classic Navajo chief's blanket, woven in single strand home-spun and ravelled yarn, 82 x 62in. (Robt. W. Skinner Inc.) $30,000 £20,978

A Verneh horse blanket, the blue field with rows of stylised animals, 5ft.5in. x 4ft.7in. (Christie's) $1,163 £825

Navajo Yei rug, woven with two rows of opposing skirted Yeibachi figures in red, white and black on a natural grey ground, 66 x 96in. (Robt. W. Skinner Inc.) $950 £664

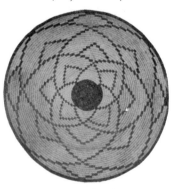

Southwestern coiled basketry tray, Apache, 22½in. diam. (Robt. W. Skinner Inc.) $1,100 £769

Navajo pictorial Germantown weaving with full yarn tassels on corners, 58 x 92in. (Robt. W. Skinner Inc.) $200 £139

Southwestern polychromed jar, Acoma, 13¼in. diam. (Robt. W. Skinner Inc.) $1,100 £769

Woodlands husk face mask, composed of bands of braided cornhusks, 11½in. high. (Robt. W. Skinner Inc.) $1,000 £699

Southwestern coiled basketry bowl, Apache, woven in devil's claw, 14½in. diam. (Robt. W. Skinner Inc.) $700 £489

Cherokee polychrome wood face mask, Boogerman Dance Mask, made by Will West Long, 16in. high. (Robt. W. Skinner Inc.) $550 £384

Plains beaded hide blanket strip, Sioux, sinew sewn, 66in. long. (Robt. W. Skinner Inc.) $1,100 £769

Southwestern American Indian tempera painting signed Robert Chee, 15½ x 18½in. (Robt. W. Skinner Inc.) $550 £384

Early 19th century Northern Plains pipe tomahawk, 18in. long. (Robt. W. Skinner Inc.) $3,400 £2,377

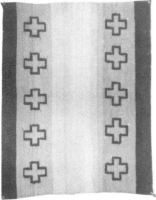

Navajo woman's manta, homespun, 33½ x 42in. (Robt. W. Skinner Inc.) $2,600 £1,818

Southwestern polychrome male figure, Yuma, attached card reads 'Bought 1892 Albuquerque, New Mexico', 8¾in. high. (Robt. W. Skinner Inc.) $650 £454

Navajo pictorial weaving, woven on a natural grey ground with geometric design motifs, 47 x 76in. (Robt. W. Skinner Inc.) $800 £559

A pair of 19th century Japanese iron stirrups abumi, inlaid overall with silver flowers and foliage, interiors of red lacquered wood. (Wallis & Wallis) $393 £275

One of a pair of officer's embossed gilt shoulder scales of the Bengal Artillery. (Wallis & Wallis) $293 £180

A post 1902 officer's gilt and silvered waist belt plate of The 22nd Frontier Force (Sam Browne's Cavalry). (Wallis & Wallis) $177 £110

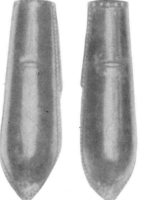

A breastplate probably adapted in the early 19th century. (Wallis & Wallis) $302 £200

A pair of 17th century Indian arm guards bazu band made for a princeling, 10in. (Wallis & Wallis) $286 £200

Part of a Japanese suit of armour. (Wallis & Wallis) $2,402 £1,550

An American cowboy leather saddle, circa 1875, body blind stamped Moran Bros., Miles City M.T. (Montana Territory). (Wallis & Wallis) $1,930 £1,350

An officer's full dress sporran of The Argyll & Sutherland Highlanders, in its tin case with chamois leather lining. (Wallis & Wallis) $668 £410

An early 19th century Indo-Persian gold damascened steel shield dhal, 13¼in.. (Wallis & Wallis) $224 £145

A 17th/18th century mail coat with short sleeves. (Christie's) $267 £190

An officer's full dress sporran of The Black Watch, gilt cantle with thistle border and St. Andrew in centre, white goatshair. (Wallis & Wallis) $164 £115

A Victorian Grenadier Guards officer's gilt and silvered waist belt clasp. (Wallis & Wallis) $122 £76

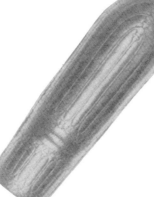

A Victorian officer's full dress sabretache of The 18th Hussars, the inner flap with trade label of Hawkes & Co., Piccadilly. (Wallis & Wallis) $830 £550

A 17th century Indian chiselled steel arm defence bazu band, 13in. (Wallis & Wallis) $91 £64

A Continental articulated breastplate, circa 1700, of swollen form with medial ridge. (Wallis & Wallis) $302 £200

A 17th century Continental breastplate with twin studs for fastening and shoulder straps. (Wallis & Wallis) $214 £150

A Victorian Cavalry officer's silver mounted full dress shoulder belt and pouch of The 20th Hussars. (Wallis & Wallis) $402 £250

One of a pair of Georgian officer's gilt bullion epaulettes of The 6th Dragoon Guards, circa 1825. (Wallis & Wallis) $374 £230

Early 17th century pikeman's breastplate together with associated simulated five lame tassets. (Christie's) $846 £600

An early 19th century Russian Bandsman's coatee of dark grey cloth with red facings, decorated with crimson and white lace. (Wallis & Wallis) $151 £100

Part of an Imperial Russian diplomatic/court uniform. (Christie's) $841 £550

A Georgian copy of a fully articulated and fluted 16th century Maximilian full suit of armour. (Wallis & Wallis) $7,150 £5,000

Rifle Volunteers (probably 4th Norfolk Rifle Vol. Corps. circa 1872) Bugle-Major's uniform. (Christie's) $336 £220

A Victorian full dress uniform of a Major-General, circa 1865. (Wallis & Wallis) $715 £500

East Suffolk Militia officer's short-tailed scarlet coatee with yellow facings and white metal domed buttons.
(Christie's) $720 £500

A retainer's suit of 19th century Japanese armour with a wakizashi in a shagreen scabbard.
(Outhwaite & Litherland)
                    $667 £460

An officer of The 2nd Bn. Highland Light Infantry's white cloth undress 'drill-jacket', together with a khaki service dress jacket.
(Christie's) $259 £180

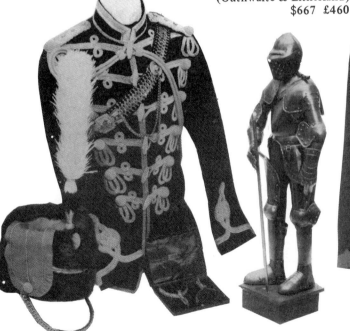

An officer's full dress uniform items of The 10th Royal Hussars, together with metal uniform case. (Christie's)
        $2,142 £1,400

A miniature suit of armour, 34in. (Wallis & Wallis)
            $402 £250

The King's (Liverpool Regt.) 6th (Rifle) Bn. officer's busby, full dress tunic, Mess jacket and waistcoat, together with Captain's service dress.
(Christie's) $720 £500

BADGES

A Victorian officer's silvered pouch belt badge of The 24th Middlesex Rifle Regt. (Wallis & Wallis) $74 £50

A bronzed cap badge of The Birmingham Electrical Engineers Vols. (Wallis & Wallis) $158 £110

A Victorian officer's darkened white metal Maltese Cross helmet plate of The West Kent Rifles. (Wallis & Wallis) $192 £130

A Victorian officer's darkened white metal helmet plate of a Vol. Bn. The Rifle Brigade. (Wallis & Wallis) $59 £40

An officer's copper, gilt, silvered and enamel shoulder belt plate of The 22nd (Cheshire) Regt., circa 1845-55. (Wallis & Wallis) $458 £310

A Victorian Glengarry of The Sussex Rifle Vols. (Wallis & Wallis)$66 £45

A Victorian officer's silvered helmet plate of The 1st Vol. Bn. The R. West Kent Regt. (Wallis & Wallis) $206 £135

A Georgian officer's copper gilt shoulder belt plate of The W(?) Volunteer Infantry. (Wallis & Wallis) $108 £75

A Victorian officer's darkened white metal helmet plate of The 5th Vol. Bn. The Manchester Regt. (Wallis & Wallis) $29 £20

BADGES

An officer's 1855 (French) pattern gilt shako plate of The 63rd (Manchester) Regt. (Wallis & Wallis) $148 £100

An Indian brass puggaree badge worn by gun lascars of the Artillery Train. (Wallis & Wallis) $57 £40

A Victorian other rank's white metal Glengarry of The 2nd Vol. Bn. The Royal Warwickshire Regt. (Wallis & Wallis) $37 £25

An other rank's die-stamped brass Albert pattern shako plate of The Royal Jersey Militia. (Wallis & Wallis) $155 £105

A Georgian officer's copper gilt rectangular shoulder belt plate of The Amounderness Local Militia. (Wallis & Wallis) $185 £125

A Victorian other rank's white metal helmet plate of The 2nd Northumberland (Percy) Artillery Vols. (Wallis & Wallis) $125 £85

An officer's hallmarked silver and enamel shoulder belt plate of The R. Lancashire Militia. (Wallis & Wallis) $310 £210

A Georgian officer's copper gilt oval shoulder belt plate of The Preston Volunteers. (Wallis & Wallis) $207 £140

A late Victorian other rank's brass helmet plate of The Canadian Medical Staff Corps. (Wallis & Wallis) $170 £115

BADGES

An officer's silvered and
enamel cap badge of The
Royal Sussex Regt., marked
'Sterling'. (Wallis & Wallis)
$51 £35

A Victorian other rank's
white metal Glengarry of The
Ross, Caithness, Sutherland &
Cromarty (Highland Rifle
Militia). (Wallis & Wallis)
$105 £70

A post-1902 officer's helmet
plate of The Royal Warwickshire Regt. (Wallis & Wallis)
$69 £47

A Victorian officer's silvered
helmet plate of The 2nd Vol.
Bn. The Sherwood Foresters.
(Wallis & Wallis) $125 £85

An officer's silver plaid
brooch of The Gordon
Highlanders. (Wallis & Wallis)
$281 £190

A Victorian other rank's
white metal Glengarry of
The 2nd Vol. Bn. The
Black Watch. (Wallis &
Wallis) $162 £110

An officer's 1878 pattern
gilt helmet plate of The
46th (South Devon) Regt.
(Wallis & Wallis)$309 £205

A Victorian officer's gilt
helmet plate of The Sussex
Artillery. (Wallis & Wallis)
$96 £65

A Victorian officer's helmet
plate of The 4th Devonshire
R.V. Corps. (Wallis & Wallis)
$51 £35

BADGES

An other rank's cap badge of The 2nd Vol. Bn. The Royal Sussex Regt. (Wallis & Wallis) $26 £18

An other rank's cap badge of The 2nd Vol. Bn. The Notts. & Derby Regt. (Wallis & Wallis) $29 £20

An other rank's cap badge of The 2nd Vol. Bn. The Worcester Regt., S. Africa 1900-02 scroll below. (Wallis & Wallis) $26 £18

An Edward VII trooper's helmet plate of H.M. Reserve Regt. of Dragoon Guards. (Wallis & Wallis) $74 £50

A George I King's Messenger's badge, by Francis Garthorne, circa 1720-23. (Phillips) $20,250 £13,500

A Victorian officer's white metal helmet plate of The Lancashire Rifle Vols. (Wallis & Wallis) $62 £42

A post-1902 other rank's white metal helmet plate of The Bearer Co., Second London Brigade (Vol. Medical Corps.) (Wallis & Wallis) $458 £310

An other rank's white metal Glengarry of The 5/9th (Artisans) Bn. Queen's Edinburgh. (Wallis & Wallis) $96 £65

A Victorian other rank's helmet plate of The Reserve Regt. of Lancers. (Wallis & Wallis) $51 £35

ARMS & ARMOUR

An other rank's cap badge of The 4th Vol. Bn. The Norfolk Regt. (Wallis & Wallis) $103 £70

A Victorian officer's gilt fur cap grenade badge of The Royal Scots Fusiliers. (Wallis & Wallis) $66 £45

An officer's bronze cap badge of The Royal Naval Air Service. (Wallis & Wallis) $216 £150

A Victorian other rank's white metal Glengarry of The 1st Northants Rifle Vols. (Wallis & Wallis) $66 £45

An officer's silvered plaid brooch of The 1st Aberdeen Rifle Vols. (Wallis & Wallis) $236 £160

An other rank's white metal Glengarry of The Royal Limerick County Militia. (Wallis & Wallis) $118 £80

A Victorian officer's silvered, gilt and enamel helmet plate of The 3rd R. Lancashire Militia. (Wallis & Wallis) $133 £90

An other rank's white metal Glengarry badge of The 4th Aberdeenshire Rifle Vol. Corps. (Wallis & Wallis) $52 £35

A pre-1881 other rank's brass Glengarry of The 42nd (R. Highlanders) Regt., white metal star and numeral. (Wallis & Wallis) $81 £55

BADGES

An other rank's white metal cap badge of The 4th Vol. Bn. The Queen's Regt. (Wallis & Wallis)$96 £65

An other rank's cap badge of The 1st Vol. Bn. The Royal Fusiliers. (Wallis & Wallis) $66 £45

An other rank's cap badge of The 1st Vol. Bn. The Royal Warwickshire Regt. (Wallis & Wallis) $37 £25

A late Victorian white metal helmet plate of The Rajputana-Merwa Railway Vol. Rifles. (Wallis & Wallis) $229 £150

An officer's silvered plaid brooch of The Black Watch. (Wallis & Wallis) $94 £64

A Victorian Glengarry badge of The Royal Herefordshire Militia. (Wallis & Wallis) $66 £45

A Victorian other rank's Glengarry of The 1st Cheshire Rifle Vols. (Wallis & Wallis) $81 £55

A military style white metal Canadian cap badge of the Carbide Chemicals Co. (Wallis & Wallis) $45 £30

A William IV officer's gilt helmet plate of The Warwickshire Yeomanry Cavalry. (Wallis & Wallis) $144 £100

DAGGERS

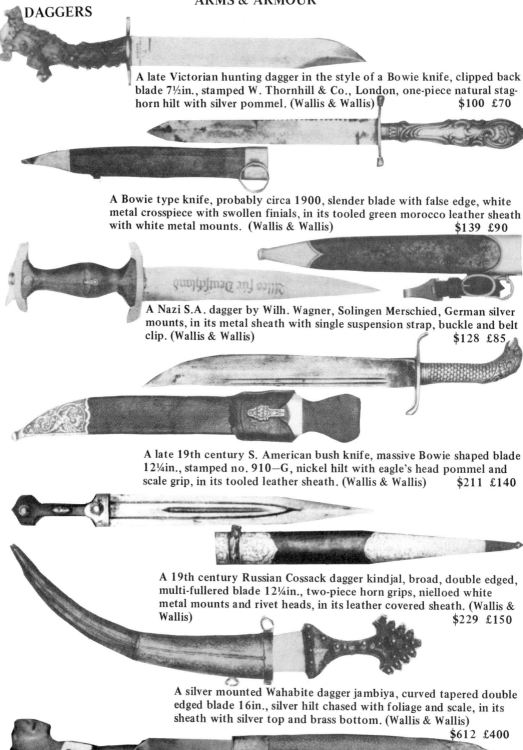

A late Victorian hunting dagger in the style of a Bowie knife, clipped back blade 7½in., stamped W. Thornhill & Co., London, one-piece natural stag-horn hilt with silver pommel. (Wallis & Wallis) $100 £70

A Bowie type knife, probably circa 1900, slender blade with false edge, white metal crosspiece with swollen finials, in its tooled green morocco leather sheath with white metal mounts. (Wallis & Wallis) $139 £90

A Nazi S.A. dagger by Wilh. Wagner, Solingen Merschied, German silver mounts, in its metal sheath with single suspension strap, buckle and belt clip. (Wallis & Wallis) $128 £85

A late 19th century S. American bush knife, massive Bowie shaped blade 12¼in., stamped no. 910—G, nickel hilt with eagle's head pommel and scale grip, in its tooled leather sheath. (Wallis & Wallis) $211 £140

A 19th century Russian Cossack dagger kindjal, broad, double edged, multi-fullered blade 12¼in., two-piece horn grips, nielloed white metal mounts and rivet heads, in its leather covered sheath. (Wallis & Wallis) $229 £150

A silver mounted Wahabite dagger jambiya, curved tapered double edged blade 16in., silver hilt chased with foliage and scale, in its sheath with silver top and brass bottom. (Wallis & Wallis) $612 £400

An Eastern dagger with jade handle, carved lion's head pommel, in shagreen sheath with engraved metal mounts, overall length, 11in. (Chancellors Hollingsworths) $168 £110

DAGGERS

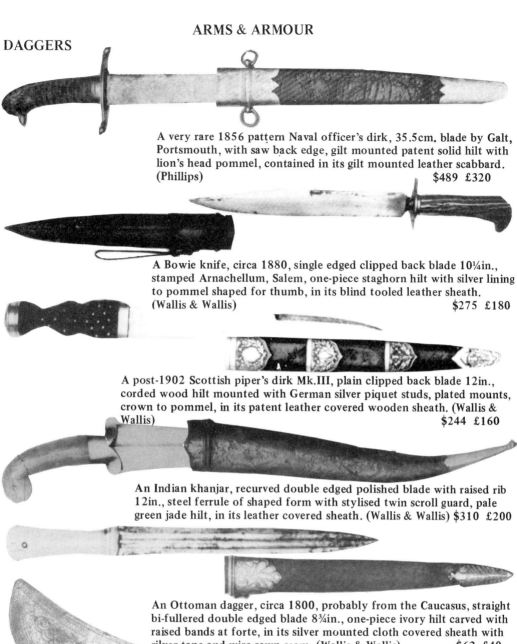

A very rare 1856 pattern Naval officer's dirk, 35.5cm. blade by Galt, Portsmouth, with saw back edge, gilt mounted patent solid hilt with lion's head pommel, contained in its gilt mounted leather scabbard. (Phillips) $489 £320

A Bowie knife, circa 1880, single edged clipped back blade 10¼in., stamped Arnachellum, Salem, one-piece staghorn hilt with silver lining to pommel shaped for thumb, in its blind tooled leather sheath. (Wallis & Wallis) $275 £180

A post-1902 Scottish piper's dirk Mk.III, plain clipped back blade 12in., corded wood hilt mounted with German silver piquet studs, plated mounts, crown to pommel, in its patent leather covered wooden sheath. (Wallis & Wallis) $244 £160

An Indian khanjar, recurved double edged polished blade with raised rib 12in., steel ferrule of shaped form with stylised twin scroll guard, pale green jade hilt, in its leather covered sheath. (Wallis & Wallis) $310 £200

An Ottoman dagger, circa 1800, probably from the Caucasus, straight bi-fullered double edged blade 8¾in., one-piece ivory hilt carved with raised bands at forte, in its silver mounted cloth covered sheath with silver tape and wire sewn seam. (Wallis & Wallis) $62 £40

A Mohammedan knife moplah from Malabar, sickle-shaped blade 12in., with chiselled decoration, bone hilt with turned and shaped brass ferrule, in its leather cover. (Wallis & Wallis) $135 £95

An 18th century Persian dagger Kard, very finely watered polished single edged hollow ground blade 8¾in., of Kirk Nardaban pattern, steel grip-strap and bolsters, two-piece polished ivory grips. (Wallis & Wallis) $100 £65

A Nazi 1st pattern Luftwaffe officer's dagger, plain blade, mounts with traces of plating, dark blue leather covered wirebound grip, in its similarly covered metal mounted steel sheath with hanging rings. (Wallis & Wallis) $170 £115

A gold mounted Arab dagger jambiya, curved double edged blade 6in., with raised rib, the entire hilt and sheath covered in sheet gold, not hallmarked. (Wallis & Wallis) $872 £610

An early 19th century Sumbawa Executioner's kris, straight double edged blade 20½in. of laminated grain, fluted scrolled top, horn hilt with swollen pommel, in its wooden sheath. (Wallis & Wallis) $193 £125

A Nazi S.A. dagger, blade retaining all original polish, with RZM mark and M.7/37, plated mounts, in its metal sheath with plated mounts and single hanging strap. (Wallis & Wallis) $198 £130

A Nazi Red Cross man's dagger, plated mounts, in its black painted metal sheath with plated mounts and leather frog, with a Nazi dress knot. (Wallis & Wallis) $185 £125

A Nazi 1933 pattern S.S. dagger, blade retaining some original polish, German silver mounts, in its German silver mounted metal sheath. (Wallis & Wallis) $428 £280

DAGGERS

A Nazi Railway protection 1935 pattern dagger, by Robt. Klaas, plated blade and mounts, spiral black grip, in its plated sheath with silvered dress knot. (Wallis & Wallis) $345 £240

A 19th century Indian double bladed dagger bichwa, recurved double edged blades 7in., brass loop shaped handle with broad ribbed knucklebow, in its green velvet sheath with brass chapes. (Wallis & Wallis) $200 £140

A Nazi Diplomat's dagger, double edged blade by Alcosa of Solingen, with trade mark, silvered brass eagle head pommel and crossguard, mother-of-pearl grips, in its plated sheath. (Wallis & Wallis) $828 £575

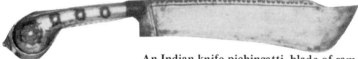

An Indian knife pichingatti, blade of ram dao form 7in., silver hilt with gold crescent pommel mount and ornamental rivet heads, silver inlaid tang sides, in its silver mounted sheath with length of silver chain. (Wallis & Wallis) $249 £165

A Nazi S.A. dagger, by Hugo Linder, German silver mounts, crosspiece stamped 16100, in its steel sheath with German silver mounts. (Wallis & Wallis)$296 £200

An Italian Fascist colonial police knife, leaf blade 7¼in., stamped at forte PC.2846, horn shaped grips, inset with oval brass cartouche of crowned eagle. (Wallis & Wallis) $193 £130

DAGGERS

A Nazi 2nd pattern Luftwaffe officer's dagger, by Holler, grey metal mounts, orange grip, in its grey metal sheath with original hanging strap and belt clip. (Wallis & Wallis) $125 £85

An early 19th century Balinese kris, straight double edged blade with narrow central fuller and etched watered pamir, one-piece bone hilt, in its two-piece carved wooden sheath. (Wallis & Wallis) $232 £150

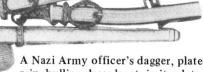

A silver mounted Nepalese kukri, blade 11½in., brass mounted bone hilt, in its leather sheath with silver mounts. (Wallis & Wallis) $200 £140

A Nazi Army officer's dagger, plated mounts, white celluloid grip, bullion dress knot, in its plated sheath with original hanging straps.   (Wallis & Wallis) $153 £100

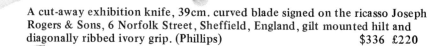

A cut-away exhibition knife, 39cm. curved blade signed on the ricasso Joseph Rogers & Sons, 6 Norfolk Street, Sheffield, England, gilt mounted hilt and diagonally ribbed ivory grip. (Phillips) $336 £220

A 19th century S. Indian dagger, recurved double edged blade 6½in., shaped horn hilt mounted with brass, incorporating grotesque animal's head pommel, with bulging eyes. (Wallis & Wallis) $211 £140

A Nazi Army officer's dagger, plated mounts, orange grip, in its plated sheath with original hanging straps and bullion dress knot. (Wallis & Wallis) $128 £85

DAGGERS

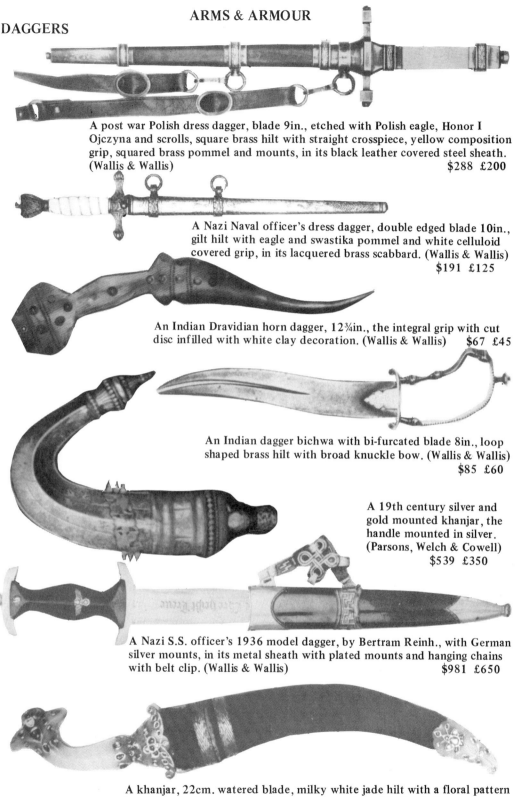

A post war Polish dress dagger, blade 9in., etched with Polish eagle, Honor I
Ojczyna and scrolls, square brass hilt with straight crosspiece, yellow composition
grip, squared brass pommel and mounts, in its black leather covered steel sheath.
(Wallis & Wallis) $288 £200

A Nazi Naval officer's dress dagger, double edged blade 10in.,
gilt hilt with eagle and swastika pommel and white celluloid
covered grip, in its lacquered brass scabbard. (Wallis & Wallis)
$191 £125

An Indian Dravidian horn dagger, 12¾in., the integral grip with cut
disc infilled with white clay decoration. (Wallis & Wallis) $67 £45

An Indian dagger bichwa with bi-furcated blade 8in., loop
shaped brass hilt with broad knuckle bow. (Wallis & Wallis)
$85 £60

A 19th century silver and
gold mounted khanjar, the
handle mounted in silver.
(Parsons, Welch & Cowell)
$539 £350

A Nazi S.S. officer's 1936 model dagger, by Bertram Reinh., with German
silver mounts, in its metal sheath with plated mounts and hanging chains
with belt clip. (Wallis & Wallis) $981 £650

A khanjar, 22cm. watered blade, milky white jade hilt with a floral pattern
in gold, cabochon rubies and diamonds, contained in its cloth covered
scabbard. (Phillips) $2,448 £1,600

HELMETS

A post-1902 officer's blue cloth spiked helmet of The Bedfordshire Regt. (Wallis & Wallis) $271 £180

A post-1902 trooper's helmet of The Life Guards, with white metal and brass helmet plate and plume. (Wallis & Wallis) $1,198 £810

A post-1902 other rank's blue cloth ball-topped helmet of The Royal Army Medical Corps. Vols. (Wallis & Wallis) $170 £115

A Prussian Jager Zu Pferd other rank's steel helmet, plated helmet plate and spike, date inside 1916. (Wallis & Wallis) $755 £500

A trooper's helmet of The 1st (Royal) Dragoons, with black hair plume and rosette. (Wallis & Wallis) $514 £360

An other rank's blue cloth spiked helmet of The 1st United States Infantry, circa 1900. (Wallis & Wallis) $158 £110

A Nazi period black patent leather covered police shako, with aluminium helmet plate and mounts. (Wallis & Wallis) $57 £38

A cabasset, circa 1600, formed in one-piece, 'pear stalk' finial to crown, brass rosettes around base. (Wallis & Wallis) $170 £110

A French grey cloth kepi of the Swiss police, Bern maker's mark inside. (Wallis & Wallis) $15 £10

A post-1902 officer's blue cloth ball-topped helmet of The Royal Army Medical Corps. Vols. (Wallis & Wallis) $236 £160

A U.S. Military Academy shako with gilt helmet plate, numeral 5 within garter, circa 1900. (Wallis & Wallis) $177 £120

An Victorian officer's blue cloth ball-topped helmet of The Vol. Medical Staff Corps. (Wallis & Wallis) $325 £220

A Bavarian Infantry officer's pickelhaube, gilt helmet plate, fluted spike and mounts. (Wallis & Wallis) $688 £450

A French grey cloth covered helmet of the Swiss police, with gilt and enamel helmet plate. (Wallis & Wallis) $33 £22

A Saxony Infantryman's pickelhaube, grey metal helmet plate, spike and mounts. (Wallis & Wallis) $286 £190

An officer's peaked forage cap of The Norfolk Regt., in its tin case. (Wallis & Wallis) $391 £240

A cabasset, circa 1600, in one-piece, 'pear stalk' finial to crown. (Wallis & Wallis) $156 £105

A French shako of the Garde Republicaine, circa 1910, black cloth with brass bound peak. (Wallis & Wallis) $43 £30

HELMETS

A Bavarian Cavalryman's NCO's pickelhaube with lacquered brass helmet plate and leather backed chinscales and mounts. (Wallis & Wallis) $436 £295

A French Mounted Gendarmerie brass helmet, circa 1900. (Wallis & Wallis) $505 £310

A Wurttemberg Infantry Reservist officer's pickelhaube with gilt helmet plate and silvered Landwehr cross. (Wallis & Wallis) $666 £450

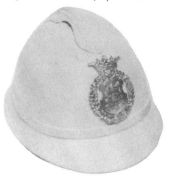

A Nazi khaki cloth covered tropical helmet, with both metal shield Army badges. (Wallis & Wallis) $83 £58

A Prussian Infantryman's Ersatz pickelhaube, gilt brass helmet plate, brass mounts and leather lining and chinstrap. (Wallis & Wallis) $177 £120

A whitened French Fire Brigade or police helmet, of military pattern. (Wallis & Wallis) $15 £10

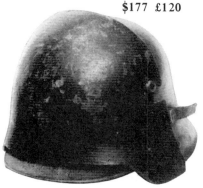

A Victorian other rank's blue cloth ball-topped helmet of The Vol. Medical Staff. (Wallis & Wallis) $177 £120

A German World War I Military 1916 steel helmet, first type triple padded lining. (Wallis & Wallis) $489 £300

A fireman's brass helmet, by Merryweather. (Wallis & Wallis) $340 £230

HELMETS

An Oldenberg Infantryman's pickelhaube, brass helmet plate with white metal arms imposed, with leather lining and chinstrap. (Wallis & Wallis) $273   £185

A post war U.S. Naval officer's peaked cap with gilt and silvered badge and gilt side buttons. (Wallis & Wallis)
$24 £16

A Prussian Reservist Artillery officer's pickelhaube, gilt helmet plate, gilt mounts and with silk lining. (Wallis & Wallis) $604 £400

A French officer's Fire Brigade helmet, blackened skull with white metal mounts, chrome and enamel coat-of-arms badge. (Wallis & Wallis) $27 £18

An Edward VII trooper's helmet of The King's Own Norfolk Imperial Yeomanry. (Wallis & Wallis) $357 £250

A khaki tropical helmet of The N. Rhodesia Police, with chromed ERII badge and dark blue puggaree. (Wallis & Wallis) $45 £30

A Bavarian Engineer officer's pickelhaube, with silvered helmet plate, spike and leather and silk lining. (Wallis & Wallis) $429 £290

A German state police black patent leather shako, bearing plate helmet plate and aluminium mounts. (Wallis & Wallis) $36 £24

A post-1902 officer's blue cloth ball-topped helmet of The Royal Army Medical Corps. (Wallis & Wallis) $207 £140

An officer's 1871 pattern helmet of The 3rd (Prince of Wales's) Dragoon Guards. (Wallis & Wallis) $1,630 £1,000

An Indian Army officer's 1871 pattern helmet of The Scinde Horse. (Wallis & Wallis) $2,689 £1,650

An other rank's helmet of The 3rd (Prince of Wales's) Dragoon Guards. (Wallis & Wallis) $554 £340

A Prussian Guard Pioneer Bn. officer's pickelhaube. (Wallis & Wallis) $1,141 £700

A plated French Sapeurs Pompiers helmet, bearing brass mounts and helmet plate. (Wallis & Wallis) $51 £34

An officer's pickelhaube of The 3rd Bn. of The 92nd Brunswick Infantry. (Wallis & Wallis) $1,304 £800

An officer's 1834 pattern helmet of The 1st or Royal Regt. of Dragoons. (Wallis & Wallis) $750 £525

A Georgian officer's 1818 Roman, pattern helmet of The 7th (or Princess Royal's) Dragoon Guards. (Wallis & Wallis) $4,238 £2,600

A Saxony Infantry officer's pickelhaube with gilt and silvered helmet plate. (Wallis & Wallis) $786 £550

HELMETS

A post-1902 trooper's lance-cap of The 16th (The Queen's) Lancers. (Wallis & Wallis)
$423 £260

A Prussian Cuirassier officer's helmet, gilt eagle badge, chinscales and German silver fluted spike. (Wallis & Wallis)
$2,502 £1,750

A late Victorian officer's lance-cap of The 9th (Queen's Royal) Lancers. (Wallis & Wallis)
$1,548 £950

A Prussian Guard Artillery officer's pickelhaube, gilt guard eagle badge with enamelled centre. (Wallis & Wallis) $1,144 £800

A French Restoration period helmet of the Garde Nationale. (Wallis & Wallis)
$1,430 £1,000

A Military 1897 Wurttemberg Infantry officer's pickelhaube, brass helmet plate, spike and mounts. (Wallis & Wallis) $684 £420

A City of London police blue cloth covered helmet, crested type with blackened brass mounts. (Wallis & Wallis) $114 £76

A French model 1845 Second Empire Dragoon officer's helmet. (Wallis & Wallis) $2,860 £2,000

An officer's 1843 pattern helmet of The 4th Royal Irish Dragoon Guards. (Wallis & Wallis)
$3,423 £2,100

ARMS & ARMOUR

Khedive's Sudan, 2 bars The
Atbara, Khartoum.
(Wallis & Wallis) $103 £70

New Zealand 1861 to 1866.
(Wallis & Wallis) $148 £100

Punjab 1849, 2 bars Mooltan,
Goojerat. (Wallis & Wallis)
$162 £110

Crimea, 4 bars Alma, Bala-
klava, Inkermann, and
Sebastopol. (Wallis &
Wallis) $244 £160

Three: Crimea, 3 bars Alma, Ink., Seb.,
Indian Mutiny, bar Central India, Turkish
Crimea, Sardinian issue. (Wallis & Wallis)
$177 £120

Punjab 1849 2 bars, Mooltan,
Goojerat, 1st Bn. 60th R.
Rifles. (Wallis & Wallis)
$170 £115

A.G.S. 1902, 2 bars Somaliland 1902-04, Jidballi.
(Wallis & Wallis) $145 £95

China 1900, no bar. (Wallis
& Wallis) $236 £160

N.G.S. 1793, 1 bar Egypt.
(Wallis & Wallis) $384 £260

MEDALS

East & West Africa medal 1887, 2 bars, 1892, 1893-4. (Wallis & Wallis) $120 £80

A.G.S. 1902, 1 bar Somaliland, 1902-04. (Wallis & Wallis) $66 £45

Indian Mutiny 1857, 2 bars Delhi, Lucknow. (Wallis & Wallis) $118 £80

Ashantee War medal 1873-74, 1 bar Coomassie. (Wallis & Wallis) $175 £115

Queen's Mediterranean medal. (Wallis & Wallis) $118 £80

Anglo-Boer War medal, 1899-1902. (Wallis & Wallis) $50 £40

M.G.S. 1793, five bars Pyrenees, Nivelle, Nive, Orthes, Toulouse. (Wallis & Wallis) $355 £240

China 1842, Wm. McCulloch, 26th Regt. Foot. (Wallis & Wallis) $229 £155

East and West Africa 1887-1900, 1 bar Benin 1897. (Wallis & Wallis) $111 £75

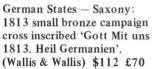

German States — Saxony: 1813 small bronze campaign cross inscribed 'Gott Mit uns 1813. Heil Germanien'. (Wallis & Wallis) $112 £70

Three: M.M. George V first type, I.G.S. 1908 1 bar Waziristan 1919-21, Army L.S. & G.C., George V Regular Army suspender. (Wallis & Wallis) $211 £130

German States — Saxony: 1814 campaign medal (private soldier's issue). (Wallis & Wallis) $128 £80

Seven: Queen's Sudan, Q.S.A. 6 bars, K.S.A. both date bars, 1914-15 star trio, Khedive's Sudan 1 bar Khartoum, together with a civic 'Victory' medal of Loughborough. (Wallis & Wallis) $257 £160

Order of the Bath, C. B. military neck badge in gilt and enamels. (Wallis & Wallis) $257 £160

Pair: Army of India, 1 bar Ava, Indian Mutiny 1 bar Central India. (Wallis & Wallis) $1,100 £675

Indian Mutiny 1857-58, no bar, together with 25 pages of service details. (Wallis & Wallis) $305 £190

MEDALS

British North Borneo 1900, bronze issue, 1 bar Tambunan. (Wallis & Wallis) $114 £70

Pair: A.G.S. 1902, 1 bar Somaliland 1908-10, N.G.S. 1917, 1 bar Persian Gulf 1909-14. (Wallis & Wallis) $171 £105

Spain: Order of Isabella the Catholic, neck badge, in gilt and enamels. (Wallis & Wallis) $67 £42

Orders and medals to Lieutenant-General Sir Robert Garrett. (Christie's) $12,672 £7,920

Naval General Service Medal 1793, 1 bar Egypt. (Wallis & Wallis) $326 £200

Pair: Crimea 3 bars, Balaklava, Inkermann, Sebastopol, Turkish Crimea. (Wallis & Wallis) $354 £220

Military General Service Medal 1793, 4 bars, Pyrenees, Nivelle, Orthes, Toulouse. (Wallis & Wallis) $391 £240

MEDALS

Military General Service
Medal 1793, 3 bars Talavera,
Salamanca, Vittoria. (Wallis
& Wallis) $391 £240

U.S.A.: silver Indian peace
medallion, obverse head of
Franklin Pierce, 14th Presi-
dent of the United States.
(Wallis & Wallis)
          $3,542 £2,200

M.G.S. 1793, 5 bars Fuentes
D'onor, Cuidad Rodrigo,
Badajoz, Salamanca,
Vittoria. (Wallis & Wallis)
          $402 £250

Coronation medal 1902,
Mayors' and Provosts' issue,
in silver. (Wallis & Wallis)
          $10 £7

Four: C.B.E., King's Police medal
George V, Jubilee 1935 and Coronation
1937. (Wallis & Wallis) $489 £300

Army of India with bar
Ava. (Wallis & Wallis)
          $181 £120

Militia Long Service medal,
Edward VII issue. (Wallis &
Wallis) $91 £60

Miniature group of four: Baltic
1854-55, Crimea, China 1857,
Turkish Crimea Sardinian issue.
(Wallis & Wallis) $273 £170

South Africa 1877-9, 1 bar
1879. (Wallis & Wallis)
          $146 £90

PISTOLS

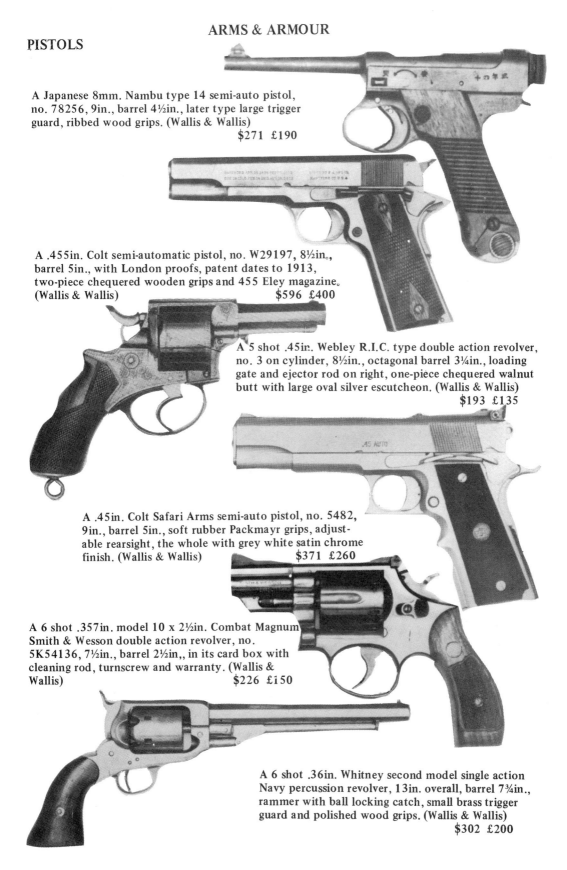

A Japanese 8mm. Nambu type 14 semi-auto pistol, no. 78256, 9in., barrel 4½in., later type large trigger guard, ribbed wood grips. (Wallis & Wallis)
$271 £190

A .455in. Colt semi-automatic pistol, no. W29197, 8½in., barrel 5in., with London proofs, patent dates to 1913, two-piece chequered wooden grips and 455 Eley magazine. (Wallis & Wallis)
$596 £400

A 5 shot .45in. Webley R.I.C. type double action revolver, no. 3 on cylinder, 8½in., octagonal barrel 3¼in., loading gate and ejector rod on right, one-piece chequered walnut butt with large oval silver escutcheon. (Wallis & Wallis)
$193 £135

A .45in. Colt Safari Arms semi-auto pistol, no. 5482, 9in., barrel 5in., soft rubber Packmayr grips, adjustable rearsight, the whole with grey white satin chrome finish. (Wallis & Wallis)
$371 £260

A 6 shot .357in. model 10 x 2½in. Combat Magnum Smith & Wesson double action revolver, no. 5K54136, 7½in., barrel 2½in,, in its card box with cleaning rod, turnscrew and warranty. (Wallis & Wallis)
$226 £150

A 6 shot .36in. Whitney second model single action Navy percussion revolver, 13in. overall, barrel 7¾in., rammer with ball locking catch, small brass trigger guard and polished wood grips. (Wallis & Wallis)
$302 £200

A .30in. Luger semi-automatic pistol by Mauser, no. 10.002421, retailed by Interarms, 10½in., barrel 6in., with wooden grips, in its factory carton with stripping tool and booklet. (Wallis & Wallis) $372 £250

A 5 shot 54-bore Adams model 1851 self-cocking percussion revolver, no. 13014, 12½in., barrel 6¾in., London proved, sprung hammer safety, one-piece chequered walnut grip with sprung cap trap. (Wallis & Wallis) $221 £155

A .450/455 centre fire double action 6-shot Webley & Scott target model revolver, no. 445960, barrel 7½in., brown bakelite grips, butt strap stamped Xlent, lanyard ring. (Wallis & Wallis) $356 £230

A .455in. Webley Mark I double action centre fire revolver, no. 1676, 9in., barrel 4in., moulded bakelite grips. (Wallis & Wallis) $166 £110

A Belgian 6 shot 11mm. double action pin fire revolver, 10½in. overall, barrel 6in., Liege proved, scroll engraved frame and cylinder, loading gate and ejector rod on right side, bag-shaped butt with chequered walnut grips. (Wallis & Wallis) $279 £180

A 6 shot 80-bore single action long spur open frame transitional percussion revolver, 11½in. overall, octagonal barrel 5¼in., engraved Reilly, New Oxford St., London, London proved. (Wallis & Wallis) $312 £210

PISTOLS

A 9mm. long barrelled Artillery Luger, no. 818 and 566, 12½in., barrel 8in., dated 1917 at breech, sights to 800 m., swivel safety, frame not slotted for shoulder stock, two-piece chequered wooden grips. (Wallis & Wallis) $196 £130

A 5 shot .31in. Nepperhan Fire Arms Co. single action percussion revolver, 11in. overall, barrel 6in., no. 1363, engraved frame, brass trigger guard, plain wood grips. (Wallis & Wallis) $302 £200

A 6 shot .44in. Smith & Wesson Russian Model single action revolver, 12¼in., barrel 7in., patent dates to 1869, spurred trigger guard, two-piece wooden grips and steel lanyard ring. (Wallis & Wallis) $241 £160

A .177in. Westley Richards 'Highest Possible' air pistol, no. 748, 11½in., barrel 9¾in. to breech, adjustable rearsight, two-piece chequered horn grips, in its original cardboard carton. (Wallis & Wallis) $267 £175

A 6 shot .36in. Colt model 1851 British Military issue single action Navy percussion revolver, 13½in. overall, barrel 7½in., no. 187145, London proved. (Wallis & Wallis) $1,023 £660

A 6 shot .36in. Savage double action Navy percussion revolver, 14½in. overall, barrel 7in., no. 6560, large trigger guard incorporating cocking lever, reciprocating cylinder and wood grips. (Wallis & Wallis) $422 £280

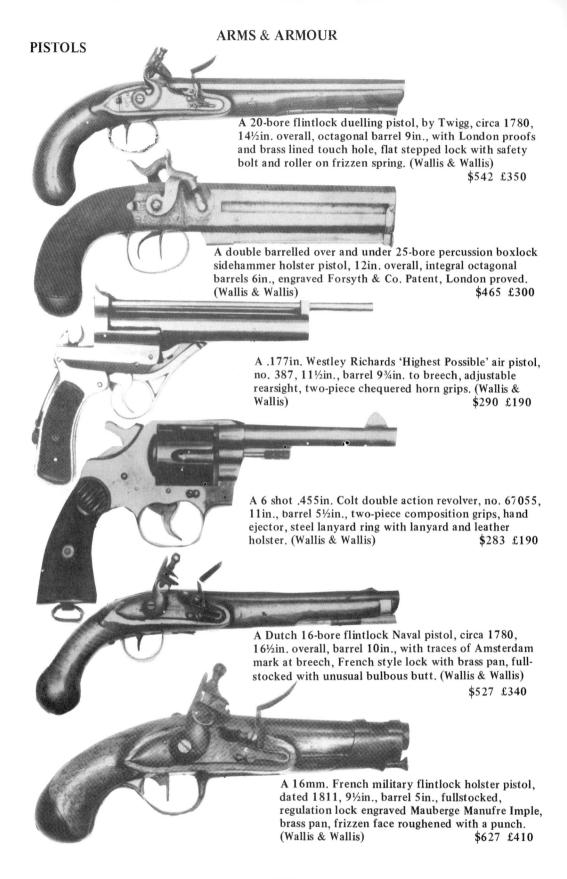

A 20-bore flintlock duelling pistol, by Twigg, circa 1780, 14½in. overall, octagonal barrel 9in., with London proofs and brass lined touch hole, flat stepped lock with safety bolt and roller on frizzen spring. (Wallis & Wallis)
$542 £350

A double barrelled over and under 25-bore percussion boxlock sidehammer holster pistol, 12in. overall, integral octagonal barrels 6in., engraved Forsyth & Co. Patent, London proved. (Wallis & Wallis) $465 £300

A .177in. Westley Richards 'Highest Possible' air pistol, no. 387, 11½in., barrel 9¾in. to breech, adjustable rearsight, two-piece chequered horn grips. (Wallis & Wallis) $290 £190

A 6 shot .455in. Colt double action revolver, no. 67055, 11in., barrel 5½in., two-piece composition grips, hand ejector, steel lanyard ring with lanyard and leather holster. (Wallis & Wallis) $283 £190

A Dutch 16-bore flintlock Naval pistol, circa 1780, 16½in. overall, barrel 10in., with traces of Amsterdam mark at breech, French style lock with brass pan, full-stocked with unusual bulbous butt. (Wallis & Wallis)
$527 £340

A 16mm. French military flintlock holster pistol, dated 1811, 9½in., barrel 5in., fullstocked, regulation lock engraved Mauberge Manufre Imple, brass pan, frizzen face roughened with a punch. (Wallis & Wallis) $627 £410

PISTOLS

A 6 shot 90-bore self-cocking open frame top snap transitional percussion revolver, 11½in. overall, octagonal barrel 5½in., Birmingham proved, with chequered wood grips. (Wallis & Wallis) $193 £130

A 5-shot .31in. Allen & Wheelock single action side hammer percussion belt revolver, 10in. overall, octagonal barrel 5in., hinged trigger guard/loading lever, plain flared wood grips. (Wallis & Wallis) $232 £150

A .455 Webley Mk. VI double action 6-shot Army revolver, barrel 6in., chequered black bakelite grips with lanyard ring, in its original leather holster, with lanyard and cleaning rod. (Wallis & Wallis) $85 £55

A 5 shot .36in. Manhattan Arms Co. single action Navy percussion revolver, no. 13020, 12in., octagonal barrel 6½in., underlever rammer, wedge frame and brass trigger guard and grip strap. (Wallis & Wallis)
$459 £300

A 6 shot 56-bore open wedge frame single action top snap transitional percussion revolver, 12in. overall, octagonal barrel 5in., Birmingham proved, chequered walnut butt with vacant escutcheon. (Wallis & Wallis) $286 £190

A 6 shot 80-bore single action long spur wedge frame percussion revolver 11in. overall, octagonal barrel 5in., engraved J. Lang, London, with chequered walnut butt. (Wallis & Wallis) $387 £260

ARMS & ARMOUR

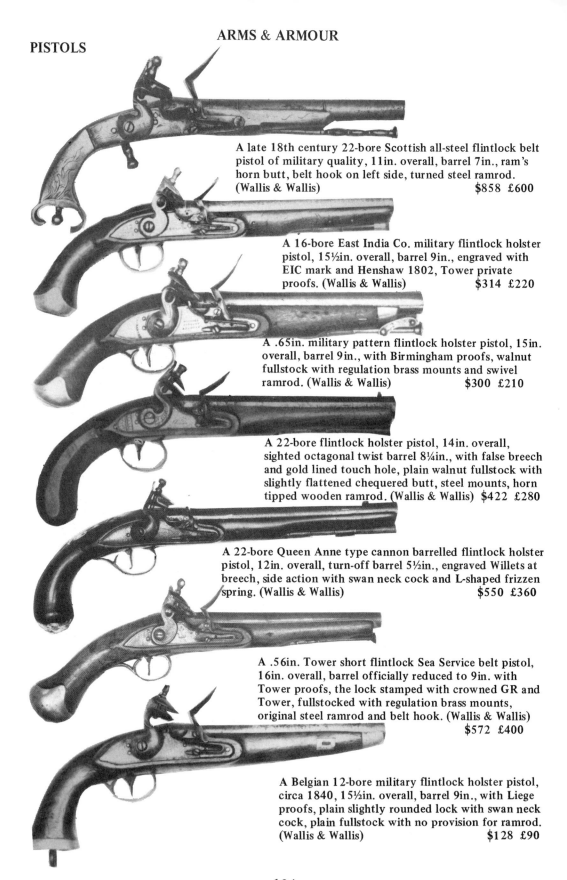

A late 18th century 22-bore Scottish all-steel flintlock belt pistol of military quality, 11in. overall, barrel 7in., ram's horn butt, belt hook on left side, turned steel ramrod. (Wallis & Wallis) $858 £600

A 16-bore East India Co. military flintlock holster pistol, 15½in. overall, barrel 9in., engraved with EIC mark and Henshaw 1802, Tower private proofs. (Wallis & Wallis) $314 £220

A .65in. military pattern flintlock holster pistol, 15in. overall, barrel 9in., with Birmingham proofs, walnut fullstock with regulation brass mounts and swivel ramrod. (Wallis & Wallis) $300 £210

A 22-bore flintlock holster pistol, 14in. overall, sighted octagonal twist barrel 8¼in., with false breech and gold lined touch hole, plain walnut fullstock with slightly flattened chequered butt, steel mounts, horn tipped wooden ramrod. (Wallis & Wallis) $422 £280

A 22-bore Queen Anne type cannon barrelled flintlock holster pistol, 12in. overall, turn-off barrel 5½in., engraved Willets at breech, side action with swan neck cock and L-shaped frizzen spring. (Wallis & Wallis) $550 £360

A .56in. Tower short flintlock Sea Service belt pistol, 16in. overall, barrel officially reduced to 9in. with Tower proofs, the lock stamped with crowned GR and Tower, fullstocked with regulation brass mounts, original steel ramrod and belt hook. (Wallis & Wallis) $572 £400

A Belgian 12-bore military flintlock holster pistol, circa 1840, 15½in. overall, barrel 9in., with Liege proofs, plain slightly rounded lock with swan neck cock, plain fullstock with no provision for ramrod. (Wallis & Wallis) $128 £90

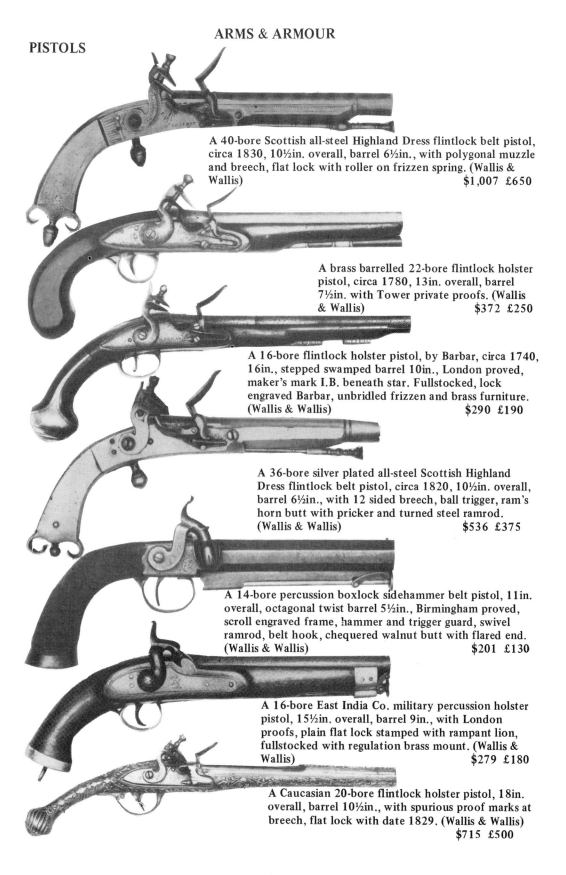

A 40-bore Scottish all-steel Highland Dress flintlock belt pistol, circa 1830, 10½in. overall, barrel 6½in., with polygonal muzzle and breech, flat lock with roller on frizzen spring. (Wallis & Wallis) $1,007 £650

A brass barrelled 22-bore flintlock holster pistol, circa 1780, 13in. overall, barrel 7½in. with Tower private proofs. (Wallis & Wallis) $372 £250

A 16-bore flintlock holster pistol, by Barbar, circa 1740, 16in., stepped swamped barrel 10in., London proved, maker's mark I.B. beneath star. Fullstocked, lock engraved Barbar, unbridled frizzen and brass furniture. (Wallis & Wallis) $290 £190

A 36-bore silver plated all-steel Scottish Highland Dress flintlock belt pistol, circa 1820, 10½in. overall, barrel 6½in., with 12 sided breech, ball trigger, ram's horn butt with pricker and turned steel ramrod. (Wallis & Wallis) $536 £375

A 14-bore percussion boxlock sidehammer belt pistol, 11in. overall, octagonal twist barrel 5½in., Birmingham proved, scroll engraved frame, hammer and trigger guard, swivel ramrod, belt hook, chequered walnut butt with flared end. (Wallis & Wallis) $201 £130

A 16-bore East India Co. military percussion holster pistol, 15½in. overall, barrel 9in., with London proofs, plain flat lock stamped with rampant lion, fullstocked with regulation brass mount. (Wallis & Wallis) $279 £180

A Caucasian 20-bore flintlock holster pistol, 18in. overall, barrel 10½in., with spurious proof marks at breech, flat lock with date 1829. (Wallis & Wallis) $715 £500

ARMS & ARMOUR

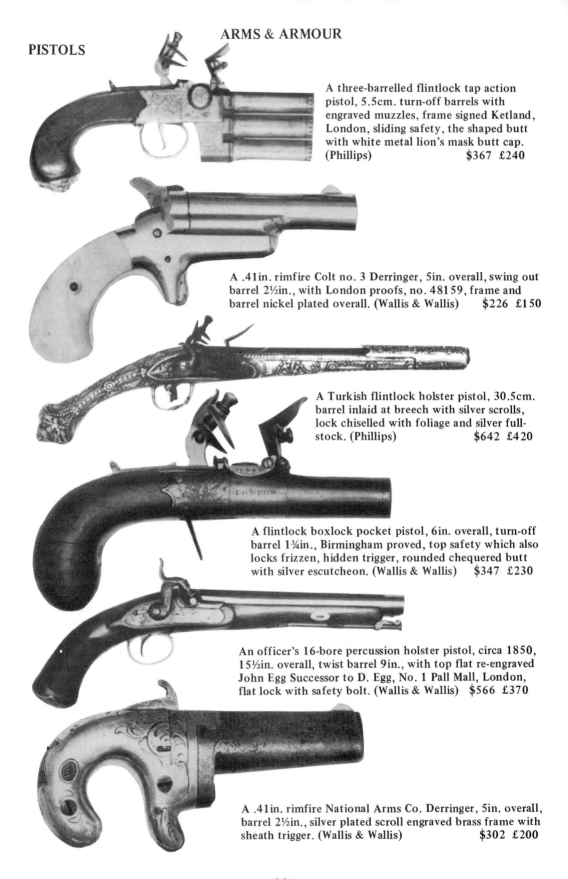

A three-barrelled flintlock tap action pistol, 5.5cm. turn-off barrels with engraved muzzles, frame signed Ketland, London, sliding safety, the shaped butt with white metal lion's mask butt cap. (Phillips) $367 £240

A .41in. rimfire Colt no. 3 Derringer, 5in. overall, swing out barrel 2½in., with London proofs, no. 48159, frame and barrel nickel plated overall. (Wallis & Wallis) $226 £150

A Turkish flintlock holster pistol, 30.5cm. barrel inlaid at breech with silver scrolls, lock chiselled with foliage and silver full-stock. (Phillips) $642 £420

A flintlock boxlock pocket pistol, 6in. overall, turn-off barrel 1¾in., Birmingham proved, top safety which also locks frizzen, hidden trigger, rounded chequered butt with silver escutcheon. (Wallis & Wallis) $347 £230

An officer's 16-bore percussion holster pistol, circa 1850, 15½in. overall, twist barrel 9in., with top flat re-engraved John Egg Successor to D. Egg, No. 1 Pall Mall, London, flat lock with safety bolt. (Wallis & Wallis) $566 £370

A .41in. rimfire National Arms Co. Derringer, 5in. overall, barrel 2½in., silver plated scroll engraved brass frame with sheath trigger. (Wallis & Wallis) $302 £200

PISTOLS

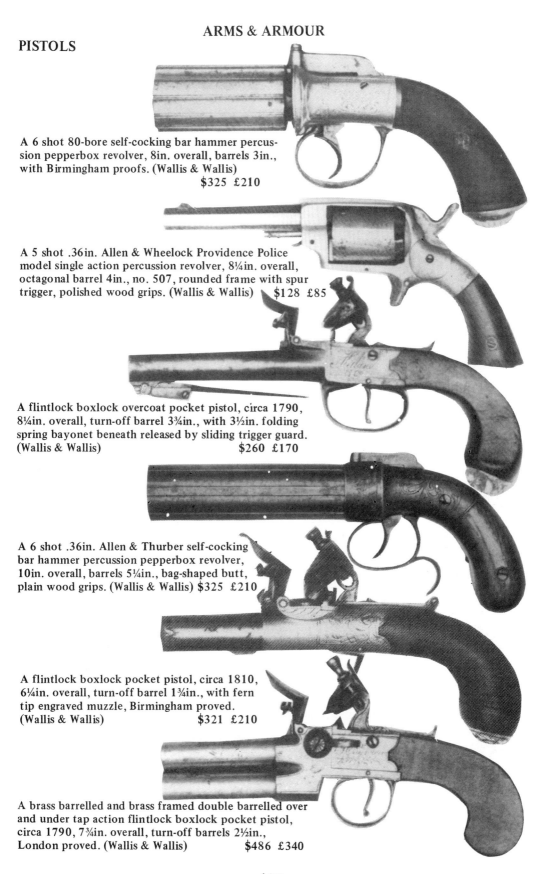

A 6 shot 80-bore self-cocking bar hammer percussion pepperbox revolver, 8in. overall, barrels 3in., with Birmingham proofs. (Wallis & Wallis)
$325 £210

A 5 shot .36in. Allen & Wheelock Providence Police model single action percussion revolver, 8¼in. overall, octagonal barrel 4in., no. 507, rounded frame with spur trigger, polished wood grips. (Wallis & Wallis) $128 £85

A flintlock boxlock overcoat pocket pistol, circa 1790, 8¼in. overall, turn-off barrel 3¾in., with 3½in. folding spring bayonet beneath released by sliding trigger guard. (Wallis & Wallis) $260 £170

A 6 shot .36in. Allen & Thurber self-cocking bar hammer percussion pepperbox revolver, 10in. overall, barrels 5¼in., bag-shaped butt, plain wood grips. (Wallis & Wallis) $325 £210

A flintlock boxlock pocket pistol, circa 1810, 6¼in. overall, turn-off barrel 1¾in., with fern tip engraved muzzle, Birmingham proved. (Wallis & Wallis) $321 £210

A brass barrelled and brass framed double barrelled over and under tap action flintlock boxlock pocket pistol, circa 1790, 7¾in. overall, turn-off barrels 2½in., London proved. (Wallis & Wallis) $486 £340

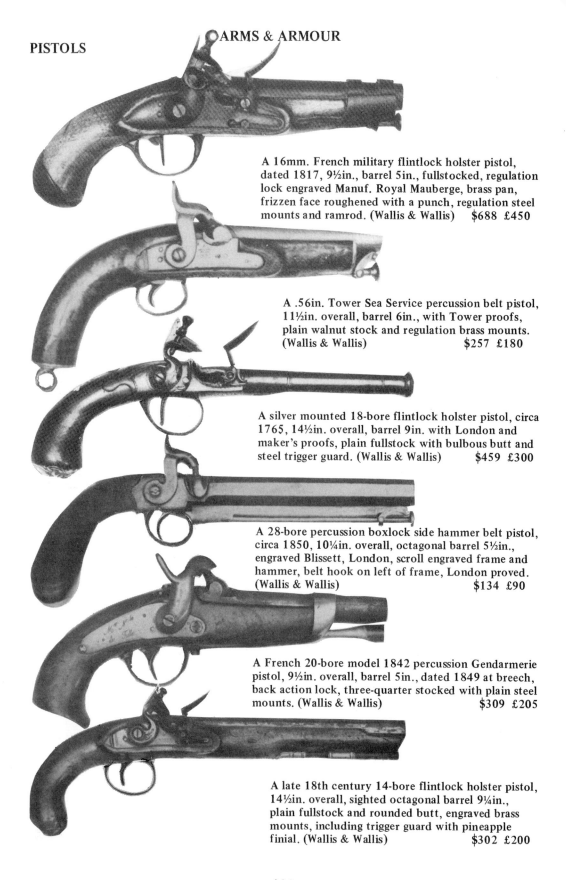

A 16mm. French military flintlock holster pistol, dated 1817, 9½in., barrel 5in., fullstocked, regulation lock engraved Manuf. Royal Mauberge, brass pan, frizzen face roughened with a punch, regulation steel mounts and ramrod. (Wallis & Wallis) $688 £450

A .56in. Tower Sea Service percussion belt pistol, 11½in. overall, barrel 6in., with Tower proofs, plain walnut stock and regulation brass mounts. (Wallis & Wallis) $257 £180

A silver mounted 18-bore flintlock holster pistol, circa 1765, 14½in. overall, barrel 9in. with London and maker's proofs, plain fullstock with bulbous butt and steel trigger guard. (Wallis & Wallis) $459 £300

A 28-bore percussion boxlock side hammer belt pistol, circa 1850, 10¼in. overall, octagonal barrel 5½in., engraved Blissett, London, scroll engraved frame and hammer, belt hook on left of frame, London proved. (Wallis & Wallis) $134 £90

A French 20-bore model 1842 percussion Gendarmerie pistol, 9½in. overall, barrel 5in., dated 1849 at breech, back action lock, three-quarter stocked with plain steel mounts. (Wallis & Wallis) $309 £205

A late 18th century 14-bore flintlock holster pistol, 14½in. overall, sighted octagonal barrel 9¼in., plain fullstock and rounded butt, engraved brass mounts, including trigger guard with pineapple finial. (Wallis & Wallis) $302 £200

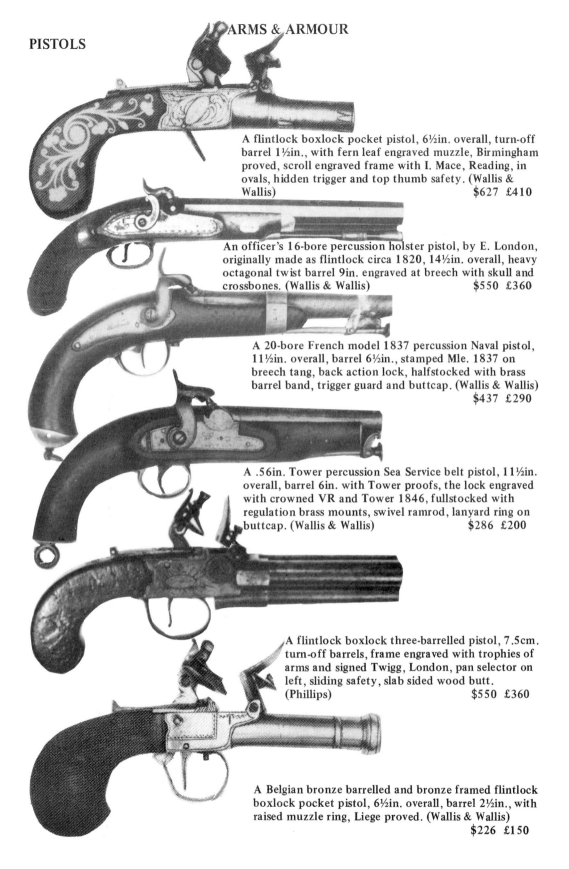

A flintlock boxlock pocket pistol, 6½in. overall, turn-off barrel 1½in., with fern leaf engraved muzzle, Birmingham proved, scroll engraved frame with I. Mace, Reading, in ovals, hidden trigger and top thumb safety. (Wallis & Wallis) $627 £410

An officer's 16-bore percussion holster pistol, by E. London, originally made as flintlock circa 1820, 14½in. overall, heavy octagonal twist barrel 9in. engraved at breech with skull and crossbones. (Wallis & Wallis) $550 £360

A 20-bore French model 1837 percussion Naval pistol, 11½in. overall, barrel 6½in., stamped Mle. 1837 on breech tang, back action lock, halfstocked with brass barrel band, trigger guard and buttcap. (Wallis & Wallis) $437 £290

A .56in. Tower percussion Sea Service belt pistol, 11½in. overall, barrel 6in. with Tower proofs, the lock engraved with crowned VR and Tower 1846, fullstocked with regulation brass mounts, swivel ramrod, lanyard ring on buttcap. (Wallis & Wallis) $286 £200

A flintlock boxlock three-barrelled pistol, 7.5cm. turn-off barrels, frame engraved with trophies of arms and signed Twigg, London, pan selector on left, sliding safety, slab sided wood butt. (Phillips) $550 £360

A Belgian bronze barrelled and bronze framed flintlock boxlock pocket pistol, 6½in. overall, barrel 2½in., with raised muzzle ring, Liege proved. (Wallis & Wallis) $226 £150

POWDER FLASKS

A gun sized copper powder flask, 6¼in., plain lacquered body, nozzle adjustable from 2 to 2¾ drams. (Wallis & Wallis) $114 £70

An early 18th century Scandinavian carved powder horn, 8½in. overall. (Wallis & Wallis) $843 £590

A copper pocket powder flask, 3½in., shaped body, brass top fixed nozzle with gnurled band. (Wallis & Wallis) $105 £65

An 18th century staghorn powder flask, 10½in. overall, with two horn hanging loops. (Wallis & Wallis) $178 £125

A 19th century copy of a German 17th century musketeer's triangular powder flask, 11in. high. (Wallis & Wallis) $28 £20

A 17th century Italian fluted steel powder flask, 7in. overall. (Wallis & Wallis)
$471 £330

A 3-way copper pistol flask of the type cased with late duelling pistols. (Wallis & Wallis) $154 £95

A Spanish 18th century powder flask, made from a section of Ibex or similar horn, 10½in. overall. (Wallis & Wallis) $114 £80

A copper gun sized powder flask, 8in., patent brass top, graduated nozzle. (Wallis & Wallis) $171 £105

A copper powder flask 'Panel' (R.504), lacquered brass universal pattern charger unit. (Wallis & Wallis) $113 £75

An early 19th century brass mounted rifleman's powder horn, 11in. overall, charger for 1 to 4 drams. (Wallis & Wallis) $45 £32

An engraved bone Continental powder flask, circa 1600, 6¾in. tall. (Wallis & Wallis) $326 £200

An 18th century engraved bone powder flask, 8¼in. overall, with six hanging rings. (Wallis & Wallis) $150 £105

A large copper gun sized powder flask, 8¼in., embossed overall with basket weave, nozzle graduated 3 to 4 drams. (Wallis & Wallis) $89 £55

An 18th century staghorn powder flask, 9in. overall, wooden charger and iron hanging loops. (Wallis & Wallis) $114 £80

A pistol sized copper powder flask, 4¾in., lacquered brass top stamped 'Dixon & Sons', with adjustable nozzle. (Wallis & Wallis) $122 £75

An 18th century staghorn powder flask, 7½in. overall, with small down turned nozzle and iron hanging loops. (Wallis & Wallis) $42 £30

A 17th century Italian brass mounted steel powder flask, 7in. overall, with belt hook. (Wallis & Wallis) $343 £240

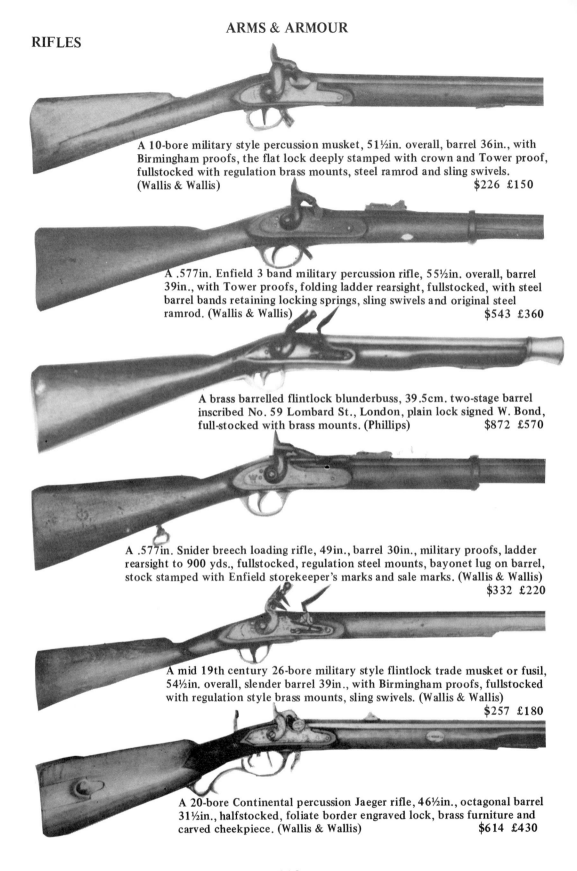

A 10-bore military style percussion musket, 51½in. overall, barrel 36in., with Birmingham proofs, the flat lock deeply stamped with crown and Tower proof, fullstocked with regulation brass mounts, steel ramrod and sling swivels. (Wallis & Wallis) $226 £150

A .577in. Enfield 3 band military percussion rifle, 55½in. overall, barrel 39in., with Tower proofs, folding ladder rearsight, fullstocked, with steel barrel bands retaining locking springs, sling swivels and original steel ramrod. (Wallis & Wallis) $543 £360

A brass barrelled flintlock blunderbuss, 39.5cm. two-stage barrel inscribed No. 59 Lombard St., London, plain lock signed W. Bond, full-stocked with brass mounts. (Phillips) $872 £570

A .577in. Snider breech loading rifle, 49in., barrel 30in., military proofs, ladder rearsight to 900 yds., fullstocked, regulation steel mounts, bayonet lug on barrel, stock stamped with Enfield storekeeper's marks and sale marks. (Wallis & Wallis) $332 £220

A mid 19th century 26-bore military style flintlock trade musket or fusil, 54½in. overall, slender barrel 39in., with Birmingham proofs, fullstocked with regulation style brass mounts, sling swivels. (Wallis & Wallis) $257 £180

A 20-bore Continental percussion Jaeger rifle, 46½in., octagonal barrel 31½in., halfstocked, foliate border engraved lock, brass furniture and carved cheekpiece. (Wallis & Wallis) $614 £430

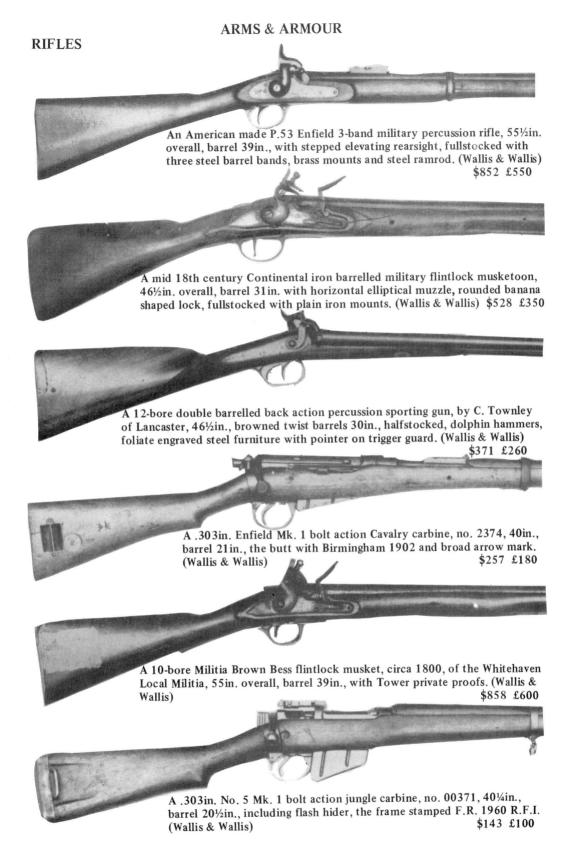

An American made P.53 Enfield 3-band military percussion rifle, 55½in. overall, barrel 39in., with stepped elevating rearsight, fullstocked with three steel barrel bands, brass mounts and steel ramrod. (Wallis & Wallis)
$852 £550

A mid 18th century Continental iron barrelled military flintlock musketoon, 46½in. overall, barrel 31in. with horizontal elliptical muzzle, rounded banana shaped lock, fullstocked with plain iron mounts. (Wallis & Wallis) $528 £350

A 12-bore double barrelled back action percussion sporting gun, by C. Townley of Lancaster, 46½in., browned twist barrels 30in., halfstocked, dolphin hammers, foliate engraved steel furniture with pointer on trigger guard. (Wallis & Wallis)
$371 £260

A .303in. Enfield Mk. 1 bolt action Cavalry carbine, no. 2374, 40in., barrel 21in., the butt with Birmingham 1902 and broad arrow mark. (Wallis & Wallis)
$257 £180

A 10-bore Militia Brown Bess flintlock musket, circa 1800, of the Whitehaven Local Militia, 55in. overall, barrel 39in., with Tower private proofs. (Wallis & Wallis)
$858 £600

A .303in. No. 5 Mk. 1 bolt action jungle carbine, no. 00371, 40¼in., barrel 20½in., including flash hider, the frame stamped F.R. 1960 R.F.I. (Wallis & Wallis)
$143 £100

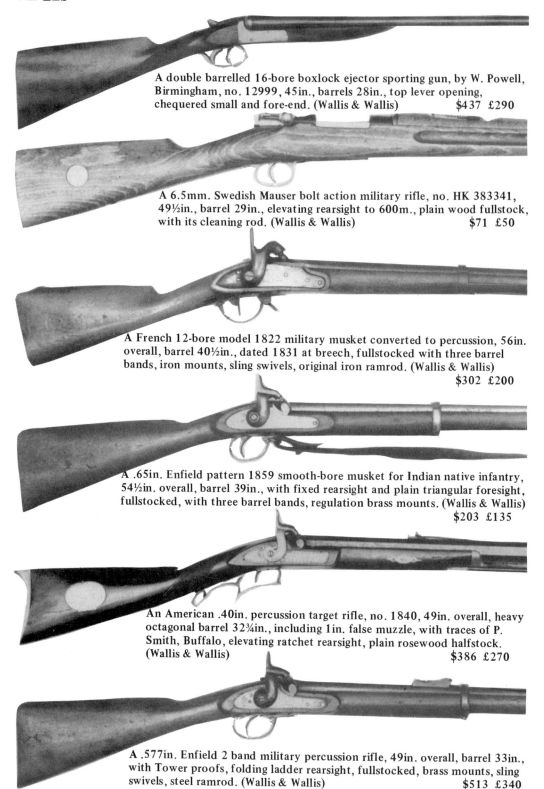

A double barrelled 16-bore boxlock ejector sporting gun, by W. Powell, Birmingham, no. 12999, 45in., barrels 28in., top lever opening, chequered small and fore-end. (Wallis & Wallis) $437 £290

A 6.5mm. Swedish Mauser bolt action military rifle, no. HK 383341, 49½in., barrel 29in., elevating rearsight to 600m., plain wood fullstock, with its cleaning rod. (Wallis & Wallis) $71 £50

A French 12-bore model 1822 military musket converted to percussion, 56in. overall, barrel 40½in., dated 1831 at breech, fullstocked with three barrel bands, iron mounts, sling swivels, original iron ramrod. (Wallis & Wallis) $302 £200

A .65in. Enfield pattern 1859 smooth-bore musket for Indian native infantry, 54½in. overall, barrel 39in., with fixed rearsight and plain triangular foresight, fullstocked, with three barrel bands, regulation brass mounts. (Wallis & Wallis) $203 £135

An American .40in. percussion target rifle, no. 1840, 49in. overall, heavy octagonal barrel 32¾in., including 1in. false muzzle, with traces of P. Smith, Buffalo, elevating ratchet rearsight, plain rosewood halfstock. (Wallis & Wallis) $386 £270

A .577in. Enfield 2 band military percussion rifle, 49in. overall, barrel 33in., with Tower proofs, folding ladder rearsight, fullstocked, brass mounts, sling swivels, steel ramrod. (Wallis & Wallis) $513 £340

A double barrelled 12-bore Needham's Patent breech loading needle
fire sporting gun, no. 1082, 47½in., twist barrels, 28¾in. to breeches,
halfstocked, foliate engraved furniture, engraved silver escutcheon,
chequered small and bolted fore with horn tip. (Wallis & Wallis)
$765 £500

A .577in. Enfield 3-band military percussion rifle, 54in. overall, barrel 39in.,
with elevating rearsight, fullstocked with brass mounts, sling swivels and
original steel ramrod. (Wallis & Wallis) $443 £310

A double barrelled 21-bore percussion rifle, 72cm. damascus
sighted barrels, signed John Dickson & Son, 60 Princes Street,
Edinburgh, folding leaf rear sights to 200 yds., complete with
its brass tipped wooden ramrod, in its oak case. (Phillips)
$994 £650

A .177in. Britannia barrel break air rifle, no. 513, 36in., barrel 21in., stamped
with 30 to 60 yds. on leaf rearsight. (Wallis & Wallis) $196 £130

An American .38in. percussion 'Plains' sporting or target rifle, circa
1840, 49in. overall, heavy octagonal barrel 33in., with fixed sights
and stamped at breech H. Jarecki Erie PA. (Wallis & Wallis)
$357 £250

A 20-bore double barrelled French silver mounted flintlock sporting gun, 48in.,
barrels 31½in., halfstocked, locks engraved Dupont a Paris, with Canon Tordu
faintly on barrels. Silver furniture hallmarked with maker's mark LD. (Wallis &
Wallis) $943 £660

ARMS & ARMOUR

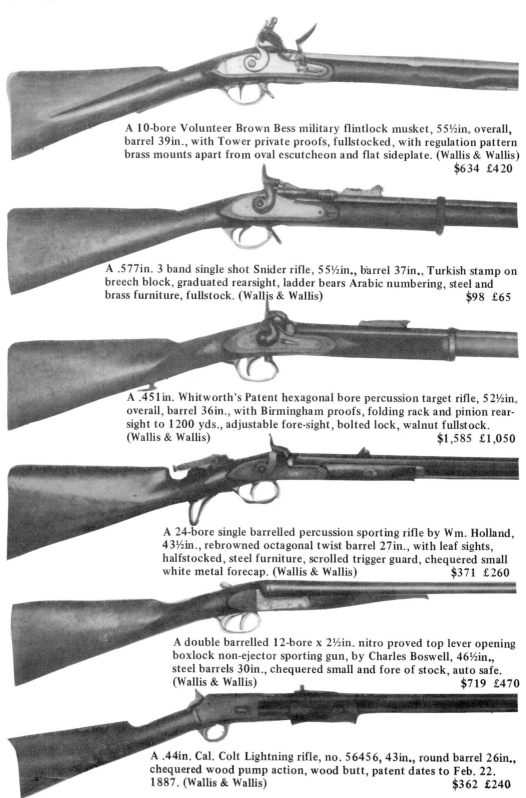

A 10-bore Volunteer Brown Bess military flintlock musket, 55½in. overall, barrel 39in., with Tower private proofs, fullstocked, with regulation pattern brass mounts apart from oval escutcheon and flat sideplate. (Wallis & Wallis)
$634 £420

A .577in. 3 band single shot Snider rifle, 55½in., barrel 37in., Turkish stamp on breech block, graduated rearsight, ladder bears Arabic numbering, steel and brass furniture, fullstock. (Wallis & Wallis)
$98 £65

A .451in. Whitworth's Patent hexagonal bore percussion target rifle, 52½in. overall, barrel 36in., with Birmingham proofs, folding rack and pinion rearsight to 1200 yds., adjustable fore-sight, bolted lock, walnut fullstock. (Wallis & Wallis)
$1,585 £1,050

A 24-bore single barrelled percussion sporting rifle by Wm. Holland, 43½in., rebrowned octagonal twist barrel 27in., with leaf sights, halfstocked, steel furniture, scrolled trigger guard, chequered small white metal forecap. (Wallis & Wallis)
$371 £260

A double barrelled 12-bore x 2½in. nitro proved top lever opening boxlock non-ejector sporting gun, by Charles Boswell, 46½in., steel barrels 30in., chequered small and fore of stock, auto safe. (Wallis & Wallis)
$719 £470

A .44in. Cal. Colt Lightning rifle, no. 56456, 43in., round barrel 26in., chequered wood pump action, wood butt, patent dates to Feb. 22. 1887. (Wallis & Wallis)
$362 £240

RIFLES

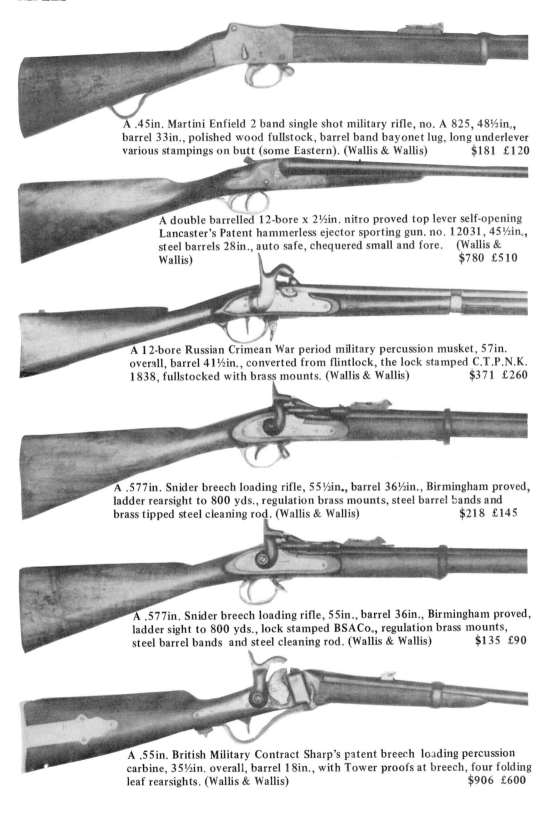

A .45in. Martini Enfield 2 band single shot military rifle, no. A 825, 48½in.,
barrel 33in., polished wood fullstock, barrel band bayonet lug, long underlever
various stampings on butt (some Eastern). (Wallis & Wallis) $181 £120

A double barrelled 12-bore x 2½in. nitro proved top lever self-opening
Lancaster's Patent hammerless ejector sporting gun. no. 12031, 45½in.,
steel barrels 28in., auto safe, chequered small and fore.   (Wallis &
Wallis) $780 £510

A 12-bore Russian Crimean War period military percussion musket, 57in.
overall, barrel 41½in., converted from flintlock, the lock stamped C.T.P.N.K.
1838, fullstocked with brass mounts. (Wallis & Wallis) $371 £260

A .577in. Snider breech loading rifle, 55½in., barrel 36½in., Birmingham proved,
ladder rearsight to 800 yds., regulation brass mounts, steel barrel bands and
brass tipped steel cleaning rod. (Wallis & Wallis) $218 £145

A .577in. Snider breech loading rifle, 55in., barrel 36in., Birmingham proved,
ladder sight to 800 yds., lock stamped BSACo., regulation brass mounts,
steel barrel bands and steel cleaning rod. (Wallis & Wallis) $135 £90

A .55in. British Military Contract Sharp's patent breech loading percussion
carbine, 35½in. overall, barrel 18in., with Tower proofs at breech, four folding
leaf rearsights. (Wallis & Wallis) $906 £600

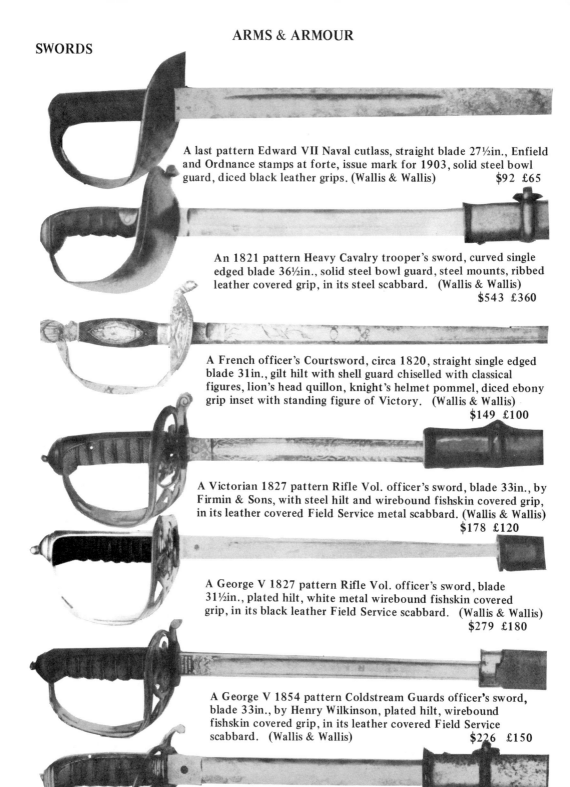

A last pattern Edward VII Naval cutlass, straight blade 27½in., Enfield and Ordnance stamps at forte, issue mark for 1903, solid steel bowl guard, diced black leather grips. (Wallis & Wallis) $92 £65

An 1821 pattern Heavy Cavalry trooper's sword, curved single edged blade 36½in., solid steel bowl guard, steel mounts, ribbed leather covered grip, in its steel scabbard. (Wallis & Wallis) $543 £360

A French officer's Courtsword, circa 1820, straight single edged blade 31in., gilt hilt with shell guard chiselled with classical figures, lion's head quillon, knight's helmet pommel, diced ebony grip inset with standing figure of Victory. (Wallis & Wallis) $149 £100

A Victorian 1827 pattern Rifle Vol. officer's sword, blade 33in., by Firmin & Sons, with steel hilt and wirebound fishskin covered grip, in its leather covered Field Service metal scabbard. (Wallis & Wallis) $178 £120

A George V 1827 pattern Rifle Vol. officer's sword, blade 31½in., plated hilt, white metal wirebound fishskin covered grip, in its black leather Field Service scabbard. (Wallis & Wallis) $279 £180

A George V 1854 pattern Coldstream Guards officer's sword, blade 33in., by Henry Wilkinson, plated hilt, wirebound fishskin covered grip, in its leather covered Field Service scabbard. (Wallis & Wallis) $226 £150

An 1821 pattern Militia Artillery officer's sword, curved fullered polished blade 35½in., regulation steel hilt, woven wirebound sharkskin covered grip, in its steel scabbard with two hanging rings. (Wallis & Wallis) $128 £90

Late 19th century American Society sword, curved fullered single edged blade, 27½in., copper gilt triple bar guard, lion's head pommel, wirebound sharkskin covered grip, in its steel scabbard. (Wallis & Wallis)

$153 £100

A Victorian officer's sword of The 6th Dragoon Guards, as carried 1877-1912, curved blade 34in., pierced steel guard and mounts, copper wirebound fishskin covered grip, in its steel scabbard. (Wallis & Wallis)

$543 £360

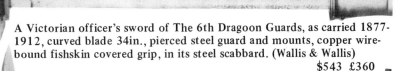

A French ANXI Cuirassier sword, straight double fullered blade 38½in., with spear point, brass hilt with triple bar guard, brass wirebound leather covered grip, in its steel scabbard. (Wallis & Wallis)

$188 £125

A Victorian trooper's sword of The 3rd Bengal Cavalry, straight single edged blade 35in., stamped Wilkinson, Pall Mall, diced black leather grip, in its leather scabbard with steel mounts. (Wallis & Wallis)

$310 £200

An Elizabeth II R.A.F. officer's sword, blade 32in., by Wilkinson Sword, gilt hilt, eagle's head pommel, bullion dress knot, gilt wirebound fishskin covered grip, in its leather scabbard with three gilt mounts. (Wallis & Wallis)

$271 £180

A French 1822 pattern Heavy Cavalry trooper's sabre, slightly curved blade 39in., broad and short fullers, brass hilt with triple bar guard, ribbed leather covered grip, in its steel scabbard. (Wallis & Wallis)

$181 £120

A George V R.A. officer's sword, blade 34in., by Henry Wilkinson, no. 53269, with wirebound fishskin covered grip in its leather covered Field Service scabbard. (Wallis & Wallis)

$163 £110

An o-wakizashi, signed Nobutaka (of Owari, late 16th century), 51cm. long, koshirae, pine-needle design saya with three ribbed shakudo seme and elongated kojiri. (Christie's) $1,504 £1,045

A Bronze Age sword, 26in. overall, swollen blade of elliptical section with stepped edges, incomplete tang pierced for attachment. (Wallis & Wallis) $446 £310

A 14th century katana attributed to Tegai Kanenaga of Yamato, 68.3cm. long, the saya with horn kojiri and koiguchi. (Christie's) $3,168 £2,200

A handachi wakizashi, the blade inscribed Suishinshi Hakuyu Nyudo Masahide saku, 49.5cm. long, koshirae, mijingai-nuri saya with impressed brown leather koshimaki and sahari-ishimeji fittings. (Christie's) $4,435 £3,080

A daisho with fine Higo-style koshirae, probably by Bizen Kiyomitsu, with a date, Teiwa ninen (1346), but 16th century, 71.5cm. long. (Christie's) $7,128 £4,950

A tachi with unsigned 19th century Bizen blade, 70.7cm. long, with shari-nashiji scabbard with aoimon and umemon, with silvered metal mounts and gilt crane menuki. (Christie's) $4,118 £2,860

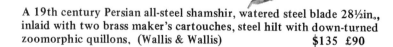

A 19th century Persian all-steel shamshir, watered steel blade 28½in., inlaid with two brass maker's cartouches, steel hilt with down-turned zoomorphic quillons. (Wallis & Wallis) $135 £90

A Bronze Age sword, 16½in. overall, tapered blade of elliptical section with stepped edges, swollen tang retaining two large bronze rivets for retaining hilt. (Wallis & Wallis) $864 £600

SWORDS

A wakizashi, by Yokoyama Sukenaga, dated Tempo kunen (1838), 48.6cm. long, with kuroronuri saya and brocade bag. (Christie's) $6,019 £4,180

A Bronze Age sword, 16½in. overall, very slightly swollen blade with raised broad flattened rib, swollen tang with eroded areas representing twin rivet holes. (Wallis & Wallis) $446 £310

Late 16th century katana with fine shakudo fittings, 68.1cm. long, koshirae, kuroronuri saya decorated with a dragon in hiramakie and with mokkogata shakudo-nanakoji tsuba. (Christie's) $3,009 £2,090

A silver mounted dha, 54cm. blade, silver wrapped hilt with bands of filigree decoration, large fluted silver pommel, contained in its wood scabbard. (Phillips) $367 £240

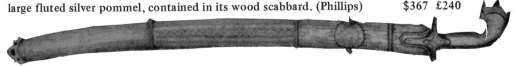

A 19th century Saudi Arabian saif with curved steel blade, the silver mounted hilt and scabbard with formal engraving, overall 34in. (Parsons, Welch & Cowell) $616 £400

Late 14th century sun-nobi tanto blade with carved ebony and ivory koshirae, inscribed Hiromitsu, but probably Soshu school, 34.7cm. long, the saya, 19th century. (Christie's) $1,425 £990

An Indian shamsir, 76cm. blade damascened in silver at the forte with foliage, gilt metal hilt, contained in its gilt scabbard. (Phillips) $198 £130

Early 17th century o-wakizashi, signed Kanesaki (of Mino), 52.6cm. long, with kuroronuri saya decorated in hiramakie with three tiny frogs in flight from a large serpent, the hilt with buffalo horn kashira and shiiremono fuchi. (Christie's) $1,425 £990

ARMS & ARMOUR

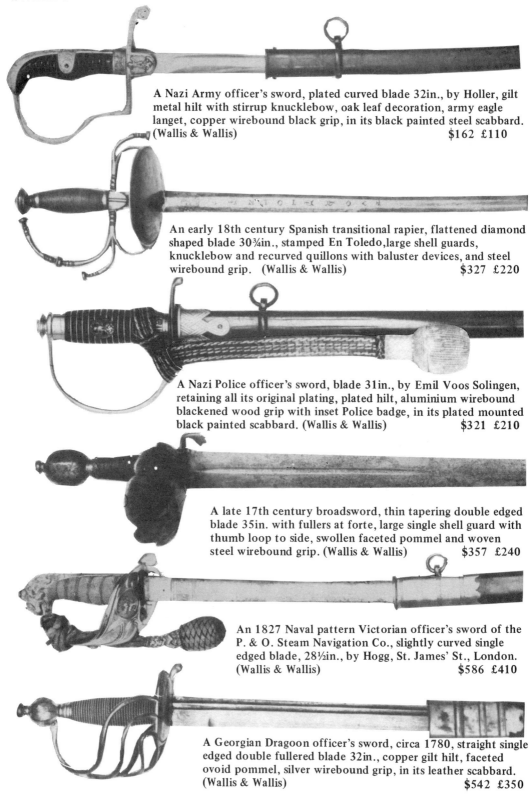

A Nazi Army officer's sword, plated curved blade 32in., by Holler, gilt metal hilt with stirrup knucklebow, oak leaf decoration, army eagle langet, copper wirebound black grip, in its black painted steel scabbard. (Wallis & Wallis) $162 £110

An early 18th century Spanish transitional rapier, flattened diamond shaped blade 30¾in., stamped En Toledo,large shell guards, knucklebow and recurved quillons with baluster devices, and steel wirebound grip. (Wallis & Wallis) $327 £220

A Nazi Police officer's sword, blade 31in., by Emil Voos Solingen, retaining all its original plating, plated hilt, aluminium wirebound blackened wood grip with inset Police badge, in its plated mounted black painted scabbard. (Wallis & Wallis) $321 £210

A late 17th century broadsword, thin tapering double edged blade 35in. with fullers at forte, large single shell guard with thumb loop to side, swollen faceted pommel and woven steel wirebound grip. (Wallis & Wallis) $357 £240

An 1827 Naval pattern Victorian officer's sword of the P. & O. Steam Navigation Co., slightly curved single edged blade, 28½in., by Hogg, St. James' St., London. (Wallis & Wallis) $586 £410

A Georgian Dragoon officer's sword, circa 1780, straight single edged double fullered blade 32in., copper gilt hilt, faceted ovoid pommel, silver wirebound grip, in its leather scabbard. (Wallis & Wallis) $542 £350

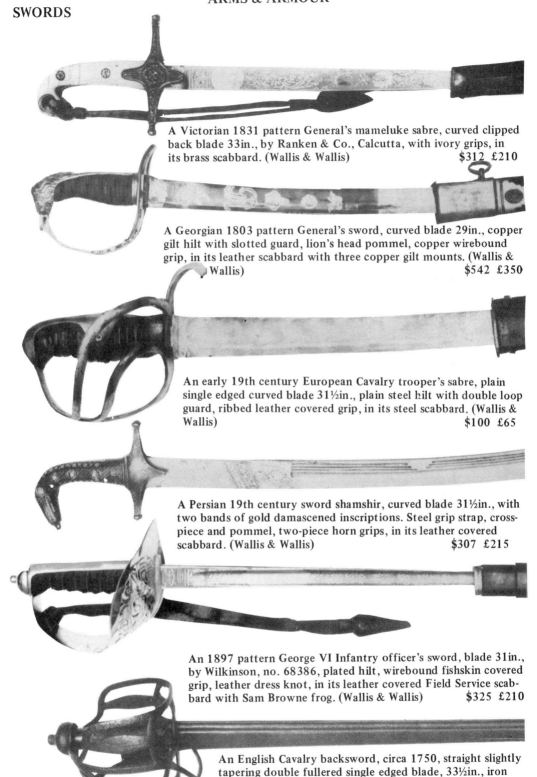

A Victorian 1831 pattern General's mameluke sabre, curved clipped back blade 33in., by Ranken & Co., Calcutta, with ivory grips, in its brass scabbard. (Wallis & Wallis) $312 £210

A Georgian 1803 pattern General's sword, curved blade 29in., copper gilt hilt with slotted guard, lion's head pommel, copper wirebound grip, in its leather scabbard with three copper gilt mounts. (Wallis & Wallis) $542 £350

An early 19th century European Cavalry trooper's sabre, plain single edged curved blade 31½in., plain steel hilt with double loop guard, ribbed leather covered grip, in its steel scabbard. (Wallis & Wallis) $100 £65

A Persian 19th century sword shamshir, curved blade 31½in., with two bands of gold damascened inscriptions. Steel grip strap, crosspiece and pommel, two-piece horn grips, in its leather covered scabbard. (Wallis & Wallis) $307 £215

An 1897 pattern George VI Infantry officer's sword, blade 31in., by Wilkinson, no. 68386, plated hilt, wirebound fishskin covered grip, leather dress knot, in its leather covered Field Service scabbard with Sam Browne frog. (Wallis & Wallis) $325 £210

An English Cavalry backsword, circa 1750, straight slightly tapering double fullered single edged blade, 33½in., iron basket guard with plain pommels, flattened circular panels and wooden grip. (Wallis & Wallis) $447 £300

ARMS & ARMOUR

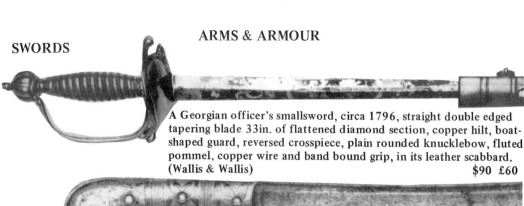

A Georgian officer's smallsword, circa 1796, straight double edged tapering blade 33in. of flattened diamond section, copper hilt, boat-shaped guard, reversed crosspiece, plain rounded knucklebow, fluted pommel, copper wire and band bound grip, in its leather scabbard. (Wallis & Wallis) $90 £60

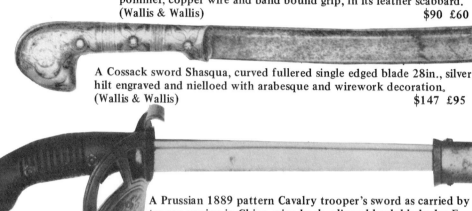

A Cossack sword Shasqua, curved fullered single edged blade 28in., silver hilt engraved and nielloed with arabesque and wirework decoration. (Wallis & Wallis) $147 £95

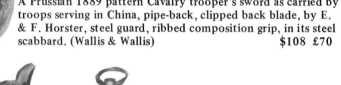

A Prussian 1889 pattern Cavalry trooper's sword as carried by troops serving in China, pipe-back, clipped back blade, by E. & F. Horster, steel guard, ribbed composition grip, in its steel scabbard. (Wallis & Wallis) $108 £70

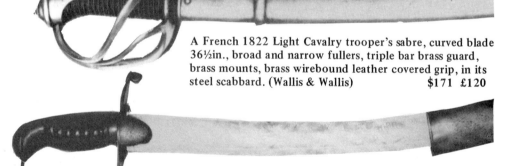

A French 1822 Light Cavalry trooper's sabre, curved blade 36½in., broad and narrow fullers, triple bar brass guard, brass mounts, brass wirebound leather covered grip, in its steel scabbard. (Wallis & Wallis) $171 £120

A 1796 Georgian Light Cavalry officer's sabre, curved blade 32½in., with plain steel stirrup hilt, copper wirebound leather covered grip, in its steel scabbard. (Wallis & Wallis) $134 £90

A gold damascened Tulwar, straight single edged blade 30½in., chiselled with pairs of animals in low relief with damascened details, iron hilt damascened with flowers and foliage, in its green velvet scabbard. (Wallis & Wallis) $170 £110

TSUBAS

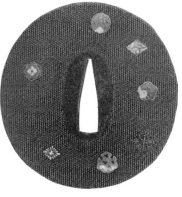

An oval iron tsuba, carved in low relief with a flowering cherry tree inlaid with gold and silver flowers and buds, 7.8cm. (Wallis & Wallis)
$126 £85

A circular Shakudo Daimyo-Nanakoji tsuba, signed Hirata Narisuke, 7.3cm. diam. (Christie's) $2,376 £1,650

A pierced and carved iron tsuba, depicting the 'Four Princes', bamboo, chrysanthe-mum, plum and orchid, 7.2cm. (Wallis & Wallis) $119 £80

An 18th century circular Awa-Shoami tsuba, kiri and tendrils in gilt nunome-zogan, 8.2cm. diam., and another. (Christie's)
$601 £418

A square pierced iron tsuba, carved overall with shells in low relief, 7.1cm. (Wallis & Wallis) $89 £60

An early 19th century circular copper Migakiji tsuba, signed Sakai Yoshitsugu, 7.6cm. diam. (Christie's) $792 £550

An oval pierced iron Chochu tsuba, carved with an assort-ment of leaves within bamboo rim, 8.5cm. (Wallis & Wallis)
$126 £85

A 19th century iron Aorigata Tsuchimeji tsuba with indented corners decorated in silver and gilt takazogan, 7.6cm. (Christie's) $1,584 £1,100

An 18th century circular iron tsuba, cherry blossoms and other designs in yosukashi with gilt detail, 7.8cm. diam. (Christie's) $792 £550

TSUBAS

A 19th century Aorigata iron tsuba, signed Hojusai Masakage, 7.3cm. (Christie's) $1,742 £1,210

A 17th century Hayashi tsuba, the ume-no-ki or plum tree design with gilt-nunome-zogan, 7.5cm. diam. (Christie's) $601 £418

A rounded square Shibuichi-Migakiji tsuba, circa 1800, 6.9cm. (Christie's) $871 £605

An 18th century circular iron tsuba, signed Bushu ju Masatsune, 7.5cm. diam., and a 17th century tsuba. (Christie's) $601 £418

A 17th/18th century oval copper Shoami tsuba, 6.9cm. (Christie's) $285 £198

A circular pierced iron Sukashi tsuba, signed Masatsune, chiselled with corn, 7.7cm. (Wallis & Wallis) $149 £100

A 19th century circular iron Migakiji tsuba, 7.4cm. diam., and an iron tsuba. (Christie's) $475 £330

A late Kamiyoshi style tsuba, hanagiri and ume in yosukashi, 8cm. diam., and a mokkogata tsuba. (Christie's) $506 £352

An oval iron tsuba, carved in relief with a flowering lotus in a stream, 8.2cm. (Wallis & Wallis) $126 £85

TSUBAS

A 16th/17th century pierced circular iron tsuba, Kyoto School, 8.1cm. (Wallis & Wallis) $119 £80

A 19th century oval Shakudo-Nanakoji tsuba, 7.2cm. (Christie's) $1,346 £935

An 18th century Rokumokko iron tsuba, six butterflies in ikizukashi, 8.1cm. diam., and an oval iron tsuba. (Christie's) $300 £209

A circular pierced iron Akasaka sukashi tsuba, depicting Lake Biwa beneath the moon, 7.8cm. (Wallis & Wallis) $104 £70

A circular pierced iron choshu tsuba, chiselled with chrysanthemum growing by a fence, 8.6cm. (Wallis & Wallis) $149 £100

A circular pierced iron tsuba, carved with thistles and an insect, 7.6cm. (Wallis & Wallis) $74 £50

A pierced iron tsuba, signed Bushu ju Masakuni, chiselled with flowering cherry blossom, 7.6cm. (Wallis & Wallis) $149 £100

A 19th century oval iron tsuba, ikizukashi, signed Choshu Hagi ju Tomoaki, 7cm., and a circular Shoami tsuba, and an oval iron Namban tsuba.(Christie's) $601 £418

A 19th century oval copper Ishimeji tsuba with fitted silver rim, 7.5cm. (Christie's) $712 £495

A Japanese polearm yari, trident head 18.4cm., signed Bushu Noju, Masakane Suki, tempered, the wings pierced for suspension of prayers.   Overall length 97in., top inlaid with mother-of-pearl segments and with copper mounts. (Wallis & Wallis) $157 £110

An early 19th century Persian qjar chiselled steel axe, 29¼in., crescent head 8in. chiselled on each side with large cartouche of Islamic script, Steel haft of alternate octagonal and roped sections with bulbous finials. (Wallis & Wallis) $164 £115

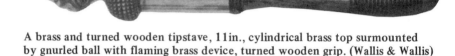

A brass and turned wooden tipstave, 11in., cylindrical brass top surmounted by gnurled ball with flaming brass device, turned wooden grip. (Wallis & Wallis) $226 £150

A Nazi Wehrmacht dress bayonet, plated blade 9½in., by Horster, plated mounts, stylised 'eagle's head' pommel, staghorn grip, in its black painted steel scabbard with leather frog. (Wallis & Wallis) $103 £70

A French partizan, circa 1700, 55½in., head 13½in., central blade with raised ribs, down turned and upturned crescents, wavy side pieces. The steel haft is a 42in. barrel from a Brown Bess. (Wallis & Wallis) $128 £90

An early Fiji missile club ulas, 15in., of patinated hardwood, with swollen head, slightly flared grip, carved with zig-zag decoration in relief. (Wallis & Wallis) $54 £38

A 19th century Persian steel axe, 30in., crescent head 7¼in., chiselled with cartouches of Islamic script. Steel haft filed with faceted and whorled sections. (Wallis & Wallis) $244 £160

A Nazi Police dress bayonet, plated blade 12½in., by Carl Eickhorn, white metal mounts, staghorn grips with police emblem, 'eagle's head' pommel, in its leather scabbard with white metal mounts and a dress knot. (Wallis & Wallis) $192 £130

WEAPONS

An 18th century Indian 'Elephant knife' bhuj from Sind, 25¼in. overall, broad recurved blade 7½in. with false edge, on its steel haft, the copper gilt lotus pommel unscrews to reveal an 11in. stiletto.   (Wallis & Wallis) $260 £170

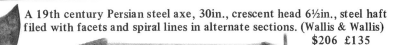

A 19th century Persian steel axe, 30in., crescent head 6½in., steel haft filed with facets and spiral lines in alternate sections. (Wallis & Wallis)
$206 £135

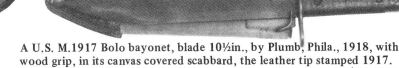

A U.S. M.1917 Bolo bayonet, blade 10½in., by Plumb, Phila., 1918, with wood grip, in its canvas covered scabbard, the leather tip stamped 1917. (Wallis & Wallis) $96 £65

A Victorian universal pattern painted Police truncheon, 18½in., with post 1837 crowned Royal Arms and 'Police'. (Wallis & Wallis)$42 £28

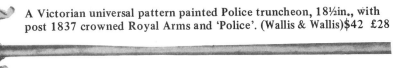

A 19th century Persian qjar etched steel axe, 34in., crescent head 8¼in., etched with two mounted horsemen clashing with shamshirs, dhals, axes, severed limbs. Square section top spike, hollow zoomorphic backpiece, steel haft with swollen pommel.   (Wallis & Wallis) $114 £80

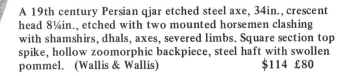

An 18th century Austrian parade lance, leaf shaped head 8¼in. etched Vivat Gothenburg above the Imperial eagle, baluster socket with long straps on later 42in. section of haft. (Wallis & Wallis) $151 £100

A William IV turned wooden tipstave, 13¾in., black painted with gilt and red WR, crowned IV. (Wallis & Wallis) $72 £48

A sword bayonet for the Jacobs double barrelled rifle, double edged, fullered blade, 30in., pierced steel guard, double hole in quillon, diced leather grips. (Wallis & Wallis) $351 £230

ARMS & ARMOUR

A 19th century Sudanese mace Shishpar, 19½in., of all steel construction, six bladed swollen head with top spike. Octagonal haft with crocodile skin covered pommel. (Wallis & Wallis) $130 £85

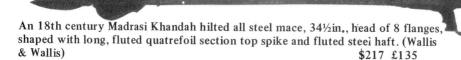

An 18th century Madrasi Khandah hilted all steel mace, 34½in., head of 8 flanges, shaped with long, fluted quatrefoil section top spike and fluted steel haft. (Wallis & Wallis) $217 £135

An old Maori carved wood club meri, 14½in., the back carved with a standing figure in the round, with protruding tongue pointing sideways. (Wallis & Wallis) $293 £205

A German target crossbow, heavy steel bow of 89.5cm. span, walnut stock with brass mounts including scroll trigger guard, peephole rear sight, double set triggers, 83.5cm. overall. (Phillips) $581 £380

A Maori hand club Meri or Patu, made from the jaw bone of sperm whale, 14¾in., thin swollen blade with thickened flared grip, pierced for wrist cord. (Wallis & Wallis) $511 £330

A model cannon, turned bronze barrel 7½in., engraved 'Relic of Royal George. Sunk 1782 Raised 1840', swollen muzzle and cascabel. (Wallis & Wallis) $128 £80

An 18th century Fiji missile club Ulas, 16½in., swollen multi-ribbed head with bulbous top, flared grip. (Wallis & Wallis) $163 £100

An African Shona knife, 15in., straight double edged blade 10in., with off-set sides, wooden hilt and sheath with carved geometric decoration, woven brass wire bindings. (Wallis & Wallis) $81 £50

A clockwork wheeled toy of a bisque swivel headed ballerina of Parisienne type, French, circa 1880, 17in. high. (Christie's)
$2,112 £1,320

An automaton figure of a clown with painted composition face and black and white costume, 18in. high, with glass dome. (Christie's)
$2,044 £1,430

Late 19th century 'Boy Feeding Pig' automaton, the bisque head marked Jumeau SGDG 4, 18¾in. high. (Robt. W. Skinner Inc.)
$2,600 £1,805

A clockwork cabbage automaton containing a white rabbit, French, circa 1900, 6½in. high. (Christie's)
$475 £297

A 20th century singing bird automaton, Switzerland, box height 1¾in. and 4.1/8in. wide. (Robt. W. Skinner Inc.)
$600 £419

A gilt metal and composition bird-cage containing a feathered bird automaton on a perch, 12½in. high. (Christie's)
$1,232 £770

A singing bird automaton with clock, Swiss, probably by Jacquet Droz, circa 1785, 20in. high. (Christie's)
$44,000 £30,703

A 19th century clockwork lady knitting automaton, Germany, 21in. high. (Robt. W. Skinner Inc.)
$1,800 £1,250

Mid 19th century Swiss musical automaton of singing birds, on oval base, 60cm. high. (Christie's)
$1,980 £1,381

A George III inlaid mahogany barometer, by P. Cattaneo, late 18th century, 38in. high. (Christie's)

$1,045 £682

A 19th century mahogany stick barometer, the plate signed Burton, London, 41½in. high. (Christie's)

$2,310 £1,500

A mid Victorian papier-mache barometer, 38in. high. (Christie's)

$471 £330

A 19th century mahogany wheel barometer, the 10in. dial signed Lione & Somalvico, 44in. high. (Christie's)

$693 £450

A late 18th century mahogany stick barometer, the brass plate signed Watkins, London, 94cm. high. (Phillips)

$1,116 £720

A Sheraton period wheel barometer, by J. B. Roncheti. (Woolley & Wallis)

$5,904 £4,100

An early 19th century crossbanded mahogany and boxwood strung stick barometer, signed Pozzi & Co., 97cm. high. (Phillips)

$542 £350

An early 19th century mahogany wheel barometer, the 8½in. diam. dial signed Negretty & Co. (Phillips)

$651 £420

A late 19th century rosewood wheel barometer, level signed D. Osborn, 38in. high. (Christie's) $700 £500

A late Georgian mahogany stick barometer, the silvered plate signed Gally, Cambridge, 39in. high. (Christie's) $847 £550

A late 19th century rosewood wheel barometer, the 10in. dial signed Crosta & Co., London, 40¾in. high. (Christie's) $292 £190

A 19th century Standard Station barometer, engraved no. 282, Burrow, Malvern. (Phillips) $434 £280

A 19th century French crossbanded mahogany wheel barometer, Paris 1740, 110cm. high. (Phillips) $1,162 £750

Late 18th century mahogany stick barometer, plate signed G. Adams, 39¼in. high. (Christie's) $1,694 £1,100

An early 19th century mahogany Sheraton shell wheel barometer, 8in. diam. silver dial signed Lione, Somalvico & Co., 100cm. high. (Phillips) $457 £320

A 19th century mahogany stick barometer, signed O. Cornitti & Son Fecit, London, 95cm. high. (Phillips) $1,085 £700

Capt. W. V. Legge: A History of the Birds of Ceylon, 34 hand-coloured lithographs, quarto, 1880. (Phillips) $1,680 £1,050

Mattheus Seutter: Atlas of the World, 62 hand-coloured maps, folio, Augsberg, circa 1740. (Phillips) $2,560 £1,600

Ludolphus de Saxonia — Dat Boeck vanden Leuen ons Liefs heren Jhesu Cristi, folio, Zwolle, Pieter van Os, 20th Nov., 1495. (Phillips) $18,000 £12,500

Capt. Robert Melville Grindlay: Scenery Costume and Architecture on the Western Side of India, folio, R. Ackermann, 1826. (Phillips) $2,880 £1,800

John Watson Stewart, The Gentleman's and Citizen's Almanack, g.e., Dublin, T. and J. W. Stewart, 1755. (Phillips) $1,015 £720

C. Dickens: Great Expectations, 3 vols., 1st Edn., 32pp. of advertisements, original cloth gilt, 1861. (Phillips) $19,200 £12,000

Autograph album containing the signatures of important late 19th/early 20th century musicians, composers and performers. (Phillips) $2,000 £1,250

E. Dodwell: Views in Greece, 30 hand-coloured views, folio, 1821. (Phillips) $6,400 £4,000

James Scott of Edinburgh Binding, The Holy Bible containing the Old and New Testaments, London, J. Baskett, 1741 bound with Psalms of David, Edinburgh, A. Kincaid, 1772. (Phillips) $1,762 £1,250

T. H. Fielding and J. Walton: A Picturesque Tour of the English Lakes, quarto, R. Ackermann, 1821. (Phillips) $880 £550

The Sporting Magazine: 156 vols. plus index, t.e.g. 1792-1870. (Phillips) $12,000 £7,500

Sydenham Edwards: The new Flora Britannica, 61 hand-coloured plates, quarto, 1812. (Phillips) $1,680 £1,050

Louis Renard: Atlas de la Navigation et du Commerce, 28 charts, Amsterdam 1715. (Phillips) $7,520 £4,700

A 17th century miniature Book of Psalms with embroidered cover, England, 2 x 3¼in. (Robt. W. Skinner Inc.) $2,000 £1,398

W. Daniell and R. Ayton: A Voyage Round Great Britain, 8 volumes in 4, 2 vols. of plates, folio, 1814-26. (Phillips) $19,200 £12,000

J. Gardner — A Pocket Guide to the English Traveller, 100 copper plates, oblong 8vo, 1719. (Woolley & Wallis) $994 £650

W. Camden: Brittania, engraved title, 57 maps, folio, London, 1610. (Phillips) $3,040 £1,900

Doves Press, Alfred Lord Tennyson, Seven Poems and two Translations, Limited Edition, by Cobden-Sanderson, signed and dated 1903. (Phillips) $1,128 £800

T. S. Eliot: The Waste Land,
Ltd. Edn., No. 92 of 300,
Officina Bodoni, 1961.
(Phillips) $992 £620

The Bible bound with Book
of Common Prayer, engraved
title dated 1672, printed title
1679. (Phillips)
$3,200 £2,000

Eragny Press, R. Browning,
Some Poems, Limited Edition
of 215 col. woodcut front, by
L. Pissarro, 1904. (Phillips)
$846 £600

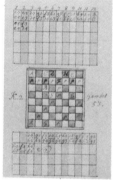

Koch and Kellermeistern von
Allen Speison Getrenken,
title printed in red and black
woodcuts, Frankfurt, 1554.
(Phillips) $4,160 £2,600

Gianutio (Horatio): Libro nel
Quale si tratta della Maniera
di Giuocara Scacchi, modern
vellum, Turin, A. de Bianchi,
1597. (Phillips) $3,200 £2,000

Greco Gioachino, 1600-c.1634,
Manuscript entitled 'The Royall
Game of Chess', comprising 95
games executed in pen, ink and
green wash. (Phillips)
$1,408 £880

Vale Press, R. Browning,
Dramatic Romances and
Lyrics, Limited Edition of
210, 1899. (Phillips)
$958 £680

James Scott of Edinburgh
Binding, The Holy Bible
bound with Psalms of David,
dark blue morocco gilt, g.e.,
Edinburgh, A. Kincaid, 1772.
(Phillips) $1,410 £1,000

Napoleonic Broadsides, small
folio, 31 satirical broadsides
concerning the outbreak of
war in 1803. (Woolley &
Wallis) $887 £580

J. Toland, The Life of John Milton, red morocco gilt, London, A. Millar, 1761. (Phillips) $1,240 £880

Henry J. Elwes: A monograph of the Genus Lilium, 48 hand-coloured plates by W. H. Fitch, folio, 1880. (Phillips) $6,400 £4,000

Historical Gossip about Golf and Golfers, Edinburgh, 1863. (Phillips) $17,920 £11,200

P. Vergilius Maro: The Pastorals, 2 vols., 3rd Edn., editor R. J. Thornton, half calf, 1821. (Phillips) $3,040 £1,900

W. L. Buller: History of the Birds of New Zealand, 1st Edition, 35 coloured plates, by J. G. Keulemans, London, 1873, 1 volume. (Prudential Fine Art) $2,184 £1,300

Omar Khayyam, Rubaiyat, trans. E. Fitzgerald, 16 colour plates, by W. Pogany, g.e. by Riviere, circa 1930. (Phillips) $987 £700

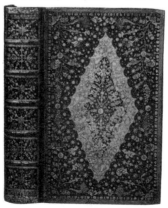

Lopez de Sigura (R.R.): Il Givoco de gli Scacchi . . . First Italian Edn., trans. G. D. Tarsia, woodcut initials, small 4to, Venice, 1584. (Phillips) $1,120 £700

Irish Binding: Book of Common Prayer, contemporary red morocco, lined case, Cambridge, John Baskerville, 1760. (Phillips) $1,434 £880

J. B. Selves, Tableau des Desordres dan l'Administration de la Justice, green morocco gilt with arms of C. A. Regnier, Paris, 1812. (Phillips) $535 £380

'Science revealing herself to Nature', a bronze figure cast from a model by E. Barrias, 60cm. high. (Christie's) $4,910 £3,410

A 19th century French bronze group of two snipe, signed J. Moigniez, with a golden patina, 24cm. high. (Christie's) $1,116 £770

The racing driver, a bronze figure cast from a model by Saalmann, stamped Echte Bronze, 28.5cm. high. (Christie's) $2,376 £1,650

'Sheltering from the Rain', a bronze and ivory group cast and carved from a model by D. Chiparus, 26cm. high. (Christie's) $2,534 £1,760

A late 19th century French bronze statuette of Phryne, signed P. Campagne, 60cm. high. (Christie's) $3,030 £2,090

A late 19th century French bronze statuette of Diana, signed Denecheau, 60cm. high overall. (Christie's) $6,380 £4,400

The Waiter, a bronze figure cast from a model by Engelhart, inscribed 1904, 26.5cm. high. (Christie's) $475 £330

A 19th century French bronze model of a prancing stallion, cast from a model by C. Fratin, 26cm. high. (Christie's) $2,233 £1,540

Water Carrier, a bronze figure cast from a model by Franz Seifert, 25.8cm. high. (Christie's) $601 £418

A bronze figure of Eve, incised Oliver Sheppard, 1924, 51cm. high. (Phillips) $1,950 £1,300

A mid 19th century French bronze group of a child with a swan, signed J. Pradier, 83.5cm. high. (Christie's)
$7,656 £5,280

A late 19th century Italian bronze statuette of a youth seated on a bollard, signed Ch. Brunin, Roma, 60cm. high. (Christie's)
$1,355 £935

A late 19th century English bronze bust of G. F. Watts, signed and dated A. Gilbert, 1888, 16.5cm. high. (Christie's) $1,276 £880

One of a set of four ormolu and simulated bronze wall lights of Empire style, fitted for electricity, 17in. high. (Christie's) $1,652 £1,080

A late 19th century French bronze bust of Napoleon as Emperor, signed and dated on the side R. Colombo, 1885, 48.5cm. high. (Christie's) $2,392 £1,650

Dancer with Tambourine, a gilt bronze figure cast from a model by Agathon Leonard, 55.5cm. high. (Christie's) $5,702 £3,960

A mid 19th century English bronze statuette of the Duke of Wellington on Horseback, cast from a model by Alfred, Count d'Orsay, 41cm. high. (Christie's) $1,355 £935

A late 19th century French bronze statuette of Hebe, signed Steiner, 94cm. high. (Christie's) $3,828 £2,640

'Exotic Dancer', a gilt bronze and ivory figure cast and carved from a model by A. Gory, 37.5cm. high. (Christie's) $3,304 £2,160

'Danseuse de Thebes', a bronze and ivory figure cast and carved from a model by C. J. Roberte Colinet, 25.8cm. high. (Christie's) $12,393 £8,100

Mandolin Player, a bronze and ivory figure cast and carved from a model by F. Preiss, signed, 59cm. high. (Christie's)
$31,395 £20,520

A 19th century animalier group of a stag, doe and fawn, on oblate ovoid base, incised Barye and F. Barbedienne Fondeur, 27cm. high. (Phillips) $2,160 £1,500

A bronze figure, cast from a model by Bruno Zach, 15½in. high. (Christie's)
$1,368 £950

A Lorenzl gilt bronze dancing girl, poised on one leg, 15in. high. (Christie's) $1,238 £820

A bronze and ivory bust cast and carved from a model by P. Mengin, 8½in. (Christie's) $332 £220

Pair of 19th century bronze and ormolu three-light figural candelabra, 55cm. high. (Phillips) $1,512 £1,050

A bronze figure cast from a model by F. Liebermann, depicting a putto astride a cockerel, 40cm. high. (Christie's) $1,487 £972

An Art Deco bronze group
of a male and female nude,
65cm. high. (Christie's)
$3,304 £2,160

'Nubian Dancer', a bronze
and ivory dancing girl, cast
and carved after a model by
D. H. Chiparus, 15½in. high.
(Christie's) $18,120 £12,000

'Oriental Dancer', a bronze
figure cast from a model by
C. J. Roberte Colinet, 19½in.
high. (Christie's)
$2,718 £1,800

'Maid of Orleans', a bronze
figure cast after a model
by Raoul Larche, 14in. high.
(Christie's) $906 £600

A bronze group cast from a
model by Guirande of a
dancing lady, 62.9cm. high.
(Christie's) $2,313 £1,512

A bronze figural lamp, cast
from a model by O. S. W.
Schimmelpfennig, 9¼in. high.
(Christie's) $785 £520

A large Lorenzl silvered bronze
figure of a dancing girl, 28½in.
high. (Christie's)
$2,718 £1,800

Pair of Regency ormolu and bronze
candlesticks with Chinamen holding
nozzles, on white marble pedestals,
8½in. high. (Christie's) $1,435 £990

Flute Player, a bronze and
ivory figure cast and carved
from a model by F. Preiss,
48.5cm. high. (Christie's)
$28,090 £18,360

A gilt bronze figure of a girl with a dog in her arms, on variegated square marble base, 30cm. high. (Christie's) $2,534 £1,760

A 19th century animalier bronze figure of a mountain goat, incised J. Moigniez, 26cm. high. (Phillips) $990 £660

'Dancer with Thyrsus', a bronze figure cast from a model by Pierre le Faguays, 27.2cm. high. (Christie's) $1,742 £1,210

A bronze hunting group 'Gone Away', 51cm. high, the base incised Elkington. (Phillips) $5,100 £3,400

One of a pair of ormolu candlesticks, the shafts formed as kneeling naked maidens with lion skin cloaks, circa 1830, 10in. high. (Christie's) $1,404 £918

A late 19th century English silvered bronze group of Adam and Eve After the Fall, cast from a model by Chas. Bell Birch, dated 1875, 40cm. high overall. (Christie's) $1,515 £1,045

La Sibylie, a bronze bust cast from a model by E. Villanis, with Societe des Bronzes de Paris foundry mark, 72cm. high. (Christie's) $3,484 £2,420

One of a pair of Regency ormolu and bronze twin-light candelabra, 13in. high. (Christie's) $1,982 £1,296

One of a set of three William IV bronze argand lamps with flame finials, fitted for electricity, 28¼in. high. (Christie's) $3,139 £2,052

A late 19th/early 20th century French bronze statue of Diana the Huntress, the base signed Mercie, 111cm. high. (Christie's) $12,760 £8,800

A 19th century animalier bronze figure of a chamois, incised J. Moigniez, 24cm. high. (Phillips) $600 £400

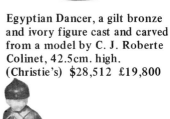

Egyptian Dancer, a gilt bronze and ivory figure cast and carved from a model by C. J. Roberte Colinet, 42.5cm. high. (Christie's) $28,512 £19,800

A late 19th century Spanish bronze group of an Arab with two lion cubs, signed Vallmitjana abarca, 36cm. high. (Christie's) $1,276 £880

One of a pair of 19th century French bronze torcheres of Cupid and Psyche, 94cm. high. (Christie's) $6,061 £4,180

Morning Walk, a parcel gilt bronze and ivory group cast and carved after a model by A. Becquerel, 26.8cm. high. (Christie's) $1,900 £1,320

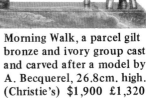

A bronze group cast from a model by C. Kauba, on a variegated square marble base, signed, 14.3cm. high. (Christie's) $554 £385

One of a pair of early 19th century bronze and ormolu candelabra, the glass sconces hung with pendant lustre drops, 31cm. high. (Phillips) $930 £620

One of a pair of mid 19th century bronze candlesticks, the shafts modelled as up-turned sea serpents, 10½in. high. (Christie's) $1,321 £864

A painted bronze and ivory figure, 'Hoop Girl', 20.50cm. high, inscribed F. Preiss. (Phillips) $1,872 £1,300

A bronze model of a seated hare, signed Hisatoshi, 24cm. high. (Christie's)
$1,093 £770

A gilt bronze and ivory figure, modelled as an Egyptianesque girl, inscribed Bohm fec, 33cm. high. (Phillips) $5,328 £3,700

A late 19th/early 20th century French parcel gilt bronze group of tigers, signed E. Drouot, 35 x 64cm. (Christie's) $1,914 £1,320

Late 19th century bronze pear-shaped vase, signed on the base Masai koku and sealed Maruki sei, 48.6cm. high. (Christie's)
$3,436 £2,420

A 19th century French bronze model of a Senegalese lion with an antelope, signed E. Delabrierre, 46 x 80cm. (Christie's) $3,987 £2,750

A bronze and ivory figure cast and carved after a model by D. H. Chiparus, 16in. high. (Christie's) $6,930 £4,500

A small bronze ship's bell, almost certainly of European origin, circa 1750, 10.5cm. high. (Christie's)
$3,004 £1,951

'Diana', a bronze figure cast after a model by Raphael Monti, 13¾in. high. (Christie's) $528 £350

BRONZE

A bronze figure, modelled
as a maiden, 30.3cm. high,
signed Mars Vallet. (Phillips)
$3,456 £2,400

A painted bronze and ivory
group, 'Towards The Unknown
(Valkyrie)', 32.50cm. high,
inscribed on rockwork Cl. J. R.
Colinet. (Phillips)
$2,160 £1,500

A painted bronze and ivory
figure, 'Sonny Boy', 20.50cm.
high, inscribed F. Preiss.
(Phillips) $2,160 £1,500

A painted bronze and ivory
figure, 'Le Grand Ecart
Respectueux', 21.50cm. high,
inscribed P. Philippe. (Phillips)
$3,312 £2,300

A bronze model of a fox,
modelled in stylised fashion,
35cm. high, stamped on
reverse Seiden-Stucker.
(Phillips) $432 £300

A late 19th/early 20th century
French bronze group of two
alsations, signed J. Joire,
49 x 66cm. (Christie's)
$2,233 £1,540

A gilt bronze figure of a girl,
'Modern Venus', cast from a
model by C. J. R. Colinet,
47cm. high. (Phillips)
$4,320 £3,000

A Byzantine bronze plaque
of almost heart-shape, with
a large loop for suspension,
18.5cm. high. (Phillips)
$306 £200

A 20th century seated bronze
study of Lucifer, 8¼in. high.
(Christie's) $539 £350

One of a pair of late Regency patinated bronze and ormolu urns, 11in. high. (Christie's) $2,831 £1,980

A bronze group of two hounds on leafy oval base, by P. J. Mene, 18in. long. (Graves Son & Pilcher) $1,585 £1,050

A bronze figure of a naked man, 'The Sluggard', cast after a model by Frederic Lord Leighton, 56.5cm. high. (Phillips) $4,608 £3,200

A painted bronze and ivory figural lamp, 'Oriental Waiter', 48cm. high, signed on base F. Preiss. (Phillips) $2,880 £2,000

A Tiffany Studios bronze and glass inkwell, 18cm. diam., stamped Tiffany Studio New York, 69391. (Phillips) $518 £360

One of a pair of ormolu three-branch wall lights, fitted for electricity, 22in. high. (Christie's) $2,655 £1,870

Pierrot, a bronze and ivory figure cast and carved after a model by Gibbert, 15.4cm. high. (Christie's) $5,287 £3,456

A 17th/18th century inlaid bronze two-handled archaistic vessel, gui, 41cm. wide. (Christie's) $1,573 £1,100

A 19th century French bronze model of a charging bull, cast from a model by Antoine-Louis Barye, 19 x 30cm. (Christie's) $3,366 £2,200

One of a pair of Louis XVI bronze and ormolu figural candelabra, 70cm. high. (Phillips) $4,608 £3,200

Late 19th century bronze model of a rhinoceros on marble stand, 48cm. long. (Christie's) $4,998 £3,520

One of a pair of 19th century large bronze garden vases, 77.5cm. high. (Christie's) $2,030 £1,430

One of a set of five ormolu twin-branch wall lights of Louis XVI design, 25in. high. (Christie's) $6,560 £4,620

One of a pair of patinated bronze models of lions, early 19th century, 11½in. wide. (Christie's) $1,551 £1,100

'The Swing', a bronze and ivory figure cast and carved from a model by Jaeger, 10½in. high. (Christie's) $1,963 £1,300

An early 20th century French bronze group of two horses, cast from a model by P. Tourgueneff, 41 x 58cm. (Christie's) $1,683 £1,100

A bronze group cast from a model by A. Boucher of three athletic youths, signed and with Siot-Paris foundry stamp, 50cm. high. (Christie's) $5,289 £3,456

A gilt bronze figure of a crouching lion, Tang Dynasty, 8cm. wide. (Christie's) $9,438 £6,600

A bronze of 'Faneur', after Charles-Octave Levy, Salon de Beaux-Art, 1885, 22.5/8in. high. (Robt. W. Skinner Inc.) $700 £486

One of a pair of bronze deer with brown patina, 34½in. high. (Christie's) $2,860 £1,866

An English bronze statuette of Peter Pan, cast from a model by Sir G. Frampton, the base dated GF 1915, 48cm. high. (Christie's) $15,147 £9,900

A bronze flattened pilgrim vase, bienhu, Warring States/ Han Dynasty, 37cm. wide. (Christie's) $2,516 £1,760

A bronze group of a man and a poodle, 59cm. high, inscribed D. de Chemellier. (Phillips) $936 £650

A 19th century inlaid bronze charger, Japan, 12.5/8in. diam. (Robt. W. Skinner Inc.) $650 £451

A bronze group of two crows perched on a tree stump, Meiji period, 58.5cm. high. (Christie's) $3,124 £2,200

Huntress, a silvered bronze figure cast from a model by G. None, Paris, 34cm. high. (Christie's) $1,887 £1,320

Bronze standing figure of a satyr, 2ft. tall. (Lots Road Galleries) $1,440 £1,000

An Art Deco bronze and
ivory Grecian figure on
marble plinth, 11¾in. high.
(Capes, Dunn & Co.)
$841   £580

A bronze and ivory figure of
a dancer cast and carved from
a model by Gerdago, 10½in.
high. (Christie's)
$6,160   £4,000

A gilt bronze and ivory figure
cast and carved from a model
by Lorenzl, 11in. high.
(Christie's) $800   £520

An archaic bronze food vessel,
gui, Shang Dynasty, 22.5cm.
diam., wood stand, fitted box.
(Christie's) $117,975 £82,500

A 20th century English bronze
statuette of The Sluggard, cast
from a model by F. Leighton,
51.5cm. high. (Christie's)
$5,386   £3,520

An archaic bronze bell, nao,
mid-1st Millenium B.C.,
40cm. high, fitted box, wood
stand and bell striker.
(Christie's) $3,146 £2,200

One of a pair of 19th century
French bronze figures depicting a fisher girl and hunter,
signed Boyer, 14in. high.
(Capes, Dunn & Co.)$725 £500

Lioness, a bronze figure cast
after a model by Demetre
Chiparus, 57.8cm. long.
(Christie's) $1,494 £1,045

One of two bronze models of
athletes on rectangular bases,
8.75in. and 9.5in. high.
(Woolley & Wallis) $437 £290

A 19th century French bronze group of a Satyr with Nymph and Baby Satyr, in the style of Clodion, 68cm. high. (Christie's) $2,019 £1,320

A 16th/17th century late Ming bronze group cast as Budai, 32.5cm. wide. (Christie's) $2,831 £1,980

A Preiss bronze and ivory figure, 'Grecian with Torch', on marble base, 11in. high. (Capes, Dunn & Co.) $1,595 £1,100

Late 19th century Austrian bronze of a Bedouin on Camel, 10in. high. (Robt. W. Skinner Inc.) $700 £486

An early 19th century ormolu table cruet on four dolphin supports, 48cm. high. (Phillips) $1,285 £850

A gilt bronze and ivory group cast and carved from an original by A. Hussmann, 18.50cm. high. (Phillips) $1,080 £750

A green patinated bronze figure, modelled as a faun holding a panther cub, cast from a model by M. Hoffman, 44.50cm. high, circa 1915. (Phillips) $1,152 £800

A painted bronze and ivory figure, 'Hush', 42cm. high, inscribed D. H. Chiparus. (Phillips) $3,888 £2,700

Europa and the Bull, a bronze figure cast from a model by H. Muller, 25.4cm. high. (Christie's) $1,022 £715

A 13th/14th century Korean gilt bronze figure of a standing Buddha, Koryo Dynasty, 21.5cm. high. (Christie's) $4,719 £3,300

A 19th century French bronze relief of a startled stallion, cast from a model by C. Fratin, 26 x 37cm. (Christie's) $2,624 £1,650

Mid 19th century bronze of a boy playing catchball, 'Preparing to Throw', cast from a model by J. Durham, 37.5cm. high. (Christie's) $1,262 £825

Late 19th century champleve enamel on bronze covered jar, China, 17.3/8in. high. (Robt. W. Skinner Inc.) $600 £416

One of a pair of Charles X ormolu five-light candelabra, 32½in. high. (Christie's) $3,124 £2,200

A late 19th century French or Italian bronze equestrian statuette of Napoleon, cast from a model by Pinedo, 40cm. high. (Christie's) $1,262 £825

A 20th century English bronze bust of the Viscount Northcliffe, cast from a model by Courtnay Pollack, 52cm. high. (Christie's) $639 £418

One of a pair of 17th/18th century partially gilt bronze censers and covers, 32cm. high. (Christie's) $7,550 £5,280

A bronze finish spelter hall lamp of a Teutonic knight in 16th century armour, 4ft.4in. high. (Woolley & Wallis) $720 £500

One of a pair of bronze models of athletes running and throwing the discus, 8.5in. and 9.5in. high. (Woolley & Wallis)
$392 £260

A 19th century French bronze group of a Greek shepherd teaching a child to play the flute, cast from a model by Coinchon, 41.5 x 34cm. (Christie's) $757 £495

A silvered bronze group, 'Carthage', after a model by T. Riviere, 56cm. high. (Phillips) $2,880 £2,000

A late 19th century French bronze model of The Vaineueur Du Derby, cast from a model by P. J. Mene, 26 x 24cm. (Christie's)
$2,524 £1,650

A painted bronze and ivory figure, 'Champagne Dancer', 41.50cm. high, inscribed on bronze F. Preiss. (Phillips)
$3,600 £2,500

A 19th century English bronze model of a stag eating oak leaves off a withered tree, from the Coalbrookdale Foundry, 40 x 46cm. (Christie's) $1,093 £715

Early 20th century bronze bust of Woman, signed Wigglesworth, stamped Gorham Co. Founders, 13¾in. high. (Robt. W. Skinner Inc.)
$800 £555

An early 19th century French romantic bronze portrait plaque of Albert Bertin, cast from a model by A. Etex, 43 x 32cm. (Christie's)
$1,514 £990

Late 19th century bronze lobed koro on karashishi mask and scroll tripod feet, 61cm. high. (Christie's)
$1,405 £990

An Art Deco bronze figure, by Fesler Felix, modelled as a naked girl with an elaborate headdress and belt, 37cm. high. (Phillips) $319 £220

A late 19th century French bronze statuette of a Huntsman with a Pointer, cast from a model by Pierre Jules Mene, 47cm. high. (Christie's) $3,366 £2,200

Mid 19th century bronze of a boy playing catchball, 'Preparing to Catch', cast from a model by J. Durham, 40cm. high. (Christie's) $1,262 £825

A late 19th century French bronze model of a lioness carrying a cub in her mouth, cast from a model by A. N. Cain, 61 x 84cm.(Christie's) $4,880 £3,190

A painted bronze and ivory figure, 'Oriental Dancer', 40.20cm. high, inscribed on the marble Chiparus. (Phillips) $6,624 £4,600

A 19th century cast bronze figure of horse and dog, 'Angelo' on base, signed P. Lenordez, France, 20.1/8in. long. (Robt. W. Skinner Inc.) $950 £659

One of a pair of late 19th century bronze baluster vases, decorated in iroe hirazogan and takazogan, 32.5cm. high. (Christie's) $702 £495

A late 19th century English bronze statue of Physical Energy, by G. F. Watts. (Christie's) $42,075 £27,500

Bear Hug, a bronze figure cast after a model by F. Rieder, 30.8cm. high. (Christie's) $2,044 £1,430

A French bronze group of the Accolade, after Pierre-Jules Mene, 43.5 x 69cm. (Christie's) $4,785 £3,300

Early 20th century large bronze architectural ornament, America, 65in. wide. (Robt. W. Skinner Inc.) $2,200 £1,527

A bronze figure of a panther cast from a model by M. Prost, dark patina, 18.7cm. high. (Christie's) $1,404 £918

Pair of early 20th century Tiffany bronze dore and opalene jewel pricket candlesticks, 12.3/8in. high. (Robt. W. Skinner Inc.) $2,800 £1,958

A pair of large bronze models of standing geese, 58cm. and 78cm. high. (Christie's) $2,030 £1,430

'Dancer with Thyrsus', a parcel gilt bronze figure cast after a model by Pierre Le Faguays, 27.6cm. high. (Christie's) $2,313 £1,512

Late 19th century cast bronze of hunting dog, signed Dubucand, France, 11in. long. (Robt. W. Skinner Inc.) $200 £138

Pair of late 18th century Italian neo-classical gilt metal candlesticks, possibly Torinese, 21in. high. (Christie's) $1,874 £1,320

A bronze oxyrhynchus fish with uraeus and horned solar disc, a suspension loop behind, 9cm. long, Late Period. (Phillips) $229 £150

A late 19th century French bronze statuette of Mercury asleep, monogrammed and dated CCH 1898, 107cm. long. (Christie's)
$3,190 £2,200

Late 19th century bronze model of a prowling tiger on wood stand, 53cm. long. (Christie's) $859 £605

An early Victorian bronze inkstand with two vase-shaped inkwells, one glass liner cracked, 17in. wide. (Christie's) $413 £270

One of a pair of inlaid bronze mask and ring handles, Warring States/Western Han Dynasty, the masks 9.5cm. wide, the rings 9cm. diam. (Christie's)$86,515 £60,500

A pair of bronze models of seated rats holding chestnuts, signed on the bases, Shosai chu, Meiji period, approx. 17cm. long. (Christie's)
$1,562 £1,100

Pair of Regency ormolu and bronze candelabra, each with chinoiserie figures holding parasol nozzles, 11½in. high. (Christie's) $7,656 £5,280

One of a pair of ormolu three-branch wall lights in the rococo taste, 26½in. high. (Christie's)
$2,343 £1,650

'A Savage Drinking from a Stream', a bronze figure cast from a model by J. De Roncourt, 81.2cm. wide. (Christie's) $1,258 £880

One of a pair of bronze and marble bookends in the form of kneeling nudes, 5½in. high. (Capes, Dunn & Co.)
$108 £75

A George III mahogany brass bound bucket, the tapering side with a door and carrying handle, 13¼in. high. (Christie's) $702 £418

A George III oval mahogany Irish peat bucket with swing handle and liner, 14in. wide. (Prudential Fine Art) $873 £520

One of two Regency brass bound mahogany peat buckets with ribbed bodies and brass handles, 15½in. high. (Christie's) $4,804 £2,860

A George III mahogany brass bound peat bucket with brass liner, 11¾in. high. (Christie's) $1,730 £1,210

A George III mahogany brass bound coal bucket of navette shape, the slatted sides with swing handle and liner, 14½in. wide. (Christie's) $3,102 £2,200

A George III brass bound mahogany coal bucket with brass handle and liner, 13in. wide. (Christie's) $786 £550

A Regency mahogany brass bound peat bucket with tapering sides and carrying handle with later tin liner, 16in. high. (Christie's) $1,663 £990

One of a pair of George III mahogany brass bound plate buckets with later tin liners, 15in. diam. (Christie's) $1,573 £1,100

One of two George III brass bound mahogany buckets of navette form with detachable brass liners, 13½in. high. (Christie's) $1,848 £1,100

Victorian amboyna veneered sewing box, inlaid with mother-of-pearl stringing, 12 x 9in. (Peter Wilson) $197 £140

Shaker butternut sewing box, the drawers with ebonised diamond escutcheon and turned ivory pull, New England, circa 1820, 7½in. wide. (Robt. W. Skinner Inc.) $7,750 £5,166

A Regency tortoiseshell tea caddy with gilt metal lion handles, 12½in. wide. (Christie's) $660 £462

A large 18th century lac burgaute peach-shaped box and cover inlaid in shell, 43.5cm. wide. (Christie's) $1,179 £825

A mid Victorian black, gilt and mother-of-pearl japanned papier-mache purdonium, 20in. wide, and another. (Christie's) $1,573 £1,100

A Victorian brass and velvet 'perambulator' sewing box, possibly America, circa 1880, 7½in. long. (Robt. W. Skinner Inc.) $400 £258

Early 19th century Chinese Export black and gold lacquer games box, 15in. wide. (Christie's) $1,551 £1,100

A George III partridgewood tea caddy with Lever patent lock, 9½in. high. (Christie's) $1,337 £935

Early 19th century roironuri suzuribako, decorated in gold hiramakie, takamakie and hirame, 24.8 x 22.9cm. (Christie's) $7,497 £5,280

157

Mid 19th century black painted chest, the interior lined with mid 19th century newspaper, New England, 19¼in. wide. (Christie's) $1,540 £1,016

A wooden, painted gesso and gilded casket, by W. Cayley-Robinson, 35cm. wide. (Phillips) $1,224 £850

A mid Victorian black and gilt japanned papier-mache cigar box with hinged lid, 7¾in. wide. (Christie's) $125 £88

One of a set of eight Regency parcel gilt and scarlet japanned tea cannisters, 18in. high. (Christie's) $7,550 £5,280

Birmingham tortoiseshell snuff box with gilt metal mounts, 2½in. diam., circa 1800. (Peter Wilson) $98 £70

One of a pair of Federal mahogany and mahogany veneer inlaid knife boxes, America or England, circa 1790, 14½in. high. (Robt. W. Skinner Inc.) $950 £664

A 17th century needlework casket, all decorated with silver wire and silkwork, 23cm. wide. (Phillips) $1,368 £950

A 19th century French gold mounted tortoiseshell jewel casket, 5in. high. (Christie's) $8,250 £5,811

Early 19th century wallpaper hat box, 'A Peep at the Moon', America, 12½in. high, 17in. wide. (Robt. W. Skinner Inc.) $200 £129

A Victorian walnut dome top tea caddy with ornate brass key escutcheon, cartouche and corners, 8.7in. wide. (Woolley & Wallis) $230 £160

Regency Tole Peinte coal bin on claw feet. (Lots Road Galleries) $720 £500

A 19th century pine Scandinavian bride's box, 11½in. high, 21½in. wide. (Christie's) $495 £323

One of a pair of George III black shagreen cutlery boxes, one with gilt fittings, the other with silvered fittings, 13½in. high. (Christie's) $660 £432

A Regency tortoiseshell veneered rectangular tea chest with wire inlay, 7in. long. (Woolley & Wallis) $445 £295

A George III fruitwood tea caddy formed as an apple, 5in. high. (Christie's) $1,179 £825

A Regency gilt metal mounted scarlet leather casket, each of the doors with a musical Chinaman, 12in. wide. (Christie's) $1,318 £935

One of a pair of George III mahogany cutlery urns, the foliate domed covers with urn finials, 29½in. high. (Christie's) $3,412 £2,420

A 17th century needlework casket, the front and side panels of raised and stuffed stumpwork, England, 10¾in. wide. (Robt. W. Skinner Inc.) $2,600 £1,818

A Flemish gilt metal mounted ebony casket with partly fitted interior, 17in. wide. (Christie's) $2,811 £1,980

A George III satinwood and marquetry tea caddy with divided interior, 8in. wide. (Christie's) $792 £518

A 17th century German black painted and parcel gilt strongbox with carrying handles, 27in. wide. (Christie's)
$781 £550

A 19th century suzuribako decorated in gold and silver hiramakie, nashiji and hirame on a maki-bokashi ground, 26 x 23.1cm. (Christie's) $5,467 £3,850

A George III treen (applewood) tea caddy formed as a large apple with hinged cover and ebonised stem, 6in. high. (Christie's) $4,653 £3,300

A late 16th century French walnut and parcel gilt casket with fitted interior, 20in. wide. (Christie's)
$2,811 £1,980

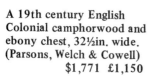

A 19th century English Colonial camphorwood and ebony chest, 32½in. wide. (Parsons, Welch & Cowell)
$1,771 £1,150

A Norwegian painted pine scala, 19in. wide. (Christie's)
$281 £198

An early Victorian gentleman's dressing case, the contents hallmarked, maker Thos. Diller, London, 1840, 11oz. weighable silver. (Woolley & Wallis)
$923 £620

An early Victorian black, gilt and mother-of-pearl japanned papier-mache tea caddy, 15¾in. wide. (Christie's) $975 £582

A Regency rosewood and boulle tea caddy of sarcophagus shape, the interior with blue glass mixing bowl 12½in. wide. (Christie's) $239 £165

Mid 19th century chinoiserie decorated lacquer sewing box, containing ivory implements, China, 14½in. wide. (Robt. W. Skinner Inc.) $550 £384

Upson family tole document box, the front and sides with floral band decoration, Conn., circa 1820, 9¼in. long. (Robt. W. Skinner Inc.) $1,000 £699

A mid Victorian black and gilt japanned tole purdonium, with shovel, 12½in. wide. (Christie's) $597 £418

An Indo-Chinese gilt lacquer box profusely decorated in alto relievo, 2ft.4in. wide. (Capes, Dunn & Co.) $522 £360

A Regency black japanned tole coal box on cabochon feet, 24in. wide. (Christie's) $629 £440

A Victorian brass bound coromandel wood dressing case, the silver mounts mostly by C. Rawlings and Wm. Summers, 1845, two bottle tops 1853, case 15 x 10¾in. (Christie's) $2,359 £1,650

A George III satinwood, marquetry and painted octangular tea caddy with hinged top, 6½in. wide. (Christie's) $957 £626

A Zeiss Ikon Miroflex, 9 x 12cm. format, with 15cm. f 4.5 Tessar lens, 19cm. long, circa 1935. (Christie's) $77 £53

A Leica IIIg camera No. 686682 with a Leitz Summaron f3.5 3.5cm. lens, a Leitz Elmar lens, a Soogz lens hood, an Ablon trimming template and a Tuvoo Universal viewfinder. (Christie's) $655 £440

A Newmand & Sinclair 35mm. cinematograph camera No. 616 with accessories. (Christie's) $418 £260

A 9 x 12cm. ?Ernemann tropical folding plate camera in brass reinforced teak casing with Bolter and Stammer, Hanover label, with lens and Compur shutter. (Christie's) $154 £104

A tropical Contess-Nettel 10 x 15cm. Deck-Rullo camera with teakwood body, circa 1927. (Christie's) $737 £495

A Thornton-Pickard half-plate Ruby camera with a Ross 8½ x 6½ rapid symmetrical No. 39577, d.d.s., focusing cloth in canvas case. (Christie's) $147 £99

A panoramic camera, the Eastman Kodak No. 4 Panoram-Kodak, model D, circa 1910, 10¼in. long. (Christie's) $55 £38

A chrome Nikon S2 camera no. 6175567, with a black Nikkor-S f1.4 5cm. lens, with two others. (Christie's) $524 £352

An Eastman Kodak Co. No. 2 Brownie camera Model D in original maker's box, made circa 1901-33. (Christie's) $65 £44

A Le Coultre Compass camera No. 2629 with a CCL 3B Anastigmat f3.5 35mm. with plate back and roll film back. (Christie's) $983 £660

A Zeiss Ikon Contax I camera No. AU80899 with a Zeiss Tessar f2.8 5cm. lens. (Christie's) $557 £374

An Andre Debrie 16mm. Sinmor professional cine camera Model No. 46 Series C, with accessories. (Christie's) $998 £620

A Wratten & Wainwright 13 x 18cm. tailboard camera with a Ross 8 x 5 Rapid symmetrical lens. (Christie's) $311 £209

A brass reproduction Petzval-Type daguerreotype camera, signed Voigtlander & Sohn in Wien, no. 084, circa 1956, 12¼in. long. (Christie's) $2,530 £1,765

A Rectaflex Rotor three-lens turret 35mm. s.l.r. camera. (Christie's) $983 £660

A Zeiss Ikon 4.5 x 6cm. Ermanox Reflex camera No. M99925 with a Carl Zeiss-Ernemann Ernostar lens, lens cap and two s.m.s. in fitted case. (Christie's) $2,093 £1,300

A 10 x 12in. brass and mahogany field camera with an alloy-bound Marion & Co. No. 5 Rectilinear and Waterhouse stops, all in a case.(Christie's) $278 £187

A 10 x 12in. G. Hare tailboard camera in brass and mahogany with red square cut bellows with a Gasc & Charconnet, Paris, 7in. lens, together with another three. (Christie's) $245 £165

An Ilford Witness camera no. 5226, with a Dallmeyer Super-Six anastigmat f1.9 2in. lens. (Christie's) $688 £462

A 45 x 107mm. Ica Poly-skop camera with a pair of Zeiss Tessar lens, in a fitted case. (Christie's) $138 £93

The Al-Vista Panoramic camera by the Multi Scope & Film Co., 11in. long, circa 1900. (Christie's) $77 £53

A Kodak Ltd. Boy Scout Kodak camera in green enamelled finish No. 99805. (Christie's) $131 £88

A Zeiss-Ikon/Ica Polyskop camera No. J91894 with a pair of Zeiss Tessar f4.5 6.5cm. lens. (Christie's) $299 £154

A red-dial Leica IIIf camera No. 795893 with self-timer and other accessories, all in a Leitz fitted case.(Christie's) $901 £605

A Voigtlander 4¼ x 1.5/8in. Verascope-style leather covered stereo camera with a pair of Heliar f4.5 lens, in fitted case. (Christie's) $154 £104

A 7¼ x 7¼in. sliding box wet-plate camera and a Jamin, Paris, lens with rack and pinion focusing and metal lens cap. (Christie's) $1,449 £900

A Marion & Co. 1¼ x 1¼in. Metal Miniature camera with a Petzval-type lens. (Christie's) $2,130 £1,430

A double stroke Leica M3 camera No. 785381, with four lenses and accessories. (Christie's) $1,065 £715

A Multiscope and Film Co. No. 4B Al-Vista Panoramic camera with lens No. 3054, in leather case. (Christie's) $262 £176

A quarter-plate Sinclair Una hand and stand camera with a Newman & Sinclair 'Accurate' shutter and Goetz Celor lens. (Christie's) $573 £385

A mid 19th century Bohemian cranberry pink six-light chandelier made for the Indian or Turkish market, 48in. high. (Christie's) $11,781 £7,700

Late 19th century six-light antler chandelier, 48in. high. (Christie's) $1,178 £770

An Art Deco glass and chromium plated metal chandelier of star form, circa 1930, 71cm. wide. (Christie's) $26,928 £18,700

A late Regency ormolu three-light chandelier with ostrich feather corona, fitted for electricity, 22½in. high. (Christie's) $1,240 £880

An ormolu six-light chandelier of Regence style, 27½in. high. (Christie's) $1,874 £1,320

Late 19th century Meissen six-light chandelier, fitted for electric light, 74cm. high. (Christie's) $4,375 £2,860

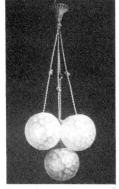

A French Art Deco spelter chandelier, the opalescent glass shades moulded with cell pattern, 72cm. high. (Christie's) $792 £550

A 17th century brass six-branch chandelier with scrolled branches, fitted for electricity, 20in. high. (Christie's) $4,404 £3,080

Early 19th century parcel gilt and ebonised six-light chandelier, 33½in. high. (Christie's) $3,722 £2,640

AMERICAN

Teco pottery brown moulded vase, bullet shape on four elongated V feet, Illinois, 1909, 8½in. high. (Robt. W. Skinner Inc.)
$1,800 £1,259

Saturday evening girl's decorated cream pitcher, Boston, circa 1910, signed S.E.G., 191-5-10 I.G., 3in. high. (Robt. W. Skinner Inc.) $850 £594

Late 19th century Dedham pottery mottled pink vase, incised H.R. Jr., for Hugh Robertson, 8¾in. high. (Robt. W. Skinner Inc.)
$1,200 £839

Late 19th century majolica garden seat, 17¾in. high, 12in. diam. (Robt. W. Skinner Inc.) $950 £664

One of a pair of Tucker porcelain pitchers, Phila., 1826-39, 9in. high. (Christie's) $2,420 £1,565

Early 20th century Dedham crackleware metal shape vase, 8½in. high. (Robt. W. Skinner Inc.) $1,100 £769

Van Briggle pottery copper clad vase, Colorado, 5½in. high. (Robt. W. Skinner Inc.)
$1,200 £839

Late 19th century Dedham pottery experimental vase, pink star drip design on green, 10¼in. high. (Robt. W. Skinner Inc.)
$5,500 £3,846

Late 19th century Walley pottery 'Devil' mug, impressed WJW, 5½in. high, 4in. diam. (Robt. W. Skinner Inc.) $350 £245

AMERICAN

Roseville decorated matt umbrella stand, Ohio, circa 1910, no. 724, 20in. high. (Robt. W. Skinner Inc.)
$1,300 £909

Early 20th century Saturday evening girl's decorated pitcher, Boston, signed S.E.G. 276-1-10, 9½in. high. (Robt. W. Skinner Inc.)
$4,000 £3,426

Grueby pottery two-colour butterscotch vase, Boston, circa 1905, 11in. high. (Robt. W. Skinner Inc.)
$2,300 £1,608

A porcelain pitcher, by The Union Porcelain Works, Greenpoint, N.Y., designed by Karl Mueller, circa 1880, 9¼in. high. (Christie's)
$2,420 £1,565

Early 20th century Dedham pottery rabbit figural flower frog, 6¼in. high. (Robt. W. Skinner Inc.) $700 £490

Early 20th century Dedham pottery large milk pitcher, Rabbit pattern, 8½in. high. (Robt. W. Skinner Inc.)
$325 £227

Late 19th century Dedham pottery volcanic oxblood vase, 7.1/8in. high. (Robt. W. Skinner Inc.)
$6,600 £4,615

Late 19th century Chelsea Keramic Art Works oxblood vase, 8¼in. high. (Robt. W. Skinner Inc.) $650 £454

Wheatley pottery vase, Ohio, circa 1905, matt green in Grueby manner, 10¾in. high. (Robt. W. Skinner Inc.)
$650 £455

Late 17th century Arita blue and white oviform ewer with loop handle, the silver mount 19th century, 25cm. high. (Christie's)
$1,718 £1,210

A European silver mounted Arita teapot and domed cover decorated in iron-red, green and black enamels, circa 1700, 19.6cm. long. (Christie's)
$859 £605

One of a pair of 19th century Arita blue and white globular bottle vases, 62.5cm. high. (Christie's) $18,744 £13,200

An ormolu mounted Japanese Arita baluster jar and cover painted in the Imari palette, the porcelain late 17th century, 35 in. high. (Christie's)
$5,935 £4,180

A large Arita polychrome model of Buddha, Meiji period, 46cm. high. (Christie's) $624 £440

Late 17th century Arita oviform ewer with loop handle decorated in underglaze blue, 21cm. high. (Christie's) $1,405 £990

Late 17th/early 18th century Arita octagonal blue and white vase and cover, 56cm. high. (Christie's) $1,874 £1,320

An 18th century Japanese Arita charger, 18in. diam. (Dreweatts) $1,224 £800

An Arita globular apothecary bottle decorated in underglaze blue, iron-red, green, yellow and black enamels, circa 1680, 27.3cm. high. (Christie's) $4,686 £3,300

BELLEEK

A Belleek oval basket with pierced trellis sides and everted looped rim, first period, 27cm. wide. (Christie's) $470 £280

A Belleek porcelain trefoil basket, osier pattern, 5in. diam. (Hobbs & Chambers) $238 £150

A Belleek basket and cover of oval shape with three strand basket weave base, 8½in. wide. (Peter Wilson) $1,510 £1,000

A Belleek cornucopia vase on shell moulded base, 9¼in. high. (Christie's) $382 £242

Late 19th century Belleek figure of a young lady dressed in a classical style pink robe, 14¼in. high. (Outhwaite & Litherland) $1,131 £780

A Belleek Parian bust of 'Clytie', the socle with Belleek black printed marks, first period, 29.5cm. high. (Christie's) $1,280 £800

A Belleek Parian figure entitled 'The Prisoner of Love', after the model by G. Fontana, 65cm. high. (Christie's) $7,114 £4,620

A Belleek porcelain nautilus shell vase, 9in. high. (Christie's) $146 £93

A Belleek figure of 'Erin Awakening from her Slumbers', modelled by Wm. B. Kirk, 42.5cm. high. (Phillips) $2,016 £1,400

Late 19th century Berlin bowl and cover, blue sceptre mark, 10.5in. diam. (Woolley & Wallis) $858 £600

A KPM wall plate, with hand-painted decoration of a bare-breasted Junoesque figure, blue printed KPM mark, 40.5cm. diam. (Christie's) $578 £378

A Berlin faience 'Schnabel-kanne' with original pewter mounts, attributed to the Wolbeer factory, dated AB 1712, 37cm. high. (Phillips) $5,852 £3,800

A Berlin green-ground ovi-form pot pourri vase, circa 1810, 31cm. high. (Christie's) $5,970 £4,146

A Berlin rectangular plaque painted with Diana and Bacchus, impressed sceptre and KPM marks, circa 1865, 27.5 x 22cm. (Christie's) $2,524 £1,650

One of a pair of late 18th century Berlin ornithological wall pockets, 21cm. high. (Christie's) $3,142 £2,182

A Berlin rectangular plaque painted after Domenichino with a portrait of Sybil, circa 1865, 14.5 x 11cm. (Christie's) $757 £495

A Berlin iron-red ground two-handled cup, cover and stand, blue sceptre mark, circa 1830. (Christie's) $1,515 £1,045

A Berlin rectangular plaque painted after Holbein, impressed KPM and sceptre marks, circa 1865, 25 x 18.5cm. (Christie's) $1,276 £880

BOW

A Bow figure of a recumbent lion painted in 'Muses' style with streaked and washed brown fur, circa 1750, 9.5cm. wide. (Christie's)
$5,068 £3,520

One of a pair of Bow figures of a gardener and companion , circa 1762, 20cm. high. (Christie's) $1,029 £715

A Bow blue and white cylindrical piggin, 6.5cm. diam., and a spoon, 9.5cm. long, circa 1760. (Christie's)
$760 £528

A Bow plate printed with Aeneas and Anchises fleeing from Troy, 1756-58, 7½in. diam. (Dreweatts)
$2,030 £1,400

A Bow octagonal plate printed in Venetian or brick red with 'The Young Archers', 7in. diam. (Dreweatts) $2,218 £1,530

A Bow sweetmeat figure modelled as a monkey seated beside a rococo scroll moulded bowl, circa 1758, 14cm. high. (Christie's) $1,029 £715

One of a pair of Bow candlesticks, each modelled as Cupid with a dog at his side, anchor and dagger marks in iron-red, circa 1770, 26.5cm. high. (Christie's) $1,584 £1,100

A Bow figure of Air modelled as a nymph in pale blue lined yellow shawl, circa 1758, 23.5cm. high. (Christie's)
$1,346 £935

A pair of Bow candlestick figures of a gallant and his companion, 10½in. high. (Graves Son & Pilcher)
$936 £620

A Bristol delft posset pot and cover decorated in the Chinese style with flowers in blue, circa 1710-30, 8in. high. (Dreweatts) $2,320 £1,600

A Bristol delft polychrome farmhouse plate painted with a cockerel, circa 1740, 18cm. diam. (Christie's) $1,219 £792

A Bristol polychrome posset pot and cover decorated in the Chinese style with flowers in red, blue and green, circa 1710-30, 9in. high. (Dreweatts) $4,640 £3,200

Two Bristol delft dishes, the centres painted with a bird perched on a branch, circa 1740, approx. 33cm. diam. (Christie's) $1,029 £715

A Bristol campana shaped vase with double rope twist handles and frilled rim, circa 1750, 6¾in. high. (Dreweatts) $3,335 £2,300

A Bristol delft circular dish, the centre painted with an Oriental lady, blue 7 mark, circa 1740, 33cm. diam. (Christie's) $1,425 £990

A Bristol delft blue-dash Adam and Eve small charger, circa 1710, 30.5cm. diam. (Christie's) $1,188 £825

A Bristol delft blue and white cylindrical mug with broad strap handle, circa 1730, 12cm. high. (Christie's) $1,355 £880

A large Bristol delft dish, decorated in blue with two figures in a punt, circa 1760, 13in. diam. (Dreweatts) $377 £260

BRITISH

A creamware globular teapot and cover with entwined strap handle, painted in the manner of D. Rhodes, circa 1770, 14.5cm. high. (Christie's) $3,484 £2,420

Victorian majolica strawberry dish moulded in the form of two nests holding sugar bowl and creamer, 10¾in. wide. (Hobbs & Chambers) $231 £150

A Linthorpe 'Peruvian' vessel, designed by Dr. C. Dresser, 17cm. high, impressed 296. (Phillips) $1,296 £900

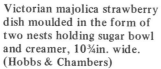

Bennington scroddled ware wash bowl and pitcher, bowl 13½in. diam., pitcher 10.7/8in. high, 1853-58. (Robt. W. Skinner Inc.) $300 £200

An English rectangular plaque, painted by James Rouse, signed and dated 1830, with Lord Byron watching Mary Anne Chaworth, 11.5 x 14.5cm. (Phillips) $708 £460

One of a pair of late 19th/ early 20th century porcelain wine coolers, English, 8.7/8in. high. (Christie's) $660 £430

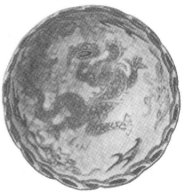

A flambe pottery bowl, by Bernard Moore, 8¼in. diam., and a Chinese carved wood stand. (Reeds Rains) $356 £230

A Caughley eye bath, printed in blue with portions of the 'Fisherman' pattern, 5.5cm. high. (Phillips) $1,001 £650

A Crown Ducal 'Manchu' pattern bowl, designed by Charlotte Rhead, 25.5cm. diam. (Phillips) $137 £95

CHINA

A pottery model of a pig,
designed by Louis Wain,
12cm. high, impressed Rd.
no. 033320, Made in England.
(Phillips) $130 £90

A Bretby tobacco jar and
cover, inscribed 'Nicotiank',
16.5cm. high. (Phillips)
                    $94 £65

A Linthorpe pottery jug
designed by Christopher
Dresser, 9in. high, and a
dish. (Christie's) $230 £160

A Linthorpe pottery vase, designed by
C. Dresser, the central neck surrounded
by five onion shaped forms, 4in. high.
(Christie's) $604 £420

A John Hassell 'Egg Man', modelled as a
policeman, Boy Scout and country yokel,
6in. high. (Christie's) $226 £150

A Brannam pottery figure
of a standing frog holding
a giant lily leaf, in shades of
blue and green, 12¼in. high.
(Christie's) $792 £550

An inscribed globular buff-
ground jug with scroll handle,
painted in the manner of
Absolon of Yarmouth, circa
1790, 10cm. high. (Christie's)
                    $633 £440

A Foley 'Intarsio' tobacco
jar and cover, 14.3cm. high,
no. 3458, Rd. no. 364386
(SR). (Phillips) $203 £140

BRITISH

A George IV yellow ground jug, printed in red and coloured, depicting 'A Visit from Richmond to Carlton House', 15.5cm. high. (Phillips) $847 £550

A ceramic sculpture of a ram, by Rosemary Wren, 13.5cm. high. (Christie's) $54 £38

A pearlware inscribed oviform jug with loop handle, painted in the manner of Absolon of Yarmouth, circa 1790, 18.5cm. high. (Christie's) $2,851 £1,980

Five pieces of Gray's pottery advertising Ross's Soft Drinks, decorated in several colours. (Lots Road Galleries) $171 £120

A Caughley baluster shaped jug with scroll handle and mask spout, 7in. high, C mark in blue. (Dreweatts) $348 £240

A Portobello money box in the form of a Wesleyan Chapel, flanked by two putti, 16.5cm. high. (Phillips) $924 £600

An English porcelain candlestick figure of 'Girl on a Horse' type modelled as an exotic pheasant, circa 1765, 21cm. high. (Christie's) $3,960 £2,750

CHINA

A Yorkshire pearlware sauce-boat in the form of a duck, circa 1790, 19cm. long. (Christie's) $1,188 £825

A Carlton Ware Limited Edition punch bowl, moulded in relief with a frieze of Henry VIII, his wives and children, 21cm. high. (Phillips) $489 £340

A Longton Hall white figure of a recumbent horse of Snowman type, circa 1750, 17cm. wide. (Christie's) $1,267 £880

An English majolica ware model of a dolphin forming the base for a table or lamp, 93cm. high. (Phillips) $1,386 £900

Three of five Art Deco Ashtead pottery wall plates. (Phillips) $337 £269

A creamware inscribed oviform jug with the inscription Jane Strickelton Armley followed by a rhyme, probably Leeds, circa 1800, 13cm. high. (Christie's) $348 £242

A Linthorpe pottery moon-flask, designed by C. Dresser, 7½in. high. (Christie's) $136 £95

One of a pair of English porcelain groups of leopards and cubs naturally coloured, circa 1835, 11cm. wide. (Christie's) $2,534 £1,760

Part of a Susie Cooper pottery fruit set, comprising a bowl, 22.4cm. diam., and twelve plates, 22.6cm. diam. (Phillips) $145 £100

CANTON

One of a pair of Canton famille rose two-handled vases with pelican handles. (Christie's) $632 £400

Early 19th century Chinese Canton decorated famille verte bowl, 11.5in. diam. (Woolley & Wallis)
$573 £370

A Canton famille rose two-handled vase with a linen fold body and neck, 25in. high. (Christie's)$758 £480

A Cantonese vase of ovoid form with Buddhist lion handles, 86cm. high, Daoguang. (Osmond Tricks) $832 £520

Pair of Cantonese famille rose vases of ovoid form with Buddhist lion handles, 37cm. high, Daoguang. (Osmond Tricks) $960 £600

One of a pair of 19th century Canton baluster vases, 24in. high. (Parsons, Welch & Cowell) $935 £560

A Beijing or Canton enamel and gilt bronze two-handled tripod censer and pierced domed cover, Qianlong seal mark, 40cm. high.(Christie's) $2,671 £1,870

A Canton enamel octagonal boxed supper set and cover, mid Qing Dynasty, 34cm. wide. (Christie's) $666 £447

A Canton coffee pot, the domed cover with gilt finial, 9¾in. high. (Reeds Rains) $418 £270

CARDEW

An Abuja stoneware casserole and cover, by Michael Cardew, with two strap handles, circa 1960, 31.2cm. diam. (Christie's) $1,156 £756

An Abuja stoneware teapot with screw top, by Michael Cardew, circa 1958, 10cm. high. (Christie's) $627 £410

A stoneware deep footed bowl, by Michael Cardew, circa 1975, 33.2cm. wide. (Christie's) $597 £418

A stoneware stemmed bowl, by Michael Cardew, with crescent lug handles, circa 1975, 17.1cm. high. (Christie's) $141 £99

An earthenware dish, by Michael Cardew, impressed MC and Winchcombe Pottery seals, circa 1930, 35.1cm. diam. (Christie's)$660 £462

A large stoneware oviform jar, by Michael Cardew, with four lug handles and short cylindrical neck, circa 1970, 39.6cm. high. (Christie's) $627 £410

An early earthenware motto jug, by Michael Cardew, circa 1925, 15.5cm. high. (Christie's) $578 £378

An Abuja stoneware slip-glazed plate, by Michael Cardew, covered in a dark brown glaze over an olive-green celadon, 25.7cm. diam. (Christie's) $148 £97

A stoneware two-handled crock and cover, by Michael Cardew, circa 1975, 38.5cm. high. (Christie's) $865 £605

CARDEW

A stoneware deep bowl, by Michael Cardew, impressed MC and Wenford Bridge seals, circa 1970, 28.7cm. diam. (Christie's) $660 £462

One of a pair of Abuja stoneware circular dishes and covers, by Michael Cardew, circa 1960, 10.5cm. diam. (Christie's) $148 £97

A large earthenware bowl, by Michael Cardew, covered in a brown glaze stopping short of the foot, circa 1930, 37.2cm. diam. (Christie's) $495 £324

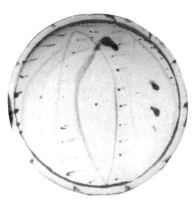

One of a pair of stoneware plates, by Michael Cardew, circa 1979, 24.4cm. diam. (Christie's) $314 £220

An Abuja stoneware oviform jar with three lug handles, by Michael Cardew, circa 1960, 19.5cm. high. (Christie's) $743 £486

A stoneware plate, by Michael Cardew, with panels of sgraffito, blue and iron-brown painted decoration against a greyish-white ground, circa 1970, 26.9cm. diam. (Christie's) $180 £118

One of a pair of Abuja stoneware soy sauce pots with screw covers, by Michael Cardew, circa 1959, 9.5cm. high. (Christie's) $330 £216

An earthenware ewer, by Michael Cardew, 26cm. high, also a basin en suite, circa 1935. (Christie's) $471 £330

An earthenware motto jug, by Michael Cardew, circa 1925, 18cm. high. (Christie's) $943 £660

A Chelsea peach-shaped cream jug with puce stalk handle, circa 1750, 11cm. wide. (Christie's)
$6,019 £4,180

A Chelsea figure of a standing cow, her coat with purple markings, red anchor mark, circa 1756, 11.5cm. wide. (Christie's) $2,692 £1,870

A Chelsea fluted oval salt or strawberry dish, incised triangle mark, 1745-49, 12.3cm. wide. (Christie's)
$2,851 £1,980

A Chelsea 'crayfish' salt after a silver original by N. Sprimont, painted in the workshop of Wm. Duesbury, 1745-49, 12.5cm. wide. (Christie's)
$20,592 £14,300

A scent bottle of 'Girl in a Swing' type modelled as a youth and companion, the base inscribed C'est L'Amour Qui m'Inspire, circa 1755, 10.5cm. high. (Christie's)
$2,534 £1,760

A Chelsea peach-shaped dish painted in the Kakiemon palette, circa 1750, 20cm. wide. (Christie's)
$4,435 £3,080

A Chelsea shell salt, painted in the workshop of Wm. Duesbury, incised triangle mark, 1745-49, 7.5cm. wide. (Christie's) $2,692 £1,870

A pair of Chelsea masqueraders, gold anchor marks at back, circa 1765, 30cm. high. (Christie's) $2,059 £1,430

A Chelsea fluted teabowl painted in a vivid Kakiemon palette with birds perched and in flight, 1750-52, 5cm. high. (Christie's)
$1,900 £1,320

A Chelsea Hans Sloane botanical dish of lobed heart shape, 27cm. long, red anchor mark. (Phillips) $2,926 £1,900

A Chelsea group of two goats, painted in the workshop of Wm. Duesbury, raised red anchor mark, circa 1751, 16.5cm. wide. (Christie's) $14,256 £9,900

A Chelsea mottled claret-ground shaped oval dish, 33.5cm. wide, and another 34cm. wide, circa 1760. (Christie's) $1,900 £1,320

A Chelsea acanthus leaf moulded cream jug with bamboo styled handle, crown and trident mark in blue, circa 1749, 8.4cm. high. (Christie's) $6,336 £4,400

Pair of Chelsea figures of Great Spotted Cuckoos, one with raised red anchor mark, circa 1750, 19cm. high. (Christie's) $6,652 £4,620

A scent bottle of 'Girl in a Swing' type modelled as Wm. Shakespeare, circa 1755, 8.5cm. high. (Christie's) $570 £396

A Chelsea peach-shaped cream jug painted in the Vincennes style with a bouquet of flowers, circa 1750, 11cm. wide. (Christie's) $6,652 £4,620

Pair of Chelsea Derby candlestick figures of a gallant and his companion, 6½in. and 6in. high, no nozzles. (Graves Son & Pilcher) $830 £550

A Chelsea chicken box and a cover, circa 1756, 9cm. wide. (Christie's) $1,267 £880

181

CHELSEA

A Chelsea double scent bottle modelled as a parrot and a rooster, circa 1755, 7cm. high. (Christie's) $2,692 £1,870

A Chelsea cinquefoil teabowl painted in the Kakiemon palette with The Lady in a Pavilion Pattern, 1750-52, 5.5cm. high. (Christie's) $1,504 £1,045

A 'Girl in a Swing' gold mounted cylindrical etui, 1751-54, 11.5cm. high. (Christie's) $2,851 £1,980

A Chelsea lobed teaplant beaker painted in a vivid famille rose palette, 1745-49, 7.5cm. high. (Christie's) $5,702 £3,960

A Chelsea decagonal plate painted in a Kakiemon palette with phoenix perched and in flight, circa 1752, 19.5cm. diam. (Christie's) $2,534 £1,760

A Chelsea acanthus leaf moulded white chocolate pot on four feet, 1745-49, 24cm. high overall. (Christie's) $1,346 £935

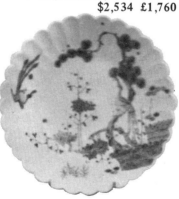

A Chelsea gold mounted scent bottle naturalistically modelled as a pineapple, circa 1755, 6.5cm. high. (Christie's) $1,584 £1,100

A Chelsea fluted saucer dish painted in a vivid Kakiemon palette with phoenix perched and in flight, circa 1752, 18cm. diam. (Christie's) $9,820 £6,820

A Chelsea cane handle modelled as a lady's head, 1745-49, 7cm. high. (Christie's) $2,217 £1,540

CHELSEA

A copper gilt mounted etui of 'Girl in a Swing' type, circa 1755, 12.5cm. long. (Christie's) $1,188 £825

A Chelsea flared fluted beaker painted in the Kakiemon palette, 1750-52, 7cm. high. (Christie's) $1,742 £1,210

One of a pair of Chelsea gold mounted scent bottles modelled as a friar and nun, circa 1756, 9cm. high. (Christie's) $1,188 £825

A Chelsea goat and bee jug of conventional type, incised triangle mark, 1745-49, 11cm. high. (Christie's) $5,385 £3,740

A Chelsea silver shaped plate painted in the Kakiemon palette with The Red Tiger Pattern, 1750-52, 23cm. diam. (Christie's) $6,336 £4,400

A Chelsea flared and fluted coffee cup with scroll handle, circa 1750, 7.5cm. high. (Christie's) $2,692 £1,870

Late 19th century Chelsea Keramic Art Works square moulded vase, 7½in. high, 4in. diam. (Robt. W. Skinner Inc.) $450 £315

A Chelsea plate with Gotszkowsky erhabene Blumen, circa 1753, 24cm. diam. (Christie's) $633 £440

A Chelsea gold mounted scent bottle naturalistically modelled as a peach, circa 1755, 7cm. high. (Christie's) $1,188 £825

CHINESE

A large Chinese bottle-shaped porcelain vase, 25in. high. (Parsons, Welch & Cowell) $477 £310

A rose-verte armorial dish, circa 1735, 14in. diam. (Christie's) $3,436 £2,420

A 17th century Dehua blanc-de-chine figure of Guandi, 24cm. high, fitted box. (Christie's) $2,044 £1,430

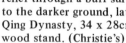

One of a pair of 19th century rose medallion garden seats, China, 19in. high. (Robt. W. Skinner Inc.) $5,250 £3,671

A Yue Yao circular box and cover, Five Dynasties, 7cm. diam. (Christie's) $1,494 £1,045

A slate panel carved in high relief through a buff surface to the darker ground, late Qing Dynasty, 34 x 28cm., wood stand. (Christie's) $1,258 £880

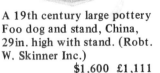

A dragon saucer dish painted in iron-red and gilt, unenclosed Guangxu six-character mark and of the period, 34cm. diam. (Christie's) $943 £660

A 19th century large pottery Foo dog and stand, China, 29in. high with stand. (Robt. W. Skinner Inc.) $1,600 £1,111

A large Export armorial dish painted in shades of blue, yellow, iron-red, green and gilt, circa 1740, 17in. diam. (Christie's) $4,686 £3,300

CHINESE

A flambe glazed bottle vase, impressed Qianlong seal mark and of the period, 45.5cm. high. (Christie's)
$4,719 £3,300

A Doucai saucer dish, Qianlong seal mark and of the period, 52cm. diam. (Christie's)
$13,370 £9,350

A transitional Wucai gu-shaped beaker vase, circa 1640, 41.2cm. high. (Christie's) $2,831 £1,980

An 11th/12th century Annamese jar and shallow domed cover, Thanh Hoa, 21cm. high. (Christie's)
$597 £418

Pair of modern Chinese ducks, on punchwork base, each 9½in. high. (Christie's) $440 £287

A phosphatic-splashed oviform ewer, Tang Dynasty, 16cm. high. (Christie's)
$4,719 £3,300

One of four late 18th century Chinese Export soup plates, 8.7/8in. diam. (Christie's)
$1,870 £1,220

A 17th/18th century Dehua blanc-de-chine figure of Guanyin, 40cm. high. (Christie's) $2,674 £1,870

An Annamese blue and white dish, 15th century, 15in. diam. (Christie's)
$1,327 £935

CHINESE

Early 19th century Oriental Export porcelain punch bowl, China, rim diam. 14¾in., 6in. high. (Robt. W. Skinner Inc.)
$2,100 £1,468

One of a pair of Doucai bowls, Daoguang seal marks and of the period, 14.3cm. diam. (Christie's) $3,146 £2,200

19th century Chinese square cut corner 'Thousand Butterfly' porcelain salad bowl, 10¼in. diam. (Robt. W. Skinner Inc.) $750 £500

One of a pair of Oriental square porcelain vases, 12in. high. (Chancellors Hollingsworths) $275 £180

A straw-glazed and painted figure of a richly caparisoned horse, Sui Dynasty, 32cm. high. (Christie's)
$5,033 £3,520

A flambe glazed rectangular pear-shaped vase, impressed Qianlong seal mark and of the period, 30cm. high. (Christie's) $1,415 £990

One of a pair of blue and white baluster vases with elephant handles, 14th century, 21.9cm. high. (Christie's) $4,876 £3,410

One of a pair of blue and white armorial dishes, circa 1752, 13¼in. diam. (Christie's)
$14,839 £10,450

One of a pair of 19th century rose Mandarin porcelain temple jars with mask and ring handles, China, 17½in. high. (Robt. W. Skinner Inc.)
$1,600 £1,066

CLARICE CLIFF

A Clarice Cliff Latona pottery oviform vase, painted with green, purple, white and orange flowers, 16.5cm. high. (Phillips) $216 £150

A large Clarice Cliff circular plaque from a design by Frank Brangwyn, in polychrome, 17in. diam., painted inscription No. 3. (Christie's) $2,416 £1,600

A Clarice Cliff Bizarre pottery mask, kite-shaped, 28cm. long. (Christie's) $1,793 £1,100

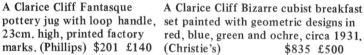

A Clarice Cliff Fantasque pottery jug with loop handle, 23cm. high, printed factory marks. (Phillips) $201 £140

A Clarice Cliff Bizarre cubist breakfast set painted with geometric designs in red, blue, green and ochre, circa 1931. (Christie's) $835 £500

A Clarice Cliff Fantasque pottery vase, painted in brown, black green, yellow and orange with a cottage and trees, 20.3cm. high. (Phillips) $216 £150

A Clarice Cliff 'Fantasque' pottery vase of flared form, 13.9cm. high, together with a Presnec pot and cover. (Phillips) $182 £120

A Clarice Cliff 'Inspiration' charger, 'The Knight Errant', 45.5cm. high. (Phillips) $1,728 £1,200

A Clarice Cliff Fantasque lotus jug, 25cm. high, printed factory marks. (Phillips) $648 £450

COALPORT

A Coalport (John Rose) oviform vase, painted with a silhouette portrait of George III, circa 1810, 20.5cm. high. (Christie's) $443 £308

A Coalport blue and white oval two-handled soup tureen and cover, transfer-printed with pagodas on river islands, circa 1800, 37cm. wide. (Christie's) $474 £308

One of a pair of Coalport oviform jugs, circa 1800, 20cm. high. (Christie's) $1,439 £935

A Coalport (John Rose & Co.) Great Exhibition plate, 1851, 26cm. diam. (Christie's) $1,267 £880

A Coalport spirally moulded oviform jug, circa 1800, 22.5cm. high. (Christie's) $406 £264

One of a pair of Coalport iron-red-ground flared bucket-shaped flower pots and stands, painted by Thos. Baxter, circa 1805, approx. 13cm. high. (Christie's) $3,801 £2,640

COPELAND

Copeland bust of Comte d'Orsay. (Lots Road Galleries) $86 £60

Bust of Venus. (Lots Road Galleries) $72 £50

A white bust of a gentleman. (Lots Road Galleries) $50 £35

HANS COPER

A stoneware goblet form vase, by Hans Coper, circa 1975, 13.7cm. high. (Christie's) $5,977 £4,180

A black glazed stoneware stemmed cup form, by Hans Coper, circa 1960, 13.1cm. high. (Christie's) $3,578 £2,460

A stoneware goblet-shaped vase, by Hans Coper, with waisted oval section rim, circa 1970, 24.9cm. high. (Christie's) $9,583 £6,264

A stoneware black bulbous bottle, by Hans Coper, circa 1965, 14.7cm. high. (Christie's) $8,651 £6,050

A waisted cylindrical stoneware vase, by Hans Coper, circa 1958, 17.3cm. high. (Christie's) $3,965 £2,592

A stoneware shouldered bottle vase, by Hans Coper, circa 1970, 20.8cm. high. (Christie's) $8,262 £5,400

A stoneware goblet vase, by Hans Coper, circa 1952, 15.2cm. high. (Christie's) $5,505 £3,850

A stoneware spherical vase, by Hans Coper, with horizontal flange, 1951, 19cm. high. (Christie's) $11,566 £7,560

A monumental stoneware 'thistle' vase, by Hans Coper, circa 1965, 57.4cm. high. (Christie's) $44,044 £30,800

DELFT

A Bristol delft dish, decorated in green, red and blue with the Mimosa pattern, circa 1740, 13¾in. diam. (Dreweatts) $282 £195

A delft posset pot with scroll handles, the waisted body decorated in blue, circa 1720, 5½in. high. (Dreweatts) $275 £190

A delft plate, the cartouche enclosing the initials G H E and date 1714, 8½in. diam., English or Dutch. (Dreweatts) $362 £250

An English delft pierced basket of circular shape raised on bun feet, probably Wincanton or Bristol, 27cm. diam. (Phillips) $3,850 £2,600

Mid 18th century Dutch Delft polychrome equestrian figure of Prince William of Orange, blue script mark of De Lampetkan, 15cm. high. (Christie's) $475 £330

Late 17th century London delft blue-dash tulip charger, 34cm. diam. (Christie's) $1,188 £825

Early 18th century Delft Dore circular plate, iron-red APK, 146, 614 mark of Pieter Adriaenson Koeks, 24.5cm. diam. (Christie's) $1,346 £935

A London delft dry drug jar, circa 1720, 6in. high. (Dreweatts) $507 £350

Early 18th century Delft Dore circular dish, iron-red APK mark of P. A. Koeks, 30.5cm. diam. (Christie's) $3,801 £2,640

DELFT

An English delft oak leaf charger with blue-dash rim edged with a yellow band, 34cm. diam. (Phillips) $1,771 £1,150

A Dutch Delft polychrome shaped plaque modelled and painted with a bird perched in a cage, mid 18th century, 34.5 x 42.5cm. (Christie's) $3,960 £2,750

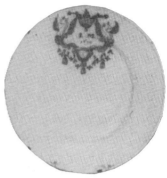

A delft plate decorated in blue with a cartouche over the rim, Dutch or English, 1698, 10in. diam. (Dreweatts) $435 £300

An English delft polychrome Royal portrait plate, William and Mary, 22cm. diam. (Phillips) $3,234 £2,100

Early 18th century Dutch Delft blue and white seated Magot, 18cm. high. (Christie's) $1,188 £825

A London delft blue-dash oak leaf charger, circa 1675, 33.5cm. diam. (Christie's) $4,118 £2,860

A large delft dish, decorated in blue, green and brown, probably Brislington, circa 1730, 13in. diam. (Dreweatts) $188 £130

One of a pair of London delft blue and white wet-drug jars, named for S. E. Spin, Ceru and S. Papau.Err, circa 1740, 17cm. high. (Christie's) $665 £462

Early 18th century Delft Dore circular plate, iron-red APK monogram of Pieter A. Koeks, 23cm. diam. (Christie's) $3,168 £2,200

DERBY

A Derby figure of Jupiter, scantily draped in a turquoise-lined pink flowered cloak, circa 1765, 27.5cm. high. (Christie's) $1,188 £825

Part of a Derby dessert service painted in the manner of Wm. Cotton, Robert Bloor & Co., circa 1815. (Christie's) $2,851 £1,980

A Derby hairdressing group, modelled as a gallant beside a lady dressing her hair, crown, crossed batons and D mark in iron-red, circa 1830, 18cm. high. (Christie's) $633 £440

A Derby 'dry-edge' group of a goat and kid, decorated in the workshop of Wm. Duesbury, Andrew Planche's period, circa 1752, 12cm. wide. (Christie's) $6,652 £4,620

A Derby seamstress group, modelled as a gallant standing beside a maid repairing his stockings, Robert Bloor & Co., circa 1830, 16.5cm. high. (Christie's) $712 £495

Part of a Crown Derby china teaset, Japan pattern with rouge-de-fer blue, gilt and green decoration, 58 pieces. (Graves Son & Pilcher) $1,585 £1,050

A Derby shoe-black group, modelled as a gallant, his shoes being polished by a maid, incised No. 81, Robert Bloor & Co., circa 1830, 18.5cm. high. (Christie's) $950 £660

A Derby baluster pot pourri vase and pierced domed cover, Wm. Duesbury & Co., circa 1760, 19cm. high. (Christie's) $633 £440

A Derby sweetmeat figure modelled as a lady seated, Wm. Duesbury & Co., circa 1760, 17cm. high. (Christie's) $823 £572

DERBY

A Derby figure of Jupiter holding a thunderbolt, circa 1770, 29cm. high.
(Christie's) $712 £405

One of a pair of Derby fluted lozenge-shaped dishes, the centres painted in the manner of Steele with fruit, circa 1810, 28.5cm. wide.
(Christie's) $1,584 £1,100

A Derby figure of John Milton leaning on a pile of books, Wm. Duesbury & Co., circa 1765, 29cm. high.
(Christie's) $570 £396

A Crown Derby squat vase and cover with two mask handles, circa 1884, 5in. high, printed mark in blue.
(Dreweatts) $290 £200

A Derby owl, its plumage in yellow, brown and pink perched astride a tree-stump, circa 1765, 6.5cm. high.
(Christie's) $1,108 £770

A Derby white 'dry-edge' figure of Winter modelled as a scantily draped putto, Andrew Planche's period, circa 1752, 10.5cm. high.
(Christie's) $712 £495

A Derby figure of Shakespeare in yellow-lined purple cloak, Wm. Duesbury & Co., circa 1765, 27.5cm. high.
(Christie's) $570 £396

One of a pair of Derby pear-shaped vases and covers of tapering form, Wm. Duesbury & Co., circa 1760, 18cm. high. (Christie's)
               $1,188 £825

A Derby white figure of St. Philip, Wm. Duesbury & Co., circa 1760, 25.5cm. high.
(Christie's) $871 £605

DOULTON

A Royal Doulton vase by
Mark V. Marshall, incised
artist's monogram JMJ
247, circa 1910, 51cm.
high. (Christie's)
$7,603 £5,280

A Royal Doulton miniature
face mask, 'Jester', possibly
HN1611, 7.7cm. long, c.m.
(Phillips) $886 £620

A Doulton stoneware vase
designed by F. Butler,
47.8cm. high. (Christie's)
$1,321 £864

A Royal Doulton Flambe
model of a bulldog, 14.2cm.
high, c.m.l. & c., impressed
date 10.26, no. 135.
(Phillips) $1,430 £1,000

A Royal Doulton earthenware
figure, 'One of the Forty',
possibly HN646, designed by
H. Tittensor, 18.1cm. high,
c.m.l. & c., shape no. 319.
(Phillips) $2,431 £1,700

A Royal Doulton Chang
jar and cover, by Harry Nixon,
8in. high. (Christie's)
$1,008 £700

A Royal Doulton stoneware
garden ornament, by Francis
C. Pope, 48.5cm. high, c.m.l.
(Phillips) $228 £160

A Doulton ewer and biscuit
barrel, both with plated lids.
(Lots Road Galleries)
$115 £80

A Doulton Lambeth stone-
ware jug decorated by H. and
F. Barlow and Mark V.
Marshall, 24.5cm. high, r.m.
& e. (Phillips) $886 £620

DOULTON

A Doulton Lambeth vase, by
Emily Stormer, 24.5cm. high,
c.m. dated 1877, artist's
monogram numbered 825.
(Phillips) $200 £140

One of a pair of Royal Doulton
Lambeth stoneware baluster
vases, by H. Barlow and Florence
Roberts, 27.4cm. high, c.m.l. &
c., dated shield 1902. (Phillips)
                        $715 £500

A Royal Doulton face mask,
'Jester', probably HN1630,
28.5cm. long, c.m.l.& c.,
date code for 1937, incised
933. (Phillips) $200 £140

A Royal Doulton Cecil Aldin
Series Ware jardiniere, the
decoration from the 'Old
English Scenes', 18cm. high,
c.m.l. & c. (Phillips)
          $243 £170

A Royal Doulton model,
'Kingfisher', 10.5cm. high,
c.m.l. & c. (Phillips)
          $42 £30

A Royal Doulton Flambe
model of an elephant,
16.8cm. high, c.m.l. & c.,
signed Noke. (Phillips)
          $157 £110

A Royal Doulton stoneware
model of a dog, by Gilbert
Bayes, 49.5cm. high.
(Phillips) $858 £600

A Royal Doulton figure of a
bulldog draped in the Union
Jack, 7in. high, printed
marks. (Christie's)
          $748 £520

A Doulton Lambeth Silicon
Ware oviform vase, by Edith
D. Lupton and Ada Dennis,
20.5cm. high, dated 1885.
(Phillips) $271 £190

DOULTON

A Royal Doulton pottery character jug modelled as The Gondolier, 8in. high, D6589. (Christie's)
$377 £250

Royal Doulton Flambe Buddha, signed Noke, 8in. high. (Hobbs & Chambers) $576 £400

Royal Doulton pottery musical character jug modelled as Owd Mac, 6¼in. high, D5889. (Christie's)
$679 £450

A Doulton Lambeth stoneware vase, by Mark V. Marshall, 25cm. high, r.m. artist's monogram no. 3. (Phillips) $386 £270

A Royal Doulton 'Tango' pattern porcelain part coffee set, coffee pot, 20.75cm. high, c.m.l. & c., impressed dates 1.1.35 and 2.1.35. (Phillips)
$314 £220

A Doulton Lambeth Faience tile panel, 61.5 x 20.6cm., printed c.m. on reverse of each. (Phillips)$314 £220

A Royal Doulton blue and white oval plaque, printed with a mother and child picking flowers, 14in. wide. (Christie's) $332 £220

A Royal Doulton pottery character jug modelled as The White Haired Clown, 6¼in. high, D6322. (Christie's) $755 £500

A Royal Doulton Flambe figure modelled as a seated Buddha, 6¾in. high, possibly by C. J. Noke. (Christie's)
$875 £580

DOULTON

A Royal Doulton figure, 'The Ballet Dancer', probably designed by L. Harradine, 19cm. high, c.m.l. & c., date code for 1943. (Phillips) $1,029 £720

A Doulton stoneware jardiniere with moulded decoration of a band of masks of comedy and tragedy, 19cm. high. (Christie's) $660 £432

A Royal Doulton figure, 'Teresa', HN1683, designed by L. Harradine, 14cm. high, c.m.l. & c., date code for 1936, introduced 1935, withdrawn 1938. (Phillips) $1,144 £800

A Doulton Burslem porcelain fruit set, by Walter Slater, each piece painted in natural colours with dandelion buds and clocks, flowers and leaves, b.r.m. & c., England, Rd. no. 72067. (Phillips) $572 £400

Royal Doulton Dewar's whisky moonflask, printed design no. 181, circa 1919, 8in. high. (Peter Wilson) $282 £200

A Royal Doulton Holbein Ware plaque, by Walter Nunn, 11.4 x 18.3cm. image area, c.m.l. & c. (Phillips) $572 £400

A Doulton Lambeth Faience moonflask, decorated by Hannah Barlow, 9½in. high. (Christie's) $504 £350

DOULTON

A Doulton Lambeth jug, by Arthur B. Barlow, 17cm. high, o.m. dated 1873, artist's monogram no. 777. (Phillips) $171 £120

One of a pair of Royal Doulton Cecil Aldin Titianian glazed Series Ware vases, 15.5cm. high, c.m.l. & c., printed D 4525. (Phillips) $157 £110

A Doulton Lambeth stoneware garden seat, possibly designed by Mark V. Marshall, 51.5cm. high. (Phillips) $1,287 £900

A Royal Doulton Flambe model of a pair of penguins, 15cm. high, c.m.l. & c. (Phillips) $114 £80

A Royal Doulton face mask, 'Sweet Anne', HN1590, design attributed to L. Harradine, 20.2cm. long, c.m.l. & c., impressed date 4.7.33. (Phillips) $357 £250

A Royal Doulton advertising model of a bulldog, 14.7cm. high, c.m.l. & c., Rd. no. 645658. (Phillips) $858 £600

A Royal Doulton miniature face mask, possibly by L. Harradine, HN1614, 7cm. high, c.m. (Phillips) $429 £300

A Doulton Lambeth figural group by George Tinworth, 14.1cm. high, r.m., dated 1881. (Phillips) $943 £660

'The Red-Haired Clown', a Royal Doulton character jug, 6¼in. high, and Mr. Pickwick, 4in. high. (Christie's) $1,728 £1,200

DOULTON

A Doulton Lambeth stone-
ware biscuit barrel, by
Florence and Lucy Barlow,
20cm. high, r.m. 1883.
(Phillips) $686 £480

A Royal Doulton figure,
'Folly', HN1750, designed
by L. Harradine, 25cm. high,
c.m.l. & c., date code for
1937, introduced 1936,
withdrawn 1949. (Phillips)
$715 £500

A Royal Doulton Chang vase,
by Henry Noke, covered
overall in a thick trailing
multi-coloured glaze, 7½in.
high. (Dreweatts)
$1,044 £720

A Royal Doulton figure,
'Doreen', 5¾in. high.
(Outhwaite & Litherland)
$507 £350

A Royal Doulton pottery
musical jug modelled as
Old Charley, 6in. high,
D5858. (Christie's)
$528 £350

A large Royal Doulton Flambe
model of a fox, glazed in black
and red, 23.6cm. high, c.m.l. &
c., signed Noke. (Phillips)
$171 £120

A Royal Doulton earthenware
globular vase, 21.8cm. high,
c.m.l. & c. (Phillips) $78 £55

Royal Doulton 'Fox in Red
Frock Coat', HN100, 16cm.
high, c.m.l. & c. (Phillips)
$300 £210

A Royal Doulton miniature
face mask, 'Jester', possibly
HN1609, 7.5cm. long, c.m.
(Phillips) $1,029 £720

An earthenware bowl with rounded triangular rim, by Gertrud and Otto Natzler, circa 1950, 22cm. diam. (Christie's) $1,074 £702

An earthenware model of a toad, by Edwin Beer Fishley, 12.9cm. wide. (Christie's) $188 £132

An earthenware bowl form, by Gordon Baldwin, covered in a white slip, 44cm. wide. (Christie's) $593 £388

One of a pair of earthenware dishes painted in iron-red and black with three blackbirds, 12in. diam. (Lawrence Fine Art) $613 £396

A 20th century earthenware pottery figure of a female in period costume, 13in. high. (Peter Wilson) $91 £65

A Weimar ceramic earthenware cake plate, 31cm. diam., together with another 28cm. diam. (Phillips) $144 £100

An earthenware food warmer of globular shape, 9in. high. (Lawrence Fine Art) $443 £286

A Satsuma type earthenware bowl, the interior and exterior painted with mille fleurs, seal mark, 5in. diam. (Lawrence Fine Art) $562 £363

An orange earthenware hand-built globular vase, by M. A. N. Odundo, 25cm. high. (Christie's) $413 £270

EARTHENWARE

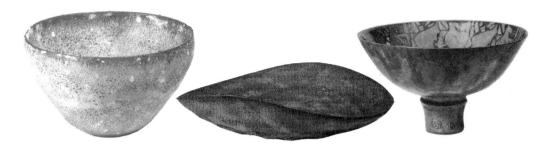

A circular earthenware bowl, by Gertrud and Otto Natzler, circa 1950, 14.5cm. diam. (Christie's) $660 £432

A circular earthenware dish, by Gertrud and Otto Natzler, circa 1950, 34cm. diam. (Christie's) $1,321 £864

An earthenware stemmed bowl, by Sutton Taylor, 29.2cm. diam. (Christie's) $283 £198

A Weimar ceramic earthenware cake plate, 22.8cm. diam., together with eight others, various. (Phillips) $216 £150

One of a pair of Weimar ceramic earthenware vases, 25.5cm. high, impressed 2800. (Phillips) $216 £150

A Webb & Co. earthenware wall plaque, artist's signature E. H. Hammond, 36.5cm. wide. (Christie's) $237 £165

A St. Ives earthenware jug with strap handle terminating in a scroll, 21.5cm. high. (Christie's) $82 £54

An Italian earthenware cylindrical vase in the style of Gio Ponti, 29.5cm. high. (Christie's) $314 £220

An earthenware mug, by Thos. Samuel Haile, circa 1940, 16.2cm. high. (Christie's) $173 £121

EUROPEAN

Mid 18th century Dutch flattened pear-shaped scent bottle and flower stopper, perhaps Weesp or Lossdrecht, 7cm. high. (Christie's) $407 £283

A laminated porcelain bowl, by Marion Gaunce, in light blue, purple and black bands, 9.7cm. high. (Christie's) $330 £216

Royal Copenhagen poly-chromed porcelain fairytale group, marked August 10, 1955, 9.1/8in. high. (Robt. W. Skinner Inc.)$850 £590

Royal Copenhagen poly-chromed porcelain fairytale group, marked June 10, 1955, 8in. high. (Robt. W. Skinner Inc.) $850 £590

Early 20th century Gouda pottery decorated vase, signed Herat, Holland, 16in. high. (Robt. W. Skinner Inc.) $150 £104

A porcelain circular landscape dish, by Ljerka Njers, dated 86, 32.7cm. diam. (Christie's) $408 £286

An Argentaware green-ground charger, silver inlaid with a design of fish, Gustavsberg mark, a vase and an ashtray. (Lots Road Galleries) $302 £200

Royal Copenhagen poly-chromed porcelain fairytale group, Denmark, marked April 25, 1955, 8.5/8in. high. (Robt. W. Skinner Inc.) $800 £555

A porcelain circular landscape dish, by Ljerka Njers, the un-glazed body textured with muslin, 25.9cm. diam. (Christie's) $279 £183

EUROPEAN

A deep porcelain bowl, by
Mary Rich, impressed M
seal, 23.6cm. diam.
(Christie's) $197 £129

A two-handled vase with octagonal
panelled neck, highlighted in two
tones of blue, 12in. high. (Woolley
& Wallis) $69 £45

A Lenzburg oval two-handled
tureen and cover, manganese
CB/21 . . and B. ./2 marks,
Hunerwadel factory, circa
1765, 30cm. wide. (Christie's)
$950 £660

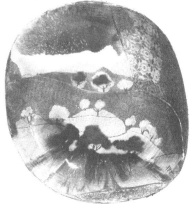

Continental square section
pottery vase painted with
Art Nouveau style maiden,
12in. high. (Peter Wilson)
$56 £40

An irregular slab built porcelain
landscape dish, by Ljerka Njers,
textured and decorated with
muslin and lace, 37.1cm. wide.
(Christie's) $396 £259

A Wiener Keramik figure of
a putto, designed by M.
Powolny, 40.5cm. high.
(Christie's) $3,304 £2,160

A Warsaw (Belvedere)
saucer dish, 23cm. diam.
(Christie's) $3,142 £2,182

An 18th century model of
a roistering Dutchman
seated astride a Dutch gin
cask, 37cm. high. (Christie's)
$21,868 £15,400

A Puente Del Arzobispo
circular dish painted blue,
ochre and manganese, circa
1650, 25.5cm. diam.
(Christie's) $348 £242

A famille rose punch bowl, circa 1765, 13½in. diam. (Christie's) $2,697 £2,090

One of a pair of 19th century large famille rose urns on pierced wooden stands, 23½in. high. (Christie's) $1,980 £1,292

A Chinese famille rose and blue and white bowl, 5¾in., seal mark of Daoguang and of the period. (Dreweatts) $1,040 £680

A famille rose armorial oblong octagonal dish, circa 1775, 12¾in. wide. (Christie's) $2,499 £1,760

One of two late 19th century famille rose covered jars, 6¾in. high. (Christie's) $660 £430

A Chinese famille rose, shaped oval meat dish, Qianlong, 17in. long. (Dreweatts) $1,595 £1,100

A famille rose armorial dish painted at the centre with a coat-of-arms and crest, circa 1730, 11in. diam. (Christie's) $1,093 £770

A famille rose gilt ground wig stand and cover, gilt Jiaqing seal mark and of the period, 27.9cm. high. (Christie's) $2,831 £1,980

Late 18th century famille rose Canton enamel circular segmented supper set formed as eight fan-shaped dishes, 18in. diam. (Christie's) $1,015 £715

FAMILLE VERTE

A 19th century Chinese baluster vase decorated with famille verte panels of figures on a powder-blue-ground, 24in. high. (Dreweatts) $551 £380

A famille verte oval incense basket and cover with high strap handle, Kangxi, 12.5cm. wide. (Christie's) $3,360 £2,000

A famille verte square bottle, Kangxi, 8¼in. high, fitted as a lamp. (Christie's) $749 £528

A famille verte saucer dish painted with rockwork issuing flowering peony and camellia, Kangxi, 27cm. diam. (Christie's) $1,260 £750

A famille verte pear-shaped vase, reverse painted with a long-tailed bird on rockwork, Kangxi, 19.5cm. high. (Christie's) $1,848 £1,100

One of a pair of famille verte saucer dishes, Chenhua six-character marks within a double circle, early 18th century, 39cm. diam. (Christie's) $12,584 £8,800

An 18th century famille verte rouleau vase, 44cm. high. (Christie's) $2,831 £1,980

A 19th century Chinese famille verte plaque, 17 x 12.5in. (Woolley & Wallis) $372 £240

An 18th/19th century famille verte group formed as a large Buddhistic lion, 12½in. high. (Christie's) $499 £352

FRENCH

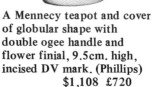

Mid 18th century Aire Faience blue and white trompe l'oeil waved circular dish, 24cm. diam. (Christie's) $3,142 £2,182

A Mennecy teapot and cover of globular shape with double ogee handle and flower finial, 9.5cm. high, incised DV mark. (Phillips) $1,108 £720

One of a pair of French Faience oval two-handled glass coolers, circa 1760, 28cm. wide. (Christie's) $1,130 £785

A Moustiers shaped circular plate, manganese GOL and cross mark of Olerys and Laugier, circa 1740, 25cm. diam. (Christie's) $1,130 £785

A pair of Mennecy figures of a young man and woman, circa 1740, 17.5cm. high. (Christie's) $2,851 £1,980

Mid 18th century Rouens Faience circular plate of panier de fleurs pattern, 24.5cm. diam. (Christie's) $1,632 £1,134

A Chantilly Kakiemon square box and cover, iron-red hunting horn mark, circa 1740, 25cm. high. (Christie's) $23,760 £16,500

One of a pair of Vincennes two-handled small seaux in the Meissen style, blue interlaced L marks enclosing dots, circa 1752, 13.5cm. wide. (Christie's) $15,048 £10,450

A Mennecy white pot pourri vase, incised DV mark on base, circa 1740, 12cm. high. (Christie's) $285 £198

FRENCH

One of a pair of documentary Vincennes white hunting groups, La Chasse au Sanglier and La Chasse au Loup, after Oudry, modelled by J. Chabry, circa 1752, 31.5cm. and 32cm. wide. (Christie's) $134,640 £93,500

A Vincennes bleu lapis conical teapot, blue interlaced L marks and painter's mark of Thevenet, circa 1753, 11cm. high. (Christie's) $1,742 £1,210

A Moustiers shaped oval dish painted in shades of manganese with Berainesque dwarves, birds and a fox, circa 1740, 33cm. diam. (Christie's) $1,884 £1,309

A St. Cloud white beaker, cover and saucer with silver gilt mounts, circa 1730. (Christie's) $950 £660

An Art Deco porcelain spirit flask and stopper, 'Joueur de Golfeur', 27.5cm. high. (Phillips) $391 £270

A Vincennes circular bowl, blue crowned interlaced Ls enclosing the Bourbon fleur-de-lys, circa 1752, 32.5cm. diam. (Christie's) $11,880 £8,250

A large turquoise glazed ceramic frog, 65cm. high, probably French from Sarreguemines. (Phillips) $1,123 £780

Late 17th century garniture of three Nevers bleu persan vases, 37cm. and 59cm. high. (Christie's) $7,128 £4,950

One of a pair of Vincennes bleu lapis pots and covers, circa 1754, 7cm. high. (Christie's) $792 £550

A Kloster-Veilsdorf figure of Cadi-Leskier, modelled by Pfranger, circa 1770, 14cm. high. (Christie's)
$5,028 £3,492

A Nymphenburg shaped octa-foil saucer dish from the Hof service, impressed P2, circa 1760, 27cm. diam. (Christie's) $4,085 £2,837

A German white figure of a young boy, probably Wegley or Cassel, circa 1765, 10cm. high. (Christie's) $158 £110

A Ludwigsburg rococo oval two-handled tureen and cover, blue crowned inter-laced C mark and impressed IP, circa 1765, 32cm. wide. (Christie's) $3,801 £2,640

A Weimar ceramic porcelain oviform chocolate jug, 19cm. high, printed factory mark Leuchtenburg. (Phillips) $72 £50

An 18th century German porcelain gold mounted rectangular snuff box and cover with waisted sides, 8.5cm. wide. (Christie's)
$4,118 £2,860

A Furstenberg figure of a bird seller modelled by Desoches, blue script F mark, circa 1775, 16cm. high. (Christie's) $1,584 £1,100

A German porcelain wine barrel supported on a wood stand, circa 1880, the barrel 30cm. wide. (Christie's)
$1,512 £1,045

A pair of late 19th century German figures of a gardener and companion, overglazed blue crossed swords mark and incised numerals, 46cm. high. (Christie's) $558 £385

GERMAN

A Cassel white figure of a putto standing nude with loin cloth on tree-stump base, incised IR on base, circa 1770, 9.5cm. high. (Christie's) $1,900 £1,320

A Bayreuth blue and white circular dish, circa 1730, 22cm. diam. (Christie's) $1,193 £829

A Frankenthal Janus-headed figure, blue crowned CT and AB monogram marks, incised S2, circa 1765, 17cm. high. (Christie's) $1,346 £935

Late 18th century German oblong octagonal snuff box and cover, probably Nymphenburg, 8cm. wide. (Christie's) $6,019 £4,180

A German Faience enghalskrug of baluster form, the front with initials 'IGS 1730', 34.5cm. high. (Phillips) $5,236 £3,400

A Niderviller Faience shaped hexafoil dish, circa 1775, 25cm. diam. (Christie's) $8,170 £5,674

A Hochst group of the garlanded sleeper, modelled by J. P. Melchior, blue wheel mark and incised SX, circa 1770, 19cm. wide. (Christie's) $3,960 £2,750

A Kelsterbach pipe bowl with silver mounts and hinged cover, 1767-68, 7cm. high. (Christie's) $3,142 £2,182

A Frankenthal chinoiserie group of lovers, blue crowned CT mark and 74, 17cm. wide. (Christie's) $1,029 £715

GERMAN

A Hochst figure of a young girl holding a basket of pears, modelled by J. P. Melchior, circa 1770, 13cm. high, and another of a girl holding a basket of apples, 10cm. high. (Christie's) $871 £605

A Frankenthal group of a seated young man and two young women, modelled by K. G. Luck, dating from 1778, 23cm. wide. (Christie's)
                     $3,960 £2,750

A Hochst figure of a boy in white tunic with puce edging, modelled by J. P. Melchior, blue wheel mark, circa 1770, 14.5cm. high. (Christie's)
          $1,267   £880

A Hochst figure of a boy holding a dog by its tail, modelled by J. P. Melchior, blue wheel mark, circa 1770, 13.5cm. high. (Christie's)
                     $1,267 £880

A Hochst baluster coffee pot and cover, blue wheel mark and incised IN, circa 1765, 18cm. high. (Christie's)
                     $1,346 £935

A Ludwigsburg chinoiserie group, modelled by J. Weinmuller, incised Geer mark, circa 1770, 34cm. high. (Christie's)
          $2,534   £1,760

A Hochst figure of a young boy, modelled by J. P. Melchior, blue wheel mark, circa 1770, 14cm. high. (Christie's) $1,188 £825

A Furstenberg arched rectangular tea caddy, impressed no. 2, circa 1770, 10.5cm. high, silver cover. (Christie's)
                     $1,108 £770

A Hochst figure of a boy eating cherries, modelled by J. P. Melchior, traces of blue mark and incised P No. 1, circa 1770, 11.5cm. high. (Christie's) $871 £605

GERMAN

A Hochst figure of a girl, in puce-edged white clothes, modelled by J. P. Melchior, blue wheel mark and incised HM monogram and no. 176, circa 1770, 14.5cm. high. (Christie's) $792 £550

A Frankenthal group, modelled by K. G. Luck, blue crowned CT mark, circa 1770, 14cm. high. (Christie's)
$2,692 £1,870

A Hochst figure of a nymph, emblematic of intelligence, impressed 2H and iron-red painter's mark IZ of J. Zeschinger, circa 1753/4, 16cm. high. (Christie's)
$633 £440

A Ludwigsburg figure of Arion, blue interlaced L mark and impressed I.L.F. 53. and with iron-red painter's mark of Sausenhofer, circa 1765, 15cm. high. (Christie's) $380 £264

A Hochst baluster hot-milk jug and cover with artichoke finial, incised HI on base, circa 1760, 14.5cm. high. (Christie's) $570 £396

A Furstenberg figure of a stonemason standing, blue script F mark, circa 1775, 11cm. high. (Christie's)
$443 £308

A Hochst figure of a boy, modelled by J. P. Melchior, blue wheel mark and incised HI and other marks, circa 1765, 17.5cm. high. (Christie's) $3,009 £2,090

A Furstenberg group of Perseus, modelled by Desoches, blue script F mark, circa 1780, 26.5cm. high. (Christie's)
$554 £385

A Ludwigsburg standing figure of Flora, circa 1775, 26.5cm. high. (Christie's)
$253 £176

Late 19th century German figure of a monkey, decorated in grey and yellow glazes, 46cm. high. (Christie's) $638 £440

A Frankenthal group of a performing bear dancing to a hurdy-gurdy played by one of two boys, circa 1770, 19.5cm. high. (Christie's)
$4,399 £3,055

A Hochst figure of a young man, modelled by J. P. Melchior, incised HM monogram and No. 3, circa 1765, 16cm. high. (Christie's)
$1,742 £1,210

A Limbach group of a family, puce LB monogram mark, circa 1775, 23cm. high. (Christie's) $443 £308

A Siegburg pale grey stoneware schnelle with hinged pewter cover, dated 1566, 21cm. high, (repair to base). (Christie's)
$1,188 £825

A Frankenthal group of a young woman embracing an elderly man, modelled by K. G. Luck, circa 1778, 15.5cm. high. (Christie's)
$3,168 £2,200

A Frankenthal figure of a horn player, modelled by Konrad Link, blue crowned CT monogram mark and date mark for 1767, 16.5cm. high. (Christie's) $3,168 £2,200

A German porcelain rectangular plaque painted with a portrait of Ruth, circa 1880, 20.5 x 13.5cm. (Christie's)
$757 £495

A Ludwigsburg figure of Columbine from the Commedia dell'Arte modelled by Franz Anton Pustelli, circa 1760, 10.5cm. high. (Christie's)
$3,142 £2,182

GERMAN

A Furstenberg figure of
Bagolin modelled by A. S.
Laplau, circa 1775, 12cm.
high. (Christie's)
$3,456 £2,400

A Nymphenburg oil and
vinegar stand with two bottles
and hinged covers, circa 1765,
the bottles 18cm. high.
(Christie's) $12,571 £8,730

A Ludwigsburg figure of a
youth seated on a rocky out-
crop, circa 1770, 19cm. high.
(Christie's) $665 £462

A Frankenthal group of four
putti emblematic of the
Seasons, blue crowned CT
mark and dating for 1779,
16.5cm. high. (Christie's)
$1,188   £825

Late 17th century Frankfurt
blue and white enghalskrug,
24cm. high. (Christie's)
$1,267 £880

A Ludwigsburg group of two
putti, blue interlaced C's and
impressed IO marks, circa
1765, 17cm. high.
(Christie's) $554 £385

An Art Deco Schwarzburger
Werkstatten porcelain figure,
56cm. high, signed O. Kramer
.29. (Phillips) $1,872 £1,300

An Erfurt cylindrical tankard
with pewter foot, circa 1740,
20.5cm. high. (Christie's)
$1,346 £935

A Rosenthal porcelain figure,
'Korean Dancer', designed by
C. Holzer-Defanti, 40cm. high,
printed factory marks for
1929. (Phillips) $576 £400

GOLDSCHEIDER

A Goldscheider figure, from a model by Lorenzl, 13in. high. (Christie's) $226 £150

A wall mask attributed to Goldscheider, modelled as the head of a young girl, orange and green on a flesh-coloured ground, 27.3cm. high. (Christie's) $158 £110

A Goldscheider pottery figure of a dancing girl, designed by Lorenzl, 16in. high. (Christie's) $1,057 £682

A Goldscheider pottery figure, modelled as a sailor holding a girl, 30cm. high. (Christie's) $537 £330

A Goldscheider pottery 'Negro' wall mask, 26.5cm. high. (Phillips) $228 £150

An Art Nouveau Goldscheider pottery figure, modelled as a girl wearing long flowing robes, designed by E. Tell, 65cm. high. (Phillips) $691 £480

'Butterfly Girl', a Goldscheider figure after a model by Lorenzl, 7in. high. (Christie's) $634 £420

A Goldscheider pottery double face wall plaque, the two females in profile, 12in. high. (Christie's) $596 £385

A Goldscheider pottery group after a model by Lorenzl, of a flamenco dancer and a guitar player, 17in. high. (Christie's) $893 £580

GOSS & CRESTED CHINA

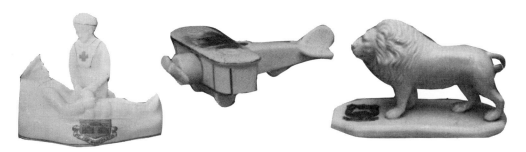

An Arcadian Nurse and Wounded Tommy, 108mm. long, with Arms of City of Winchester. (Goss & Crested China Ltd.) $114 £75

Shelley Bi-plane, No. 344, with fixed propeller, 150mm. long, bearing a transfer of Peterborough. (Goss & Crested China Ltd.) $99 £65

A lion standing with Wembley Exhibition arms, date 1924-5, 135mm. long. (Goss & Crested China Ltd.)
$405 £265

A three-handled loving cup, 5in. high. (Christie's)
$143 £99

A Savoy Stokes Bomb, 95mm. (Goss & Crested China Ltd.)
$306 £200

Jersey fish basket, arms of Saltash, large size, 58mm. (Goss & Crested China Ltd.)
$24 £16

Parian bust of W. H. Goss, impressed legend and printed mark, 6½in. high. (Christie's) $159 £110

Portland Lighthouse with black band, arms of Leeds, 120mm. high. (Goss & Crested China Ltd.)
$107 £70

Roman Tetinae, International League Model for 1924, printed mark. (Christie's)
$72 £50

GOSS & CRESTED CHINA

A Third Period, Churchill Toby jug, dated 1927, 164mm. high. (Goss & Crested China Ltd.) $175 £115

British Hall at the Wembley Exhibition, by Carlton China, 110mm. long. (Goss & Crested China Ltd.) $55 £36

A Third Period coloured figurine, Edyth. (Goss & Crested China Ltd.) $260 £170

'Sandbach Crosses' by Goss, 10½in. high. (Peter Wilson) $183 £130

Manx cottage nightlight, fully coloured, 122mm. long. (Goss & Crested China Ltd.) $229 £150

A triple bag centrepiece, 200mm. high. (Goss & Crested China Ltd.) $198 £130

First Period terracotta 'Keystone of the Kingdome', life size head of Lord Beaconsfield, dated 1876. (Goss & Crested China Ltd.) $612 £400

A Windsor kettle, the favourite of Queen Charlotte, 170mm. high. (Goss & Crested China Ltd.) $168 £110

A windmill with revolving sails, 103mm. high, by Carlton. (Goss & Crested China Ltd.) $24 £16

GOSS & CRESTED CHINA

An Arcadian grandfather clock with Shakespeare verse, 108mm. high. (Goss & Crested China Ltd.) $16 £10

A girl playing with bucket and spade and a boy playing with a model yacht, some colouring, by Grafton China, nos. 564 and 563, 85mm. high. (Goss & Crested China Ltd.) $122 £80

A Greek amphora vase, the International League model for 1921, 138mm. high. (Goss & Crested China Ltd.) $91 £60

Carlton advertising piece for Pear's soap, 110mm. high. (Goss & Crested China Ltd.) $122 £80

Bell Hotel, Abel Fletcher's House, 85mm. wide, fully coloured by Willow Art. (Goss & Crested China Ltd.) $84 £55

An Arcadian village pump with trough, 90mm. high. (Goss & Crested China Ltd.) $8 £5

King Richard's Well Cover at Market Bosworth, 100mm. high. (Goss & Crested China Ltd.) $328 £215

Welsh Tea Party group by Willow Art, with arms of Aberystwyth, 50mm. high. (Goss & Crested China Ltd.) $38 £25

A Second Period (1881-1934) milk jug, 67mm. high, with nobility arms. (Goss & Crested China Ltd.) $15 £10

A grey pottery horse torso and head formed in two parts, Han Dynasty, 53cm. long. (Christie's) $11,011 £7,700

A green-glazed pottery hill jar and cover on three bear feet, Han Dynasty, 23cm. high. (Christie's) $1,179 £825

A large painted grey pottery horse torso and head, Han Dynasty, 48.5cm. long. (Christie's) $22,022 £15,400

A grey earthenware door post, Warring States/Han Dynasty, 82cm. high. (Christie's) $2,988 £2,090

A green-glazed pottery vase moulded with taotie and fixed ring handles, Han Dynasty, 33cm. high. (Christie's) $2,145 £1,500

A massive green-glazed red pottery watch-tower, in four sections, Han Dynasty, 134cm. high. (Christie's) $22,022 £15,400

A painted grey pottery cocoon-shaped jar, some earth encrustation, Han Dynasty, 26.5cm. wide. (Christie's) $1,101 £770

A green-glazed red pottery jar, Han Dynasty, 36cm. high. (Christie's) $2,359 £1,650

A green-glazed red pottery hill jar and related cover, Han Dynasty, 22cm. high. (Christie's) $943 £660

IMARI

An Imari circular deep bowl decorated in various coloured enamels and gilt on underglaze blue, Meiji period, 25cm. diam. (Christie's) $1,405 £990

One of a pair of Imari models of a man partly clad in a kimono seated astride a large carp, circa 1700, approx. 26cm. long. (Christie's) $5,935 £4,180

Late 19th century Imari deep bowl decorated in typical colours and gilt on underglaze blue, 25cm. diam. (Christie's) $749 £528

An 18th century Imari figure of an actor decorated in various coloured enamels and gilt on underglaze blue, 47cm. high. (Christie's) $2,186 £1,540

One of a pair of Imari models of a cockerel and hen, Genroku period, 28cm. and 24cm. high. (Christie's) $6,996 £4,406

An 18th century Imari globular bottle vase with tall neck, 23.5cm. high. (Christie's) $2,098 £1,320

An Imari oviform jar and cover decorated in iron-red enamel and gilt on underglaze blue, Genroku period, 48cm. high. (Christie's) $3,847 £2,420

Late 19th century Genroku style Imari dish decorated in various enamels on underglaze blue, 57cm. diam. (Christie's) $11,715 £8,250

An Imari model of a bijin decorated in coloured enamels on underglaze blue, Genroku period, 38cm. high. (Christie's) $4,547 £2,860

IMARI

One of a pair of Imari jars and covers, Genroku period, 53cm. high. (Christie's) $7,810 £5,500

A Japanese Imari soup plate painted with 'La Dame au Parasol', circa 1735, 9¼in. diam. (Christie's) $2,186 £1,540

Late 17th/early 18th century moulded Imari pear-shaped coffee pot, 44cm. high. (Christie's) $1,874 £1,320

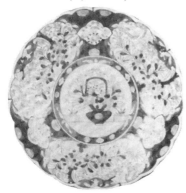

A large Imari plaque with a scalloped border, decorated in underglaze blue and over glaze red and green enamels, 16in. diam. (Outhwaite & Litherland) $232 £160

Late 17th century Ko-Imari koro modelled as a kirin, 23cm. high. (Christie's) $2,343 £1,650

A large Imari dish decorated in iron-red, green, aubergine, black enamels and gilt on underglaze blue, Genroku period, 53.5cm. diam. (Christie's) $6,560 £4,620

One of a pair of Imari Tokkuri decorated in typical colours and gilt, 23cm. high. (Christie's) $1,249 £880

Large Imari porcelain jardiniere, Japan, 18in. high, 21¼in. diam. (Robt. W. Skinner Inc.) $1,700 £1,180

Late 17th century Imari gin cask modelled as a bijin seated on a stylised cart, 40cm. high. (Christie's) $4,061 £2,860

IMARI

One of a pair of Japanese Imari bottle vases, circa 1900, 12in. high. (Peter Wilson) $1,128 £800

Late 18th/early 19th century Imari foliate rimmed blue and white bowl, 37cm. diam. (Christie's) $1,874 £1,320

Late 17th century Imari conical coffee pot with loop handle, 34cm. high. (Christie's) $1,562 £1,100

Late 19th century Imari dish painted in underglaze blue, iron-red, coloured enamels and gilt, 78.6cm. diam. (Christie's) $4,373 £3,080

One of a pair of late 17th century Imari trumpet-shaped beaker vases, 30cm. high. (Christie's) $3,436 £2,420

An Imari dish decorated in iron-red, green, black, aubergine enamels and gilt on underglaze blue, Meiji period, 53cm. diam. (Christie's) $2,499 £1,760

One of a pair of Imari models of leaping carp, Genroku period, 25cm. high. (Christie's) $4,998 £3,520

Late 19th century Imari foliate rimmed jardiniere, 38cm. high. (Christie's) $2,186 £1,540

One of a pair of late 17th century Imari models of a cockerel and hen with a chick, 16cm. high. (Christie's) $3,748 £2,640

ITALIAN

A Deruta majolica albarello, inscribed 'Ghoma di Lava', on a scroll surrounded by grotesques and leaf forms, 18.5cm. high. (Phillips) $492 £320

A Faenza circular tondino of Cardinal's hat form, circa 1525, 25cm. diam. (Christie's) $21,384 £14,850

A 17th century Castel Durante baluster armorial pharmacy bottle, 22cm. high. (Christie's)
$2,534 £1,760

Early 18th century Castelli circular tondo painted with St. Francis of Assisi, 20cm. diam., (minor rim chip). (Christie's) $506 £352

A 16th/17th century Italian majolica blue glazed, two-handled baluster vase with dolphin handles, 27cm. high. (Christie's) $1,267 £880

An 18th century Castelli circular tondo, 24.5cm. diam., (rim chips). (Christie's)
$554 £385

A Doccia baluster coffee pot and cover with bird's head mask spout, circa 1780, 22cm. high. (Christie's)
$443 £308

A Savona or Albissola majolica syrup jar, from the workshop of Luigi Levantino, with short spout and loop handle, 19cm. high. (Phillips) $739 £480

A Le Nove white group of a dancing gallant and companion, circa 1780, 16cm. high. (Christie's) $538 £374

ITALIAN

A Montelupo majolica circular dish, painted in blue, ochre and green with an equestrian figure, 32cm. high. (Phillips) $770 £500

A Doccia teacup and saucer, circa 1765. (Christie's) $475 £330

A Montelupo majolica circular dish, with an equestrian figure carrying a flag, 31.5cm. diam. (Phillips) $847 £550

Late 16th century Palermo waisted albarello, 26.5cm. high. (Christie's) $792 £550

A pair of mid 18th century Castelli circular tondi, 20cm. diam. (Christie's) $2,692 £1,870

A dated Montelupo albarello of dumb-bell shape, the reverse dated 1561, 21cm. high. (Phillips) $847 £550

Late 18th century bassano shaped circular dish, 34cm. diam. (Christie's) $1,193 £829

A Montelupo wet drug jar with ovoid body and two green dolphin handles, 33cm. high. (Phillips) $1,047 £680

A Savona blue and white pierced tazza, blue lighthouse mark, circa 1700, 35.5cm. diam. (Christie's) $1,108 £770

Mid 18th century Castelli documentary circular plate painted with Lot and his daughters, 17.5cm. diam. (Christie's) $316 £220

A Capodimonte oviform teapot with scroll handle and spout, blue fleur-de-lys mark, circa 1750, 14.5cm. wide. (Christie's)
$1,188 £825

A Gubbio lustre tondino, painted in red and yellow lustre and in green and blue, circa 1530, 22cm. diam. (Christie's) $7,603 £5,280

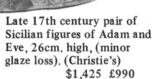

Early 17th century Palermo oviform vase, 27.5cm. high. (Christie's) $1,188 £825

Late 17th century pair of Sicilian figures of Adam and Eve, 26cm. high, (minor glaze loss). (Christie's)
$1,425 £990

A Castelli rectangular plaque painted with Abraham sacrificing a lamb, circa 1720, 27 x 20.5cm. (Christie's)
$1,425 £990

A Gubbio lustre plate painted in ruby lustre, blue and green, circa 1530, 25cm. diam. (Christie's) $14,256 £9,900

A 1950's Italian china Galle figure of a kneeling semi-dressed female figure, 18in. high. (Reeds Rains)
$775 £500

Late 18th century Castelli circular plate, blue G.M. mark, 18cm. diam. (Christie's) $348 £242

A porcellanous stem dish, by Shoji Hamada, the cup with pentafoil bowl, circa 1922, 7.8cm. high. (Christie's) $1,817 £1,188

A Kakiemon model of a bijin decoated in iron-red, blue, green, yellow and black enamels, circa 1680, 36cm. high. (Christie's) $14,058 £9,900

A Kakiemon bowl with moulded rim, circa 1680, 21.5cm. diam. (Christie's) $15,620 £11,000

A Kakiemon oviform ewer of Islamic form, Kanbun/ Empyo period (1663-81), 33cm. high. (Christie's) $11,715 £8,250

One of a pair of Kakiemon-type foliate blue and white shallow dishes, late 17th century, 34cm. diam. (Christie's) $15,391 £9,680

A Kakiemon model of a standing bijin decorated in iron-red, blue, green, aubergine and black enamels and gilt, circa 1680, 41cm. high. (Christie's) $7,870 £4,950

A stoneware bottle-shaped vase, by Shoji Hamada, circa 1930, 37.4cm. high. (Christie's) $1,982 £1,296

Late 19th century Satsuma hexagonal oviform jar on tripod feet, 22.5cm. high. (Christie's) $4,547 £2,860

A Kakiemon hexagonal jar and domed cover, Empo/ Jokoyo period (1673-1687), 32cm. high. (Christie's) $96,195 £60,500

JAPANESE

A stoneware press moulded rectangular bottle, by Shoji Hamada, covered in panels of tenmoku and dark turquoise glaze, circa 1960, 25.1cm. high. (Christie's) $1,982 £1,296

A stoneware jug, by Shoji Hamada, covered in a greyish-green glaze decorated in iron-brown brushwork with scrolling foliage, circa 1922, 8.3cm. high.(Christie's) $231 £151

Late 19th century Kinkozan tapering cylindrical vase decorated in various colours and gilt on glazed blue, 24.5cm. high. (Christie's) $1,562 £1,100

A stoneware bowl on shallow foot, by Shoji Hamada, covered in a tenmoku glaze with brushwork decoration, circa 1921, 18cm. diam. (Christie's) $908 £594

A stoneware bottle vase, by Shoji Hamada, covered in a lustrous black glaze with areas of running iron-brown, circa 1922, 24.6cm. high. (Christie's) $578 £378

Late 19th century Kyoto square dish with canted corners, 15.7cm. sq. (Christie's) $937 £660

A stoneware carved jar and cover, by Shoji Hamada, circa 1922, 10.5cm. high. (Christie's) $908 £594

A 19th century Kiyomizu rounded rectangular koro, 23cm. high. (Christie's) $546 £385

A stoneware globular vase with two strap lug handles, by Shoji Hamada, circa 1922, 15.9cm. high. (Christie's) $527 £345

JAPANESE

A small stoneware jar, by Shoji Hamada, circa 1920, 7.3cm. high. (Christie's) $263 £172

Late 19th century Seifu blue and white plate, 21cm. diam. (Christie's) $702 £495

Late 18th century bowl and cover modelled as a seashell with smaller shells, probably Hirado, 14.4cm. wide. (Christie's) $656 £462

Late 19th century Shofu oviform vase with everted rim, 22cm. high. (Christie's) $343 £242

A stoneware moulded rectangular tray, by Shoji Hamada, with printed label Made in Japan, circa 1960, 2.5cm. (Christie's) $743 £486

A stoneware press moulded rectangular bottle vase, by Shoji Hamada, circa 1960, 23.5cm. high. (Christie's) $7,931 £5,184

A Raku roughly potted jar and cover, by Keiko Hasegawa, 19.8cm. high. (Christie's) $527 £345

A 19th century large Kyoto-Satsuma oviform vase, signed Nihon Kyoto Kinkozan zo, 83cm. high. (Christie's) $3,124 £2,200

One of a pair of late 19th century Hirado saucer-shaped dishes, each decorated in Kutani style, 61.2cm. diam. (Christie's) $5,467 £3,850

A George Jones game-pie dish and cover, impressed maker's monogram GJ, George Jones within crescent moon and registration lozenge for 1873, 37cm. long. (Christie's) $2,871 £1,980

A George Jones strawberry set, comprising a tray and two detachable containers, impressed maker's monogram GJ and registration lozenge for 1875, 23cm. high. (Christie's) $925 £638

A George Jones sweetmeat dish, moulded monogram GJ and Stoke-on-Trent and impressed registration lozenge for 1868, 30cm. diam. (Christie's) $1,036 £715

A George Jones flower holder modelled as three wicker baskets, with moulded registration lozenge for 1872, 27.8cm. high. (Christie's) $765 £528

Pair of George Jones majolica garden seats of cylindrical form, circa 1874, 18.1/8in. high. (Robt. W. Skinner Inc.) $9,500 £5,937

A George Jones figure of a camel, impressed with monogram GJ and Kumassie, 23.2cm. high. (Christie's) $1,515 £1,045

A George Jones majolica ware punch bowl, modelled as Mr. Punch, 21.5cm. diam. (Phillips) $1,800 £1,250

A George Jones vase, the handles formed as be-ribboned rams' heads, moulded maker's monogram GJ and Stoke-on-Trent, 34cm. high. (Christie's) $1,595 £1,100

A George Jones majolica cheese dome and stand. (Dreweatts) $604 £360

KANGXI

An Imperial famille verte coral-red ground bowl, underglaze blue Kangxi yuzhi mark within a double square and of the period, 11cm. diam. (Christie's) $26,880 £16,000

A famille verte bowl and cover, Kangxi, 13.5cm. wide, wood stand. (Christie's) $1,176 £700

A famille verte bowl, encircled Kangxi six-character mark and of the period, 14.8cm. diam. (Christie's) $685 £460

A blue and white and underglaze copper red fish bowl, Kangxi, 40cm. diam. (Christie's) $3,775 £2,640

An iron-red and gilt oviform vase with slender trumpet neck, Kangxi, 28cm. high. (Christie's) $303 £204

A famille verte saucer dish, . encircled Kangxi six-character mark and of the period, 24.8cm. diam. (Christie's) $2,856 £1,700

A famille verte saucer dish, painted in the Kangxi manner, encircled Tongzhi six-character mark and of the period, 18.6cm. diam. (Christie's) $247 £166

A blue and white vase, with period six-character Kangxi mark, 14½in. high. (Christie's) $1,210 £789

A blue and yellow saucer dish, Kangxi six-character mark and of the period, 25.1cm. diam. (Christie's) $2,359 £1,650

A porcelain circular box and cover, by Bernard Leach, with St. Ives seals, 7.8cm. wide. (Christie's)
$1,188 £777

A stoneware tea caddy, by Bernard Leach, circa 1970, 16cm. high. (Christie's)
$440 £308

A circular stoneware plate with everted rim decorated by Bernard Leach, 39.2cm. diam., circa 1954. (Christie's) $2,643 £1,728

A tall stoneware jug, by Bernard Leach, with ribbed rim and strap handle, 28.8cm. high. (Christie's)
$495 £324

An oviform stoneware vase, by Bernard Leach, impressed BL and St. Ives seals, circa 1960, 27.6cm. high. (Christie's) $2,045 £1,430

A tapering stoneware cylindrical vase, by Bernard Leach, circa 1960, 34.2cm. high. (Christie's) $1,074 £702

A stoneware rectangular slab bottle, by Bernard Leach, impressed St. Ives seal, circa 1960, 19.5cm. high. (Christie's) $826 £540

A porcelain footed bowl, by Bernard Leach, circa 1955, 25.7cm. diam. (Christie's)
$3,775 £2,640

A stoneware rectangular slab bottle, by Bernard Leach, circa 1965, 19cm. high. (Christie's) $865 £605

LEACH

A stoneware cut-sided bowl, by Bernard Leach, circa 1965, 25cm. wide. (Christie's) $1,415 £990

An early stoneware rectangular tea caddy, by Bernard Leach, circa 1925, 15.2cm. high. (Christie's) $503 £352

A stoneware teabowl, by Bernard Leach, circa 1969, 14.1cm. diam. (Christie's) $707 £495

A stoneware pilgrim plate with everted rim, decorated by Bernard Leach, 32.2cm. diam. (Christie's) $6,940 £4,536

A stoneware 'Leaping Deer' vase, by Bernard Leach, impressed St. Ives seal, 35cm. high. (Christie's) $7,435 £4,860

A circular stoneware plate with everted rim, decorated by Bernard Leach, circa 1957, 32cm. diam. (Christie's) $826 £540

A stoneware oviform vase, by Bernard Leach, circa 1957, 32cm. high. (Christie's) $1,074 £702

A stoneware rectangular slab bottle, by Bernard Leach, circa 1960, 18.5cm. high. (Christie's) $2,674 £1,870

A tall stoneware elongated oviform vase with flattened sides, by Bernard Leach, circa 1960, 18.5cm. high. (Christie's) $1,258 £880

LENCI

A Lenci centrepiece modelled as a young naked girl, 46cm. high. (Christie's)
$1,258 £880

A Lenci figure modelled as a naked girl reclining on a tartan blanket, black painted Lenci marks, 30.7cm. long. (Christie's) $1,258 £880

A Lenci ceramic figure, the young girl in geometric patterned dress, 9½in. high, painted marks. (Christie's)
$422 £280

LIVERPOOL

A Liverpool delft blue and white globular bottle painted with a mother and child in a garden, circa 1760, 24cm. high. (Christie's) $762 £495

Late 18th century Naval Liverpool pitcher, England, 11in. high (several chips on rim and a crack on spout seams). (Robt. W. Skinner Inc.) $2,100 £1,400

A Liverpool Herculaneum green-ground tapering oviform vase, circa 1810, 24cm. high. (Christie's) $931 £605

One of four late 18th century Liverpool dinner plates, 10in. diam. (Robt. W. Skinner Inc.)
$550 £366

A Christian Liverpool bottle vase of plain pear shape with a slightly flared rim, 28cm. high. (Phillips)
$1,925 £1,250

An inscribed Liverpool delft puzzle jug, the rim with three spouts and hollow handle, circa 1750, 8in. high. (Dreweatts) $3,190 £2,200

LOWESTOFT

A Lowestoft creamboat of low Chelsea ewer shape, painted in blue with floral swags, 5.5cm. high. (Phillips) $246 £160

A Lowestoft cream jug of barrel shape, painted in underglaze blue with a diaper and scroll cartouche, 7cm. high. (Phillips) $554 £360

A Lowestoft teapot and cover, printed in underglaze blue with the 'Pagoda and Man Crossing a Bridge' pattern, the cover with the 'Wolf and Exotic Bird', 10.5cm. high. (Phillips) $847 £550

A Lowestoft cream jug of slender pear shape, painted by the Tulip Painter, 8.5cm. high. (Phillips) $585 £380

An inscribed Lowestoft 'trifle' mug with single-spur handle, 14cm. high. (Phillips) $7,700 £5,000

A Lowestoft 'pencilled' cream jug of slender shape, painted with a scene of a chinaman crossing a bridge, 9cm. high. (Phillips) $446 £290

A Lowestoft sparrow-beak jug, painted in underglaze blue with a bold flower spray, 8.5cm. high. (Phillips) $215 £140

A Lowestoft sparrow-beak jug, painted in colours with a floral spray with scattered sprigs, 8.5cm. high. (Phillips) $354 £230

A Lowestoft sparrow-beak jug, painted in blue with pagodas and flowering plants, 9cm. high. (Phillips) $215 £140

LUSTRE

Queen Caroline: a small lustre pottery cream jug, printed in black with portrait and national flora, 8cm. high.
(Phillips) $480 £300

A Zsolnay Pecs lustre group, modelled as two polar bears on a large rock in a green and blue golden lustre, 4½in. high.
(Christie's) $400 £250

A Pilkington Royal Lancastrian lustre vase, designed by W. Crane and painted by Wm. S. Mycock, 27cm. high.
(Phillips) $1,584 £1,100

Early 19th century Sunderland lustre pottery jug, 4¾in. high. (Reeds Rains)
$131 £85

A Sunderland lustre oviform jug, 9½in. high, circa 1830.
(Christie's) $496 £320

A Pilkington's Lancastrian jar and cover, the body decorated by Richard Joyce, 6in. high, date mark for 1911. (Christie's)
$576 £400

A Pilkington Lancastrian baluster vase with everted rim, decorated by Walter Crane, 26.6cm. high.
(Christie's) $792 £550

Pair of mid 19th century copper lustre jugs with blue band decoration and painted figures of Queen Victoria and Prince Albert, 5½in. high. (Reeds Rains) $372 £240

A lustre Pilkington 'Royal Lancastrian' oviform vase, painted by Richard Joyce, 30.5cm. high. (Phillips)
$960 £600

MARTINWARE

A Martin Bros. stoneware bird, 27.5cm. high, the head dated 1891 and the base 1890. (Phillips) $2,880 £2,000

A large Martin Bros. stoneware jardiniere of tapering cylindrical shape, 32cm. high. (Christie's) $960 £600

A Martin Bros. stoneware bird with detachable head, 9¾in. high, London and Southall, 1902. (Reeds Rains)
$6,975 £4,500

A Martinware stoneware gourd vase, the oviform body incised and cross hatched at the neck with green, 9½in. high. (Christie's)
$547 £380

A Martin Bros. stoneware double face jug in buff coloured glaze, 7in. high, London and Southall, 1903. (Reeds Rains)
$1,395 £900

A Martinware stoneware single handled jug, the incised decoration in shades of brown, green and blue on a cream ground, 8¾in. high. (Christie's) $316 £220

A Martin Bros stoneware two-handled spirit flask, 9½in. high, London and Southall, 1901. (Reeds Rains)
$1,085 £700

A Martin Bros. stoneware model of a bird, 36cm. high, the head only dated 1898. (Phillips) $4,896 £3,400

A Martin Bros. stoneware jug painted with fish and sea monsters on mottled blue ground, 10¼in. high, London and Southall 1897. (Reeds Rains) $1,085 £700

235

MASON'S

Part of a Mason's Ironstone dinner service, pattern no. 2604, approx. 90 pieces, retailed by Higginbotham and Son, Dublin. (Worsfolds) $5,232 £3,250

A Mason's ironstone circular jardiniere, the handles in the form of bears, 42cm. diam. (Phillips) $1,152 £800

A Mason's patent ironstone jug decorated in the Chinese taste, 32cm. high. (Lawrence Fine Art) $672 £400

Mason's style jug and foot bath. (John D. Fleming & Co.) $1,411 £850

A comprehensive Mason's ironstone dinner service, decorated in famille rose style, 72 pieces. (Phillips) $6,468 £4,200

MEISSEN

A Meissen circular saucepan with shaped handle, circa 1740, 18.5cm. wide. (Christie's) $712 £495

A Meissen snuff box and cover, modelled as a recumbent pug-dog, with contemporary copper gilt mounts, circa 1755, 8cm. long. (Christie's)
$10,296 £7,150

A Meissen circular bowl, blue crossed swords mark and Pressnummer 21, circa 1750, 16.5cm. diam. (Christie's) $871 £605

A Meissen chinoiserie plate, the centre painted by C. F. Herold, circa 1728, 22cm. diam. (Christie's)
$13,828 £9,603

A Meissen small Kakiemon hexagonal baluster vase, circa 1735, 10cm. high. (Christie's) $5,970 £4,146

A Meissen ornithological sugar basin and cover, Pressnummer 6, 1745-50, 11.5cm. diam. (Christie's)
$2,136 £1,484

A Meissen rectangular tea caddy and cover painted in Silbermalerei with chinoiserie figures, circa 1740, 13.5cm. high. (Christie's)
$4,713 £3,273

A Meissen group of a pug bitch suckling her puppy, after a model by Kaendler, 21.5cm. high, crossed swords mark. (Phillips) $677 £440

One of a pair of Meissen baluster pots and covers, one with Pressnummer 37, circa 1740, 9cm. high. (Christie's) $3,456 £2,400

MEISSEN

A Meissen figure of a Chinese boy, modelled by J. J. Kaendler, with fixed head, blue crossed swords mark at back, circa 1750, 22cm. high. (Christie's) $2,376 £1,650

A Meissen small octagonal dish from the Christie Miller Service, blue crossed swords mark and Pressnummer 22, circa 1742, 17.5cm. wide. (Christie's) $11,880 £8,250

A Meissen Kakiemon baluster jug with scroll handle and foliage spout, blue crossed swords marks, circa 1730, 20cm. high. (Christie's) $2,217 £1,540

A Meissen chinoiserie arbour group, modelled by P. Reinicke, blue crossed swords mark on base, circa 1750, 19cm. high. (Christie's) $3,960 £2,750

A Meissen white figure of Neptune, modelled by J. G. Kirchner, blue crossed swords mark at back, circa 1728-32, 33cm. high. (Christie's) $15,048 £10,450

A Meissen circular two-handled tureen and cover with Frauenkopf scroll handles, circa 1730, 32.6cm. high. (Christie's) $6,336 £4,400

One of a pair of Meissen figures of cedar waxwings, modelled by J. J. Kaendler, circa 1745, 24cm. high. (Christie's) $4,752 £3,300

One of a pair of Meissen Imari circular tureens and covers, blue crossed swords marks and K. for Kretschmar, circa 1735, 24.5cm. diam. (Christie's) $6,019 £4,180

One of two Meissen figures of children dressed as hunchbacks, Pressnummer 24 to each figure, circa 1745, 13cm. high. (Christie's) $3,168 £2,200

A Meissen topographical oviform coffee pot and cover, painted with views in Dresden and Schandau, circa 1815, 19.5cm. high. (Christie's) $717 £495

One of six Meissen Hausmalerei shaped circular plates painted by F. F. Meyer von Pressnitz, blue crossed swords mark and Pressnummer 22, circa 1740, 23.5cm. diam. (Christie's) $9,504 £6,600

A Meissen figure of a nodding Chinese boy, modelled by J. J. Kaendler, blue crossed swords mark at back, circa 1750, 22cm. high. (Christie's) $1,900 £1,320

A Meissen gold Chinese baluster hexagonal tea caddy and cover, the cover with chinoiserie figures, circa 1725, 10cm. high. (Christie's) $5,385 £3,740

A Meissen porcelain figure of a cockatoo, modelled by Paul Walther, one claw damaged, circa 1920, 47cm. high. (Christie's) $1,742 £1,210

A Meissen figure of a Bolognese terrier, blue crossed swords and incised numeral marks, circa 1880, 23cm. high. (Christie's) $574 £396

A Meissen figure of a mandolin player, blue crossed swords mark at back, circa 1745, 20.5cm. high. (Christie's) $2,376 £1,650

A Meissen oval snuff box and cover with copper gilt mount, circa 1760, 6.5cm. wide. (Christie's) $5,544 £3,850

A Meissen standing figure of Hercules, blue crossed swords mark at back, circa 1750, 12cm. high. (Christie's) $221 £154

MEISSEN

A Meissen figure of a Dutchman in dancing attitude, circa 1740, 17cm. high. (Christie's) $506 £352

A Meissen model of a town house of two storeys and an attic, circa 1748, 18cm. high. (Christie's) $6,913 £4,801

A Meissen figure of an Austrian fusilier, blue crossed swords mark at back, circa 1765, 23.5cm. high. (Christie's) $3,168 £2,200

A Meissen group of Bacchus, blue crossed swords and dot and 3 mark, circa 1770, 22cm. high. (Christie's) $792 £550

A Meissen Fabeltiere baluster candlestick, blue crossed swords mark and impressed Former's marks, circa 1735, 24cm. high. (Christie's) $5,970 £4,146

A Meissen baluster hot milk jug and cover with contemporary silver hinge, circa 1740, 14cm. high.(Christie's) $1,571   £1,091

A Meissen Jagd cup and cover, circa 1733, 42cm. high. (Christie's) $20,113 £13,968

A Meissen fluted large saucer dish with scalloped rim, circa 1735, 15.5cm. diam. (Christie's) $1,884 £1,309

A Meissen figure of a lemon-seller from the Cris de Paris series, circa 1755, 13.5cm. high. (Christie's) $1,188 £825

MEISSEN

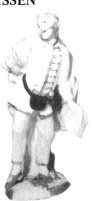

A Meissen figure of Scapin from the Commedia dell' Arte Series modelled by J. J. Kaendler and P. Reinicke, circa 1744, 13.5cm. high. (Christie's) $5,068 £3,520

A Meissen yellow-ground cylindrical chocolate pot and cover, Pressnummer 21, circa 1740, 15cm. high. (Christie's) $2,010 £1,396

A Meissen figure of a bread seller, modelled by P. Reinicke and J. J. Kaendler, circa 1755, 19.5cm. high. (Christie's) $3,484 £2,420

A Meissen turquoise-ground baluster hot milk jug and cover, circa 1740, gilder's mark C. (Christie's) $1,507 £1,047

A Meissen chinoiserie two-handled pilgrim flask/scent bottle, the sides painted by J. G. Horoldt, circa 1728, 9cm. high. (Christie's) $5,028 £3,492

A Meissen group of four children scantily clad, blue crossed swords and incised numeral and impressed marks, circa 1880, 17cm. high. (Christie's) $1,093 £715

A Meissen figure of an oarsman, blue crossed swords, star and 4 mark at back, circa 1780, 13.5cm. high. (Christie's) $1,188 £825

A Meissen Kakiemon plate painted with the Flying Fox and Brocade pattern, circa 1740, 24cm. diam. (Christie's) $2,010 £1,396

A Meissen figure of a gardener, blue crossed swords at back and impressed 1756, 11cm. high. (Christie's) $237 £165

MEISSEN

A Meissen circular sugar
bowl and cover, gilt 85
mark, circa 1740, 10cm.
diam. (Christie's)
$2,010 £1,396

A Meissen blue and white
baluster teapot and domed
cover, the porcelain 1725-30,
the gilding almost contemporary, 18cm. wide.
(Christie's) $2,010 £1,396

A Meissen cartouche-
shaped snuff box and
cover, the interior of the
base entirely gilt, circa
1730, 7.5cm. wide.
(Christie's)
$7,128 £4,950

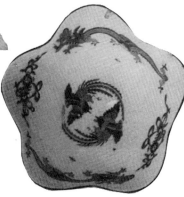

A Meissen Hausmalerei
shell-shaped bowl, painted
by F. F. Mayer von Press-
nitz, circa 1750, 19cm. wide.
(Christie's) $1,130 £785

A Meissen figure of Cupid,
blue crossed swords, impressed
and incised numeral marks,
circa 1880, 19.5cm. high.
(Christie's) $673 £440

A Meissen pentagonal saucer
painted with the Red Dragon
pattern, circa 1730.
(Christie's) $691 £480

A Meissen rectangular tea
caddy and cover, circa 1735,
in fitted case, 11cm. high.
(Christie's) $3,456 £2,400

A Meissen group of Europa
and the Bull, circa 1880,
22.5cm. high. (Christie's)
$1,093 £715

A Meissen circular sugar
bowl and cover with
flower-bud finial, blue
crossed swords mark, circa
1750, 10.5cm. diam.
(Christie's) $1,029 £715

MEISSEN

A Meissen chinoiserie oval sugar box and cover, blue crossed swords mark and incised W, circa 1730, 12cm. wide. (Christie's)
$16,342 £11,349

A Meissen KPM chinoiserie baluster teapot and domed cover, circa 1723-25, 15.5cm. wide. (Christie's)
$11,314 £7,857

A Meissen cartouche-shaped snuff box and cover, circa 1745, 7.5cm. wide. (Christie's) $8,712 £6,050

A Meissen KPM chinoiserie two-handled bowl and cover, circa 1725, 13cm. wide. (Christie's) $26,399 £18,333

A Meissen group of nude girls standing beside a tree stump, circa 1880, 18.5cm. high. (Christie's) $673 £440

A Meissen rectangular waisted snuff box and cover, with hinged silver mount, circa 1760, 8cm. wide. (Christie's)
$2,851 £1,980

A Meissen dish with barbed rim, circa 1735, 37.5cm. diam. (Christie's)
$1,571 £1,091

A Meissen chinoiserie hot milk jug and cover, circa 1735, in fitted case, 15cm. high. (Christie's)
$2,387 £1,658

A Meissen saucer dish from the Bamberg Service, blue crossed swords and K mark for Kretschmar, circa 1730, 21.5cm. diam. (Christie's)
$2,059 £1,430

Early/mid 18th century blue and white moonflask moulded and painted in early Ming taste, 31cm. high. (Christie's) $1,887 £1,320

One of a pair of Ming blue and white vases, meiping, circa 1500, 24.5cm. high. (Christie's) $3,932 £2,750

A late Ming blue and white frog kendi modelled as a seated frog, Wanli, 16cm. high. (Christie's) $2,202 £1,540

A late Ming blue and white barrel-shaped garden seat with lion mask handles, Wanli, 38cm. high. (Christie's) $3,146 £2,200

A late Ming blue and white saucer dish with foliate rim, Wanli, 52cm. diam. (Christie's) $3,775 £2,640

A late Ming blue and white gu-shaped vase, Wanli, 9¾in. high. (Christie's) $1,483 £1,045

A late Ming blue and white baluster jar, encircled Wanli six-character mark and of the period, 34cm. high. (Christie's) $14,943 £10,450

A Ming blue and white stem cup, encircled Wanli six-character mark at the centre and of the period, 10cm. diam. (Christie's) $14,157 £9,900

A late Ming polychrome square table screen probably for the Japanese market, Tianqi, 17.4cm. sq. (Christie's) $4,089 £2,860

MINTON

A Minton parian figure of Florinda, after John Bell, 13¼in. high, 1848. (Parsons, Welch & Cowell) $138 £90

A Minton mushroom teapot, gourd-shaped, yellow body with naturalistic polychrome colouring, impressed Minton with date code for 1862, 14.8cm. high. (Christie's) $638 £440

A Minton parian figure of Dorothea, after John Bell, 13¾in. high, registration tablet for 1872. (Parsons, Welch & Cowell) $323 £210

Minton Art Deco hexagonal garden seat, 18in. tall, marked No. 1364. (Worsfolds) $604 £400

A Minton centrepiece with flower form base divided into six segmented compartments, date code for 1865, 36.5cm. high. (Christie's) $4,785 £3,300

A Minton majolica vase, impressed Minton 1558 date code for 1870, 17.9cm. high. (Christie's) $538 £352

A majolica teapot in the form of a monkey, probably Minton, 10¼in. high. (Reeds Rains) $518 £360

Pair of Minton candlesticks, impressed Minton and with date code for 1862, 41.2cm. high. (Christie's) $1,116 £770

A Minton vase, designed by Dr. C. Dresser, U-shaped on four splayed feet, 19.2cm. high. (Christie's) $1,817 £1,188

MINTON

A Minton jug, impressed
Minton 474 and with date
code for 1870, 32cm. high.
(Christie's) $797 £550

A large Minton oval platter
on four bracket feet, glazed
in green, yellow, brown and
white, impressed Minton
927 O and date code for
1870, 61cm. long.
(Christie's) $1,595 £1,100

One of a pair of Minton jugs,
each one impressed Minton
596, one with date code for
1867, one for 1870, 24.5cm.
high. (Christie's) $319 £220

A Minton figure modelled as
a bare-foot maiden in a full-
length robe, naturalistic polychrome colouring, impressed
date code for 1857, 44.7cm.
high. (Christie's) $717 £495

A large Minton jardiniere
with bearded ram's head
handles, aubergine with
naturalistic polychrome
colouring, date code for
1851, 36cm. high.
(Christie's) $1,276 £880

A Minton jardiniere and stand,
designed by Albert Carrier de
Belleuse, jardiniere impressed
Mintons 990 and with date
code for 1872, base impressed
Minton 2227, 168cm. high.
(Christie's) $19,140 £13,200

One of a pair of garden seats
modelled as crouching monkeys holding coconuts and
supporting cushions on their
heads, 46.5cm. high.
(Christie's) $15,950 £11,000

A Minton plant trough, rectangular shape with rounded
bottom on attached bracket
support, 35.8cm. high.
(Christie's) $10,367 £7,150

One of a pair of Minton
vases of swollen baluster
shape, impressed Minton
827 and 827A, 35.5cm. high.
(Christie's) $2,233 £1,540

MINTON

A Minton two-handled vase, naturalistic polychrome colouring on pale blue ground, impressed Minton and with date code for 1870, 40.7cm. high. (Christie's)
$1,276 £880

A Minton fish platter and cover, the cover modelled as a carp, impressed Mintons 1979 and with date code for 1903, 61cm. long.(Christie's)
$3,030 £2,090

One of a pair of Minton 'Tower' jugs, impressed 1231 and with date codes for 1868(?), 34.5cm. high. (Christie's) $957 £660

A Minton sweet chestnut dish and spoon, impressed marks Minton 594N and date mark for 1867, 24.5cm. diam. (Christie's) $1,515 £1,045

A Minton jardiniere with a moulded frieze of figures, pale blue and white with a pink interior, impressed Minton 534, 29cm. high. (Christie's) $957 £660

A Minton porcelain figure of a putto seated upon a conch shell, impressed Mintons 1539 and with date code for 1873, 43.5cm. high. (Christie's) $1,435 £990

A Minton wall plaque, ochre and cobalt blue on a turquoise ground, impressed Minton 1668 and with date code for 1873, 51cm. long. (Christie's)
$829 £572

A Minton figure modelled as a boy in rustic garb, his arm round the neck of a donkey, impressed Minton 196, 20cm. high. (Christie's) $478 £330

One of a pair of Minton pedestal form garden seats, naturalistic polychrome colouring on an olive ground, 43cm. high. (Christie's)
$3,190 £2,200

MOORCROFT

A Moorcroft wheatear motif vase with green and purple tones on an off-white ground, 13½in. high. (Locke & England) $691 £480

A Moorcroft pottery dark pink glazed box and cover, designed for Liberty & Co., 3¾in. high. (Christie's) $422 £264

A Moorcroft pottery vase, the body decorated in the leaf and blackberry pattern, 6in. high. (Christie's) $115 £72

A Moorcroft 'Spanish' pattern pot pourri of oviform with screw cover, 10.2cm. high. (Phillips) $261 £180

A Moorcroft MacIntyre Florian ware four-piece teaset, in shades of blue and white, teapot, 4½in. high. (Christie's) $387 £242

One of a pair of Moorcroft Art pottery vases, painted with red and ochre poppies, 10½in. high. (Biddle & Webb) $662 £460

A Moorcroft two-handled box and cover, decorated in the 'Claremont' pattern, 6½in. high. (Christie's) $691 £480

A pair of Moorcroft vases, bodies painted in the pomegranate pattern, 15in. high, impressed marks, signed in green. (Christie's) $716 £462

A Wm. Moorcroft pottery circular plaque, trailed and enamelled with anemonies in red and yellows on a yellow ground with blue centre. (Biddle & Webb) $631 £410

One of two blue and white sauceboats of European silver shape, circa 1750, 21cm. wide. (Christie's) $6,009 £3,902

One of twelve provincial blue and white bowls painted with a stylised landscape, circa 1750, 15cm. diam. (Christie's) $1,638 £1,064

One of twelve blue and white bowls painted with the 'Scholar on Bridge' pattern, circa 1750, 19cm. diam. (Christie's) $4,643 £3,015

One of twelve plates painted with the 'Boatman and Six-Flower Border' pattern, circa 1750, 23cm. diam. (Christie's) $3,003 £1,951

A Martaban olive-brown glazed oviform jar, circa 1750, 29cm. high. (Christie's) $3,012 £1,956

One of two blue and white dishes, the borders each with three clusters of flowering branches, circa 1750, 42cm. diam. (Christie's) $15,295 £9,932

One of two blue and white oval butter tubs and shallow domed covers, circa 1750, 11.5cm. wide. (Christie's) $8,739 £5,675

One of four Chinese Imari spittoons, circa 1750, 12.3cm. diam. (Christie's) $4,096 £2,660

A blue and white oblong octagonal tureen and cover, circa 1750, 33.5cm. wide. (Christie's) $6,009 £3,902

A blue and white chamber pot painted with peony and bamboo issuing from rockwork, circa 1750, 18.5cm. diam. (Christie's)
$2,293 £1,489

One of two enamelled globular teapots and shallow domed covers, circa 1750, 21.5cm. wide. (Christie's)
$1,529 £993

A blue and white bowl-shaped jug, the handle with a flower spray at right angles to the spout, circa 1750, 21cm. wide. (Christie's) $2,293 £1,489

One of twelve blue and white plates painted with 'The Boatman and Six-Flower Border' pattern. (Christie's)
$8,194 £5,321

A copper red and celadon glazed figure of a standing dignitary, circa 1750, 18.3cm. high. (Christie's)
$30,045 £19,510

A large blue and white deep dish painted with four fantailed fish, circa 1750, 45cm. diam. (Christie's)
$10,924 £7,094

  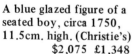

A blue glazed figure of a seated boy, circa 1750, 11.5cm. high. (Christie's)
$2,075 £1,348

A blue and white oval tureen, cover and stand, heavily encrusted, circa 1750, the stand 41cm. wide. (Christie's)
$4,643 £3,015

A blue and white 'piggy-back' group formed as a standing lady and a small boy, circa 1750, 19.8cm. high. (Christie's) $14,203 £9,223

NANKING

One of two blue and white circular tureens and shallow domed covers, circa 1750, 23.5cm. wide. (Christie's) $14,203 £9,223

One of two blue and white globular teapots and shallow domed covers, circa 1750, 21cm. wide. (Christie's) $3,277 £2,128

One of two chamber pots, circa 1750, 15.5cm. wide, 12.5cm. diam. (Christie's) $3,754 £2,438

Part of a set of twelve Chinese Imari teacups and saucers painted with the 'Chrysanthemum Rock' pattern, circa 1750. (Christie's) $12,018 £7,804

A white glazed figure of a pheasant, circa 1750, 26.3cm. high. (Christie's) $2,621 £1,702

One of two underglaze blue and gilt dishes painted with the 'Three Pavilions' pattern, circa 1750, 39.5cm. diam. (Christie's) $6,009 £3,902

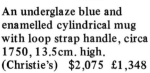

An underglaze blue and enamelled cylindrical mug with loop strap handle, circa 1750, 13.5cm. high. (Christie's) $2,075 £1,348

One of two blue and white spittoons, the interior with a border of trellis pattern, circa 1750, 12.6cm. diam. (Christie's) $3,277 £2,128

One of two cylindrical condiment jars and shallow domed covers, with a wide loop handle, circa 1750, 11.5cm. wide. (Christie's) $6,009 £3,902

PARIS

A Paris tea kettle, cover and stand, iron-red monogram mark of Louis-Stanislas-Xavier, circa 1780, 30cm. wide. (Christie's) $2,387 £1,658

One of a pair of Paris centre-pieces, modelled as biscuit figures of Cupid, circa 1820, 32.5cm. high. (Christie's) $957 £660

A Paris gold-ground cabinet-cup and saucer, circa 1815. (Christie's) $1,178 £770

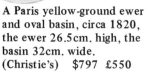

A Paris (Schoelcher) tea service in the Empire taste, the salmon-pink grounds painted in sepia with vases of fruit flanked by putti seated on foliage scrolls and anthemion on wide bands beneath richly gilt borders, the interiors richly gilt, puce script marks, circa 1820. (Christie's) $4,147 £2,860

One of a pair of late 19th century Paris porcelain urns, 10½in. high. (Christie's) $440 £287

A Paris yellow-ground ewer and oval basin, circa 1820, the ewer 26.5cm. high, the basin 32cm. wide. (Christie's) $797 £550

A Paris porcelain coffee pot of pear form with strap handle, 9½in. high. (Christie's) $323 £209

PRATTWARE

A Pratt type Toby jug modelled as a rotund gentleman seated, entitled 'Tobey', 9¾in. high, circa 1790. (Christie's) $930 £600

A Prattware flask of circular form with a portrait of The Duke of York and the reverse Louis XVI and Marie Antoinette, 5in. high, circa 1794. (Christie's) $186 £120

A Prattware Toby jug, his pipe by his left side, 24cm. high. (Phillips) $720 £500

A Prattware oval jug moulded with two bust portraits of The Miser, 5½in. high, circa 1795. (Christie's) $281 £176

A pair of Prattware oval plaques, moulded in relief with busts of Louis XVI and Queen Marie Antoinette, 18cm. high. (Phillips) $631 £410

Early 19th century Prattware figure of a young maiden with hand outstretched, 9½in. high. (Reeds Rains) $217 £140

A Prattware model of a Gothic Chapel with central tower and spire, 24cm. high. (Phillips) $893 £580

A Prattware oval plaque, moulded in high relief with two lions coloured in ochre and brown, 28.5cm. long. (Phillips) $800 £520

A Prattware cottage money box in the form of a two-storeyed house with blue tiled roof, 12.5cm. high. (Phillips) $646 £420

LUCIE RIE

An early and unique porcelain dish, by Lucie Rie, circa 1954, 14cm. diam. (Christie's) $660 £432

A porcelain inlaid sgraffito cylindrical vase, by Lucie Rie, circa 1955, 21cm. high. (Christie's)
$3,635 £2,376

A stoneware bottle vase, by Lucie Rie, covered in a light slate-blue pitted glaze with iron-coloured flecks, circa 1960, 22.6cm. high. (Christie's) $1,569 £1,026

A stoneware dish, by Lucie Rie, with loop handle, circa 1955, 19.5cm. diam. (Christie's) $396 £259

A stoneware vase, by Lucie Rie, covered in a thick and pitted turquoise glaze with bronze-coloured flecks, circa 1958, 23.5cm. high. (Christie's) $908 £594

An earthenware bowl with pulled lip, by Lucie Rie and Hans Coper, circa 1949, 26cm. diam. (Christie's)
$826 £540

A stoneware bottle vase, by Lucie Rie, covered in a greenish-white pitted glaze, circa 1960, 20cm. high. (Christie's) $1,074 £702

A porcelain sgraffito conical bowl, by Lucie Rie, impressed LR seal, circa 1957, 10.2cm. diam. (Christie's)
$1,487 £972

A porcelain sgraffito bottle vase, by Lucie Rie, circa 1955, 23.9cm. high. (Christie's) $3,304 £2,160

LUCIE RIE

A monumental stoneware bottle vase, by Lucie Rie, covered in a pitted matt mottled white glaze with chocolate-coloured flecks, circa 1972, 33.2cm. high. (Christie's) $5,948 £3,888

A porcelain rounded bowl, by Lucie Rie, covered in a yellow uranium glaze with a matt manganese rim border, circa 1960, 22.1cm. diam. (Christie's) $1,487 £972

A compressed cylindrical vase, by Lucie Rie, impressed LR seal, circa 1955, 22.4cm. high. (Christie's)
$1,652 £1,080

A porcelain fluted bowl, by Lucie Rie, covered in a pale turquoise glaze under a mottled grey-brown glaze, circa 1975, 22.6cm. diam. (Christie's) $527 £345

A flattened cylindrical porcelain vase, by Lucie Rie, covered in a mottled pastel pink, blue and brown glaze, circa 1967, 13.5cm. high. (Christie's) $991 £648

A porcelain deep bowl, by Lucie Rie, covered in a matt white glaze with green/black mottled spiral, circa 1968, 15.7cm. diam. (Christie's)
$826 £540

A white glazed porcelain bottle vase, by Lucie Rie, with raised spot decoration covered in a matt white glaze, circa 1974, 23.9cm. high. (Christie's) $5,783 £3,780

A stoneware teapot and cover, by Lucie Rie, with cane handle, 15.2cm. high. (Christie's) $462 £302

A porcelain bottle vase, by Lucie Rie, covered in a thick matt manganese glaze, circa 1957, 20.1cm. high. (Christie's) $1,156 £756

LUCIE RIE

A squat stoneware bottle vase, by Lucie Rie, covered in thick pitted greyish white glaze with traces of lavender-blue, circa 1970, 16.5cm. high. (Christie's) $1,404 £918

A stoneware footed bowl, by Lucie Rie, covered in a white glaze, 15cm. wide.
(Christie's) $396 £259

A porcelain bottle vase, by Lucie Rie, circa 1982, 24.2cm. high. (Christie's)
$2,831 £1,980

A porcelain sgraffito and inlaid bottle vase, by Lucie Rie, circa 1972, 16.3cm. high. (Christie's)
$1,179 £825

An early sgraffito stoneware vase, by Lucie Rie, circa 1953, 22.6cm. high. (Christie's) $6,292 £4,400

A stoneware sgraffito bottle vase, by Lucie Rie, circa 1972, 24.6cm. high. (Christie's)
$2,123 £1,485

A monumental tall stoneware tapering cylindrical vase, by Lucie Rie, circa 1955, 36.5cm. high. (Christie's)
$1,569 £1,026

A stoneware cylindrical vase, by Lucie Rie, circa 1972, 13.1cm. high. (Christie's)
$393 £275

A large stoneware sgraffito goblet shaped vase, by Lucie Rie, with cylindrical flower holder, circa 1955, 19.8cm. high. (Christie's)
$1,569 £1,026

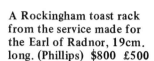

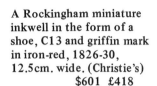

A Rockingham miniature
inkwell in the form of a
shoe, C13 and griffin mark
in iron-red, 1826-30,
12.5cm. wide. (Christie's)
$601 £418

A Rockingham model of a
dog recumbent on a maroon
coloured base, 9.5cm. long.
(Phillips) $928 £580

A Rockingham toast rack
from the service made for
the Earl of Radnor, 19cm.
long. (Phillips) $800 £500

A Rockingham plate, the
centre painted with fruit and
flowers, puce griffin mark
and pattern no. 562, circa
1835, 23.5cm. diam.
(Christie's) $348 £242

A documentary Rockingham
biscuit figure of Paysan
Basque Des Environs De
Bayonne, 1829, 21cm. high.
(Christie's) $633 £440

A Rockingham plate, the
centre painted by J. Wager
Brameld with Cole Titmouse
and Goldfinch, circa 1835,
23cm. diam. (Christie's)
                $760 £528

A Rockingham biscuit
figure of a Tyrolean girl,
incised no. 13, circa 1830,
18.5cm. high. (Christie's)
                $871 £605

A Rockingham green-ground
bombe-shaped rectangular
inkstand, puce griffin mark,
circa 1835, 31cm. wide.
(Christie's) $4,118 £2,860

A Rockingham figure of a
cobbler, after the model by
Cyffle, incised no. 39, 1826-
30, 14.5cm. high. (Christie's)
                $1,188 £825

A Rockingham onion-shaped table scent bottle and stopper, C12 in red, puce griffin mark, circa 1835, 15cm. high. (Christie's) $554 £385

A Rockingham figure of a shepherd, incised no. 4, 1826-30, 21.5cm. high. (Christie's) $554 £385

A Rockingham pastille burner, the cover with C12 in iron-red, the stand with red griffin mark, 1826-30, 9.5cm. high. (Christie's) $475 £330

A Rockingham spill vase painted with a church in a mountainous wooded river landscape, C8 in gold and puce griffin mark, circa 1835, 11.5cm. high. (Christie's) $633 £440

A Rockingham blue-ground pin tray, the centre painted in the manner of Edwin Steele, circa 1835, 9.5cm. wide. (Christie's)
        $506 £352

A Rockingham green-ground cylindrical vase, painted by John Randall, C13 in red, puce griffin mark, circa 1835, 11cm. high. (Christie's)
        $950 £660

A Rockingham cabinet cup and stand with two gilt scroll handles, circa 1835, the stand 11.5cm. diam., the cup 10cm. high. (Christie's)
        $760 £528

A Rockingham biscuit bust of Frederick Augustus, Duke of York, circa 1827, 16.5cm. high. (Christie's)
        $1,108 £770

A Rockingham cylindrical patch box and screw-on cover painted in the manner of Edwin Steele, 1826-30, 10cm. diam. (Christie's)
        $1,188 £825

ROOKWOOD

Rookwood standard glaze ewer with sterling silver overlay, Ohio, 1892, 10¼in. high. (Robt. W. Skinner Inc.) $2,800 £1,958

Rookwood pottery tall portrait vase, Cincinnati, 1894, decorated with figure entitled 'Spirit of the Summit', 14½in. high. (Robt. W. Skinner Inc.) $4,100 £2,867

Rookwood standard glaze jug, with Palmer Cox figure, Ohio, 1891, artist's initials H.E.W., 6in. high. (Robt. W. Skinner Inc.) $950 £664

Rookwood standard glaze vase with sterling silver overlay, Ohio, 1892, initialled K.C.M. for Kate C. Matchette, 6½in. high. (Robt. W. Skinner Inc.) $2,300 £1,608

Rookwood pottery scenic vellum plaque, signed C. Schmidt, 1921, 12½ x 8½in. (Robt. W. Skinner Inc.) $800 £560

A Rookwood earthenware vase, decorated by Leonore Asbury, sizemark XXI and Rookwood mark for 1914, 21cm. high. (Christie's) $408 £286

Rookwood pottery silver overlay vase, initialled HEW for Harriet Eliz. Wilcox, 1894, 5.5/8in. high. (Robt. W. Skinner Inc.) $1,300 £909

One of a pair of Rookwood stoneware bookends, modelled as sphinx holding books, light brown glaze, 18cm. high. (Christie's) $190 £132

A Rookwood silver overlay vase, impressed artist's monogram SS, 12.5cm. high. (Christie's) $792 £550

ROYAL DUX

A Royal Dux bust, the young Art Nouveau maiden gazing to the left, raised pink triangle mark, 20in. high. (Christie's) $943 £660

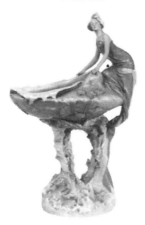

A Royal Dux centrepiece with figure of a water nymph kneeling on an abalone shell, 15½in. high. (Reeds Rains) $387 £250

A Royal Dux group of a flute player and dancer both wearing Orientally inspired costume, 12in. high, raised pink triangle mark. (Christie's) $261 £170

A Royal Dux porcelain group of classical figures, the boy in wolf-skin, and girl wearing a gown, 26in. high. (Dacre, Son & Hartley) $1,094 £760

Pair of small Royal Dux figures. (Cooper Hirst) $527 £340

A Royal Dux porcelain group of a peasant man and woman, on leaf decorated base, 22¾in. high. (Dacre, Son & Hartley) $432 £300

RUSSIAN

A biscuit group of three tipsy men standing on an oval base, by Gardner, printed and impressed marks, 23.5cm. high. (Phillips) $1,078 £700

A biscuit figure of a man fishing through ice, by Gardner, printed and impressed marks, 26.5cm. high. (Phillips) $492 £320

A biscuit group of two bearded men, by Gardner, printed and impressed marks, 22cm. high. (Phillips) $677 £440

SATSUMA

Late 19th century Satsuma
model of a recumbent
karashishi, 34cm. long.
(Christie's) $1,874 £1,320

Late 19th century Satsuma
teapot and cover modelled
as a stylised bird, 18cm. long.
(Christie's) $1,249 £880

A 19th century Satsuma
shaped oval box and cover,
signed Tokozan, 24cm. wide.
(Christie's) $1,562 £1,100

Late 19th century Satsuma
trumpet-shaped two-handled
vase decorated in various
coloured enamels and gilt,
37.5cm. high. (Christie's)
        $4,897 £3,080

Late 19th century large
oviform Satsuma vase in
various coloured enamels and
gilt, 48cm. high. (Christie's)
        $7,810 £5,500

One of a pair of Satsuma
vases, Japan, circa 1880,
14½in. high. (Robt. W.
Skinner Inc.) $300 £193

Late 19th century Satsuma
model of a courtier, signed
Dai Nihon, 22.5cm. high.
(Christie's) $1,311 £825

A Japanese Satsuma bowl
painted with panels of
figures at various pastimes,
4¾in. diam. (Christie's)
        $474 £300

Late 19th century Satsuma
temple jar with carved teak
cover, Japan, 13.1/8in. high.
(Robt. W. Skinner Inc.)
        $950 £659

A Sevres baluster cream jug, blue interlaced L marks enclosing the date letter N for 1766, 12.5cm. high. (Christie's) $285 £198

One of three 19th century Sevres porcelain gilt mounted jardinieres, one oval 10½in. wide and a pair of cache pots, 6in. diam. (Reeds Rains) $961 £620

A Sevres circular sugar bowl and cover, blue interlaced L marks enclosing the date letter O for 1767, 11cm. high. (Christie's) $380 £264

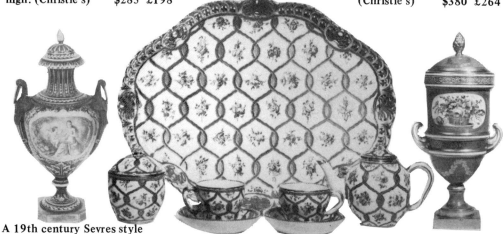

A 19th century Sevres style ormolu mounted covered urn, France, 32½in. high. (Robt. W. Skinner Inc.) $2,600 £1,805

A Sevres Dejeuner comprising a teapot and cover, circular sugar bowl and cover, four cups and saucers and a tray, date letter D for 1756 on the tray. (Christie's) $3,960 £2,750

One of a pair of Sevres apple-green ground vases and covers, circa 1770, 35cm. high. (Christie's) $5,068 £3,520

A Sevres blue-ground baluster jug and cover with gilt metal mount, blue interlaced L marks enclosing the date letter H for 1760, 19cm. high. (Christie's) $1,267 £880

A Sevres two-handled seau a liqueur rond, blue inter-laced L marks enclosing the date letter U for 1773, 13cm. high. (Christie's) $3,801 £2,640

One of a pair of Sevres apple-green ground baluster pot pourri vases and covers, date letter K for 1763, 22cm. high. (Christie's) $10,296 £7,150

SEVRES

A Sevres green-ground circular sugar bowl and cover, blue interlaced L's enclosing the date letter I for 1761 and the painter's mark Aloncle, 12cm. high. (Christie's) $554 £385

A Sevres oviform teapot and cover with gilt dentil rims, circa 1765, 16cm. wide. (Christie's)
          $475 £330

A large Sevres (hard-paste) two-handled blue nouveau and Louis XVI ormolu jardiniere, date letter GG for 1784, 52cm. wide. (Christie's)
          $41,184 £28,600

A Sevres hop-trellis fluted cup and saucer, circa 1765. (Christie's) $475 £330

A Sevres pattern gilt metal mounted, royal blue ground, two-handled pot pourri vase and domed cover, circa 1888, 29in. high. (Christie's)
    $2,073   £1,430

A Sevres hard-paste cup and saucer, blue crowned interlaced L mark enclosing date letter U for 1773. (Christie's)
          $554 £385

One of a pair of late 19th century Sevres pattern oval pot pourri vases and covers with winged caryatid handles, imitation interlaced L marks, 40.5cm. high. (Christie's) $1,914 £1,320

A Sevres hard-paste green-ground soup tureen and cover, gilt interlaced L marks and HP mark of Prevost, circa 1785, 30cm. wide. (Christie's)
          $1,584 £1,100

One of a pair of late 19th century Sevres pattern royal blue-ground oviform vases and fixed covers with gilt bronze mounts, 42cm. high. (Christie's) $1,116 £770

A Sevres two-handled seau a bouteille, blue interlaced L marks enclosing the date letter D for 1756 and with painter's mark of Rosset, 23cm. wide. (Christie's)
$1,506 £902

A Sevres shaped oval basin, date letter F for 1758, 31.5cm. wide. (Christie's) $1,194 £715

A Sevres shaped circular plate made to match 'des Asturies' service, 24cm. diam. (Christie's) $1,469 £880

A Sevres bleu celeste square tray with pierced scroll border, circa 1757, 14.8cm. sq. (Christie's) $1,469 £880

A Sevres bleu nouveau coffee cup and saucer, painter's mark of Morin, date letter N for 1766. (Christie's)
$1,561 £935

A Sevres mocha set, blue interlaced L marks enclosing the date letter G for 1759 and painter's mark of Catrice. (Christie's) $734 £440

One of two Sevres two-handled feuille-de-choux seaux a bouteille, with painter's marks of Tardy and Tandart, 26cm. wide. (Christie's) $1,837 £1,100

A Sevres pattern royal blue-ground jewelled coffee can and saucer, imitation interlaced L marks, circa 1865. (Christie's) $398 £275

A Sevres rose pompadour square tray, blue interlaced L marks enclosing the date letter E for 1757 and painter's mark of Noel, 14.5cm. sq. (Christie's)
$6,492 £3,850

A Jian Yao deep bowl with russet streaks over a black glaze thinning to a chocolate-brown at the rim, S. Song Dynasty, 12.9cm. diam. (Christie's) $1,258 £880

A Ding Yao bottle potted in the form of a contemporary metal prototype, N. Song Dynasty, 25cm. high, fitted box. (Christie's) $94,380 £66,000

A Jun Yao bowl, the sides under a lightly-crackled lavender glaze, S. Song Dynasty, 11.3cm. diam. (Christie's) $3,932 £2,750

A Cizhou carved oviform jar, Song Dynasty, 26cm. high, fitted box. (Christie's) $7,865 £5,500

A Ding Yao dish carved with a feathery lotus spray and scrolling leaves, N. Song Dynasty, 20.7cm. diam., fitted box. (Christie's) $23,595 £16,500

A Cizhou small baluster jar, Song Dynasty, 12.3cm. high, fitted box. (Christie's) $3,932 £2,750

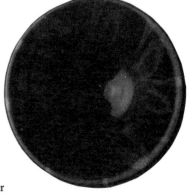

A Ding Yao dish, Northern Song Dynasty, 11.2cm. diam., fitted box. (Christie's) $1,047 £703

A Yingqing fluted baluster vase with S-scroll handles on the flaring neck, Song Dynasty, 17.2cm. high. (Christie's) $629 £440

A Henan black glazed conical bowl, Song Dynasty, 14cm. diam., fitted box. (Christie's) $1,333 £895

A Spode blue-ground garniture of five vases painted with pink and gilt flowering prunus branches, puce marks and pattern no. 3975, circa 1820. (Christie's) $760 £528

George III Spode part tea service, each piece hand-enamelled on a white ground showing thumb nail decoration , heightened in gilt. (Peter Wilson) $719 £510

A Spode pearlware Greek Pattern part dinner service printed in blue and iron-red with classical figures at various pastimes within shaped cartouches reserved on berried-foliage grounds, circa 1810. (Christie's) $30,096 £20,000

Late 18th century Spode blue and white pottery oval footbath, 18in. wide. (Reeds Rains) $1,267 £880

A Spode miniature teapot and cover with gilt spout, red mark and pattern no. 1166, circa 1820, 5cm. high. (Christie's) $677 £440

A Spode circular box and cover, pattern no. 1166, circa 1820, 7.2cm. diam. (Christie's) $1,270 £825

A Staffordshire figure of a sheep, recumbent to the left, circa 1780, 15cm. wide. (Christie's) $443 £308

Staffordshire soup tureen, England, circa 1845, marked 'Texian Campaigne', with ladle and undertray, J.B. mark on base, 10in. high. (Robt. W. Skinner Inc.) $3,900 £2,727

A Staffordshire saltglaze globular teapot and cover, painted in the famille rose palette, circa 1750, 10.5cm. high. (Christie's) $712 £495

A 19th century Staffordshire pottery portrait figure of Wm, Shakespeare, 9in. high. (Reeds Rains) $139 £90

A Brownfield teaset, comprising a platter, teapot, sugar bowl, milk jug, four cups and saucers, platter 41cm. diam. (Christie's) $303 £209

One of a pair of early 19th century Staffordshire pottery figures of putti, 6in. high. (Reeds Rains) $201 £130

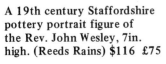

A 19th century Staffordshire pottery portrait figure of the Rev. John Wesley, 7in. high. (Reeds Rains) $116 £75

Pair of mid 19th century Staffordshire pottery equestrian groups of the Prince and Princess of Wales, 7½in. high. (Reeds Rains) $279 £180

A Staffordshire figure of Napoleon on a floral encrusted rocky plinth, 8½in. high, circa 1825. (Christie's) $154 £100

STAFFORDSHIRE

CHINA

A Staffordshire pearlware figure of a girl, circa 1790, 17cm. high. (Christie's) $316 £220

A Staffordshire saltglaze agateware cat, with irregular blue markings and brown striations, circa 1750, 13.5cm.high. (Christie's) $2,692 £1,870

A Staffordshire Toby jug, smoking a pipe and holding a jug, circa 1770, 23.5cm. high. (Christie's) $2,217 £1,540

A Staffordshire saltglaze octagonal plate, transfer-printed in iron-red with the fable of The Lion and The Fox. (Christie's) $4,118 £2,860

A Staffordshire figure of an Alcibiades hound, on a black marbled base edged in green and turquoise, circa 1810, 42cm. high. (Christie's) $2,059 £1,430

A 19th century Staffordshire 'cottage' ornament, modelled as a double fronted house, 10in. high. (Parsons, Welch & Cowell) $83 £54

A Staffordshire saltglaze bear-jug and cover, circa 1755, 24cm. long. (Christie's) $3,009 £2,090

An amusing Staffordshire sheep creamer, their fleeces washed in ochre, 10.5cm. long. (Phillips) $1,540 £1,000

A Staffordshire porcellaneous pastille burner in two sections, modelled as a hexagonal cottage, 11cm. high. (Phillips) $308 £200

STAFFORDSHIRE

A jardiniere modelled as a rectangular plant holder of wooden slats, impressed Brown, Westhead Moore, 33cm. high. (Christie's) $2,392 £1,650

A Staffordshire saltglaze solid agateware cat, circa 1750, 12.5cm. high. (Christie's) $3,484 £2,420

A Staffordshire figure of a boy leaning against a tree-stump with a dog at his side, circa 1790, 16.5cm. high. (Christie's) $348 £242

A 19th century Staffordshire 'cottage' ornament in the form of a double turreted chapel, 9in. high. (Parsons, Welch & Cowell) $55 £36

A Staffordshire saltglaze pear-shaped cream jug and cover, painted in a bright famille rose palette, circa 1750, 12.5cm. high. (Christie's) $1,267 £880

A Staffordshire saltglaze plate, transfer-printed in iron-red with the fable of the Two Travellers and The Bear. (Christie's) $712 £495

One of a pair of Queen Anne silver mounted stoneware tankards, attributed to Staffordshire, 13cm. and 13.5cm. high. (Phillips) $1,416 £920

A Staffordshire small oval combined patchbox and nutmeg grater, with gilt metal mounts, circa 1765, 1.7/8in. long. (Christie's) $629 £440

A Staffordshire group of a sheep and a lamb standing calmly together on a shaped rectangular base, 10cm. high. (Phillips) $616 £400

STONEWARE

A Rhenish stoneware baluster tankard with English silver neck mount, circa 1700, 19cm. high. (Christie's) $554 £385

A small stoneware inkpot, by Shoji Hamada, 1923, 5.4cm. high. (Christie's) $1,101 £770

A stoneware four gallon crock, by J. Norton & Co., Vermont, circa 1880, 14in. high. (Robt. W. Skinner Inc.) $1,700 £1,096

A stoneware asymmetrical bulbous vase, by Jennifer Lee, covered in a matt oatmeal glaze, 19.5cm. high. (Christie's) $90 £59

A stoneware plate, by Henry Hammond, covered in a grey pitted and fleck glaze with iron-brown brushwork, circa 1958, 26cm. diam. (Christie's) $214 £140

A stoneware footed vase, by Ewen Henderson, circa 1972, 27cm. high. (Christie's) $707 £495

A celadon stoneware globular vase, by Norah Braden, covered in a greyish-green glaze with wax resist decoration, 21cm. high. (Christie's) $578 £378

A stoneware sake bottle vase, by S. Ichino, impressed Ichino character and St. Ives seals, 17.4cm. high. (Christie's) $47 £33

A stoneware pinched and coiled bulbous vase, by Betty Blandino, impressed BB seal 1985, 31cm. high. (Christie's) $247 £162

STONEWARE

A Bunzlau brown stoneware heptagonal flask with pewter mounts and cover, 1643, 18.5cm. high. (Christie's) $1,346 £935

A large Abuja stoneware bowl, by Alhassan Tanko, 36cm. diam. (Christie's) $330 £216

'Dark Sky with Clouds', a stoneware vase form, by Ivo Mosley, 40.4cm. high. (Christie's) $440 £308

Mid 19th century three gallon stoneware jug, stamped 'S. Hart — Fulton', 13½in. high. (Robt. W. Skinner Inc.) $425 £283

A stoneware mug, by Katharine Pleydell-Bouverie, impressed Cole, circa 1930, 11.5cm. high. (Christie's) $157 £110

A massive stoneware asymmetrical vase, by Ewen Henderson, with everted rim, 56cm. high. (Christie's) $1,569 £1,026

A stoneware spherical bottle by the Mashiko School, 21.3cm. high. (Christie's) $97 £64

A stoneware figure of an eagle, inscribed M. Schilkin, Arabia, 44.2cm. high. (Christie's) $125 £88

A stoneware elongated oviform asymmetrical vase, by Jennifer Lee, 20.6cm. high. (Christie's) $35 £23

Stoneware butter churn, marked 'John Burger, Rochester', circa 1860, 19in. high. (Robt. W. Skinner Inc.)
$29,000 £20,279

A stoneware press-moulded jar and cover, by S. Ichino, covered in a semi-translucent olive-green glaze, 20cm. high. (Christie's) $47 £33

A Siegburg grey stoneware schnelle, dated 1576, 27cm. high. (Christie's)
$3,168 £2,200

A large slab-built stoneware vase, inscribed James Tower 85, 54.6cm. high. (Christie's)
$550 £385

One of a pair of stoneware candlesticks, 22cm. and 21.5cm. high, registration lozenge for 1876, silver collars, London, 1884. (Phillips) $290 £200

A Nottingham stoneware puzzle-jug with a lustrous brown glaze, incised date 1715, 12cm. high. (Christie's)
$3,484 £2,420

A German Westerwald stoneware jug, circa 1750, 22cm. high. (Christie's)
$6,009 £3,902

A spherical stoneware bowl, by Val Barry, covered in a greenish-grey matt glaze, with brown speckling, 18.7cm. high. (Christie's)
$231 £151

A stoneware double gourd-shaped bottle vase, by Poh Chap Yeap, circa 1975, 16.6cm. high. (Christie's)
$78 £55

STONEWARE

A European stoneware grey glazed slender baluster jug with plain loop handles, circa 1750, 26cm. high. (Christie's) $1,091 £709

A stoneware press-moulded rectangular bottle, by Shoji Hamada, circa 1967, 20.1cm. high. (Christie's) $2,516 £1,760

A Westerwald armorial blue and grey stoneware baluster jug with hinged pewter cover, 25cm. high. (Christie's) $871 £605

Late 17th century Westerwald grey stoneware cylindrical tankard, 15cm. high, (hair crack in base). (Christie's) $665 £462

A stoneware crane-necked bottle vase, by Hiroyuki Ichino, 28.2cm. high. (Christie's) $503 £352

'Chest', a large slab-built stoneware vase, incised James Tower 83, 54cm. high. (Christie's) $865 £605

A stoneware pilgrim flask, by Malcolm Pepper, circa 1975, 32.8cm. high. (Christie's) $188 £132

'Swan Pot', a stoneware jug, by Vicki Read, painted artist cypher and dated 72 Winslow, 26.4cm. high. (Christie's) $114 £75

A Westerwald blue and grey stoneware oviform tankard, circa 1800, 35.5cm. high. (Christie's) $396 £275

A stoneware rounded rectangular bowl, by Karl Scheid, dated 67, 19.5cm. wide. (Christie's) $495 £324

A Yixing brown stoneware globular teapot and domed cover, circa 1750, 19cm. wide. (Christie's) $2,183 £1,418

A stoneware deep bowl, by John Ward, with foliate rim, 36.2cm. diam. (Christie's) $197 £129

A massive stoneware flattened bottle, by Joanna Constantinidis, impressed C seal 1982, 54.5cm. high. (Christie's) $1,101, 770

Pair of late 19th century almost life-sized stoneware models of a courtier and a courtesan, probably Kyoto ware, 149cm. high. (Christie's) $10,153 £7,150

A Henri van de Velde stoneware amphora vase, covered in a sang-de-boeuf translucent glaze separating in parts to reveal beige-coloured body, 23.5cm. high. (Christie's) $8,712 £6,050

An early marbled stoneware lamp holder formed as a wide flanged recessed dish, Tang Dynasty, 11cm. diam. (Christie's) $2,516 £1,760

A Yixing pale brown stoneware rectangular cylindrical teapot, circa 1750, 22.5cm. wide. (Christie's) $2,456 £1,596

A stoneware chamberstick, by K. Pleydell-Bouverie, 8.9cm. high, and a bowl, circa 1975, 5.9cm. high. (Christie's) $70 £49

CHINA

A yellow and amber-glazed shallow cup, Tang Dynasty, 10cm. diam. (Christie's) $1,573 £1,100

A buff pottery figure of an expectant mother, Tang Dynasty, 25.5cm. high. (Christie's) $1,101 £770

A large glazed tripod globular jar of Yue type, Tang Dynasty, 28cm. wide, 23.5cm. high. (Christie's) $6,606 £4,620

A painted red pottery figure of a camel, Tang Dynasty, 48.6cm. high. (Christie's) $1,887 £1,320

A pair of large Sancai standing figures of Court Dignitaries, Tang Dynasty, approx. 85cm. high. (Christie's) $29,887 £20,900

An unglazed russet pottery standing camel, Tang Dynasty, 63cm. high. (Christie's) $5,033 £3,520

A phosphatic-splashed black-glazed wrist rest, Tang Dynasty, 11cm. wide. (Christie's) $1,573 £1,100

A Sancai buff pottery figure of a standing horse, Tang Dynasty, 47cm. high. (Christie's) $23,595 £16,500

A green and white-glazed stoneware ewer with double loop handle, Tang Dynasty, 21.5cm. high. (Christie's) $2,831 £1,980

TERRACOTTA

CHINA

A 19th century terracotta garden ornament, probably France, 25½in. diam., 25½in. high. (Robt. W. Skinner Inc.) $750 £520

A pair of 19th century Continental terracotta figures of a peasant girl and a boy, 90cm. and 91cm. high. (Phillips) $2,700 £1,800

A black glazed terracotta teapot and cover, printed in yellow and decorated in enamels and gilt, 16cm. high. (Phillips) $80 £50

A late 18th century French terracotta bust of a man wearing The Order of St. Esprit, in the style of Pajou, 20in. high. (Christie's) $2,811 £1,980

A set of three black glazed terracotta jugs of graduated size, printed in yellow with portraits and vases of enamelled flowers. (Phillips) $160 £100

A terracotta wall bracket in the form of a grotesque boar's head, 53cm. high. (Phillips) $540 £360

VENICE

An 18th century Venice (Cozzi) white veilleuse, cover and stand, 27cm. high. (Christie's) $1,267 £880

A Venice (Cozzi) teabowl and saucer, iron-red anchor marks, circa 1775. (Christie's) $1,346 £935

Late 16th century Venice Istoriato two-handled, ovi-form vase and tall waisted cover, 44cm. high, overall. (Christie's) $950 £660

VIENNA

A Vienna (Du Paquier) deep shaped quatrefoil dish painted in Schwartzlot, circa 1730, 22cm. diam. (Christie's) $1,382 £960

A Vienna group of a shepherdess, blue beehive marks, circa 1770, 16.5cm. wide. (Christie's) $506 £352

One of a pair of late 19th century Vienna plaques, painted by F. Koller, 19in. diam. (Woolley & Wallis) $1,430 £1,000

A Vienna red lacquer oval snuff box and cover, circa 1800, 17.5cm. wide. (Christie's) $8,712 £6,050

A Vienna ceramic centrepiece, by George Klimt, 20cm. wide. (Christie's) $235 £165

A Vienna pink-ground oval snuff box and cover, with copper gilt mount, blue beehive mark, circa 1780, 8.5cm. wide. (Christie's) $871 £605

A Vienna (Du Paquier) plate painted in underglaze blue, enamel colours and silver, circa 1730, 23cm. diam. (Christie's) $1,884 £1,309

A Vienna figure of Venus, impressed beehive mark, circa 1760, 15cm. high.(Christie's) $627 £436

A Vienna (Du Paquier) lobed circular dish, circa 1730, 34.5cm. diam. (Christie's) $6,652 £4,620

WEDGWOOD

A Wedgwood polished black basalt intaglio seal, 3.5cm. diam. (Phillips) $662 £460

A Wedgwood three-colour jasper dice-pattern cylindrical jardiniere, 9cm. high, and a stand, circa 1790. (Christie's) $1,439 £935

A Wedgwood lilac and white jasper teacup and saucer, circa 1790. (Christie's) $609 £392

A Wedgwood & Bentley black basalt oviform two-handled vase and cover, circa 1775, 40cm. high. (Christie's) $2,851 £1,980

One of a pair of Wedgwood solid lilac jasper cylindrical vases moulded in white relief with Corinthian columns, circa 1785, about 15.5cm. high. (Christie's) $950 £660

A Wedgwood black basalt encaustic-decorated oviform two-handled vase painted with Jupiter, circa 1800, 30cm. high. (Christie's) $1,101 £715

A Wedgwood caneware oviform jug and cover, 22cm. high, and a saucer dish, circa 1815. (Christie's) $931 £605

Pair of Wedgwood caneware oviform vases, impressed marks and B, circa 1815, 16cm. high. (Christie's) $287 £187

A Wedgwood garden seat of rounded hexagonal shape, impressed Wedgwood, 46cm. high. (Christie's) $1,355 £935

WEDGWOOD

A Wedgwood creamware pierced circular basket and stand painted in puce camaieu by J. Bakewell, circa 1768, basket 18.5cm. diam. (Christie's) $2,710 £1,760

A Wedgwood salmon platter, naturalistic colouring on a brown ground, impressed Wedgwood, 64cm. long. (Christie's) $1,595 £1,100

A Wedgwood oval medallion, modelled by Wm. Hackwood, 2.5cm. diam. (Phillips)
$748 £520

A Wedgwood black basalt encaustic decorated vase, painted in red and enriched in white with Apollo and Diana, late 18th century, 24cm. high. (Christie's)
$2,217   £1,540

One of a pair of Wedgwood black basalt tritons, impressed lower-case mark and K, circa 1785, 28cm. high. (Christie's)
$3,726 £2,420

A 19th century Wedgwood jasper model of the Portland Vase, 10½in. high. (Reeds Rains) $792 £550

One of a pair of Wedgwood & Bentley black basalt oviform two-handled vases and covers, circa 1775, 38cm. high. (Christie's) $11,088 £7,700

Pair of Wedgwood black basalt encaustic decorated oviform two-handled vases and one cover, circa 1800, 37.5cm. high. (Christie's) $5,702 £3,960

One of a pair of Wedgwood & Bentley black basalt ewers with dolphin handles, circa 1775, 41.5cm. and 42.5cm. high. (Christie's) $4,752 £3,300

WEDGWOOD

Wedgwood pearlware nautilus compote and undertray, circa 1872, 9in. high, 10¾in. long. (Robt. W. Skinner Inc.) $650 £398

A Wedgwood/Whieldon hexagonal teapot and cover in chinoiserie style, 16cm. high. (Phillips) $2,400 £1,500

A Wedgwood green and white jasper cylindrical teapot and cover, circa 1800, 9.5cm. high. (Christie's) $542 £352

A Wedgwood & Bentley 'porphyry' vase and cover, the shield-shaped body applied with gilt mounting, 47.5cm. high. (Phillips) $6,468 £4,200

Pair of Wedgwood black basalt encaustic decorated vases, painted in red with Hercules and Hercules seated on a lion skin before a sphinx, 18th century, 24cm. high. (Christie's) $4,435 £3,080

One of a pair of Wedgwood black basalt wine and water ewers after the models by J. Flaxman, date code for 1868, 39cm. high. (Christie's) $2,032 £1,320

Late 19th century Wedgwood blue ground jasper jardiniere, 10in. diam. (Peter Wilson) $190 £135

An Art Deco Wedgwood animal figure, modelled as a duiker, designed by J. Skeaping, 23.5cm. high. (Phillips) $187 £130

Pair of Wedgwood cream glazed octagonal plates each painted by E. Lessore, 8¾in. diam. (Christie's) $400 £250

WEDGWOOD

A Wedgwood creamware globular teapot and cover, painted in the atelier of D. Rhodes, circa 1770, 13.5cm. high. (Christie's)
$3,726 £2,420

Stilton cheese dish and cover in the style of Wedgwood, circa 1900, 12in. high. (Lots Road Galleries)
$160 £100

A Wedgwood blue and white jasper cylindrical teapot and cover, circa 1790, 10.5cm. high. (Christie's) $847 £550

One of a pair of Wedgwood blue and white jasper cylindrical altar vases, circa 1785, 13.5cm. high. (Christie's)
$1,016 £660

A Wedgwood black basalt encaustic decorated vase, painted in red and enriched in white with a lady and attendants, late 18th century, 24cm. high. (Christie's) $2,217 £1,540

A large Wedgwood black basalt pot pourri vase and cover with loop handles, 12in. high. (Parsons, Welch & Cowell) $784 £490

A Wedgwood caneware custard cup and cover with rope twist handle, 7.5cm. high. (Phillips) $1,040 £650

A Wedgwood 'Fairyland' lustre 10in. circular bowl of inverted bell shape. (Parsons, Welch & Cowell)
$1,312 £820

An Art Deco Wedgwood animal figure, modelled as a fallow deer, designed by J. Skeaping, 21.5cm. high. (Phillips) $230 £160

WEDGWOOD

A Wedgwood green and white jasper teabowl and saucer, circa 1790. (Christie's)
$1,101 £715

WHIELDON

A Whieldon wall pocket of waisted form moulded with bearded mask beneath a manganese glaze, circa 1760, 22.5cm. high. (Christie's)
$1,585 £1,100

One of two Wedgwood caneware flared circular flower-bowls and pierced liners, circa 1815, 20.5cm. and 18.5cm. high. (Christie's)
$542 £352

A Whieldon spirally moulded wall pocket, circa 1750, 24cm. high. (Christie's)
$2,059 £1,430

A Wedgwood lustre charger, by Alfred and Louise Powell, 31.5cm. wide. (Christie's) $380 £264

Late 18th century Whieldon pattern square shaped pottery tea caddy, 4in. high. (Reeds Rains) $259 £180

WOOD

A Ralph Wood Toby jug, in brown jacket and hat, circa 1770, 25cm. high. (Christie's)
$1,346 £935

A Ralph Wood figure of a recumbent ram, on an oval green rockwork base moulded with foliage, circa 1770, 18.5cm. wide. (Christie's)
$3,801 £2,640

A Ralph Wood Toby jug of conventional type, circa 1770, 25.5cm. high. (Christie's) $2,692 £1,870

WORCESTER

One of a pair of Royal Worcester vases and covers, by A. Lewis, in the Hadley style, shape no. 1911, date codes for 1904, 30cm. high. (Phillips) $800 £520

A Worcester partridge tureen and cover, circa 1765, 15cm. wide. (Christie's)
$1,185 £770

A Royal Worcester ovoid vase and cover, by John Stinton, shape no. G998, date code for 1907, 33cm. high. (Phillips)
$1,262 £820

An ormolu mounted Worcester vase and cover, 45cm. high, square mark in blue, the porcelain circa 1770, the mounts probably early 19th century. (Phillips) $2,079 £1,350

A Worcester baluster mug transfer-printed in black by R. Hancock with Parrot Pecking at Fruit, circa 1760, 12cm. high. (Christie's)
$5,759 £3,740

One of a pair of late 19th century Worcester porcelain vases, Grainger period, 9.3/8in. high. (Christie's)
$550 £358

Royal Worcester Persian ewer, cream ground with gilt painted and polychrome enamelled decoration, date mark code for 1886. (Peter Wilson) $380 £270

A Worcester small cylindrical mug transfer-printed in black by R. Hancock with The King of Prussia, date 1757, 9cm. high. (Christie's)
$1,185 £770

One of a pair of Royal Worcester vases and covers, painted by R. Sebright, 13½in. high. (Reeds Rains)
$576 £400

WORCESTER

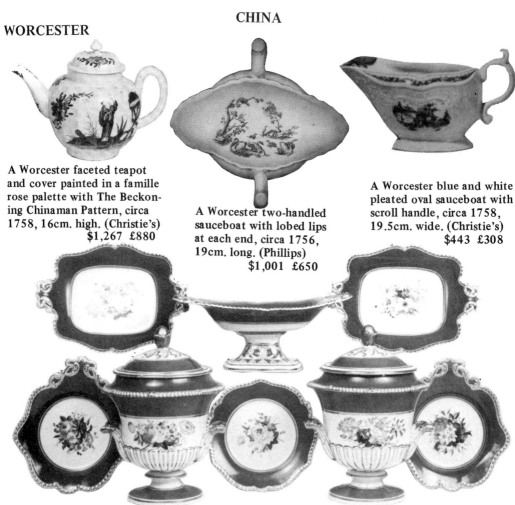

A Worcester faceted teapot and cover painted in a famille rose palette with The Beckoning Chinaman Pattern, circa 1758, 16cm. high. (Christie's) $1,267 £880

A Worcester two-handled sauceboat with lobed lips at each end, circa 1756, 19cm. long. (Phillips) $1,001 £650

A Worcester blue and white pleated oval sauceboat with scroll handle, circa 1758, 19.5cm. wide. (Christie's) $443 £308

A Chamberlain's Worcester green-ground part dessert service, the centres painted with bouquets within gilt wells, within apple-green borders and shaped gilt gadrooned rims, impressed marks and script marks in red, circa 1830. (Christie's) $2,851 £1,980

A Royal Worcester oviform ewer, the body painted by John Stinton, date code for 1911, pattern no. 1309, 41cm. high. (Christie's) $1,504 £1,045

Two of four Royal Worcester 'ivory' wall brackets emblematic of the Seasons, circa 1880, approx. 26cm. high. (Christie's) $1,029 £715

A Royal Worcester vase, by George Owen, shape no. 1527, date code for 1922, 11cm. high. (Phillips) $3,080 £2,000

WORCESTER

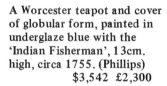

A Worcester blue and white moulded oval sauceboat, blue crescent mark, circa 1768, 20cm. wide. (Christie's) $601 £418

A Worcester teapot and cover of globular form, painted in underglaze blue with the 'Indian Fisherman', 13cm. high, circa 1755. (Phillips) $3,542 £2,300

A Worcester tapering ovi-form teapot and cover with faceted spout and scroll handle, circa 1758, 14cm. high. (Christie's) $1,267 £880

A Flight, Barr & Barr Worcester armorial vase and cover, attributed to Thos. Baxter, 19cm. high. (Phillips) $4,928 £3,200

A Worcester blue-ground small mug painted with exotic birds, blue crescent mark, circa 1770, 8.5cm. high. (Christie's) $1,504 £1,045

A Chamberlain's Worcester coral-red-ground crested jug painted with a view of Worcester, circa 1805. (Christie's) $1,425 £990

A Royal Worcester melon-shaped biscuit barrel and stand, circa 1895. (Coles, Knapp & Kennedy) $332 £220

A Worcester, Flight, Barr & Barr, urn-shaped two-handled vase and cover, circa 1820, 46cm. high. (Christie's) $2,376 £1,650

A Chamberlain's Worcester armorial plate, decorated with the arms of Allan, 9¼in. diam. (Dreweatts) $348 £240

285

WORCESTER

A Worcester cos lettuce leaf moulded sauceboat, the stalk handle with fruit and foliage terminal, circa 1760, 18.5cm. wide. (Christie's) $633 £440

One of a pair of Worcester partridge tureens and covers, circa 1760, 18cm. wide. (Christie's) $2,371 £1,540

One of a pair of Worcester yellow-ground pierced oval two-handled baskets, blue square seal marks, circa 1768, 18.5cm. wide. (Christie's) $6,969 £4,840

A Worcester blue-scale tapering hexagonal vase and domed cover, circa 1770, 33cm. high. (Christie's) $8,470 £5,500

A Worcester blue and white bottle and a basin transfer-printed with The Pinecone and Foliage pattern, circa 1775, bottle 22cm. high, basin 27.5cm. diam. (Christie's) $1,439 £935

A Worcester blue-ground inverted baluster vase painted by J. H. O'Neale, circa 1770, 34cm. high. (Christie's) $3,049 £1,980

A Hadleys Worcester vase painted by J. W. Sedgley, printed green mark and date code for 1905, 10in. high. (Outhwaite & Litherland) $290 £200

A Worcester quartrefoil two-handled basket, pierced cover and stand, circa 1760, basket 20cm. wide. (Christie's) $1,524 £990

Royal Worcester vase and cover painted by Ricketts, 11in. high. (Reeds Rains) $713 £460

Late 19th century Dresden Christmas ornament of a silver two-wheeled basket cart drawn by Billy goat, 3¾in. long. (Robt. W. Skinner Inc.) $450 £312

Late 19th century Dresden Christmas ornament, white poodle with red silk ribbon, 3¼in. long. (Robt. W. Skinner Inc.) $225 £156

Late 19th century Dresden Christmas ornament of a silver cannon on wheeled carriage, 3½in. long. (Robt. W. Skinner Inc.) $200 £138

Late 19th century Dresden Christmas ornament of a three-masted ship, 4½in. high, 4.7/8in. long. (Robt. W. Skinner Inc.) $190 £131

Late 19th century Dresden Christmas ornament of a silver champagne bottle candy container, 3.5/16in. high. (Robt. W. Skinner Inc.) $100 £69

Late 19th century Dresden Christmas ornament of a rooster, brown wash over gold, 3.1/8in. high. (Robt. W. Skinner Inc.) $140 £97

Late 19th century Dresden Christmas ornament of a sitting silver retriever, 2¾in. high. (Robt. W. Skinner Inc.) $300 £208

Late 19th century Dresden Christmas ornament of a gold and rose iridescent cockatoo in a hoop, 3.3/8in. high. (Robt. W. Skinner Inc.) $175 £121

Late 19th century Dresden Christmas ornament of a silver three-quarter flat jockey on horse, 2in. high. (Robt. W. Skinner Inc.) $150 £104

BRACKET CLOCKS

A George III mahogany striking bracket clock, by Ellicott, London, 16in. high. (Christie's) $3,146 £2,200

A George III bracket clock with enamel dial, by Robt. Henderson, 15½in. high. (Graves Son & Pilcher) $10,570 £7,000

A Regency mahogany and gilt brass mounted bracket clock, the brass dial signed Robt. Wood, London, 43cm. high. (Phillips) $1,740 £1,200

A Regency mahogany striking bracket clock, the painted dial signed Collett, Chelsea, 15½in. high. (Christie's) $1,630 £1,080

An 18th century Austrian ebonised quarter striking bracket clock with gilt metal handle, 12in. high. (Christie's) $2,359 £1,650

A late 17th century ebony veneered bracket timepiece, by Henry Jones, London, 36cm. high. (Phillips) $5,472 £3,800

A Georgian fruitwood bracket clock, signed on a cartouche Henry Heve, London, 43cm. high. (Phillips) $2,448 £1,700

A late Stuart tortoiseshell veneered case for a miniature bracket clock, 10in. high. (Christie's) $1,415 £990

An 18th century ebonised and gilt brass mounted quarter chiming bracket clock, signed Wm. Webster, 52cm. high. (Phillips) $4,176 £2,900

BRACKET CLOCKS

A scarlet lacquer striking bracket clock, the brass dial signed Jas. Smith, London, 20in. high. (Christie's) $1,540 £1,074

Late 18th century George III mahogany bracket clock for the Canadian market, signed Fras. Dumoulin a Montreal, 16½in. high including handle. (Christie's) $2,640 £1,842

A George II striking mahogany bracket clock, date aperture and plaque signed Tho. Hall, Rumsey, 19½in. high. (Christie's) $2,692 £1,870

A Queen Anne ebonised timepiece bracket clock, signed Fromanteel, London, 14¼in. high. (Christie's) $2,988 £2,090

An early George III 8-day bracket clock with verge striking movement by Wm. Allam, 15.5in. high. (Woolley & Wallis) $11,808 £8,200

Late 18th century ebonised striking bracket clock, signed A. Van Eeden, Haarlem, 20in. high. (Christie's) $1,650 £1,151

A mid Georgian ebonised striking bracket clock, the dial signed Stepn. Rimbault, London, 19½in. high. (Christie's) $2,283 £1,512

An 18th century ebonised bracket clock, signed S. de Charmes, London, 39cm. high. (Phillips) $1,872 £1,300

A Georgian ebonised bracket clock, signed Tho. Wagstaffe, London, 50cm. high. (Phillips) $1,872 £1,300

BRACKET CLOCKS

A late Georgian mahogany musical bracket clock, chime/not chime lever signed Rivers & Son, Cornhill, London, 24in. high. (Christie's) $4,566 £3,024

A Regency ebonised bracket clock, the dial signed W. French, Royal Exchange, London, 40cm. high. (Phillips) $1,267 £880

A George II green japanned striking bracket clock, the dial signed Fra Dorrell, London, 18¼in. high. (Christie's) $9,306 £6,600

A William III ebonised quarter striking bracket clock, with gilt metal handle to ogee basket top, 14in. high, excluding later feet. (Christie's) $2,359 £1,650

A Regency period bracket clock, the brass inlaid lancet case of Egyptian styling, circa 1810, 20in. high. (Reeds Rains) $2,015 £1,300

A George III mahogany bracket clock, the arched brass dial signed Benjn. Ward, London, 52cm. high. (Phillips) $4,350 £3,000

A Regency mahogany bracket clock, Gothic shaped case, by Payne, London, 24in. high. (Coles, Knapp & Kennedy) $1,887 £1,250

Early 19th century George III mahogany striking bracket clock, signed Edw. Tomlin, Royal Exchange, London, 15½in. high. (Christie's) $2,200 £1,535

An 18th century ebony and gilt brass mounted bracket clock, signed on a cartouche Cha: Cabrier, London, 57cm. high. (Phillips) $3,168 £2,200

BRACKET CLOCKS

An Austrian fruitwood quarter striking bracket clock, signed B. Schmidt, 20in. high. (Christie's) $1,346 £935

A George III ebonised miniature striking bracket clock, signed Williams, 168 Shoreditch on Arabic chapter disc, 14½in. high overall. (Christie's)
$3,775 £2,640

A mid Georgian scarlet japanned quarter striking, musical and automaton bracket clock in the style of G. Grendey, 37in. high. (Christie's) $77,550 £55,000

A documentary Louis XIV bronze mounted tortoiseshell religieuse, signed Gaudron a Paris, the case inscribed L.B., circa 1710, 18in. high. (Christie's) $5,500 £3,837

A 19th century rosewood and inlaid bracket timepiece, 32cm. high. (Phillips)
$748 £520

A Charles II ebonised striking bracket clock, backplate signed R. Pingo Neare The Pallmall, Londini in a lambrequin, 13½in. high. (Christie's)
$2,988 £2,090

An early George III padouk-wood automaton organ clock, by Wm. Vale, London, 37in. high. (Christie's)
$12,692 £8,800

An early George III ebon-ised striking bracket clock with brass handle, dial signed Sam. Toulmin, Strand, London, 18½in. high. (Christie's)
$1,258 £880

A Continental tortoiseshell bracket timepiece, basically circa 1700, 16in. high. (Christie's) $2,186 £1,540

CARRIAGE CLOCKS

A brass grande sonnerie carriage clock with split compensated balance to lever platform, 5¾in. high. (Christie's) $943 £660

A gilt metal grande sonnerie oval carriage clock with enamel dial, 6.1/8in. high. (Christie's) $2,516 £1,760

A gilt metal striking carriage clock by Paul Garnier, one-piece case with lifting front glass, 5in. high. (Christie's) $2,044   £1,430

A gilt metal striking carriage clock with decorative swagged Arabic chaptered enamel dial, 6½in. high. (Christie's)
$629 £440

A 19th century English time-piece, the backplate signed French Royal Exchange, London, 17.5cm. high. (Phillips) $7,540 £5,200

A silver plated striking carriage clock with split compensated balance to gilt lever platform, 6½in. high. (Christie's)
$865 £605

A gilt metal striking carriage clock, inscribed Examined by Dent and with presentation inscription dated 1877, 7in. high. (Christie's)
$755 £528

A 19th century English gilt brass quarter striking carriage clock, the dial signed James McCabe, Royal Exchange, London 2677, 19cm. high. (Phillips)
$4,350 £3,000

A French 19th century gilt brass carriage clock, bearing the Drocourt trademark, and signed for Klaftenberger, Paris, 17cm. high. (Phillips)
$493 £340

CARRIAGE CLOCKS

A gilt metal striking carriage clock for the Chinese market, stamp of Japy Freres, 5¾in. high. (Christie's) $1,022 £715

A gilt metal striking oval carriage clock with uncut bimetallic balance to silvered lever platform, plain oval case, 5½in. high. (Christie's) $865 £605

A gilt brass quarter striking carriage clock with cut bimetallic balance to lever platform, 6in. high. (Christie's) $786 £550

An English striking carriage clock, mottled plates signed Chas. Frodsham, 9in. high. (Christie's) $7,827 £5,184

A Franche Comte gilt metal striking carriage clock for the Chinese market, 6½in. high. (Christie's) $1,022 £715

A gilt metal and enamel striking carriage clock, ivorine dials within multi-coloured champleve enamel mask, 7in. high. (Christie's) $3,617 £2,530

An ormolu quarter striking pendule d'officier with Turkish chaptered enamel dial signed Courvoisier et Compe., 8½in. high. (Christie's) $2,359 £1,650

A brass cased quarter striking carriage clock, the backplate signed L. Leroy & Cie, 6in. high. (Christie's)
$1,304 £864

A 19th century French gilt brass carriage clock, the enamel dial signed for J. F. Bautte, Geneve, 17cm. high. (Phillips) $2,900 £2,000

293

CARRIAGE CLOCKS

A gilt brass grande sonnerie carriage clock, 7¾in. high. (Christie's) $2,200 £1,535

A gilt metal striking oval carriage clock for the Oriental market, stamp of Japy Freres, 6in. high. (Christie's) $1,900 £1,320

A gilt metal striking carriage clock, stamp of Henri Jacot, 5¾in. high. (Christie's) $1,267 £880

An oval engraved gilt brass grande sonnerie carriage clock, 7½in. high. (Christie's) $2,420 £1,688

A French gilt brass carriage clock, the lever movement striking on a gong, 21cm. high. (Phillips) $1,324 £920

A Victorian brass inlaid, rosewood carriage clock, dial signed Craighead & Webb, 9¼in. high. (Christie's) $2,217 £1,540

An early multi-piece striking carriage clock with lever narrow platform, strike and alarm on bell, 5¾in. high. (Christie's) $815 £540

A Swiss gilt brass striking carriage clock with chronometer escapement, circa 1830, 7in. high. (Christie's) $9,350 £6,524

A 19th century French brass carriage clock, signed on the backplate Ollivant & Botsford, Paris & Manchester, 17cm. high. (Phillips) $464 £320

CARRIAGE CLOCKS

A gilt metal striking carriage clock with modern lever platform, stamp of Henri Jacot, 4¾in. high. (Christie's) $950 £660

A brass striking carriage clock with strike/repeat on gong, stamp of Henri Jacot, 4.7/8in. high. (Christie's) $570 £396

A French brass carriage timepiece, the enamel dial signed Le Roy & Fils, in a gorge case, 9.5cm. high. (Phillips) $633 £440

A lacquered brass grande sonnerie carriage clock, 7in. high. (Christie's) $1,320 £921

Breguet Neveu & Compie., No. 3992: a silver quarter striking carriage clock with alarm, 5½in. high. (Christie's) $33,264 £23,100

A lacquered brass petite sonnerie carriage clock with enamel dial, corniche case, 5¼in. high. (Christie's) $865 £605

A gilt metal striking carriage clock with centre seconds for the Chinese market, 6in. high. (Christie's) $1,022 £715

A gilt metal strking oval carriage clock with scroll handle and on rosso antiquo marble stand, 5½in. high, excluding stand. (Christie's) $2,044 £1,430

A lacquered brass grande sonnerie carriage clock with calendar, by Drocourt, No. 12276, 7in. high. (Christie's) $2,640 £1,842

LANTERN CLOCKS

An early 18th century brass lantern clock, dial signed Smorthwait in Colchester, 37cm. high. (Phillips) $1,824 £1,200

A George I bracket timepiece movement, backplate signed L. Bradley, London, dial 6in. x 8¼in. (Christie's) $1,312 £800

A 17th century Stuart brass and steel lantern clock, by J. Ebsworth 'in Bethlehem', London, 'fecit', 16in. high. (Robt. W. Skinner Inc.) $1,400 £875

A late 17th century brass lantern clock, the dial signed Edward Stanton, London, 39cm. high. (Phillips) $1,872 £1,300

A 19th century Japanese lantern clock with red enamel dial, 28cm. high. (Phillips) $3,360 £2,100

An 18th century Continental brass lantern clock of small size, 27cm. high. (Phillips) $1,656 £1,150

A brass lantern clock, dial signed Lawrence Debnam in Froome, 34cm. high. (Phillips) $1,520 £1,000

Mid 18th century brass lantern clock for the Turkish market, signed Isaac Rogers, London, 14in. high. (Christie's) $935 £652

An Edwardian lantern clock in the 17th century taste, London, 1902, 6½in. high. (Christie's) $1,241 £748

LANTERN CLOCKS

A brass lantern clock, signed
Thomas Knifton in Lothbury,
London, 15in. high.
(Christie's) $3,643 £2,530

A Japanese brass lantern clock,
the posted frame 30-hour iron
movement with double foliot
verge escapement, 11½in. high.
(Christie's) $2,120 £1,404

An English lantern clock,
dial signed Nicholas Coxeter,
14½in. high. (Christie's)
$6,160 £3,850

A N. European striking
lantern clock, dated 1672,
8in. high. (Christie's)
$2,992 £1,870

A Germanic iron chamber
clock, the posted frame
30-hour movement with
fabricated wheels, 22in.
high. (Christie's)
$4,118 £2,860

A Japanese striking lantern
clock with alarm, 15in.
high. (Christie's)
$3,872 £2,420

A lantern clock with engraved
dial plate, 15in. high.
(Christie's) $1,496 £935

A brass lantern clock with
pendulum verge escapement,
signed Stephen Tracy, London,
15in. high. (Christie's)
$1,015 £715

A late Stuart brass quarter
chiming carillon lantern
clock, dial signed Edw.
Hemins of Bister, 15in. high.
(Christie's) $6,160 £3,850

LONGCASE CLOCKS

A late Stuart walnut and marquetry longcase clock, dial signed Peter Mallett, London, 7ft.6in. high. (Christie's)
$11,088 £7,700

An 18th century mahogany longcase clock, by Charles Haley. (Parsons, Welch & Cowell)
$2,038 £1,350

A Georgian mahogany longcase clock, signed Wm. Webster, London, 91in. high. (Christie's)
$1,718 £1,210

A late Georgian mahogany longcase clock, dial signed Robert Martin, Glasgow, 6ft. 11in. high. (Christie's)
$943 £660

George III oak longcase clock, by J. Ivory, Dundee, 7ft. 6in. high. (Capes, Dunn & Co.)
$1,007 £696

A 17th century walnut month going longcase clock, by John Knibb, Oxford, 2.08m. high. (Phillips)
$18,720 £13,000

Federal mahogany inlaid tall case clock, by J. Bailey, Mass., circa 1790, 93in. high. (Robt. W. Skinner Inc.)
$18,000 £12,587

A Georgian mahogany longcase clock, the 12in. dial signed Will. Phelps, Putney, 2.28m. high. (Phillips)
$4,176 £2,900

LONGCASE CLOCKS

Federal cherry inlaid tall case clock, back of dial inscribed 'Wm. Prescott', circa 1790, 91¾in. high. (Robt. W. Skinner Inc.)
$12,000 £8,391

A George III mahogany longcase clock, the silvered chapter ring signed Rich. Penny, London, 2.08m. high. (Phillips)
$1,885 £1,300

A George III Lancashire mahogany longcase clock, signed H. Fisher, Preston, 7ft.5in. high. (Christie's)
$2,851 £1,980

A late Stuart Provincial walnut longcase clock, dial signed Thos. Cruttenden in Yorke, 6ft. 11½in. high. (Christie's)
$3,460 £2,420

An early George III dark green japanned longcase clock, dial signed Benjamin Baddy, London, 8ft. 7in. high. (Christie's)
$18,612 £13,200

A George II green and chinoiserie lacquered longcase clock, by Wm. Lambert, London, 7ft.2in. high. (Capes, Dunn & Co.)
$1,377 £950

A 19th century mahogany regulator, the dial signed James, Saffron Walden, 1.87m. high. (Phillips)
$4,320 £3,000

A 19th century mahogany regulator with 12in. circular painted dial, 2.09m. high. (Phillips)
$3,456 £2,400

LONGCASE CLOCKS

Mid 18th century
George III mahogany
tall case clock, signed
'Isaac Hewlett, Bristol',
93.1/8in. high.
(Christie's)
$5,500 £3,589

A Chippendale maho-
gany tall case clock,
works by Thos.
Stretch, Phila., circa
1750-65, 92½in.
high. (Christie's)
$16,500 £10,769

A Chippendale maho-
gany tall case clock,
dial signed by Thos.
Wagstaffe, London,
case Phila., 1760-90,
87¾in. high.
(Christie's)
$19,800 £13,064

A mid Georgian
black japanned
longcase Act of
Parliament clock,
31in. dial signed
Will. Threlkeld,
London, 6ft.10in.
high. (Christie's)
$2,202 £1,540

Mid 18th century
Dutch floral marquetry
longcase clock, signed
Lourens Eichelar, 8ft.
5in. high. (Christie's)
$6,050 £4,221

George III mahogany
longcase clock with
swan-neck pediment,
7ft.10in. high. (Hobbs
& Chambers)
$886 £620

An 18th century
walnut longcase clock,
by Marm'd. Storr.
(Parsons, Welch &
Cowell)
$3,020 £2,000

An 18th century
mahogany longcase
clock, signed G.
Binch, Manchester,
94in. high. (Reeds
Rains)
$1,440 £1,000

LONGCASE CLOCKS

A George II burr walnut calendar longcase clock, the dial signed George Merttins, Londini, 8ft. high. (Christie's)
$7,128 £4,950

A George III Salisbury mahogany veneered 8-day longcase clock, the dial inscribed Edw. Marsh, 7ft.8in. high. (Woolley & Wallis)
$2,288 £1,600

A George III Lancashire mahogany longcase clock, the dial signed Saml. Collier, Eccles, 8ft. 2in. high.(Christie's)
$3,960 £2,750

A George III Scottish mahogany longcase clock, the brass dial signed Jas. Mylne, Montrose, 7ft.3in. high. (Christie's)
$2,217 £1,540

A George III mahogany 8-day striking longcase clock, dial inscribed Jno. Morse, 6ft.9in. high. (Woolley & Wallis)
$3,718 £2,600

A Chippendale walnut tall case clock, dial signed by Thos. Crow, Delaware, circa 1770, 89¼in. high. (Christie's)
$6,820 £4,410

The Longstreet Family Federal inlaid mahogany tall case clock, dial signed by Aaron Lane, circa 1790, 94in. high.(Christie's)
$41,800 £27,579

A George III mahogany veneered 8-day striking longcase clock, inscribed James Vigne, London, 8ft.2in. high.(Woolley & Wallis)
$4,320 £3,000

LONGCASE CLOCKS

A William and Mary
walnut and marque-
try month going
longcase clock, the
11¼in. dial signed
Wm. Jourdain, 7ft.
3in. high. (Christie's)
$13,861 £9,180

A Chippendale maho-
gany tall case clock,
dial signed by Joseph
Hollingshead, circa
1750, 93½in. high.
(Christie's)
$3,850 £2,694

Late 19th century
mahogany quarter
chiming longcase
clock, signed Maple
& Co., London,
2.54m. high. (Phillips)
$3,625 £2,500

An 18th century wal-
nut longcase clock,
brass dial signed Hen.
Massey, London,
2.46m. high. (Phillips)
$2,610   £1,800

A George III maho-
gany longcase clock,
the dial signed Rich.
Winch, Hackney,
2.46m. high.
(Phillips)
$2,610 £1,800

Walnut tall case clock, New
England, circa 1780, 88in.
high, back of dial inscribed
'G.R.'. (Robt. W. Skinner
Inc.) $2,000 £1,333

A Georgian maho-
gany longcase clock,
the brass dial signed
Thos. Nevitt, 2.14m.
high. (Phillips)
$3,190 £2,200

A Georgian maho-
gany quarter chim-
ing longcase clock,
the dial signed Wm.
Dutton, London,
2.09m. high.
(Phillips)
$9,860 £6,800

LONGCASE CLOCKS

An American carved walnut longcase regulator, signed Howard & Davis, Makers — Boston, circa 1851, 8ft.0½in. high. (Christie's)
$24,200 £16,886

A Continental 18th century mahogany longcase clock with 11in. brass dial, 2.62m. high. (Phillips)
$1,740 £1,200

A late 17th century walnut and panel marquetry longcase clock, signed Jos. Buckingham in ye Minories, 2.16m. high. (Phillips)
$8,410 £5,800

A 19th century mahogany longcase clock, the dial signed Barraud, Cornhill, London, 1.98m. high. (Phillips)
$841 £580

A George III mahogany longcase clock, dial signed Wm. Farrar, Pontefract, 8ft.2in. high. (Christie's)
$1,573 £1,100

A 19th century mahogany longcase clock, signed Simmons, Coleman St., 2.01m. high. (Phillips)
$2,465 £1,700

An early 18th century walnut longcase clock, signed Dan. Delander, London, 2.54m. high. (Phillips)
$5,510 £3,800

Country cherry tall case clock, by A. & C. Edwards, Mass., circa 1794, 92in. high. (Robt. W. Skinner Inc.)
$1,000 £666

LONGCASE CLOCKS

Early 19th century Country Federal cherry tall case clock, by R. Whiting, Conn., 89in. high. (Robt. W. Skinner Inc.)
$2,300 £1,533

Country painted pine tall clock, by Simeon Crane, Mass., circa 1810, 86¼in. high. (Robt. W. Skinner Inc.) $5,750 £3,833

Federal cherry inlaid tall case clock, probably Conn., circa 1790, 93in. high. (Robt. W. Skinner Inc.) $4,000 £2,666

A George III style mahogany longcase clock, dial plate signed Henry Jarman, London, 7ft.10½in. high. (Christie's)
$3,460 £2,420

A Dutch walnut longcase clock, dial signed Andris Vermeulent, Amsterdam, 7ft. high. (Christie's)
$4,404 £3,080

Federal birch inlaid tall case clock, New England, circa 1780, 90in. high. (Robt. W. Skinner Inc.)
$3,200 £2,133

A walnut longcase clock, the chapter ring signed Edn. Stanton, London, 6ft.4in. high. (Christie's)
$5,218 £3,456

An Art Nouveau oak longcase clock, by J. Gruber, 253cm. high. (Christie's)
$3,304 £2,150

LONGCASE CLOCKS

A George I walnut longcase clock, by Jos. Windmills, London, 7ft.8in. high. (Christie's) $10,696 £7,480

A Queen Anne walnut year-going longcase clock, by Daniel Quare, London, 7ft.6in. high. (Christie's) $31,460 £22,000

A Federal inlaid cherrywood tall case clock, dial signed by Seth Thomas, Conn., circa 1800, 90in. high. (Christie's) $8,250 £5,773

A Charles II walnut and parquetry long-case clock, 10in. dial signed C. Gretton, London, 6ft.3in. high. (Christie's) $9,438 £6,600

A green japanned longcase clock, the brass dial signed Jos. Windmills, London, 8ft.4in. high. (Christie's) $3,261 £2,160

A Charles II wal-nut month-going longcase clock, dial signed Thos. Tompion, 6ft.4in. high. (Christie's) $66,066 £46,200

A Federal inlaid maho-gany tall case clock, dial signed by Wm. Cummens, Mass., circa 1800, 96in. high. (Christie's) $16,500 £11,546

A Chippendale cherry-wood tall case clock, dial signed by Thos. Harland, Conn., circa 1775, 95in. high. (Christie's) $12,100 £8,467

MANTEL CLOCKS

An ormolu strut clock, in the manner of Thos. Cole, the silvered dial signed Hunt & Roskell, London, 5½in. high. (Christie's) $1,223 £810

A German gilt brass square timepiece alarm signed Ang. Metzke Soran, 3¼in. square. (Christie's) $3,424 £2,268

Federal mahogany pillar and scroll clock, E. Terry & Sons, Conn., circa 1825, 31in. high. (Robt. W. Skinner Inc.) $650 £454

A Victorian strut clock with enamel dial signed Baudin Freres, Geneve, 8in. high. (Christie's) $792 £550

A George III gilt metal alabaster and white mantel clock, the backplate signed J. Burrows, Goodge Street, London, 19in. high. (Christie's) $495 £324

Mid 19th century Black Forest carved walnut figural clock, 28¾in. high. (Robt. W. Skinner Inc.) $2,900 £2,027

Federal mahogany pillar and scroll clock, by Ephraim Downes, Conn., circa 1825, 31in. high. (Robt. W. Skinner Inc.) $750 £524

An electric mantel timepiece, the movement with enamel dial signed Dollond, London, 44cm. high. (Phillips) $864 £600

A gilt metal clock, by Thos. Cole, London, simulating a watchstand in the form of a miniature chiffonier set, 5¼in. high. (Christie's) $6,197 £4,104

MANTEL CLOCKS

Federal mahogany pillar and scroll clock, by Ephraim Downs for G. Mitchell, Conn., circa 1820, 31in. high. (Robt. W. Skinner Inc.) $850 £566

An early English alarm 'table' clock, the movement signed Eduardus East, Londini, 3¾in. diam. of dial. (Christie's)
$10,600 £7,020

A small timepiece contained in an amboyna veneered lancet case with brass outline, by Thos. Cole, 10in. high. (Woolley & Wallis)
$1,800   £1,250

A 19th century French ormolu and enamel mantel clock, the case decorated with polychrome champleve enamel, 24cm. high. (Phillips) $406 £280

A Regency English bronze and gilt bronze mantel timepiece, 30cm. high. (Phillips) $648 £450

An Empire ormolu mantel clock, the steel dial signed Le Roy & fils Hrs du roi, 25in. high. (Christie's)
$1,405 £990

A Regency variegated wood mantel timepiece, signed Davd. Magson, 12¾in. high. (Christie's) $823 £572

Mid 19th century red marble and patinated gilt bronze industrial clock, French, 17in. high. (Christie's) $2,200 £1,535

An Empire ormolu mantel clock with enamel dial signed Le Roy Hr. du Roi a Paris, 14½in. high. (Christie's)
$1,015 £715

MANTEL CLOCKS

A 19th century French ormolu and champleve enamel mantel clock, the gilt dial signed for Howell & James, 43cm. high. (Phillips) $870 £600

Mid 19th century ormolu mantel clock with circular dial, 17½in. high. (Christie's) $797 £550

An Alfred Dunhill Art Deco marble mantel clock and cigarette case, 23.7cm. high. (Christie's) $871 £605

Empire mahogany carved mantel clock, by Eli Terry & Son, Conn., circa 1825, 31in. high. (Robt. W. Skinner Inc.) $1,000 £666

A 19th century French ormolu and porcelain mantel clock, the enamel dial signed Grohe A Paris, 28cm. high. (Phillips) $696 £480

A Meissen clockcase with a seated figure of Cupid, blue crossed swords and incised numeral marks, circa 1880, 30cm. high. (Christie's) $1,084 £748

A 19th century French ormolu and bronze mantel clock, the dial with enamel numerals, 58cm. high. (Phillips) $1,015 £700

A Belgian incised black slate perpetual calendar mantel clock, 16¾in. high. (Christie's) $1,262 £770

A 19th century French ormolu and porcelain mounted mantel clock, 41cm. high. (Phillips) $754 £520

MANTEL CLOCKS

A French 19th century bronze ormolu and red marble mantel clock, the enamel dial signed Guibal A Paris, 57cm. high.   (Phillips)
$2,175 £1,500

A glass and ormolu oval four-glass clock with gong strike, the chapter ring signed Franz Wiess & Sohne Wien, 13in. high. (Christie's)
$2,609 £1,728

A 16th century gilt metal table clock, by Hans Gruber, the whole case well engraved, 23cm. high. (Phillips)
$6,380 £4,400

A Japanese gilt brass striking spring clock, the case engraved with stylised flowers and with turned angle columns, 6in. high. (Christie's)
$1,956 £1,296

Early 19th century Sicilian coral mantel clock with enamel dial, 21in. high. (Christie's) $2,552 £1,760

An ormolu mounted boulle mantel clock, the enamel dial signed Grohe Paris, 11½in. high. (Christie's) $792 £495

A Paris (Jacob Petit) clock-case and stand of scroll outline, blue JP marks, circa 1835, 37cm. high overall. (Christie's) $1,196 £825

Mantel clock on D-shaped marble base, the clock face surmounted by a bronzed group of lovers. (Lots Road Galleries)
$703 £460

An ormolu and white marble four glass clock with perpetual calendar and moonphase dial below time dial, 16¾in. high. (Christie's) $5,348 £3,740

MANTEL CLOCKS

An early Anglo-Flemish weight driven clock, circa 1600, 19cm. high. (Phillips) $1,087 £750

An enamelled Art Deco timepiece, retailed through Fortnum & Mason, London, 23.5cm. wide, when open, with Swiss 8-day movement. (Phillips) $1,224 £850

French ormolu mounted boulle bracket clock in Louis XV style, with strike. (Worsfolds) $1,170 £775

A 17th century gilt brass table clock, the rectangular case surmounted by a bell, 17cm. high. (Phillips) $3,190 £2,200

A Lalique square-shaped clock, Inseparables, the clear and opalescent glass decorated with budgerigars, 11cm. high. (Christie's) $1,584 £1,100

An Empire ormolu mounted mahogany mantel clock, the dial signed Gaston Jolly a Paris, 16in. high. (Christie's) $1,015 £715

A 16th century gilt metal drum clock, 6cm. diam., together with an alarm mechanism of drum form. (Phillips) $2,175 £1,500

A 17th century South German gilt metal quarter striking table clock, the movement signed J. O. H., for Johann Ott. Halaicher, 13.5cm. sq. (Christie's) $3,484 £2,420

A 19th century ebonised mantel clock, the dial signed James McCabe, Royal Exchange, London, 1717, 26cm. high. (Phillips) $1,872 £1,300

MANTEL CLOCKS

An ormolu mounted boulle bracket clock, the chapter ring signed J. Gudin a Paris, 41½in. high. (Christie's) $2,499 £1,760

A Regency bronze and ormolu mantel clock with enamel dial, 14½in. wide. (Christie's) $3,567 £2,530

A gilt metal strut clock attributed to Thos. Cole, 5¼in. high. (Christie's) $1,425 £990

A Federal mahogany pillar and scroll clock, by E. Terry & Sons, circa 1835, 31in. high. (Robt. W. Skinner Inc.) $1,200 £774

A Charles X ormolu mantel clock with glazed circular dial, 19in. high. (Christie's) $1,483 £1,045

An Empire mahogany mantel clock, bearing partial label of Forestville Mfg. Co., circa 1830, 32in. high. (Robt. W. Skinner Inc.) $325 £209

Mid 19th century silvered bronze and ormolu mantel clock, the backplate signed Le Roy a Paris, 26½in. high. (Christie's) $1,093 £715

A Meissen clockcase of shaped outline, the movement with circular dial, blue crossed swords mark, circa 1880, 31cm. high. (Christie's) $2,356 £1,540

A Galle carved and acid-etched clock, 13cm. high. (Christie's) $4,089 £2,860

311

MANTEL CLOCKS

An early 17th century crucifix clock with detachable base, signed under the countwheel B.R. 1631, 35cm. high. (Phillips)
$7,250 £5,000

A 19th century French gilt brass and champleve enamel four glass mantel clock, 25cm. high. (Phillips)
$696 £480

Late 19th century lacquered brass and painted metal lighthouse clock, probably French, 22in. high. (Christie's) $2,200 £1,535

An Empire ormolu mantel clock, the dial signed F. B. Adams, London, 17in. high. (Christie's) $1,249 £880

A 19th century French white marble and ormolu mantel clock, 51cm. high. (Phillips)
$691 £480

A 19th century mechanical organ automaton with clock, 26in. high. (Christie's)
$13,200 £9,210

A Black Forest trumpeter clock, the two-train movement striking on a wire gong and playing a fanfare, 48in. high. (Christie's) $2,618 £1,700

A Regency bronze and gilt bronze mantel timepiece, 31cm. high. (Phillips)
$1,425 £990

A 19th century French ormolu mantel clock with circular enamel dial, 35cm. high, together with a base. (Phillips) $580 £400

MANTEL CLOCKS

Mid 19th century banjo time-piece with alarm, signed A. Willard, Jnr., Boston, 33½in. high. (Christie's)
$11,000 £7,675

William IV period mahogany four glass mantel clock, by W. J. Thomas, London, 12½in. high. (Reeds Rains)
$892 £620

A Federal mahogany veneer lighthouse clock, by Simon Willard, Mass., circa 1825, 27½in. high. (Christie's)
$110,000 £72,578

An Empire white marble clock, signed Robin, H. de l'Empereur, circa 1810, 17¾in. high. (Christie's)
$1,650 £1,151

A French late 19th century champleve bronze and glass mantel clock, 15½in. high. (Robt. W. Skinner Inc.)
$1,200 £839

Early 19th century Empire pendule a cercle tournant, signed J. J. Lepaute, 19in. high. (Christie's)
$16,500 £11,513

A 19th century Austrian silver and lapis lazuli decora-tive mantel timepiece, 22cm. high. (Phillips) $3,744 £2,600

A French Empire ormolu mantel clock, the move-ment mounted on a chariot, 44cm. high. (Phillips)
$1,728 £1,200

An ormolu mantel clock, the glazed dial signed Gosselin a Paris, 16¾in. high. (Christie's) $1,093 £770

MANTEL CLOCKS

A Fin De Siecle silvered and parcel gilt brass windmill clock, 18½in. high. (Christie's) $1,443 £880

An Empire ormolu mantel clock surmounted with a winged putto striking metal on an anvil at a forge, 12½in. wide. (Christie's) $1,408 £880

A Louis XVI ormolu mounted marble pendule a cercle tournant, signed Ant. Coliau a Paris, 15½in. high. (Christie's) $4,400 £3,070

An Empire ormolu mantel clock with circular enamel dial set within a plinth with Apollo and his lyre, 20½in. high. (Christie's) $1,584 £990

Federal mahogany shelf clock, by Aaron Willard, Mass., circa 1825, 34in. high. (Robt. W. Skinner Inc.) $7,500 £5,244

An Empire bronze and ormolu mantel clock, the enamel dial signed Lemoine a Paris, 24¼in. high. (Christie's) $2,640 £1,650

A Regence ormolu mounted boulle bracket clock, dial signed Mynuel a Paris, 32in. high. (Christie's) $2,464 £1,540

Late 19th century gilt and patinated bronze and marble industrial clock, probably French, 14½in. high. (Christie's) $1,650 £1,151

An Empire ormolu mantel clock with glazed dial in tapering plinth case surmounted by an oil lamp, 15in. high. (Christie's) $2,816 £1,760

SKELETON CLOCKS

A small skeleton timepiece, on mahogany base with glass dome, 11in. high. (Christie's) $1,144 £715

A Victorian brass 'Strutt' epicyclic skeleton clock, slate base with plaque signed W. Wigston, Derby, No. 51, W. Strutt Esq. Inv., 10¼in. high. (Christie's) $4,089 £2,860

A brass skeleton timepiece with spring detent escapement on oval white marble base, 17in. high excluding dome. (Christie's) $2,200 £1,535

A Eureka electric striking clock, signed Eureka Clock Co. Ltd., London, 11in. high overall. (Christie's) $2,516 £1,760

A quarter chiming skeleton clock, the pierced plates of open and angular design, 21in. high. (Christie's) $3,261 £2,160

A brass chiming skeleton clock, on oval oak base with glass dome, English, circa 1900, 24in. high including dome. (Christie's) $5,500 £3,837

A Victorian brass skeleton clock, 12½in. high, with glass dome. (Christie's) $3,968 £2,420

An early Victorian brass striking skeleton clock, signed Harrison Darlington, 12¼in. high, excluding dome. (Christie's) $2,164 £1,320

A brass skeleton timepiece with coup perdu escapement, on oval base with two plinths, 14in. high. (Christie's) $1,650 £1,151

WALL CLOCKS

An Ithaca walnut calendar clock, 1866, 45in. long. (Robt. W. Skinner Inc.) $1,600 £1,032

A Louis XVI ormolu cartel clock, the enamel dial signed Brille a Paris, 14in. high. (Christie's) $7,040 £4,400

A George III black lacquered and chinoiserie decorated tavern wall timepiece, signed Frans. Perigal, London, 1.44m. high. (Phillips) $1,305 £900

A cherry wall regulator timepiece, by Seth Thomas Clock Co., Conn., circa 1880, 36in. long. (Robt. W. Skinner Inc.) $650 £419

French 18th century wall clock with dual striking, by Basnard. (John D. Fleming & Co.) $398 £240

A Dutch marquetry 'Koortstaartklok' with automaton, 19th century, 39in. high. (Christie's) $2,059 £1,430

A George III giltwood cartel clock with later white dial and timepiece movement, 30in. high. (Christie's) $1,240 £880

An Austrian Biedermeier mahogany quarter striking wall clock, 41½in. high. (Christie's) $2,376 £1,650

An 18th century Continental carved giltwood cartel clock, 64cm. high. (Christie's) $1,185 £780

WALL CLOCKS

An ormolu cartel clock of Louis XVI style, the enamel dial signed Guibal, Paris, 26in. high. (Christie's) $757 £495

A Georgian giltwood wall dial clock, the 14in. enamel dial signed Geo. Yonge, London, 24in. diam. (Christie's) $2,217 £1,540

Late 19th century walnut regulator timepiece, by the Chelsea Clock Co., Mass., 35in. high. (Robt. W. Skinner Inc.) $850 £590

The Col. Isaac Gardiner Reed Presentation banjo clock, by Aaron Willard, 1812-16, 35½in. high, including eagle. (Christie's) $121,000 £84,675

An 18th century Dutch 'Stoelklok', 71cm. high. (Christie's) $1,033 £680

A French cartel clock with eight day movement, 9½in. high. (Capes, Dunn & Co.) $174 £120

A Federal mahogany gilt-wood and eglomise banjo clock, Mass., 1815-25, 40in. high. (Christie's) $1,430 £943

An 8-day fusee wall clock in mahogany case, the cream painted dial inscribed 'Ganthony'. (Woolley & Wallis) $1,065 £740

Late 19th century walnut regulator timepiece, by The E. Howard Watch & Clock Co., Boston, 40in. high. (Robt. W. Skinner Inc.) $900 £625

A gilt metal and leather covered verge watch, inscribed Quare, London, 2567, 60mm. diam. (Phillips) $580 £400

An 18ct. gold hunter-cased keyless chronograph, the movement signed J. W. Benson, No. 2516, London, 54mm. diam. (Phillips) $1,740 £1,200

A silver pair cased verge watch, the movement signed Tho. Tompion, London, 2631, 55mm. diam. (Christie's) $4,240 £2,808

A late 17th century silver pair cased verge watch, signed Tho. Tompion, London 0292, 57mm. diam. (Phillips) $2,610 £1,800

A Continental gold verge watch, the bridge-cock movement with gold dial and serpentine hands, 55mm. diam. (Christie's) $503 £352

A French gold quarter repeating musical cylinder watch with plain balance, musical disc and gilt cuvette, 59mm. diam. (Christie's) $3,617 £2,530

An 18ct. gold keyless lever chronograph, the movement signed Nicole & Capt., London, Patent No. 7255, 48mm. diam. (Phillips) $754 £520

A gold keyless lever watch, signed Geo. Edward & Sons on ½-plate gilt movement jewelled to the third, 53mm. diam. (Christie's) $943 £660

An 18th century silver pair cased verge watch, signed G. Bryan, London, 399, 50mm. diam. (Phillips) $609 £420

WATCHES

A gold hunter-cased chrono-meter, the enamel dial signed French Royal Exchange, London 18567, 51mm. diam. (Christie's) $1,467 £972

An 18ct. gold hunter-cased keyless lever watch, signed Nicole & Capt., London, Patent No. 2932, 44mm. diam. (Phillips) $464 £320

A French gold and enamel verge watch, the bridge-cock movement signed Hessen a Paris, 38mm. diam. (Christie's) $815 £540

A Continental gold and enamel quarter repeating watch, the movement with ruby cylinder escapement, 37mm. diam. (Phillips) $1,305 £900

A silver cased pocket chrono-meter by John Arnold, London, 50mm. diam. (Christie's) $13,046 £8,640

A gold minute repeating lever watch, the ¾-plate movement signed Jos. Penlington, Liverpool, No. 12937, 51mm. diam. (Christie's) $2,446 £1,620

A platinum keyless lever dress watch, by Cartier, the signed silver dial with sweep minute hand and with aperture for the hours, 45mm. diam. (Phillips) $2,030 £1,400

A gold pocket chrono-meter, the fusee movement signed Wm. Pickman, with enamel dial and gold hands, 54mm. diam. (Christie's) $1,258 £880

A French gold and gem set verge watch, the case with three-colour decoration set with turquoise and rubies, 42mm. diam. (Phillips) $522 £360

An 18ct. gold openface quarter repeating verge watch with jacquemarts, Swiss, signed on the cuvette Breguet & Fils, no. 23592, 55mm. diam. (Christie's) $2,640 £1,842

An 18ct. gold openface dress watch, signed Patek Philippe & Co., Geneva, no. 188192, 42mm. diam. (Christie's) $880 £614

A two-colour gold openface dress watch, signed Patek Philippe & Co., no. 817759, 45mm. diam. (Christie's) $1,210 £844

An enamelled platinum open-face dress watch, signed Patek Philippe & Co., Geneva, no. 810822, 39mm. diam. (Christie's) $1,320 £921

A nielloed silver sector watch, signed Record Watch Co., Tramelan, 60mm. wide. (Christie's) $1,320 £921

A platinum openface dress watch, signed Patek Philippe & Co., Geneva, no. 890237, 43mm. diam. (Christie's) $1,265 £882

A 14ct. gold openface pocket watch, 'Paul Breguette', 17-jewel, in a polished gold case. (Robt. W. Skinner Inc.) $125 £86

An 18th century gold pair cased pocket watch, the fusee movement inscribed John Walker, Newcastle upon Tyne 736. (Parsons, Welch & Cowell) $862 £560

A gold pair cased verge watch, signed Jams. Hagger, London 200, 54mm. diam. (Christie's) $3,643 £2,530

Late 19th century 14ct. gold openface calendar watch, Swiss, 50mm. diam. (Christie's) $495   £345

An 18ct. gold openface lever watch, signed Patek Philippe & Co., no. 135231, 45mm. diam. (Christie's)
     $1,540   £1,074

A 14ct. gold openface lever watch, signed Patek Philippe & Co., Geneva, no. 89566, 50mm. diam. (Christie's)
     $1,045   £729

An enamelled platinum openface dress watch, signed Patek Philippe & Co., Geneva, no. 814228, 42mm. diam. (Christie's) $1,210   £844

Breguet No. 58: a gold quarter repeating duplex watch, gilt Lepine calibre, 44mm. diam. (Christie's) $3,168   £2,200

An openface platinum dress watch with 19-jewel movement with gold train, signed Audemars Piguet & Co., no. 36541, 43mm. diam. (Christie's) $990   £690

An 18ct. gold openface dress watch, signed Patek Philippe & Co., Geneva, no. 892815, 47mm. diam. (Christie's)
     $1,320   £921

An openface gun metal calendar watch with damascened bar pattern lever movement, 62mm. diam. (Christie's) $165   £115

A late 18th century gold and enamel verge watch, the movement signed Gregson A Paris 13123, 50mm. diam. (Phillips) $792   £550

WATCHES

A silver fusee lever watch with winding indicator, signed Smith & Son, London, the case, London, 1899, 52mm. diam. (Christie's) $1,100 £767

A gold hunter-cased cylinder watch, the movement signed Vulliamy, London ruim, 50mm. diam. (Christie's) $619 £410

14ct. gold hunting case pocket watch, 'Elgin', jewelled gilt movement and white porcelain dial. (Robt. W. Skinner Inc.) $225 £156

A slender gold stem wind open faced lever pocket watch, signed Cartier, Paris, 45mm. diam. (Reeds Rains) $1,147 £740

A Swiss gold, enamel and gem set verge watch, the bridgecock movement signed Fres. Bordier, Geneve No. 35751, 44mm. diam. (Christie's) $950 £660

A small 18ct. gold openface five-minute repeating split-second chronograph, signed Tiffany & Co., the movement by P. Philippe, no. 111758, 42mm. diam. (Christie's) $4,950   £3,454

A gold miniature keyless lever watch, the steel bar movement jewelled to the centre and signed for Tiffany & Co., N.Y., 27mm. diam. (Phillips) $493 £340

An 18th century silver and horn pair cased verge watch, signed Conrs. Dunlop, London 3451, the inner case marked London 1762, 52mm. diam. (Phillips) $2,016 £1,400

14ct. gold hunting case pocket watch, 'Elgin', lever set jewelled nickel movement and white porcelain dial. (Robt. W. Skinner Inc.) $550 £381

WATCHES

A Swiss gilt metal and enamel verge watch, wound through Arabic enamel dial, 54mm. diam. (Christie's) $633 £440

A gold hunter-cased quarter repeating calendar watch, signed L. A. Favre Brandt, Geneve, 53mm. diam. (Christie's) $1,760 £1,228

An 18ct. gold openface centre seconds watch, signed Patek Philippe & Co., Geneva, no. 185202, 46mm. diam. (Christie's) $2,200 £1,535

A French gold jump hour cylinder watch with plain balance and gold cuvette inscribed Breguet A Paris No. 8416, 50mm. diam. (Christie's) $2,202 £1,540

A Continental gold quarter repeating ruby cylinder watch, 49mm. diam. (Christie's) $871 £605

A gilt metal pair cased verge stop watch, signed James Wild, Soho, 56mm. diam. (Phillips) $273 £190

A French gold, enamel and pearl verge watch, the bridge-cock movement signed Martin A Paris 11750, 37mm. diam. (Christie's) $2,217 £1,540

An 18ct. gold openface dress watch, with nickel 17-jewel lever movement, signed Vacheron & Constantin, Geneva, no. 486697, 48mm. diam. (Christie's) $880 £614

A gun metal double dial calendar watch with white enamel dial, 52mm. diam. (Christie's) $385 £268

WRISTWATCHES

A gold self-winding wristwatch with centre seconds,
signed Rolex Oyster Perpetual.
(Christie's) $1,760 £1,228

A platinum wristwatch with
17-jewel movement and
sapphire crown, signed
Breguet, no. 4300.
(Christie's) $2,200 £1,535

An 18ct. gold wristwatch
with nickel 18-jewel cal.
27-AM400 movement,
signed Patek Philippe & Co.,
no. 731479. (Christie's)
$1,100 £767

An 18ct. gold wristwatch
with nickel 18-jewel cal. 23-
300 movement, signed Patek
Philippe & Co., no. 781179.
(Christie's) $1,210 £944

A gold self-winding wristwatch with calendar, signed
Lucien Picard, Seashark, with
textured 14ct. gold bracelet.
(Christie's) $495 £345

A gold wristwatch, signed
Breguet, no. 3150, with
leather strap and 18ct. gold
deployant buckle. (Christie's)
$2,200 £1,535

A Swiss gold wristwatch,
gold cuvette inscribed in
Russian, the dial signed
in Cyrillic Pavel Buhre,
39mm. diam. (Christie's)
$1,584 £1,100

A gold wristwatch with nickel
17-jewel movement, signed
Gruen Watch Co., Curvex
Precision. (Christie's)
$330 £230

An 18ct. gold wristwatch,
signed Patek Philippe & Co.,
retailed by Cartier, with
fitted box. (Christie's)
$1,430 £997

WRISTWATCHES

A gold wristwatch with nickel 21-jewel movement, signed Lord Elgin, with 14ct. gold bracelet. (Christie's)
$418 £291

A gentleman's gold wrist-watch, the movement with 17 rubies, signed Rolex Precision. (Christie's)
$629 £440

An 18ct. gold wristwatch with nickel 17-jewel move-ment, signed Vacheron & Constantin, no. 421150. (Christie's) $2,200 £1,535

A gold self-winding wristwatch with centre seconds, signed Rolex Oyster Perpetual. (Christie's) $990 £690

A gold wristwatch with nickel 18-jewel cal. 23-300 move-ment, signed Patek Philippe & Co., no. 782328, and a 14ct. gold watch signed Omega. (Christie's) $1,760 £1,228

An 18ct. gold self-winding wristwatch, signed Patek Philippe & Co., no. 116018, with signed 18ct. gold buckle to leather strap. (Christie's)
$1,540 £1,074

A gold wristwatch, signed Audemars Piguet, no. 58098, with nickel 18-jewel move-ment. (Christie's)
$935 £652

A gold self-winding wrist-watch, signed Piaget, no. 7311215, the leather strap with 18ct. gold buckle. (Christie's) $825 £575

An 18ct. gold wristwatch, signed West End Watch Co., with nickel movement jewelled through the centre. (Christie's)
$660 £460

Late 19th century cloisonne enamel globular jar and shallow domed cover, 59.5cm. high. (Christie's) $5,935 £4,180

A cloisonne enamel and gilt bronze tripod censer and domed cover, Qianlong/ Jiaqing, 39cm. high. (Christie's) $2,516 £1,760

A Japanese cloisonne enamel baluster vase decorated with butterflies in flight, 4¾in. high. (Christie's) $3,168 £2,200

Late 19th century Japanese cloisonne urn of baluster form, 19¼in. high. (Christie's) $2,090 £1,364

A cloisonne enamel and gilt bronze vessel and cover, ding, Qianlong, 49.5cm. high. (Christie's) $5,977 £4,180

A 17th century cloisonne enamel Hu vase, 48cm. high. (Christie's) $2,516 £1,760

A cloisonne enamel circular box and flat cover, Qianlong, 32.7cm. diam., wood stand. (Christie's) $3,460 £2,420

One of a pair of Japanese cloisonne vases, 10in. high. (Reeds Rains) $518 £360

Japanese cloisonne octagonal wall plaque, circa 1900, 24in. diam. (Peter Wilson) $1,762 £1,250

A 16th century Ming cloisonne enamel globular tripod censer, 12.8cm. diam. (Christie's) $2,831 £1,980

Cloisonne vase decorated with dragons on a dark-blue field, converted to a reading lamp, 19in. high. (Peter Wilson) $158 £100

A Namikawa compressed globular tripod censer and domed cover, circa 1900, 10.3cm. diam. (Christie's) $3,124 £2,200

One of a pair of Japanese cloisonne vases, each painted with panels of cockerels and hens and birds in flight, 6¼in. high. (Christie's) $632 £400

Pair of rounded rectangular enamelled cloisonne vases, Meiji period wood stands, 30.4cm. high. (Christie's) $879 £550

A fine Ando cloisonne enamel slender oviform vase with short flaring neck, Meiji period, 24.3cm. high. (Christie's) $1,249 £880

A cloisonne enamel foliate shaped box and cover, Meiji period, 9cm. wide. (Christie's) $234 £165

A tall cloisonne vase decorated in various coloured enamels on a dark blue ground with a spray of tiger lilies, late 19th century, 33cm. high. (Christie's) $781 £550

A cloisonne enamel candle holder formed as a standing elephant, late Qing Dynasty, overall 33cm. wide. (Christie's) $3,775 £2,640

A brass bowl, the outer rim decorated with a Moorish design, possibly Turkish, 8½in. diam., and another. (Christie's)　$156　£93

Pair of Federal brass andirons, Phila., 1800-10, 29in. high. (Christie's) $3,050　£2,012

An early 17th century South German gilt brass and copper miniature casket, signed Michel Mann, 7.3cm. wide. (Phillips)　$4,608　£3,200

One of two pairs of brass candlesticks, early 19th century, 9½ and 10¾in. high. (Robt. W. Skinner Inc.) $375　£234

A Nara period copper gilt square plaque decorated in repousse with Amida, 7th/ 8th century, 11.3 x 11.3cm. (Christie's)　$13,992　£8,800

Early 20th century hammered copper bird cage on stand, 74in. high. (Robt. W. Skinner Inc.)　$275　£192

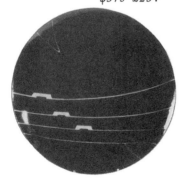

A Robin Banks enamelled copper charger, RB mono-gram 1986, 39.4cm. diam. (Christie's)　$302　£198

A Dutch or Flemish 16th century brass candlestick, 18.8cm. high. (Phillips) $792　£550

A gilt copper turret of hexa-gonal form, probably Tuscan 15th century. (Phillips) $576　£400

An oval brass planter with gadroon embossed decoration, 13in. high. (Peter Wilson) $300 £190

A pair of brass and iron knife-blade andirons, American, circa 1800, 22¼in. high. (Christie's) $880 £539

Early 19th century copper coal helmet, also a matching shovel, 17½in. high. (Peter Wilson) $616 £390

A Benham & Froud brass and copper adjustable floor oil lamp, 175cm. high. (Christie's) $364 £253

A brass alms dish with raised central dome, 17th century, 17½in. diam. (Christie's) $776 £462

A set of three George III brass fire-irons, 31¼in. long. (Christie's) $775 £550

One of a pair of brass and enamelled andirons, 26in. high. (Christie's) $3,344 £2,200

An urn-shaped lidded coal bin fitted with two lion mask ring handles, 18in. high. (Peter Wilson) $189 £120

Pair of early 19th century brass andirons, New York, signed Bailey, 21½in. high. (Robt. W. Skinner Inc.) $1,400 £875

An 18th century Spanish brass flagon, 8.5in. high. (Woolley & Wallis) $403 £280

Pair of Perry & Co. brass candlesticks, designed by Dr. C. Dresser, with wood handles, 5½in. (Christie's) $1,661 £1,100

One of a pair of copper and brass vacuum flasks with handles, attributed to W. A. S. Benson, 48cm. high. (Christie's) $364 £253

Pair of early 18th century Continental brass candlesticks, 9in. high. (Christie's) $3,080 £2,032

Gustav Stickley hammered copper umbrella holder, circa 1905, no. 273, 27¼in. high. (Robt. W. Skinner Inc.) $700 £490

Benedict Art Studios hammered copper wall plaque, N.Y., circa 1907, 15in. diam. (Robt. W. Skinner Inc.) $800 £560

Mid 19th century copper jelly mould, 5in. diam. (Peter Wilson) $155 £110

One of a pair of 19th century brass atheniennes, supported on four ram's head monopodiae on square bases, 45cm. high. (Phillips) $1,944 £1,350

A late 19th century English brass doorway, each door 209 x 77.5cm. (Christie's) $23,925 £16,500

Large 19th century brass planter with bird's head ring handles, China, 28in. diam. (Robt. W. Skinner Inc.) $950 £659

A 19th century firegrate with brass detail. (Lots Road Galleries) $331 £230

Early 20th century Arts & Crafts hammered copper wood box with loop handles, 23½in. wide. (Robt. W. Skinner Inc.) $750 £524

Pair of early 18th century brass tapersticks, English, 4½in. high. (Christie's) $2,310 £1,524

A Regency copper oval samovar, the domed cover with a sphinx finial, 13in. high. (Woolley & Wallis) $317 £210

Pair of Federal brass andirons and matching tools, 1800-20, 17in. high. (Christie's) $1,045 £675

An early 20th century English copper electrotype bust of Eliza Macloghlin, cast by A. Toft from a model by Sir A. Gilbert, dated 1906, 40.5cm. high. (Christie's) $15,950 £11,000

Mid 19th century copper jelly mould with fluted column decoration, 6in. diam. (Peter Wilson) $155 £110

Pair of 18th century brass table candlesticks with baluster stems, 11in. high. (Hobbs & Chambers) $172 £120

A pair of late 19th century Chinese lady's stilted shoes of red silk with blue silk border. (Phillips) $226 £150

A 16th century man's embroidered cap embellished with sequins and gold lace trim, England, 8in. high. (Robt. W. Skinner Inc.) $10,000 £6,993

A late 19th century Chinese child's robe of terracotta silk, embroidered in coloured silks. (Phillips) $573 £380

A gentleman's banyan of printed worsted, circa 1820's. (Phillips) $1,057 £750

Three-quarter length wrap-over mink coat, silk lined. (Peter Wilson) $705 £500

A late 19th century two-piece gown of mauve, grey and orange silk brocade of striped design, circa 1880. (Phillips) $241 £160

A late 19th century Chinese waistcoat of brown worsted, the black silk border embroidered in blue and ivory silk. (Phillips) $131 £100

A noh costume, Karaori, decorated in various colours on gold twill-weave ground, late Edo period. (Christie's) $26,554 £18,700

A Moroccan Western Atlas cloak of black wool, of semi-circular form, with narrow hood. (Phillips) $282 £200

A late 19th century Chinese robe of blue silk, embroidered in coloured silks and applied gold thread. (Phillips) $1,057   £700

A Nigerian Haussa robe of indigo cotton embroidered in pale blue with knives, roundels and knots. (Phillips) $169 £120

A noh costume, Karaori, late Edo period. (Christie's) $14,839 £10,450

A mid 19th century dress of cream and brown wool printed in mainly red, green and orange. (Phillips) $253 £180

A 19th century black silk uchikake richly embroidered in gold and colour. (Christie's) $4,373 £3,080

A two-piece gown of ivory silk brocaded in lime and pink silk, maker's label G. Worth, Paris, circa 1900. (Phillips) $1,963 £1,300

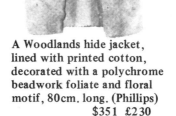

An embroidered vest and pair of embroidered shoes, 18th century, the vest with floral sprays on ivory silk. (Robt. W. Skinner Inc.) $800 £559

A Woodlands hide jacket, lined with printed cotton, decorated with a polychrome beadwork foliate and floral motif, 80cm. long. (Phillips) $351 £230

A late 18th century gentleman's double-breasted waistcoat of yellow silk brocade. (Phillips) $119 £85

V.A.A.A.C.C.C. Team 1892: An Australian navy-blue velvet and gold braid cap for 1892. (Phillips) $336 £200

An inscription from an Edwardian two-handled silver tray for Teignbridge Cricket Club, 70cm. long. (Phillips) $1,512 £900

A 19th century Staffordshire pottery mug, 8cm. high. (Phillips) $67 £40

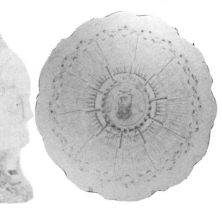

A Royal Worcester porcelain plate, the centre printed in gilt with signatures of the Australian Touring Side, 1964, 27cm. diam. (Phillips)
                    $168 £100

A pair of Continental porcelain figures of Young England and His Sister, approx. 32cm. high. (Phillips) $756 £450

A Coalport porcelain plate commemorating W. G. Grace's century of centuries, 23cm. diam. (Phillips) $218 £130

J. Wisden: Cricketers' Almanack 1864-1985, bound in blue calf and gilt with Scarborough Cricket Club badge on front cover. (Phillips)
            $16,800 £10,000

Sir Jeremiah Colman: The Noble Game of Cricket, pub. 1941, ltd. edn. of 150. (Phillips) $772 £460

The Canterbury Cricket Week. Volume First, pub. 1865. (Phillips) $436 £260

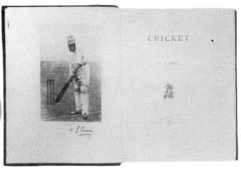

A Minton pottery ashtray for M.C.C. 1787-1937, 13.5cm. (Phillips) $100 £60

W. G. Grace: Cricket, pub. 1891, crown quarto edn. de luxe. (Phillips) $436 £260

A Staffordshire pottery mug, decorated with cricket figures in white relief and silver lustre, 10cm. high. (Phillips) $184 £110

Henry Scott Tuke, by W. G. Grace, 1905, sketch in charcoal, 20 x 26cm. (Phillips) $3,696 £2,200

The Cricket Match Played at Toronto, Canada, 1872, lithograph designed by R. Smith, 90 x 50cm. (Phillips) $1,596 £950

A Minton pottery jug for M.C.C. 1787-1937, 19cm. high. (Phillips) $252 £150

A Minton pottery tankard for M.C.C. 1787-1937, 13cm. high. (Phillips) $218 £130

J. Nyren: The Young Cricketer's Tutor, pub. 1833. (Phillips) $285 £170

A Robinson & Leadbetter parian bust of W. G. Grace, 17cm. high. (Phillips) $1,260 £750

DOLLS

An Armand Marseille bisque-headed 'dollie', wood and composition ball jointed body, 24in. high. (Hobbs & Chambers) $285 £170

Early 20th century Lehmann waltzing doll, head with EPL trademark, 9in. high. (Robt. W. Skinner Inc.) $900 £625

A Chad Valley painted felt portrait doll modelled as the Princess Elizabeth, circa 1938, 18in. high, together with another and a koala bear. (Christie's) $471 £308

A pink china shoulder headed doll, the kid body with wooden limbs, 15in. high, circa 1840. (Christie's) $471 £330

A set of composition dolls representing the Dionne quintruplets with doctor and nurse, 7½in. high, the adults 13in. high, by Madame Alexander. (Christie's) $639 £418

A bisque-headed character doll, marked 1488 Simon & Halbig 4, 12½in. high. (Christie's) $2,359 £1,650

A Simon & Halbig bisque headed doll with composition ball jointed body, 24in. high. (Hobbs & Chambers) $489 £340

A bisque headed character baby doll, 9in. high, marked 142 2/0 by Kestner. (Christie's) $302 £198

Early 20th century Armand Marseille bisque headed Floradora doll, 14in. high. (Hobbs & Chambers) $187 £130

A bisque headed child doll, 8½in. high, marked 1078 S&H. (Christie's) $403 £264

A bisque headed character baby doll, 27in. high, marked SFBJ252 Paris 12. (Christie's) $2,356 £1,540

A bisque headed character baby doll moulded as an Oriental, 9¼in. high, marked 3/0. (Christie's) $639 £418

A French mechanical walking doll, the bisque head with blonde mohair wig, 38cm. high. (Phillips) $1,047 £680

A composition portrait doll modelled as Shirley Temple, 13½in. high, marked S.T. 5/0 CB Germany. (Christie's) $370 £242

Simon & Halbig/Kammer & Reinhardt bisque-headed doll, 1914-27, 26in. high. (Hobbs & Chambers) $789 £470

Late 19th century Heubach 12-Koppelsdoft bisque headed doll, impressed AWW, Germany, 32in. high. (Hobbs & Chambers) $857 £568

A bisque headed doll, C1912, by Franz Schmidt, 12½in. high. (Hobbs & Chambers) $446 £310

A bisque-headed bebe, the jointed body dressed in pink, 19in. high, marked on the head 8 and with the Schmitt of Paris shield mark on bottom. (Christie's) $2,988 £2,090

A bisque-headed child doll, 22in. high, marked Handwerck 109-11 Halbig on the shoes, NAPAUD 32 rue du 4 Septembre. (Christie's) $1,179 £825

A brown bisque-headed baby doll with brown composition baby's body, 14½in. high, marked AM341/ 2.5K. (Christie's) $314 £220

A bisque-headed bebe, marked SteA.2 and written in red Steiner A.S.G.D.G. Paris Bourgoin jeun, and a wig, 18in. high. (Christie's) $2,359 £1,650

A set of Chad Valley Snow White and the seven dwarfs. Snow White with painted cloth face, fixed blue glass eyes and velvet limbs, 17in. high, the dwarfs in original clothes, 9½in. high. (Christie's) $440 £308

A bisque-headed character doll, marked SFBJ236 Paris 6 and embossed 21, 14in. high. (Christie's) $786 £550

A bisque-headed bebe, the fixed wrist jointed composition body dressed in blue, impressed SteA.1, 16in. high. (Christie's) $2,674 £1,870

A bisque-headed doll with composition body, 17in. high, impressed SFBJ60 Paris O. (Outhwaite & Litherland) $290 £200

A composition headed Japanese doll with closed mouth, inset eyes and black hair wig, 16½in. high, and a composition headed Gosho Ningo. (Christie's) $235 £165

A bisque-headed character child doll, 23in. high, marked K*R Simon and Halbig 117n58, and a boy doll, 22in. high. (Christie's) $1,337 £935

A bisque-headed bebe with jointed composition body, mark 7 stamped in blue on the body Bebe Jumeau Depose, 15in. high. (Christie's) $1,494 £1,045

A bisque headed character doll with a quantity of other items, including bedding, shoes, a parasol, a box of washing items and twenty-three changes of clothes, 14½in. high, marked F.S. and Co., 1272/352 Deponiert. (Christie's) $1,337 £935

A bisque-headed character boy doll, impressed 7 3072 and with JDK sticker on the body, 20in. high. (Christie's) $865 £605

A bisque shoulder headed doll with closed mouth, solid pate and kid body with bisque arms, 14½in. high. (Christie's) $503 £352

A bisque shoulder headed doll, the stuffed body with bisque limbs, 11½in. high, circa 1860. (Christie's) $1,022 £715

A German oblong enamel snuff box, the white ground body painted in puce with battle scenes, circa 1760, 3¼in. long. (Christie's) $1,321 £864

A German oblong enamel box commemorating the Treaty of Hubertsburg, circa 1763, 3¼in. long. (Christie's) $1,074 £702

A German oblong enamel snuff box with engraved gilt metal mounts, circa 1765, 3¼in. long. (Christie's) $991 £648

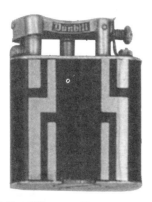

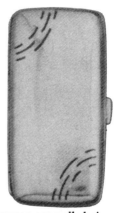

A Dunhill enamelled cigarette lighter, 5cm. high, stamped with maker's marks and Pat. No. 143752. (Phillips) $403 £280

Pair of Staffordshire white ground enamel candlesticks, circa 1770, 10.5/8in. high. (Christie's) $1,487 £972

A German enamelled cigarette case, 8.5 x 4.5cm., stamped 800 with crescent and crown and with Austrian import marks. (Phillips) $57 £40

A George III oblong enamel 'New Year's Gift' calendar snuff box in the style of Anthony Tregent, London, 1757, 3¼in. long. (Christie's) $1,022 £715

A Staffordshire oblong enamel tea caddy with gilt metal mounts, circa 1765, 4.3/8in. long. (Christie's) $1,487 £972

A Staffordshire small rectangular enamel snuff box, inscribed on the interior 'Vole Amour a mon Secours', circa 1765, 1¾in. long. (Christie's) $943 £660

An officer's silver (not hall-marked) and enamel cap badge of The Irish Guards. (Wallis & Wallis) $103 £70

A 19th century enamel nef, the hull and sails decorated with the Rape of Europa and other classical scenes, 20cm. long, probably Vienna. (Phillips) $864 £600

A Staffordshire small oval enamel snuff box of tub form, with crimped gilt metal mounts and shaped thumbpiece, circa 1770, 2.5/8in. long. (Christie's) $629 £440

A Staffordshire oblong white ground enamel snuff box with engraved gilt metal mounts, circa 1770, 3½in. long. (Christie's) $1,101 £770

A Staffordshire small oval enamel snuff box, the gilt metal mounts with zig-zag ornament, circa 1765, 1.7/8in. long. (Christie's) $865 £605

A German oblong white ground enamel snuff box, painted in the manner of David Chodowiecki, the scenes mostly after Boucher, Berlin, circa 1760, 3¼in. long. (Christie's) $3,775 £2,640

A plique-a-jour circular box and cover decorated in trans-lucent enamels, 5.8cm. diam., stamped on base 925. (Phillips) $230 £160

A German circular gold mounted enamel snuff box with waisted sides, circa 1760, 2¼in. diam. (Christie's) $2,643 £1,728

A Staffordshire oval enamel snuff box of tub-shape, with crimped gilt metal mounts, circa 1770, 2.5/8in. long. (Christie's) $597 £418

A Flemish fan with ivory sticks, the guards inlaid with mother-of-pearl and decorated with silver pique, 26.5cm, long. (Phillips)
$479 £340

An ivory brise fan painted and lacquered with a classical scene, 8½in., circa 1730. (Christie's)
$3,933 £2,640

A late 18th century Italian fan with pierced ivory sticks, 28cm. long. (Phillips)
$535 £380

La Contre Revolution, a printed fan edged with green silk fringe, 11in., French, circa 1790. (Christie's)
$901 £605

A French painted pierced ivory brise fan with tortoiseshell guards decorated with silver pique, early 18th century, 21cm. long. (Phillips)
$479 £340

A fan, the dark leaf painted with a Biblical scene of figures drinking from a mountain torrent, 10¼in., Italian, circa 1770, in silk covered box. (Christie's) $1,147 £770

A late 18th century fan with carved, pierced and silvered ivory sticks, 24.5cm. long, and a box. (Phillips) $155 £110

An early 19th century fan with carved shaped ivory sticks, the vellum leaf painted with Flora attended by maidens and suitors, 28cm. long. (Phillips) $513 £340

An early 18th century Flemish fan, the carved ivory sticks decorated with silver pique and mother-of-pearl cloute, 27cm. long. (Phillips) $120 £80

An ivory brise fan painted with a lady fishing, 9in., circa 1730. (Christie's) $5,736 £3,850

Early 18th century ivory brise fan, the leaf painted with convivial figures in a garden, 8in. (Christie's) $3,605 £2,420

A fan, the leaf painted with the return of a hero, the verso with chinoiserie, 10in., French, circa 1760, in glazed case. (Christie's) $3,278 £2,200

A French fan, the leaf painted with elegant figures in a park, the mother-of-pearl sticks carved, pierced and gilt with figures in Turkish dress, 11in., circa 1760. (Christie's) $2,950 £1,980

A fan, the leaf painted with a court scene, 10in., circa 1770. (Christie's) $655 £440

A fan, the mother-of-pearl sticks carved with the departure of a hero, 10½in., circa 1760. (Christie's) $1,966 £1,320

A fan, the ivory sticks carved, pierced and gilt with the Altar of Love, 10½in., Italian, circa 1780. (Christie's) $1,346 £935

Scottish, Commercial Fire and Life Insurance, copper, oval, raised figure of Caledonia. (Phillips) $316 £220

Liverpool Fire Office, lead, liver bird and torse raised on circular section, 'Liverpool' raised on panel below and impressed with policy no. 426. (Phillips) $1,152 £800

Aberdeen Fire and Life Insurance Co., stamped lead, oval, raised arms of the city with motto 'Bon Accord'. (Phillips) $2,160 £1,500

Albion Fire and Life Insurance, cast iron, circular, raised 'Albion Fire Office', with raised border, issued circa 1810-28. (Phillips) $316 £220

Westminster Insurance, lead, open portcullis with Prince of Wales' feathers above, policy no. 20867 on panel below. (Phillips) $504 £350

West of Scotland Insurance, 1823-38, stamped lead, circular, raised crown in centre. (Phillips) $316 £220

Hercules Fire Insurance, cast iron, 'Hercules Fire Office' raised on ornate shield. (Phillips) $288 £200

Royal Exchange Assurance, lead, raised Royal Exchange building, policy no. 570 on panel below, issued circa 1721. (Phillips) $6,336 £4,400

Berkshire, Gloucestershire and Provincial Life and Fire Assurance, 1824-31, copper, castle raised on oval. (Phillips) $230 £160

North British Insurance, copper, St. Andrew and saltire cross raised in centre, 'North British' raised on panel below. (Phillips) $288 £200

Dundee Assurance, lead, raised arms of the city, impressed policy no. 3294. (Phillips) $1,152 £800

East Kent and Canterbury Economic Fire Assurance, 1824-28, tinned iron, oval. (Phillips) $374 £260

Hampshire and South of England Insurance, 1841-47, copper, rose and crown raised on centre. (Phillips) $273 £190

Eagle Insurance, stamped lead, raised with eagle standing on rock, 'Safety' raised on panel below. (Phillips) $1,180 £820

Edinburgh Friendly Assurance, heavy lead, policy no. 1805 pierced through panel below. (Phillips) $1,584 £1,100

Bristol Crown Fire Office, lead, crown raised in high relief, 'Bristol' raised on panel below. (Phillips) $489 £340

The General Insurance Company of Ireland, lead, rectangular, raised phoenix, torse and borders, policy no. 2036 on panel below. (Phillips) $1,152 £800

London Assurance, lead, seated figure of Britannia with shield, spear and harp, 'London' raised on panel below, issued cira 1805-07. (Phillips) $604 £420

BEDS

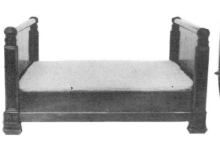

A mahogany lit a bateau, three-quarter size, circa 1830, 43½in. high. (Robt. W. Skinner Inc.) $1,000 £694

Late 19th century ebonised Bentwood cradle, Europe, 52in. long. (Robt. W. Skinner Inc.) $900 £625

An Empire mahogany lit en bateau with box spring mattress, 48in. wide, 86in. long. (Christie's) $4,686 £3,300

A George III mahogany four-post bedstead, 5ft.2in. wide, 6ft.9in. long, 7ft.6in. high. (Parsons, Welch & Cowell) $6,680 £4,000

A mahogany four-post bed with box spring and mattress covered in pale green repp, 18th century and later, 82½in. long. (Christie's) $10,367 £7,150

A giltwood four-post bed with padded arched head-rest, box-spring and mattress, circa 1830, 64in. wide, (Christie's) $10,153 £7,150

A parcel gilt and cream-painted four-post bed, with padded headboard and yellow repp pleated hang-ings, box spring and mattress, 83.5in. wide. (Christie's) $1,652 £1,080

A George III painted cradle with ogee-arched hood and cane-filled sides, 41in. long. (Christie's) $1,328 £827

A Renaissance Revival walnut and burl veneer bed and chest, bearing the label 'E. D. Trymby's, Phila., Penn.', (Robt. W. Skinner Inc.) $3,500 £2,250

BEDS

Painted Empire maple masonic bed, N.Y., circa 1830, 54in. wide. (Robt. W. Skinner Inc.) $600 £419

An oak bed with panelled headboard on square legs with rollers, late 16th century, 52in. wide. (Christie's) $3,344 £2,200

An Empire mahogany bed, the head and foot-end inlaid with brass musical trophies, 43¾in. wide. (Christie's) $1,562 £1,100

A late Federal carved cherrywood four-post bedstead, probably New York, circa 1825, 53¼in. wide. (Christie's) $6,050 £3,991

A mahogany four-post bed with box-spring and mattress, 59in. wide. (Christie's) $2,772 £1,650

A Regency parcel gilt and fruitwood four-post bed, 43½in. wide, 96in. high. (Christie's) $6,198 £3,850

A Regency mahogany and brass campaign bed, with inscribed brass plaque 'Butler's Patent, Catherine St.', 26in. wide. (Christie's) $6,375 £3,960

A rococo Revival walnut bed, America, circa 1860, 91in. high, 74in. long. and a chest. (Robt. W. Skinner Inc.) $2,700 £1,741

A Federal carved mahogany four-post bedstead, Mass., circa 1820, 76in. long, 47¼in. wide. (Christie's) $6,600 £4,354

BOOKCASES

A Regency mahogany dwarf bookcase with four graduated shelves above a drawer, 30in. wide. (Christie's)
$2,851 £1,980

A satinwood dwarf bookcase on moulded base with brass paw feet, 55½in. wide. (Christie's) $5,583 £3,960

A Regency ormolu mounted, parcel gilt and rosewood dwarf bookcase with specimen marble top, 18in. wide. (Christie's) $4,032 £2,860

A mahogany breakfront bookcase with moulded dentilled overhanging cornice, 71½in. wide. (Christie's)
$3,102 £2,200

An oak breakfront bookcase, by A. W. N. Pugin and John Webb, now painted white, 98in. wide. (Christie's)
$9,438 £6,600

A George III mahogany breakfront bookcase on splayed bracket feet, 74½in. wide. (Christie's) $11,011 £7,700

A Victorian oak breakfront library bookcase, the top section enclosed by four glazed panel doors, 88in. wide. (Christie's)
$2,175 £1,500

A Regency mahogany breakfront bookcase with raspberry moire silk lined interior, 108in. wide. (Christie's)
$24,816 £17,600

A late Federal tiger maple bookcase, in two parts, possibly New York, 1810-20, 52½in. wide.(Christie's)
$7,150 £4,717

BOOKCASES

A George III mahogany bookcase with a pair of glazed cupboard doors enclosing shelves, 49in. wide. (Christie's) $6,979 £4,950

A Regency purpleheart pedestal bookcase with square 17th century Italian marble top formed in two segments, 23in. sq. (Christie's) $31,460 £22,000

A George IV rosewood dwarf bookcase with adjustable open shelves, 44in. wide. (Christie's) $1,258 £880

An early Victorian oak bookcase in the Gothic style, 92in. wide, 93in. high. (Christie's) $5,049 £3,300

A 19th century mahogany breakfront cabinet with dentil cornice, 79in. wide. (Dreweatts) $2,610 £1,800

A Georgian mahogany breakfront library bookcase on a plinth base, 2.56m. wide. (Phillips) $18,460 £13,000

A German walnut and marquetry bookcase, the open shelves lined with rust-coloured velveteen, basically mid 18th century, 64½in. wide. (Christie's) $5,467 £3,850

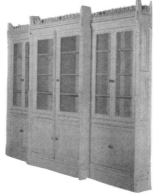

An early Victorian oak breakfront bookcase, by A. W. N. Pugin and John Webb, now painted white, 146in. wide. (Christie's) $7,078 £4,950

A George III mahogany bookcase, banded with satinwood, 53in. wide. (Christie's) $28,314 £19,800

BOOKCASES

A George III mahogany break-front bookcase with a pair of glazed cupboard doors, 97½in. wide. (Christie's) $8,262 £5,400

Gustav Stickley open slat-sided bookshelf, circa 1909, 27in. wide. (Robt. W. Skinner Inc.) $800 £560

A George III carved maho-gany bookcase on stand with scroll carved hairy paw feet, 1.56m. wide. (Phillips) $3,600 £2,400

Georgian two-part mahogany bookcase with two glazed doors above two panelled doors, 7ft.10in. high. (Lots Road Galleries) $3,825 £2,500

Gustav Stickley two-door bookcase, gallery top over doors with eight panes each, circa 1903-4, no. 716, 42in. wide. (Robt. W. Skinner Inc.) $4,500 £3,147

One of a pair of dwarf maho-gany reproduction bookcases with Empire style mounts. (Lots Road Galleries) $362 £240

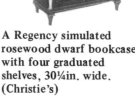

L. & J. G. Stickley two-door bookcase, style no. 645, circa 1912, 49in. wide. (Robt. W. Skinner Inc.) $2,500 £1,748

A Regency simulated rosewood dwarf bookcase with four graduated shelves, 30¼in. wide. (Christie's) $4,957 £3,240

Gustav Stickley leaded two-door bookcase, designed by Harvey Ellis, circa 1904, no. 716, 42¾in. wide. (Robt. W. Skinner Inc.) $2,200 £1,539

BOOKCASES

A Gustav Stickley oak book-case, the door with wrought iron lock plate and drop loop handle, 98cm. wide. (Christie's) $1,982 £1,296

An Isokon book stand, white painted natural wood, with sloping book compartments, 40.3cm. high. (Christie's) $330 £216

A mid Georgian mahogany bookcase with pair of glazed doors with egg-and-dart carved astragals, 73½in. wide. (Christie's) $11,962 £8,250

A large Regency mahogany breakfront bookcase, the base with six panelled cup-board doors, 176in. wide. (Christie's) $6,061 £4,180

Gustav Stickley two-door bookcase, gallery top, eight panes in each door, circa 1912, 48in. wide. (Robt. W. Skinner Inc.) $1,900 £1,329

Gustav Stickley leaded single door bookcase, designed by Harvey Ellis, circa 1904, no. 700, 36in. wide. (Robt. W. Skinner Inc.) $7,500 £5,245

Gustav Stickley two-door bookcase, circa 1910, no. 716, gallery above eight-pane doors, 42in. wide. (Robt. W. Skinner Inc.) $1,900 £1,329

L. & J. G. Stickley narrow bookcase with adjustable shelves, circa 1912, no. 652, 22in. wide. (Robt. W. Skinner Inc.) $1,700 £1,189

Onondaga double door book-case, by L. & J. G. Stickley, circa 1902-04, 56½in. high. (Robt. W. Skinner Inc.) $1,900 £1,328

BOOKCASES

A set of George III pierced fret side mahogany wall shelves, 19in. wide. (Woolley & Wallis)
$815 £540

A mid Victorian gilt metal mounted satinwood and walnut dwarf bookcase, 109in. wide. (Christie's)
$5,662 £3,960

A Regency simulated rosewood hanging open bookshelf, 57cm. wide, 75cm. high. (Phillips) $2,698 £1,900

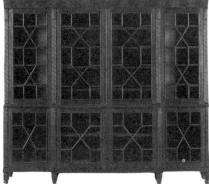

Late 18th/early 19th century George III mahogany two-part bookcase cabinet in two sections, 23¼in. wide. (Christie's) $5,500 £3,589

A late Federal mahogany breakfront bookcase, Phila., 1815-20, 108in. wide. (Christie's)
$28,600 £18,870

An early Victorian oak bookcase, by A. W. N. Pugin and John Webb, now painted white, 75½in. wide. (Christie's)
$7,078 £4,950

A Regency rosewood bookcase, the upper part with open shelves, the lower part with two glazed doors. (Lots Road Galleries)
$1,872 £1,300

A George III mahogany bookcase, the glazed doors enclosing shelves, 43½in. wide. (Christie's)
$3,932 £2,750

A Regency mahogany bookcase in the Gothic style, 29in. wide. (Christie's)
$7,755 £5,500

BUREAU BOOKCASES

An early 18th century walnut and featherstrung bureau cabinet, 1.07m. wide. (Phillips) $11,628 £7,600

Mid 18th century Italian scarlet and gold lacquer bureau cabinet on cabriole legs and hoof feet, 37in. wide. (Christie's) $3,124 £2,200

A William and Mary walnut banded pollard elm bureau cabinet, 39½in. wide. (Christie's) $12,408 £8,800

A George III mahogany bureau bookcase, the sloping flap enclosing a fitted interior, 43½in. wide. (Christie's) $5,174 £3,080

A Scandinavian green painted and parcel gilt secretaire bookcase, basically late 18th century, 47in. wide. (Christie's) $3,124 £2,200

Edwardian mahogany inlaid bureau bookcase, shell inlay on fall-front, 35in. wide. (Peter Wilson) $1,185 £750

A Victorian painted and decorated pine secretary bookcase, Heywood Bros., painting attributed to E. and T. Hill, circa 1860, 49in. wide. (Christie's) $11,000 £7,257

A George II padoukwood bureau cabinet, the sloping flap enclosing ten drawers, 34in. wide. (Christie's) $8,530 £6,050

A George III mahogany bureau bookcase, the leather lined flap enclosing a fitted interior, 50in. wide. (Christie's) $9,740 £6,050

BUREAU BOOKCASES

A Chippendale walnut bookcase desk, in two sections,
Mass., 1760-80, (Christie's)
$6,050 £3,912

A mahogany bureau bookcase,
the fall-flap enclosing a fitted
interior, 34in. wide.
(Christie's) $3,509 £2,420

A George III rosewood and
mahogany bureau bookcase,
the fall-flap enclosing a
fitted interior, 45in. wide.
(Christie's) $7,177 £4,950

A Queen Anne walnut bureau
bookcase with candle slides,
41½in. wide. (Christie's)
$14,734 £10,450

A Chippendale style faded
mahogany bureau bookcase
on ogee bracket feet, 4ft.
wide. (Woolley & Wallis)
$3,861 £2,700

A George II mahogany bureau
cabinet, the fall front enclosing a fitted interior with
drawers, 1.04m. wide.
(Phillips) $7,200 £5,000

A Chippendale block front
desk and bookcase in two
sections, Mass., 1760-80,
40½in. wide. (Christie's)
$38,500 £25,128

An 18th century Anglo-
Dutch kingwood, burr yew-
wood and amboyna oyster
veneered bureau cabinet,
1.98m. high. (Phillips)
$4,350 £2,900

A George III mahogany
bureau bookcase, the leather-
lined fall-flap enclosing a
fitted interior, 49in. wide.
(Christie's) $5,104 £3,520

BUREAU BOOKCASES

A late 18th/early 19th century Italian scarlet lacquer and gilt bureau cabinet, 89cm. wide. (Phillips) $10,080 £7,000

A George I walnut and parcel gilt bureau cabinet inlaid with feather banding, 39¼in. wide. (Christie's)
$62,040 £44,000

A Regency mahogany bureau cabinet, the George III base with sloping lid above two short and three long drawers, 45in. wide. (Christie's) $1,900 £1,242

A late 17th/early 18th century walnut crossbanded bureau cabinet, with fitted interior, 1.25m. wide. (Phillips) $8,928 £6,200

A George III mahogany bureau bookcase, 46in. wide, 96½in. high. (Christie's) $3,460 £2,420

A Queen Anne walnut bureau bookcase with a partly-fitted interior, 41½in. wide. (Christie's) $40,326 £28,600

A George III mahogany bureau bookcase, the fall-flap opening to reveal a fitted interior, 3ft.8in. wide. (Woolley & Wallis)
$4,176 £2,900

A Queen Anne walnut cross-banded and featherstrung bureau cabinet in three sections, 1.08m. wide. (Phillips)
$44,640 £31,000

A walnut bureau cabinet with a pair of mirror glazed doors, 32½in. wide. (Christie's) $7,078 £4,950

BUREAUX

A George I walnut bureau inlaid with featherbandings, with later fitted interior, 36in. wide. (Christie's) $2,718 £1,800

A Chippendale maple slant-front desk, New England, 1760-90, 37½in. wide. (Christie's) $3,300 £2,177

A Chippendale walnut slant-front desk with fitted interior, Rhode Island, 1760-90, 40¼in. wide. (Christie's) $3,850 £2,540

A Chippendale walnut slant-front desk with a fitted interior, Penn., dated 1779, 41½in. wide. (Christie's) $17,600 £11,612

Mid 18th century George III mahogany slant-front desk, 36¼in. wide. (Christie's) $4,950 £3,230

Federal cherry drop-front desk with fitted interior, New England, circa 1800, 39½in. wide. (Robt. W. Skinner Inc.) $1,600 £1,066

Mid 18th century German rococo miniature walnut veneer slant-front bureau, 18¼in. wide. (Christie's) $1,760 £1,148

A Chippendale maple slant-front desk, attributed to Nathaniel Dominy IV or V, Long Island, N.Y., 1760-80, 36¼in. wide. (Christie's) $9,900 £6,532

A George I walnut bureau with leather lined flap enclosing a fitted interior, 36in. wide. (Christie's) $6,292 £4,400

BUREAUX

A Chippendale walnut slant top desk on claw and ball feet, probably Penn., circa 1780. (Robt. W. Skinner Inc.) $10,000 £6,993

An Edwardian inlaid mahogany cylinder bureau with decorated urn front, 30in. wide. (Coles, Knapp & Kennedy) $792 £525

An 18th century Dutch marquetry inlaid bombe bureau veneered in mahogany, 4ft.1in. high. (Woolley & Wallis) $6,292 £4,400

Chippendale tiger maple slant top desk with fall-front, New England, circa 1780, 42in. wide. (Robt. W. Skinner Inc.) $8,250 £5,769

An early 18th century small walnut bureau. (Parsons, Welch & Cowell) $6,191 £4,100

A George I walnut bureau with later leather lined flap enclosing a fitted interior, 35½in. wide. (Christie's) $3,102 £2,200

A Queen Anne walnut bureau with fall-front and stepped fitted interior, 28¾in. wide. (Coles, Knapp & Kennedy) $10,570 £7,000

Late 18th century George III mahogany slant-top desk with fitted interior, 39in. wide. (Christie's) $4,950 £3,230

Chippendale tiger maple desk, Rhode Island, circa 1770, exterior with original worn red paint, 36in. wide. (Robt. W. Skinner Inc.) $36,000 £25,174

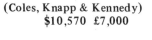

BUREAUX

A Queen Anne maple slant front desk, New England, 1750-60, 40in. wide. (Christie's) $6,050 £4,233

A cedar wood and walnut bureau, the sloping flap enclosing a fitted interior, the sides with carrying handles, 22½in. wide. (Christie's) $1,156 £756

Mid 18th century Chinese Export padoukwood bureau with four serpentine drawers, the back inscribed TH52, 39¾in. wide. (Christie's) $17,061 £12,100

An inlaid walnut slant front desk, by Thos. Cooper, Long Island, 1770, 40in. wide. (Christie's) $26,400 £18,474

A Federal mahogany eagle-inlaid slant front desk, 1790-1810, 44¾in. wide. (Christie's) $6,600 £4,618

Chippendale mahogany slant top desk on ogee bracket feet, Mass., circa 1780, 41in. wide. (Robt. W. Skinner Inc.) $6,000 £4,195

A Chippendale mahogany reverse-serpentine slant front desk, labelled by Stone and Alexander, Boston, circa 1790, 42in. wide. (Christie's) $13,200 £9,237

Late 18th century Italian satinwood and marquetry bureau, 50in. wide. (Christie's) $9,372 £6,600

A walnut bureau inlaid with feather banding, the sloping flap enclosing a fitted interior, 30in. wide. (Christie's) $1,337 £935

BUREAUX

A George I walnut bureau, the leather lined crossbanded sloping flap enclosing a fitted interior, 38in. wide. (Christie's) $15,950 £11,000

Gustav Stickley drop-front desk with cabinet doors, circa 1902-04, 32¾in. wide. (Robt. W. Skinner Inc.) $3,700 £2,587

A late George III mahogany cylinder bureau with tambour shutter enclosing a fitted interior, 42in. wide. (Christie's) $1,694 £1,100

A William and Mary burr walnut bureau, the sloping flap enclosing a fitted interior, 38¼in. wide. (Christie's) $9,251 £6,380

A George I walnut bureau, the quarter baize lined flap inlaid with chevron banding enclosing a fitted interior, 29¼in. wide. (Christie's) $13,959 £9,900

A George III mahogany bureau, the leather lined crossbanded sloping flap enclosing a fitted interior, 37in. wide. (Christie's) $1,487 £972

An early Georgian walnut and featherbanded bureau on bracket feet, 33in. wide. (Christie's) $6,048 £4,200

Federal mahogany inlaid cylinder desk on flared French feet, Maryland, circa 1790, 44in. wide. (Robt. W. Skinner Inc.) $6,000 £4,195

An early Georgian yewwood bureau with leather lined crossbanded sloping flap, 37½in. wide. (Christie's) $5,505 £3,850

Late 17th century German walnut and marquetry cabinet, 55¼in. wide. (Christie's) $1,718 £1,210

A Charles II black and gold lacquer cabinet-on-stand decorated with chinoiserie scenes, 40½in. wide. (Christie's) $20,163 £14,300

A Spanish walnut cabinet on splayed feet, 29in. wide. (Christie's) $2,030 £1,430

A William and Mary oyster-veneered walnut cabinet with fitted interior, formerly surrounding a cupboard, lacking stand, 40½in. wide. (Christie's) $1,487 £972

A William and Mary walnut, floral marquetry and inlaid cabinet-on-stand, on later supports, 1.14m. wide. (Phillips) $7,920 £5,500

A mid 17th century oak side cabinet with inset grey fossil marble top, 52½in. wide. (Christie's) $3,635 £2,376

A decorated pine side cabinet designed and painted by H. Von Herkomer, 95cm. wide. (Phillips) $2,304 £1,600

Mid 18th century French chestnut side cabinet, 49in. wide. (Christie's) $2,030 £1,430

A mahogany Chippendale style cabinet in the Gothic manner, on octagonal reeded supports, 38in. wide. (Outhwaite & Litherland) $17,255 £11,900

CABINETS

Late 17th century Portuguese rosewood sewing cabinet carved with ripple mouldings, 21½in. wide. (Christie's) $3,124 £2,200

A George III mahogany music cabinet with adjustable top, opening to reveal four sloping flaps, 26in. wide. (Christie's) $4,561 £3,190

A George I black lacquer cabinet-on-stand, 53½in. wide. (Christie's) $7,444 £5,280

A late 18th century Milanese rosewood cabinet, with quartered chevron veneered top and front, 47½in. wide. (Dreweatts) $1,160 £800

An Arts & Crafts painted cabinet and bookshelves (top missing), the figures drawn by M. Reed, 61cm. wide. (Phillips) $460 £320

A Regency brass inlaid rosewood side cabinet with mirror glazed panelled doors, 48½in. wide. (Christie's) $13,183 £9,350

A bamboo and lacquer cabinet with central mirror to the back, the door panels decorated with Chinese warriors. (Lots Road Galleries) $483 £320

A Regency rosewood dwarf cabinet with Bramah lock, 36in. wide. (Christie's) $1,318 £935

One of a pair of Regency ormolu mounted rosewood side cabinets, the doors with pleated cafe-au-lait silk ground, 19in. wide. (Christie's) $3,877 £2,750

CABINETS

One of a pair of Regency
rosewood and parcel gilt
dwarf cabinets attributed
to Wm. Marsh, 50¼in. wide.
(Christie's)
$77,550 £55,000

A 19th century gilt brass
mounted black lacquered
cabinet on stand, Japan,
32½in. wide. (Robt. W.
Skinner Inc.) $2,200 £1,527

A 17th century ormolu
mounted ebonised and
Japanese lacquer side cabinet
with red marble top, 52in.
wide. (Christie's)
$23,265 £16,500

A 19th century carved, painted
and parcel gilt cabinet, China,
44¼in. wide. (Robt. W. Skinner
Inc.) $2,100 £1,458

Grain painted pine lawyer's
cabinet, the panel doors
opening to reveal thirty-eight
compartments, New England,
circa 1800, 33in. wide. (Robt.
W. Skinner Inc.)
$2,500 £1,748

A late 17th/early 18th century Italian ebonised, tortoiseshell and gilt metal
mounted cabinet on later
stand, 2.05m. high x 1.72m.
wide. (Phillips)
$14,400 £10,000

An early Georgian walnut
cabinet in two sections
inlaid with chevron banding,
119cm. wide. (Christie's)
$44,044 £30,800

Early 20th century Jacobean
style cabinet on stand,
America, 48in. wide. (Robt.
W. Skinner Inc.) $900 £625

A Charles II oak cabinet
on square feet, 43in. wide.
(Christie's) $1,573 £1,100

CABINETS

One of a pair of Regency mahogany wall cabinets with glazed fronts, 12½in. wide. (Christie's) $2,044 £1,430

A mid Victorian ebony and ivory inlaid display cabinet of concave semi-circular shape, designed by O. Jones, 110in. wide. (Christie's) $30,294 £19,800

A late Victorian black and gilt japanned papier-mache purdonium, on later rosewood bracket feet, 18¾in. wide. (Christie's) $1,573 £1,100

One of a pair of Regency mahogany dwarf cabinets, the top crossbanded and edged with satinwood, 33in. wide. (Christie's) $32,571 £23,100

Late 19th century Russian oak cabinet, 33½in. wide, 99in. high. (Christie's) $1,598 £1,045

One of a pair of rosewood dwarf cabinets with specimen marble tops, 29½in. wide. (Christie's) $7,865 £5,500

An Italian walnut cabinet with a fall-front panel enclosing a fitted interior, the carvings late 17th century, 27¾in. wide. (Christie's) $1,874 £1,320

A Renaissance Revival inlaid rosewood cabinet, America, circa 1870, 36½in. wide. (Robt. W. Skinner Inc.) $1,900 £1,319

An ebonised and ivory inlaid side cabinet, the design attributed to T. E. Colcutt, 137cm. wide. (Phillips) $1,008 £700

A late 17th/early 18th century Chinese coromandel lacquer cabinet on carved giltwood stand, 60cm. wide. (Phillips) $1,584 £1,100

An early Victorian oak cabinet, by A. W. N. Pugin and John Webb, 52in. wide. (Christie's) $3,775 £2,640

A Swiss walnut and marquetry cistern cabinet, basically late 17th century, 31in. wide. (Christie's) $3,436 £2,420

An early Victorian oak cabinet fitted with a pair of gothic panelled doors enclosing seventeen drawers, 43¾in. wide. (Christie's) $943 £660

An Art Deco Epstein & Goldbart cocktail cabinet, mahogany veneered in sycamore, fitted interior, 60½in. high. (Christie's) $770 £500

One of a pair of Regency brass inlaid rosewood side cabinets with mottled black marble tops, 26½in. wide. (Christie's) $5,583 £3,960

Late 19th century Kinji cabinet decorated in gold hiramakie, hirame and nashiji and inlaid in Shibayama style, 20.8cm. high. (Christie's) $5,935 £4,180

A Portuguese rosewood cabinet-on-stand with five short and two long drawers, basically late 17th century, 25¼in. wide. (Christie's) $2,343 £1,650

A 19th century large dark reddish-brown nashiji cabinet, 114 x 96 x 46.5cm. (Christie's) $17,182 £12,100

CABINETS

A Queen Anne walnut and crossbanded miniature bureau on stand of a later date, 41cm. wide. (Phillips) $3,168 £2,200

Regency satinwood and ebony collector's cabinet, the ebony handles with ivory centres, 38in. wide. (Christie's) $17,061 £12,100

A mid 18th century carved mahogany breakfront china cabinet on later stand, in the Chippendale manner, 1m. wide. (Phillips) $3,900 £2,600

An early Victorian ormolu mounted ebony and pietra dura side cabinet, 43in. wide. (Christie's) $6,699 £4,620

An Italian walnut pedestal cabinet on bracket feet, 21in. wide. (Christie's) $1,405 £990

An ormolu mounted mahogany cabinet, the base with a pair of shibayama lacquer panel doors, 48¼in. wide. (Christie's) $7,177 £4,950

One of a pair of Regency ormolu mounted and parcel gilt dwarf rosewood cabinets, the doors backed with pleated green silk, 36in. wide. (Christie's) $21,714 £15,400

A scarlet and black lacquer cabinet-on-stand, the cabinet 17th century and later, 41in. wide. (Christie's) $3,190 £2,200

An Art Deco cocktail bar trolley, the bar handle flanked by two inset clear and satin glass panels by Lalique, 88cm. wide. (Christie's) $9,914 £6,480

Late 18th century George III mahogany cabinet, 63in. wide. (Christie's) $7,150 £4,666

Late 19th century pine tall cabinet, probably New York, 26½in. wide. (Christie's) $1,100 £674

A Regency ormolu mounted rosewood breakfront dwarf cabinet, the doors backed with pleated silk, 60¼in. wide. (Christie's) $13,042 £9,250

A Goanese ivory inlaid ebony cabinet-on-stand, the cabinet late 17th century, 19in. wide. (Christie's) $4,752 £2,970

An Italian ebony and pietra dura cabinet-on-stand with three-quarter balustraded gallery, 47in. wide. (Christie's) $29,920 £18,700

One of a pair of Empire ormolu mounted cabinets, 25¾in. wide. (Christie's) $11,440 £7,150

Early 17th century Tuscan walnut cabinet with moulded overhanging cornice, 64in. wide. (Christie's) $6,688 £4,180

Victorian gilt bronze and porcelain mounted walnut side cabinet, circa 1860, 59½in. wide. (Robt. W. Skinner Inc.) $1,400 £915

An Edwardian rosewood inlaid side cabinet, 54in. wide. (Peter Wilson) $1,185 £750

CANTERBURYS

Early 19th century mahogany swept top music canterbury, 22in. wide. (Dreweatts) $899 £620

Regency rosewood canterbury with rectangular top and pierced undulating splayed gallery, 27½in. wide. (Christie's) $2,481 £1,760

A George IV rosewood music canterbury, 20½in. wide. (Christie's) $2,296 £1,375

A George III satinwood canterbury, the hinged top with three-quarter gallery. (Christie's) $11,632 £8,250

Late 18th century George III mahogany canterbury, 19½in. long, 21in. high. (Robt. W. Skinner Inc.) $850 £555

A George IV mahogany and rosewood canterbury with gilt metal gallery, 51cm. wide, stamped Wilkinson. (Phillips) $6,420 £4,200

A Regency rosewood canterbury on baluster legs, 20½in. wide. (Christie's) $4,247 £2,970

A Victorian figured walnut canterbury stand, the top with three-quarter gallery, 22in. wide. (Christie's) $1,056 £660

A carved rosewood canterbury, England, circa 1875, 20½in. wide. (Robt. W. Skinner Inc.) $950 £664

DINING CHAIRS

One of a set of five Regency stained beechwood dining chairs covered with green and pink glazed chintz, and another of later date. (Christie's) $1,483 £1,045

Two of a set of seven George III design mahogany dining chairs. (Woolley & Wallis) $2,880 £2,000

One of a set of six Victorian mahogany balloon-back dining chairs with stuff over seats. (Hobbs & Chambers) $1,296 £900

A carved gilt and gesso side chair in the George I style, the vase splat depicting the child Zeus. (Phillips) $497 £350

Two of a set of six Regency period mahogany dining chairs, the padded seats covered in differing classical design needlework. (Woolley & Wallis) $3,289 £2,300

A Queen Anne carved walnut side chair, Penn., 1740-60, 40½in. high. (Christie's) $3,960 £2,560

One of an assembled set of six Chippendale maple side chairs, New England, 1760-80, 40½in. high. (Christie's) $1,980 £1,280

Two of a set of fourteen mahogany dining chairs of George III style, the seats covered in red leatherette. (Christie's) $9,123 £5,380

One of a pair of late 18th/early 19th century Dutch walnut veneered and marquetry balloon-back dining chairs in the Queen Anne taste. (Phillips) $823 £580

DINING CHAIRS

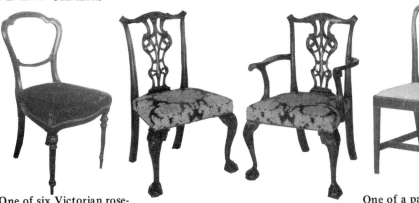

One of six Victorian rosewood balloon-back chairs
with upholstered seats.
(Reeds Rains)
$1,267 £880

Two of a set of ten George III
style mahogany dining chairs.
(Christie's) $4,089 £2,860

One of a pair of mid 18th
century George III carved
mahogany side chairs,
37¾in. high. (Christie's)
$1,760 £1,148

One of a pair of Chippendale
carved mahogany side chairs,
Phila., 1765-85, 39in. high.
(Christie's) $104,500 £68,949

Two of a set of six Stickley Bros.
dining chairs, including one
armchair, circa 1908. (Robt. W.
Skinner Inc.) $850 £594

An early Victorian child's
black, gilt and mother-of-
pearl japanned correction
chair. (Christie's)
$173 £121

One of a set of five late
Federal mahogany side chairs,
probably Phila., 1800-10,
31in. high. (Christie's)
$2,860 £1,887

Two of a set of ten mahogany
dining chairs in Georgian style,
with drop-in seats. (Woolley &
Wallis) $3,565 £2,300

A Charles Thompson, Chippendale, carved mahogany side
chair, Phila., 1765-80, 38¼in.
high, 23½in. wide. (Christie's)
$341,000 £224,991

DINING CHAIRS

One of a pair of George II mahogany dining chairs on cabriole legs and scrolled toes, 21¾in. wide. (Christie's) $8,530 £6,050

One of a pair of Louis XVI elm chaises with oval backs and serpentine seats. (Christie's) $2,343 £1,650

One of a set of five late 18th century George III mahogany shield back side chairs, 37in. high. (Robt. W. Skinner Inc.) $700 £489

One of a set of three George III mahogany dining chairs with shield-shaped backs and trailing flowerhead crestings, stamped HM. (Christie's) $3,877 £2,750

One of a set of six George III mahogany dining chairs with bowed drop-in seats covered with floral chintz. (Christie's) $8,065 £5,720

One of a set of four George III satinwood dining chairs upholstered in aubergine watered silk. (Christie's) $3,722 £2,640

One of two 19th century maple Shaker slat-back tilter chairs, Conn., 40¾in. high. (Robt. W. Skinner Inc.) $1,000 £699

One of a set of twelve grained beech frame sabre leg side chairs with brass mounts and mouldings. (Woolley & Wallis) $4,752 £3,300

A Queen Anne maple side chair, Newport, Rhode Island, 1750-65, 37¾in. high. (Christie's) $2,640 £1,847

DINING CHAIRS

One of a set of five
Dutch walnut dining chairs
with eared serpentine drop-
in seats. (Christie's)
$5,618 £3,672

One of four Louis XV carved
and cream decorated side
chairs, having bowed seats on
moulded cabriole legs.
(Phillips) $3,744 £2,600

One of a pair of cherry Queen
Anne side chairs with upholstered seats, Conn. River
Valley, circa 1750, 39¾in.
high. (Robt. W. Skinner Inc.)
$2,900 £2,027

One of a set of seven
George III mahogany dining
chairs, including a pair of
armchairs, with drop-in
seats. (Christie's)
$4,957 £3,240

One of a set of three Regency
simulated rosewood dining
chairs mounted with gilt
metal, the split-cane seat on
sabre legs. (Christie's)
$382 £264

One of a set of eight mahogany dining chairs with waved
ladder backs. (Christie's)
$3,412 £2,420

One of a set of six black
painted Windsor side chairs,
each stamped 'J. R. Hunt,
Maker', circa 1820.
(Christie's) $3,520 £2,322

One of a set of eight white painted
frame side chairs covered in late
18th/early 19th century tapestry.
(Woolley & Wallis) $5,285 £3,500

One of a pair of Chippendale
mahogany side chairs, Mass.,
1760-90, 36½in. high.
(Christie's) $17,600 £11,487

DINING CHAIRS

One of a pair of Regency mahogany hall chairs with scallop shell backs and solid moulded seats on sabrè legs. (Christie's) $1,276 £880

Two of a set of eight George III mahogany dining chairs, including two open armchairs. (Christie's) $7,444 £5,280

One of a set of six George III mahogany dining chairs with buttoned squabs covered in yellow silk. (Christie's) $3,877 £2,750

One of a set of six late Victorian ormolu mounted satinwood, mahogany and marquetry boudoir chairs. (Christie's) $3,509 £2,420

Two of a set of seven Gustav Stickley V-back dining chairs, circa 1907, 35½in. high. (Robt. W. Skinner Inc.) $2,300 £1,608

One of a pair of George IV mahogany hall chairs with gothic arched panelled backs. (Christie's) $629 £440

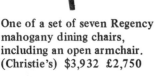

One of a set of seven Regency mahogany dining chairs, including an open armchair. (Christie's) $3,932 £2,750

Two of a set of eight William and Mary style walnut dining chairs, the legs with Spanish scroll feet. (Christie's) $1,463 £950

One of a set of eight George I walnut dining chairs, the drop-in seat covered in floral petit point needlework. (Christie's) $147,345 £104,500

DINING CHAIRS

One of a set of eight Austrian early 19th century elm dining chairs upholstered in cotton. (Christie's) $3,905 £2,750

Two of a set of eight mahogany dining chairs of mid Georgian design, including two open armchairs. (Christie's) $6,975 £4,500

Mid 17th century Italian walnut side chair, together with a walnut low table, 19in. wide. (Christie's) $1,093 £770

One of three transitional Queen Anne mahogany side chairs, Essex County, circa 1770, 38in. high. (Robt. W. Skinner Inc.) $10,000 £6,666

Two of a set of eight George III mahogany dining chairs, including two armchairs. (Christie's) $12,584 £8,800

One of a set of six Victorian walnut framed dining chairs. (Lots Road Galleries) $1,573 £1,100

One of a pair of George III mahogany dining chairs, the serpentine seats covered in close-nailed floral needlework. (Christie's) $1,861 £1,320

Two of a set of eight Chippendale design mahogany dining chairs, including two elbow chairs. (Parsons, Welch & Cowell) $3,311 £2,150

One of a pair of William and Mary walnut side chairs, covered in ivory damask, on turned baluster legs. (Christie's) $1,473 £1,045

DINING CHAIRS

One of a pair of Chippendale mahogany side chairs, Salem, circa 1770-85, 37in. high. (Christie's)
$22,000 £15,395

Two of a set of eight Regency mahogany dining chairs, including two armchairs, on sabre legs. (Christie's)
$9,814 £6,480

One of a set of six Regency ebonised and parcel gilt dining chairs with split cane seats and buttoned squabs. (Christie's) $13,370 £9,350

Shaker maple and ash side chair, Mass., circa 1850, 39¾in. high. (Robt. W. Skinner Inc.)$700 £489

Two of a set of eight Georgian mahogany dining chairs with brass inlaid cresting rails. (Graves Son & Pilcher)
$6,040 £4,000

Shaker child's maple ladder-back tilter side chair, Conn., circa 1840, 32in. high. (Robt. W. Skinner Inc.)
$1,200 £839

One of a pair of George III giltwood side chairs covered in close-nailed red damask, 35½in. high. (Christie's) $1,982 £1,296

Two of a set of fourteen George III mahogany ladderback dining chairs, including a pair of armchairs, with leather upholstered seats. (Christie's) $10,081 £7,150

One of a set of eighteen William IV mahogany side chairs, the backs and seats covered in close-nailed red leather. (Christie's)
$34,122 £24,200

DINING CHAIRS

One of a set of eight George III mahogany dining chairs, the padded seats covered in close-nailed yellow brocade. (Christie's) $13,959 £9,900

Two of a set of eight George III mahogany dining chairs with stuffed saddle seats in brass studded leather. (Dreweatts) $4,930 £3,400

One of a pair of George II mahogany side chairs, the seat covered with later petit point floral needlework. (Christie's) $8,530 £6,050

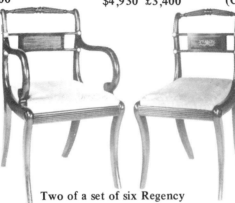

One of a set of four Victorian chairs. (Lots Road Galleries) $394 £280

Two of a set of six Regency mahogany dining chairs on sabre legs, together with a pair of arm-chairs of a later date. (Christie's) $4,957 £3,240

A carved mahogany Chippen-dale side chair, Phila., 1760-75, 24in. wide. (Christie's) $242,000 £169,351

A Louis XV beechwood chaise with close-nailed cartouche-shaped back, covered in blue cut-velvet. (Christie's) $937 £660

Two of a set of ten George III mahogany dining chairs, includ-ing two elbow chairs. (Dreweatts) $6,670 £4,600

One of a pair of George III mahogany side chairs with oval padded backs and bowed seats upholstered in pale green silk. (Christie's) $2,016 £1,430

DINING CHAIRS

One of a set of six Regency mahogany dining chairs, the toprails incised with key-pattern and ebonised. (Christie's) $5,287 £3,456

Federal mahogany inlaid shield-back side chair, Mass., circa 1800, 38¼in. high. (Robt. W. Skinner Inc.) $1,700 £1,188

One of a pair of mid Georgian mahogany dining chairs with paper scroll toprails and pierced splats. (Christie's) $2,974 £1,944

A George III mahogany dining chair with bow shaped toprail and vase shaped splat. (Christie's) $991 £648

One of a set of four 18th century painted turned slat-back side chairs, New England, 40in. high. (Robt. W. Skinner Inc.) $3,250 £2,272

A Chippendale carved walnut side chair, with shell-carved cabriole legs, Phila., 1760-80. (Christie's) $3,080 £2,155

One of a set of eight Regency mahogany dining chairs, including an open armchair, with drop-in seats. (Christie's) $4,089 £2,860

A French Art Nouveau oak dining chair, designed by C. Plumet and A. Selmersheim. (Phillips) $489 £340

One of a set of ten Regency simulated rosewood dining chairs with caned seats. (Christie's) $2,636 £1,870

DINING CHAIRS

A George III mahogany
dining chair with bowed
padded seat. (Christie's)
$1,551 £1,100

One of a pair of Queen Anne
fruitwood side chairs with
drop-in needlework seats.
(Christie's) $2,233 £1,540

One of a pair of scarlet
lacquered chairs of Queen
Anne design on cabriole
legs and pad feet.
(Christie's) $2,230 £1,458

One of a set of eight Regency
mahogany dining chairs, and
a similar pair of armchairs.
(Christie's) $3,146 £2,200

One of a set of nine George
III mahogany dining chairs
with close-nailed red leather
covered seats. (Christie's)
$13,959 £9,900

One of a set of six Regency
rosewood (part simulated)
dining chairs with brass inlaid
toprails. (Phillips)
$1,275 £850

One of a set of twelve
William IV carved mahogany
dining chairs with stuff over
seats. (Phillips)
$8,064 £5,600

One of a pair of Louis XV
beechwood chaises with
cartouche-shaped backs
and serpentine seats.
(Christie's) $1,405 £990

An Empire mahogany chaise
with padded seat covered in
green velour. (Christie's)
$437 £308

DINING CHAIRS

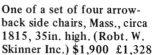

One of a pair of mid Victorian black, gilt and mother-of-pearl japanned papier-mache occasional chairs. (Christie's) $1,258 £880

Two of a set of eight William IV mahogany dining chairs, including a pair of armchairs. (Reeds Rains) $4,320 £3,000

One of a set of four arrow-back side chairs, Mass., circa 1815, 35in. high. (Robt. W. Skinner Inc.) $1,900 £1,328

A Chippendale mahogany side chair on cabriole legs, Mass., 1760-90, 38in. high. (Christie's) $2,200 £1,451

Two of a set of seven George III carved mahogany shield back dining chairs and one later copy, England, circa 1780. (Robt. W. Skinner Inc.) $6,900 £4,825

One of a set of six mid 18th century Portuguese carved hardwood dining chairs in the rococo taste. (Phillips) $4,260 £3,000

One of a pair of William and Mary bannister-back maple side chairs, New England, 1710-40. (Christie's) $1,650 £1,088

Two of a set of seven Regency mahogany dining chairs, including a pair of armchairs, and a single chair of later date. (Christie's) $4,963 £3,520

A Chippendale mahogany side chair, Mass., 1760-90, 39¼in. high. (Christie's) $1,430 £943

DINING CHAIRS

One of a set of four late George III inlaid mahogany side chairs, 34¾in. high. (Christie's) $5,500 £3,589

Two of a set of six Regency period mahogany dining chairs. (Woolley & Wallis) $2,288 £1,600

One of a set of four Victorian mahogany dining chairs with trafalgar seats. (Hobbs & Chambers) $561 £390

One of an assembled pair of 18th century 'York' maple side chairs, New England, 41in. high. (Christie's)$770 £500

Two of an assembled set of nine English, 19th century, elm and beech wheelback Windsor chairs, approx. 34in. high. (Christie's) $4,620 £3,015

One of two Shaker cherry ladder-back side chairs, New Hampshire, circa 1840. (Robt. W. Skinner Inc.) $5,250 £3,500

A Chippendale mahogany side chair on cabriole legs, probably New Jersey, 1760-90, 38¾in. high. (Christie's) $4,400 £2,903

Two of a set of five late 18th century George III elmwood dining chairs, 37in. high. (Christie's) $3,850 £2,512

One of a set of eleven Regency carved mahogany dining chairs with slip-in horsehair seats. (Phillips) $6,816 £4,800

379

EASY CHAIRS

A mid Victorian walnut open armchair, the cartouche-shaped padded back with gros and petit point needlework panel. (Christie's)
$1,276 £880

A blue PVC inflatable armchair. (Christie's)
$578 £378

A George III parcel gilt and white painted open armchair with oval back, upholstered in puce silk. (Christie's)
$1,551 £1,100

A George III mahogany open armchair covered in red velvet. (Christie's)
$1,730 £1,210

One of a pair of George III mahogany open armchairs, covered in buff linen, 23¾in. wide. (Christie's)
$5,428 £3,850

A Queen Anne style easy chair, upholstered in a red, white and blue bargello patterned fabric. (Christie's)
$1,540 £1,005

A George III mahogany library armchair with padded back, arm supports and bowed seat upholstered in maroon damask. (Christie's)
$2,636 £1,870

An early George II mahogany library armchair upholstered in floral yellow damask, on cabriole legs and scrolled feet. (Christie's)
$8,932 £6,160

A George I mahogany library armchair upholstered in white linen, on cabriole legs and pad feet. (Christie's)
$2,326 £1,650

EASY CHAIRS

One of a pair of George III grey painted open armchairs covered in pale blue watered cotton, 24in. wide. (Christie's) $2,636 £1,870

A Gothic Revival walnut chair, America, circa 1870, 39in. wide, and matching arm couch, 87in. long. (Robt. W. Skinner Inc.) $1,700 £1,180

One of a pair of Louis XVI walnut fauteuils, covered in close-nailed floral needlework. (Christie's) $2,343 £1,650

One of a pair of Chippendale style easy chairs, 50in. high. (Christie's) $2,640 £1,723

An upholstered oak armchair with cut out sides, circa 1905, 28¾in. wide. (Robt. W. Skinner Inc.) $1,000 £699

One of two George III mahogany library armchairs with padded rectangular backs, arm supports and seats. (Christie's) $4,032 £2,860

A George III mahogany open armchair, lacking upholstery. (Christie's) $1,887 £1,320

Late 18th century George III library chair on Marlborough legs, 40in. high. (Christie's) $2,860 £1,866

One of a set of four George III gilded mahogany open armchairs in the Louis XVI style. (Christie's) $13,959 £9,900

A George III parcel gilt and white painted open armchair, covered in a blue, white and grey floral brocade. (Christie's) $1,008 £715

An early George III giltwood bergere upholstered in aqua-marine silk. (Christie's) $1,163 £825

One of a pair of mid 18th century walnut open arm-chairs, possibly German. (Christie's) $6,284 £4,400

One of a pair of mahogany open armchairs covered in olive-green linen. (Christie's) $3,460 £2,420

One of a pair of early Victorian rosewood armchairs, each with a spoon-shaped back and serpen-tine seat, on cabriole legs. (Christie's) $4,712 £3,080

One of a set of six George III parcel gilt and cream painted open armchairs covered in pale green mercerised cotton. (Christie's) $32,571 £23,100

A Federal mahogany wing chair with serpentine crest, New York, 1790-1810, 47in. high. (Christie's) $825 £544

An inlaid rosewood curule-type armchair, attributed to Pottier and Stymus, circa 1870, 34in. high, 31in. wide. (Robt. W. Skinner Inc.) $1,100 £763

One of a pair of George III style wing chairs, together with a matching footstool. (Christie's) $3,080 £2,010

EASY CHAIRS

Late 18th century stained beechwood fauteuil upholstered in yellow striped cotton. (Christie's) $468 £330

A George III carved, and later gilded, elbow chair with stuffover serpentine seat. (Phillips) $426 £300

One of a pair of mid 19th century ebonised Gothic Revival armchairs, America, 57in. high. (Robt. W. Skinner Inc.) $900 £625

An early Georgian walnut wing armchair on cabriole legs and pad feet headed by shells. (Christie's) $3,722 £2,640

A George III mahogany bergere with later brass feet and castors. (Christie's) $9,438 £6,600

An early Georgian walnut wing armchair, the back and out-scrolled arms and bowed seat upholstered in floral moquette. (Christie's) $3,460 £2,420

Mid 19th century Louis XV style tapestry upholstered miniature giltwood bergere, France, 19in. wide. (Robt. W. Skinner Inc.) $2,250 £1,573

A George III mahogany dining armchair with high curved back, out-scrolled arms and squab.(Christie's) $1,887 £1,320

One of a set of six mid 18th century Italian parcel gilt and green painted open armchairs. (Christie's) $14,839 £10,450

EASY CHAIRS

One of a pair of late 18th/
early 19th century carved
hardwood fauteuils in the
Louis XV style. (Phillips)
$460 £320

A George III parcel gilt open
armchair with oval padded
back and bowed seat in sky-
blue satin. (Christie's)
$1,473 £1,045

A Regency mahogany side
chair after a design by Thos.
Hope, with buttoned scroll
back and seat in a moulded
frame. (Christie's)
$5,423 £3,740

One of a pair of George III
giltwood library armchairs,
upholstered in mustard-yellow
cut velvet. (Christie's)
$29,469 £20,900

A Chippendale period
carved mahogany library
open armchair of Gains-
borough type in the French
taste. (Phillips)
$5,700 £3,800

One of two Regency maho-
gany bergeres with caned backs,
sides and seats. (Christie's)
$10,857 £7,700

A mid Georgian mahogany
wing armchair upholstered
in pale yellow floral damask.
(Christie's) $2,313 £1,512

A Regency mahogany library
bergere upholstered in
buttoned pale green leather.
(Christie's) $2,202 £1,540

An early Georgian walnut
wing armchair with high
back, upholstered in close-
nailed scarlet velvet.
(Christie's) $7,444 £5,280

EASY CHAIRS

A walnut wing armchair with waved seat-rail on cabriole legs. (Christie's)
$3,190 £2,200

One of a pair of giltwood bergeres, covered in green floral glazed cotton, circa 1830, possibly Scandinavian. (Christie's) $2,811 £1,980

A Georgian carved and ebonised elbow chair, in the manner of John Linnell. (Phillips) $489 £340

One of two George III mahogany library armchairs with padded backs, arms and seats, one re-railed, one partly re-railed. (Christie's)
$3,304 £2,160

A William IV library armchair, the back, arms and seat upholstered in pale green leather. (Christie's)
$697 £495

A George III mahogany arm-chair of Gainsborough type, with a stuff over floral gros point needlework back and seat. (Phillips) $1,440 £1,000

A George III mahogany frame library tub-shaped bergere on ring-turned tapered legs. (Phillips)
$2,250 £1,500

A Regency beechwood bergere, on ring turned tapering legs, lacking candle arms. (Christie's)
$1,179 £825

A Queen Anne walnut wing armchair covered in cream linen on cabriole legs. (Christie's) $4,963 £3,520

EASY CHAIRS

One of a set of five George III
stripped beechwood open
armchairs. (Christie's)
$7,550 £5,280

One of a pair of Barcelona
chairs, designed by Mies
van der Rohe, with stainless
steel, X-shaped frames.
(Christie's) $1,108 £770

One of a pair of early George
III giltwood open armchairs
with cartouche shaped padded
backs, arm rests and seats.
(Christie's) $38,775 £27,500

One of a pair of giltwood
bergeres of Louis XV style,
seats covered in 18th century Beauvais tapestry.
(Christie's) $5,582 £3,850

Mid 18th century ebonised
mahogany open armchair
with high removable panel
back. (Christie's)
$5,423 £3,740

One of a pair of Louis XVI
style carved and polished
beech frame fauteuils.
(Lots Road Galleries)
$570 £380

An early George III maho-
gany open armchair after a
design by T. Chippendale.
(Christie's)
$49,632 £35,200

A Regency mahogany
reading chair with deeply
buttoned green leather
upholstery and yoke
shaped toprail. (Christie's)
$826 £540

A George III mahogany
library armchair upholstered
in needlework, partly re-
railed. (Christie's)
$6,380 £4,400

EASY CHAIRS

A Louis XVI stained beech-wood bergere, the back, seat and squab covered in plum velvet. (Christie's) $1,874 £1,320

A mid Victorian walnut folding armchair with button upholstered slung seat and back, on sabre legs. (Christie's) $957 £660

Part of a Louis XVI style salon suite of settee, six elbow chairs and two side chairs. (Lots Road Galleries) $3,600 £2,400

A mid Victorian walnut tub armchair with padded back and seat, on cabriole legs. (Christie's) $1,196 £825

One of a pair of George III giltwood open armchairs with oval padded backs and bowed seats. (Christie's) $991 £648

A parcel gilt and beechwood fauteuil of neo-classical design, on spirally-turned tapering legs. (Christie's) $2,073 £1,430

A walnut wing armchair, the seat upholstered in yellow floral damask, on shell cabriole legs and claw and ball feet. (Christie's) $1,817 £1,188

A hall porter's mahogany chair with arched buttoned olive green leather canopy seat and arms, 31in. wide. (Christie's) $3,257 £2,310

One of a pair of early George III mahogany library chairs covered in close-nailed and buttoned yellow damask. (Christie's) $37,224 £26,400

ELBOW CHAIRS

One of a pair of early George III mahogany open armchairs in the Gothic style, 23½in. wide. (Christie's)
$29,469 £20,900

Early 19th century Empire painted and parcel gilt armchair, Europe, 35in. high. (Robt. W. Skinner Inc.)
$850 £590

One of a set of nine mahogany Chippendale style open armchairs, 43in. high. (Christie's)
$5,500 £3,589

A Chippendale walnut armchair, Phila., 1760-80, 38in. high. (Christie's)
$1,430 £924

One of a set of six Regency parcel gilt, painted and simulated rosewood dining chairs, and four en suite of a later date. (Christie's) $8,179 £5,720

An American Arts & Crafts stained oak rocking chair, in the manner of David Kendal for Phoenix Furniture. (Phillips) $129 £90

A Regency mahogany bergere, the cane-filled back and arms with two pale green leather squab cushions. (Christie's)
$2,831 £1,980

Gustav Stickley revolving office chair, no. 361, circa 1904, signed with decal in a box, 28in. wide. (Robt. W. Skinner Inc.)
$1,300 £909

L. & J. G. Stickley slat-sided armchair, circa 1912, style no. 408, 26½in. diam. (Robt. W. Skinner Inc.)
$1,200 £839

ELBOW CHAIRS

A satinwood bergere of George III design with caned back, sides and seat with a rust squab cushion. (Christie's) $702 £495

A mid Victorian black, gilt and mother-of-pearl japanned papier-mache open armchair. (Christie's) $1,101 £770

A George III painted satin-wood open armchair uphol-stered in cream silk. (Christie's) $1,628 £1,155

A George III mahogany elbow chair, the drop-in seat covered in needlework. (Woolley & Wallis) $403 £280

One of a pair of early 19th century yew and elm Windsor armchairs. (Christie's) $2,340 £1,550

A George III mahogany open armchair, and another similar. (Christie's) $865 £605

One of a pair of Finimar laminated birchwood open armchairs designed by Alvar Alto. (Christie's) $2,044 £1,430

Late 19th century Victorian steer horn armchair, uphol-stered in maroon velvet, America. (Robt. W. Skinner Inc.) $1,300 £909

One of a pair of Federal style mahogany lolling chairs, 41¼in. high. (Christie's) $3,520 £2,297

ELBOW CHAIRS

A Queen Anne walnut corner chair, Penn., 1735-60, 25in. wide. (Christie's)
$3,300 £2,309

A walnut rocking chair, by G. Hunzinger, N.Y., circa 1876, 32in. high. (Robt. W. Skinner Inc.) $250 £174

One of a set of three Adam period carved giltwood elbow chairs with stuffover bowed seats. (Phillips)
$6,816 £4,800

One of a set of eight Regency carved mahogany dining chairs, including a pair of scroll arm elbow chairs. (Phillips)
$5,112 £3,600

One of a set of ten Renaissance Revival walnut dining chairs, circa 1870, 37in. high. (Robt. W. Skinner Inc.)
$1,700 £1,096

One of a set of four Regency ebonised and gilt decorated elbow chairs painted en grisaille. (Phillips)
$9,230 £6,500

A laminated mahogany armchair, circa 1900, 45in. high. (Robt. W. Skinner Inc.)
$550 £354

Fancy wicker armchair, by Heywood Bros. & Co., Mass., 39in. high. (Robt. W. Skinner Inc.) $1,300 £838

A George I carved red walnut corner chair on cabriole legs with shell pendant ornament and pointed pad feet. (Phillips) $2,272 £1,600

ELBOW CHAIRS

One of a set of three George III satinwood open armchairs with shield-shaped backs and triple bar splats. (Christie's)
$15,510 £11,000

A Bentwood rocking recliner, with adjustable back, Austria, circa 1890. (Robt. W. Skinner Inc.) $550 £354

A George IV mahogany armchair with channelled scroll back, stamped W. Hodge, 36½in. high. (Christie's)
$2,809   £1,836

One of a pair of Sheraton ebonised and gilt decorated elbow chairs with cane seats. (Phillips) $3,692 £2,600

An Adam period giltwood frame armchair with padded shield-shaped back. (Woolley & Wallis) $2,880 £2,000

One of a set of six Regency mahogany dining chairs, including one armchair inscribed Young upholsterer, 1809 Wm. Teiocks frame maker. (Christie's)
$7,975   £5,500

One of a set of four early Victorian oak open armchairs by Bell & Coupland, Preston. (Christie's)
$11,781 £7,700

One of two Dutch Colonial hardwood burgomaster chairs with drop-in seats. (Christie's) $5,467 £3,850

One of a set of twelve Regency mahogany dining chairs, including a pair of elbow chairs. (Phillips)
$6,816 £4,800

ELBOW CHAIRS

One of a set of eight
George III carved mahogany
dining chairs, including a
pair of elbow chairs.
(Phillips) $5,760 £4,000

Ash and pine bowback
Windsor armchair, New
England, circa 1780,
36½in. high. (Robt. W.
Skinner Inc.) $850 £566

A George III mahogany
open armchair with waved
toprail and pierced interlaced splat. (Christie's)
$1,196 £825

Early 19th century maho-
gany bergere on reeded
front legs. (Lots Road
Galleries) $372 £240

One of a pair of walnut
Jacobean-style high-backed
elbow chairs, carved fretwork.
(Lots Road Galleries)
$558 £360

One of a set of ten hand
carved mahogany chairs,
the backs of 16th century
design. (Lots Road
Galleries) $1,364 £880

One of a set of six Gustav
Stickley dining chairs, including
one armchair, circa 1907, 18in.
wide. (Robt. W. Skinner Inc.)
$3,200 £2,238

One of a set of eight 19th
century Anglo-Colonial carved
rosewood elbow chairs.
(Phillips) $15,120 £10,500

One of a set of eight Regency
mahogany dining chairs,
including a pair of elbow
chairs, stamped HP. (Phillips)
$5,760 £4,000

ELBOW CHAIRS

A George III mahogany 'cockpen' open armchair with pierced trelliswork back and arms. (Christie's) $1,982 £1,296

Gustav Stickley 'rabbit ear' armchair, 1901-02, signed, 41½in. high. (Robt. W. Skinner Inc.) $550 £385

A Chippendale carved mahogany elbow chair with shaped toprails, and another elbow chair of later date. (Phillips) $2,448 £1,700

An Italian Directoire white painted and parcel gilt elbow chair. (Phillips) $2,592 £1,800

One of a pair of mahogany open armchairs with cartouche-shaped, moulded solid backs, one stamped Koopman & Co. (Christie's) $4,626 £3,024

A mid Georgian mahogany open armchair, the slightly arched back with solid splat and drop-in seat. (Christie's) $578 £378

Painted bowback Windsor armchair, Connecticut, circa 1780, 38in. high. (Robt. W. Skinner Inc.) $1,400 £933

One of a set of four mahogany armchairs with leather upholstered toprails and leather seats. (Christie's) $908 £594

One of a pair of Regency mahogany Windsor armchairs with moulded scrolled toprails and spindle filled backs centred by scrolling solid splats. (Christie's) $6,380 £4,400

ELBOW CHAIRS

One of a pair of George III
mahogany armchairs with
bowed padded seats.
(Christie's) $2,016 £1,430

One of a pair of Spanish
walnut open armchairs,
partly 17th century.
(Christie's) $3,436 £2,420

One of a pair of avodire and
painted open armchairs,
each with a shield-shaped
back. (Christie's)
$4,404 £3,080

One of a pair of George III
mahogany open armchairs
with close-nailed yellow
brocade covered seats.
(Christie's) $7,755 £5,500

An Empire ormolu mounted
mahogany fauteuil, the back
and seat upholstered with
distressed silk. (Christie's)
$3,280 £2,310

One of a pair of Sheraton
style elbow chairs, the back
panels embossed with putti.
(Lots Road Galleries)
$270 £180

Gustav Stickley mahogany
bow armchair, circa 1907,
no. 336, 36in. high. (Robt.
W. Skinner Inc.)
$1,600 £1,110

A James II walnut caned
chair with cartouche
shaped back and X-framed
seat, stamped EW.
(Christie's) $826 £540

One of a pair of walnut open
armchairs of late 17th century style, covered in ivory
and plum velvet. (Christie's)
$2,811 £1,980

ELBOW CHAIRS

A George III mahogany open armchair with shield-shaped back and pierced splat. (Christie's) $2,831 £1,980

Late 17th century Flemish elm and beechwood open armchair covered in floral needlework. (Christie's) $937 £660

One of a set of eight Regency mahogany dining chairs, including a pair of elbow chairs. (Phillips) $4,050 £2,700

One of a set of six George III carved mahogany dining chairs in the Sheraton taste, including one elbow chair. (Phillips) $2,850 £1,900

An Arts & Crafts inlaid oak elbow chair, the central back splat inlaid with a flower motif in pewter and wood. (Phillips) $172 £120

An early 19th century Russian birch open armchair with pigskin covered seat. (Christie's) $2,343 £1,650

Part of a suite of Scandinavian cream and green painted furniture in the revived neo-classical style, circa 1880. (Christie's) $3,905 £2,750

A carved walnut armchair, by G. Hunzinger, N.Y., circa 1869, 32¾in. high. (Robt. W. Skinner Inc.) $400 £279

A mid Victorian open armchair of Gothic style with drop-in seat. (Christie's) $1,473 £1,045

ELBOW CHAIRS

An early 18th century
German giltwood fauteuil,
the back and seat upholstered
in patterned cut-velvet.
(Christie's) $1,874 £1,320

One of a set of seven George
III mahogany dining chairs
in the Hepplewhite taste,
including one elbow chair.
(Phillips) $3,300 £2,200

Late 18th century Italian
green painted and parcel
gilt armchair, upholstered
in green and white striped
silk. (Christie's) $781 £550

A bowback Windsor armchair
with saddle seat, New England,
circa 1780, 37¼in. high.
(Robt. W. Skinner Inc.)
        $2,600 £1,818

One of a pair of oak Bentwood open armchairs, each
bearing a label 'Patent Pending
25597/1932, Regd Design 781,
637. (Phillips) $489 £340

A George III beechwood
open armchair with oval
padded back and bowed
seat, formerly caned.
(Christie's) $743 £486

L. & J. G. Stickley tall back
armchair, with spring cushion
seat, no. 837, circa 1907,
44in. high. (Robt. W. Skinner
Inc.) $500 £350

One of a pair of Regency
simulated bronze and parcel
gilt bergeres after a design
by George Smith, 24in. wide.
(Christie's) $80,652 £57,200

One of a set of six Wiener
Werkstatte black stained
limed oak dining chairs,
designed by J. Hoffmann.
(Christie's)
        $25,344 £17,600

ELBOW CHAIRS

One of a pair of Dutch mahogany and marquetry open armchairs, together with a double chairback settee. (Christie's) $3,905 £2,750

One of a set of twelve Chippendale style carved mahogany armchairs, 39½in. high. (Christie's)
$15,400 £10,051

A mahogany open armchair of George I design, with leather upholstered seat. (Christie's) $1,551 £1,100

One of a pair of parcel gilt and green painted open armchairs. (Christie's)
$1,171 £825

An American Arts & Crafts oak reclining chair with reclining mechanism, in the manner of A. H. Davenport of Boston. (Phillips)
$216 £150

One of a pair of George III cream and brown painted open armchairs, the caned seat with squab cushion. (Christie's) $4,342 £3,080

An early Georgian walnut open armchair, the back and seat covered in yellow damask. (Christie's) $2,831 £1,980

A late 18th/early 19th century ash and elm chair with wide seat and turned legs. (Dreweatts) $986 £680

One of a pair of George III mahogany library armchairs covered in close-nailed blue suede. (Christie's)
$23,265 £16,500

CHESTS-OF-DRAWERS

A George III mahogany chest with later rectangular top, 47in. wide. (Christie's) $1,258 £880

Mid 18th century Italian walnut and marquetry chest inlaid with scrolling foliage, 57in. wide. (Christie's) $3,748 £2,640

A Federal mahogany veneered bowfront chest-of-drawers, on bracket feet, circa 1805-20, 41½in. wide. (Christie's) $3,080 £2,155

A Federal mahogany bow-front chest-of-drawers, Mass., 1800-15, 40¾in. wide. (Christie's) $1,100 £725

Victorian satinwood and mahogany chest with poker-work inlay. (Lots Road Galleries) $620 £400

A Federal inlaid cherrywood chest-of-drawers, probably New Hampshire, 1800-10, 38in. wide. (Christie's) $4,180 £2,757

A Federal inlaid mahogany and maple veneered chest-of-drawers, probably Boston, 1800-15, 43¾in. wide. (Christie's) $5,500 £3,628

A George III mahogany veneered serpentine chest-of-drawers on French feet, 37in. wide. (Christie's) $2,200 £1,435

A late Federal grain painted chest-of-drawers, Mass., 1810-30, 41in. wide. (Christie's) $4,400 £2,903

CHESTS-OF-DRAWERS

A Chippendale mahogany reverse serpentine chest-of-drawers, Mass., 1760-90, 41½in. wide. (Christie's) $9,900 £6,532

An American mahogany upright chest, the top with brass spindle half gallery, 28in. wide. (Christie's) $1,101 £770

A Queen Anne walnut chest, the drawers with brass drop handles, on bun feet, 3ft.7in. wide. (Hobbs & Chambers) $786 £550

A Victorian walnut chest, the drawers with wood knob handles, 3ft.11in. wide. (Hobbs & Chambers) $343 £240

Wellington chest in three sections, with side locking stiles and carrying handles to each section. (Lots Road Galleries) $1,440 £1,000

A Regency satinwood inlaid mahogany chest-of-drawers, 47in. wide. (Robt. W. Skinner Inc.) $750 £520

Classical Revival mahogany and mahogany veneer bureau, circa 1815, 48in. wide. (Robt. W. Skinner Inc.) $2,700 £1,800

A mahogany chest with serpentine front eared top and on spreading ogee bracket feet, 40½in. wide. (Christie's) $3,460 £2,420

A Federal cherry bowfront bureau, circa 1790, 40in. wide. (Robt. W. Skinner Inc.) $2,400 £1,548

CHESTS-OF-DRAWERS

A Chippendale pine chest-of-drawers, New England, 1760-80, 40in. wide. (Christie's) $880 £569

A Chippendale mahogany chest-of-drawers, New England, 1780-1800, 33½in. wide. (Christie's) $4,620 £3,015

A Jacobean style oak and walnut chest fitted with four long drawers, 41in. wide. (Christie's) $1,415 £990

A Federal cherrywood serpentine chest-of-drawers, New England, 1790-1810, 42in. wide. (Christie's) $4,620 £3,048

A Chippendale walnut tall chest-of-drawers on ogee bracket feet, Penn., 1760-90, 43in. wide. (Christie's) $3,300 £2,177

A George I burr walnut bachelor's chest with cross-banded double hinged top, 34in. wide. (Christie's) $29,469 £20,900

A 19th century mahogany campaign chest, the drawers with brass inset handles, 3ft. wide. (Hobbs & Chambers) $1,008 £700

A William and Mary painted pine blanket chest, Conn., 1720-40, 41in. wide. (Christie's) $9,350 £6,169

A Federal inlaid mahogany bowfront chest-of-drawers, New Hampshire, 1790-1810, 40in. wide. (Christie's) $6,600 £4,307

CHESTS-OF-DRAWERS

A Queen Anne walnut, cross-banded and featherstrung bachelor's chest, on bracket feet, 71cm. wide. (Phillips) $7,810 £5,500

A William and Mary marquetry and oyster walnut chest, 39in. wide. (Christie's)$7,865 £5,500

A Chippendale mahogany chest-of-drawers, New England, 1760-80, 42in. wide. (Christie's) $2,420 £1,579

A Louis Philippe mahogany, marble top chest-of-drawers, circa 1840, 44½in. wide. (Robt. W. Skinner Inc.) $600 £416

Chippendale walnut tall chest-of-drawers with old brass pulls, Penn., circa 1780, 38in. wide. (Robt. W. Skinner Inc.) $4,000 £2,666

A late 17th century oak chest with four long graduated drawers on side runners, 3ft. 2in. wide. (Woolley & Wallis) $772 £540

Federal mahogany and mahogany veneer bowfront chest-of-drawers, New England, circa 1800, 41in. wide.) (Robt. W. Skinner Inc.) $1,500 £1,000

Mid 19th century Napoleon III carved mahogany chest-of-drawers, 51½in. wide. (Robt. W. Skinner Inc.) $450 £312

An early George III mahogany chest on later ogee bracket feet, 31½in. wide. (Christie's) $2,030 £1,430

CHESTS-OF-DRAWERS

Chippendale four-drawer maple chest, New England, circa 1780, 36in. wide. (Robt. W. Skinner Inc.)
$900 £620

Late 19th century wood tansu in two parts, 118.5cm. wide. (Christie's)
$1,405 £990

A George III mahogany chest of four long graduated drawers, 31in. wide. (Christie's) $2,202 £1,540

A George III mahogany chest with four graduated long drawers on ogee bracket feet, 38in. wide. (Christie's) $1,982 £1,296

Chippendale tiger maple chest, New England, circa 1780, 37in. wide. (Robt. W. Skinner Inc.)
$6,500 £4,545

A Federal inlaid mahogany bowfront chest-of-drawers, Massa., 1795-1810, 42in. wide. (Christie's)
$1,650 £1,154

Child's Empire stencil decorated chest-of-drawers, New England, circa 1820, 17¾in. wide. (Robt. W. Skinner Inc.)
$950 £664

An unusual George III mahogany bachelor's chest with twelve short drawers, 39¼in. wide. (Christie's)
$4,785 £3,300

A George III mahogany campaign secretaire chest with crossbanded top above a fall-front writing drawer, 34in. wide. (Christie's)
$2,831 £1,980

CHESTS-OF-DRAWERS

A George III satinwood bow-fronted chest, the top cross-banded with rosewood, 42in. wide. (Christie's)
$15,510   £11,000

Decorated blanket chest, Albany County, N.Y., circa 1840, 41¾in. wide. (Robt. W. Skinner Inc.)
$9,000   £6,293

Shaker birch chest-of-drawers, probably New England, circa 1840, 38½in. wide. (Robt. W. Skinner Inc.) $1,100   £769

An oak Norfolk style chest-of-drawers with brass handles and escutcheons, 30in. wide. (Worsfolds) $2,340   £1,550

George III mahogany chest-of-drawers with replaced bail handles, England, circa 1770, 46¼in. wide. (Robt. W. Skinner Inc.) $500   £349

A George III mahogany bow-fronted chest of four graduating drawers, 27¾in. wide. (Christie's) $3,146   £2,200

George III mahogany chest-of-drawers with writing slide, England, circa 1770, 37¼in. wide. (Robt. W. Skinner Inc.)
$2,800   £1,958

An early Georgian burr walnut chest with four crossbanded graduated drawers, 26in. wide. (Christie's) $22,022   £15,400

Federal mahogany inlaid bow-front chest-of-drawers, N.Y., circa 1790, 41¼in. wide. (Robt. W. Skinner Inc.)
$2,200   £1,538

FURNITURE

A George II mahogany chest with four graduated long drawers, 30in. wide. (Christie's) $2,044 £1,430

Chippendale cherry serpentine chest-of-drawers with old brasses, Conn., circa 1780, 34½in. wide. (Robt. W. Skinner Inc.) $6,000 £4,000

A walnut and oyster-veneered chest decorated and inlaid with boxwood lines, part 18th century, 37in. wide. (Christie's) $3,542 £2,300

A George III mahogany serpentine chest, with writing slide and four graduated long drawers, 37in. wide. (Christie's) $1,982 £1,296

A William and Mary walnut and seaweed marquetry chest-on-stand, on later bun feet, 98cm. wide. (Phillips) $3,456 £2,400

A George III mahogany serpentine chest with four graduated long drawers, 40in. wide. (Christie's) $6,514 £4,620

Chippendale cherry chest-of-drawers with five thumb-moulded drawers, 38¼in. wide, circa 1790. (Robt. W. Skinner Inc.) $1,400 £933

A Chippendale blue painted maple chest-of-drawers, New England, circa 1780-1810, 41½in. wide. (Christie's) $5,500 £3,848

Painted Country Chippendale chest-of-drawers, New England, 36½in. wide. (Robt. W. Skinner Inc.) $2,500 £1,666

FURNITURE

A George III mahogany serpentine fronted chest-of-drawers with chased brass handles, 36½in. wide. (Dreweatts) $4,205 £2,900

A Chippendale mahogany serpentine chest, the top containing a brushing slide, 1.03m. wide. (Phillips) $2,850 £1,900

A mahogany bachelor's chest with crossbanded rounded rectangular top, basically 18th century, 30in. wide. (Christie's) $20,735 £14,300

George II mahogany bachelor's chest, the top with a baize-lined dressing slide, 31in. wide. (Christie's) $1,914 £1,320

A late Georgian mahogany bowfront chest crossbanded and inlaid with boxwood lines, 36in. wide. (Christie's) $725 £500

A bachelor's walnut chest with crossbanded hinged top, 31in. wide. (Christie's) $2,946 £2,090

Federal mahogany inlaid bowfront chest with original brass pulls, circa 1790, 40in. wide. (Robt. W. Skinner Inc.) $2,300 £1,608

Chippendale walnut inlaid tall chest, Penn., 1805, 39in. wide. (Robt. W. Skinner Inc.) $5,000 £3,496

Federal bird's-eye maple and birch chest-of-drawers, probably New Hampshire, circa 1820, 37¾in. wide. (Robt. W. Skinner Inc.) $1,600 £1,118

CHESTS-ON-CHESTS

A George III mahogany tallboy on ogee bracket feet, 43¾in. wide. (Christie's) $3,877 £2,750

An early George II mahogany tallboy, the base with three graduated long drawers on bracket feet, 41¼in. wide. (Christie's) $2,359 £1,650

A mid Georgian mahogany tallboy on ogee bracket feet, 44in. wide, 73in. high. (Christie's) $1,982 £1,296

A George I walnut tallboy with moulded cornice, 45½in. wide. (Christie's) $7,975 £5,500

An early Georgian walnut tallboy on later bracket feet, 41½in. wide. (Christie's) $7,975 £5,500

A mid Georgian walnut secretaire-tallboy with later back, 41½in. wide. (Christie's) $4,131 £2,700

A Chippendale maple chest-on-chest, in two parts, probably New Hampshire, 1760-90, 38½in. wide.(Christie's) $13,200 £8,709

A Chippendale inlaid walnut tall chest-of-drawers, Penn., 1760-90, 44½in. wide. (Christie's) $3,520 £2,322

A George III mahogany secretaire tallboy, 42½in. wide, 72½in. high. (Christie's) $2,988 £2,090

CHESTS-ON-CHESTS

An early Georgian walnut and oak tallboy on bracket feet, 41½in. wide. (Christie's) $2,809 £1,836

A Chippendale maple chest-on-chest, in two parts, New England, 1760-90, 37½in. wide. (Christie's) $26,400 £17,418

A Queen Anne walnut tallboy with chamfered cavetto cornice, 42in. wide. (Christie's) $32,571 £23,100

Chippendale cherry flat top chest-on-chest, Conn., circa 1770, 38¼in. wide. (Robt. W. Skinner Inc.) $11,500 £7,666

A Queen Anne cherrywood high chest-of-drawers, in two sections, New England, 1740-60, 71½in. high. (Christie's) $11,000 £7,697

George III carved mahogany chest-on-chest, England, circa 1770, 42in. wide. (Robt. W. Skinner Inc.) $1,700 £1,188

A George III mahogany tallboy with key-pattern cornice, 44½in. wide. (Christie's) $2,831 £1,980

Late 18th century George III inlaid mahogany chest-on-chest, England, 44½in. wide. (Robt. W. Skinner Inc.) $2,200 £1,538

One of a pair of figured walnut tallboys inlaid with feather-banding, possibly German, 41¼in. wide. (Christie's) $13,959 £9,900

CHESTS-ON-STANDS

A Queen Anne burr walnut chest-on-stand with feather banded top, 40¾in. wide. (Christie's) $3,460 £2,420

A Queen Anne mahogany high chest-of-drawers in two sections, Boston, circa 1755, 38in. wide. (Christie's)$46,200 £30,154

A Queen Anne walnut chest-on-stand inlaid with fruitwood compass medallions, 42in. wide. (Christie's) $2,478 £1,620

A William and Mary style burr walnut veneered chest-on-stand inlaid with geometric chequered boxwood lines, 44in. wide. (Christie's) $2,156 £1,400

A William and Mary walnut and marquetry chest-on-stand, 38½in. wide. (Christie's) $3,828 £2,640

A William and Mary kingwood oyster veneered and rosewood banded chest-on-stand, the stand circa 1840, 49½in. wide. (Christie's) $4,785 £3,300

A George I pale walnut chest-on-stand, on cabriole legs and pad feet, the stand partly re-veneered and with replaced back, 39¼in. wide. (Christie's) $2,313 £1,512

A Queen Anne maple and walnut chest-on-frame, in two sections, N.Y. State, 1740-80, 38¼in. wide. (Christie's) $8,250 £5,773

A Queen Anne inlaid walnut high chest-of-drawers, in two sections, Mass., 1730-40, 39¼in. wide. (Christie's) $49,500 £32,660

CHESTS-ON-STANDS

A Chippendale walnut high chest-of-drawers on stand, Penn., 1760-90, 43in. wide. (Christie's) $17,600 £11,612

Queen Anne walnut and maple highboy on four cabriole legs, New England, circa 1770, 38in. wide. (Robt. W. Skinner Inc.) $13,000 £9,090

A Queen Anne walnut chest-on-stand with two short and three graduated long drawers, 40in. wide. (Christie's) $9,570 £6,600

A walnut chest-on-stand, the cupboard door enclosing a fitted interior, flanked by six drawers, 37½in. wide. (Christie's) $1,735 £1,134

An Anglo-Dutch early 18th century walnut and inlaid chest-on-stand. (Parsons, Welch & Cowell) $785 £520

A William and Mary walnut chest-on-stand with two short and three long graduated drawers, 38½in. wide. (Christie's) $1,887 £1,320

A Queen Anne cherrywood high chest-of-drawers, Long Island, 1735-70, 40½in. wide. (Christie's) $11,000 £7,179

A Queen Anne style walnut veneered highboy on hipped cabriole legs with Spanish type feet, England, 62¼in. high. (Robt. W. Skinner Inc.) $1,400 £979

A George I walnut and elm chest-on-stand, 38½in. wide. (Christie's) $2,988 £2,090

One of a pair of late Victorian ebonised chiffoniers banded with amboyna, 35¾in. wide. (Christie's) $3,190 £2,200

A rococo Revival rosewood veneered etagere, America, circa 1860, 51in. wide. (Robt. W. Skinner Inc.) $1,300 £909

A Regency period mahogany chiffonier, the drawers with brass knob handles, 3ft.3in. wide. (Woolley & Wallis) $2,867 £1,850

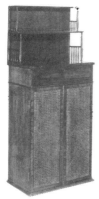

A Regency mahogany chiffonier, the two-tiered superstructure with baluster supports and gallery, 24in. wide. (Christie's) $2,552 £1,760

A mid 19th century rosewood secretaire chiffonier of reverse breakfront form, 7ft.2in. wide. (Parsons, Welch & Cowell) $2,233 £1,450

A Regency rosewood secretaire chiffonier with shelf and mirror superstructure, 27in. wide. (Graves Son & Pilcher) $987 £650

A George IV rosewood chiffonier, the shelved back inset with a mirror plate, 44in. wide. (Christie's) $1,309 £850

A Renaissance Revival walnut carved sideboard, the panelled back with two oval mirrors, possibly New York, circa 1860, 89½in. high. (Robt. W. Skinner Inc.) $3,300 £2,129

Early 19th century rosewood chiffonier with two frieze drawers above two panelled doors. (Lots Road Galleries) $703 £460

George III mahogany tray-top night cupboard, 1ft.8in. wide. (Hobbs & Chambers) $800 £500

One of a pair of late 18th century North Italian, Milanese, walnut and ivory bedside commodes, 24¼in. wide. (Christie's) $17,600 £11,000

A George III mahogany bedside commode with rectangular tray top, 21in. wide. (Christie's) $1,108 £660

A Biedermeier mahogany pedestal cupboard with D-shaped top and frieze drawer above a cupboard door and base drawer, 23½in. wide. (Christie's) $1,056 £660

A pair of walnut bedside tables with rectangular tops and waved three-quarter galleries, 16¼in. wide. (Christie's) $3,896 £2,420

A Biedermeier mahogany pedestal cabinet, the swivelling door enclosing three shelves, 25½in. wide. (Christie's) $1,056 £660

A Renaissance Revival walnut demi-commode, 20in. wide. (Robt. W. Skinner Inc.) $750 £483

A set of Regency mahogany bedside steps with three leather lined treads, a door and a drawer, 28½in. wide. (Christie's) $1,839 £1,210

Table de nuit, Continental brass inlaid with a drawer, cupboard and marble top, 1ft.8in. wide. (Lots Road Galleries) $672 £420

COMMODE CHESTS

A George III mahogany serpentine commode, 50½in. wide. (Christie's) $8,530 £6,050

An 18th century Dutch coromandel and satinwood veneered serpentine commode of slight bombe outline, 1.20m. wide. (Phillips) $2,272 £1,600

An 18th century Maltese walnut veneered serpentine commode, 5ft.5in. wide. (Woolley & Wallis) $1,860 £1,200

A late 18th century walnut crossbanded and parquetry demi-lune commode in the Louis XVI taste, 1.04m. wide, possibly Italian. (Phillips) $5,814 £3,800

A D-shaped figured oak commode with two pannelled doors on gadrooned bun feet, 41½in. wide. (Christie's) $1,500 £1,000

A George III mahogany veneered demi-lune commode, crossbanded, 3ft.7in. wide. (Woolley & Wallis) $1,208 £800

A Dutch mahogany and marquetry commode of bombe form with shaped serpentine top, 35in. wide. (Christie's) $5,632 £3,520

A 20th century inlaid fruit-wood demi-lune commode, with semi-circular variegated onyx top, 48in. wide. (Robt. W. Skinner Inc.) $1,200 £833

A Dutch ormolu mounted mahogany and marquetry commode on cabriole legs. (Christie's) $4,928 £3,080

COMMODE CHESTS

An ormolu mounted king-wood commode of Louis XV style with serpentine breccia marble top, 48in. wide. (Christie's) $2,871 £1,980

An ormolu mounted king-wood and marquetry commode of Louis XVI design, with breakfront Carrara marble top, stamped five times Wassmus, 50in. wide. (Christie's) $5,104 £3,520

A Dutch mahogany and marquetry commode on later feet, 49in. wide. (Christie's) $6,560 £4,620

A Kingwood breakfront commode with later eared white marble top, basically late 18th century, 37½in. wide. (Christie's) $3,124 £2,200

A George III mahogany small commode, the serpentine top geometrically veneered and crossbanded, 29½in. wide. (Christie's) $8,870 £5,280

A 19th century French parquetry inlaid commode cabinet, 2ft.2½in. wide. (Geering & Colyer) $403 £280

Mid 18th century Portuguese rosewood commode of serpentine outlines with box-wood stringing, 51in. wide. (Christie's) $4,686 £3,300

Late Empire figured maho-gany marble top commode, circa 1830, 47¾in. wide. (Robt. W. Skinner Inc.) $1,100 £763

Late 17th century Italian rosewood commode profusely inlaid with ivory, mother-of-pearl and pewter, 60in. wide. (Christie's) $7,029 £4,950

CORNER CUPBOARDS

A Federal walnut corner cupboard, probably Kentucky, 1800-20, 50in. wide. (Christie's) $2,860 £1,754

George III mahogany bow-front corner cabinet, 44in. high. (Lots Road Galleries) $604 £420

A 19th century Continental painted corner cupboard, 81in. high, 41in. wide. (Christie's) $3,850 £2,512

George III mahogany standing corner cupboard, 36in. wide. (Reeds Rains) $694 £460

A George III mahogany encoignure in the Louis XV style, of bombe shape with serpentine top, 30½in. wide. (Christie's) $9,861 £6,050

A satinwood and mahogany inlaid bowfront display cabinet, 31in. wide. (Christie's) $968 £605

George III inlaid mahogany bow-fronted corner cupboard, 2ft.7in. wide. (Hobbs & Chambers) $832 £520

An Edwardian Sheraton design bowfront standing corner cupboard, 29in. wide. (Lalonde Fine Art) $2,604 £1,550

An early Georgian walnut hanging cupboard, the panelled door enclosing shaped shelves. (Christie's) $2,217 £1,320

CORNER CUPBOARDS

Federal pine corner cupboard, possibly Penn., circa 1820, 56in. wide. (Robt. W. Skinner Inc.)
$2,100 £1,400

A Chippendale pine hanging corner cupboard, Penn., 1760-85, 46in. high, 26½in. wide. (Christie's)
$1,430 £1,000

Grain painted pine and poplar corner cupboard, possibly Pennsylvania, circa 1830, 83in. high, 55½in. wide. (Robt. W. Skinner Inc.)
$3,500 £2,187

A George III style mahogany standing corner display cabinet inlaid with urns, 33½in. wide. (Christie's)
$1,280 £800

An early Georgian oak hanging cupboard, 22in. wide. (Christie's)
$702 £418

One of a pair of 19th century N. Italian marquetry and walnut bowfront corner cabinets, 2.45m. high, 82cm. wide. (Phillips) $9,180 £6,000

A mahogany inlaid corner cupboard with glazed astragal door. (Dee & Atkinson) $392 £260

A mid Georgian oak corner cupboard, 40in. wide, 86½in. high. (Christie's)
$3,511 £2,090

George III oak corner cupboard on stand with original brass fittings. (Hobbs & Chambers)
$328 £230

CUPBOARDS

An early George III maho-
gany bedside cupboard,
22in. wide. (Christie's)
$1,861 £1,320

A 17th century oak cupboard,
38in. wide. (Christie's)
$4,804 £2,860

A small oak court cupboard,
basically early 17th century,
27½in. wide. (Christie's)
$11,088 £6,600

A Georgian mahogany linen
press with dentilled moulded
cornice, 4ft. wide. (Parsons,
Welch & Cowell)
$1,760 £1,100

A 16th/17th century Spanish
walnut cupboard with two
pairs of panelled doors, 37½in.
wide. (Christie's) $4,250 £2,530

Country Federal walnut step-
back cupboard, circa 1820,
46in. wide, 85½in. high.
(Robt. W. Skinner Inc.)
$1,900 £1,187

A 19th century American
pine step-back cupboard,
54 in. wide. (Christie's)
$2,090 £1,351

An oak and fruitwood food
cupboard inlaid with geo-
metric lozenge patterns, late
16th/early 17th century,
35¾in. wide. (Christie's)
$7,022 £4,180

Federal cherry and mahogany
veneer mantel cupboard,
Penn., circa 1820, 13½in.
wide. (Robt. W. Skinner Inc.)
$750 £468

CUPBOARDS

A Spanish elm cupboard with two doors pierced with gothic lancets, 25in. wide. (Christie's) $8,870 £5,280

A George III mahogany bedside cupboard on square moulded legs, 21in. wide. (Christie's) $1,258 £880

A walnut court cupboard, in the manner of A. W. Pugin, 147cm. wide. (Christie's) $1,267 £880

An 18th century carved pine tall cupboard on replaced ball feet, 44in. wide. (Robt. W. Skinner Inc.) $1,000 £699

An oak cupboard, partly 16th century with restorations, 35in. wide. (Christie's) $6,468 £3,850

One of a pair of Austrian oak and leaded glass cupboards, 197.9cm. high, 103.6cm. wide. (Christie's) $1,226 £858

Two-part poplar cupboard, the drawers with brass bail handles, New Jersey, circa 1810, 45in. wide. (Robt. W. Skinner Inc.) $2,700 £1,800

Painted pine chimney cupboard, Mass., circa 1810, 25in. wide, 78in. high. (Robt. W. Skinner Inc.) $5,700 £3,986

Early 19th century oak, mahogany cupboard on bracket feet, 50in. wide. (Peter Wilson) $423 £300

DAVENPORTS

A George IV rosewood veneered davenport, the sliding top with a pierced brass gallery, 19.5in. wide. (Woolley & Wallis)
$1,389 £920

A mid Victorian mahogany davenport of gothic style, 30in. wide. (Christie's)
$3,825 £2,640

A Victorian walnut davenport, with fret gallery above a writing slide and two small drawers, four side drawers, 22in. wide. (Dreweatts)
$2,218 £1,450

Victorian rosewood davenport, sloping top, fitted interior and four drawers. (Hobbs & Chambers) $1,113 £700

Victorian ebonised davenport with maple banding and incised decoration. (Lots Road Galleries) $474 £310

Mid 19th century Victorian burl walnut davenport desk, 23in. wide. (Robt. W. Skinner Inc.) $800 £522

A Victorian burr walnut veneered piano top davenport with fitted interior, 22in. wide. (Woolley & Wallis)
$2,004 £1,200

A 19th century Irish inlaid yew davenport with fitted interior, 25½in. wide. (Reeds Rains)
$3,168 £2,200

A Regency rosewood davenport with three-quarter gilt metal gallery and leather lined flap, 20½in. wide. (Christie's) $3,542 £2,200

DAVENPORTS

A rosewood and marquetry inlaid davenport, in the manner of T. Turner of Manchester. (Geering & Colyer)
$1,144 £800

Victorian carved and brass inlaid mahogany davenport desk, America, 19th century, 29¼in. wide. (Robt. W. Skinner Inc.) $1,100 £674

A 19th century Burmese carved teak davenport, 26in. wide. (Dacre, Son & Hartley)
$775 £500

A Regency mahogany davenport with sliding leather lined sloping flap, enclosing a fitted interior, 20in. wide. (Christie's) $6,353 £4,180

Early Victorian burr walnut davenport with sliding top, after a design by W. Smee & Sons, London, circa 1850, 1ft.10in. wide. (Capes, Dunn & Co.) $3,024 £1,800

A Victorian walnut davenport, with pierced brass gallery and rising surface, 2ft.10in. wide. (Geering & Colyer)
$1,185 £775

An early Victorian rosewood davenport with pierced three-quarter gallery, with Bramah locks, 21¼in. wide. (Christie's) $3,326 £1,980

A mid Victorian burr walnut davenport with serpentine piano lid, 39in. wide. (Locke & England)
$1,800 £1,250

A George IV pollard oak davenport with three-quarter pierced brass gallery and leather lined flap, 19½in. wide. (Christie's) $2,674 £1,870

DISPLAY CABINETS

An Art Nouveau inlaid mahogany vitrine, 114.7cm. wide. (Christie's) $1,074 £702

A mid Victorian ormolu mounted figured walnut side cabinet, 72in. wide. (Christie's) $5,049 £3,300

An Art Nouveau mahogany display cabinet in Scottish style, with bevelled mirror top above a single leaded glass door, 54in. wide. (Christie's) $1,001 £650

A Louis XIV fruitwood and walnut cabinet with later moulded cornice, possibly German, 29in. wide. (Christie's) $4,928 £3,080

An Edwardian mahogany display cabinet in two parts with swan-neck pediment, blind fret carving and urn finials. (Lots Road Galleries) $1,887 £1,250

One of a pair of ormolu mounted tulipwood display cabinets, 21¾in. wide, 57½in. high. (Christie's) $7,337 £5,060

A mid Victorian oak and marquetry cabinet, 55in. wide, 85in. high. (Christie's) $3,828 £2,640

A Louis Majorelle Art Nouveau walnut and rosewood vitrine, 188cm. high. (Phillips) $3,744 £2,600

Late 18th century Dutch walnut and marquetry display cabinet, 60in. wide. (Christie's) $17,182 £12,100

DISPLAY CABINETS

A 19th century Chinese hardwood display cabinet, 32in. wide. (Woolley & Wallis) $883 £570

An Edwardian satinwood and marquetry china cabinet in the Sheraton taste, 1.10m. wide. (Phillips) $5,760 £4,000

An English Art Nouveau mahogany display cabinet with bevelled mirror back, 71in. high x 53in. wide. (Christie's) $1,479 £980

A Christopher Pratt & Sons inlaid mahogany display cabinet, 192.6cm. high. (Christie's) $1,262 £825

A scarlet boulle and ebonised breakfront vitrine cabinet, 64in. wide. (Christie's) $3,509 £2,420

Late 18th century Louis XVI carved and painted demi-lune vitrine, France, 27½in. wide. (Robt. W. Skinner Inc.) $1,400 £972

An ormolu mounted kingwood vitrine cabinet with serpentine breccia marble top, 35in. wide. (Christie's) $2,871 £1,980

One of a pair of mid Victorian ormolu mounted satinwood side cabinets, 36in. wide. (Christie's) $4,342 £3,080

A mahogany serpentine front standing corner cabinet with astragal glazed upper section, on ogee bracket feet, 194cm. high. (Osmond Tricks) $928 £580

DRESSERS

An early Georgian oak high dresser, the moulded cornice with three shelves on shaped trestle supports, 61 in. wide. (Christie's) $11,088 £6,600

Late 18th/early 19th century oak shelf rack, 41in.wide. (Peter Wilson) $758 £480

Late 18th century oak three-drawer dresser with rack, 74in. long. (Peter Wilson) $2,054 £1,300

Mid 18th century George II oak Welsh dresser, 58½in. long. (Robt. W. Skinner Inc.) $2,700 £1,764

A carved oak Victorian dresser with three drawers in base, 6ft.2in. wide. (Jacobs & Hunt) $800 £500

Late 18th century oak, mahogany banded dresser with rack, 72in. wide. (Peter Wilson) $1,480 £1,050

A Charles II oak low dresser, 88½in. wide. (Christie's) $14,784 £8,800

An oak Welsh dresser on square tapering legs, 6ft. wide. (Woolley & Wallis) $2,736 £1,900

An oak low dresser, the frieze with three fielded drawers, 71½in. wide. (Christie's) $2,956 £1,760

DUMB WAITERS

A late Georgian mahogany two-tier dumb waiter, 41½in. high. (Christie's) $924 £550

A Regency ormolu mounted mahogany dumb waiter, 27in. diam., 42¾in. high. (Christie's) $8,530 £6,050

A George III satinwood and mahogany two-tier dumb-waiter with circular cross-banded tray top, 22½in. wide. (Christie's) $3,987 £2,750

A Regency mahogany two-tier dumbwaiter, 36½in. high. (Christie's) $1,108 £660

A George III mahogany two-tier dumb waiter on tripod support, 2ft.1½in. diam., circa 1760. (Christie's) $1,150 £700

George III mahogany dumb-waiter with three graduated dished shelves, circa 1770, 42½in. high. (Robt. W. Skinner Inc.) $1,100 £718

A mid Georgian mahogany three-tier dumbwaiter with graduated shelves, 43in. high. (Christie's) $1,948 £1,210

A Regency ormolu mounted mahogany dumb waiter, 26¼in. diam., 45¼in. high. (Christie's) $6,979 £4,950

A William IV mahogany three-tier dumb waiter, 150cm. high. (Phillips) $2,240 £1,400

A mahogany partner's desk
with red leather lined top,
71½in. wide. (Christie's)
$2,016 £1,430

Mid 18th century George III
crescent-shaped mahogany
desk, 81½in. wide. (Christie's)
$13,200 £8,615

A George II mahogany
partner's desk with leather
lined top and nine drawers,
57½in. wide. (Christie's)
$19,387 £13,750

A mahogany pedestal desk
with gilt-tooled green leather
lined top, 33in. wide.
(Christie's) $1,240 £880

A George II mahogany kneehole desk with arched apron
and six short drawers about
a recessed enclosed cupboard,
83cm. wide. (Phillips)
$2,850 £1,900

A George III mahogany kneehole dressing chest with crossbanded hinged top, 41½in.
wide. (Christie's)
$2,831 £1,980

A George III mahogany
partner's pedestal desk, the
top with inset baize top, 4ft.
5in. wide. (Woolley & Wallis)
$13,680 £9,500

A William and Mary figured
walnut kneehole desk inlaid
with feather banding, 33¾in.
wide. (Christie's)
$6,606 £4,620

A late Victorian oak library
desk, the moulded leather
lined top above a kneehole,
113in. wide. (Christie's)
$2,831 £1,980

KNEEHOLE DESKS

Early 19th century mahogany partner's desk with leather lined top and six frieze drawers, 60in. wide. (Christie's) $2,831 £1,980

Early Victorian oak partner's desk, the lock stamped Clarke & Simmons, Birmingham, 71½in. wide. (Christie's) $20,163 £14,300

A mid Victorian mahogany partner's desk with green leather lined top, 65in. wide. (Christie's) $4,962 £3,520

A figured walnut kneehole desk crossbanded and inlaid with feather-banding, basically 18th century, 32½in. wide. (Christie's) $4,466 £3,080

A George III mahogany cylinder desk with three-quarter pierced ormolu gallery, 47½in. wide. (Christie's)
      $13,557 £9,350

A George III mahogany military dressing table, the hinged top enclosing a fitted interior, 36in. wide. (Christie's) $2,326 £1,650

A Heal's sycamore kneehole desk, the rectangular top with semi-circular end, 133.4cm. wide. (Christie's)
      $633 £440

A mahogany kneehole desk with chequer pattern inlay, 41½in. wide. (Christie's)
      $1,240 £880

A George I burr walnut kneehole desk with hinged top enclosing a fitted interior with dressing mirror and lidded compartments, 36in. wide. (Christie's)
      $32,571 £23,100

An early George III mahogany lowboy on cabriole legs and pad feet, 32in. wide. (Christie's) $5,583 £3,960

An early 18th century gilt and gesso japanned side table on cabriole legs, 82cm. wide. (Phillips) $12,780 £9,000

An 18th century Scottish red walnut lowboy with carved and scrolled kneehole, 33½in. wide. (Christie's) $2,808 £1,950

A burr walnut lowboy, featherbanded in ash with quarter veneered moulded top, 33½in. wide, basically late 17th century. (Christie's) $2,265 £1,500

An early Georgian walnut side table with arched and waved frieze, 29in. wide. (Christie's) $6,609 £4,320

Early 18th century walnut lowboy, 29½in. wide. (Christie's) $2,400 £1,500

An early Georgian oak side table, the frieze with three drawers on lappeted club legs and pad feet, 34in. wide. (Christie's) $1,706 £1,210

An early Georgian oak lowboy on cabriole legs and trifid feet, 31¼in. wide. (Christie's) $1,504 £990

A 19th century Dutch walnut and foliate marquetry lowboy, 27in. wide. (Christie's) $1,510 £1,000

SCREENS

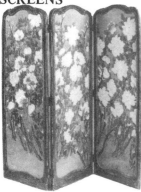

A giltwood three-leaf screen with arched panels applied with silk and painted with paeonies and foliage, each leaf 59 x 22½in. (Christie's) $4,576 £2,860

Late 19th century fundame two-leaf table screen inlaid in Shiba-yama style, signed Nobuyuki, each leaf 25 x 14cm. (Christie's) $3,148 £1,980

An ebonised and marquetry four-leaf screen inlaid in satinwood, beechwood, walnut and stained fruitwood, 190cm. high, 141cm. wide. (Christie's) $2,356 £1,540

An Empire mahogany cheval firescreen, the screen filled with distressed silk, 24in. wide. (Christie's) $492 £308

An Arts & Crafts mahogany four-fold embroidered screen, 152cm. high. (Christie's) $1,262 £825

A Louis XVI grey painted firescreen with rectangular silk panel, 17¼in. wide. (Christie's) $1,672 £1,045

An Aesthetic Movement ebonised and painted three-leaf screen, 134.2cm. wide, 143.9cm. high. (Christie's) $1,262 £825

One of two similar mid Georgian mahogany pole-screens, 56in. high. (Christie's) $924 £550

Late 19th century two-leaf table screen, each leaf 33 x 15.5cm. (Christie's) $3,847 £2,420

FURNITURE

SCREENS

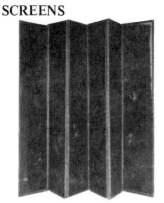

A Dutch painted leather six-leaf screen, late 18th century, each leaf 95½ x 21½in. (Christie's) $2,044 £1,430

An early Victorian rosewood firescreen with glazed panel, 40in. wide, 63in. high. (Christie's) $826 £540

A painted leather four-leaf screen, each leaf 66 x 19½in. (Christie's) $1,914 £1,320

A mahogany pole screen with acorn finial, the adjustable panel with a spray of flowers, 23in. wide. (Christie's) $620 £440

An 18th century Chinese coromandel lacquer twelve-leaf screen, each leaf 19in. wide, 93½in. high. (Christie's) $58,938 £41,800

An Arts & Crafts oak firescreen, the framework enclosing a panel of Morris & Co. fabric woven with 'The Tulip and Rose', 55.5cm. high. (Phillips) $273 £190

A Regency mahogany four-leaf screen, the divided panels with Chinese wallpaper, slightly distressed, each leaf 78 x 21½in. (Christie's) $12,393 £8,100

A painted Japanese two-part folding screen, gouache and silver leaf, circa 1860, 55 x 49½in. (Robt. W. Skinner Inc.) $3,400 £2,377

A Dutch painted leather four-leaf screen decorated with parrots and exotic birds, each leaf 84¼ x 20in. (Christie's) $1,258 £880

428

SCREENS

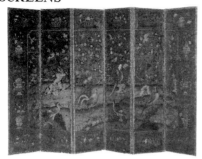

An 18th century Dutch polychrome painted leather six-leaf screen, each leaf 22in. wide, 84in. high. (Christie's) $29,887 £20,900

A Chippendale mahogany polescreen, Mass., 1765-85, 58in. high. (Christie's) $4,950 £3,230

A Regency black and gold lacquer six-leaf screen, each leaf 108 x 23¾in. (Christie's) $9,616 £6,820

A mid Victorian black, gilt and mother-of-pearl japanned firescreen, 52in. high. (Christie's) $2,674 £1,870

A Chinese six-leaf coromandel screen, the panels early 19th century, each leaf 78 x 21½in. (Christie's) $4,147 £2,860

A silk-embroidered firescreen, attributed to Morris & Co., 97.5cm. high. (Christie's) $316 £220

A 19th century spinach-green jade and hardwood four-leaf screen, each leaf 211 x 43cm. (Christie's) $13,370 £9,350

Early 19th century Dutch painted four-leaf screen, one panel distressed, each panel 72 x 21in. (Christie's) $2,643 £1,728

An Indian hardwood three-leaf screen, each leaf 76 x 32in. (Christie's) $774 £506

An early Georgian walnut secretaire, the convex frieze drawer and fall-flap inlaid with chevron lines, 43½in. wide. (Christie's) $3,304 £2,160

A mid 19th century ormolu mounted mahogany secretaire with griotte marble top, 50in. wide. (Christie's) $4,783 £3,300

A walnut and yewwood secretaire cabinet, 41½in. wide. (Christie's) $3,146 £2,200

A Renaissance Revival walnut butler's secretary, circa 1860, 40¾in. wide. (Robt. W. Skinner Inc.) $1,900 £1,225

Gustav Stickley oak and wrought iron secretary, designed by Harvey Ellis, circa 1904, 56in. wide. (Robt. W. Skinner Inc.) $13,000 £9,090

An ormolu mounted, parquetry and marquetry secretaire a abattant of Louis XVI style, on toupie feet, 30in. wide. (Christie's) $2,392 £1,650

Late Empire figured mahogany secretary on scroll feet, circa 1835, 46¼in. wide. (Robt. W. Skinner Inc.) $950 £659

A Louis XVI tulipwood and chequer inlaid secretaire a abattant with later gilt metal ornament, 97cm. wide. (Phillips) $1,950 £1,300

A Georgian mahogany secretaire press. (Parsons, Welch & Cowell) $1,283 £850

SECRETAIRE BOOKCASES

A Federal mahogany secretary, in three sections, 1800-15, 41½in. wide. (Christie's) $7,150 £5,003

A Regency mahogany secretaire cabinet, the base with baize-lined secretaire with burr elm fitted interior, 48½in. wide. (Christie's) $5,783 £3,780

George III mahogany secretaire bookcase, circa 1800, 42½in. wide. (Robt. W. Skinner Inc.) $2,600 £1,699

A George III carved mahogany secretaire bookcase, 2.45m. high, 1.34m. wide. (Phillips) $7,344 £4,800

A George III mahogany secretaire cabinet on bracket feet, 48in. wide. (Christie's) $10,164 £6,050

A Regency yewwood and laburnum crossbanded secretaire bookcase, 1.74m. high, 95cm. wide. (Phillips) $5,184 £3,600

A George III mahogany secretaire cabinet, 49½in. wide. (Christie's) $14,784 £8,800

A Regency mahogany secretaire bookcase, the base with fall-front fitted writing drawer, 47½in. wide. (Christie's) $6,688 £4,400

George III mahogany secretaire bookcase, circa 1810, 44in. wide. (Robt. W. Skinner Inc.) $1,100 £718

431

SECRETAIRE BOOKCASES

Mid 18th century George III mahogany butler's secretary desk in two sections, 46in. wide. (Christie's) $6,600 £4,307

A mahogany secretaire bookcase, inlaid with boxwood lines and having satinwood banded borders, 19th century, 43½in. wide. (Christie's) $3,770 £2,600

A George III mahogany secretaire cabinet with a pair of glazed cupboard doors, 46½in. wide. (Christie's) $3,257 £2,310

A George III satinwood Weeks secretaire cabinet, the fall-flap enclosing a fitted interior, 38½in. wide. (Christie's) $24,816 £17,600

A Federal inlaid mahogany breakfront secretary bookcase, Salem, Mass., 1795-1800, 67in. wide. (Christie's) $275,000 £181,445

A Chippendale carved maple desk and bookcase, Rhode Island, 1750-80, 82in. high, 38in. wide. (Christie's) $26,400 £17,418

A Federal secretary bookcase, in three sections, N.Y., 1800-10, 37in. wide. (Christie's) $28,600 £20,014

Late 18th century George III mahogany secretary bookcase, 77½in. wide. (Christie's) $26,400 £17,231

A George III secretaire bookcase, the top section enclosed by two glazed Gothic astragal doors, 43in. wide. (Christie's) $4,350 £3,000

SECRETAIRE BOOKCASES

A Regency mahogany secretaire cabinet with a pair of gothic pattern glazed doors, 43in. wide. (Christie's) $2,871 £1,980

A Federal mahogany inlaid desk/bookcase, probably Mass., circa 1800, 37½in. wide. (Robt. W. Skinner Inc.) $3,300 £2,307

A George III satinwood secretaire bookcase with circular enamelled ring handles, 30¾in. wide. (Christie's) $65,142 £46,200

A George III satinwood secretaire bookcase banded with mahogany and inlaid with boxwood lines, trade label of George Simson, 33¾in. wide. (Christie's) $26,367 £18,700

A George III mahogany secretaire cabinet with a pair of gothic glazed doors enclosing later shelves, 44in. wide. (Christie's) $4,785 £3,300

A George III mahogany and burr yew secretaire cabinet, 41½in. wide. (Christie's) $13,959 £9,900

A George III mahogany secretaire bookcase with a pair of gothic glazed doors, 46in. wide. (Christie's) $2,946 £2,090

A Georgian carved mahogany secretaire breakfront library bookcase in the Chippendale taste, 2.20m. wide. (Phillips) $11,520 £8,000

A George III mahogany secretaire bookcase with original brass swan neck handles, 3ft.8in. wide. (Woolley & Wallis) $4,576 £3,200

433

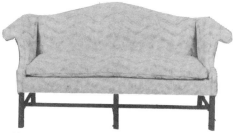

A Chippendale style stained maple sofa on moulded Marlborough legs, 76in. long. (Christie's)　　$2,860　£1,866

Late 18th century carved fruitwood settee, 82in. long. (Robt. W. Skinner Inc.) $800　£559

A Victorian walnut chaise longue with buttoned graduated back panel, 83in. long. (Christie's)　　$2,015　£1,300

A Victorian chaise longue with carved mahogany show wood frame and cabriole legs and gold damask cover. (Lots Road Galleries)　　$870　£580

A Regency ebonised and gilt decorated sofa of chaise longue design with upholstered panel back and scroll ends, having cushion seat and bolster. (Phillips)　　$5,396　£3,800

A Federal upholstered mahogany sofa on turned reeded legs with birch inlay, Mass., 1790-1810, 79in. wide. (Christie's)　　$12,100　£7,897

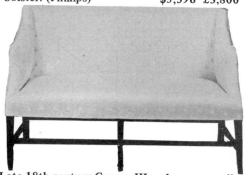

Late 18th century George III mahogany small sofa on square tapering legs, on brass cuffs, 50in. wide. (Christie's)　　$3,520　£2,297

A Louis XVI white painted banquette with rectangular back, bowed seat and squab covered in blue floral chintz, 53in. wide. (Christie's)　　$1,483　£1,045

SETTEES & COUCHES

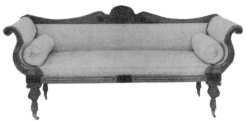

Classical Revival teak sofa with carved lyre legs terminating in turned feet with brass cap castors, China, circa 1840, 86in. long. (Robt. W. Skinner Inc.) $2,000 £1,398

Late 18th century Louis XVI painted canape, repainted white and gilt, probably Sweden, 86in. long. (Robt. W. Skinner Inc.) $500 £349

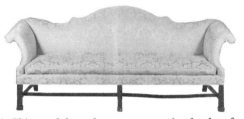

A Chippendale mahogany serpentine-back sofa on Marlborough legs with blocked feet joined by stretchers, Phila., 1765-85, 109½in. wide. (Christie's) $605,000 £423,379

A Federal carved mahogany sofa, attributed to the shop of Duncan Phyfe, N.Y., 1800-20, 80in. wide. (Christie's) $49,500 £32,660

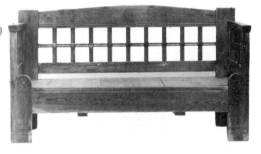

A Chippendale style stained maple sofa on moulded Marlborough legs, upholstered in ivory striped damask, 76in. long. (Christie's) $3,300 £2,153

Pine bench, probably circa 1900. (Lots Road Galleries) $371 £260

An ebonised sofa with rectangular back, sides and seat covered in a floral brocade with wild animals, 60in. wide. (Christie's) $1,494 £1,045

A George III mahogany frame settee with a stuff over back and seat. (Phillips) $1,584 £1,100

SETTEES & COUCHES

A Victorian carved walnut and upholstered double chair-back settee, 5ft.9in. wide. (Parsons, Welch & Cowell) $2,112 £1,320

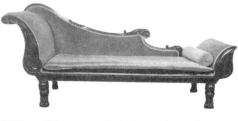

William IV rosewood chaise with scroll carved arm and back rail, lotus carved foot, 86in. long. (Reeds Rains) $835 £580

A mahogany daybed upholstered in blue moire, 65in. long, the castors and leg stamped Howard & Sons Ltd., London. (Christie's) $1,278 £825

A George I walnut and beechwood settee covered in petit and gros point floral needle-work, 64in. wide. (Christie's)
$58,938 £41,800

A William and Mary walnut sofa with high double-arched winged back, outscrolled arms and two squab cushions covered in floral needlework. (Christie's) $4,620 £2,750

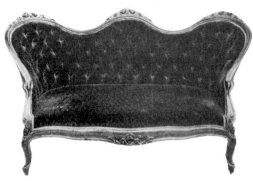

A rococo Revival walnut settee on scroll feet, America, circa 1860, 72in. long. (Robt. W. Skinner Inc.) $750 £524

An Indian white marble bench on baluster legs and square feet, 49in. wide. (Christie's)
$5,049 £3,300

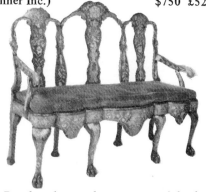

A Dutch walnut and marquetry triple chair-back settee with waved arched toprail and three solid splats, 62in. wide. (Christie's)
$3,520 £2,200

SETTEES & COUCHES

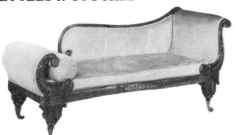

A George IV brass inlaid mahogany and rosewood chaise longue with scrolling padded back, sides and foot rest, 82in. wide. (Christie's) $1,817 £1,188

A carved mahogany tete-a-tete with scrolled and carved back over S-shaped arms above round upholstered seat, America, circa 1900, 41½in. long. (Robt. W. Skinner Inc.)
$550 £354

A giltwood daybed in the Theban style, 79½in. wide. (Christie's) $18,876 £13,200

A Biedermeier satin-birch sofa with padded rectangular box back, 72in. wide. (Christie's)
$2,288 £1,430

A George III carved mahogany scroll end sofa in the French taste, on cabriole legs with scroll feet, 2.15m. wide. (Phillips) $4,032 £2,800

A George II elm double chair-back settee with rectangular back and pierced strapwork splats, the padded drop-in seat covered with brown repp, 45in. wide. (Christie's) $1,651 £1,155

A Windsor bench on bamboo turned legs joined by swelled H-stretchers, 75in. long. (Christie's) $825 £533

A mid Victorian centre sofa covered in buttoned green velvet with deep fringe on tapering ebonised baluster legs, 40in. wide. (Christie's) $3,304 £2,160

SIDEBOARDS

A mahogany sideboard with serpentine top and ledge back, 56½in. wide. (Christie's)
$5,582 £3,850

George III inlaid mahogany sideboard, the bowfronted top with satinwood crossbanding, 52in. wide. (Robt. W. Skinner Inc.)
$2,400 £1,678

A George III mahogany sideboard with four short and two cellaret drawers, 46in. wide. (Christie's) $1,395 £990

Gustav Stickley eight-legged sideboard, circa 1904, no. 817, with plate rack, 70in. wide. (Robt. W. Skinner Inc.) $7,000 £4,895

A Regency mahogany breakfront sideboard, inlaid with ebonised lines, the top with a later superstructure with four tambour shutters, possibly Scottish, 84in. wide. (Christie's) $1,982 £1,296

A Federal inlaid carved mahogany sideboard with serpentine top, attributed to Ephraim Haines, Phila., 1800-15. (Christie's)
$9,350 £6,543

SIDEBOARDS

A Sheraton period bowfronted mahogany sideboard, the top with brass rail and rosewood edge bands, 7ft. wide. (Parsons, Welch & Cowell) $3,542 £2,300

A Federal inlaid mahogany sideboard, with serpentine-shaped top, 1790-1815, 73½in. wide. (Christie's) $5,500 £3,848

A 19th century mahogany sideboard, the bow fronted top inlaid with a broad satinwood band and two floral and foliate roundels, 6ft. wide. (Parsons, Welch & Cowell) $3,542 £2,300

A Regency mahogany breakfront sideboard inlaid with ebonised lines, 84½in. wide. (Christie's) $2,233 £1,540

A George III mahogany sideboard with serpentine crossbanded top, the double-arched centre with a drawer flanked by two deep drawers, 72in. wide. (Christie's) $25,520 £17,600

A George III mahogany sideboard crossbanded with rosewood and inlaid with chevron lines, 73½in. wide. (Christie's) $21,714 £15,400

SIDEBOARDS

A Regency mahogany sideboard, inlaid with bands of brass ovals on an ebonised ground, 88½in. wide. (Christie's)
$19,828 £12,960

Mid 18th century inlaid mahogany sideboard table on moulded Marlborough legs, 70in. wide. (Christie's) $7,700 £5,025

A Renaissance Revival walnut and burl veneer marble top sideboard, bearing label 'E. D. Trymby's, Philadelphia', circa 1860, 56in. wide. (Robt. W. Skinner Inc.) $1,200 £774

Mid 19th century rosewood marble top sideboard, Lewis McKee & Co., Conn., 60in. wide. (Robt. W. Skinner Inc.) $650 £451

A Regency mahogany sideboard with breakfront D-shaped crossbanded top, 63½in. wide. (Christie's) $1,887 £1,320

Mid 18th century George III inlaid mahogany demi-lune sideboard, 54in. wide. (Christie's)
$4,180 £2,728

Late Georgian figured mahogany breakfront sideboard with lion mask ring handles, 5ft.7in. wide. (Capes, Dunn & Co.) $1,051 £725

A George III mahogany, tulipwood crossbanded and inlaid sideboard with arched apron and fan spandrels, 1.53m. wide. (Phillips)
$6,300 £4,200

SIDEBOARDS

A Regency mahogany pedestal sideboard with crossbanded moulded top with rounded inset centre, 97in. wide. (Christie's)
$10,740 £7,020

A George III mahogany sideboard with double bowed top, the tablet-centred frieze flanked by two later baize-lined drawers and two deep drawers, 82in. wide. (Christie's)
$7,601   £4,968

Part of a French Art Deco walnut veneered diningroom suite, comprising a dining table, six chairs and two sideboards, 184cm. and 143cm. long respectively. (Phillips)
$748 £520

A mahogany bow-fronted sideboard inlaid with boxwood lines, a brass backrail and arched kneehole, 50in. wide. (Christie's)
$1,520 £1,000

A late George III mahogany bowfront sideboard on ring turned tapering legs and feet, 72½in. long. (Christie's) $1,887 £1,320

A Sheraton period mahogany veneered bow-fronted sideboard with satinwood line inlay and stringing, 4ft.9in. wide. (Woolley & Wallis)
$5,863 £4,100

A George III mahogany sideboard crossbanded with rosewood, 71¾in. wide. (Christie's)
$7,865 £5,500

William IV mahogany pedestal sideboard with shaped gallery, three drawers and two side cupboards and cellarette, 7ft. wide. (Hobbs & Chambers) $338 £220

FURNITURE

A Federal birch candlestand, original red stain finish, New England, circa 1790, 26¾in. high. (Robt. W. Skinner Inc.) $1,900 £1,328

L. & J. G. Stickley open magazine rack, circa 1910, 42in. high, 21in. wide. (Robt. W. Skinner Inc.) $1,100 £769

A mid 19th century French bronze tripod with inset circular green marble top, 34½in. high. (Christie's) $4,785 £3,300

A Gufram hat-stand, designed by Guido Drocco and Franco Mello, modelled as a cactus plant, 1971, 174.5cm. high. (Christie's) $4,296 £2,808

A George IV mahogany library bookstand with a panelled fall-flap, 45½in. wide. (Christie's) $1,156 £756

Chippendale cherry candlestand, probably Rhode Island, circa 1770, 25½in. high. (Robt. W. Skinner Inc.) $750 £524

An early Victorian coat stand, by John Webb, on bracket base with metal liner, 64in. wide. (Christie's) $2,044 £1,430

A pair of Venetian painted and gilded Blackamoor torcheres, 85in. high. (Christie's) $11,715 £8,250

One of a pair of ormolu mounted cloisonne etageres, each with two rectangular tiers, 20¼in. wide. (Christie's) $5,948 £3,888

STANDS

One of a pair of walnut torcheres with lobed tray-tops and hexagonal shaped shafts, 10in. wide, 30½in. high. (Christie's)
$1,156 £756

Painted Tramp art stand with drawers, possibly New York, 1820-40, 17½in. wide. (Robt. W. Skinner Inc.)
$300 £200

Chippendale cherry candle-stand, the shaped top with ovolo corners, circa 1780, 26in. high. (Robt. W. Skinner Inc.)
$2,500 £1,748

A Chippendale style mahogany urn table, 25in. high. (Christie's) $646 £420

An early 18th century Italian carved giltwood stand with a simulated green marble top, 1.10m. high. (Phillips)
$1,200 £800

Gustav Stickley inlaid tiger maple open music stand, circa 1904, no. 670, signed with Eastwood label, 39in. high. (Robt. W. Skinner Inc.)
$7,250 £5,069

A George II grained pine pedestal, 53¼in. high. (Christie's)
$10,081 £7,150

A pair of late 18th century Italian parcel gilt and green painted torcheres, 69½in. high. (Christie's)
$7,810 £5,500

A Victorian mahogany folio stand with brass ratcheted adjustable open slatted slopes, 76cm. high. (Phillips)
$2,550 £1,700

STANDS

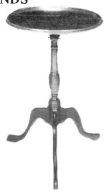

A Federal mahogany tilt-top candlestand, American, 1790-1810, 26½in. high. (Christie's) $990 £646

A Federal inlaid mahogany corner stand, New York, 1790-1810, 23in. wide. (Christie's) $8,580 £5,661

A Federal inlaid cherrywood candlestand, Connecticut River Valley, 1790-1810, 26¾in. high. (Christie's) $13,200 £8,615

A George III style mahogany urn stand, 27in. high, 12in. wide. (Christie's) $1,045 £682

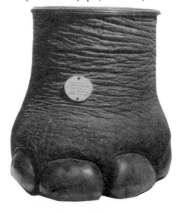

An elephant's foot wastepaper basket with rosewood rim and ivory plaque, 11in. high. (Christie's) $697 £495

A Thonet stained beechwood plant stand, the design attributed to Josef Hoffmann, 119cm. high. (Christie's) $865 £605

Country Chippendale cherry octagonal top candlestand, probably Conn., circa 1760, 24.7/8in. high, 17¼in. diam. (Robt. W. Skinner Inc.) $1,500 £1,000

A Federal inlaid mahogany corner stand, the top with a pierced brass gallery, probably New York, 1800-15, 34½in. high. (Christie's) $2,860 £1,887

A William IV walnut pedestal teapoy, the interior fitted with two cannisters and two glass mixing bowls, stamped Gillow, 28½in. high. (Christie's) $1,057 £700

444

STANDS

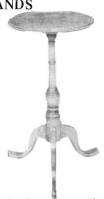

A Federal maple candlestand, with circular dished top, New England, 1790-1810, 28½in. high, 17¼in. diam. (Christie's) $5,500 £3,589

One of a pair of mid Victorian oak and ebonised umbrella stands in the Gothic taste, 66in. wide. (Christie's) $1,009 £660

A carved mahogany galleried kettle stand, the top with open baluster gallery, 30cm. diam., 75cm. high. (Phillips) $2,272 £1,600

An ormolu mounted king-wood and marquetry pedestal, with mottled purple marble top, stamped Bertram & Son, 46in. high. (Christie's) $1,355 £935

A pair of parcel gilt and painted Blackamoors of a negro and negress, 76¼in. high. (Christie's) $7,029 £4,950

A George III mahogany reading stand, the adjustable top with hinged ratcheted slope, 70cm. high. (Phillips) $4,320 £3,000

An early Victorian walnut pedestal teapoy, the hinged panel lid enclosing a fitted interior, 19½in.diam. (Christie's) $431 £280

Limbert octagonal plant stand, style no. 251, circa 1910, 24¼in. high. (Robt. W. Skinner Inc.) $1,000 £699

A mid Victorian black and mother-of-pearl japanned papier-mache music stand, 17¾in. diam. (Christie's) $613 £429

A Regency mahogany reading stand with adjustable top, 30½in. wide. (Christie's) $1,381 £858

Limbert round tall pedestal, circa 1906, no. 267, 32½in. high, 14in. diam. (Robt. W. Skinner Inc.) $900 £630

A mid Victorian walnut music stand, the slope on an adjustable brass shaft, 23in. wide. (Christie's) $1,003 £660

An early Victorian walnut folio stand with pierced adjustable twin-flap top, 28in. wide. (Christie's) $5,313 £3,300

A painted and parcel gilt Blackamoor torchere, carved as a negress, 62½in. high. (Christie's) $2,343 £1,650

Late 19th century Eastlake folio stand. (Lots Road Galleries) $1,152 £720

A Regency rosewood double-sided music stand, the sides with candle sconces, 48in. high. (Christie's) $3,344 £2,200

An open-sided music stand, possibly by Stickley Bros., circa 1907, 39in. high. (Robt. W. Skinner Inc.) $400 £245

A maple black painted and decorated candlestand, New England, circa 1775-1800, 26in. high. (Christie's) $660 £426

STOOLS

A Federal carved mahogany window seat, attributed to the shop of Duncan Phyfe, N.Y., 1810-20, 40in. wide. (Christie's) $26,400 £17,418

Late Regency rosewood framed window seat with swept rail ends, 42in. wide. (Lots Road Galleries) $648 £450

An early Victorian stool on cabriole legs, 26in. wide. (Woolley & Wallis) $437 £290

A mahogany stool with padded octangular drop-in seat, on cabriole legs, 21in. wide. (Christie's) $1,478 £880

A George II mahogany foot-stool, the upholstered seat on cabriole legs, 22in. wide. (Christie's) $1,320 £861

A Napoleon III giltwood stool, designed by A. M. E. Fournier, 29½in. diam. (Christie's) $3,960 £2,750

An Edwardian mahogany framed stool with floral tapestry covered pad seat, 23in. wide. (Anderson & Garland) $464 £290

A giltwood stool with square seat covered in patterned velvet, 24½in. sq. (Christie's) $1,178 £770

A George I red walnut stool with a slip-in seat and shaped apron, on cabriole legs. (Phillips) $4,828 £3,400

A cream painted and parcel gilt stool, the oval seat upholstered in a pale blue and white cotton, 33½in. wide. (Christie's) $3,124 £2,200

One of a pair of mid 19th century giltwood tabourets, covered in pink silk with gold stencilled dots, 21in. diam. (Christie's) $3,030 £2,090

A Louis Philippe giltwood stool in the manner of A. M. E. Fournier, with square crimson velvet seat, 21¼in. wide. (Christie's) $4,785 £3,300

A George III beechwood stool with concave-fronted rectangular seat covered in close-nailed crimson velvet, 20½in. wide. (Christie's) $1,573 £1,100

An oak stool on solid notched ends, circa 1600, 20¼in. wide. (Christie's) $1,179 £825

A Biedermeier mahogany tabouret with padded seat, stamped G. Jacob with a fleur-de-lys, 24in. wide. (Christie's) $2,030 £1,430

A George II walnut and parcel gilt stool on cabriole legs, 24½in. wide. (Christie's) $14,734 £10,450

One of a pair of oak stools, each with a squab, Italian or Spanish, 23½in. wide. (Christie's) $937 £660

A walnut stool, the drop-in seat with gros and petit point needlework, 22in. wide. (Christie's) $826 £540

STOOLS

A George III mahogany window seat, the seat and arms upholstered in pale pink floral damask, 30in. wide. (Christie's) $930 £660

Gustav Stickley spindle-sided footstool, circa 1907, no. 395, 15in. high. (Robt. W. Skinner Inc.) $150 £105

A George III mahogany window seat with serpentine seat covered in gold damask, 37in. wide. (Christie's) $13,183 £9,350

One of a pair of mahogany stools, the seats with petit point needlework sprays on a camel-coloured ground, the cabriole legs carved with clasps and claw-and-ball feet. (Christie's) $5,582 £3,850

Late 17th century oak coffin stool, initialled WC, 18½in. wide. (Christie's) $2,044 £1,430

A Spanish brass and wrought-iron faldistorio, partly 17th century. (Christie's) $3,436 £2,420

A Regency parcel gilt and simulated rosewood X-framed stool, the seat with a squab cushion covered in striped silk, 35in. wide. (Christie's) $3,146 £2,200

A Louis Philippe giltwood stool, in the manner of A. M. E. Fournier, with deep buttoned red velvet seat, 20in. diam. (Christie's) $2,552 £1,760

A Liberty & Co. walnut 'Thebes' stool, the square seat strung with brown hide. (Christie's) $1,267 £880

SUITES

Part of a seven-piece Renaissance Revival walnut and burl veneer parlour set, consisting of sofa, 73in. long, two armchairs and four side chairs, America, circa 1860. (Robt. W. Skinner Inc.) $2,300 £1,483

A mid 19th century suite of giltwood seat furniture, comprising: a settee and four open arm elbow chairs on fluted and turned legs. (Parsons, Welch & Cowell) $12,525 £7,500

A 19th century suite of Louis XV-style giltwood seat furniture, comprising a canape and four fauteuils, upholstered in 19th century Aubusson tapestry. (Robt. W. Skinner Inc.)
$2,600 £1,699

SUITES

Part of a mid 19th century Spanish giltwood suite of furniture comprising: a settee with cartouche-shaped back and serpentine seat covered in close-nailed brown leather, painted with flowers on a trellis ground and four side chairs, the settee 85in. wide. (Christie's)
$4,375 £2,860

Part of a four-piece Harden & Co. livingroom set, comprising: settee, rocker and two armchairs, settee 54in. wide, circa 1910. (Robt. W. Skinner Inc.) $1,800 £1,104

Part of a suite of giltwood seat furniture of Louis XV design comprising: four fauteuils and a canape, each upholstered in floral Aubusson tapestry. (Christie's) $9,130 £5,500

A Federal mahogany card table, the top with canted corners, N.Y., 1800-20, 35in. wide. (Christie's) $2,200 £1,539

A Chippendale carved mahogany card table, Phila., 1765-85, 36in. wide. (Christie's) $8,800 £5,743

A Federal inlaid mahogany card table with hinged, shaped top, Mass., 1790-1810, 37in. wide. (Christie's) $6,600 £4,354

An early Georgian mahogany tea table with D-shaped folding top, 30in. wide. (Christie's) $2,326 £1,650

A Federal inlaid mahogany card table with D-shaped top, E. Mass., 1790-1810, 35½in. wide. (Christie's) $2,860 £1,887

A William and Mary black and gold japanned card table decorated with chinoiserie, 30in. wide. (Christie's) $6,979 £4,950

A mahogany and burr walnut tea table with folding semi-circular top, 34in. wide. (Christie's) $781 £550

George III style mahogany galleried tea table on three carved ogee legs, England, 27½in. wide. (Robt. W. Skinner Inc.) $1,000 £699

A Federal mahogany inlaid card table with hinged top, Mass., 1810-25, 36in. wide. (Christie's) $1,650 £1,088

CARD & TEA TABLES

A Federal inlaid cherrywood card table with hinged D-shaped top, 1800-10, 35¾in. wide. (Christie's)
$9,350 £6,543

Queen Anne painted tiger maple tea table, probably Rhode Island, circa 1760, 34in. long. (Robt. W. Skinner Inc.) $40,000 £27,972

Early 19th century gilt metal mounted mahogany card table with D-shaped folding top, 42¾in. wide. (Christie's)
$1,874 £1,320

A Regency brass inlaid rose-wood card table, 35½in. wide. (Christie's) $3,412 £2,420

One of a pair of mid Victorian walnut and marquetry card tables, 34in. wide. (Christie's) $8,751 £5,720

An 18th century mahogany card table, top with needle-work inset, Boston. (Robt. W. Skinner Inc.)
$8,250 £5,769

A mahogany card table, the baize-lined eared top with candle sconces and guinea-wells, 35in. wide. (Christie's)
$3,828 £2,640

Late 18th century Louis XVI brass bound mahogany demi-lune card table, 42½in. diam., open. (Robt. W. Skinner Inc.)
$500 £349

A Federal inlaid mahogany circular card table, with hinged D-shaped top, Massa., 1790-1810, 36in. wide. (Christie's) $7,700 £5,388

CARD & TEA TABLES

One of a pair of William IV rosewood card tables, each with fold-over top, 36in. wide. (Christie's)
$1,661 £1,100

A Chippendale tilt-top mahogany tea table, Mass., 1760-80, 32in. diam. (Christie's)
$4,400 £2,871

A classical carved mahogany card table, N.Y., 1815-25, 36¼in. wide. (Christie's)
$1,760 £1,231

A Queen Anne mahogany porringer-top tea table, Rhode Island, 1740-70, 33in. wide. (Christie's)
$19,800 £12,923

A George III mahogany card table, the baize-lined eared top with one frieze drawer, 34in. wide. (Christie's)
$3,509 £2,420

A George III carved mahogany card table, the baize-lined hinged top with egg and dart edge, the hinges engraved G. Tibats, 91cm. long. (Phillips)
$1,950 £1,300

One of a pair of Regency rosewood card tables, banded with maple, 36in. wide. (Christie's) $3,190 £2,200

A Chippendale walnut circular tilt-top tea table, Phila., 1760-85, 33¾in. diam. (Christie's)
$8,800 £5,743

A late Federal carved mahogany card table, New York, 1815-25, 36in. wide. (Christie's) $990 £640

CARD & TEA TABLES

A Regency mahogany card
table inlaid with ebonised
lines, the canted, folding
top enclosing a well, 35¾in.
wide. (Christie's)
$1,861 £1,320

A George III mahogany tea
table with eared folding top
and frieze drawer, 34in. wide.
(Christie's) $2,674 £1,870

Mid 18th century George III
walnut 'Isle of Man' tilt-top
tea table, 31¾in. diam.
(Christie's) $4,620 £3,015

An early George III maho-
gany card table on cabriole
legs, 35½in. wide.
(Christie's)
$17,061 £12,100

A George II walnut and
mahogany tea table with
later semi-circular folding
top enclosing a well, 30½in.
wide. (Christie's)
$1,735 £1,134

Classical Revival carved
mahogany card table, circa
1810, 25¾in. wide. (Robt.
W. Skinner Inc.) $550 £366

A Federal inlaid mahogany
card table, with hinged top,
Massa., 1790-1810, 34¾in.
wide. (Christie's)
$6,050 £4,233

A Chippendale mahogany
tilt-top tea table, probably
Newport, Rhode Island,
1760-80, 30¾in. diam.
(Christie's) $1,100 £725

A Chippendale mahogany
tilt-top tea table, Mass.,
1770-85, top 30.1/3 x 30in.
(Christie's)
$28,600 £20,014

CARD & TEA TABLES

One of a pair of classical carved mahogany card tables, each with D-shaped moulded edge and hinged rotating top, Boston, circa 1820, 34½in. wide. (Christie's) $2,200 £1,539

A George III satinwood and banded D-shaped tea table with boxwood and ebony stringing, 38in. wide. (Dreweatts) $5,220 £3,600

A Regency rosewood card table with fold-over top, 35¼in. wide. (Coles, Knapp & Kennedy) $1,359 £900

One of a pair of mahogany card tables, the baize-lined D-shaped tops crossbanded with rosewood, 39¼in. wide. (Christie's) $4,626 £3,024

A Chippendale mahogany card table, the top with outset porringer corners, 1750-80, 35in. wide. (Christie's) $14,300 £9,435

A laburnum and walnut card table, the baize-lined top with candle roundels and guinea wells, 34in. wide. (Christie's) $11,165 £7,700

A George III satinwood veneered half-round card table, the top crossbanded in rosewood, 3ft.2in. wide. (Woolley & Wallis) $2,088 £1,450

A late Federal carved mahogany card table, Mass., 1810, 20, 36in. wide. (Christie's) $2,750 £1,778

A Federal inlaid mahogany card table on square tapering legs with line inlay and castors, 35¾in. wide. (Christie's) $1,430 £924

CENTRE TABLES

A Regency rosewood and parcel gilt centre table with circular tip-up top, 47½in. diam. (Christie's)
$10,081 £7,150

An early Victorian rosewood pedestal centre table, 52in. diam., labelled Improved Circular Log Table. (Christie's) $1,317 £850

A George IV pollard oak centre table with tip-up top, 50in. diam. (Christie's)
$3,460 £2,420

A Scandinavian green and cream painted centre table in the revived neo-classical style, circa 1880, 47in. diam. (Christie's) $4,373 £3,080

A mid Victorian figured walnut and silver gesso centre table with eared shaped, tip-up top, 60in. wide. (Christie's)
$1,861 £1,320

An elm and oak centre table, on turned baluster legs joined by square stretchers, 55in. wide. (Christie's)
$1,573 £1,100

A marble centre table with circular moulded specimen marble top, 48¼in. diam. (Christie's)$16,830 £11,000

A George IV mahogany and specimen marble centre table, the top bearing label Philippo Lopes, 19½in. diam. (Christie's)
$2,233 £1,540

A walnut centre table with octagonal moulded specimen marble top, 47in. wide. (Christie's) $5,935 £4,180

A mid Victorian gilt metal mounted amboyna and marquetry centre table, 42¼in. wide. (Christie's)
$3,366 £2,200

A William IV walnut centre table with octagonal specimen marble top bordered with black limestone, stamped Eastmure, 45in. wide. (Christie's)
$43,428 £30,800

A German walnut centre table on shackled slave legs, 51in. wide. (Christie's)
$4,712 £3,080

A George III sycamore centre table with waved crossbanded top centred by an amboyna oval, edged with chequered stringing, on cabriole legs, 23¾in. wide. (Christie's)
$3,030 £2,090

An early Victorian walnut centre table in the manner of Baldock, 35½in. diam. (Christie's) $4,375 £2,860

A Renaissance Revival walnut centre table, with variegated red and white marble insert, circa 1860, 36in. wide. (Robt. W. Skinner Inc.) $550 £354

A mid Victorian mahogany and marquetry centre table, 58in. wide. (Christie's)
$4,375 £2,860

An early Victorian ebonised and parcel gilt centre table with Italian scagliola top, 36¼in. diam. (Christie's)
$9,306 £6,600

A gilt and green japanned centre table on cabriole legs, possibly German, 41in. wide. (Christie's) $2,811 £1,980

CENTRE TABLES

A Dutch oyster-veneered walnut and marquetry centre table, the top 17th century, 45½in. wide. (Christie's) $4,061 £2,860

Renaissance Revival inlaid walnut centre table, circa 1870, 42¼in. wide. (Robt. W. Skinner Inc.) $1,600 £1,111

An ormolu centre table in the style of Weisweiler, with inset marble top, 38in. wide. (Christie's) $7,656 £5,280

A Napoleon III ormolu and purple quartz centre table, twice stamped Monbro, 32in. wide. (Christie's) $15,152 £10,450

An ormolu mounted tulip-wood and ebony centre table with inset breccia marble top, 28.5in. wide. (Christie's) $4,785 £3,300

A Scandinavian cream painted and parcel gilt centre table with tray top inset with twelve Dutch Delft tiles, 24in. wide. (Christie's) $781 £550

A Victorian pollard oak and painted centre table, the top on a naturalistic bullrush pedestal, 28¾in. diam. (Christie's) $15,730 £11,000

A George II mahogany centre table with rounded rectangular tray top, 30¼in. wide. (Christie's) $1,101 £770

A Regency rosewood, satinwood, mahogany and amboyna centre table, 26in. diam. (Christie's) $1,817 £1,188

FURNITURE

A Regency serpentine gilt console table with green marble top, 44in. wide. (Morphets) $2,160 £1,350

A Regency simulated rosewood and parcel gilt console in the manner of Thos. Hope, 89cm. wide. (Phillips) $9,230 £6,500

One of a pair of giltwood console tables in the manner of Thos. Johnson, 49¾in. wide. (Christie's) $20,163 £14,300

A giltwood console table with verde antico marble top, circa 1830, 28¾in. wide. (Christie's) $2,516 £1,760

Pair of early 19th century Danish parcel gilt and cream painted pier glasses and console tables, 28¼in. wide, 109½in. high. (Christie's) $7,040 £4,400

Late 18th century George III mahogany inlaid console table, 42in. wide. (Christie's) $2,640 £1,723

A Classical Revival brass inlaid mahogany console table, 36in. wide. (Robt. W. Skinner Inc.) $1,300 £812

A 19th century giltwood and gesso serpentine fronted console table. (Parsons, Welch & Cowell) $800 £500

A George II pine console table with moulded white and grey marble top, 48½in. wide. (Christie's) $50,204 £30,800

CONSOLE TABLES

One of a pair of mahogany console tables with D-shaped tops, 58in. wide. (Christie's) $2,974 £1,944

An 18th century giltwood console table, 52¼in. wide. (Christie's) $5,428 £3,850

A George III pine console table with later D-shaped mahogany top, 59in. wide. (Christie's) $2,148 £1,404

A George III satinwood and marquetry half-round pier table surmounted by a grey-viened white marble top, 92cm. wide. (Phillips) $2,250 £1,500

A Venetian parcel gilt and ebonised console table with eared serpentine white marble top supported by a blackamoor, 31in. wide. (Christie's) $4,785 £3,300

Classical Revival mahogany and mahogany veneer pier table with white marble top, possibly New York, circa 1825, 36½in. wide. (Robt. W. Skinner Inc.) $1,300 £866

Late 18th century Italian parcel gilt and black painted console table with inset jasper top, 29½in. wide. (Christie's) $4,061 £2,860

An 18th century Italian carved giltwood console table with a serpentine sienna marble top, 1.46m. long. (Phillips) $1,650 £1,100

An Empire mahogany and gilt metal mounted console table, 44in. wide. (Christie's) $2,019 £1,320

DINING TABLES

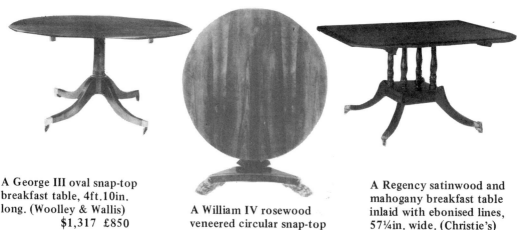

A George III oval snap-top
breakfast table, 4ft.10in.
long. (Woolley & Wallis)
$1,317 £850

A William IV rosewood
veneered circular snap-top
breakfast table, 4ft. diam.
(Woolley & Wallis)
$1,267 £880

A Regency satinwood and
mahogany breakfast table
inlaid with ebonised lines,
57¼in. wide. (Christie's)
$5,505 £3,850

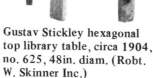

A mahogany drum table with
circular red leather lined top,
42in. diam. (Christie's)
$3,932 £2,750

Gustav Stickley hexagonal
top library table, circa 1904,
no. 625, 48in. diam. (Robt.
W. Skinner Inc.)
$5,700 £3,986

A rosewood and brass inlaid
breakfast table in the Regency
taste, 1.24m. diam. (Phillips)
$4,500 £3,000

A Regency mahogany break-
fast table with circular tip-up
top, 50½in. diam.(Christie's)
$3,412 £2,420

A George III satinwood and
inlaid breakfast table, crossbanded in tulipwood, with
oval snap top, 1.23m.
(Phillips) $12,070 £8,500

A George III mahogany
breakfast table, the crossbanded top with satinwood
banding, 54¾in. wide.
(Christie's) $3,139 £2,052

DINING TABLES

A Regency mahogany break-fast table with tip-up top, 53in. long. (Christie's) $1,249 £880

A Regency circular mahogany and brass inlaid breakfast or dining table. (Parsons, Welch & Cowell) $1,585 £1,050

A Regency mahogany break-fast table on ring-turned baluster shaft, branded W. & C. Wilkinson, 59½in. diam. (Christie's) $12,760 £8,800

Round oak pedestal base dining table, signed with metal tag, circa 1908, 54in. diam. (Robt. W. Skinner Inc.) $1,400 £979

A George III mahogany library table with circular gilt tooled leather-lined top, 46in. diam. (Christie's) $4,625 £3,190

A 19th century mahogany ebony strung and brass mounted drum top library table, 1.01m. diam. (Phillips) $3,456 £2,400

A mahogany drum top library table, the top with tooled leather inset, the drawers stamped A. Blain, Liverpool, 47in. diam. (Parsons, Welch & Cowell) $2,464 £1,600

An early Victorian mahogany veneered circular snap-top breakfast table, 4ft.7in. diam. (Woolley & Wallis) $1,180 £820

An early Victorian mahogany drum table, the circular top lined in tooled brown leather, 53in. diam. (Christie's) $1,224 £800

DINING TABLES

A Regency rosewood brass inlaid centre table with circular tip-up top, 48½in. diam. (Christie's) $8,065 £5,720

Mid Victorian oak dining table carved in Elizabethan style, extending with six leaves to 17ft.8in. (Lots Road Galleries) $1,920 £1,200

A mid Victorian burr walnut breakfast table with quarter veneered inlaid marquetry tilt-top, 60in. diam. (Christie's) $3,586 £2,200

A George III mahogany library table with leather lined circular top, 39in. diam. (Christie's) $5,977 £4,180

A Georgian mahogany circular snap-top dining table, 5ft.2in. diam. (Prudential Fine Art) $8,640 £5,400

A Victorian coromandel ebonised and parcel gilt loo table, 48in. diam. (Christie's) $1,208 £800

A Regency mahogany breakfast table with oval tip-up top, 60in. wide. (Christie's) $3,460 £2,420

A Renaissance Revival walnut and burl veneer dining table, the base separates to accommodate nine leaves, circa 1860. (Robt. W. Skinner Inc.) $2,000 £1,290

A mahogany breakfast table with crossbanded circular top, 58in. diam. (Christie's) $1,848 £1,100

DINING TABLES

A George III mahogany breakfast table with tip-up top, 60in. wide. (Christie's) $3,511 £2,090

An early Victorian mahogany dining table, extending to 93in., including two extra leaves. (Christie's) $2,103 £1,375

A Regency satinwood breakfast table, the top crossbanded with rosewood, 53¼in. wide. (Christie's) $15,708 £9,350

A George IV rosewood dining table on pedestal with tripod base, 4ft. diam. (Worsfolds) $1,001 £650

A 19th century Celonise ebony centre table with peacock octagonal tilt-top, 39in. wide. (Christie's) $5,280 £3,300

A late George III mahogany library table with leather lined oval top and six frieze drawers, 49in. wide. (Christie's) $14,058 £9,900

George III mahogany two pedestal dining table, circa 1800, 123in. long. (Robt. W. Skinner Inc.) $3,300 £2,156

A George IV mahogany breakfast table, the tilt top on a quadripartite turned support, 56in. wide. (Christie's) $847 £550

A George IV mahogany twin pedestal 'D' end dining table, including an extra leaf, 1.89 x 1.19m. extended. (Phillips) $7,344 £4,800

A Queen Anne carved and inlaid walnut dressing table, New Hampshire, circa 1735-60, 36in. wide. (Christie's) $88,000 £61,582

A late Chippendale mahogany dressing table with tripartite top, probably Rhode Island, 1780-1800, 31.1/8in. wide. (Christie's) $7,700 £5,388

Late 18th century Italian kingwood, marquetry and painted dressing table, 45¼in. wide. (Christie's) $2,811 £1,980

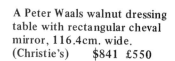

A Liberty oak dressing table with adjustable mirror, 132.6cm. wide with flaps extended. (Christie's) $660 £432

A George III mahogany breakfront dressing table, the divided top with three tambour shutters, 62½in. wide. (Christie's) $1,663 £990

A Peter Waals walnut dressing table with rectangular cheval mirror, 116.4cm. wide. (Christie's) $841 £550

A Chippendale carved walnut dressing table, Phila., 1765-85, 36in. wide. (Christie's) $253,000 £155,215

Mid 19th century carved walnut marble top shaving stand, America, 58¼in. high. (Robt. W. Skinner Inc.) $1,200 £833

Queen Anne tiger maple dressing table, circa 1760, 28½in. wide. (Robt. W. Skinner Inc.) $4,000 £2,500

DRESSING TABLES

A George III mahogany veneered dressing table, the drawers with original brass plate paterae embossed handles, 3ft.2in. wide. (Woolley & Wallis) $2,574 £1,800

A Regency mahogany dressing table with three drawers and an arched kneehole frieze, 3ft.3in. wide. (Woolley & Wallis) $1,912 £1,250

A George III rectangular mahogany kneehole dressing table, 49 x 32½in. high. (Anderson & Garland) $2,160 £1,350

Part of an Edwardian satinwood bedroom suite, the dressing table 51in. wide, 10 pieces. (Christie's) $2,015 £1,300

Late 18th century Scandinavian mahogany and parquetry dressing table, 33½in. wide. (Christie's) $3,124 £2,200

An Art Nouveau mahogany and inlaid dressing table with cartouche-shaped bevelled swing-frame mirror, 122cm. wide. (Phillips) $748 £520

A George III tulipwood bonheur-du-jour with leather lined writing slide, 30in. wide. (Christie's) $4,032 £2,860

Late 18th century George III mahogany dressing table, the hinged top opens to reveal a fitted interior, 24in. wide. (Robt. W. Skinner Inc.) $950 £664

A Sheraton period mahogany tulipwood crossbanded and chequerstrung serpentine front enclosed dressing table, 75cm. wide. (Phillips) $2,880 £2,000

DROP-LEAF TABLES

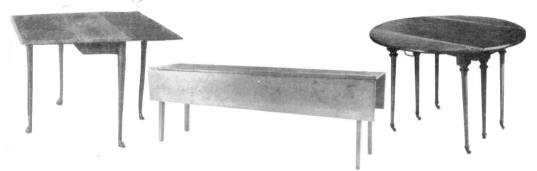

Mid 18th century George III mahogany drop-leaf table, 36in. wide. (Christie's) $1,760 £1,148

Painted pine drop-leaf harvest table, New England, circa 1800, 41½in. wide, open, 84¾in. long. (Robt. W. Skinner Inc.) $2,100 £1,400

A Louis XVI provincial walnut dining table on six turned tapering legs, 42¾in. wide. (Christie's) $2,343 £1,650

An Empire cherry and bird's-eye maple drop-leaf table, New England, circa 1825, 74in. long, open. (Robt. W. Skinner Inc.) $1,200 £774

Chippendale walnut drop-leaf table, circa 1780, 38½in. wide. (Robt. W. Skinner Inc.) $700 £489

A George III mahogany oval twin-flap top dining table, 4ft.11in. x 5ft.4in. (Woolley & Wallis) $4,147 £2,900

A Federal tiger maple dining table with shaped leaves, New England, circa 1820, 49½in. long, open. (Robt. W. Skinner Inc.) $1,900 £1,328

Late Federal rosewood veneer, gilt and brass inlaid breakfast table, attributed to Charles-Honore Lannuier, N.Y., circa 1815, 46in. long, extended. (Christie's) $71,500 £47,175

Queen Anne tiger maple drop-leaf table, New England, circa 1780, 16¾in. wide (closed). (Robt. W. Skinner Inc.) $1,500 £1,000

DROP-LEAF TABLES

A George III mahogany single drop-leaf occasional table, with a rectangular hinged top, 84 x 64cm. extended. (Phillips) $1,275 £850

A Queen Anne walnut drop-leaf dining table, the cabriole legs with peaked knees, New England, circa 1740-70, top 51½ x 46½in. (Christie's) $9,900 £6,928

A Federal mahogany dining table with four swing legs, Boston, 1810-25, 62½in. long. (Christie's) $4,950 £3,464

A Federal mahogany breakfast table with D-shaped leaves, 1800-15, 45in. wide, open. (Christie's) $3,080 £2,155

A Spanish walnut drop-leaf table, 32½in. wide. (Christie's) $1,874 £1,320

A Federal inlaid mahogany breakfast table, circa 1790-1810, 39¼in. wide. (Christie's) $6,600 £4,618

An Empire cherry dining table, possibly New York, circa 1825, 45½in. wide. (Robt. W. Skinner Inc.) $600 £387

Federal mahogany dining table, the large drop-leaves with rounded and moulded edge, N.Y., circa 1800, 65in. wide, open. (Robt. W. Skinner Inc.) $8,000 £5,594

A Chippendale mahogany drop-leaf dining table, Townsend School, 1760-80, 43in. deep. (Christie's) $28,600 £20,014

GATELEG TABLES

A Charles II oak gateleg table with oval twin-flap top, some later supports and later bun feet, 71½in. wide, open. (Christie's) $5,742 £3,960

An oak and grained elm gateleg table with oval twin-flap top and one frieze drawer, mid 17th century, 68in. wide, open. (Christie's) $6,198 £3,850

A mid Georgian red walnut gateleg table with oval twin-flap top on scroll headed cabriole legs, 57in. wide, open. (Christie's)
$4,404 £3,080

An oak gateleg table with oval twin-flap top, 17th century, 56½in. long. (Christie's)
$1,683 £1,100

A George II mahogany gateleg side table, the top with one flap, 26½in. wide. (Christie's)
$2,478 £1,620

Mid 17th century small oak gateleg table with oval twin-flap top, possibly Dutch, 32¼in. wide, open. (Christie's) $2,956 £1,760

A late 17th century oak oval twin-flap top gateleg table, the friezes with a drawer each end, 4ft.6in. x 5ft. (Woolley & Wallis)
$4,342 £2,600

Yewwood topped gateleg dining table, oval, on turned and knopped supports, 4ft.1½in. x 3ft.6in. (Hobbs & Chambers)
$2,184 £1,300

GATELEG TABLES

An oak gateleg dining table with oval twin-flap top, part 17th century, 80in. long. (Christie's) $1,600 £1,000

A mid Georgian mahogany gateleg table with oval twin-flap top, on club legs and pad feet, 56in. wide, open. (Christie's) $3,146 £2,200

George II mahogany gateleg table, England, circa 1750, 57½in. long. (Robt. W. Skinner Inc.) $1,600 £1,045

Late 17th century oak gateleg table with oval twin-flap top and frieze drawer, possibly Dutch, 49½in. wide. (Christie's)
                                    $3,141 £1,870

A Jacobean oak oval top gateleg table, two drawers, carried on double baluster legs, 57in. wide. (Christie's) $2,880 £2,000

An oak gateleg dining table, the planked oval folding top with two frieze drawers, extending to 63in., basically late 17th century. (Christie's) $1,667 £1,150

A 17th century oak gateleg table, the oval twin-flap above an end drawer, 38½in. long. (Christie's) $800 £500

Late 17th century William and Mary gateleg table, England, 60¼in. long, extended. (Robt. W. Skinner Inc.) $650 £454

A mahogany dining table of early Georgian style in two sections, each drop-leaf section with twin-flap rectangular top, 96in. long. (Christie's)
$13,175 £8,500

A George IV mahogany extending dining table, the top with two drop leaves on seven turned and ribbed tapering legs, 132in. long extended. (Christie's) $4,719 £3,300

A Federal three-part mahogany dining table on square tapering legs with stringing, American, 1790-1810, 154¾in. long. (Christie's)
$12,100 £7,983

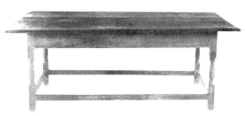

William and Mary walnut tavern table, the top with breadboard ends, Pennsylvania, circa 1740, 71½in. long. (Robt. W. Skinner Inc.)
$3,900 £2,600

A Regency mahogany and ebony strung D-end dining table in three sections, centre section with reconstruction, 1.87 x 1.22m. extended. (Phillips) $5,184 £3,600

A George III mahogany bow-ended sectional dining table, 4ft.5in. x 7ft.2in. (Woolley & Wallis) $4,032 £2,800

One of a pair of George III giltwood side tables designed by Robt. Adam and made by S. Alken, 65½in. long. (Christie's)
$403,260 £286,000

A Regency mahogany drop-leaf table on turned tapering ribbed legs, 70½in. long. (Christie's) $4,963 £3,520

LARGE TABLES

Large Queen Anne style mahogany oval drop-leaf table, 83¼in. long. (Robt. W. Skinner Inc.) $2,600 £1,818

Early 20th century mahogany library table with leather inset top, by Waring & Gillows, 8ft. x 4ft. (Peter Wilson) $1,128 £800

A Regency mahogany twin pedestal dining table, on ring turned column and quadruped hipped splayed legs, 2.41 x 1.33m. overall. (Phillips) $5,184 £3,600

A George III mahogany serpentine serving table with fluted frieze, 103in. long. (Christie's) $13,370 £9,350

A William IV oak extending dining table, with three leaves, 53¼in. wide, 99½in. long. (Christie's) $4,342 £3,080

A George III yewwood serpentine serving table with eared top and fluted frieze flanked and divided by roundels, 83½in. long. (Christie's) $11,797 £8,250

A George III oval snap-top dining table with a reeded edge, 4ft.1in. x 5ft.8in. (Woolley & Wallis) $4,896 £3,400

A Georgian D-ended mahogany dining table, the friezes with rosewood bands, 8ft.8in. long. (Parsons, Welch & Cowell) $1,540 £1,000

A mahogany three-pillar dining table, the rounded rectangular top with a reeded edge, 150in. long, including two leaves. (Christie's) $2,416 £1,600

A Wiener Werkstatte black stained limed oak table designed by J. Hoffmann, 224.7cm. long. (Christie's) $10,281 £7,140

A George III Irish mahogany drop-leaf dining table of 'Hunt' or 'Wake' type, 2.75 x 1.36m. (Phillips) $22,720 £16,000

A George III mahogany D-end dining table in three sections, the centre with two flaps above a plain frieze on square tapering legs, 106in. (Christie's) $3,190 £2,200

A George III style mahogany three-pillar dining table with D-ended top, 140in. x 46in. (Christie's) $3,775 £2,640

A George III mahogany side table of Adam design, 60in. wide. (Dreweatts) $5,800 £4,000

An oak draw-leaf table on baluster turned legs joined by box stretcher, basically 17th century, 72in. wide, extended. (Christie's) $1,573 £1,100

An early Victorian figured mahogany extending dining table, the oval ends with five extra leaves, stamped Cope & Collinson, 12ft.4in. long, extended. (Woolley & Wallis) $4,433 £3,100

LARGE TABLES

A mid Victorian burr walnut dining table on fluted and turned twin-column supports and scrolled feet, 96in. long. (Christie's)
$2,988 £2,090

An early 19th century D-ended mahogany dining table. (Parsons, Welch & Cowell)
$3,020 £2,000

A George III giltwood side table with D-shaped white marble top, 62¼in. wide. (Christie's) $15,510 £11,000

A Regency rosewood veneered platform base extending dining table, the splayed legs with brass sabots on castors, 4ft.2in. x 8ft.4in. extended. (Woolley & Wallis) $3,289 £2,300

A late George III mahogany twin-pedestal dining table, 105½ x 48in., including three extra leaves. (Christie's) $7,755 £5,500

One of a pair of George III mahogany serpentine serving tables, 67in. wide. (Christie's) $17,303 £12,100

A Regency ormolu mounted mahogany break-front serving table, 81in. wide. (Christie's)
$13,370 £9,350

A George III mahogany dining table with wide darker mahogany borders, fully extended 122in. (Graves Son & Pilcher) $2,642 £1,750

OCCASIONAL TABLES

One of a pair of parcel gilt and rosewood tripod tables with leather lined tops, 16¼in. diam. (Christie's) $2,988 £2,090

A mahogany circular snap-top galleried occasional table, 32in. diam. (Woolley & Wallis) $1,872 £1,300

A 19th century carved rosewood, brass embellished and inlaid marble top occasional table. (Phillips) $3,124 £2,200

A Regency ormolu mounted mahogany and bronze gueridon in the manner of Thos. Hope, 21¼in. diam., 32¼in. high. (Christie's) $49,632 £35,200

A brushed steel and chromium-plated table, the design attributed to Ringo Starr, 121.5cm. wide, 66cm. high. (Christie's) $314 £220

An ormolu gueridon in the manner of Weisweiler with pink granite top, stamped P. Sormani, Paris, 19¾in. diam. (Christie's) $20,196 £13,200

A George III satinwood tripod table, the tip-up top crossbanded with tulipwood, 21½in. wide. (Christie's) $13,959 £9,900

A Chippendale period mahogany snap-top table, 34½in. diam. (Parsons, Welch & Cowell) $1,232 £800

An early Victorian black and gilt japanned papier-mache pedestal table, 24in. wide. (Christie's) $7,078 £4,950

OCCASIONAL TABLES

A George III mahogany tripod table with scalloped circular tip-up top, 25½in. diam. (Christie's) $4,342 £3,080

A George III satinwood, sycamore and marquetry tripod table with circular tip-up top, 29½in. diam. (Christie's) $5,505 £3,850

A George II mahogany tripod table with circular piecrust top, 18in. diam. (Christie's) $1,318 £935

A Regency penwork and ebonised table, the octangular top with a temple in a land-scape, 18½in. wide. (Christie's) $2,831 £1,980

A George III mahogany tripod table with octagonal tilt-top, 47in. wide. (Christie's) $3,460 £2,420

A Victorian walnut occasional table, labelled Plucknett & Steevens, Cabinet Makers & Upholsterers, Warwick & Leamington, 28in. high. (Christie's) $1,178 £770

Early 19th century rosewood tripod table, the top centred by a glazed panel enclosing a Viennese porcelain plate, 13in. sq. (Christie's) $7,735 £5,500

A Georgian mahogany tripod table. (Lots Road Galleries) $573 £380

An early Victorian oak occasional table with cross-banded circular top, 21.5in. diam. (Christie's) $1,473 £1,045

OCCASIONAL TABLES

One of a pair of ebonised tripod tables with concave-sided rectangular eared tops, on bobbin-turned shafts and scrolling legs with brass bun feet, 17½in. wide.(Christie's) $3,030 £2,090

A Regency mahogany table with rectangular top and ring-turned tapering legs, 24in. wide. (Christie's) $660 £432

A rosewood occasional table with rectangular specimen marble top and ripple-moulded edge, 18in. wide. (Christie's) $2,073 £1,430

An Italian specimen marble low table on gilt metal ring-turned ribbed tapering legs, 30¾in. diam. (Christie's) $5,582 £3,850

A mahogany tripod table, the octagonal top centred by a fan roundel with pierced fluted gallery, 27in. wide. (Christie's) $1,404 £918

William and Mary oval top painted tavern table, New England, circa 1740, 29in. wide. (Robt. W. Skinner Inc.) $6,750 £4,500

An Emile Galle fruitwood and marquetry table a deux plateaux, 52.5cm. wide. (Christie's) $858 £561

A laminated beechwood two-tier low circular table designed by Gerald Summers for The Makers of Simple Furniture, 73.3cm. diam. (Christie's) $2,478 £1,620

A Majorelle marquetry beech occasional table, the trefoil top inlaid in tulip and rose-wood, 74.8cm. high. (Phillips) $748 £520

OCCASIONAL TABLES

One of a pair of rosewood occasional tables, edged with brass, 16½in. wide. (Christie's) $8,772 £6,050

Country Chippendale maple table, New England, circa 1780, 26in. wide. (Robt. W. Skinner Inc.) $1,900 £1,266

A late 18th century Russian mahogany, tulipwood cross-banded and ormolu mounted oval occasional table, 50cm. long. (Phillips) $2,100 £1,400

An early Victorian ebony and marquetry octagonal library table by Edward Holmes Baldock, banded with kingwood, 58in. wide. (Christie's) $11,165 £7,700

Chippendale mahogany serpentine top tip table, Mass., circa 1780, 32½in. diam. (Robt. W. Skinner Inc.) $2,000 £1,333

Early 19th century Chinese Export black and gold lacquer tripod table, 45¼in. diam. (Christie's) $9,251 £6,380

A George II mahogany tripod table with circular tray top, 9¾in. diam. (Christie's) $1,116 £770

A John Penn Chippendale carved mahogany slab-top table, with grey and white inset marble top, 44¾in. wide, 1765-1775. (Christie's) $605,000 £423,379

A Regency rosewood drum table inlaid with boxwood lines, with circular green leather lined top, 24in. wide. (Christie's) $8,530 £6,050

OCCASIONAL TABLES

A mahogany tric-trac table of Louis XVI style, the leather lined reversible tray top with ebony and fruitwood chess players, 44½in. wide. (Christie's) $2,871 £1,980

A Chippendale cherrywood tilt-top stand, Mass., 1780-1800, 28in. high, 18¼in. wide. (Christie's) $1,760 £1,231

A Chippendale cherrywood side table, probably Conn., 1760-90, 34in. wide. (Christie's) $880 £569

A late 18th/early 19th century Chinese coromandel and lacquer occasional table, 47cm. sq. (Phillips) $1,207 £850

An Art Deco coffee table, circular parquetry top on four scrolling wrought iron legs, 79.6cm. diam. (Christie's) $660 £432

Country Federal maple and mahogany veneer tray table, with original red translucent stain finish, circa 1820, 28in. high. (Robt. W. Skinner Inc.) $8,000 £5,594

A mahogany tripod table, the circular tilting top with scalloped edge, 25in. diam. (Christie's) $924 £550

L. & J. G. Stickley oak server with open plate rack, circa 1912, no. 750, 48in. wide. (Robt. W. Skinner Inc.) $500 £350

A late Victorian mahogany specimen marble occasional table, 21in. wide. (Christie's) $2,831 £1,980

OCCASIONAL TABLES

A George II mahogany tripod table with hexagonal tip-up top, 26½in. wide.(Christie's) $3,102 £2,200

Gustav Stickley cut-corner library table, 1902-04, 48in. wide. (Robt. W. Skinner Inc.) $750 £524

A nest of three satinwood quartetto tables, the tops crossbanded with rosewood and with ebonised low galleries, one 19in., one 14½in. (Christie's) $4,342 £3,080

A George III mahogany urn table with square rosewood banded top, 11½in. sq. (Christie's) $1,730 £1,210

A Chippendale period carved mahogany half round side table of Director design, 1.29m. wide. (Phillips) $5,760 £4,000

A black lacquer and simulated bamboo two-tier occasional table, 23¼in. wide. (Christie's) $1,771 £1,100

A set of four mahogany quartetto tables with twin-turned spreading trestle ends, 11½in. to 18in. (Christie's) $2,171 £1,540

A Georgian mahogany snap-top table, on turned column and tripod, 2ft.11in. diam. (Hobbs & Chambers) $257 £180

A mahogany occasional table with circular galleried top and fluted frieze, 23¼in. diam. (Christie's) $471 £330

PEMBROKE TABLES

A George III mahogany Pembroke table with twin-flap top and pierced fretwork frieze, 41½in, wide, open. (Christie's)
$18,612 £13,200

Federal cherry Pembroke table with drop-leaf top, New England, circa 1790, 36in. wide. (Robt. W. Skinner Inc.) $900 £600

An 18th century mahogany Pembroke table with cross-banded serpentine twin-flap top, 32¾in. wide, open. (Christie's) $2,326 £1,650

A George III mahogany and marquetry Pembroke table, the oval top inlaid with a musical trophy, 38in. wide, open. (Christie's)
$1,861 £1,320

A small Regency mahogany Pembroke table, the top crossbanded with satinwood, on baluster shaft and quadripartite legs, 34in. wide. (Christie's)$1,321 £864

A George III mahogany and satinwood Pembroke table, 38in. wide. (Christie's)
$6,204 £4,400

A George III mahogany Pembroke table, the oval twin-flap top crossbanded in satinwood, 36½in. wide, open. (Christie's)
$2,481 £1,760

A Federal inlaid mahogany Pembroke table, the oval top with two drop-leaves, 1795-1825, 29½in. wide. (Christie's) $2,200 £1,539

A George III mahogany Pembroke table crossbanded with rosewood, 37in. wide, open. (Christie's)
$4,653 £3,300

PEMBROKE TABLES

An early George III mahogany Pembroke table with serpentine twin-flap top, 34in. wide, open. (Christie's) $1,735 £1,134

A Chippendale mahogany Pembroke table, Rhode Island, 1760-90, 42½in. wide. (Christie's) $1,650 £1,088

A Regency mahogany Pembroke table with rosewood banded twin-flap top, 37¼in. wide. (Christie's) $471 £330

A George III mahogany Pembroke table, the top crossbanded with tulipwood, 35½in. wide. (Christie's) $2,233 £1,540

A 19th century satinwood and decorated Pembroke table, 99 x 80cm. extended. (Phillips) $5,680 £4,000

A George III mahogany Pembroke table, the oval twin-flap top crossbanded in satinwood, 36½in. wide, open. (Christie's) $2,313 £1,512

A George III inlaid mahogany oval Pembroke table, 92 x 74cm. extended. (Phillips) $6,248 £4,400

A Federal inlaid mahogany Pembroke table, the oval top with two drop leaves, 1790-1810, 39¼in. wide, open. (Christie's) $8,800 £5,800

A painted satinwood Pembroke table, the oval twin-flap top crossbanded with rosewood, 36in. wide, open. (Christie's) $6,606 £4,620

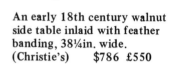

A laburnum and walnut side table with associated oyster-veneered top, basically late 17th century, 35¾in. wide. (Christie's) $5,020 £3,080

A maple side table, the design attributed to Ico Parasi, with plate glass top, 128.1cm. wide. (Christie's) $2,217 £1,540

An early 18th century walnut side table inlaid with feather banding, 38¼in. wide. (Christie's) $786 £550

A late Victorian cast iron side table with associated specimen marble top on scrolling foliate trestle-ends, 43in. wide. (Christie's) $3,932 £2,750

An early Georgian walnut side table on cabriole legs and pad feet, 27½in. wide. (Christie's) $2,148 £1,404

Classical Revival pier table, possibly Boston, circa 1830, minus marble top, 39in. wide. (Robt. W. Skinner Inc.) $1,600 £1,118

A Regency black painted and gilded side table in the Brighton Pavilion taste, 38in. wide. (Christie's) $6,813 £4,180

A Regency mahogany side table on ring-turned tapering legs, 22in. wide. (Christie's) $393 £275

A William and Mary oak side table banded with walnut and inlaid with boxwood lines, 25¾in. wide. (Christie's) $1,982 £1,296

SIDE TABLES

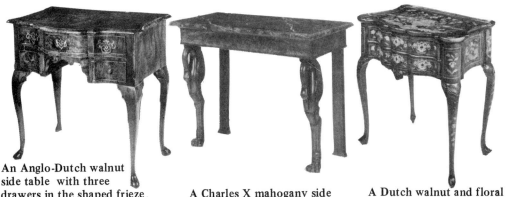

An Anglo-Dutch walnut side table with three drawers in the shaped frieze, on cabriole legs and hoof feet, 30½in. wide. (Christie's) $3,139 £2,052

A Charles X mahogany side table with red-veined black marble top. (Christie's) $4,686 £3,300

A Dutch walnut and floral marquetry side table of serpentine outlines, 30½in. wide. (Christie's) $3,124 £2,200

A Regency amboyna and yewwood side table with two frieze drawers, 35½in. wide. (Christie's) $2,313 £1,512

A George III sycamore and marquetry side table, the top inlaid with a parrot on a branch, 22in. wide. (Christie's) $3,190 £2,200

A George III mahogany side table with rounded rectangular top and two frieze drawers, 32in. wide. (Christie's) $1,258 £880

A Dutch walnut and floral marquetry side table, 33¾in. wide. (Christie's) $2,811 £1,980

An early Georgian walnut side table with crossbanded quartered rectangular top and three drawers, 25in. wide. (Christie's) $1,652 £1,080

An early Georgian walnut side table, the top with later carved border, 30in. wide. (Christie's) $1,569 £1,026

SIDE TABLES

A George III rosewood and marquetry side table in the manner of Pierre Langlois, 50½in. wide. (Christie's) $13,183 £9,350

A George III Irish carved mahogany folding top table, 1.17m. wide. (Phillips) $5,040 £3,500

A late George III mahogany bowfront side table, 29½in. wide. (Christie's) $830 £550

A George I mahogany side table on lapetted turned spreading legs and pad feet, 30in. wide. (Christie's) $2,016 £1,430

A George III mahogany side table with rectangular moulded top, 36in. wide. (Chrstie's) $707 £495

One of a pair of Queen Anne gilt gesso side tables on cabriole legs and foliate pad feet, 29in. wide. (Christie's) $46,530 £33,000

A George III mahogany side table with serpentine top, 34¾in. wide. (Christie's) $2,636 £1,870

A giltwood side table with rectangular eared verde antico marble top, 40¼in. wide. (Christie's) $11,797 £8,250

An Irish walnut side table with serpentine marble top, basically mid 18th century, 41½in. wide. (Christie's) $5,273 £3,740

SIDE TABLES

A Regency rosewood side table with one drop-leaf, 52in. wide. (Christie's) $3,102 £2,200

A George III mahogany serving table, the top outlined with boxwood, 63in. wide.(Christie's) $3,190 £2,200

A George III mahogany and giltwood pier table, 45in. wide. (Christie's) $10,857 £7,700

A George III mahogany and cream painted serving table with three-quarter brass gallery, 66in. wide. (Christie's) $7,444 £5,280

A George III painted satinwood small side table, the top with a low gallery, 20½in. wide. (Christie's) $7,755 £5,500

A George I walnut side table with four drawers around an arched kneehole, 32in. wide. (Christie's) $15,510 £11,000

One of a pair of early George III giltwood side tables each with a serpentine eared Portor marble top, 48in. wide. (Christie's) $58,938 £41,800

A 19th century Anglo-Indian carved hardwood side table, 52in. wide. (Parsons, Welch & Cowell) $708 £460

An early George III mahogany side table with later rectangular serpentine marble top, 51in. wide. (Christie's) $7,931 £5,184

SOFA TABLES

A satinwood sofa table with rounded rectangular twin-flap top, on trestle ends and splayed feet, 56in. wide, open. (Christie's)
$1,036 £715

A Regency rosewood sofa table, the top with rope-twist brass border, 58in. wide, open. (Christie's)
$2,871 £1,980

A George III satinwood sofa table banded with partidge-wood and inlaid with ebonised lines, 58½in. wide, open. (Christie's) $24,816 £17,600

A mid 19th century satinwood and inlaid sofa table with a hinged top crossbanded in kingwood, 1.41m. x 64cm. (Phillips) $2,130 £1,500

A George III mahogany sofa table, the twin-flap top crossbanded with rosewood, 54in. wide, open. (Christie's)
$2,831 £1,980

A sofa table veneered and decorated as satinwood and painted with a design of flowers and ribbon border, 5ft. long, extended. (Lots Road Galleries)
$1,650 £1,100

A George III mahogany sofa table with twin-flap cross-banded top above two frieze drawers, 57½in. wide, open. (Christie's) $3,987 £2,760

A Regency brass inlaid roswood sofa table with twin-flap top and ebonised border, 61¼in. wide, open. (Christie's) $10,224 £7,150

A George III mahogany sofa table crossbanded with rose-wood and inlaid with box-wood lines, 59in. wide, open. (Christie's) $4,032 £2,860

SOFA TABLES

A Regency mahogany sofa
table with twin-flap top and
reeded edge, 58¾in. wide,
open. (Christie's)
$9,306 £6,600

A Regency rosewood and
brass inlaid sofa table,
stamped T. Sharples,
Liverpool, 1.66m. x 69cm.
(Phillips) $6,624 £4,600

A Regency mahogany sofa
table with twin-flap top
and reeded edge, 57¼in. wide.
(Christie's) $2,202 £1,540

An Empire ormolu mounted
mahogany sofa table, possibly
Sweden, circa 1815, 39¼in.
wide. (Robt. W. Skinner Inc.)
$1,600 £1,118

A William IV rosewood sofa
table, stamped T. & A. Blain,
Liverpool, 58in. wide.
(Christie's) $4,785 £3,300

Regency rosewood sofa
table, 58in. wide, open.
(Worsfolds)
$6,468 £4,200

A Regency mahogany and
ebony strung sofa table, the
hinged top crossbanded in
satinwood and rosewood,
1.48m. x 71cm. (Phillips)
$2,448 £1,700

A Regency rosewood sofa
table with twin-flap top and
three frieze drawers, 73in.
wide. (Christie's)
$7,444 £5,280

A Regency mahogany sofa
table with twin-flap top above
two frieze drawers, 52in. wide.
(Christie's) $3,567 £2,530

WORKBOXES & GAMES TABLES

A George III satinwood work table with a fitted frieze drawer and slide hung with a pleated green silk work basket, 19¼in. wide. (Christie's) $1,355 £935

A Regency padoukwood games table, the satinwood banded twin-flap top with reversible centre section, 43in. wide, open. (Christie's) $13,183 £9,350

A Federal walnut and maple work table, New England, 1815-25, 20in. wide. (Christie's) $990 £692

A late Federal mahogany work table, New York, 1815-25, 23in. wide. (Christie's) $3,300 £2,177

A Victorian walnut and parcel gilt etched pedestal games table with inset octagonal specimen marble top, 33in. wide. (Christie's) $3,460 £2,420

A Federal mahogany work table, the drawer fitted with compartments, Penn., 1810-20, 18¾in. wide. (Christie's) $3,300 £2,177

A Victorian papier-mache games table, the revolving top inlaid for chess in mother-of-pearl, stamped Jennens & Bettridge, 67cm. wide. (Phillips) $3,692 £2,600

Regency rosewood games table with tooled red leather top and fitted backgammon drawer. (Lots Road Galleries) $3,410 £2,200

A George III Scottish black and gold lacquer work table, stamped Bruce & Burns, Edin., 18½in. wide. (Christie's) $991 £648

WORKBOXES & GAMES TABLES

Early 19th century Shaker pine and maple work table, probably New England, 36in. high. (Robt. W. Skinner Inc.) $2,000 £1,398

A Chinese Export lacquer games table, the top with reversible lift-out centre enclosing chess squares and a backgammon board, circa 1820, 35½in. wide. (Christie's) $2,974 £1,944

A Regency satinwood games and work table with lift-out top crossbanded with rosewood and inlaid on the reverse with a chessboard, 20in. wide. (Christie's) $4,404 £3,080

A George IV rosewood sewing table with velvet-lined swivelling hinged top, with pleated olive simulated-silk basket, 21in. wide. (Christie's) $957 £660

Federal cherry inlaid work table, New Jersey, circa 1815, 27in. high. (Robt. W. Skinner Inc.) $1,600 £1,118

A Victorian figured walnut games/sewing table with serpentine front and ends, 23in. wide. (Peter Wilson) $1,057 £750

A mid Victorian black, gilt and mother-of-pearl japanned papier-mache pedestal work table, 18½in. wide.(Christie's) $943 £660

An early 19th century Chinese Export lacquer games table with twin-flap top, 39in. wide, open. (Christie's) $1,551 £1,100

A mid Victorian black, gilt and mother-of-pearl japanned papier-mache pedestal table, 24½in. wide. (Christie's) $1,258 £880

WORKBOXES & GAMES TABLES

An Empire mahogany and mahogany veneer work table, circa 1830, 20½in. wide. (Robt. W. Skinner Inc.)
$225 £145

A Jaipur marble games table, top inlaid with polychrome marbles, including lapis lazuli and coloured quartz, 25½in. sq. (Christie's)
$3,146 £2,200

A Regency penwork games table, on spirally-turned shaped ebonised shaft, 21½in. wide. (Christie's)
$2,044 £1,430

Late 18th century Anglo-Indian ivory work table with oval hinged top, Vizagapatam, 24¼in. wide. (Christie's)$26,367 £18,700

A classical mahogany work table with hinged top enclosing a compartmented interior, New York, 1815-25, 27in. wide. (Christie's)
$12,100 £7,983

A George III mahogany work table inlaid with boxwood stringing, 17¾in. wide. (Christie's) $1,651 £1,155

A Regency ormolu mounted rosewood work table with pierced galleried hinged top, 16¼in. wide. (Christie's)
$1,730 £1,210

A George III mahogany work table, the top with adjustable slide to the back filled with sky blue moire silk, 25½in. wide. (Christie's)
$4,653 £3,300

A mid Victorian black, gilt and mother-of-pearl japanned papier-mache games table, 19¾in. diam. (Christie's)
$1,101 £770

A George III satinwood work table, the kidney-shaped quartered top crossbanded with rosewood, 32½in. wide. (Christie's) $13,183 £9,350

A Regency mahogany games table inlaid with ebonised lines and with reversible centre section, 42½in. high. (Christie's) $15,510 £11,000

A William IV burr elm work table, the folding top with rosewood banded borders, 33½in. wide. (Christie's) $1,386 £900

A George III satinwood work table with twin-flap octangular top crossbanded with rosewood, 21¼in. wide. (Christie's) $8,065 £5,720

Early 20th century Regency brass and ebony inlaid work table, England, 23½in. wide. (Robt. W. Skinner Inc.) $1,300 £909

A 19th century walnut and fruitwood pictorial marquetry games table, 25in. diam. (Christie's) $2,016 £1,430

A Regency beechwood and oak work table with crossbanded, twin-flap rounded top, 25½in. wide. (Christie's) $797 £550

An early 19th century Chinese Export black lacquer work table, the top enclosing a fitted interior, 26in. wide. (Christie's) $1,036 £715

A George III tulipwood work table of tricoteure form, 23¼in. wide. (Christie's) $7,755 £5,500

FURNITURE

A Regency ormolu mounted
rosewood writing table in
the manner of John McLean,
42¼in. wide. (Christie's)
$55,836 £39,600

Federal mahogany and mahogany veneer desk, possibly
New York, circa 1820, 50½in.
wide. (Robt. W. Skinner Inc.)
$600 £400

A Robert Thompson 'Mouse-
man' oak writing desk, signed
with a carved mouse, 182.5cm.
wide. (Christie's) $554 £385

A Federal inlaid mahogany
writing desk, with hinged
lid, 1790-1810, 29.7/8in.
wide. (Christie's)
$1,650 £1,154

A Victorian walnut roll-top
desk, Winneberger, Penn.,
circa 1890, 40½in. wide.
(Robt. W. Skinner Inc.)
$1,100 £709

A George III mahogany
writing table with leather
lined, kidney-shaped top,
40in. wide. (Christie's)
$3,102 £2,200

Mid 18th century George III
mahogany writing table,
44in. wide. (Christie's)
$6,600 £4,307

A Dutch walnut and floral
marquetry bureau de dame
of serpentine outline, 35in.
wide. (Christie's)
$3,436 £2,420

A Regency maple and rose-
wood marquetry library
table, on standard end
supports, 1.30m. (Phillips)
$8,064 £5,600

WRITING TABLES & DESKS

A Regency mahogany writing table with green leather lined top, the ends with brass balustrade galleries, 42in. wide. (Christie's) $2,202 £1,540

A Regency ormolu mounted mahogany and ebonised Carlton House desk with Bramah locks, 57in. wide. (Christie's)
$93,060 £66,000

A George III mahogany veneered rectangular writing table with inset gilt tooled green leather top, 3ft.3in. long. (Woolley & Wallis)
$1,550 £1,000

A Louis XV/XVI transitional period parquetry, marquetry and ormolu decorated bureau a cylindre veneered in tulipwood, kingwood and purpleheart, 1.44m. wide. (Phillips) $10,650 £7,500

A lady's oak desk with fall-front, circa 1890, 28½in. wide. (Robt. W. Skinner Inc.)
$500 £320

A mid Victorian ormolu mounted walnut and tulipwood writing table with leather lined top, 43in. wide. (Christie's) $8,530 £6,050

A walnut bureau-on-stand with baize-lined sloping flap enclosing a fitted interior, 21in. wide. (Christie's) $1,239 £810

A Regency mahogany writing table with leather lined top, the panelled frieze with five drawers, 54¾in. wide. (Christie's) $5,033 £3,520

A George III satinwood writing table with leather lined easel top and slide, 23½in. wide. (Christie's)
$7,755 £5,500

A Louis XIV marquetry
bureau mazarin, the top with
brass edge, 1.17m. wide.
(Phillips) $18,000 £12,500

A Heal's oak writing desk,
designed by Ambrose Heal,
152.3cm. wide. (Christie's)
$3,801 £2,640

A 19th century scarlet tortoiseshell and brass marquetry
bureau mazarin in the manner
of Boulle, 1.22m. wide.
(Phillips) $5,680 £4,000

A Federal inlaid mahogany
writing desk, 1790-1810,
29in. wide. (Christie's)
$2,860 £2,001

A rococo walnut marquetry
lady's desk, bombe and serpentine case with fall-front,
Italy, 31in. wide. (Robt. W.
Skinner Inc.) $1,400 £979

A mid Victorian ormolu
mounted rosewood and
satinwood writing table,
on cabriole legs, 32½in.
wide. (Christie's)
$2,233 £1,540

A Regency pollard oak and
parcel gilt writing table, the
top centred by a hinged easel,
31in. wide. (Christie's)
$2,791 £1,980

Late 19th century Wooton's
Patent desk of walnut and
burr walnut, 39½in. wide.
(Christie's) $6,380 £4,400

A George III satinwood
cylinder desk with tambour
shutter enclosing a fitted
interior, 39¼in. wide.
(Christie's)
$40,326 £28,600

WRITING TABLES & DESKS

A Spanish walnut writing table with hinged top, basically 17th century, 51in. wide. (Christie's) $10,934 £7,700

A George III mahogany architect's desk with rectangular sloping double-flap top, 54in. wide. (Christie's) $3,509 £2,420

An early Victorian rosewood library writing table with inset gilt tooled red leather top, 64in. long. (Christie's) $3,460 £2,420

Louis XV walnut and parquetry bureau a pente on cabriole legs, 36in. wide. (Robt. W. Skinner Inc.) $1,200 £833

A Japanese red and black lacquer cylinder pedestal desk, inlaid with mother-of-pearl and inset with gold lacquer panels, 1.04. wide. (Phillips) $6,900 £4,600

Late 18th century Louis XVI walnut veneered bureau plat, 43in. wide. (Robt. W. Skinner Inc.) $1,100 £763

Late 19th century lady's rosewood veneered cylinder bureau with inlaid marquetry sprays of flowers and stringing, 32in. wide. (Woolley & Wallis) $1,144 £800

A Victorian walnut and ebonised kidney-shaped writing table, by Gillow & Co., 6555, 45½in. wide. (Christie's) $1,015 £700

A George III mahogany cylinder bureau with tambour shutter enclosing a fitted interior, 21in. wide. (Christie's) $6,380 £4,400

A late 17th century brass mounted kingwood coffre fort, the interior with a well, two drawers and two compartments, 11½in. wide. (Christie's) $1,015 £715

An early Victorian oak coffer, the panels 16th century, 65in. wide. (Christie's) $4,712 £3,080

A Chippendale walnut blanket chest, Penn., probably 1782, 54½in. wide. (Christie's) $1,870   £1,308

William and Mary child's blanket chest, New England, circa 1740, 28in. wide. (Robt. W. Skinner Inc.) $5,500 £3,846

A Louis Vuitton cabin trunk covered in brown hide secured by brass pins and mounted with brass lock plate, 114cm. wide. (Christie's) $1,404 £918

Late 18th century painted pine blanket chest on straight bracket feet, Penn., 33¼in. wide. (Christie's) $3,850 £2,540

A Chippendale painted pine blanket chest, attributed to the Himmelberger Shop, circa 1790, 51in. wide. (Christie's) $11,000 £7,257

Late 18th century elm chest with panelled front and plank top, 52in. long. (Peter Wilson) $282 £200

TRUNKS & COFFERS

Late 16th century Momoyama period small coffer with hinged domed cover, 28.5 x 17 x 13cm. (Christie's) $781 £550

An Italian walnut cassone with hinged top, 17th century and later, 67½in. wide. (Christie's) $2,499 £1,760

An iron-bound round topped coffer chest, inscribed 'Clara Angela from Men Anno 1744 21 January'. (Worsfolds) $604 £400

Mid 18th century black and gold lacquer coffer, mounted with shaped and engraved gilt brass angles and lock-plate, 56in. wide. (Christie's) $15,510 £11,000

A 17th century oak coffer with moulded hinged top and panel front, 61cm. wide. (Phillips) $3,168 £2,200

Painted pine dower chest, the moulded lift lid above dovetailed case with deep well above three drawers, Penn., dated 1829, 47in. wide. (Robt. W. Skinner Inc.) $850 £594

An Italian walnut cassone, partly 17th century, 80in. wide. (Christie's) $6,248 £4,400

A Chinese Export black and gold lacquer coffer decorated with foliage and with hinged lid, 36in. wide. (Christie's) $1,321 £864

TRUNKS & COFFERS

Pine and white cedar board chest, the lift top with snipe hinges, probably Mass., circa 1700, 51in. wide. (Robt. W. Skinner Inc.)
$2,700 £1,888

Items of vintage leather luggage, including two trunks, hat box, picnic case and others. (Lots Road Galleries) $400 £250

A George III mahogany chest with hinged lid, 52½in. wide. (Christie's) $1,320 £825

A Momoyama period black lacquer domed chest in hiramakie and takamakie and inlaid in shell, circa 1600, 52cm. wide. (Christie's)
$3,124 £2,200

Late 17th century Flemish leather covered coffer banded with pierced metal strapwork, 43½in. wide. (Christie's) $2,288 £1,430

A large rectangular roironuri chest decorated in gold and brown hiramakie with mon, engraved gilt kanagu, late Edo period, 120 x 61 x 74cm. (Christie's) $3,498 £2,200

Early 18th century oak chest with panelled top enclosing an interior fitted with a well and two small drawers, 55½in. wide. (Christie's) $1,771 £1,100

A putty painted pine blanket box, New England, late 18th century, 47in. wide. (Robt. W. Skinner Inc.) $1,700 £1,062

WARDROBES & ARMOIRES

A bachelor's mahogany wardrobe, the doors opening to reveal four sliding trays, 52in. wide. (Outhwaite & Litherland) $1,334 £920

A 17th century Flemish rosewood and ebony armoire with massive bun feet, 91in. wide. (Christie's) $3,436 £2,420

A Dutch fruitwood armoire with a pair of shaped panelled doors, 76in. wide, 96in. high. (Christie's) $7,040 £4,400

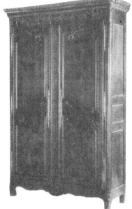

A Louis XV provincial oak armoire on scrolled feet, 57½in. wide. (Christie's) $2,288 £1,430

A 17th century Dutch walnut and ebony armoire, 76in. wide. (Christie's) $1,874 £1,320

Mid 18th century French provincial oak armoire with moulded foliate cornice, 64in. wide, 88in. high. (Christie's) $6,688 £4,180

Late 18th century George III inlaid mahogany linen press on bracket feet, 47½in. wide. (Christie's) $4,950 £3,230

An 18th century French provincial oak armoire, 6ft. 2in. wide. (Capes, Dunn & Co.) $1,522 £1,050

Mid 18th century French provincial oak armoire, 62in. wide, 89in. high. (Christie's) $3,168 £1,980

WARDROBES & ARMOIRES

A George III gentleman's mahogany wardrobe with gilt brass cast swag handles, 4ft.2in. wide. (Woolley & Wallis) $1,268 £840

A William and Mary gumwood kas in two sections, New York, 1725-55, 54in. wide. (Christie's) $4,180 £2,757

A Regency mahogany clothes press, the panelled doors enclosing four slides and two drawers, 56½in. wide. (Christie's) $3,828 £2,640

A 17th century Flemish oak press in two parts, 53½in. wide. (Christie's) $3,748 £2,640

An 18th century Dutch walnut armoire, the bombe lower part fitted with three drawers, 1.83m. wide. (Phillips) $3,124 £2,200

Gustav Stickley two-door wardrobe, panelled doors opening to pull-out shelves, 1904, 33in. wide. (Robt. W. Skinner Inc.) $1,500 £1,049

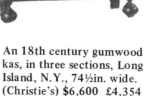

George III pine linen press, the drawers with replaced brass bail handles, England, circa 1800, 46in. wide. (Robt. W. Skinner Inc.) $1,500 £1,048

An 18th century gumwood kas, in three sections, Long Island, N.Y., 74½in. wide. (Christie's) $6,600 £4,354

Late 18th century French provincial oak armoire on squat cabriole legs, 59¾in. wide. (Christie's) $3,748 £2,640

WARDROBES & ARMOIRES

A French provincial fruitwood armoire on squat cabriole legs, 61in. wide. (Christie's) $2,343 £1,650

A George III mahogany clothes press on bracket feet, 50in. wide, 71in. high. (Christie's) $1,487 £972

A George III satinwood clothes press, the sides cross-banded with rosewood, 51½in. wide, 77¼in. high.(Christie's) $21,714 £15,400

A Louis XV cherrywood armoire with moulded chamfered cornice, 56in. wide. (Christie's) $5,935 £4,180

A Regency mahogany break-front wardrobe, 102in. wide. (Christie's) $6,292 £4,400

George III mahogany linen press, the panelled doors enclosing sliding trays, 4ft. x 7ft.6in. high. (Hobbs & Chambers) $1,258 £880

An 18th century South German figured and burr walnut armoire, 74in. wide. (Christie's)$20,306 £14,300

An 18th century German walnut veneered and marquetry armoire, 78in. wide. (Robt. W. Skinner Inc.) $15,500 £10,839

A George III mahogany clothes press with a pair of shaped panelled doors enclosing slides, 47in. wide. (Christie's) $2,148 £1,404

503

WASHSTANDS

A late George III inlaid mahogany corner washstand, 38½in. high, 22in. wide. (Christie's) $1,540 £1,005

A Regency period faded mahogany veneered toilet stand, 21in. wide. (Woolley & Wallis) $334 £200

A George III Sheraton design gentleman's washstand, 28in. wide. (Locke & England) $1,224 £850

A George III mahogany toilet stand inlaid with satinwood bands and geometric boxwood lines, 24¼in. wide. (Christie's) $620 £440

A Classical Revival mahogany washstand, probably Boston, circa 1815, 17½in. diam. (Robt. W. Skinner Inc.) $16,500 £10,312

Shaker pine, tiger maple and butternut washstand, 20¼in. wide. (Robt. W. Skinner Inc.) $10,000 £6,993

A George III Sheraton design mahogany serpentine front washstand, 17½in. wide. (Lalonde Fine Art) $571 £340

A mahogany washstand with small shelf, two drawers and pot shelf, 26 x 18 x 29in. high. (County Group) $273 £170

A Regency oval two-tier washstand, the top tier with open centre, 24½in. wide. (Christie's) $1,293 £770

WHATNOTS

One of a pair of George IV rosewood whatnots with bead-and-reel-moulded tops, 53½in. high. (Christie's) $7,975 £5,500

A snuff and gold lacquer etagere, the two shelves with pierced strapwork galleries, 28½in. long. (Christie's) $2,956 £1,760

Napoleon II ebonised and marquetry three-tier whatnot, 18¼in. wide. (Robt. W. Skinner Inc.) $475 £291

Regency rosewood whatnot, oblong, the three tiers with three-quarter spindle galleries, 1ft.2in. wide. (Hobbs & Chambers) $1,221 £820

A George IV mahogany serving whatnot, the three-quarter galleried tiers joined by baluster supports, 40½in. wide. (Christie's) $1,240 £880

A Regency mahogany two-tier whatnot with easel top and ribbed supports, 21in. wide. (Christie's) $3,102 £2,200

A Regency brass three-tier whatnot with rosewood shelves, 15 x 28in. high. (Dreweatts) $4,437 £2,900

A gilt metal mounted mahogany etagere with two tiers crossbanded with satinwood and centred by a shell medallion, 23½in. wide. (Christie's) $1,415 £990

Victorian figured walnut whatnot, three tier, on scroll feet, 2ft.5in. wide. (Hobbs & Chambers) $571 £340

505

A George III brass bound mahogany cellarette with a lead lined interior, 18½in. wide. (Christie's)
$7,022 £4,180

A Regency mahogany sarcophagus wine cooler with detachable divided tin liner, 33in. wide. (Christie's)
$1,735 £1,134

A George III mahogany cellarette with hinged lid enclosing a divided interior, 16¾in. wide. (Christie's)
$1,551 £1,100

A Federal inlaid walnut cellarette on stand, 1790-1810, 42½in. high, 18½in. wide. (Christie's)
$2,640 £1,707

A Regency mahogany wine cooler with lead lined interior, formerly with a lid, 39in. wide. (Christie's)
$5,667 £3,520

A George III mahogany and satinwood moulded octagonal cellarette on contemporary stand, 46cm. high. (Phillips)
$2,400 £1,600

A Regency mahogany and parcel gilt wine cooler with hinged lid enclosing a tin liner, 26¼in. wide. (Christie's) $2,202 £1,540

A George III mahogany wine cooler, the lined oval body banded in brass, 28in. wide. (Christie's)
$4,228 £2,800

A William IV mahogany sarcophagus-shaped wine cooler with lead lined interior, 27½in. wide. (Christie's) $1,328 £825

WINE COOLERS

A Regency mahogany sarcophagus shaped wine cooler with lead lined interior, on paw feet, 29½in. wide. (Christie's) $3,800 £2,484

A Regency mahogany and inlaid cellarette of boat design, with triple hinged top, 1.02m. wide. (Phillips) $6,532 £4,600

A late Regency mahogany sarcophagus-shaped wine cooler with lid enclosing a lead lined interior, 29½in. wide. (Christie's) $1,887 £1,320

A Regency mahogany cellarette with hinged octagonal top and tin lined interior, 22in. wide. (Christie's) $1,069 £748

A Regency mahogany wine cooler with bronze lion-mask ring handles, on paw feet, 17in. wide. (Christie's) $1,036 £715

A George III mahogany wine cooler with octagonal hinged lid enclosing a metal liner, 19½in. wide. (Christie's) $4,653 £3,300

A large Regency mahogany and ebonised wine cooler in the manner of Gillows, with a lead lined divided interior, 33in. wide. (Christie's) $4,963 £3,520

A George III brass bound mahogany hexagonal cellarette, 28in. high, 17in. wide. (Christie's) $4,400 £2,871

A George III brass bound mahogany wine cooler with arched brass carrying handle and lead lined interior, 13in. wide. (Christie's) $10,081 £7,150

Mid 18th century Central
European 'milchglas'
armorial flared beaker,
14.5cm. high. (Christie's)
$1,082 £660

A 17th/18th century Venetian
'Calcedonia' bell-shaped beaker
of blue, green and brown
marblised glass, 9cm. high.
(Christie's) $665 £462

A Bohemian blue overlay
engraved beaker perhaps by
A. Pfeiffer, Karlsbad, circa
1840, 13cm. high.
(Christie's) $811 £495

A Bohemian 'Zwischensilber-
glas' beaker, circa 1730,
9cm. high. (Christie's)
$2,376 £1,650

Four Lobmeyr beakers, the
bowls fluted, enamelled with
cartouches portraying ladies
and gentlemen in 18th century
costume, 4in. high. (Christie's)
$400 £250

A Bohemian portrait beaker,
the bowl engraved in the
manner of Biemann, circa
1840, 13cm. high.
(Christie's) $1,984 £1,210

A Bohemian 'Zwischengoldglas'
and polychrome beaker, circa
1735, 10cm. high. (Christie's)
$2,851 £1,980

One of a pair of Lobmeyr
beakers, decorated with
Arabic script in blue and red
on a gilt ground, 4in. high.
(Christie's) $319 £209

A Bohemian 'Zwischengoldglas'
flared beaker, by Johann
Mildner, 1790, 10.5cm. high.
(Christie's) $1,584 £1,100

BOTTLES

GLASS

A late Victorian cut glass square cologne bottle with a silver openwork mount by William Comyns, 5½in. high. (Christie's)
$600   £385

Three Vistosi tall bottle vases, designed by Peter Pelzel, circa 1960, 43.5cm., 41cm. and 34cm. (Christie's) $2,112 £1,320

A 19th century overlaid cranberry glass scent bottle and stopper decorated with a painted oval portrait of a lady, 5¾in. high. (Dacre, Son & Hartley) $193 £125

An oil or vinegar bottle with a beaded stopper, 15cm. high, and a finger bowl, 12cm. (Phillips) $277 £180

A set of three Bristol green spirit bottles and stoppers, with cut shoulders and canted corners, gilt with Rum, Shrub and Brandy, 20cm. high. (Lawrence Fine Art)
$672   £400

A German silver gilt mounted ruby glass pilgrim bottle, by Tobias Baur, Augsburg, circa 1690, 12¼in. high. (Christie's) $36,179 £25,300

Mid 17th century Netherlands turquoise serving bottle with gilt metal domed cover, chain and collar attachment, 18.5cm. high. (Christie's) $4,510 £2,750

A Lalique clear and frosted glass bottle and stopper, the cylindrical body moulded with thorny branches, 4¼in. high. (Christie's) $550 £385

Mid 17th century Netherlands turquoise serving bottle, the globular body with kick-in base, 19.5cm. high. (Christie's)
$3,968 £2,420

Saint-Vincent, a Lalique amber plafonnier, the circular bowl in clear and satin-finished glass moulded with bands of scrolling fruit laden vines, 34.6cm. wide. (Christie's) $792 £550

Probably mid 19th century cut glass barber's bowl, 26.5cm. diam. (Christie's) $165 £115

A Dale Chihuly basket set, composed of a blown glass bowl with four other free blown 'squashed' bowl shapes, 37.9cm. diam. of large bowl. (Christie's) $4,296 £2,808

  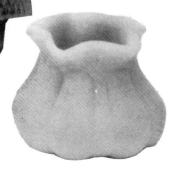

A Burmese satin finished toothpick holder, Boston & Sandwich Glass Co., Mass., circa 1885, 1.7/8in. high. (Robt. W. Skinner Inc.) $200 £139

An Irish cut glass oval fruit bowl with alternate prismatic-cut turnover rim, circa 1800, 32.5cm. wide. (Christie's) $1,188 £825

An Irish cut glass circular fruit bowl, circa 1800, 25cm. diam. (Christie's) $601 £418

A Dale Chihuly basket set, composed of a large blown glass bowl with four other free blown 'squashed' bowl shapes, 1980, 37cm. diam. of large bowl. (Christie's) $4,957 £3,240

A Lalique bowl, clear and pale green glass, 9.5cm. high. (Christie's) $165 £108

An amethyst glass bowl and cover, the design attributed to Josef Hoffmann, 12.5cm. high. (Christie's) $1,573 £1,100

BOWLS

A Tiffany 'Favrile' bowl, the gold and violet iridescent glass wheel engraved with maple leaves, 30cm. wide. (Christie's) $1,101 £770

A Galle enamelled bowl, boat-shaped with frilly rim, engraved Galle signature incorporating mushroom, 29cm. wide. (Christie's)
$1,742 £1,210

A Lalique bowl, jade green opalescent glass moulded with budgerigars, 24cm. diam. (Christie's)
$3,643 £2,530

Late 19th century two-part cut glass punch bowl, America, 14½in. high, 14¾in. diam. (Robt. W. Skinner Inc.)
$900 £629

Early 18th century engraved 'Goldrubinglas' bowl and cover, Bohemia, 15cm. high. (Christie's) $1,425 £990

A Daum bowl, the white, green and red mottled glass acid-etched with primroses and foliage, 13.9cm. high. (Christie's) $865 £605

A Venetian enamelled shallow bowl, decorated in iron-red, white and blue, circa 1500, 16cm. high. (Christie's)
$1,900 £1,320

A Daum acid etched cameo bowl, the clear glass etched with poppies heightened with gilt decoration, 25cm. wide. (Christie's) $707 £495

Glossy Burmese bowl, star shaped form with fluted, ruffled rim, circa 1890, 2¼in. high. (Robt. W. Skinner Inc.) $200 £139

A Christopher Williams dust bowl, engraved The Glasshouse 1986, 30.5cm. diam. (Christie's) $706 £462

'Jardiniere Acanthus', a Lalique canoe-shaped bowl in clear and satin finished glass, 45.4cm. long. (Christie's) $693 £453

A Lalique plafonnier, the hemispherical bowl of yellow frosted glass moulded with peaches and leaves, 38cm. wide. (Christie's)
                    $1,108 £770

A Diana Hobson pate-de-verre bowl form, 1986. (Christie's) $2,356 £1,540

An Irish cut glass punch bowl in the form of an urn, circa 1800, 32cm. high. (Christie's) $950 £660

'Limbo for Three', a David Prytherch sculpture bowl form, 1986, 38cm. high. (Christie's) $5,049 £3,300

One of a pair of white overlay ruby flash bowls, 9in. diam. (Christie's)
            $504 £330

A Jacobite two-handled glass bowl with rose and thistle engraved emblems, 9in. high. (Prudential Fine Art)
            $756 £450

A Steven Newell bowl with decoration of Adam and Eve, 1986, 23.5cm. high. (Christie's) $3,702 £2,420

CANDLESTICKS

Pair of 20th century Colred cut glass candlesticks, European, 14¼in. high. (Robt. W. Skinner Inc.) $500 £326

A Tiffany 'Favrile' glass candlestick in iridescent gold, 4½in. high. (Du Mouchelles) $300 £180

Two of a set of four dwarf candlesticks, each with an alternative pink or clear glass shade decorated with flowers and foliage, 9.5in. high. (Christie's) $240 £150

Pair of 19th century opalene crystal candlesticks, 15½in. high. (Du Mouchelles) $800 £481

A cut glass candlestick with cylindrical nozzle, circa 1800, 25cm. high. (Christie's) $285 £198

A pair of ormolu and cut glass candlesticks with petal nozzles. 12½in. high. (Christie's) $1,416 £880

A faceted taperstick, the slender diamond-cut column with base knob supporting a cylindrical fluted nozzle, circa 1780, 16.5cm. high. (Christie's) $411 £286

Pair of early 20th century Dominick & Haff sterling silver and cut glass candlesticks, threaded into Classical Revival bases, 13½in. high. (Robt. W. Skinner Inc.) $1,200 £736

Mid 18th century moulded pedestal stemmed candlestick, 25.5cm. high. (Christie's) $871 £605

DECANTERS

One of a pair of George III decanters with bull's eye lozenge stoppers, late 18th century. (Woolley & Wallis) $543 £360

A James Powell decanter, clear glass, with pear-shaped stopper, 32cm. high. (Christie's) $201 £132

Early 20th century kew blas decanter, Union Glass Co., Mass, 13½in. high. (Robt. W. Skinner Inc.) $250 £163

An English Jeroboam decanter, the reverse engraved March 8th 1791, 38cm. high. (Phillips) $1,925 £1,250

An Orrefors decanter and stopper, by Nils Landberg. (Christie's) $2,516 £1,760

One of a pair of early 19th century dark emerald green cut glass decanters and stoppers of slender club shape, 30.5cm. high. (Christie's) $792 £550

A Netherlands blue-tinted decanter, the metal mounted cork stopper secured by a chain, 25cm. high. (Phillips) $2,772 £1,800

One of a pair of cylindrical decanters and shaped spiral stoppers, 10½in. high. (Christie's) $81 £55

A Bohemian engraved and cut decanter, circa 1730, 27.5cm. high. (Christie's) $475 £330

DISHES

A Lalique frosted grey green glass boat-shaped dish, 18in. long. (Dacre, Son & Hartley) $586 £360

Lalique amber glass shell duck ashtray, 2¾in. high. (Reeds Rains) $186 £120

A Lalique glass circular dish, the sides and centre decorated with moulded daisy stems, ¡3¼in. wide. (Dacre, Son & Hartley) $326 £200

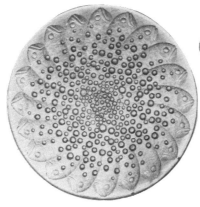

Mid 18th century moulded pedestal stemmed sweetmeat glass, 16.5cm. high. (Christie's) $601 £418

A large Lalique circular, blue opalescent dish, moulded on the underside with carp among bubbles, 35cm. diam. (Christie's) $1,188 £825

A Liberty pewter and Clutha glass dish on stand, designed by A. Knox, 6½in. high. (Christie's) $589 £418

An 18th century cut glass turnover fruit dish, 9in. high. (Prudential Fine Art) $705 £420

An Irish cut centre dish, the bowl of canoe shape, circa 1800, 35cm. wide. (Christie's) $1,984 £1,210

Mid 16th century Venetian bucket or aspersory with rope twist loop handle, 18.5cm. diam. (Christie's) $1,584 £1,100

Bohemian gold decorated cobalt blue glass punch set, late 19th century, 9½in. high. (Robt. W. Skinner Inc.) $900 £548

A Victorian liqueur set with crimped heart-shaped tray, by Heath & Middleston, Birmingham, 1891, the liqueur bottle 8¼in. high, 12.75oz. free. (Christie's) $480 £300

Part of an Art Deco liqueur set, consisting of an engraved glass decanter and stopper, the semi-circular body black, 8¼in. high, and five glasses en suite, 3½in. high, and another three decanters and seven glasses similar. (Christie's) $924 £600

A Japanese cocktail set decorated in high relief with iris, circa 1900. (Phillips) $1,640 £1,000

A Schott & Gen 'Jena er Glas' clear glass tea-set, designed by Wm. Wagenfeld, teapot, cover and filter, 11cm. high. (Phillips) $316 £220

FLASKS

'Rosace Figurines', a Lalique frosted glass circular scent flask and stopper, 11cm. high. (Phillips) $668 £400

A 17th century spirit flask (Tonnelet) of barrel shape, Low Countries or France, 11.5cm. wide. (Christie's) $631 £385

A Nuremburg metal mounted engraved serving bottle, circa 1700, 27.5cm. high. (Christie's) $1,267 £880

A 17th/18th century South German pewter mounted spirit flask, 15.5cm. high. (Christie's) $3,066 £1,870

Mid 18th century Venetian enamelled small scent flask from the atelier of O. Brussa, 11cm. high. (Christie's) $2,525 £1,540

A Netherlands diamond engraved, pewter mounted, green tinted serving bottle, inscribed B. Boers, Warmont, 12 April 1690, 25cm. high. (Christie's) $3,960 £2,750

An 18th century Central European enamelled pewter mounted rectangular spirit flask, 20cm. high. (Christie's) $541 £330

A 17th century Bohemian enamelled small pewter mounted blue flask, 8cm. high. (Christie's) $4,118 £2,860

A 16th century Bohemian enamelled flask, the body painted in colours, 16.5cm. high, together with another 15cm. high, 1595. (Christie's) $1,533 £935

GOBLETS

An incised twist goblet of emerald green tint, circa 1760, 14cm. high. (Christie's)　$760　£528

A Bohemian engraved and stained ruby goblet, circa 1860, 23cm. high. (Christie's)　$792　£550

One of a set of six large Vedar goblets with cylindrical stems and hemispherical bowls, 8in. high. (Christie's)
$1,510　£1,000

Early 18th century German engraved double bowled goblet, 18.5cm. high. (Christie's)　$665　£462

A Netherlands or Rhenish roemer, the egg-shaped bowl and hollow stem applied with irregular prunts, 15.5cm. high. (Phillips)
$246　£160

A semi-polychrome enamelled opaque twist goblet with ogee bowl, circa 1775, 17.5cm. high. (Christie's) $2,217　£1,540

A N. Bohemian (Haida) engraved amber flash goblet and cover, perhaps by F. Egermann Jnr., circa 1845, 44.5cm. high. (Christie's)
$4,118　£2,860

A Wiener Werkstatte glass goblet, the design attributed to Dagobert Peche, 8.4cm. high. (Phillips)　$316　£220

A 17th century Facon-De-Venise serpent stemmed goblet, Venice or Netherlands, 31cm. high. (Christie's)
$2,534　£1,760

GOBLETS

Late 17th century Netherlands diamond engraved goblet, 14.5cm. high. (Christie's) $2,217 £1,540

A Bohemian dated green and enamelled goblet and cover, the fluted bowl decorated in silver, 1841, 25.5cm. high. (Christie's)
$1,584 £1,100

A Bohemian engraved ruby and clear glass goblet in the manner of Karl Pfohl, circa 1855, 22cm. high. (Christie's) $1,029 £715

A James Powell flower-form goblet, milky vaseline-coloured glass, 30.5cm. high. (Christie's) $1,404 £918

One of a pair of champagne coupes, by Hans Christiansen, 17cm. high. (Christie's)
$1,575 £1,100

Late 17th century Facon-De-Venise diamond engraved serpent stemmed goblet, 18cm. high. (Christie's)
$871 £605

A Silesian mercantile goblet and cover perhaps for the Dutch market, circa 1745, 27cm. high. (Christie's)
$6,652 £4,620

One of a set of six Tiffany 'Favrile' champagne coupes, 15cm. high. (Christie's)
$2,359 £1,650

A Potsdam armorial goblet and cover, circa 1720, 41cm. high. (Christie's)
$1,029 £715

Glossy Burmese moulded cream pitcher, Boston & Sandwich Glass Co., 1885, 3¼in. high. (Robt. W. Skinner Inc.) $350 £244

Smith Bros. enamel decorated creamer, Mass., circa 1890, 3.3/8in. high. (Robt. W. Skinner Inc.) $150 £104

A cut glass tapering claret jug with domed hinged cover, 8¾in. high. (Christie's) $166 £99

A Bohemian dated enamelled jug with applied loop handle 1601, 15cm. high. (Christie's) $2,851 £1,980

An oviform water jug with applied scroll handle, 6½in. high. (Christie's) $53 £33

A 16th/17th century Spanish serving vessel of green tint, 25.5cm. high. (Christie's) $475 £330

Crown Milano enamel decorated cream pitcher, Mt. Washington Glass Co., circa 1893, 4¼in. high. (Robt. W. Skinner Inc.) $450 £314

A Victorian silver mounted cut glass claret jug, by Hirons, Plante & Co., Birmingham, 1866, 12in. high. (Christie's) $1,584 £1,100

A Victorian plain bellied glass claret jug, by M. G., London, 1883, 7¼in. high. (Christie's) $576 £400

JUGS

Wheeling peach blow drape pattern pitcher, Hobbs, Brockunier & Co., circa 1886, 4½in. high. (Robt. W. Skinner Inc.) $325 £212

An enamelled glass jug with stopper, by Galle, decorated with enamelled hearts and a dwarf playing a violin, 20cm. high. (Christie's) $633 £440

A Victorian silver mounted dimple glass claret jug, London, 1894, 6¾in. high. (Christie's) $269 £187

Late Victorian cut glass claret jug, by John Round, Sheffield, 1898, 10in. high. (Woolley & Wallis) $633 £440

An oviform wrythen-moulded cream jug, 3½in. high, and another with globular body. (Christie's) $89 £55

A 17th/18th century Spanish amethyst jug, 22.5cm. high. (Christie's) $316 £220

Threaded art glass pitcher, tinted in cranberry and amber, circa 1890, 8½in. high. (Robt. W. Skinner Inc.) $225 £157

A diamond quilted satin glass creamer, probably England, circa 1880, 3¾in. high. (Robt. W. Skinner Inc.) $250 £174

An amberina miniature cream pitcher, New England Glass Co., Mass., circa 1880, 2½in. high. (Robt. W. Skinner Inc.) $225 £157

A Lalique plafonnier, the circular bowl in clear and satin finished glass moulded with bands of fan motifs, 37.4cm. diam. (Christie's) $1,569 £1,026

A Lalique frosted glass figure on bronze base, Suzanne, 23cm. high without base. (Christie's) $6,019 £4,180

A Lalique press-papier in clear and satin-finished glass moulded as a reclining Indian sacred bull, 5.2cm. high. (Christie's) $712 £495

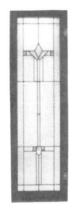

Early 19th century glass and ormolu table centrepiece of eight pieces. (Hobbs & Chambers) $633 £440

One of a pair of early 20th century prairie school-style leaded glass windows, 58in. high, 18in. wide. (Robt. W. Skinner Inc.) $375 £262

Two plate glass Royal Warrant Holder's display signs, bearing the coat of arms of H.M. Queen Alexandra, 18½ x 18in. (Christie's) $393 £275

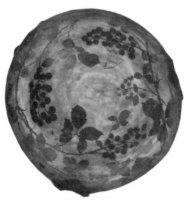

'Cote d'Azur Pullman Express', a Lalique figure, the clear satin finished glass moulded as a naked maiden, 16.8cm. high. (Christie's) $4,404 £3,080

A large Daum cameo glass hanging lampshade of shallow domed form, 46cm. diam., signed. (Phillips) $3,024 £2,100

A 19th century Continental soda glass lace maker's lamp, of baluster form, 22cm. high. (Phillips) $293 £180

MISCELLANEOUS

A Colin Reid cast glass sculptural form, 37cm. high. (Christie's) $3,366 £2,200

Pair of 19th century cut glass lustres, 11½in. high. (Du Mouchelles) $700 £421

A cut glass cruet in the form of an open tourer motor car, 9in. long. (Christie's) $147 £95

A Salviati glass sculpture designed by Livio Seguso, 1960, 61.5cm. high. (Christie's) $629 £440

A 19th century Chinese painting on glass with a group of richly clad children playing with flowers, one with a model goldfish, 28½in. wide. (Christie's) $991 £648

One of two early 20th century prairie school-style leaded glass windows, 20½ x 53½in., and five smaller, 18 x 18¾in. (Robt. W. Skinner Inc.) $1,100 £769

One of a set of six wine glass coolers. (Worsfolds) $107 £70

A late 19th century leaded stained and coloured glass window, signed W. J. McPherson, Tremont St., Boston, Mass. (Robt. W. Skinner Inc.) $800 £490

A cameo glass urn, inscribed Le Verre Francais, 11½in. high. (Christie's) $767 £495

GLASS

A Kaziun poinsettia paperweight, Mass., 2¼in. diam. (Robt. W. Skinner Inc.) $1,600 £1,111

A St. Louis coloured-ground pom-pom weight, set on a pink cushion with swirling white threads, 6.9cm. diam. (Christie's) $1,267 £880

A St. Louis signed and dated concentric millefiori mushroom weight, 8cm. diam. (Christie's) $4,118 £2,860

A St. Louis faceted upright bouquet weight, 5.8cm. diam. (Christie's) $269 £187

A Baccarat snake weight, the pink reptile with green spine markings, 7.9cm. diam. (Christie's) $4,752 £3,300

A Kaziun Morning Glory paperweight, Mass., 2.1/16in. diam. (Robt. W. Skinner Inc.) $1,000 £694

A St. Louis fuchsia weight, the flower resting on a cushion of white spiral latticinio thread, 8cm. diam. (Christie's) $2,851 £1,980

A Clichy initialled 'barber's pole' concentric millefiori weight, 6.8cm. diam. (Christie's) $1,584 £1,100

Mid 19th century Sandwich cherry paperweight, probably by Nicholas Lutz, 2.15/16in. diam. (Robt. W. Skinner Inc.) $700 £489

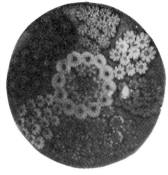

A Clichy swirl weight with alternate pink and white staves radiating from a central red, white and green cane, 5.5cm. diam. (Christie's) $760 £528

A Clichy pink-ground patterned millefiori weight, 8.3cm. diam. (Christie's) $950 £660

A Kaziun pansy paperweight, Mass., signed with gold K on bottom, 2.1/8in. diam. (Robt. W. Skinner Inc.) $750 £520

A Baccarat blue and white flower weight on a star-cut base, 6.7cm. diam. (Christie's) $554 £385

A Kaziun snake paperweight, Mass., 1940's, signed with gold K on bottom, 2.5/16in. diam. (Robt. W. Skinner Inc.) $1,200 £833

A Baccarat garlanded butterfly weight, the insect with purple body, blue eyes and marblised wings, 8cm. diam. (Christie's) $2,217 £1,540

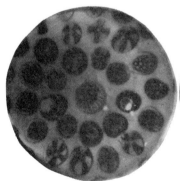

A Clichy 'Sodden Snow' ground concentric spaced millefiori weight, 9cm. diam. (Christie's) $348 £242

A St. Louis blue dahlia weight on a cushion of white spiral latticinio thread, 7.7cm. diam. (Christie's) $918 £638

A Baccarat mushroom weight on a star-cut base, 8cm. diam. (Christie's) $792 £550

A St. Louis three-dimensional fuschia weight, 7cm. diam. (Christie's) $1,584 £1,100

A Baccarat 'thousand-petalled' rose weight, 7cm. diam. (Christie's)
$3,484 £2,420

A Kaziun pedestal rose, Mass., signed with gold K on bottom, 2in. high. (Robt. W. Skinner Inc.) $500 £347

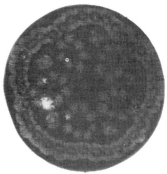

A Baccarat close millefiori mushroom weight on a star-cut base, 8cm. diam. (Christie's) $475 £330

A St. Louis faceted upright bouquet weight, 6.5cm. diam. (Christie's)
$1,346 £935

A Clichy blue-ground patterned millefiori weight on a translucent cobalt blue ground, 8cm. diam. (Christie's) $633 £440

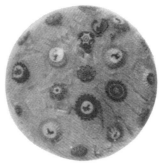

A Baccarat yellow and red flower weight, 6.5cm. diam. (Christie's)
$2,217 £1,540

A Baccarat dated scattered millefiori weight, 7.7cm. diam. (Christie's)
$1,029 £715

A Baccarat double-clematis weight on a star-cut base, 6.5cm. diam. (Christie's)
$633 £440

SCENT BOTTLES

Jade glass ovoid perfume flask and stopper, the moulded body decorated with fish, 7in. high. (Peter Wilson) $331 £210

A Spode globular table scent bottle and stopper, circa 1820, 8.5cm. high. (Christie's) $406 £265

An Apsley Pellatt emerald green cut glass scent bottle and stopper, circa 1825, 14cm. high. (Christie's) $316 £220

A large Victorian porcelain scent bottle of circular shape, by Sampson Mordan, 1885, 5.8cm. diam. (Phillips) $256 £170

A London or South Stafford-shire scent bottle moulded as The Tyrolean Dancers, circa 1770, 3½in. high. (Christie's) $1,859 £1,155

An Orrefors perfume bottle and stopper, designed by E. Hald, engraved H 193 24 B9, 15cm. high. (Christie's) $633 £440

Mid 18th century Venetian lattimo scent bottle of flattened tear-drop form, 10cm. high. (Christie's) $475 £330

Galle cameo glass perfume bottle and mushroom stopper, 4½in. wide, 3¾in. high. (Capes, Dunn & Co.) $739 £440

A Galle flask-shaped scent bottle, the neck with a gilt band, rim chip, 12.5cm. high. (Christie's) $570 £396

A plated amberina tumbler, New Bedford Glass Co., Mass., circa 1886, 3¾in. high. (Robt. W. Skinner Inc.) $850 £555

Late 16th century enamelled armorial 'Stangenglas', S. German or Hall, 26cm. high. (Christie's) $1,900 £1,320

A Bohemian engraved cylindrical tumbler, circa 1825, 10cm. high. (Christie's) $760 £528

A Bohemian 'Zwischengoldglas' flared tumbler, circa 1730, 9cm. high. (Christie's) $950 £660

A tumbler, 9cm. high, together with a pair of cylindrical mugs with loop handles, 6cm. high. (Phillips) $308 £200

A Bohemian cut glass coin tumbler, circa 1830, 12.5cm. high. (Christie's) $538 £374

Green opaque art glass tumbler, New England Glass Co., Mass., 1887, 3.7/8in. high. (Robt. W. Skinner Inc.) $450 £314

A German enamelled 'Stangenglas' for Augustus Sudoflen, Saxony or Bohemia, 1658, 23cm. high. (Christie's) $3,960 £2,750

A plated amberina tumbler, New Bedford Glass Co., Mass., circa 1886, 3¾in. high. (Robt. W. Skinner Inc.) $1,000 £699

TUMBLERS

A Viennese transparent enamelled topographical 'ranftbecher' attributed to Anton Kothgasser, circa 1830, 12cm. high. (Christie's) $7,128 £4,950

A German 'Reichsadler' humpen of greenish-grey tint, Bohemia, dated 1601, 28.5cm. high. (Christie's) $12,672 £8,800

A peachblow agata tumbler, New England Glass Co., Mass., circa 1887, 3.5/8in. high. (Robt. W. Skinner Inc.) $475 £332

A Viennese gold-ground enamelled 'ranftbecher', attributed to Anton Kothgasser, circa 1830, 11cm. high. (Christie's) $6,652 £4,620

A Viennese transparent enamelled 'ranftbecher', the body painted with three playing-cards from a Tarot pack, circa 1830, 11cm. high. (Christie's) $7,603 £5,280

A German enamelled 'Reichsadler' humpen of greenish metal, dated 1678, Bohemia, 28cm. high. (Christie's) $2,851 £1,980

A Viennese transparent enamelled topographical tumbler, attributed to G. Samuel Mohn, 1815-20, 9cm. high. (Christie's) $3,484 £2,420

Late 16th century enamelled armorial 'Stangenglas', S. German or Hall, 27.5cm. high. (Christie's) $1,900 £1,320

A N. Bohemian transparent enamelled armorial tumbler, circa 1835, 12cm. high. (Christie's) $1,900 £1,320

A Galle cameo glass vase of
flared cylindrical shape,
31.5cm. high, signed with
sinuous cameo 'Galle'.
(Phillips) $4,032 £2,800

'Camargue', a Lalique frosted
glass vase, moulded with
horses in amber stained
cartouches, 28.5cm. high.
(Christie's) $4,561 £3,190

A Le Verre Francais overlay
and acid etched vase, the
white and amber mottled
glass decorated with amethyst
stylised tulips, 39.5cm. high.
(Christie's) $314 £220

A Sabino blue opalescent
glass elongated vase, 29.2cm.
high. (Christie's) $393 £275

An 18th century Spanish
four-handled vase of transparent greenish tint, 22cm.
high, and another, 21cm.
high. (Christie's)
          $285 £198

Lalique smokey-grey flared
vase, cobweb design in
relief, 9½in. high. (Capes,
Dunn & Co.)
          $1,595 £1,100

A Vallerysthal enamelled
and acid etched vase,
24.9cm. high. (Christie's)
          $629 £440

Early 20th century cut glass
flower centre, America,
9.1/8in. high. (Robt. W.
Skinner Inc.) $800 £559

An artistic Galle 'verrerie
parlante' vase, engraved
Galle expos 1900, 41.5cm.
high. (Christie's)
          $75,504 £52,800

VASES

A tall Le Verre Francais overlay acid etched vase, the milky-white and yellow mottled glass overlaid with mottled green, brown and orange glass, 48cm. high. (Christie's) $629 £440

A Lalique baluster vase, the clear satin finished glass moulded with bands of roses with blue staining, 23.6cm. high. (Christie's) $660 £462

A Galle double overlay carved and acid etched landscape vase, the yellow glass overlaid with amethyst trees, 32cm. high. (Christie's) $3,932 £2,750

'Chamois', an amber Lalique vase, the green stained clear and satin finished glass moulded with stylised antelopes, 12cm. high. (Christie's) $1,101 £770

A French glass vase of elliptical section, 24.5cm. high, stamped with poincon and maker's mark JM in lozenge. (Phillips) $547 £380

A Russian cameo glass vase, the milky-white martele glass overlaid with amber stylised leaves, 17cm. high. (Christie's) $1,179 £825

A Galle carved and acid-etched vase, the amber glass overlaid with green oak leaves and acorns, 40cm. high. (Christie's) $1,415 £990

'Soucis', a Lalique blue opalescent glass vase in clear and satin finished glass, 17.2cm. high. (Christie's) $826 £540

A Nuutajarvi Notsjo vase, designed by Gunnel Nyman, 38.8cm. high. (Christie's) $503 £352

A Galle acid etched and enamelled soli-fleur glass vase, the cylindrical body with ribbed and splayed base, 31.6cm. high. (Christie's) $1,487 £972

A Galle cameo vase with carved and acid etched deco-ration of a lakeside scene, the yellow glass overlaid with brown, 26.5cm. high. (Christie's) $2,478 £1,620

A tall Galle double overlay landscape vase, the matt pale white ground overlaid in brown, green and amber polished glass with daffodils, 41.8cm. high. (Christie's) $2,478 £1,620

A vase attributed to Barovier, of flattened urn shape, 29.1cm. high. (Christie's) $1,569 £1,026

An Aureliano Toso vase of asymmetric double-gourd shape, clear glass with thin white latticinio stripes, 27.4cm. high. (Christie's) $2,217 £1,540

A Galle blowout vase with flowering clematis in shaded purple on a yellow ground, 25.5cm. high. (Christie's) $5,287 £3,456

A Daum cameo vase, the matt yellow, amethyst and green ground overlaid in shaded claret-coloured glass, 26.3cm. high. (Christie's) $4,626 £3,024

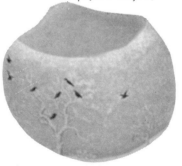

A Daum enamelled and acid etched vase of rounded cube form, enamelled in white, black and grey, with black-birds in winter landscape, 15.2cm. diam. (Christie's) $2,534 £1,760

A tall Daum cameo vase with bulbous neck, with Cross of Lorraine, 50.2cm. high. (Christie's) $1,652 £1,080

VASES

A Daum cameo vase of tall cylindrical shape with slightly everted rim and compressed globular base, 29.1cm. high. (Christie's) $4,461 £2,916

A green Lalique vase, Epicea, with moulded overall decoration of palm fronds, 23.5cm. high. (Christie's) $3,484 £2,420

A Galle acid etched and enamelled vase with cylindrical body and spreading base, 34.9cm. high. (Christie's) $991 £648

A Schneider vase, the mottled orange, yellow and blue glass blown through a wrought-iron mount, 29.3cm. high. (Christie's) $428 £280

'Fountainebleu', a Lalique blue glass vase, the body moulded with fruit-laden trailing vines, 17.4cm. high. (Christie's) $1,487 £972

A Venini 'vetro a file' vase, the russet coloured glass internally decorated with grey veining inlaid with purple rafia. (Christie's) $1,074 £702

A Galle triple cameo fire-polished vase, waisted and flaring cylindrical shape, 49.1cm. high. (Christie's) $3,304 £2,160

A handkerchief vase, attributed to Venini, cased glass with alternating vertical stripes in yellow and purple latticinio, 14.7cm. high. (Christie's) $578 £378

A Tiffany Jack-in-the-Pulpit vase, deep purple and gold iridescent glass, 33cm. high. (Christie's) $3,139 £2,052

533

Mid 19th century engraved opaque white glass vase, 24in. high. (Woolley & Wallis) $1,172 £820

'Marise', a Lalique opalescent glass vase, the body moulded with shoals of fish, 9½in. high. (Christie's) $2,079 £1,350

A Daum glass vase, 39.3cm. high, signed 'Daum Nancy' in gilt on base. (Phillips) $3,600 £2,500

A Loetz orange glass vase, designed by M. Powolny, 8in. high. (Christie's) $231 £150

A Val Saint Lambert elongated baluster enamelled and acid etched vase, 40.1cm. high. (Christie's) $3,303 £2,310

A Galle double overlay carved vase, the shaded grey and green glass overlaid with dark amethyst and violet bindweeds, 13.5cm. high. (Christie's) $786 £550

A Le Verre Francais overlay acid etched vase, the pinkish-white mottled glass overlaid with amethyst stylised chrysanthemums, 32cm. high. (Christie's) $786 £550

'Alicante', a Lalique blue opalescent vase, satin finished glass moulded with a band of six parakeet heads among wheatears, 25.7cm. high. (Christie's) $5,348 £3,740

A Daum cameo and engraved martele baluster vase, engraved Daum Nancy with Cross of Lorraine, 25.4cm. high. (Christie's) $2,674 £1,870

VASES

A Tiffany 'Favrile' vase, the bowl of milky-white glass shading to yellow decorated with lime-green striated feathers, 26cm. high. (Christie's) $2,059 £1,430

A Galle double overlay carved and acid-etched vase, the milky-white glass decorated with dark brown pine trees, 15cm. high. (Christie's) $943 £660

Mother-of-pearl art glass vase in Federzeichnung design, circa 1900, patent 9159, (English control marks), 11½in. high. (Robt. W. Skinner Inc.)
$950 £664

One of a pair of Galle fire-polished urn-shaped vases, one vase inscribed with Galle depose, 26.9cm. high. (Christie's) $3,139 £2,052

A Galle double overlay carved and acid-etched vase, the shaded green, white and pink glass overlaid with brown and green trees, 47cm. high. (Christie's) $4,089 £2,860

A Kosta vase, designed by Vicke Lindstrand, bottle-shaped, circa 1955, 32.5cm. high. (Christie's) $629 £440

A Loetz white metal mounted baluster vase, the metallic orange glass with pulled loop metallic green and white decoration, 19.1cm. high. (Christie's) $918 £638

'Six Figurines et Masques', a Lalique opalescent vase moulded with nude females, 25cm. high. (Christie's)
$3,146 £2,200

A 20th century Steuben cased glass vase, Corning, N.Y., emerald green to white to gold Aurene interior, 10in. high. (Robt. W. Skinner Inc.)
$600 £416

A Daum vase with cameo-cut and enamel painted winter landscape on acid treated matt pale amber ground, 25cm. high. (Christie's) $1,504 £1,045

A Barovier patchwork vase, clear and amber-coloured glass outlined in a darker amber, 18cm. high. (Christie's) $2,534 £1,760

A Galle double overlay carved and acid etched vase, the light green glass overlaid with ferns in shades of green and light brown, 41cm. high. (Christie's) $2,376 £1,650

A Lalique blue opalescent vase, Ceylan, the satin-finished glass moulded with band of budgerigars, 24.2cm. high. (Christie's) $1,742 £1,210

A Galle vase, pale amber-coloured glass with gold foil inclusions overlaid with white and blue, 18.5cm. high. (Christie's) $3,168 £2,200

An Orrefors vase, wheel-engraved in neo-classical style, etched signature Orrefors 1930 S Gate 238 E.W., 17.5cm. high. (Christie's) $601 £418

A Galle marqueterie-sur-verre vase of cylindrical shape, engraved Galle etude, circa 1895, 19.5cm. high. (Christie's) $15,840 £11,000

A small Daum carved and acid etched vase of boat shape, engraved signature Daum Nancy with the Cross of Lorraine, 10.5cm. high. (Christie's) $3,801 £2,640

A Daum internally decorated engraved and applied glass vase of slender shouldered form and bulbous flaring neck, 35cm. high. (Christie's) $79,200 £55,000

VASES

A Galle internally decorated vase, the amber-coloured glass decorated with dark red streaks, engraved Cristallerie de Galle, 20cm. high. (Christie's)
$3,168   £2,200

A D'Argental cameo bowl with trefoil rim, overlaid in claret-coloured glass with water-lily and lily-pad on a pond against a pale amber ground, 16cm. diam. (Christie's) $950 £660

A Galle carved and fire-polished vase, the glass shading from purple to milky white and amber with silver foil inclusions, 32.5cm. high. (Christie's) $9,504 £6,600

A Galle etched and double overlay glass vase, the aquamarine glass overlaid in white and brown and etched with penguins, 20.3cm. high. (Christie's) $17,424 £12,100

A Galle double overlay martele carved and acid etched vase of goblet shape, 15.5cm. high. (Christie's)
$12,672 £8,800

A Cenedese vase, milky glass partly overlaid with white, the decoration and rim in deep amethyst-coloured glass, 34cm. high. (Christie's) $1,188 £825

'Roses de France', a Galle internally decorated, applied martele and overlay glass vase of pear shape, 19.2cm. high. (Christie's)
$76,032 £52,800

A Lalique amber oviform vase, Gros Scarabees, engraved signature R. Lalique, France, No. 892, 29.4cm. high. (Christie's)
$9,504 £6,600

A clear glass vase, the cylindrical shape pulled out on one side to form two oval prunts, engraved Vistosi 1970, 28.5cm. high. (Christie's) $1,029 £715

A tall Galle double overlay landscape baluster vase with everted rim and circular base, 45.9cm. high. (Christie's) $6,606 £4,620

A Muller carved vase, the clear and satin finished glass deeply carved with a reclining tiger, 18.5cm. high. (Christie's) $597 £418

A Gabriel Argy-Rousseau tall pate-de-verre vase, 26cm. high. (Christie's) $7,078 £4,950

Royal Flemish enamel decorated glass vase, Mt. Washington Glass Co., circa 1885, 6.7/8in. high. (Robt. W. Skinner Inc.) $1,100 £769

A Loetz iridescent glass vase, the silvery-purple and green glass with tall tapering neck, 35.8cm. high. (Christie's) $1,258 £880

A Galle double overlay carved blowout vase, the amber glass overlaid with fruiting vines, 27.5cm. high. (Christie's) $7,078 £4,950

A tall Legras acid etched vase, the milky-white and blue glass with trapped air inclusions, 41cm. high. (Christie's) $629 £440

An Orrefors vase, designed by Ingeborg Lunam, shaped like a giant bubble, 40cm. high. (Christie's) $786 £550

A Loetz vase, the textured clear glass with gold iridescence on an amber ground, 20cm. high. (Christie's) $220 £154

VASES

A Galle cameo vase, the matt amber ground overlaid in shaded claret-coloured glass, 45.5cm. high. (Christie's) $5,033 £3,520

'Palissy', a Lalique green tinted vase, the satin finished glass moulded with snail shells, 15.8cm. high. (Christie's) $251 £176

A G. Argy-Rousseau pate-de-verre vase, numbered 16485, 26.5cm. high. (Christie's) $7,550 £5,280

A Galle cameo glass moon-shaped vase, 7in. high. (Reeds Rains) $1,440 £1,000

One of a pair of Moser vases, the clear and amethyst tinted glass carved and engraved with flowers, 26.5cm. high. (Christie's) $471 £330

Burmese satin finish enamel decorated vase, Mt. Washington Glass Co., Mass., circa 1890, 4¾in. high. (Robt. W. Skinner Inc.) $325 £227

A Galle carved acid etched and fire-polished vase, 23.5cm. high. (Christie's) $2,831 £1,980

'Gui', a Lalique vase, the clear satin finished glass with tur-quoise staining moulded with branches of mistletoe, 17.2cm. high. (Christie's) $220 £154

Late 17th/early 18th century Facon-De-Venise filigree vase, 20.5cm. high. (Christie's) $823 £572

WINE GLASSES

One of a pair of ogee shaped wine glasses, 5¼in. high. (Christie's) $191 £121

An opaque twist wine glass, the ogee bowl on double series stem and plain foot, 6¼in. high. (Christie's) $627 £385

A facet stem wine glass of Jacobite significance, 5¾in. high. (Christie's) $152 £94

Late 17th century Bohemian Facon De Venise wine goblet, 16.5cm. high. (Phillips) $800 £500

A moulded pedestal stemmed champagne glass with ogee bowl, circa 1750, 16cm. high. (Christie's) $475 £330

An air-twist wine glass, 5¼in. high, and another 6in. high. (Christie's) $196 £132

A cut cased wine glass, by E. Bakalowits, Vienna, 8in. high, circa 1908. (Giles Haywood) $1,440 £1,000

An engraved opaque twist cordial glass, the funnel bowl with stylised hatched and foliate border, circa 1765, 16.5cm. high. (Christie's) $443 £308

A mercury twist cordial glass of Jacobite significance and drawn trumpet shape, circa 1750, 17cm. high. (Christie's) $506 £352

WINE GLASSES

An opaque twist wine glass with ogee bowl, 5¼in. high, and another of similar type. (Christie's) $251 £154

A wine glass, the opaque twist stem with a pair of six-ply spiral bands outside lace twist, 13.5cm. high. (Phillips)
$492 £320

An opaque twist wine glass, the ogee bowl with hammered flute to the lower part on double series stem, 6¼in. high. (Christie's)
$233 £143

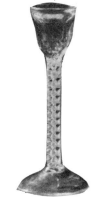

An armorial wine glass of drawn trumpet shape, circa 1740, 18cm. high. (Christie's) $2,217 £1,540

A dark green tinted wine glass with ribbed cup-shaped bowl, circa 1765, 12.5cm. high. (Christie's)$950 £660

An opaque twist deceptive cordial glass, the ogee bowl on a double-series stem and conical foot, circa 1765, 17.5cm. high. (Christie's)
$1,504 £1,045

The 'Breadalbane' Amen glass, the bowl engraved in diamond point, 1745-50, 20cm. high. (Christie's)
$41,184 £28,600

One of a set of five ogee shaped drinking glasses, 6in. high. (Christie's) $590 £374

Mid 18th century mercury twist Jacobite cordial glass with bucket bowl, 17cm. high. (Christie's) $871 £605

A Continental jewelled gold and enamel snuff box, unmarked, 3.1/8in. long. (Christie's) $49,572 £32,400

Late 19th century Australian gold inkstand formed as a possum climbing over a tree trunk, unmarked, 12in. long overall, 41oz. (Christie's) $14,045 £9,180

A French gold mounted marquetry snuff box by Alexandre Leferre, Paris, circa 1840, 3¼in. long. (Christie's) $13,219 £8,640

An early 19th century Swiss gold musical fob seal, maker's initials JJ.H. (Christie's) $1,652 £1,080

A gold and enamel mounted nephrite vinaigrette, probably 19th century, 3¼in. high. (Christie's) $1,321 £864

A George II small shaped oblong gold patch box with mirrored interior, circa 1740, 2in. long. (Christie's) $991 £648

An Omar Ramsden 9ct. beaten gold cigarette case with cut steel relief decoration, gold mark for 1922, 11.3 x 8.8cm. (Christie's) $950 £660

A two-colour gold and amethyst table seal, the citrine matrix with crest and initials, circa 1830, 2¾in. high. (Christie's) $1,900 £1,242

A Louis XVI vari-coloured gold automaton musical snuff box, the lady tight-rope walker on the cover dances to the music, circa 1780, 3.1/8in. long. (Christie's) $99,144 £64,800

A Louis XV rectangular gold and mother-of-pearl snuff box, the panels engraved in the manner of J. B. Oudry, Paris, 1745/6, 3¼in. long. (Christie's) $14,871 £9,720

A gold fob seal, the cornelian base inscribed 'Registrar of Colonial Slaves', circa 1820, small chip. (Christie's) $693 £453

An oblong gold mounted Cairngorm snuff box, circa 1820, possibly Scottish, in slip case, 2¾in. long. (Christie's) $5,618 £3,672

18ct. gold purse, 'Buccellate', Italy, with diamond set thumbpiece, 131gr. (Robt. W. Skinner Inc.) $1,700 £1,180

A 19th century large shaped oblong gold vinaigrette, the lid set with malachite, 1.7/8in. long. (Christie's) $1,074 £702

A 19th century miniature gold mounted mother-of-pearl bureau, in fitted case, 5.1/8in. high. (Christie's) $4,957 £3,240

A Swiss oval gold and enamel snuff box, by J. Georges Remond & Compagnie, the painting on cover by Adam f., circa 1790-1800, 3½in. long. (Christie's) $9,914 £6,480

A George III small enamelled gold scent bottle, in fitted leather case, circa 1775, 2in. high. (Christie's) $3,139 £2,052

A gold mounted agate scent bottle case, containing two 18th century scent bottles, the case 19th century, 2¾in. high. (Christie's) $2,974 £1,944

A small gold and enamel mounted two-handled jasper cup with pierced scroll handles, circa 1625, with later French control mark, 3½in. diam. (Christie's)$5,977 £4,180

A gold, turquoise and diamond lady's mesh evening purse, 10.5cm. across, stamped 9ct., import marks for London 1905. (Phillips) $604 £420

A George III oval gold snuff box, by Elias Russell, London, 1777, 2.7/8in. long. (Christie's) $10,224 £7,150

A gold and enamel musical watch key, the music played on single comb. (Christie's) $2,044 £1,430

A circular gold mounted micro-mosaic box, 2.7/8in. diam. (Christie's) $14,045 £9,180

A gold mounted bloodstone table seal, the stem formed as a hand, 1830, 3.5/8in. high. (Christie's) $1,982 £1,296

A gold mounted amethystine quartz snuff box, modelled as the head of a gryphon, 2.1/8in. long. (Christie's) $5,505 £3,850

A George II gold mounted etui, circa 1750, 3¾in. high. (Christie's) $3,139 £2,052

An Irish circular gold Freedom Box, by Abraham Tuppy, Dublin, 1780, 2½in. diam. (Christie's) $5,033 £3,520

A Swiss shallow octagonal gold and enamel snuff box, by Francois Joanin, with Russian control marks, Geneva, circa 1820, 3½in. long. (Christie's) $4,719 £3,300

An archaic gold crescent-shaped ornament, Sino-Siberian/Warring States, 21.6cm. wide. (Christie's) $34,606 £24,200

A Swiss octagonal gold and enamel snuff box, circa 1820, with incuse maker's initials H?, in fitted case, 3in. long. (Christie's) $3,460 £2,420

A 19th century Swiss gold musical seal with chased foliage handle. (Christie's) $1,573 £1,100

An archaic gold arch-shaped ornament with repousse decoration, Warring States, 6.5cm. wide. (Christie's) $2,831 £1,980

A 17th century gold bar, salvaged from the Santa Margarita, 9in. long, 824.5 grams. (Christie's) $10,740 £7,020

A George III oblong engine turned gold snuff box, by A. J. Strachan, London, 1808, 18ct., 3¼in. long. (Christie's) $7,865 £5,500

Three gold stone set keys formed respectively as the head of a hound, fox and unicorn. (Christie's) $943 £660

A George I oblong gold snuff box, circa 1715, 3.1/8in. long. (Christie's) $22,022 £15,400

A top hat of brown felt, with black ribbon, by A. Giessen, Delft, circa 1870. (Christie's) $688 £462

A boy's cap of black mole-skin with peak of patent leather, circa 1845. (Christie's) $114 £77

A top hat of black beaver, with black silk ribbon, 7in. high, circa 1840. (Christie's) $360 £242

A mourning bonnet of black crepe, circa 1830. (Christie's) $163 £110

A top hat of grey beaver, possibly 1829, labelled M. Strieken, 8in. high. (Christie's) $1,065 £715

A bonnet of black satin trimmed with a large bow and rouleaux, circa 1830. (Christie's) $360 £242

A top hat of grey beaver with narrow ribbon of cream ribbed silk, 5½in. high, circa 1830. (Christie's) $426 £286

A pearl grey bowler hat, made in Italy by Borsalino for Cecil, 112 rue de Richelieu, circa 1800, together with two others and a bowler. (Christie's) $65 £44

A top hat of grey beaver, 7½in. high, circa 1830. (Christie's) $426 £286

A 17th century rhinoceros horn libation cup, 16cm. wide. (Christie's)
$876 £588

A 16th/17th century rhino-ceros horn libation cup, 16cm. wide. (Christie's)
$3,460 £2,420

A 17th century rhinoceros horn libation cup carved as a half-open hibiscus flower, 14.7cm. wide. (Christie's)
$2,044 £1,430

A 17th century rhinoceros horn libation cup, the handle pierced and carved as groups of chilong, 17cm. wide. (Christie's) $8,651 £6,050

Part of a set of twelve Victorian silver mounted horn beakers, maker's initials H.W.D., London, 1877, together with a horn claret jug, 11½in. high. (Christie's) $1,346 £880

A 17th/18th century rhino-ceros horn libation cup with pierced pine handle, 13cm. wide. (Christie's)
$4,089 £2,860

A 17th century rhinoceros horn libation cup, 18.5cm. diam., wood stand. (Christie's) $3,146 £2,200

A 17th/18th century rhino-ceros horn libation cup, show-ing a scene from 'The Romance of the Western Chamber', 13cm. wide. (Christie's) $1,299 £872

A 17th/18th century rhino-ceros horn libation cup with pierced pine-trunk handle, 16.7cm. wide. (Christie's)
$4,404 £3,080

Late 18th century four-case inro, fundame compartments, signed Jokasai, with red agate ojime attached. (Christie's) $4,719 £3,300

A 19th century bamboo Kodansu inro, signed Toyo and Kao, with a bone ojime attached. (Christie's) $2,516 £1,760

A 19th century five-case inro, signed Yoyusai, and Kao. (Christie's) $4,719 £3,300

Early 19th century four-case Nashiji inro, unsigned. (Christie's) $503 £352

Late 19th century boxwood three-case inro formed as a terrapin, signed Chuichi. (Christie's) $3,146 £2,200

A 19th century four-case Roiro inro with fundame compartments, signed Koma Kyuhaku saku. (Christie's) $4,719 £3,300

A 19th century five-case Roiro inro, fundame compartments, with an attached coral ojime. (Christie's) $2,359 £1,650

Early 19th century three-case inro decorated in hiramakie, kirikane and heidatsu with a mountainous landscape. (Christie's) $2,359 £1,650

A 19th century four-case Kinji inro, signed Kakosai, with a spherical Kinji ojime. (Christie's) $4,719 £3,300

An 18th/19th century five-case Somada inro with compartments in nashiji, unsigned. (Christie's)
$2,359 £1,650

A 19th century small Roiro two-case inro of fluted fan-shaped form, unsigned. (Christie's) $755 £528

A 19th century four-case inro with a spherical red glass ojime and a manju netsuke. (Christie's) $6,292 £4,400

Early 19th century five-case Fundame inro, signed Hirose Nagaharu. (Christie's)
$786 £550

Early 19th century four-case inro, signed Toju, with a soft metal mokume ojime attached. (Christie's) $4,719 £3,300

A 19th century five-case Kinji inro, signed Kakosai Shozan, with red tsubo seal and attached agate ojime. (Christie's) $4,404 £3,080

A 19th century five-case inro, signed Kajikawa saku, with an ojime and a wood manju netsuke. (Christie's)
$6,292 £4,400.

A seven-case inro with gyobu nashiji compartments, unsigned, with coral ojime attached. (Christie's) $2,359 £1,650

A 19th century three-case Kamakura-Bori inro with a glass ojime and a manju netsuke. (Christie's)
$4,719 £3,300

A 17th/18th century three-case Samegawa-Togidashi inro, unsigned, with a spherical shell ojime attached. (Christie's) $865 £605

Early 19th century four-case kinji inro, nashiji interiors, signed Shokosai. (Christie's) $1,718 £1,210

A 19th century four-case Roiro inro, signed with two red lacquer seals Shiomi Masanari, and with a glass ojime. (Christie's) $3,932 £2,750

A four-case kinji inro, signed Kakosai Teimin, with hard-stone ojime and ivory manju netsuke, signed Shibayama. (Christie's) $1,483 £1,045

A 19th century three-case inro with nashiji compartments, unsigned. (Christie's) $1,101 £770

Late 18th/early 19th century five-case roironuri inro, signed Kajikawa saku. (Christie's) $1,327 £935

Early 19th century four-case kinji inro decorated in gold, red and black hiramakie and takamakie, signed Kajikawa. (Christie's) $1,483 £1,045

A 19th century three-case Roiro inro, signed Jokasai, with a coral ojime attached. (Christie's) $5,505 £3,850

Late 19th century three-case yoroigata inro, modelled as an o-yoroi set up on an armour box. (Christie's) $7,497 £5,280

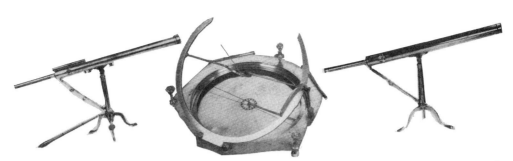

A mid 19th century brass astronomical refracting telescope, signed Carpenter & Westley, London, 95cm. long. (Phillips) $2,635 £1,700

A large brass equatorial Universal dial, Indian, possibly Jaipur, probably 19th century, 29in. long. (Christie's)
$1,760 £1,228

A 19th century lacquered brass astronomical refracting telescope, signed Baker, London, 79cm. long. (Phillips) $744 £480

An early 19th century brass single draw monocular, signed Berge, London late Ramsden, with ivory body tube, 10cm. long, in case. (Phillips) $124 £80

A lacquered brass precision balance, the beam stamped To Weigh/To Grain, No. 5962, with electrical attachments in a glazed mahogany case, 14¾in. wide. (Christie's)
$278 £176

Pajot's midwifery forceps, signed Charriere a Paris, late 19th century, 34cm. long. (Christie's) $286 £199

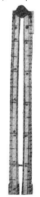

An early 19th century pocket drawing instrument set, in silver mounted shagreen case, 13cm. long. (Phillips) $310 £200

A Regency mahogany new terrestrial globe, signed by Cruchley, 20in. diam., 47in. high. (Christie's)
$7,444 £5,280

An early 18th century ivory and brass folding 12in. rule, together with an 8in. boxwood rule and a shaped 3in. rule. (Phillips) $108 £70

An early 19th century brass astronomical refracting achromatic telescope, signed Dollond, London, 107cm. long. (Phillips) $2,790 £1,800

A late 18th century brass ellipsograph, signed J. & W. Watkins, London, in T-shaped mahogany case. (Phillips)　$728　£470

A 19th century anodised brass Troughton & Simms double frame sextant, the index arm with 8in. radius. (Phillips)　　$806　£520

A mid 19th century 12in. celestial globe, with printed coloured and varnished paper gauze, Wyld Globe of the Heavens .. published by James Wyld, Charing Cross East 1869. (Phillips)　　　$1,007　£650

Early 19th century Nuremburg microscope, the base impressed I M, 33cm. high. (Christie's)　　　　　　　$880　£614

A 16th/17th century Italian ship's drycard compass, 11cm. diam. (Phillips)　　　　　　$6,200　£4,000

A 19th century brass three-draw monocular, signed Dollond, with ivory body tube, 10.5cm. long, in case. (Phillips)　　　$248　£160

A brass Brewster's law apparatus to produce polarised light, signed Deleuil a Paris, circa 1850, 30.5cm. high. (Christie's)　　　　　　　$825　£575

A late 18th century lacquered brass Ramsden theodolite, 29cm. high. (Phillips)　　　　　　$1,007　£650

A 19th century lacquered brass four prism spectroscope, signed John Browning, 32cm. high, in mahogany case. (Phillips) $1,550 £1,000

A late 19th century 14in. Betts's Portable Terrestrial Globe, by George Philip & Son Ltd. (Phillips) $279 £180

A brass graphometer with case, signed Martin au Temple a Paris, circa 1760, 28cm. diam. (Christie's) $1,760 £1,228

An American celestial globe on stand, signed Wilson's New Thirteen Inch Celestial globe, by C. Lancaster, N.Y., 1845, 13in. diam. (Christie's) $825 £575

A mid 19th century miniature terrestrial globe, by Malby & Co., 1½in. diam. (Phillips) $341 £220

Probably 19th century large brass drum microscope, 36cm. high. (Christie's) $220 £153

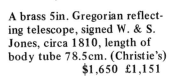

An early 19th century 3in. pocket globe, 'A Correct Globe with the New Discoveries', contained in a simulated fishskin covered case. (Phillips) $1,085 £700

A brass 5in. Gregorian reflecting telescope, signed W. & S. Jones, circa 1810, length of body tube 78.5cm. (Christie's) $1,650 £1,151

A 19th century gilt brass nocturnal, probably French, 95mm. diam. (Christie's) $880 £614

One of a pair of Regency terrestrial and celestial globes, dated March 1816, 24in. diam., 43in. high.(Christie's) $21,714 £15,400

An early marine chronometer by John Arnold & Son, with 4½in. circular silvered dial, in mahogany box. (Phillips) $11,600 £8,000

An early 19th century lacquered brass Culpeper-type compound monocular microscope, signed F. Day, 41cm. high. (Phillips) $1,162 £750

A lacquered brass compound monocular microscope, by Powell & Lealand, 1901, 49cm. high, in case. (Phillips) $4,650 £3,000

An ivory diptych dial, with the thrush trademark of Hans Troschel, Nuremburg, dated 1649, 4¼in. long. (Christie's) $2,420 £1,688

An orrery on turned mahogany stand with three scroll feet, French, circa 1810, 53cm. high. (Christie's) $2,420 £1,688

An 18th century boxwood nocturnal, probably English, 8¼in. long. (Christie's) $1,980 £1,381

A hydraulic tourniquet on octagonal mahogany base, circa 1830, 54cm. high. (Christie's) $605 £422

A mid 19th century lacquered brass compound monocular microscope, signed Dollond, 38cm. wide. (Phillips) $1,860 £1,200

Thomas' forceps, with ebony grips, circa 1860, 29.5cm. long. (Christie's) $132 £92

A small 18th century silver perpetual calendar, one volvelle engraved with days of the week, the other with hours of the day and months, 2.5cm. wide. (Phillips) $248 £160

A Malby's 1858 terrestrial globe on a mahogany tripod stand with turned shaft, 40½in. high. (Christie's) $2,711 £1,870

An ivory diptych magnetic Azimuth dial, signed Fait par Charles Bloud a Dieppe, late 17th century, 70mm. long. (Christie's) $990 £690

Early 19th century French papier-mache ptolemaic armillary sphere, 18½in. high. (Christie's) $2,420 £1,688

Late 19th century 'Easter Egg' globe, made in Germany for the English market, 14cm. long. (Phillips) $341 £220

An 18th century brass Butterfield dial, signed, 7.8cm. long. (Christie's) $462 £322

An American lacquered brass monocular microscope, signed E. H. & F. H. Tighe, Detroit, circa 1885, length of tube 5in. (Christie's) $605 £422

A brass air pump with bell jar, probably English, circa 1790, 43cm. long including handle. (Christie's) $880 £614

Pair of cast iron armorial andirons with scrolled feet, 19in. high. (Christie's) $440 £308

One of a pair of cast iron hall trees, America, circa 1875, 75in. high. (Robt. W. Skinner Inc.) $700 £486

Early 20th century Art Deco cast and wrought iron parcel gilt pier table, France, 53in. wide. (Robt. W. Skinner Inc.) $950 £659

A set of three polished steel fire-irons with baluster pommels, 36in. long. (Christie's) $1,144 £715

A George III steel and brass basket grate with serpentine front, 32½in. wide. (Christie's) $3,635 £2,376

Mid 19th century cast iron interior plant stand, America, 43in. high. (Robt. W. Skinner Inc.) $1,900 £1,319

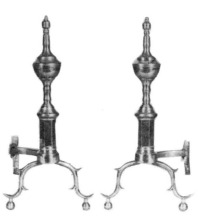

A moulded zinc polychrome tobacconist figure, Wm. Demuth, N.Y., circa 1890, 67½in. high without base. (Robt. W. Skinner Inc.) $11,000 £6,875

Pair of Federal bell metal andirons, probably New York, 1800-10, 25in. high. (Christie's) $770 £508

A wrought-iron candelabrum with triangular shaped top applied with five pricket candle sconces, 62¼in. high. (Christie's) $369 £220

Victorian polished steel coal
scuttle with a lifting flap and
shovel. (Lots Road Galleries)
$144 £90

A George III polished steel
basket grate with railed
basket, 33¼in. wide.
(Christie's) $5,893 £4,180

Mid 19th century blackened
steel basket grate, 22¼in.
wide. (Christie's)
$1,570 £935

An iron mounted oak Alms
box, the hinged lid with
chained loop handle above
coin slot, 25cm. high. (Phillips)
$748 £520

A George III steel basket grate,
26¾in. wide, 33½in. high.
(Christie's) $3,678 £2,420

An early iron bound oak octagonal Alms box, 12.5cm. high.
(Phillips) $374 £260

One of a pair of cast iron foliate
andirons, attributed to E. Gimson,
circa 1905, 22¼in. high. (Robt.
W. Skinner Inc.) $5,500 £3,846

A fully articulated russet
iron model of a crayfish,
(ebi), signed Miochin, Edo
period, 26cm. long.
(Christie's) $1,562 £1,100

An American 19th century
painted iron trade sign,
40in. high, 15in. wide.
(Christie's) $2,640 £1,619

Late 19th century ivory okimono of a seated musician, signed Kyoga, 14.9cm. high. (Christie's) $1,249 £880

Late 19th century sectional ivory carving of four bears, 26.5cm. long. (Christie's) $2,811 £1,980

One of two late 19th century ivory tusk vases, signed by Kikugawa Jorinsai Masamitsu, one 34cm., the other 31cm. high. (Christie's) $2,499 £1,760

A Tokyo School ivory group of an old fisherman with a boy on his back and another crouching at his feet, signed Gyokusui, Meiji period, 24cm. high. (Christie's) $3,436 £2,420

A 19th century French or German ivory group of a medieval woodsman and a court jester, 20cm. high. (Christie's) $7,537 £4,950

Late 19th century ivory carving of an old woman holding a boy on her back, signed Kozan, 13.8cm. high. (Christie's) $235 £165

Late 19th century ivory group of a farmer with his wife and son, 18cm. wide. (Christie's) $2,655 £1,870

Late 19th century ivory box and cover carved as Benkei seated on top of the great bell of Miidera, signed Takayuki, 24cm. high. (Christie's) $1,015 £715

Late 19th century sectional ivory okimono of Daikoku, signed Gyokuyu, 13.8cm. high. (Christie's) $624 £440

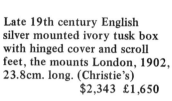

Late 19th century sectional ivory okimono of three apes playing with a biwa, signed Masaaki, 13.5cm. long. (Christie's) $755 £528

Late 19th century English silver mounted ivory tusk box with hinged cover and scroll feet, the mounts London, 1902, 23.8cm. long. (Christie's) $2,343 £1,650

Late 19th century sectional ivory carving of a drummer, signed Munehisa, 19.5cm. high. (Christie's) $1,562 £1,100

Late 19th century ivory okimono of a Chinese girl holding a boy up to her chest, another boy standing at her side riding a hobby horse, 11cm. high. (Christie's) $440 £308

Late 19th century ivory okimono of a group of five Kendo fighters in a melee, signed Ikkosai, 8.2cm. high. (Christie's) $1,337 £935

Late 19th century ivory group of a farmer with two small boys. signed Wasui, 21.5cm. high. (Christie's) $1,124 £792

A 19th century French carved ivory tankard, in the Baroque style, 26cm. high.(Christie's) $3,702 £2,420

A Japanese 19th century carved ivory okimono, 6.3/8in. high. (Robt. W. Skinner Inc.) $850 £594

'Girl with Hoop', an ivory figure carved after a model by F. Preiss, 17.5cm. high. (Christie's) $1,404 £918

An early 19th century barley-corn chess set in natural and black stained ivory, king 9.5cm., pawn 4.3cm., in contemporary penwork box. (Phillips) $832 £520

An ivory carving of a scholar reading a manuscript, signed Seiraku, Meiji period, 21cm. high. (Christie's) $624 £440

A mid 19th century Jaques Staunton ivory chess set, stained red and natural, king 10cm., pawn 4.8cm., in carton pierre box. (Phillips) $5,440 £3,400

An ivory figure of a girl, 'Invocation', carved from a model by D. Chiparus, 24.5cm. high. (Phillips) $1,584 £1,100

Late 19th century stained ivory okimono style netsuke of Kintoki astride a carp, signed Meisai. (Christie's) $390 £275

A Tokyo School ivory carving of a standing girl, signed Meido, Meiji period, 24.4cm. high. (Christie's) $937 £660

An English pattern chess set, natural and black stained, the white king signed G. Merrifield, Maker, circa 1825, king 8cm., pawn 4cm. (Phillips) $2,720 £1,700

Late 19th century ivory carving of a fisherman, signed Kyoshu, 24.4cm. high. (Christie's) $781 £550

A Jaques In Statu Quo travelling chess set of large size, the bone pegged pieces approx. 2cm., in sycamore folding board. (Phillips) $576 £360

A Lund ivory and red stained chess set, the white king signed Lund, Maker, king 10.5cm. high, pawn 4.2cm., in original fitted leather box. (Phillips) $4,000 £2,500

A Tokyo School ivory carving of a falconer, signed Korin, Meiji period, 27.5cm. high. (Christie's) $2,343 £1,650

An ivory 'Washington' chess set, stained red and natural, king 8.5cm., pawn 3.8cm., circa 1880, in tortoiseshell veneered box. (Phillips) $1,312 £820

A Tokyo School ivory carving of an old man reading a book, signed Masaaki, Meiji period, 23.1cm. high. (Christie's) $1,874 £1,320

An ivory carving of a kneeling girl, a small boy seated by her side, signed Yoshimas, Meiji period, 12.3cm. high. (Christie's) $786 £550

One of a pair of late 19th century ivory tusk vases, one signed Sasada Kanemitsu, 46.2cm. high. (Christie's) $3,436 £2,420

An early ivory rectangular plaque, Yuan/Ming Dynasty, 9cm. wide. (Christie's) $2,044 £1,430

Late 19th century ivory okimono style netsuke, signed Zenraku. (Christie's) $624 £440

A Tibetan ivory ritual phallus, possibly 16th century, 23cm. long, and a wood casket, 12.5 x 25cm. (Phillips) $690 £460

A 16th/early 17th century late Ming small flecked greyish-celadon jade model of a recumbent buffalo, 16.5cm. wide, box. (Christie's) $8,651 £6,050

A pale celadon and white flecked jade bowl, Qing Dynasty, 20.6cm. wide. (Christie's) $943 £660

A brown and grey flecked jade carving of a recumbent horse, Song Dynasty, 5.6cm. wide, wood stand. (Christie's) $346 £242

An archaic black and cream jade cylinder, cong, 3rd/2nd Millenium B.C., 11.2cm. sq. (Christie's) $15,730 £11,000

An archaic mottled celadon and brown jade blade, Shang/W. Zhou Dynasty, 17cm. wide. (Christie's) $1,101 £770

A mottled spinach and celadon jade table screen, late Qing Dynasty, 30cm. wide, wood stand. (Christie's) $1,101 £770

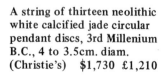

A string of thirteen neolithic white calcified jade circular pendant discs, 3rd Millenium B.C., 4 to 3.5cm. diam. (Christie's) $1,730 £1,210

A brown and celadon jade square cylinder, cong, E. Han Dynasty, 5.7cm. wide, wood stand, fitted box. (Christie's) $550 £385

A jade phoenix rhyton, Yuan Dynasty or earlier, 12.8cm. wide. (Christie's) $1,101 £770

A yellowish-green and grey jade carving of a recumbent horse, possibly Ming Dynasty, 11cm. long. (Christie's) $1,573 £1,100

An 18th century pale celadon and russet jade gourd-shaped brushwasher, 24.5cm. wide. (Christie's) $4,404 £3,080

A small russet and caramel jade crouching dog, Song Dynasty, 6.3cm. wide, box, wood stand. (Christie's) $5,662 £3,960

Pair of dark green jade figures of hawks, Qing Dynasty, 22.5cm. high. (Christie's) $786 £550

An 18th/early 19th century pale celadon jade figure of Guanyin. (Christie's) $2,359 £1,650

One of a pair of green and grey jade Buddhistic lions, carved as censers with detachable heads, 23cm. high. (Christie's) $2,988 £2,090

An 18th century pale celadon jade group of a scholar and his attendant looking up at a crane, 12.8cm. high, wood stand. (Christie's) $1,022 £715

A string of twelve neolithic calcified jade discs, from 2.5 to 1.5cm. diam., and an axe-shaped pendant, 2.5cm. long, all 3rd Millenium B.C. (Christie's) $1,337 £935

An apple-green jade pendant of triangular form carved with two boys, 3.5cm. high. (Christie's) $2,044 £1,430

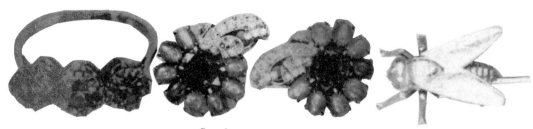

Three-stone ring with a total of 3¼ct. claw set in white metal. (Peter Wilson)
$2,961 £2,100

Sapphire and diamond ear-clips, 'Yard', the oval sapphires weighing approx. 5ct. (Robt. W. Skinner Inc.)
$5,000 £3,472

Gold stickpin, set with a large realistically rendered gold 'fly'. (Robt. W. Skinner Inc.) $250 £173

Art Deco diamond bow pin, pave-set with 105 diamonds weighing approx. 3.00ct. and highlighted by calibre cut onyx. (Robt. W. Skinner Inc.)
$3,600 £2,500

A gold, diamond and plique-a-jour pendant fashioned as a seagull in flight, 7.5cm. wide, probably French. (Phillips)
$576 £400

A Theodor Fahrner enamelled bar brooch, the ends set with coral beads, 5.2cm. long, stamped TF monogram and indistinct 925. (Phillips)
$360 £250

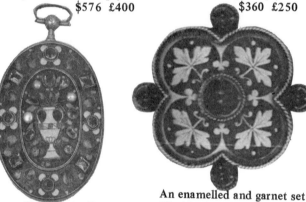

An Arts & Crafts brooch, possibly Birmingham Guild of Handicrafts, 4cm. diam. (Phillips) $108 £75

A George Hunt enamelled and gemset locket pendant of oval shape, inside is a lock of hair, 8.5cm. long. (Phillips)
$1,008 £700

An enamelled and garnet set 'Gothic' brooch, based on a design by A. W. N. Pugin, 4.5cm. across. (Phillips)
$504 £350

One of a pair of 18ct. gold earrings, composed of fluted hoops, 29.6gm. (Robt. W. Skinner Inc.) $400 £277

A gold mounted diamond set trembleuse feather brooch, converting to an aigrette, in fitted case. (Woolley & Wallis)
$4,023 £2,700

An enamelled 'wasp' pendant, holding a baroque pearl, 4.5cm. wide, stamped 900 and Depose, probably Austrian. (Phillips) $345 £240

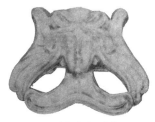

A Tiffany & Co. two-colour gold, sapphire and moonstone oval brooch, 3.3cm. across. (Phillips) $1,008 £700

A sunray brooch, centring an opal with diamond set cluster and rays, gold set, in Goldsmiths & Silversmiths case. (Woolley & Wallis) $1,490 £1,000

A Kerr gilded Art Nouveau brooch, 6.5cm. across, stamped with maker's mark, Sterling and 1702. (Phillips) $432 £300

A German 'Egyptianesque' plique-a-jour brooch, formed as a scarab, 11cm. wide. (Phillips) $547 £380

A Liberty & Co. gold sapphire and moonstone pendant, probably designed by A. Gaskin, 5cm. long, 15ct. (Phillips) $547 £380

Antique gold and diamond brooch, French hallmarks, designed as a French poodle. (Robt. W. Skinner Inc.) $1,000 £694

Enamelled diamond ring on an 18ct. gold band, English hallmark. (Robt. W. Skinner Inc.) $800 £555

A silver brooch, stamped Georg Jensen 300 and with London import marks for 1965. (Christie's) $117 £82

14ct. gold and diamond ring, the centre oval gold plaque with tiny raised 'fly' encircled in a frame of diamonds. (Robt. W. Skinner Inc.) $850 £590

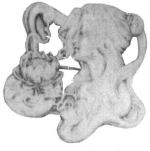

Cultured pearl and diamond necklace, 'Cartier', a double strand of 86, 9mm. pearls, the diamonds weighing approx. 2.20ct. (Robt. W. Skinner Inc.) $7,000 £4,861

Art Deco emerald and diamond ring, diamonds weighing a total of approx. 2ct. (Robt. W. Skinner Inc.) $1,100 £763

An Unger Brothers Art Nouveau brooch, 5.5cm. across, stamped 925 Sterling fine. (Phillips) $360 £250

An Arts & Crafts ring with an oval cabochon of green turquoise. (Phillips) $100 £70

An Arts & Crafts pendant, 7cm. long, engraved 1936, with chain. (Phillips) $244 £170

A Van Cleef and Arpels gold and sapphire 'Serti Invisible' ring, stamped with French gold poincon, numbered 16995. (Phillips) $8,352 £5,800

A pearl, emerald and enamelled pendant, 5.7cm. long. (Phillips) $432 £300

 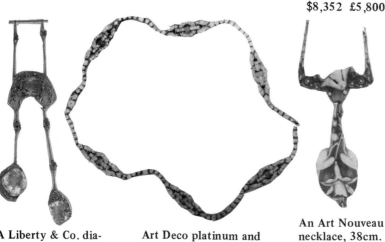  

A Liberty & Co. diamond and aquamarine negligee necklace, 39cm. long. (Phillips) $2,088 £1,450

Art Deco platinum and diamond necklace, diamonds approx. 7.25ct. (Robt. W. Skinner Inc.) $660 £458

An Art Nouveau necklace, 38cm. long, stamped H & S and 333. (Phillips) $216 £150

A gold and moonstone pendant, 4cm. long. (Phillips) $273 £190

A gold, enamel, plique-a-jour and diamond Art Nouveau necklace. (Phillips) $460 £320

A Murrle Bennett gold pendant locket, 5.5cm. long, 15ct. (Phillips) $288 £200

An Art Nouveau trefoil shaped silver and green enamel pendant. (Reeds Rains) $139 £90

A diamond and pearl set Art Nouveau pendant, 3.5cm. long. (Phillips) $417 £290

A 14ct. yellow gold ring set with a diamond weighing approx. .50ct. (Robt. W. Skinner Inc.) $250 £173

Arts & Crafts necklace, a heart shaped pendant suspended from a gold chain, hallmarked. (Robt. W. Skinner Inc.) $500 £347

A diamond and peridot necklace, chain 37.5cm. long, in fitted case for Shepheard & Co. (Phillips) $748 £520

A Gaskin Arts & Crafts pendant with central amethyst, having seed pearl and fresh-water pearl drop, 4cm. wide. (Phillips) $576 £400

Platinum, diamond and ruby earrings, the diamond cap supports a 9mm. cultured pearl. (Robt. W. Skinner Inc.) $1,800 £1,250

An Art Nouveau pin/ pendant, profile of a young girl on a plique-a-jour ground. (Robt. W. Skinner Inc.) $1,000 £694

A Theodor Fahrner Art Deco bracelet, 19cm. long. (Phillips) $1,440 £1,000

A George Hunt 'Medusa' brooch, 6cm. long, maker's mark in sheild, inscribed 'Medusa' on reverse. (Phillips) $1,440 £1,000

An apple-green jade pendant, 5cm. high, wood stand. (Christie's) $2,988 £2,090

Victorian gold earrings. (Robt. W. Skinner Inc.) $275 £190

A 14ct. yellow gold ring, mounting pave-set with 18 diamonds and 5 rubies. (Robt. W. Skinner Inc.) $475 £329

Early 20th century plique-a-jour necklace and earrings. (Robt. W. Skinner Inc.) $325 £227

Bi-colour gold and ruby ear-clips, circa 1940, each a blossom with a cluster of rubies. (Robt. W. Skinner Inc.) $225 £156

A Jean Despres Art Deco ring fashioned in carved ivory with inner silver coloured band, set with a turquoise. (Phillips) $2,232 £1,550

A German horn comb, sur-mounted by panels of green plique-a-jour enamels amid tendrils set with marcasites, 8.5cm. wide. (Phillips) $136 £95

14ct. white gold bar set with two diamonds, each weigh-ing approx. 1ct. and high-lighted by 7 small diamonds. (Robt. W. Skinner Inc.) $2,500 £1,736

A Murrle Bennett gold and amethyst brooch, 3.2cm. wide, stamped with monogram and 9ct. (Phillips) $172 £120

Art Deco platinum and diamond jabot pin. (Robt. W. Skinner Inc.) $1,900 £1,319

A Wiener Werkstatte button brooch designed by Josef Hoffmann, circular with moulded decoration of a robin. (Christie's) $743 £486

Victorian gold and diamond pin, a fleur-de-lys pave-set with turquoise beads and diamonds. (Robt. W. Skinner Inc.) $175 £121

Gold and citrine brooch, an oval brooch set with over-lapping gold leaves high-lighted with four cultured pearls. (Robt. W. Skinner Inc.) $300 £208

An Arts & Crafts pendant, attributed to Sibyl Dunlop, with a teardrop plaque of Labradorite, 5.5cm. long. (Phillips) $403 £280

Gold and ruby earclips and pin, 'Tiffany & Co.', designed as a leaf. (Robt. W. Skinner Inc.) $650 £451

An Arts & Crafts pendant, in the manner of Omar Ramsden, set with three oval almondine garnet cabochons, 6cm. (Phillips) $230 £160

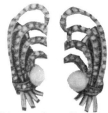

Antique rose-cut diamond earrings. (Robt. W. Skinner Inc.) $800 £555

A plique-a-jour brooch, formed as a locust, 10.6cm. long, stamped with maker's mark and 900, probably Austrian. (Phillips) $691 £480

Diamond earclips, designed as a diamond plume with a cultured pearl at the base, 18ct. white gold. (Robt. W. Skinner Inc.) $850 £590

An 18ct. gold brooch, designed as two textured gold leaves, 13.3gm.   (Robt. W. Skinner Inc.) $150 £104

Art Deco 14ct. gold, pearl and enamel pin, designed as a sailfish. (Robt. W. Skinner Inc.) $300 £208

A Victorian gold pendant set with cabochon tear-drop garnets in a petal mount with central old cut diamond. (Reeds Rains) $434 £280

A French gold, pearl and plique-a-jour circular pendant, 2cm. diam., inscribed F. Vernon. (Phillips) $216 £150

An enamelled brooch, after a design by Henri Matisse, 6cm. wide, possibly produced in the U.S.A. (Phillips) $172 £120

French gilt metal and enamel peacock feather buckle, circa 1900. (Reeds Rains) $279 £180

An Art Nouveau sapphire and diamond ring in a scrolled gold mount. (Robt. W. Skinner Inc.)$160 £111

Diamond earrings, each a cluster of diamonds in platinum top yellow gold, total weight of diamonds approx. 1.6ct. (Robt. W. Skinner Inc.) $750 £520

An Austrian silver gilt, enamel and plique-a-jour dragonfly spring clip brooch, circa 1885. (Reeds Rains) $350 £226

An early 19th century Japanese black and gold lacquer jardiniere, 20½in. diam. (Christie's) $2,674 £1,870

Late 18th/early 19th century lacquer Chinese style fan (uchiwa), 43.7cm. long. (Christie's) $3,436 £2,420

A Chinese 18th century cinnabar lacquer box of 5in. circular lobed form. (Parsons, Welch & Cowell) $217 £130

A red lacquer altar vase carved with eight Buddhist emblems, Qianlong seal mark and of the period, 24.5cm. high. (Christie's) $865 £605

A Gyobu silver rimmed tebako decorated in gold takamakie with flowering peonies, circa 1800, 27.5 x 22.5 x 16.5cm. (Christie's) $6,996 £4,400

An 18th century Export lacquer medallion, 12.6cm. high. (Christie's) $1,049 £660

Late 17th century Export lacquer cabinet, 74cm. high, with a fitted 18th century English japanned wood stand, 80cm. high. (Christie's) $6,121 £3,850

A set of three mid Victorian black and gilt japanned papiermache oval trays, the largest 31in. wide. (Christie's) $1,861 £1,320

A 19th century Chinese lacquered panel, 33 x 25in. (Dreweatts) $1,680 £1,000

A Chinese red, black and brown lacquer box and cover, 12¾in. diam., the base incised with a Qianlong six-character mark. (Christie's) $475 £330

A Korean inlaid black lacquer hinged rectangular box and cover, 17th/18th century, 21.8cm. wide. (Christie's) $2,381 £1,598

An 18th century Chinese 4½in. circular red lacquer box. (Parsons, Welch & Cowell) $73 £44

A 16th century inlaid black lacquer four-tiered box and cover, 27cm. high. (Christie's) $1,142 £767

A 19th century silver rimmed fundame tebako, fitted wood box, 24.2 x 19.1 x 12cm. (Christie's) $11,368 £7,150

A red and yellow lacquer six-tiered square box and cover, Ming Dynasty, 28.2cm. high. (Christie's) $2,381 £1,598

Early 19th century Chinese Export lacquer picnic box, 15in. wide. (Christie's) $708 £440

A black and gold lacquer tray decorated with chinoiserie figures in a landscape, 30in. wide. (Christie's) $2,675 £1,760

One of a pair of 19th century Japanese lacquer picnic baskets, 52cm. high. (Phillips) $1,453 £950

A Daum cameo table lamp
with wrought-iron, three-
branch neck mount,
44.1cm. high. (Christie's)
$8,712 £6,050

An Art Nouveau table lamp,
beaten brass inset with coloured glass, on oval wooden
base, 49cm. high. (Christie's)
$660 £432

A Tiffany three-light table
lamp, shade 40.6cm. diam.,
61.5cm. high. (Christie's)
$11,566 £7,560

A German Art Nouveau
silvered pewter nautilus
shell desk lamp, stamped
M H 20, 27cm. high.
(Christie's) $2,692 £1,870

A Galle cameo glass table
lamp with domed shade and
baluster base, 60cm. high.
(Christie's)
$11,566 £7,560

Gustav Stickley oak table
lamp with wicker shade,
circa 1910, 22in. high, 18in.
diam. (Robt. W. Skinner
Inc.) $1,100 £769

A Tiffany Studios 'lotus'
leaded glass and bronze table
lamp, 62.5cm. high.
(Christie's) $15,048 £10,450

Rudolph, a robot light fitting,
designed by Frank Clewett,
149cm. high. (Christie's)
$3,484 £2,420

Bronze table lamp with green
swirl glass and calcite shade,
probably Steuben, circa 1910,
14in. high. (Robt. W. Skinner
Inc.) $750 £524

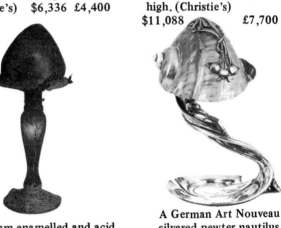

A Tiffany three-light table lamp, the bronze base bun-shaped on four ball feet, 41cm. diam. of shade, 63.5cm. high. (Christie's) $11,566 £7,560

One of a pair of Tiffany Studios three-light, lily-gold favrile glass and bronze table lamps, 33.2cm. high. (Christie's) $6,336 £4,400

A Daum overlaid and acid-etched table lamp with wrought-iron mount, 60cm. high. (Christie's) $11,088 £7,700

A Tiffany Studios bronze and glass filigree table lamp, 42.5cm. high. (Christie's) $3,643 £2,530

A Daum enamelled and acid etched cameo table lamp with three-cornered bulbous domed shade, 45.3cm. high. (Christie's) $9,583 £6,264

A German Art Nouveau silvered pewter nautilus shell desk lamp, 29.7cm. high. (Christie's) $3,326 £2,310

Hampshire pottery lamp with leaded shade, circa 1910, 19½in. high, 16in. diam. (Robt. W. Skinner Inc.) $750 £524

A 1950s solid rosewood table lamp, 45.5cm. high. (Christie's) $2,809 £1,836

Art pottery lamp with pierced copper and slag glass shade, circa 1905, 14½in. high. (Robt. W. Skinner Inc.) $600 £420

A mid 19th century gilt
metal lampe bouillotte with
green and gilt tole shade,
23½in. high. (Christie's)
$11,723 £8,256

Early 20th century Hampshire
pottery lamp with leaded
Handel shade, 21in. high,
16in. diam. (Robt. W. Skinner
Inc.) $700 £490

Roycroft hammered copper
and mica lamp, E. Aurora,
N.Y., circa 1910, no. 903,
14¾in. high. (Robt. W.
Skinner Inc.)
$1,300 £909

A patinated metal table lamp,
marked 'Benedict United
States', circa 1915, 26in.
high. (Robt. W. Skinner Inc.)
$225 £145

An Art Nouveau bronze figural
lamp, cast from a model by E.
Drouot, the young woman
personifying music, 34in. high.
(Christie's) $2,310 £1,500

A Stilnova painted metal
lamp, by Gaetano Scolari,
Italy, circa 1959, 67cm. high.
(Phillips) $174 £120

A brass and rosewood lamp
table, fitted for electricity
with fringed pleated cream
silk shade piped in red,
58in. high. (Christie's)
$1,573 £1,100

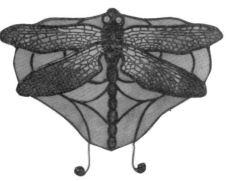

A Tiffany Studios stained glass
dragonfly lamp/pendant, 25.5cm.
wide, chain for suspension.
(Phillips) $720 £500

A Continental porcelain oil
lamp base in the form of a
white owl with glass eyes,
17½in. high. (Dreweatts)
$754 £520

A Daum cameo glass table lamp with conical shade, 51cm. high, signed. (Phillips) $4,320 £3,000

An Art Nouveau bronze and leaded glass shade on bronze base, 22½in. high. (Christie's) $1,078 £700

A Charles X gilt metal lampe bouillotte with spreading circular tole shade and ostrich feather finial, 32in. high. (Christie's) $2,967 £2,090

Early 20th century Tiffany bronze table lamp with leaded shade, 22in. high. (Robt. W. Skinner Inc.) $2,500 £1,748

An Italian glass and chromed standard lamp by Barovier and Toso, 180cm. high. (Phillips) $792 £550

Early 20th century leaded cased glass lantern in vintage pattern, 13¼in. high, 9in. wide. (Robt. W. Skinner Inc.) $450 £315

A Galle cameo glass table lamp with domed shade of amber tone, 57cm. high, signed. (Phillips) $8,352 £5,800

Grueby pottery two-colour lamp base, Boston, circa 1905, bronze foot signed Gorham Co., 18in. high. (Robt. W. Skinner Inc.) $11,750 £8,217

A Galle glass table lamp with domed shade, 52cm. high, signed in fine linear manner on shade and on base 'Galle'. (Phillips) $5,472 £3,800

A brass table lamp, the pierced and scrolled base with three urn-turned candle-cups and scrolled thumbpiece, 21½in. high. (Christie's) $385 £251

One of a pair of gilt metal and turquoise porcelain twin-branch wall lights, fitted for electricity, 11in. high. (Christie's) $393 £275

A Tiffany Studios 'Pansy' leaded glass and bronze table lamp, 54cm. high. (Christie's) $7,865 £5,500

A tall Galle cameo table lamp, the domed shade and stem overlaid with claret-coloured glass, 63.5cm. high. (Christie's) $12,584 £8,800

A Lalique table lamp, the clear satin finished glass with amber staining, 27.1cm. high. (Christie's) $3,775 £2,640

A Gabriel Argy-Rousseau pate-de-verre and wrought-iron veilleuse, the grey, blue and dark blue mottled glass moulded with stylised leaves, 25.5cm. high. (Christie's) $3,146 £2,200

One of a pair of giltwood single-branch wall appliques with frosted glass flambeaux, 21in. high. (Christie's) $503 £352

A brass and tole painted table lamp, 20in. high. (Christie's) $330 £215

A 19th century dark blue tinted lacemaker's lamp, 27cm. high. (Christie's) $554 £385

A brass table lamp, the turned standard with three scrolled arms, 24in. high. (Christie's) $770 £502

A Tiffany Studios 'Dragonfly' leaded glass and gilt bronze table lamp, 46.7cm. high. (Christie's) $24,381 £17,050

A Daum Nancy acid etched glass table lamp, France, circa 1900, 14in. high. (Robt. W. Skinner Inc.) $2,000 £1,388

An Andre Delatte cameo table lamp with metal neck mount, 52.5cm. high. (Christie's) $2,359 £1,650

An Almaric Walter pate-de-verre and wrought-iron lamp, the amber glass plaque moulded with a blue and amber mottled peacock, 27cm. high. (Christie's) $3,146 £2,200

Early 20th century pairpoint reverse painted table lamp, New Bedford, base signed and numbered 3011, 22¾in. high. (Robt. W. Skinner Inc.)
$1,500 £1,041

A brass and glass ship's lantern, with a plaque inscribed 'Samuel Hall/Ship Chandler/East Boston', mounted as a lamp, 15in. high. (Christie's) $440 £287

A Gabriel Argy-Rousseau pate-de-verre and wrought-iron veilleuse, 17.5cm. high. (Christie's) $4,404 £3,080

A Regency brass frame hall lantern with six glass panels, one a door, 26in. high. (Woolley & Wallis) $1,887 £1,250

An early 19th century English marble group of a King Charles spaniel watching a cat, by Joseph Gott, 26in. high. (Christie's) $3,460 £2,420

A 19th century French marble statue of a girl possibly representing Winter, by E. Carlier, 86cm. high. (Christie's) $2,356 £1,540

A mid 19th century English marble statue of Sabrina, the base signed Holme Cardwell Fecit Roma 1856, 101cm. high, 60cm. diam. (Christie's) $20,735 £14,300

One of a pair of carved white marble standing lions, 24½in. high. (Robt. W. Skinner Inc.) $3,300 £2,307

A late 19th century Italian marble statuette of a maiden looking at her reflection in a pool, by E. Brunelleschi, 79cm. high. (Christie's) $3,509 £2,420

A Roman marble torso of a male, 1st-2nd century A.D. (Phillips) $1,425 £950

A white marble Buddhist stele formed as Buddha, Tang Dynasty or earlier, 31cm. high. (Christie's) $4,089 £2,860

Pair of 19th century Italian marble busts representing Spring and Autumn, by A. Bottinelli, 77.5 and 70cm. high.(Christie's) $8,772 £6,050

A 19th century sculptured marble cat, America, 8¾in. high. (Robt. W. Skinner Inc.) $700 £489

Late 19th century Austrian marble figure of Diana, by Victor Tilgner, 1896, 127cm. high. (Christie's) $84,150 £55,000

An 18th century English marble group of two lions fighting, 15 x 19¾in. (Christie's) $3,775 £2,640

A 19th century white marble group of two Greco-Roman wrestlers, 20in. high, on a dark green marble pedestal, 4ft. high. (Capes, Dunn & Co.) $1,160 £800

A French 19th century marble group of Venus with Cupid asleep in her lap, by Albert E. C. Belleuse, 56 x 58cm. (Christie's) $25,245 £16,500

Pair of early 19th century Italian marble statues of Hercules and Omphale, 68cm. high. (Christie's) $1,093 £715

A late 19th century Italian coloured marble bust of Beatrice, 45cm. high. (Christie's) $3,190 £2,200

An early 20th century Italian marble bust of a classical woman in a headdress, by Clerici, 40cm. high. (Christie's) $841 £550

An agate and specimen marble chessboard with wide borders, the squares with lapis lazuli, malachite and other hard-stones and marbles, 14in. sq. (Christie's) $589 £418

One of a pair of 19th century ormolu and marble urns and covers, the ovoid bodies with twin bacchante handles, 37cm. high. (Phillips) $3,168 £2,200

MINIATURES

An American, 19th century, miniature painted bannister-back armchair, 9½in. high. (Christie's) $495 £326

A 19th century miniature grain painted bowfront chest-of-drawers, American or English, 12in. high. (Christie's) $1,210 £798

A 19th century, American, miniature classical maple fiddleback chair, 10¾in. high, 8¼in. wide. (Christie's) $550 £362

Mid 18th century miniature Chippendale cherrywood chest-of-drawers, 7¾in. high. (Christie's) $1,540 £1,016

An American, 18th century, miniature Queen Anne maple and pine slant-front desk, with a cherrywood mirror, the desk 11in. high. (Christie's) $3,520 £2,322

Late 19th century miniature Chippendale walnut slant-front desk, American, 7¼in. high. (Christie's) $1,650 £1,088

Late 18th century miniature George III mahogany side table, English, 6in. high. (Christie's) $330 £217

Late 18th century miniature Chippendale mahogany chest-on-chest, English, 16¾in. high. (Christie's) $1,870 £1,233

An American, 19th century, miniature Federal mahogany four-post bedstead with canopy, 15½in. high. (Christie's) $330 £217

A 19th century miniature green painted pine blanket chest, American, 9½in. high. (Christie's) $330 £217

Early 19th century miniature Federal mahogany oxbow chest-of-drawers, New England, 7¼in. high. (Christie's)
                    $4,400 £2,903

Early 19th century miniature Federal mahogany tilt-top tea table, American, 9in. high. (Christie's) $990 £653

A 19th century miniature Federal mahogany picture mirror, American, 9½in. high. (Christie's)
                    $1,210 £798

A 17th century miniature oak coffer of panelled construction, probably French, 35 x 21 x 23cm. (Phillips) $1,008 £700

Late 18th/early 19th century miniature Continental painted tall clock case, 17in. high. (Christie's)
$550   £362

A miniature Chippendale mahogany desk and bookcase, Rhode Island, 1760-80, 16in. high. (Christie's)
             $2,090 £1,378

Two 19th century miniature painted side chairs, American, 9¾in. and 8¼in. high. (Christie's) $528 £348

A Dutch mahogany and oak miniature clothes press, 21in. wide, 33in. high. (Christie's)
            $3,168 £1,980

One of a pair of German silvered wood girandoles, each with a cartouche-shaped plate, 32 x 19in. (Christie's) $2,499 £1,760

A 19th century Chinese Export lacquer swing-frame toilet mirror with cartouche-shaped plate, 69cm. high. (Phillips) $750 £500

A giltwood mirror with later waved rectangular plate, regilded, 53 x 24in. (Christie's) $2,171 £1,540

A grained and parcel gilt mirror with shaped rectangular plate, 53 x 42in. (Christie's) $2,637 £1,870

An early George III giltwood mirror with later circular plate, 42½ x 32¼in. (Christie's) $15,510 £11,000

An Italian giltwood mirror with later plate, the frame 17th century, 84 x 68in. (Christie's) $5,467 £3,850

A George I burr walnut and parcel gilt mirror, 49½ x 23in. (Christie's) $10,081 £7,150

A Regency giltwood convex mirror with circular plate in ebonised slip, 48 x 43½in. (Christie's) $13,183 £9,350

Mid 19th century large giltwood pier glass with rectangular plate, 103 x 66in. (Christie's) $2,326 £1,650

An early George III giltwood mirror with later plate, 33½ x 21¼in. (Christie's) $8,530 £6,050

A Regency satinwood large toilet mirror with oval swing frame, lacking plate, 25½in. wide. (Christie's) $495 £324

One of a pair of giltwood mirrors in the rococo style with cartouche-shaped plates, 35 x 21in. (Christie's) $1,022 £715

A giltwood mirror with rectangular plate in shaped frame, 45½ x 35½in. (Christie's) $4,998 £3,520

A Chippendale carved giltwood oval marginal wall mirror with contemporary plate and bird crestings, 1.06m. high. (Phillips) $7,200 £5,000

A George II silver gilt dressing table mirror, by Edward Feline, 1750, 23¾in. high, 62oz. (Christie's) $25,168 £17,600

A giltwood mirror with later arched shaped bevelled plate with mirrored slip, 54 x 33in. (Christie's) $2,343 £1,650

A Lalique hand mirror, 'Deux Chevres', 16.20cm. diam., in original fitted case. (Phillips) $1,152 £800

One of a pair of Regency giltwood pier glasses with rectangular plates in leaf moulded frames, 98 x 52½in. (Christie's) $13,959 £9,900

A George III inlaid mahogany cheval glass, 59in. high, 24in. wide. (Christie's) $2,420 £1,579

A Regency period circular carved giltwood frame convex mirror, 33in. x 3ft. 8in. (Woolley & Wallis) $1,152 £800

A Queen Anne mahogany shaving mirror, American or English, 1730-60, 24in. high. (Christie's) $1,320 £870

An early Georgian walnut mirror with later bevelled rectangular plate and gilt slip, 38¼ x 21½in. (Christie's) $2,073 £1,430

A late Federal mahogany dressing glass, Penn., 1810-20, 29½in. wide. (Christie's) $825 £544

Late 18th century neo-classical cream painted and parcel gilt mirror, 59½ x 20½in. (Christie's) $7,029 £4,950

A Federal mahogany looking glass, bears label 'Wells M. Gaylord, no. 59, Genesee St., Utica', circa 1820, 39in. high. (Robt. W. Skinner Inc.) $350 £225

A Renaissance Revival walnut and burl veneer hall tree, circa 1870, 100in. high. (Robt. W. Skinner Inc.) $1,700 £1,096

Late 18th century Chippendale mahogany mirror, 32½in. high, 18¼in. wide. (Christie's) $3,520 £2,322

A 19th century carved ivory and walnut dressing mirror, Europe, 23in. high. (Robt. W. Skinner Inc.)$950 £659

A Regency giltwood convex mirror with ebonised ribbed surround, 41 x 24in. (Christie's) $2,988 £2,090

An early George III gilt metal automaton toilet mirror, by James Cox, with musical and mechanical base, 11½in. wide. (Christie's) $89,958 £63,800

A George II gilt and gesso wall mirror with a broken pediment and cartouche cresting, 1.20m. x 63cm. (Phillips) $5,112 £3,600

A William III giltwood mirror with later oval plate, 74½ x 46in. (Christie's)
$7,550 £5,280

A Dieppe ivory mirror with rectangular arched bevelled plate, 60¼ x 34in. (Christie's) $9,372 £6,600

A Continental mirror with chamfered blue glass border, 44 x 20¼in. (Christie's)
$2,186 £1,540

A George II mahogany toilet mirror, the base with three drawers on ogee bracket feet, 17in. wide. (Christie's)
$1,861 £1,320

A German dressing table mirror of shaped outline, by Johann Christoph Berns, Magdeburg, circa 1755, 24¼in. high. (Christie's)
$9,123 £6,380

A Regency carved giltwood marginal wall mirror, 1.83 x 1.03m. (Phillips) $6,912 £4,800

A Victorian gilt pier-glass and jardiniere foyer stand, 104 x 65in. (Christie's) $924 £600

One of a pair of George I gilt gesso pier glasses, 87 x 33½in. (Christie's) $55,836 £39,600

A Regency mahogany cheval mirror, the plain frame on reeded uprights, 70½in. high, 32in. wide. (Christie's) $1,156 £756

A Regency carved giltwood convex mirror with ribband tied laurel leaf surround, 1.31m. x 78cm. (Phillips) $15,120 £10,500

One of a pair of George III giltwood mirrors with oval plates in moulded gadrooned frames, 51 x 23½in. (Christie's) $20,163 £14,300

A Chippendale mahogany mirror, American, 1760-80, 41in. high. (Christie's) $2,860 £2,001

A Regency carved giltwood girandole convex mirror with military trophy cresting, 1.10m. high. (Phillips) $6,048 £4,200

One of a pair of mid 18th century Italian giltwood girandoles with arched plates, 37½ x 10½in. (Christie's) $5,467 £3,850

A William and Mary silvered mirror in moulded frame, 60 x 20½in. (Christie's) $2,478 £1,620

A George II walnut toilet mirror, the coved base with a drawer on later bracket feet, 17¼in. wide. (Christie's) $597 £418

Late 18th century Italian giltwood mirror with shaped divided plate, 86 x 57½in. (Christie's) $10,153 £7,150

Late 18th century neo-classical parcel gilt and cream painted mirror, 54 x 19¾in. (Christie's) $6,560 £4,620

A Regency giltwood convex mirror with circular plate, 55 x 26in. (Christie's) $2,516 £1,760

A painted hall mirror in the style of Robert Mallet-Stevens, 183cm. high. (Christie's) $1,156 £756

One of a pair of 19th century carved giltwood girandole mirror frames in the Chippendale taste, 97 x 52cm. (Phillips) $12,000 £8,000

One of a pair of 19th century Irish ebonised and gilded oval mirrors, the frames applied with cabochon studs, 28½ x 22½in. (Christie's) $4,719 £3,300

Late 18th century Italian giltwood mirror, 17 x 35in. (Christie's) $2,030 £1,430

A George II walnut and parcel gilt mirror, 52 x 26½in. (Christie's) $21,714 £15,400

A Regency carved giltwood and gesso convex girandole, 1.03m. x 59cm. (Phillips) $3,168 £2,200

Queen Anne walnut mirror, original glass and backing, probably England, circa 1750, 24in. high. (Robt. W. Skinner Inc.) $425 £283

A George III giltwood mirror with later oval plate in a tied, out-scrolled rush frame, 39 x 26½in. (Christie's) $6,940 £4,536

A Dutch marquetry toilet mirror, the solid cylinder enclosing a fitted interior, 21½in. wide. (Christie's) $3,190 £2,200

A dressing glass by Howard & Co., N.Y., 1884, 33in. high, 30in. wide. (Christie's) $17,600 £12,316

One of a pair of giltwood mirrors of George III style with oval plates and urn crestings, 38½ x 18in. (Christie's) $2,791 £1,980

A George II giltwood over-mantel with later rectangular bevelled plate, 79 x 76½in. (Christie's) $17,303 £12,100

A George III giltwood mirror with later oval plate, 21½ x 32½in. (Christie's) $3,635 £2,376

A Queen Anne giltwood mirror with shaped divided partly bevelled plate, 69 x 44in. (Christie's)
$46,530 £33,000

Early 19th century Federal giltwood mirror surmounted by gold leaf eagle, 44in. high. (Robt. W. Skinner Inc.)
$1,700 £1,133

One of a pair of mid 18th century carved giltwood girandoles, probably France, 14½in. wide, sconces missing. (Robt. W. Skinner Inc.)
$700 £489

A WMF silvered pewter table mirror, stamped marks WMF, 70g., 34.9cm. high. (Christie's) $1,425 £990

Early 18th century Italian lead framed mirror, 60½ x 28in. (Christie's)
$11,715 £8,250

Mid 18th century Italian giltwood mirror with later shaped plate and moulded foliate slip, 59 x 42in. (Christie's) $1,562 £1,100

A George III giltwood mirror with later oval plate, 45¼ x 23¾in. (Christie's)
$3,257 £2,310

A Charles II giltwood mirror with later bevelled plate, 43 x 33in. (Christie's)
$1,754 £1,210

An Adam carved giltwood oval wall mirror with anthemion cresting, 1.62m. x 76cm. overall. (Phillips)
$5,184 £3,600

A Regency scarlet and gold
papier-mache tray with
everted gallery, 30in. wide.
(Christie's) $660 £462

A lead figure of a child
holding a scallop shell bowl,
40in. high. (Heathcote Ball
& Co.) $1,874 £1,150

A Regency mahogany cheese
coaster, 17in. wide.
(Christie's) $480 £286

One of a pair of rock crystal
and gilt metal pricket candlesticks, mid 19th century,
11in. high. (Christie's)
         $3,436 £2,420

A chromium plated automatic
traffic warner, inscribed Auto
Signal Pat. 375944, 42in. long.
(Christie's) $186 £120

A pair of fireside companions
painted with a boy and a girl
in 18th century costume,
42in. and 45in. high.
(Christie's) $4,347 £2,860

A Dunhill white metal and
enamelled watch lighter,
4.5cm. high. (Christie's)
         $717 £440

One of a pair of Chinese hard-
stone flowering trees in lacquer
jardinieres, 16½in. high.
(Christie's) $702 £495

A French circular medallion
enclosing black ink prints on
silk on both sides, circa 1795,
3.1/8in. diam. (Christie's)
         $597 £418

One of a pair of gilt metal six-branch candelabra of Louis XVI style, stamped AB on the bases, 20½in. high. (Christie's) $1,754 £1,210

Cast zinc St. Bernard dog figure, probably Mass., circa 1880, 45in. wide. (Robt. W. Skinner Inc.) $2,600 £1,818

One of a group of six circular gilt metal knobs with short stems and threaded fitments, circa 1780, each 2¾in. diam. (Christie's) $707 £495

A Dunhill electroplated table lighter, stamped Made in England, patent no. 143752, 9cm. high. (Christie's) $179 £110

A Shaker splint sewing basket, probably Enfield, Connecticut, 19th century, 15½in. diam. (Christie's) $880 £539

An Art Deco white metal minaudiere, shaped as a guitar, 16cm. long. (Christie's) $717 £440

One of a pair of metal mounted flambe stoneware vases, designed by Otto Eckmann, 52.2cm. high. (Christie's) $1,730 £1,210

A faience ushabti fired green and mottled black with crisp impressed inscription, 11.5cm. high, and two others, all late Dynastic Period. (Phillips) $260 £170

An American 19th century arrangement of various wax fruits on a wooden pedestal base, under a glass dome, 21in. high. (Robt. W. Skinner Inc.) $475 £332

A builder's model of the single screw cargo ship M.V. 'Deerwood' of London, built 1955 by Wm. Pickersgill & Sons Ltd., for Wm. France, Fenwick & Co. Ltd., 12½ x 53in. (Christie's) $1,530 £1,000

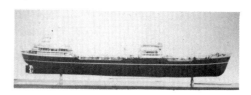

A display model of the motor tanker 'London Glory', built by Messrs. Sir James Laing & Sons Ltd., Sunderland for London & Overseas Freighters Ltd. Yard No. 793, 1952 and modelled for the builders by I. R. Amis Ltd. London, 7 x 31in. (Christie's) $1,071 £700

An exhibition standard 1:72 scale planked and fully rigged model of the French frigate 'La Venus' of circa 1782, built by P. M. di Gragnano, Naples, 31 x 44in. (Christie's) $6,885 £4,500

A 1:100 scale model of the Le Havre Pilot Boat 'Henriette', pennant No. H2, of 1866, built by M. Deveral, Folkestone, 8 x 8in. (Christie's) $336 £220

A 1:60 scale model of the late 18th century French Ceremonial Galley 'Reale de France', built by J. Cherrill, Weybridge, 25 x 42in. (Christie's) $1,377 £900

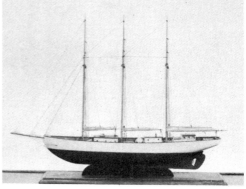

A 1:100 scale model of the three masted auxiliary schooner 'Cruz del Sur' built by W. M. Wilson, Silloth, 12 x 17½in. (Christie's) $306 £200

A 1/8in.:1ft. scale builder's model of the single screw steam newsprint carrier 'Sarah Bowater' of London, built 1955 by Denny Bros., Dumbarton for the Bowater Paper Corporation Ltd., 12 x 52in. (Christie's) $3,060 £2,000

An exhibition standard ¾in.:1ft. scale model of the steam yacht 'Turbinia', as developed to 1895 and modelled by A. Broad, Bromley, 18½ x 77in. (Christie's) $1,989 £1,300

A 1:100 scale model of a Trouville trawler of circa 1866, built by M. Deveral, Folkestone, 6 x 6½in. (Christie's) $336 £220

Late 19th century possibly builder's model of the fully rigged model of a yawl believed to be the 'Constance' of 1885, built for C. W. Prescott-Westcar by A. Payne & Sons, Southampton and designed by Dixon Kemp, 28 x 35¾in. (Christie's) $6,120 £4,000

A finely carved 'Dieppe' ivory model three masted man-of-war with spars and rigging, full suit of carved ivory sails, mounted on wood with two ship's boats, 7 x 9in. (Christie's) $994 £650

An exhibition standard 1:75 scale fully planked and rigged model of the French 60 gun man-of-war 'Le Protecteur' of circa 1760, built by P. M. di Gragnano, Naples, 31 x 38in. (Christie's) $7,650 £5,000

A builder's mirror backed half model of the schooner rigged steam yacht 'Rona', built for A. H. E. Wood Esq., by David and William Henderson & Co., 1893/4 to the order of Thomas and Campbell, designed by G. L. Watson & Co., 10 x 71in. (Christie's) $5,508 £3,600

A builder's 3/16in.:1ft. scale model of H.M.S. 'Transport Ferry No. 3016', built for the Royal Navy by R. & W. Hawthorn, Leslie & Co. Ltd., Hebburn-on-Tyne, 1945, 16 x 63½in. (Christie's) $4,590 £3,000

A 20th century carved and painted model of the paddle steamer 'City of Key West', American, in wooden and glass case, 38in. long. (Christie's) $1,210 £782

A well detailed live steam, spirit fired, radio controlled, fully planked and framed model of the Barry Pilot Cutter 'Chimaera' of circa 1918, built by Marvon Models, Doncaster, 24½ x 47in. (Christie's) $1,530 £1,000

A carved and painted model of the 'Royal Ark', by J. R. Whittemore, on a moulded wooden base, 43in. long. (Christie's) $1,980 £1,280

Late 19th century carved and painted model of the 'William Tapscot', in a glass and mahogany case, 38in. long. (Christie's) $1,540 £995

A carved and painted model of ocean liner 'Liberte', executed for the Companie Generale Transatlantique, circa 1950, in wooden and plexi-glass case, 54in. long. (Christie's) $6,050 £3,912

A builder's mirror back half model of a single screw cabin motor cruiser built by John I. Thorneycroft & Co. Ltd., London, 6 x 26in. (Christie's) $1,989 £1,300

A Voltamp gauge 2 trolley No. 2123, 0-4-4-0, circa 1913. (Christie's) $3,080 £2,159

No. 5 thin rim locomotive lettered 'B & O R.R.', circa 1907. (Christie's) $2,090 £1,465

A gauge 1 Bing locomotive 4-4-0 with 6-wheel tender, circa 1915. (Christie's) $1,430 £1,002

Carette green locomotive, 2-2-0, 4-wheel tender, alcohol burner, together with an olive 4-wheel baggage car, circa 1905. (Christie's)
$935 £655

A 'Washington Special', No. 385E locomotive with tender and cars, circa 1934. (Christie's)
$1,980 £1,387

A late 19th century 3¾in. gauge spirit fired brass model of the Great Northern Railway Stirling 2-4-0 locomotive and tender No. 152, built by H. J. Wood, London, 10¼ x 35in. (Christie's) $1,836 £1,200

A 5in. gauge model of the Great Western Railway 57XX Class 0-6-0 pannier tank locomotive No. 5702, built by C. G. Balding, Bideford, 13½ x 34in. (Christie's) $2,448 £1,600

A 7¼in. gauge model of the North Eastern Railway Class G5 0-4-4 side tank locomotive No. 505, built by D. W. Horsfall, Northowram, 20½ x 52½in. (Christie's) $3,060 £2,000

Set No. 1771RW, gauge 0 No. 1681 Hudson type locomotive 2-6-4, 8-wheel 1936 version tender and three pullmans, American Flyer Lines. (Christie's) $660 £462

A 7mm. finescale two rail electric model of the London and North Eastern Railway Class B12 4-6-0 locomotive and tender No. 8523, built by K. J. Leeming and painted by A. Brackenborough, 3½ x 16½in. (Christie's) $1,836 £1,200

A 7¼in. gauge model of the Great Western Railway Armstrong Class 4-4-0 locomotive and tender No. 8 'Gooch', built by T. Childs, Churchill, 20¼ x 88in. (Christie's)
$10,710 £7,000

An exhibition standard 5in. gauge model of the Great Western Railway River Class 2-4-0 locomotive and tender No. 69 'Avon' as running in 1906, built from builder's drawings and photographs by R. W. Gale, Newport, 14¼ x 53¼in. (Christie's) $11,475 £7,500

A well engineered 3½in. gauge model of the Great Western Railway County class 4-6-0 locomotive and tender No. 1022 'County of Northampton', 10 x 47in. (Christie's)
$2,295 £1,500

A 3½in. gauge model of the British Railways Class 7 4-6-2 locomotive and tender No. 70013 'Oliver Cromwell, built by H. C. Luckhurst, Oxley, 10¼ x 52½in. (Christie's)
$3,060 £2,000

A 5in. gauge model of the London Midland and Scottish Railway Class 2F 0-6-0 side tank locomotive No. 11270, 13 x 27½in. (Christie's) $2,907 £1,900

A 7¼in. gauge model of the London Midland and Scottish Railway Class 2F 0-6-0 side tank locomotive No. 11270, built by C. Ottaway, Chippenham, 18½ x 41in. (Christie's)
$6,885 £4,500

A 3½in. gauge model of the Southern Railway 0-4-2 side tank locomotive No. 2036, built to the designs of Juliet by M. Darlow, 1972 — 10 x 21in. (Christie's) $688 £450

A Hornby gauge 0 (3-rail) electric model of the No. 1 LNER 0-4-0 special locomotive and tender, original paintwork, (loco in original box). (Christie's) $403 £280

A well engineered 2½in. gauge model of the London Midland and Scottish Railway 4-4-0 locomotive and tender No. 1000, built to the designs of Eagle by G. Ward, 8 x 31in. (Christie's) $612 £400

An exhibition standard 5in. gauge model of the Great Northern Railway Stirling Single 4-2-2 locomotive and tender No. 53, built from works drawings and photographs by J. S. Richardson, Halifax, 14 x 56in. (Christie's) $7,650 £5,000

A finely detailed 7mm. finescale two rail electric model of the Deutches Bundesbahn 144 Bo Bo class electric outline locomotive No. E44070 built by Hego Modellbahn for the Nuremburg Toy Fair, 1976, 4 x 13½in. (Christie's)
$765 £500

A mid 19th century live steam spirit fired 4¾in. gauge brass model of the 2-2-2 locomotive and tender 'Express', built by Steven's Model Dockyard, 11¾ x 30in. (Christie's) $3,213 £2,100

A fine Marklin gauge 1 clockwork model of the LB & SCR 4-4-2 'Atlantic' tank locomotive No. 22, in original paintwork, with lamps, circa 1920 (1 loose bogie). (Christie's) $2,880 £2,000

A gauge 1 (3-rail) electric model of the G.N.R. 0-4-0 side tank locomotive No. 112, in original paintwork by Bing for Bassett-Lowke (lacks 3 buffers). (Christie's) $374 £260

An exhibition standard 5in. gauge model of the Great Western Railway Armstrong Class 4-4-0 locomotive and tender No. 14, 'Charles Saunders', built by P. J. Rich, Rhiwderin, 14 x 62in. (Christie's) $15,606 £10,200

A fine contemporary late 19th century 3¼in. gauge brass and steel spirit fired model 4-2-0 locomotive and tender, built by H. J. Wood, London, 8½ x 21½in. (Christie's) $994 £650

A 3in. scale model of a single cylinder two speed, four shaft Clayton & Shuttleworth traction engine, built by K. Prout, 31 x 56in. (Christie's) $4,284 £2,800

A model Stuart triple expansion vertical reversing marine engine built by G. B. Houghton, Rochester, 7 x 8¾in. (Christie's) $994 £650

An exhibition standard 3in. scale model of the Savage horse-drawn Electric Light Engine No. 357, built by C. J. Goulding, Newport, 27 x 47in. (Christie's) $4,284 £2,800

An early 19th century model of a single cylinder table engine, possibly by Murdock, 15½ x 10in. (Christie's) $1,377 £900

A well engineered 2in. scale model of an Aveling and Porter twin crank compound two speed, four shaft Road Roller, 19½ x 35in. (Christie's) $3,987 £2,600

Late 19th century model of the three cylinder compound vertical surface condensing mill engine 'Asia', 16¼ x 13¼in. (Christie's) $2,907 £1,900

A well presented approx. 1:20 scale model of the Weatherhill Pit Winding Engine of 1833, built by W. K. Walsam, Hayes, 19 x 14½in. (Christie's) $918 £600

A 1:20 scale brass model of the Fenton, Murray & Wood 6 N.H.P. underlever beam engine of 1806 built by G. L. Dimelow, Ashton-under-Lyne, 9¾ x 9¼in. (Christie's) $918 £600

An unusual model of a steam driven 19th century twin bore Deep Well Engine House and Pump, built by R. J. Sare, Northleach, 16½ x 18½in. (Christie's) $306 £200

An exhibition standard 2in. scale model of a Burrell 5 N.H.P. double crank compound three shaft, two speed Showman's Road Locomotive, 20 x 30½in. (Christie's) $8,415 £5,500

An ingenious and well presented model steam driven Stone Sawing Plant, built by R. J. Sare, Northleach, 13½ x 24½in. (Christie's) $489 £320

A finely engineered model twin cylinder compound undertype stationary steam engine built to the designs of A. H. Greenly, by P. C. Kidner, London, 14½ x 24½in. (Christie's) $2,295 £1,500

A contemporary early 19th century brass and wrought iron single cylinder six pillar beam engine, built by Chadburn Bros., Sheffield, 19 x 19¼in. (Christie's) $3,060 £2,000

An approx. 4in. scale Foden type twin cylinder overtype two speed steam lorry, built by A. Groves, Watford, 1937 and restored by M. Williams at the British Engineerium, Hove, 1983, 36½ x 88in. (Christie's) $7,650 £5,000

A well presented model single cylinder vertical reversing stationary engine, built from Clarkson castings, 17½ x 9¾in. (Christie's) $1,071 £700

An exhibition standard model of the three cylinder compound surface condensing vertical reversing marine engine, fitted to S.S. 'Servia', and modelled by T. Lowe, 1907, 14½ x 12½in. (Christie's) $6,120 £4,000

A sturdily constructed 2in. scale model of a Fowler twin crank compound three speed, four shaft road locomotive built by S. W. Brown, Newbury, 23 x 37in. (Christie's) $3,672 £2,400

An early 19th century small full size single cylinder six pillar beam engine, 31 x 34in. (Christie's) $1,377 £900

599

Two frogs cast iron mechanical bank, J. & E. Stevens, Co., Pat. 1882, 8¾in. long. (Robt. W. Skinner Inc.) $625 £434

Owl cast iron mechanical bank, J. & E. Stevens, Co., pat. 1880, 7.5/8in. high. (Robt. W. Skinner Inc.) $200 £138

'Bad Accident' cast iron mechanical bank, J. & E. Stevens, Co., 1891-1911, 10.3/8in. long. (Robt. W. Skinner Inc.)$1,100 £763

'Bull Dog Bank' cast iron mechanical bank, J. & E. Stevens, Co., pat. 1880, 7½in. high. (Robt. W. Skinner Inc.) $500 £347

William Tell cast iron mechanical bank, J. & E. Stevens, Co., pat. 1896, 10.5/8in. long. (Robt. W. Skinner Inc.) $600 £416

Lion and Monkeys cast iron mechanical bank, Kyser & Rex Co., Pat. 1883, 10in. long. (Robt. W. Skinner Inc.) $400 £277

'World's Fair' cast iron mechanical bank, J. & E. Stevens, Co., pat. 1893, 8¼in. long. (Robt. W. Skinner Inc.) $600 £416

'Jolly Nigger' metal money bank. (Hobbs & Chambers) $97 £68

'Chief Big Moon' cast iron mechanical bank, J. & E. Stevens, Co., pat. 1899, 10in. long. (Robt. W. Skinner Inc.) $1,200 £833

Early 19th century micro-mosaic plaque, depicting the Temple of Vesta at Tivoli, 2½in. long. (Christie's) $1,200 £810

Early 19th century circular Roman micro-mosaic decorated with a duck and duckling, the box 3in. diam. (Christie's) $1,573 £1,100

A Roman rectangular micro-mosaic panel decorated with a bull-baiting scene, circa 1800, 3in. long. (Christie's) $4,404 £3,080

Early 19th century circular Roman micro-mosaic decorated in the style of Rafaelli with a finch, the box 3in. diam. (Christie's) $1,730 £1,210

A 19th century Roman micro-mosaic panel decorated in bright colours with a bunch of flowers, approx. 8in. long. (Christie's) $5,505 £3,850

A circular tortoiseshell snuff box with detachable cover, the mosaic circa 1820, 2¾in. diam. (Christie's) $1,487 £880

A Roman micro-mosaic panel decorated with Pliny's Doves of Venus, circa 1840, 2.5/8in. long. (Christie's) $1,337 £935

A circular Roman micro-mosaic of a pannier brimming with flowers, circa 1830, the box 2¾in. diam. (Christie's) $2,674 £1,870

A 19th century Roman rectangular mosaic panel, decorated with a view of the Piazza del Popolo in Rome, 2¾in. long. (Christie's) $1,573 £1,100

Victorie (Spirit of the Wind), a Lalique glass female head car mascot, 10¼in. long. (Christie's) $2,480 £1,600

A chromium plated and enamelled Aero-Club Brooklands badge, 3¾in. high. (Onslow's) $686 £480

'Perche', a Lalique car mascot in clear and satin finished glass, moulded as a fish, 9.5cm. high. (Christie's) $1,022 £715

An 18ct. gold key-ring modelled as a Rolls-Royce radiator, 3in. overall. (Christie's) $294 £190

The Romance of a Record Breaker, by F. G. Crosby, signed and dated 1911, watercolour — 11 x 11in. (Christie's) $4,030 £2,600

A rosewood and ivory toucan radiator cap, inscribed Howett, London, 5in. high. (Christie's) $248 £160

'Sanglier', a Lalique car mascot in clear and satin finished glass, moulded as a boar, 6.5cm. high. (Christie's) $1,022 £715

Le Rire, special 13 July number, 1901 for the Paris-Berlin automobile race, brochure. (Christie's) $116 £75

'Tete de Coq', a Lalique car mascot, in clear and satin finished glass, 18cm. high. (Christie's) $2,044 £1,430

A brass Lucas King of the Road oil sidelight, stamped no. 630, 10½in. high. (Onslow's) $114 £80

A silver gilt and enamelled dashboard St. Christopher, Birmingham, 1922, 2¼in. long. (Christie's) $77 £50

A brass figure of a stylised eagle perched on a decorative base, 8in. high. (Christie's) $100 £65

'Falcon', a Lalique car mascot in clear and satin finished glass, 15.5cm. high. (Christie's) $2,674 £1,870

Racing Cars, by R. Brone, signed and dated 1969, 38½ x 39in. (Christie's)$155 £100

A silver plated R.A.C. badge, hollow, stamped B1631, 7in. high. (Onslow's) $357 £250

A brass Lucas King of the Road oil light, stamped no. 435, 12in. high. (Onslow's) $114 £80

A chromium plated and enamelled B.A.R.C. Brooklands badge, stamped 1367, 3¾in. high. (Onslow's) $572 £400

A brass car mascot of Minerva, inscribed 'Minerva P. de Soete', 6in. high. (Christie's) $403 £260

A chromium plated car mascot figure of 'Puss in Boots', 6in. high. (Christie's) $465 £300

'Pharaoh', a Red-Ashay, car mascot in clear and satin finished glass, 11.5cm. high. (Christie's) $1,321 £864

A Lalique glass car mascot, modelled as the head of a cockerel, 8½in. high. (Parsons, Welch & Cowell) $2,310 £1,500

'Saint-Christopher', a Lalique car mascot in clear and satin finished glass, with Breves Galleries Knightsbridge metal radiator mount, 22.5cm. high. (Christie's) $314 £220

Two of twenty-one R.A.C.I. dashboard plaques, late 1920's early 1930's, approx. 3 x 2in. (Christie's) $1,085 £700

A Lalique car mascot in clear and satin-finished glass, moulded as a falcon, 16.5cm. high. (Christie's) $2,217 £1,540

A nickel plated brass stylised tyre with seated speed god inside, inscribed Coffin, 6in. high. (Christie's) $620 £400

A motoring picnic hamper, four settings, marked Coracle, 22½in. long. (Christie's) $1,085 £700

'Archer', a Lalique car mascot in clear and satin finished glass, 12cm. high. (Christie's) $2,044 £1,430

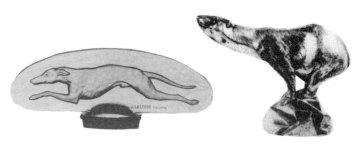

A brass stylised car mascot bust of Minerva, inscribed P. de Soete, 5½in. high. (Christie's) $589 £380

A Lalique greyhound car mascot. (Woolley & Wallis) $4,185 £2,700

A nickel plated car mascot of a polar bear standing on a stylised rock plinth, 4½in. high. (Christie's) $100 £65

A Rolls-Royce Spirit of Ecstasy car mascot, indistinctly marked Trade Mark Reg., Reg. U.S. Pat. Off., 5¾in. high. (Christie's) $248 £160

Olympia, Motor Show, Oct. 12 1933, colour lithograph poster, after A. E. Marty, 10 x 12½in. (Christie's) $248 £160

A brass Lucas King of the Road oil sidelight, stamped no. 724, 12½in. high. (Onslow's) $178 £125

A chromium plated bronze car mascot, Farman Icarus, inscribed Colin George, Made in France, circa 1922, 6in. high. (Christie's) $496 £320

A Lalique car mascot, Longchamps, in clear and satin-finished glass, 13cm. high. (Christie's) $12,672 £8,800

'Grand Libellule', a Lalique car mascot in clear and satin finished glass, 21cm. high. (Christie's) $5,783 £3,780

An Edison Home phonograph, Model A No. H104435, with B reproducer, crane 42in. long, and 25 cylinders. (Christie's) $693 £450

An interchangeable cylinder mandolin musical box on table with six eight-air cylinders, 47in. wide overall, the cylinders 11in. (Christie's) $6,160 £4,000

A Mandoline Expressive Zither musical box by P.V.F. playing twelve airs, 28in. wide, the cylinder 17¼in. long. (Christie's) $2,310 £1,500

A key-wind forte piano musical box, by Nicole Freres, No. 39788, playing twelve airs, 22in. wide, the cylinder 13 x 3¼in. diam. (Christie's) $2,618 £1,700

An HMV Automatic Model 1 gramophone No. 570 with 5a soundbox, 42in. wide, circa 1929. (Christie's) $539 £350

Late 19th century rosewood veneer and ebonised wood cylinder music box on stand, F. Conchon, Manufacturer, Switzerland, 39½in. wide. (Robt. W. Skinner Inc.) $3,700 £2,587

A G. & T. single-spring Monarch gramophone with Morning Glory horn, 24in. diam., circa 1903-04. (Christie's) $492 £320

An interchangeable cylinder music box on stand, by B. A. Bremond, circa 1875, cylinder 13in. long, table 35½in. long. (Christie's) $2,420 £1,688

A Gramophone Co. mahogany Junior Monarch ('Doric') with single-spring motor, the horn 21½in. diam., circa 1908. (Christie's) $1,001 £650

An HMV Model V mahogany horn gramophone with single-spring motor, Exhibition soundbox and fluted mahogany horn, circa 1914. (Christie's) $1,232 £800

A hidden drum, bells and castagnette musical box playing six airs, 20½in. wide, the cylinder 13in. (Christie's) $1,386 £900

A horn Pathephone with chequer-strung oak case, horn 22in. diam., (Christie's) $924 £600

Walnut cased polyphon coin-operated, wind-up gramophone with key, winder and nine discs. (Lots Road Galleries)
$1,836 £1,200

A clockwork barrel-organ, by Flight & Robson, 66½in. wide, the barrels 35 x 8in. diam., and a discus electric suction unit. (Christie's)
$8,470 £5,500

An Edison Fireside phonograph, Model A No. 31916, now with Diamond B reproducer, Model R and Model K reproducers with adapter ring. (Christie's) $646 £420

An Edison Triumph phonograph, Model A No. 45259, in 'New Style' green oak case, with 14in. witch's hat horn. (Christie's) $770 £500

A G. & T. double-spring Monarch in oak case, the oak horn 18in. diam., the gramophone circa 1906. (Christie's)
$1,232 £800

A musical box, by Baker-Troll, playing eight airs accompanied by drum, castanet and six-engraved bells, 23½in. wide. (Christie's) $3,080 £2,000

A violoncello, by Ch.
J. B. Collin-Mezin,
dated 1884, length of
back 29.7/8in.
(Christie's)
$7,865 £5,500

A violin, by Dante
and Alfredo Guastalla,
1929, length of back
14.1/8in. (Phillips)
$2,926 £1,900

A violin, by Giovanni
Battista Gaibisso,
1922, length of back
14.1/16in. (Christie's)
$4,147 £2,900

A violin, by Jean M.
Remy, Paris, circa
1810, length of back
14¼in., with two
bows in case.
(Phillips)
$1,267 £880

A viola, by Bruno
Barbieri, maker's
label Liutaio in Man-
tova Anno 1974,
length of back 15½in.
(Christie's)
$3,003 £2,100

An Italian violin, by
F. Ruggieri, length
of back 14in.
(Christie's)
$60,192 £41,800

A violin, by Paul
Bailly, circa 1890,
length of back
14.1/16in., with a
bow in case. (Phillips)
$1,872 £1,300

An Italian violin,
by Pietro Guarneri
of Mantua, 1707,
length of back 14in.
(Christie's)
$126,720 £88,000

An Italian viola, attributed to G. & L. Bisiach, 1932, length of back 16.3/8in. (Christie's)
$8,712 £6,050

A viola da gamba, labelled Joachim Tielke/in Hamburg/ An 1685, length of back 26in. (Christie's)
$47,520 £33,000

A violin, by Nicolas Aine in Mirecourt, circa 1800, length of back 14¼in. (Phillips)
$1,800 £1,250

An Austrian viola d'amore, by M. I. Stadlmann, length of back 14.13/16in. (Christie's)
$1,267 £880

A violin, by Etienne Vatelot 1946, length of back 14.1/16in. (Phillips)
$1,617 £1,050

A French violin, by Pierre Silvestre, Lyon 1850, length of back 14.1/8in. (Christie's)
$15,048 £10,450

A Neapolitan violin, by a member of the Gagliano family, circa 1780-1810, length of back 14.1/16in. (Phillips)
$10,472 £6,800

A violin, by T. Earle Hesketh in Manchester, dated 1929, length of back, 13.7/8in. (Christie's)
$1,315 £920

A viola, circa 1870,
of the Honore
Derazey School,
length of back
16.1/16in.
(Christie's)
$3,146 £2,200

A violin, by Enrico
Veronesi, 1931,
length of back
14.1/16in.
(Christie's)
$2,431 £1,700

A violin, by Carlo
Storioni, 1895,
length of back,
14¼in. (Phillips)
$893 £580

A violin, by Leon
Mougenot Gauche,
maker's label dated
1927, length of
back 14.1/8in.
(Christie's)
$1,716 £1,200

A violin, probably
the work of George
Wulme Hudson,
circa 1920, length
of back 14¼in.
(Christie's)
$1,108 £770

A violin, by A. Kloz,
dated 1789, length
of back 13.7/8in.
(Christie's)
$4,147 £2,900

An Italian violin,
unlabelled, circa
1780, length of back,
13.15/16in.
(Christie's)
$3,801 £2,640

A violin, by Job
Ardern, bearing the
label 'born 1826,
died 1912', length
of back 14.1/8in.
(Phillips) $585 £380

A viola, by Jean
Baptiste Colin,
length of back
15.13/16in., with
bow. (Phillips)
$1,617 £1,050

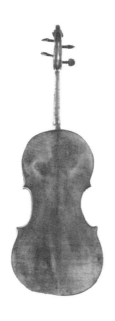

An English violoncello,
Panormo School, circa
1820, length of back
28.15/16in.
(Christie's)
$7,920 £5,500

A violin, by Pierre
Silvestre of Lyons,
circa 1850, length
of back 14.3/16in.
(Christie's)
$9,295 £6,500

A viola of the Meurot
School, Paris, circa
1910, length of back
15.5/8in., in a hide
case. (Phillips)
$1,440 £1,000

A viola, by Giovanni
Battista Gaibisso,
1915, length of back
16.7/16in. (Phillips)
$2,926 £1,900

An Italian violin, by
C. F. Landolfi, 1750,
length of back
13.7/8in. (Christie's)
$38,016 £26,400

A viola, by William
Ebsworth Hill, 1849,
length of back
16.3/8in. (Phillips)
$10,472 £6,800

A viola, by Alfred
Vincent, London,
1930, length of back
17.1/8in. (Phillips)
$2,772 £1,800

An Italian violin,
by Fratelli Melegari,
1903, length of back
14.1/8in. (Christie's)
$3,168 £2,200

A violin, by Joannes
C. Leidolf, 1748,
length of back
14.1/8in., with two
bows in case.
(Phillips)
$1,180 £820

A composite Italian
violin, length of
back 14.1/8in.
(Christie's)
$38,016 £26,400

A violin, by T. Earle
Hesketh, dated 1931,
length of back
14.1/16in., with a
nickel mounted bow.
(Christie's)
$1,716 £1,200

A violin, by Laurence
Cocker, bearing maker's
label in Derby dated
1964, length of back
14in. (Phillips)
$708 £460

An English viola,
circa 1800, labelled
Amati, length of
back 15.5/16in.
(Christie's)
$2,851 £1,980

A violin, by Giuseppe
Lucci, maker's label
Da Bagnacavallo Fece
in Roma 1978, length
of back 14.1/16in.
(Christie's)
$3,432 £2,400

A violin, by Thos.
Perry, 1785, length
of back 13.7/8in.
(Phillips)
$2,310 £1,500

An Austrian violin, by A. F. Mayr, Salzburg An 1726, length of back 13.15/16in. (Christie's) $4,435 £3,080

A violin, by Alexandre Delanoy in Bordeaux, dated 1879, length of back 14.1/8in. (Christie's) $2,431 £1,700

An English violin, by Clifford A. Hoing, 1934, length of back 14in. (Christie's) $2,059 £1,430

A violoncello, by L. M. Gauche, in Mirecourt, label dated 1912, length of back 30.1/8in. (Christie's) $6,006 £4,200

A violin, by Dr. N. Aine, circa 1830, length of back 14.1/16in. (Christie's) $2,216 £1,550

An Italian violin, by Giovanni B. Gabrielli, length of back 13.7/8in. (Christie's) $22,176 £15,400

Early 19th century Italian violoncello, length of back 29.1/8in. (Christie's) $6,019 £4,180

A viola of the Claude Pierray, Paris School, circa 1740, length of back 16.7/16in. (Christie's) $12,584 £8,800

A 19th century marine ivory netsuke of a snake passing through a gourd, signed Shuraku above a square seal. (Christie's) $1,101 £770

A well carved ivory netsuke of a branch of three fruiting kaki, signed Mitsushiro. (Christie's) $624 £440

A 19th century ivory netsuke of Kiyohime standing next to the Bell of Dojoji, signed Masanaga. (Christie's)
              $468 £330

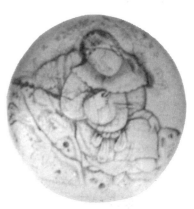

Mid 19th century wood and ivory netsuke of a kneeling karako, signed Hojitsu, Edo School. (Christie's)
              $2,186 £1,540

An 18th century ivory Chinese-style netsuke of a karashishi looking to the right, unsigned. (Christie's)
              $314 £220

A 19th century ivory manju netsuke decorated in shishiai-bori, signed Ikko, and kao. (Christie's) $393 £275

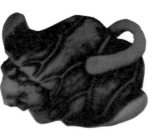

A 19th century iron kaga-mibuta netsuke decorated in iroe hirazogan and takazogan with a green frog. (Christie's)
              $593 £418

Late 18th century well carved ivory netsuke of a frog emerging from a curled lotus leaf. (Christie's)
              $1,405 £990

A 19th century wood netsuke of a snake entwined in and around a pumpkin, inscribed Tadamasa, Nagoya School. (Christie's)
              $1,405 £990

NETSUKE

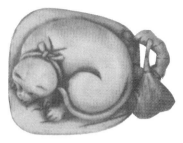 

An ivory netsuke of a cat
sleeping on a winnowing
fan, circa 1800. (Christie's)
$937 £660

A boxwood netsuke of a
chestnut, signed Toyomasa
kore o horu. (Christie's)
$1,249 £880

Late 18th century ivory
netsuke of two quail on
sprays of millet, signed
Okatomo, Kyoto School.
(Christie's) $937 £660

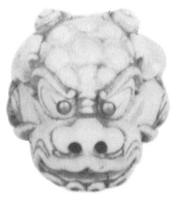  

Early 19th century ivory
netsuke of the head of a
karashishi, in the style of
Tomotada. (Christie's)
$786 £550

Mid/late 19th century ivory
netsuke of a snail crawling
over a bamboo shoot,
signed Koho. (Christie's)
$749 £528

A 19th century ivory manju
netsuke carved with a girl
kneeling beneath a pine tree,
signed Nagamitsu. (Christie's)
$468 £330

Early 19th century umoregi
and ivory netsuke of a dragon
coiled in and around rocks,
(Christie's) $3,124 £2,200

A 19th century ivory netsuke
of two of Momotaro's friends,
the monkey and the dog,
signed Tomomasa. (Christie's)
$1,887 £1,320

Late 19th century wood
netsuke of a kneeling puppe-
teer, signed Sokoku, Tokyo
School. (Christie's)
$2,030 £1,430

A 19th century boxwood netsuke of a Sennin, signed Toyomasa. (Christie's) $2,967 £2,090

Mid/late 19th century ivory netsuke of a Samurai seated next to a kneeling hunter, signed Ichijusai Seizan. (Christie's) $702 £495

Late 18th century triangular ivory netsuke of Gama Sennin, unsigned. (Christie's) $1,093 £770

Mid 19th century stained boxwood netsuke of a rat with a chestnut beneath one paw, signed Ikkan. (Christie's) $6,560 £4,620

Mid 19th century ivory manju netsuke decorated with a herdboy astride an ox, signed Kosai. (Christie's) $781 £550

Late 19th century ivory netsuke of a Noh dancer in the role of a Shojo, and another. (Christie's) $343 £242

Early 19th century wood netsuke of a seated monkey cradling one of its offspring, signed Mitsuhide, Kyoto School. (Christie's) $1,093 £770

Early 19th century ivory netsuke of one of the Three Heroes of Han, Gentoku, inscribed Tametaka, and another of a priest. (Christie's) $781 £550

A 19th century ivory netsuke of a rat on a pumpkin, signed Toshinobu. (Christie's) $1,483 £1,045

A 19th century ivory netsuke of a Shoki, the Demon Queller. (Christie's)
$702 £495

Early 19th century boxwood netsuke of Okame, signed Kokei, Tsu School. (Christie's)
$1,093 £770

A 19th century ivory netsuke of Ashinaga and Tenaga. (Christie's) $749 £528

Mid 19th century wood netsuke of Raijin, the God of Thunder, signed Tomo-kazu. (Christie's)
$5,467 £3,850

Mid 19th century ivory netsuke of a South Sea islander seated inside a lotus leaf, signed Hakusen. (Christie's) $1,483 £1,045

A 19th century wood netsuke of a fieldmouse curled into a ball, signed Masanao, Yamada School. (Christie's)
$2,499 £1,760

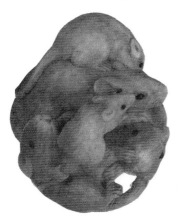

An ivory netsuke of a group of five playful rats, signed Kaigyokudo. (Christie's)
$4,061 £2,860

Mid 19th century ivory netsuke, signed Toun (Ikkosai), Edo School. (Christie's) $1,405 £990

A 19th century ivory netsuke of three Samurai in full armour in a melee, unsigned. (Christie's) $393 £275

A 19th century boxwood netsuke of a smiling karako astride a hobby horse, unsigned. (Christie's)
$503 £352

Early 19th century boxwood netsuke of a snake passing through a pumpkin, signed Tadayoshi or Tadatoshi, Nagoya School. (Christie's)
$943 £660

A 19th century red lacquer netsuke modelled as a double gourd, with silver ring attachment for suspension.
(Christie's) $298 £209

An 18th century ivory seal netsuke carved as a groom asleep next to a recumbent horse. (Christie's)
$550 £385

Early 19th century wood netsuke of a toad, signed Shigetada. (Christie's)
$550 £385

A wood netsuke of ten Noh and Kyogen masks, including Hiottoku, Hannya, Okame and a fox, unsigned, circa 1800. (Christie's) $456 £319

Late 19th century wood okimono of an ape seated on a carapace of a turtle, signed Shinpuken Masakatsu, 8.5cm. high. (Christie's)
$2,831 £1,980

A 19th century bronze kagamibuta netsuke decorated in nikubori and takabori with 'Gentoku's ride', ivory bowl. (Christie's)
$707 £495

A 19th century ivory and buffalo horn netsuke of Okame in a parody of Daruma during his nine year meditation. (Christie's)
$511 £385

A 19th century lacquer, ivory, shell and pressed horn netsuke of a performing Noh actor wearing a Sambaso dancer's outfit, unsigned. (Christie's) $550 £385

A 19th century wood netsuke of a lotus pod with ten moveable seeds, the stalk forming the himotoshi, unsigned. (Christie's) $393 £275

Late 18th century ivory netsuke of a man running and holding one hand up to his chin. (Christie's) $471 £330

Late 18th century wood netsuke of a crouching ape, unsigned. (Christie's) $393 £275

Mid 19th century ivory netsuke of a crouching karako, signed Kosai, Edo School. (Christie's) $629 £440

An ivory netsuke of three mice on a partly eaten mushroom, unsigned. (Christie's) $1,573 £1,100

A wood netsuke of a cockerel seated on a drum, signed Hori Yasumoto, circa 1800. (Christie's) $660 £462

A 19th century circular lacquered wood manju-type netsuke decorated in hiramakie and takamakie. (Christie's) $550 £385

A 19th century boxwood netsuke of a Noh mask of Okina, unsigned. (Christie's) $314 £220

Early 19th century ivory netsuke of a fish, its eyes inlaid in dark polished horn, unsigned. (Christie's) $1,337 £935

Mid 19th century ivory netsuke of a crouching karako, signed Gyokuyosai. (Christie's) $550 £385

A 19th century silvered metal kagamibuta netsuke with gilt and copper detail and ivory bowl. (Christie's) $534 £374

A 19th century ivory netsuke of a large snake gripping a toad in its tail and baring its fangs, signed Sako. (Christie's) $2,202 £1,540

An ivory netsuke of triangular section carved with a tiger among bamboo and rocks, circa 1800. (Christie's) $440 £308

A 19th century gold, silver, red and black lacquered wood netsuke of a dog, unsigned. (Christie's) $440 £308

Mid 19th century wood netsuke of an oni and a skeleton crouching on a lotus, signed Hojitsu, Edo School. (Christie's) $1,258 £880

A 19th century bronze kagamibuta netsuke with ivory bowl. (Christie's) $440 £308

A 19th century ivory netsuke of the demon Soshiki kneeling on clouds, signed Masatomo. (Christie's) $629 £440

Late 18th century ivory net-suke of a recumbent ox, signed Tomotada, Kyoto School, probably pupil's work. (Christie's) $597 £418

19th century natural double walnut netsuke with attached ojime, signed Kozan. (Christie's) $503 £352

Late 18th century ivory netsuke of a seated dog, unsigned, Kyoto School. (Christie's) $629 £440

A 19th century wood netsuke of a chestnut, one side inlaid with an ivory maggot, unsigned. (Christie's) $346 £242

Mid 19th century marine ivory okimono-style netsuke of Ashinaga and Tenaga, signed Mitsuchika. (Christie's) $550 £385

A small stained ivory okimono of the 'Disappointed Rat Catcher', signed Juzan, Meiji period, 5.8cm. long. (Christie's) $440 £308

Late 18th century ivory netsuke of a seated karashishi, in the style of Karaku, Kyoto School. (Christie's) $550 £385

A 19th century silver manju netsuke decorated in niku-bori, kebori, takabori and gold and shakudo hirazogan. (Christie's) $1,101 £770

A 19th century wood netsuke of three boys, their eyes inlaid in dark horn, metal ring attachment, unsigned. (Christie's) $283 £198

Mexico: 1916 Tesoreria General del Estado for Merida, Yucatan 2 pesos front and back proofs on card printed by the Parsons Trading Co. of New York. (Phillips) $104 £72

Canada: 1914 Banque d'Hochelaga $10 colour trial in black and blue with four cancellation holes. (Phillips) $166 £115

Mozambique: 1909 1,000 escudos overprint on 20 libras. (Phillips) $391 £270

Bank of Ireland: £5, 1916. (Phillips) $181 £125

Royal Bank: £1, 1872. (Phillips) $464 £320

Part of a set of 1902 Keeling & Cocos Islands 1/10, ¼. ½, 1, 2 and 5 rupees.(Phillips) $362 £250

Germany: 1960 5-1,000 Deutsche mark Specimen set. (Phillips) $551 £380

National Bank: £10, 1920 small size (150 x 90mm.) (Phillips) $217 £150

Channel Islands, Guernsey: £1, 1 September 1917. (Phillips) $3,190 £2,200

Uruguay: 1865 El Banco Navia 1 doblon unissued and with crayoned 'X' across lower half. (Phillips) $224 £155

Portugal: 1910 10 milreis. (Phillips) $104 £72

Columbia: 1883 El Banco Americano 100 pesos unissued and perforated 'Specimen C. Skipper & East'. (Phillips) $333 £230

Mozambique: 1921 1, 2½, 5, 10, 20 and 50 escudos Specimen notes. (Phillips) $580 £400

Portugal: 1910 50 milreis. (Phillips) $159 £110

Italy: 1947–62, 500, 1,000, 5,000 and 10,000 lire Specimens. (Phillips) $203 £140

French West Africa: 1942, 1,000 francs. (Phillips) $152 £105

A mid Victorian black and gilt japanned papier-mache tray of waved and shaped rectangular form, 23¾ x 31in. (Christie's) $2,055 £1,430

A mid Victorian black and gilt japanned papier-mache writing-slope with hinged flap, 12in. wide. (Christie's) $503 £352

An 19th century oval papier mache tray, centrally decorated after Morland, 30in. wide. (Dreweatts) $1,276 £880

An early Victorian black and gilt japanned papier-mache card box with lifting lid, 11¼in. wide. (Christie's) $550 £385

One of a pair of early Victorian papier-mache fans, both signed Jennens and Betteridge, with ring turned stained beech handles, 17½in. high. (Christie's) $414 £286

A 19th century papier-mache tray with shaped edge and a design of flowers by Evans. (Lots Road Galleries) $417 £290

A mid Victorian black, gilt and mother-of-pearl japanned papier-mache table-bureau, 14¾in. wide. (Christie's) $1,258 £880

A Regency scarlet and gilt japanned papier-mache tray, with impressed mark 'Clay King St/Covt. Garden', 20¼in. wide. (Christie's) $8,995 £6,380

One of a pair of mid Victorian black, gold japanned papier-mache spill vases, 8in. wide. (Christie's) $471 £308

A National Benzole Mixture, diamond with Mercury head petrol pump globe. (Onslow's) $214 £150

Cleveland Super Discol petrol pump globe. (Onslow's) $148 £100

Esso petrol pump globe. (Onslow's) $100 £70

A post war B.P. shield petrol pump globe. (Onslow's) $300 £210

A Redline Super, pre war petrol pump globe. (Onslow's) $185 £130

Shell petrol pump bowl. (Onslow's) $143 £100

A Shell, first design, pre war glass petrol pump globe. (Onslow's) $300 £210

Pratts petrol pump bowl, pre-war. (Onslow's) $171 £120

A Pratts post war glass petrol pump globe. (Onslow's) $429 £300

A covered sugar bowl, by
Hiram Yale & Co., 1822-31,
6in. high. (Christie's)
$330 £230

Pair of mid 19th century
fluid lamps, each with a
brass double wick holder,
6½in. high. (Christie's)
$154 £107

A globular shaped teapot, by
Israel Trask, Mass., circa 1813-
56, 7½in. high. (Christie's)
$198 £138

A beaker, by Rufus Dunham,
1837-60, marked with
Montgomery touch, 3.3/8in.
high. (Christie's) $77 £53

A circular pewter basin with
single reed brim, marked on
base with 'Love' touch,
Laughlin 868, Phila., circa
1750-1800, 8in. diam.
(Christie's) $418 £292

A mug on moulded flaring
base with double scroll
handle, by T. Boardman &
Co., N.Y., 1822-25, marked
with Laughlin touch 432,
4½in. high. (Christie's)
$495 £346

A cylindrical tankard, by
F. Bassett, N.Y., marked on
interior with Laughlin touch
468, 7in. high. (Christie's)
$8,800 £6,158

A circular salt, the rim and
footrim with a beaded
moulding, attributed to Wm.
Will, Phila., 1764-98, 2¼in.
high. (Christie's)$660 £461

A small tapering, cylindrical
pitcher, by Wm. Savage,
circa 1838, 4½in. high.
(Christie's) $275 £192

An oval shaped teapot with a domed oval cover, American, 1790-1810, 7½in. high. (Christie's) $660 £461

A pewter chamber pot, stamped with crown and other marks. (Lots Road Galleries) $115 £80

A covered sugar bowl, by G. Richardson, Rhode Island, 1830-45, 5in. high. (Christie's) $2,200 £1,539

A small covered pitcher, by Simpson & Benham, N.Y., 1845-47, 6¼in. high. (Christie's) $220 £153

A coffee pot of baluster shape with a hinged lid, by Daniel Curtiss, 1822-40, 11in. high. (Christie's) $242 £169

A mug with double scroll handle, by Boardman & Hart, N.Y., 1827-50, 4½in. high. (Christie's) $495 £346

A mug with S-scroll handle with a shell grip, by Robt. Bonynge, circa 1750-64, marked with Laughlin touch 292, 4¾in. high. (Christie's) $6,050 £4,233

Pair of mid 19th century candlesticks, American, 9¾in. high, together with a modern pair, 7in. high. (Christie's) $286 £200

A circular porringer, by S. Hamlin, marked with Laughlin touch 337, 5.5/8in. diam. (Christie's) $550 £384

A coffee pot of shaped baluster form, by Luther Boardman, Mass., 1834-37, 11in. high. (Christie's) $220 £153

A cylindrical humidor, with a domed and moulded lid with an acorn finial, 6¾in. high. (Christie's) $242 £169

A coffee pot of pyriform shape, by Roswell Gleason, Mass., 1821-71, 10¾in. high. (Christie's) $88 £61

A vase-shaped pitcher, by George Richardson, 1828-45, marked with Jacobs touch 237, 7in. high. (Christie's) $308 £215

A plate, by Frederick Bassett, N.Y., 1761-80 and 1785-99, marked with Montgomery touch, 8.3/8in. diam. (Christie's) $165 £115

A globular teapot, by Chas. Yale, Conn., 1817-35, 8in. high. (Christie's) $132 £92

A circular porringer with beaded brim and dolphin handle, by S. Danforth, marked with Laughlin touch 401, 5.5/8in. diam. (Christie's) $2,860 £2,001

A covered pitcher of baluster form, by Thos. D. and S. Boardman, 1830-50, marked with Laughlin touch 435, 10in. high. (Christie's) $330 £230

A flask with a threaded cap, by James Weekes, N.Y., 1820-43, marked with Laughlin touch, 7in. high. (Christie's) $495 £346

A lighthouse coffee pot, by G. Richardson, Boston, 1818-28, 10½in. high. (Christie's) $330 £230

A ship's hanging fluid lamp, by H. Yale and S. Curtis, N.Y., 1858-67, marked with Montgomery touch, 5in. high. (Christie's) $715 £500

A coffee pot of baluster form, by Leonard, Reed & Barton, Mass., 1835-40, 12¾in. high. (Christie's) $308 £215

A small pitcher, by Boardman & Hart, N.Y., 1830-50, marked with Laughlin touch 437, 4in. high. (Christie's) $220 £153

A circular pewter plate, by J. C. Heyne, P.A., circa 1756-80, marked with initial and Jacobs touch 169, 6.3/8in. diam. (Christie's) $5,720 £4,002

A pitcher of baluster form, by Daniel Curtiss, 1822-40, marked with Laughlin touch 523, 7¾in. high. (Christie's) $715 £500

A pewter flagon with a domed lid, by Boardman & Co., N.Y., circa 1825-30, 12.1/8in. high.(Christie's) $1,760 £1,231

A teapot of pyriform, by Luther or Thomas D. Boardman, circa 1840, 7¼in. high. (Christie's) $550 £384

A porringer, by Thos. D. and S. Boardman, CT., 1810-30, the handle marked with Laughlin touch 428, 4in. diam. (Christie's) $286 £200

A globular shaped teapot with a domed lid, by Roswell Gleason, Mass., 1830-40, with Jacobs touch 147, 7½in. high. (Christie's) $132 £92

Late 18th century porringer, New England, 4½in. diam. (Christie's) $264 £184

A globular teapot, by Thomas D. and Sherman Boardman, marked with Laughlin touch 428, 7½in. high. (Christie's) $198 £138

A WMF pewter mounted engraved green glass decanter of flaring form, 9½in. high, stamped marks. (Christie's) $196 £130

A Kayserzinn pewter teaset, the tray 18in. wide, all with stamped marks. (Christie's) $286 £190

Late 18th century porringer with dolphin handle, New London or Hartford, 5½in. diam. (Christie's) $1,210 £846

A porringer, the Old English handle marked with Laughlin touch 399, by S. Bamforth, 1795-1816, 5in. diam. (Christie's) $1,210 £846

A beaker with two incised mid-bands on a single beaded base, by T. Boardman & Co., N.Y., 1822-25, marked with Laughlin touch 425, 3in. high. (Christie's) $176 £123

A compressed globular shaped teapot, by H. B. Ward & Co., 1849 and later, 9in. high. (Christie's) $132 £92

A teapot, by Wm. Will, Phila., 1764-98, marked on inside with Laughlin touches 538 and 539, 6¼in. high. (Christie's)
$24,200 £16,935

A porringer with flowered handle, by Gershom Jones, 1774-1809, with Laughlin touch 341, 5in. diam. (Christie's) $418 £292

A teapot with a domed lid, a disc finial and an S-scroll spout, by G. Richardson, 1818-28, marked with Laughlin touch 310, 6¼in. high. (Christie's)
$308 £215

Late 18th/early 19th century beaker, American, 3in. high. (Christie's) $88 £61

A 16th century German pewter sauce plate, the reverse with wheel touchmark (of Mainz), 19.2cm. diam. (Phillips) $576 £400

A circular pewter salt, attributed to Wm. Will, Phila., 1764-98, 2¼in. high. (Christie's) $660 £461

A circular plate, by F. Bassett, N.Y., 1761-80 and 1785-99, marked with Laughlin touches 467 and 464a, 9in. diam. (Christie's)
$308 £215

A vase-shaped pitcher with a flaring rim, by Rufus Dunham, Maine, 1837-61, 6½in. high. (Christie's)
$385 £269

A beaker, by Boardman & Hart, N.Y., 1828-53, 3.1/8in. high. (Christie's)
$110 £76

A lighthouse coffee pot, by Wm. Calder, Rhode Island, 1817-56, marked with Laughlin touch 350, 11¾in. high. (Christie's) $220 £153

A porringer with everted brim and curved sides, probably by R. Lee, 1795-1816, 4½in. diam. (Christie's) $198 £138

A coffee pot of tapering, cylindrical form, by Israel Trask, Mass., circa 1825-35, marked with Jacobs touch 262, 11½in. high. (Christie's) $418 £292

A circular plate, by Thos. Danforth II or III, marked with Montgomery touch, 9½in. diam. (Christie's) $990 £692

A WMF electroplated centre-piece, modelled in full relief with a Middle Eastern lady, 19½in. high. (Christie's) $483 £320

A pewter basin, marked on the interior with two eagle touches and the 'Richmond Warranted' touch, by Thos. Danforth, Virginia, circa 1807-12, 11.7/8in. diam.(Christie's) $2,640 £1,847

A tapering, cylindrical flagon, by Boardman & Co., N.Y., 1825-27, marked 'X' and a Laughlin touch 431, 8in. high. (Christie's) $1,870 £1,308

A tapering cylindrical mug, by Frederick Bassett, N.Y., 1761-80, marked with Montgomery touch, 4½in. high. (Christie's) $935 £654

A tankard, by Thos. D. & Sherman Boardman, marked with Laughlin touch 428, 8in. high. (Christie's) $5,280 £3,694

A coffee pot of baluster form, by Roswell Gleason, 1830-40, 11½in. high. (Christie's)
$352 £246

A porringer by Wm. Calder, 1817-56, flowered handle marked with Laughlin touch 350, 4¼in. diam. (Christie's) $550 £384

A flagon with a low domed lid, attributed to Henry Will, Albany, 1775-83, 11¾in. high. (Christie's)
$16,500 £11,546

A circular pewter plate, Phila., marked on base with 'Love' touch, Laughlin 868, circa 1750-1800, 7¾in. diam. (Christie's) $242 £169

A WMF pewter mounted green glass decanter of flaring form on four leaf moulded feet, 15in. high. (Christie's)
$453 £300

A pewter circular plate, marked on base with 'Love' touch, Laughlin 868, Phila., circa 1750-1800, 8½in. diam. (Christie's) $286 £200

A lighthouse coffee pot, by Israel Trask, Mass., 1813-56, 12¼in. high. (Christie's)
$605 £423

A tapering cylindrical mug, by Henry Will, N.Y., 1761-76, marked with Laughlin touch 491, 6¼in. high. (Christie's) $1,760 £1,231

A cylindrical flagon, by Boardman & Co., N.Y., 1825-27, marked with Montgomery touch, 12½in. high. (Christie's) $2,420 £1,693

A footed, vase-shaped pitcher, by Hiram Yale & Co., 1822-31, 13½in. high. (Christie's) $495 £346

A circular porringer, by S. Hamlin, 1771-1801, handle marked with Laughlin touch 334, 4.1/8in. diam. (Christie's) $495 £346

Late 19th century tankard of pyriform, with a low domed lid, probably English, 8in. high. (Christie's) $495 £346

A tapering cylindrical tankard, by Wm. J. Ellsworth, N.Y., 1767-98, 9½in. high. (Christie's) $3,300 £2,309

A Loetz pewter mounted two-handled iridescent glass vase, 8¾in. high. (Christie's) $483 £320

A flagon with stepped domed lid, by Boardman & Co., N.Y., 1825-27, marked 'XX' and Laughlin touch 431, 12½in. high. (Christie's) $2,640 £1,847

A ship's hanging lamp, by Yale & Curtis, N.Y., 1858-67, 7.7/8in. high. (Christie's) $550 £384

An 18th century European basin, 13in. diam. (Christie's) $275 £192

One of a pair of Art Nouveau silvered pewter vases, each cast Flora, with copper liners, 41.5cm. high. (Christie's) $1,346 £935

A tapering cylindrical tankard, possibly by Parks Boyd, 7.5/8in. high. (Christie's) $4,180 £2,925

Late 18th century porringer, with beaded brim and Penn. tab handle, 5.3/8in. diam. (Christie's) $110 £76

A coffee pot of baluster form, marked 'I. Curtiss', circa 1818-25, marked with Laughlin touch 452, 10½in. high. (Christie's)
$220 £153

A flagon with a domed lid and scrolling thumbpiece, by Boardman & Co., N.Y., 1825-27, marked with Montgomery touch, 11.1/8in. high. (Christie's) $550 £384

A Liberty & Co. 'Tudric' pewter box and cover, designed by Archibald Knox, 11.9cm. high. (Christie's) $380 £264

A tankard with S scroll handle, by Parks Boyd, Phila., 1795-1819, marked with Laughlin touch 546, 7½in. high. (Christie's)
$2,090 £1,462

One of a set of mid 19th century American chalices, 8in. high. (Christie's)
$550 £384

A plate with smooth brim, by Nathaniel Austin, 1763-1807, marked with Laughlin touch 301, 8¾in. diam. (Christie's) $88 £61

One of a pair of fluid lamps, by Joshua B. and Henry H. G. Graves, circa 1850, 9in. high. (Christie's) $880 £615

PHOTOGRAPHS

Garibaldi, by Gustave Le Gray, albumen print, oval 10 x 7¾in., date 1860. (Christie's)
$169 £120

'The Everton Toffee Shop', ambrotype, approx. 8 x 9½in., photographer's label 'Lee, Portrait Rooms, Liverpool' and date April 1855. (Christie's) $105 £75

Male nude, by R. Mapplethorpe, gelatin silver print, image size, 13¾ x 13¾in., dated '78. (Christie's) $775 £550

'Fox Talbot', by John Moffat, carbon print, 17 x 12½in. (Christie's) $1,057 £750

'Top Withens, West Riding, Yorkshire, 1944', by B. Brandt, gelatin silver print, 13½ x 11¼in., printed 1970's. (Christie's)
$846 £600

'Miners returning to daylight, South Wales', by B. Brandt, gelatin silver print, 16 x 12in., 1930's. (Christie's) $634 £450

'Souvenir de St. Petersbourg', by Wm. Carrick and J. Dazario, album of 86 photographs, albumen prints, sizes from 3¾ x 2¼in. to 8½ x 10½in., 1870's. (Christie's) $634 £450

Military group portrait, daguerreotype, approx. 4 x 5in., gilt matt, folding morocco case, circa 1850. (Christie's) $705 £500

A Dexo Hoffman black and white gelatin silver print of Marilyn Monroe and Sir Lawrence Olivier, 1958. (Christie's) $382 £250

Innes of Cowie family photographs, collection of 14
albums and a book-form case
of cabinet cards, over 700
photographs, 1850-1920's.
(Christie's) $1,339 £950

Street Scene with Wine Shop,
waxed paper negative, 6.7/8
x 8¾in., and an albumen
positive print, 1850's.
(Christie's) $775 £550

Paris, after the Commune,
1871, by Franck and Liebert,
fifteen albumen prints, majority 9¾ x 7¾in., 1871.
(Christie's) $423 £300

'Man Ray et Ses Amis', port-
folio with essay by T. Baum,
4to, Paris: Filipacchi, n.d.
(Christie's) $267 £190

'Memorials of Bonnie Bonaly',
by D. O. Hill and R. Adamson,
album of twenty-seven calotypes. (Christie's)
                  $23,970 £17,000

Portraits from S. Europe, The
Middle East and Russia, an
album of 112 cartes-de-visite
and 12 cabinet portraits,
1860's. (Christie's)$987 £700

Japanese landscape, Samurai
Warriors and military life, by
F. Beato, F. C. Gould and others,
an album of ninety-nine photographs, circa 1864. (Christie's)
         $19,740 £14,000

Lady brushing her hair, by
Oscar Gustave Rejlander,
albumen print, 10 x 8in.,
circa 1860. (Christie's)
                  $197 £140

Japanese portraits, landscape
and flower studies, two albums,
each with fifty hand-tinted
albumen prints, approx. 7½ x
9¾in., late 19th century.
(Christie's) $535 £380

'The Kiss of Peace', by J. M. Cameron, albumen print, 9 x 7in., 1869. (Christie's) $634 £450

Farm Interior, by J. Whistler, salt print, 8½ x 10in, 1855-65. (Christie's) $1,692 £1,200

Lt. James Lacey Reynolds and others, four quarter-plate daguerreotypes, late 1840's and early 1850's. (Christie's) $634 £450

'Japanese Costumes', by F. Beato, Baron Von Stillfried and K. Kimbei, album of eighty-five albumen prints, 1870's. (Christie's) $1,692 £1,200

South Pacific Islands, by J. W. Lindt, an album of twenty-four photographs, albumen prints, 6 x 8in., 1880's. (Christie's) $987 £700

Royal portraits, Mr. Baldwin, Sir T. Lipton and others, by C. Van Dyk, H. Cecil and W. & D. Downey, collection of 39 portraits, gelatin silver prints and 3 carbon prints, 1929. (Christie's) $253 £180

The snake collection, by F. Downer, album of 32 cabinet cards, 1890's. (Christie's) $648 £460

'The Old Country Houses of the Old Glasgow Gentry', by Thos. Annan, 4to, 1870. (Christie's) $564 £400

'Mrs. Ewen Hay Cameron', by J. M. Cameron, albumen print, 13 x 10¼in., 1869. (Christie's) $493 £350

'Old Closes and Streets', by Thos. Annan, a series of photogravures 1868-99. (Christie's) $493 £350

The Scott Monument, by D. O. Hill and R. Adamson, calotype, 11½ x 14¾in., 1845. (Christie's)
$1,057 £750

'Salle des Statues, Vatican', by Charles Soulier, albumen print, 9¾ x 7½in., late 1860's. (Christie's) $141 £100

Lord and Lady Canning family album, by Capt. J. Constantine Stanley, an album containing 117 albumen prints, dated 1858-61. (Christie's) $12,690 £9,000

'Japan', by ?Baron Von Still-fried, album of twenty-nine hand-tinted albumen prints, 5½ x 4 to 10¼ x 8¼in., 1870's. (Christie's)
$916 £650

'The People of India', a series of photographic illustrations of the Races and Tribes of Hindustan, 1872 and 1875. (Christie's) $493 £350

Still life and wall study, by R. Mayne, two gelatin silver prints, 8¾ x 7¼in. and 10½ x 9¼in., 1950's. (Christie's)
$169 £120

'Nude, March 1952', by B. Brandt, gelatin silver print, 16 x 12in. (Christie's) $987 £700

'Old Closes and Streets of Glasgow', by T. Annan, 31 albumen prints, folio, 1868. (Christie's) $21,150 £15,000

A George III mahogany square piano with ivory keyboard, enamel plaque inscribed 'Longman, Clementi & Comp'y, London, New Patent', 5ft.5in. wide. (Woolley & Wallis) $936 £650

A Classical Revival mahogany inlaid piano-forte, Boston, circa 1825, 72½in. long. (Robt. W. Skinner Inc.) $3,400 £2,125

A Carillon of twenty-five hemispherical metal bells (glockenspiel), by H. Godden, circa 1810, overall height with stand 55in. (Phillips) $835 £500

A double-manual harpsichord, by Jacob Kirckman, 1761, 91½ x 37in. (Christie's) $123,200 £77,000

A portable table harmonium in an oak case, by Metzler & Co., circa 1845, 23¼in. wide. (Phillips) $384 £230

An English single manual harpsichord, by Jacob Kirckman, in a mahogany case, 87 x 37in. (Christie's) $24,564 £15,400

An English spinet, by Charles Haward, in a walnut case, circa 1685, 58½in. wide. (Christie's) $24,640 £15,400

A spinet shaped pianoforte by John C. Hancock, 1779, in a crossbanded mahogany case with figured walnut interior. (Christie's) $16,720 £10,450

An English grand pianoforte, by John Broadwood, in mahogany case with sycamore interior on trestle stand, 88 x 38in. (Christie's) $5,702 £3,960

A single manual harpsichord, by Jacob and Abraham Kirckman, London, 1784, 3ft.1in. wide. (Phillips) $15,030 £9,000

An English spinet in a crossbanded mahogany case, circa 1740, 74in. wide, on later stand. (Christie's) $4,576 £2,860

A W. Menzel Secessionist piano, the mahogany case with elaborate brass mounts, circa 1900, 148.1cm. wide. (Christie's) $1,029 £715

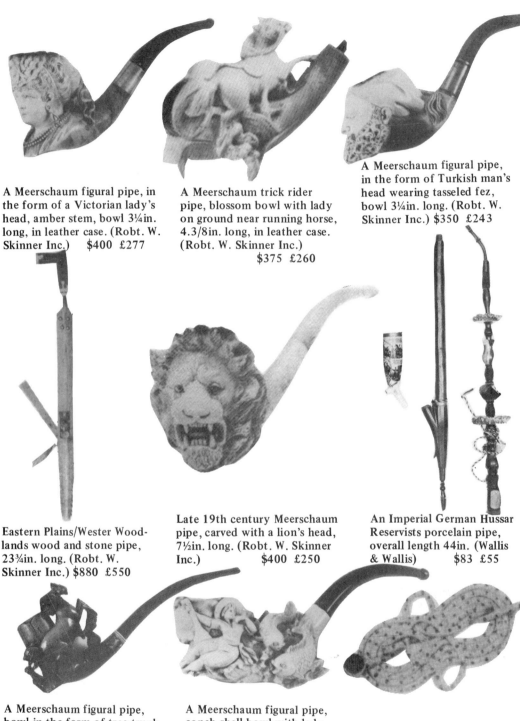

A Meerschaum figural pipe, in
the form of a Victorian lady's
head, amber stem, bowl 3¼in.
long, in leather case. (Robt. W.
Skinner Inc.) $400 £277

A Meerschaum trick rider
pipe, blossom bowl with lady
on ground near running horse,
4.3/8in. long, in leather case.
(Robt. W. Skinner Inc.)
$375 £260

A Meerschaum figural pipe,
in the form of Turkish man's
head wearing tasseled fez,
bowl 3¼in. long. (Robt. W.
Skinner Inc.) $350 £243

Eastern Plains/Wester Woodlands wood and stone pipe,
23¾in. long. (Robt. W.
Skinner Inc.) $880 £550

Late 19th century Meerschaum
pipe, carved with a lion's head,
7½in. long. (Robt. W. Skinner
Inc.) $400 £250

An Imperial German Hussar
Reservists porcelain pipe,
overall length 44in. (Wallis
& Wallis) $83 £55

A Meerschaum figural pipe,
bowl in the form of tree trunk
with rearing horse startled by
a snake, bowl 4¾in. long, in
leather case. (Robt. W.
Skinner Inc.) $750 £520

A Meerschaum figural pipe,
conch shell bowl with lady
and two dolphins, bowl
4.1/8in. long, and another.
(Robt. W. Skinner Inc.)
$475 £329

A Staffordshire pottery curled
pipe painted with blue and
yellow dashes. (Christie's)
$400 £250

A plaster bust of George II, his hair dressed with laurels. (Christie's) $707 £495

A Richard Garbe green-tinted plaster figure of a naked seated maiden, 1928, 104cm. high. (Christie's)
$1,074 £702

Pair of painted plaster book-ends, each modelled as a bowl of fruit, 8¾in. high. (Christie's) $277 £165

A Richard Garbe plaster figure of a naked maiden, 1912, 99cm. high. (Christie's) $660 £432

An English plaster panel, in oak frame carved 'Speed with the light-foot winds to run', 42.2 x 37.7cm. (Christie's)
$168 £110

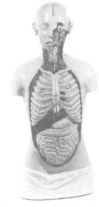

A plaster instructional torso coloured and numbered and arranged so as to dismantle for display purposes, 33in. high. (Christie's) $918 £600

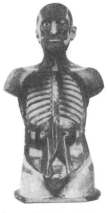

A coloured plaster instructional torso, showing muscular con-struction and some internal organs, 33in. high. (Christie's)
$94 £65

A Richard Garbe plaster figure of a naked kneeling maiden with streaming hair and flowing drapery, 102cm. high. (Christie's)
$1,239 £810

A Richard Garbe buff tinted plaster group of a seated fawn with a figure gazing up at him, 1924, 76.5cm. high. (Christie's) $495 £324

John, Lord Somers, by Susan
Penelope Rosse, on vellum,
gold frame, oval, 2¼in. high.
(Christie's) $6,292 £4,400

Barbara Villiers, Countess of
Castlemaine and Duchess of
Cleveland, by Samuel Cooper,
dated 1664, oval, 3¼in. high.
(Christie's) $55,055 £38,500

W. Leigh Symes, by Thos.
Flatman, on vellum, signed
with initial F, gilt metal
frame, oval, 2½in. high.
(Christie's) $5,641 £3,945

Queen Anne, by Christian
Richter, gilt metal frame,
oval, 3in. high. (Christie's)
$629 £440

A boy of the Blackett family,
by George Chinnery, black
wood frame, oval, 2.7/8in.
high. (Christie's)
$4,719 £3,300

Elizabeth Lindsay in white
dress, fichu and bonnet, by
Philip Jean, ormolu frame,
oval, 2.5/8in. high.
(Christie's) $755 £528

A gentleman in armour, by
John Hoskins, Jnr., on
vellum, signed with initials,
oval, 2.3/8in. high.
(Christie's) $3,775 £2,640

Frances Bankes of Kingston
Lacey, by Anthony Stewart,
ormolu frame, 3¼in. diam.
(Christie's) $3,460 £2,420

A lady seated in red chair,
Continental School, gilt
metal frame, oval, 1¾in. high.
(Christie's) $346 £242

Catherine Clopton, by C. F. Zincke, enamel, chased silver gilt frame, oval, 1.7/8in. high. (Christie's) $943 £660

Major General James Hartley, by T. Langdon, gold frame, the reverse with plaited hair, oval, 2.5/8in. high. (Christie's) $471 £330

Empress Elizabeth Alexandria of Russia, by Franz Gerhard Von Kuegelgen, signed and dated 1799, oval, 3in. high. (Christie's) $7,435 £4,860

James Syme in uniform of The 7th Light Dragoons, by H. Burch, oval, 1.5/8in. high. (Christie's) $629 £440

Sarak Otway-Cave, Baroness Braye, by Frederick Cruik-shank, gold frame, oval, 1½in. high. (Christie's) $566 £396

An officer in the scarlet uniform of The 65th Regt., by T. Wheeler, signed and dated 1841 on the reverse, oval, 2¾in. high. (Christie's)
$629 £440

A lady full face, by John Bogie, signed with initials and dated 1801, gold frame with plaited hair border, oval, 2in. high. (Christie's)
$1,022 £715

A detail of Grafton from 'Dignity' and 'Impudence', by Wm. Bishop Ford, after Sir E. Landseer, dated 1867, 18ct. gold frame, 1¾in. diam. (Christie's)
$1,101 £770

Sir Walter Scott, by Wm. Bishop Ford, enamel, signed and dated 1881 on the reverse, ormolu frame, oval, 2½in. high. (Christie's) $755 £528

A gentleman, by Jean E. P. M. Delacluze, on card, gilt metal frame, oval, 5.1/8in. high. (Christie's)
$471 £330

A lady, possibly Angelica Kauffman, by Richard Cosway, gold frame, silver mount with diamond border, oval, 1¾in. high. (Christie's) $1,573 £1,100

George, 3rd Earl of Egremont, by Thomas Day, signed and dated 1785, gold coloured frame, oval, 1¾in. high. (Christie's) $1,022 £715

A lady in decollete white dress, by Jean-Francois-Marie Huet-Villiers, gilt metal frame, oval, 2.7/8in. high. (Christie's)
$550 £385

Catharine Inglis, aged 31, by George Engleheart, gold frame, oval, 1¾in. high. (Christie's) $2,202 £1,540

William Freeman, by Christian Frederick Zincke, enamel, gilt metal frame, oval, 1.7/8in. high. (Christie's) $1,022 £715

Louis XIV wearing the sash of the Order of the St. Esprit, by Jean Petitot, enamel, gilt metal frame, oval, 1½in. high. (Christie's) $2,988 £2,090

Maria Theresa, by Le Sage, signed, gilt metal frame, 3in. diam. (Christie's)
$660 £462

An officer in scarlet uniform with white facings and gold lace, black turned wood frame, oval, 3in. high. (Christie's) $503 £352

A lady in decollete brown dress, by Susan Penelope Rosse, on vellum, gilt metal frame, with spiral cresting, oval, 1.7/8in. high. (Christie's) $1,573 £1,100

A miniature of Gurmin, George Adolph Barras, by Rodolphe Bel (Bell), on card, signed and dated 1820, oval, 4¾in. high. (Christie's) $1,258 £880

A lady in black dress, by Jacques J. G. Vidal, signed and dated 1859, oval, 2¾in. high. (Christie's) $629 £440

A lady nearly full face in white dress and fichu, by John Barry, oval, 2in. high. (Christie's) $578 £378

Major Edward John Lake, aged 13, by Herman, signed and dated 1836, 2.5/8in. high. (Christie's) $1,022 £715

Catherine Blount (Mrs. Freeman), Circle of Charles Boit, enamel, gilt metal frame, oval, 1.7/8in. high. (Christie's) $786 £550

A gentleman in blue coat, by Andrew Robertson, turned wood frame, oval, 2.7/8in. high. (Christie's) $597 £418

Lettice Knollys, The Countess of Essex, English School, circa 1720, on card, 1.7/8in. diam. (Christie's) $1,074 £702

A gentleman, by Samuel Shelley, signed on the reverse, gold frame, oval, 2¼in. high. (Christie's) $550 £385

Col. Montalba in scarlet uniform of the second Horse Guards, by John Smart, signed and dated 1771, oval, 1½in. high. (Christie's) $4,293 £2,806

A lady full face in decollete white dress, by Louis Lie Perin-Salbreux, signed, 2½in. diam. (Christie's) $1,404 £918

A gentleman with grey hair and blue eyes, wearing a black coat, by Raphael Peale, circa 1795, 2.3/8in. high. (Christie's) $1,980 £1,385

A lady facing right in white dress with lace border, by Le Chevalier De Chateaubourg, oval, 2¾in. high. (Christie's) $330 £216

A gentleman in blue coat with black collar, white waistcoat and cravat, by S. Shelley, oval, 2¾in. high. (Christie's) $462 £302

A lady with white turban, brown hair and grey dress, attributed to Henry Inman, circa 1820, 2½in. high. (Christie's) $1,320 £923

Perhaps Mr. Vavasour facing right in blue coat, by George Engleheart, signed with cursive E, oval, 3.1/8in. high. (Christie's) $1,453 £950

A gentleman with his son and daughter, attributed to Michael M. Daffinger, oval, 1¼in. high. (Christie's) $1,023 £669

A gentleman in ochre-coloured coat, by Noah Seeman, enamel, signed on the reverse N. Seeman and dated 1723, oval, 2in. high. (Christie's) $1,156 £756

Robert Parry Nesbet, M.P., by John C. D. Engleheart, oval, 3¼in. high. (Christie's) $1,982 £1,296

A lady seated before a harp, in mauve dress edged with lace, Continental School, 2½in. diam. (Christie's) $1,618 £1,058

A Sea Captain with cropped grey hair and brown eyes, American, circa 1800, 2½in. high. (Christie's) $605 £423

Mrs. Wm. Few, (Catharine Witter), by John Ramage, 1787, in a gold locket frame with half pearls, 1½in. high. (Christie's) $4,520 £3,233

A gentleman facing left in blue coat with gold buttons, white waistcoat and tied cravat, by N. Plimer, oval, 2¾in. high. (Christie's) $413 £270

A girl facing three-quarters to left in white muslin dress, by Andrew Plimer, oval, 3.1/8in. high. (Christie's) $1,321 £864

A nobleman facing left in black doublet and lace ruff, by Isaac Oliver, on card, signed with monogram, oval, 2in. high. (Christie's) $1,569 £1,026

A lady resting her elbow and head on the edge of a blue sofa, by Jeremiah Meyer, oval, 2¼in. high. (Christie's) $1,404 £918

Gustav IV Adolph, King of Sweden, by Jacob Axel Gillberg, oval, 1¼in. high. (Christie's) $578 £378

A lady nearly full face in white dress, black hat with bow, coral bead necklace, by G. Engleheart, signed and dated 1805 on the reverse, oval, 3¼in. high. (Christie's) $2,974 £1,944

A gentleman in dark brown coat, by Abraham Seaman, enamel, signed on the reverse AB Seaman, oval, 1¾in. high. (Christie's) $957 £626

A lady facing right in white dress sewn with ropes of pearls, by John Smart, signed with initials and dated 1786, oval, 1.7/8in. high. (Christie's) $8,262 £5,400

A portrait miniature of a gentleman, American, circa 1790, 1¾in. high. (Christie's) $550 £384

William Young wearing a black coat with black waistcoat, by James Peale, 1807, 2.7/8in. high. (Christie's) $5,500 £3,848

A gentleman with long grey hair, attributed to Wm. Verstille, circa 1790, oval, 1¾in. high. (Christie's) $715 £500

Edward Shaw, bust length, facing right, by Wm. Verstille, circa 1790, oval, 1.7/8in. high. (Christie's) $1,320 £923

A lady in white dress and turban headgear, by George Engleheart, oval, 3in. high. (Christie's) $1,453 £950

A gentleman wearing a dark purple coat and yellow waistcoat, by James Peale, 1791, 2½in. high. (Christie's) $7,150 £5,003

A girl in white muslin dress with lace border, yellow sash and coral bead necklace, by Andrew Plimer, oval, 3.1/8in. high. (Christie's)
$2,974 £1,944

A gentleman in crimson coat, lace cravat and powdered wig, by C. F. Zincke, enamel, oval, 1.7/8in. high. (Christie's)
$1,074 £702

Matilda Few, wearing a white dress with shirred lace collar, shoulders and bust, by N. Rogers, circa 1820, 2.7/8in. high. (Christie's)
$3,080 £2,155

Lt.-Col. Benjamin Tallmadge, wearing Continental Army uniform, by John Ramage, circa 1785, 1.7/8in. high. (Christie's) $4,400 £3,079

A gentleman, facing left, the reverse with locket of hair shaped as a feather, American, circa 1815, 2.7/8in. high. (Christie's) $605 £423

Thomas Witter with a fringe of grey hair, by John Ramage, circa 1780, 1¾in. high. (Christie's)
$1,100 £769

Samuel Foote wearing a black coat, against a shaded green field, American, circa 1800, 2¾in. high. (Christie's) $990 £692

A miniature of Mrs. Sturm, by Richard Cosway, signed and dated 1795 on reverse, oval, 3½in. high. (Christie's)
$4,626 £3,024

A nobleman in brown coat with gold frogging, by C. F. Zincke, enamel, oval, 1.7/8in. high. (Christie's)
$991 £648

George Washington, oval, bust length facing right, by Robert Field, 1800, 3in. high. (Christie's) $2,860 £2,001

A lady with curly brown hair worn up with pearls, American, circa 1795, 2.3/8in. high. (Christie's) $990 £692

Charles II in armour and lace lawn collar, by P. Jean, enamel on gold, signed, oval, 1.3/8in. high. (Christie's) $2,359 £1,650

Miss Annis, wearing a white dress with blue waist ribbon, by Lawrence Sully, circa 1800, 2½in. high. (Christie's) $2,640 £1,847

A lady facing right in violet coloured dress with lace collar, by Philip Augustus Barnard, signed and dated 1847, 3.1/8in. high. (Christie's) $495 £324

Auguste Wilhelmine von Hessen-Darmstadt, by Sebastien Gratitien, signed and dated 1789, oval, 2¼in. high. (Christie's) $743 £486

Amabel Marchioness Grey, by Philip Jean, signed with initials, black wood frame with ormolu beaded border, oval, 6in. high. (Christie's) $8,651 £6,050

A child full face in white tunic and gold loop earrings, by P. Gay, signed, 1.5/8in. diam. (Christie's) $495 £324

A lady full face in white dress with jewelled brooches at her shoulder and corsage, by Jean Baptiste Isabey, signed, oval, 5.1/8in. high. (Christie's) $10,244 £6,696

Anne Frances Barlow (nee Bockett), by George Engleheart, oval, 1¾in. high. (Christie's) $1,156 £756

A lady facing left in scarlet coat and large black hat, English School, circa 1790, oval, 2½in. high. (Christie's) $1,817 £1,188

A miniature of Anne Chetwode, by George Engleheart, dated 1787, oval, 1.7/8in. high. (Christie's) $9,088 £6,940

The Rev. Philip de la Garde (1747-98), by Philip Jean, signed and dated 1787, oval, 1.7/8in. high. (Christie's) $247 £162

A group of three children before a garden wall, by G. L. perhaps George Lawrence, signed with initials, 5in. high. (Christie's) $495 £324

A lady nearly full face in fur-bordered blue dress, by Louis Marie Sicardi, signed and dated 1789, oval, 2½in. high. (Christie's) $1,023 £669

A gentleman in blue coat with gold buttons, white waistcoat and white cravat, by George Engleheart, oval, 1.7/8in. high. (Christie's) $1,123 £734

A miniature of a child seated on a red cushion, holding a dove, French School, lock of hair reverse, 2.5/8in. diam. (Christie's) $330 £216

Miss Rachel Baldwin in white dress with lace edge, by N. Plimer, oval, 2.5/8in. high. (Christie's) $495 £324

653

L.N.E.R. Fraserburgh, Glorious Sands, Bathing, Golf, Tennis, by H. G. Gawthorn. (Onslow's) $418 £270

Shillingford Bridge, Oxfordshire, See Britain First On Shell, No. 282, by D. Adams, 30 x 45in. (Onslow's) $248 £160

Anchor Line Glasgow & New York via Londonderry, by K. Shoesmith. (Onslow's) $527 £340

L.N.E.R. Harrogate, by Frank Newbould. (Onslow's) $336 £210

Your Cue for Summer Sunshine, by Shep. S.R., quad royal, 40 x 50in. (Onslow's) $345 £240

L.N.E.R. The Norfolk Coast, by Picking. (Onslow's) $640 £400

The Glasgow Herald £650 Golf Tournament at Gleneagles Open to the World's Players May 1920, 40 x 30in., and another. (Onslow's) $93 £60

L.N.E.R. Scarborough, by Austin Cooper, 1932. (Onslow's) $573 £370

Maurice Denis: 'La Depeche — Grand Format', a chromo-lithographic poster, 145.5 x 100cm. (Phillips) $100 £70

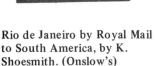

Rio de Janeiro by Royal Mail to South America, by K. Shoesmith. (Onslow's) $384 £240

S.R. Winter in the Southern Sunshine and Warmth of Bournemouth City Gaiety Amid Rural Surroundings, by H. G. Gawthorn, 1939. (Onslow's) $434 £280

L.M.S. Travel to Ireland By The Stranraer-Larne Route, by N. Wilkinson. (Onslow's) $279 £180

L.M.S. Southport, by Fortunio Matania, quad royal, 40 x 50in. (Onslow's) $720 £500

L.N.E.R. Felixstowe, by Tom Purvis. (Onslow's) $713 £460

L.M.S. Llandudno, by Chas. Pears, quad royal 40 x 50in. (Onslow's) $129 £90

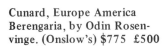

Cunard, Europe America Berengaria, by Odin Rosenvinge. (Onslow's) $775 £500

Caledonian Railway, Gleneagles For Golf 'In The Very He'rt o' Scotland', by Fred Taylor. (Onslow's) $511 £330

P.S.N.C. to South America, by K. Shoesmith. (Onslow's) $308 £220

Pierre Bonnard: Le Menu,
lithograph, circa 1925, on
Chine, signed in pencil,
309 x 273mm. (Christie's)
$1,093 £770

Sheep, Plate VI from Sheep
Album, by Henry Moore,
etching with drypoint, 1972,
on Rives, 188 x 253mm.
(Christie's) $2,534 £1,760

Three Heads of Women, by
Rembrandt Harmensz. van
Rijn, etching, 143 x 96mm.
(Christie's) $2,376 £1,650

Slippery Steps, by Sir William
Russell Flint, drypoint printed
in brown, 1929, on J. Whatman
wove paper, watermark 1831,
238 x 173mm. (Christie's)
$601 £418

El Lissitzky: Mani Leib, Ingle
Zingle Chwat, Kultur-Lige,
Warsaw, 1922, zincographs,
title page plus ten pages of text
and illustrations, 138 x 109mm.
(Christie's) $2,030 £1,430

The Holy Family with the
Butterfly, by Albrecht Durer,
engraving, 237 x 165mm.
(Christie's) $2,851 £1,980

David Hockney: Gregory,
etching printed in colours,
1974, 688 x 545mm.
(Christie's) $2,655 £1,870

Hokusai, oban yoko-e, from the series
Fugaku Sanjurokkei, Sunshu Ejiri,
signed Zen Hokusai Iitsu hitsu, 25.4 x
38.5cm. (Christie's) $2,851 £1,980

The vision of St. Francis,
etching by F. Barocci,
534 x 323mm.
(Christie's) $712 £495

David Hockney: Godetia, etching, 1973, on Arches, signed and dated, 433 x 292mm. (Christie's) $4,998 £3,520

Hokusai, oban yoko-e, from the series Fugaku Sanjurokkei, Sunshu Ejiri, signed Zen Hokusai Iitsu hitsu, 24.1 x 36.6cm. (Christie's) $3,168 £2,200

Gerald Leslie Brockhurst, Le Beguin, etching, signed in pencil, 13.8 x 11cm. (Phillips) $158 £110

Utamaro, oban tate-e, a bust portrait of the courtesan Hanaoogi, published by Omiya Gonkuro, 37.7 x 25cm. (Christie's) $3,168 £2,200

Henri Matisse: Marie-Jose en Robe jaune, aquatint printed in five colours, 1950, on Arches, 537 x 417mm. (Christie's) $43,736 £30,800

Hokusai, oban tate-e, from the series Shokoku Taki-meguri, 37.2 x 25.5cm. (Christie's) $8,712 £6,050

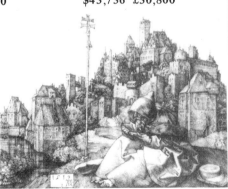

The Great War: Building Ships, by Sir M. Bone, 668 x 550mm. (Christie's) $443 £308

St. Anthony, by Albrecht Durer, engraving, 99 x 142mm. (Christie's) $3,009 £2,090

Henri de Toulouse-Lautrec: Mme. Marcelle Lender en Buste, de Trois Quarts, lithograph, 1898. (Christie's) $11,715 £8,250

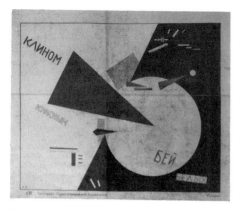

El Lissitzky: Beat the Whites with the Red Wedge, lithograph printed in red and black, 1919, on tan wove paper, 460 x 557mm. (Christie's) $29,678 £20,900

An engraving of two galleys and a man of war, after Pieter Brueghel, the Elder, 248 x 278mm. (Christie's) $2,296 £1,595

Winifred Austen, Budgerigars, aquatint printed in colours, signed and titled in pencil, 21 x 27cm. (Phillips) $230 £160

Michael Chijarev: The Progress of the Five Year Plan, offset lithograph printed in black, red, blue and yellow, 1929, on wove paper, 681 x 1018mm. (Christie's) $562 £396

Christ Healing the Sick, by Rembrandt Harmensz. van Rijn, etching with drypoint and engraving, third state (of four), 278 x 398mm. (Christie's) $4,118 £2,860

Marc Chagall: Le Jugement de Chloe, from Daphnis et Chloe, lithograph printed in colours, 1961, on Arches, signed in pencil, 427 x 641mm. (Christie's) $39,050 £27,500

A hand-coloured lithograph on paper, 'Arguing The Point', by Nathaniel Currier, N.Y., 1855. (Robt. W. Skinner Inc.) $1,000 £699

Georges Braque: Oiseau bleu et jaune, lithograph printed in colours, 1960, on Japon nacre, signed in pencil, 330 x 515mm. (Christie's) $5,935 £4,180

Paul Cezanne: Les Baigneurs, lithograph printed in colours, circa 1898, on laid paper, 419 x 528mm. (Christie's) $28,116 £19,800

Max Beckmann: Der Morgen, drypoint, 1923, on cream wove paper, signed in pencil, 258 x 308mm. (Christie's) $2,343 £1,650

Homenatge a Joan Prats, by Joan Miro, lithograph printed in colours, 1971, on Guarro wove paper, from the set of fifteen, numbered 40/75 (full edition 113), 545 x 753mm. (Christie's) $1,742 £1,210

Currier and Ives: 'Winter Morning — Feeding The Chickens', circa 1863, hand-coloured lithograph. (Robt. W. Skinner Inc.) $4,400 £3,076

Felix the Cat, one of nine original animated celluloids including The Pink Panther, Inspector Clouseau and others. (Christie's) $76 £50

Pablo Picasso: Tete de jeune Fille, lithograph, 1949, on Arches, second (final) state, signed in pencil, 397 x 298mm. (Christie's) $15,620 £11,000

Walter Richard Sickert: The Hanging Gardens, etching, published by Ernest Brown & Phillipi, 1928, 17.6 x 11cm. (Phillips) $187 £130

Eishi, oban tate-e, from the set Ukiyo Genji Hakkei, print published by Nishi-muraya Yohachi. (Christie's) $2,059 £1,430

Edvard Munch: Das kranke Madchen, drypoint, 1894, on stiff wove paper, fifth state of six, 384 x 289mm. (Christie's) $13,277 £9,350

Hiroshige, oban tate-e, from the series Meisho Edo Hyakkei, Ohashi, Atake no Yudachi, 37.4 x 25.3cm. (Christie's) $12,672 £8,800

Kathe Kollwitz: Arbeiterfrau mit Schlafenden Jungen, lithograph, 1927, on stiff wove paper, signed in pencil, 393 x 336mm. (Christie's) $5,467 £3,850

Eine Liebe, by Max Klinger, etchings, 1887, on wove paper, title and set of ten plates, from the fourth (final) edition, 695 x 534mm. (Christie's) $1,425 £990

Tsuguji Foujita: Le Chat, etching with aquatint and roulette printed in colours, circa 1925, on Chine applique, 378 x 290mm. (Christie's) $8,591 £6,050

Kasimir Malevich: Patriotic Poster against the Germans, lithograph printed in colours, 1914-15, on wove paper, 516 x 340mm. (Christie's) $4,061 £2,860

One of two original hand paintings on celluloid, from the Walt Disney film Snow White and the Seven Dwarfs, 6½ x 9½in. (Christie's) $994 £650

The Great War: Britain's Efforts and Ideals, Making Soldiers, by Sir F. Brangwyn, lithographs, 1917, set of six, five signed, 455 x 357mm. and smaller. (Christie's) $1,108 £770

Henri de Toulouse-Lautrec: Le Jockey, lithograph printed in colours, 1899, on Chine, second (final) state, 514 x 361mm. (Christie's) $28,116 £19,800

Rue de Seine, by David Hockney, etching, 1971, on J. Green, mouldmade wove paper, signed and dated '72, 537 x 434mm. (Christie's) $7,603 £5,280

Kunisada, oban tate-e, an okubi-e of the actor Onoe Matsusuke II as the carpenter Rokusaburo, 37.1 x 25.6cm. (Christie's) $91,008 £63,200

Jacques Villon' Autre Temps, 1830, drypoint with aquatint printed in colours, 1904, on wove paper, 445 x 353mm. (Christie's) $10,934 £7,700

The Great War: Britain's Efforts and Ideals, Making Sailors, by Sir F. Brangwyn, lithographs, circa 1917, set of six, 670 x 545mm. (Christie's) $396 £275

Henri de Toulouse-Lautrec: Mme. Marcelle Lender, en Buste, 1898, 249 x 215mm. (Christie's) $11,715 £8,250

Mid 19th century pieced and applique cotton quilt, American, 103½in. long, 100in. wide. (Christie's) $2,420 £1,596

An undyed linen coverlet, the whole embroidered in coloured wools with crewel work, 2.26 x 2.12m. (Phillips) $369 £240

A 19th century pieced and quilted cotton coverlet, American, 87½in. long, 71½in. wide. (Christie's) $1,430 £943

Mid 19th century appliqued quilt, the field divided into squares with a variation of the 'Rose of Sharon' pattern, 92 x 104in. (Robt. W. Skinner Inc.) $650 £406

Political patchwork quilt, American, circa 1844, 88 x 88in. (Robt. W. Skinner Inc.) $1,200 £750

Mid 19th century American pieced and appliqued quilted coverlet, worked in a Rose of Sharon variation pattern, 94 x 94in. (Christie's) $1,320 £857

Patchwork coverlet, variant of 'The Star of Bethlehem' pattern, possibly by Mrs. George R. Newton, America, circa 1856, 118in. sq. (Robt. W. Skinner Inc.) $3,200 £2,133

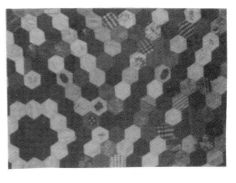

A mosaic patchwork cover composed of plain and patterned silks and velvets, E. F. Slade, March 2nd 1864, 80 x 84in. (Christie's)
$237 £165

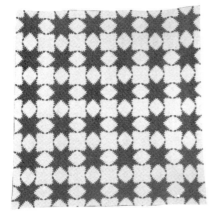

Mid 19th century American pieced and applied quilted coverlet, 88 x 87in. (Christie's)
$715 £462

Mid 19th century applique and stuffed cotton quilt, American, 77½in. long, 74in. wide. (Christie's) $1,760 £1,161

Pieced Star of Bethlehem quilt, New England, circa 1850, 90 x 92in. (Robt. W. Skinner Inc.)
$900 £562

Mid 19th century pieced and appliqued quilt top, probably Penn., 88 x 88in. (Christie's)
$2,420 £1,571

Drawings of the London & Birmingham Railway, by J. C. Bourne, London, 1939. (Onslow's) $5,760 £4,000

L.N.E.R. poster North Berwick, by Frank Newbould. (Onslow's) $728 £470

L.N.E.R. poster Then and Now, 'The Flying Scotsman', The World's Most Famous Train, by A. R. Thomson. (Onslow's) $511 £330

Views on the Manchester and Leeds Railway, a book by A. F. Tait, published by Bradshaw & Blacklock, London, 1845. (Onslow's) $2,304 £1,600

L.N.E.R. poster The Flying Scotsman's Cocktail Bar, by M. Beck. (Onslow's) $2,170 £1,400

Great Western Railway, original painted cast iron sign, 8½ x 11in. (Onslow's) $50 £35

L.N.E.R. poster Wages of Signalmen for 1 Year £1,837,647 Going On All the Time, by A. Cooper. (Onslow's) $325 £210

The Railways in Great Britain also the Line of Navigation from the Principal Sea Ports, printed cotton handkerchief, 24in. square. (Onslow's) $432 £300

George Stephenson Standing on Chat Moss, engraving by T. L. Atkinson, after John Lucas, 32 x 21in. (Onslow's) $187 £130

L.N.E.R. poster Then and Now 600 Golf Courses on the L.N.E.R. Including St. Andrews, by A. R. Thomson. (Onslow's) $434 £280

L.M.S. poster The Irish Mails, by Bryan de Grineau. (Onslow's) $279 £180

L.M.S. poster Luggage In Advance. (Onslow's) $403 £260

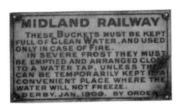

Midland Railway, red, blue and white enamel sign, 6 x 11in. (Onslow's) $25 £18

Great Eastern Railway, painted cast iron moulded coat-of-arms, 12in. diam. (Onslow's) $115 £80

Great Northern Railway, blue and white enamel sign, 5 x 8in. (Onslow's) $89 £62

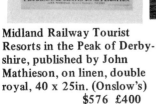

Midland Railway Tourist Resorts in the Peak of Derbyshire, published by John Mathieson, on linen, double royal, 40 x 25in. (Onslow's) $576 £400

L.M.S. Pacific, Sir Wm. Stanier FRS ascending Shap Incline, by Vic Welch, signed, gouache, on board, 13½ x 18½in. (Onslow's) $244 £170

Poster, Factories on L.N.E.R. Lines Are On The Right Lines, by A. Cooper. (Onslow's) $558 £360

L.N.E.R. poster Scotland by 'The Night Scotsman', King's Cross, by Tobt. Bartlett. (Onslow's) $1,705 £1,100

L.N.E.R. locomotive of the Coronation Streamline Engine Dominion of Canada, cast iron paperweight and inkwell model, 11½in. long. (Onslow's) $93 £65

G.E.R., black painted iron paperweight. (Onslow's) $20 £14

Poster To London by Sleeper from Edinburgh (Waverley) To King's Cross, by Alexeieff. (Onslow's) $4,960 £3,200

Highland Railway, a mahogany eight-day wall clock, dial inscribed H. Ry. Ferguson, Inverness, 58in. high. (Onslow's) $777 £540

Poster 'Mons Meg', Edinburgh Travel by L.N.E.R. East Coast Route, by F. Newbould. (Onslow's) $682 £440

Moorish Arch looking from the Tunnel, by T. T. Bury, H. Pyall and S. G. Hughes, hand-coloured aquatint, 10¼ x 13in. (Onslow's) $144 £100

Excavation of Olive Mount 4 miles from Liverpool, by T. T. Bury, H. Pyall and S. G. Hughes, hand-coloured aquatint, 10¼ x 13in. (Onslow's) $144 £100

The Tunnel, by T. T. Bury, H. Pyall and S. G. Hughes, hand-coloured aquatint, 10¼ x 13in. (Onslow's) $158 £110

Dire Straits, a presentation 'Platinum' disc, 'Brothers In Arms', the album mounted with a 'platinum' cassette above a reduction of the album cover. (Christie's) $612 £400

A copy of the Marriage Certificate of John Winston Lennon and Yoko Ono Cox, contracted at the Registrar's Office, in the City and Garrison of Gibraltar, by Governor's Special Licence, on 20th March, 1969. (Christie's) $4,590 £3,000

A coloured screen print portrait of Mick Jagger, by Andy Warhol, number 176 of 250 copies, 44 x 29in., 1975. (Christie's) $841 £550

The Beatles, 'Help', Parlophone 33½ r.p.m., mono, 1965, signed on the cover by each of The Beatles, and inscribed 'All the Best, George Harrison'. (Christie's) $1,836 £1,200

Jimi Hendrix, one of four unpublished black and white photographs taken at The Round House, Chalk Farm, London, in Feb. 1967, 14 x 9in. (Christie's) $581 £380

The Beatles, Peter le Vasseur, 'Illustration for the Beatles Song "In My Life"', dated 1969, oil on board, 8½ x 8½in. (Christie's) $994 £650

Pete Townshend's pound note suit worn in 'Tommy', circa 1975, with label 'Bermans & Nathans'. (Christie's) $2,754 £1,800

The Beatles, a signed menu for the Supper Party following Royal World Premiere "Help!". (Christie's) $642 £420

One of three Dezo Hoffman portrait photographs of The Rolling Stones, 8 x 12in., 9 x 12in. and 12 x 9½in. (Christie's) $168 £110

Dire Straits, a presentation 'Platinum' disc, 'Brothers In Arms', the album mounted above a reduction of the L.P. cover and a plaque. (Christie's) $489 £320

A set of hand 'Reindeer' bells, with red wooden handle used by John Lennon for the recording of 'Happy Christmas (War Is Over)', 1972, 12in. long.(Christie's) $1,377 £900

A promotional postcard for the release of The Move album, 'Flowers In The Rain', circa 1967. (Christie's) $306 £200

A 1966-69 Vox Mando 12 String Guitar in sunburst, serial no. 74309. (Christie's) $306 £200

George Harrison, the original artist's proof for an un-issued album cover, 'Somewhere in England', Dark Horse Records, 1981, 18½ x 26in. (Christie's) $994 £650

An early 1960's Hofner Violin (Beatle) Bass in sunburst with added Hofner style knobs, serial no. 1019. (Christie's) $382 £250

One of four polychrome Richard Avedon psychedelic posters of The Beatles, produced for the Daily Express, circa 1967, each 27½ x 19½in., together with another of the four Beatles, 15½ x 40½in. (Christie's) $428 £280

A 1976 Portative Organ by N. P. Mander Ltd., custom made for David Palmer of Jethro Tull, used on tour between 1976-80 and on the album 'Songs From The Wood'. (Christie's) $1,530 £1,000

A Corgi 'Yellow Submarine' toy, the die cast scale model with two opening hatches revealing figures of The Beatles, circa 1967, 5in. long, in original box. (Christie's) $183 £120

'Old Wrecked Car — Portugal', circa 1977, a silk screen print of a colour photograph taken by Linda McCartney, no. 5 of a limited edition of 150, 18¾ x 13in. (Christie's) $382 £250

'Our First Four', a cardboard presentation folder containing the first four 45 r.p.m. records produced by Apple Records Ltd., 13½ x 9½in. (Christie's) $336 £220

George Benson, a presentation 'Platinum' disc, 'Breezin', the album mounted above a reduction of the L.P. cover, and a plaque. (Christie's) $275 £180

A limited edition resin bronze G.R.P. bust of Jimi Hendrix, circa 1985, by J. Somerville, no. 5 of an edition of 20, 24in. high. (Christie's) $459 £300

John Lennon, a self portrait with Yoko Ono in black felt-tip pen, autographed by John and Yoko beside each appropriate caricature, 7½ x 10½in., 1969. (Christie's) $1,836 £1,200

A Mark Smith Custom electric guitar, the body and sides in mahogany with a two-piece bird's-eye maple top. (Christie's) $765 £500

Original etching and aquatint of 'The King', by David Oxtoby, signed by the artist, 27 x 21½in. (Christie's) $382 £250

A quantity of autograph material from Pink Floyd, The Who, Marvin Gaye and 'Auf Wiedersehen Pet'. (Christie's) $306 £200

A 1960's Fender Tremolux amplifier and 2 x 10in. speaker cabinet in light coloured Tolex vinyl, used on the set of the Paul McCartney Film, 'Give My Regards to Broad Street'. (Christie's) $734 £480

Early 20th century Kerman rug, the tan field with magenta lobed floral medallion, 4ft.7in. x 6ft.10in. (Robt. W. Skinner Inc.) $2,300 £1,597

Late 19th century Soumak rug with all-over pattern of stylised palmettes and geometric motifs, 8ft.11in. x 4ft.3in. (Robt. W. Skinner Inc.) $2,300 £1,597

Late 19th century East Caucasian rug, the ivory Lesghi stars on a gold field, 5ft.6in. x 3ft.9in. (Robt. W. Skinner Inc.) $2,600 £1,805

A Shirvan rug, the indigo field with six brick octagons, 6ft.7in. x 3ft.10in. (Woolley & Wallis) $1,054 £680

A Kashan rug, the ivory field with a repeated boteh design, 2.03 x 1.32m. (Phillips) $3,266 £2,300

A Derbend rug of Persian influence, dated 1923, 1.70 x 1.26m. (Phillips) $1,278 £900

Late 19th century Kazak prayer rug with blue abrashed mihrab, 4ft.8in. x 3ft.7in. (Robt. W. Skinner Inc.) $3,700 £2,569

An 18th century Anatolian Village rug, 4ft.9in. x 6ft. 10in. (Robt. W. Skinner Inc.) $23,000 £15,972

A Lesghi rug, circa 1875, 4ft.3in. x 3ft.2in. (Christie's) $3,850 £2,512

An Armenian Caucasian rug, dated 1916, 4ft.9in. x 8ft. (Robt. W. Skinner Inc.) $3,200 £2,222

A Shirvan long rug, 10ft.8in. x 4ft.9in. (Christie's) $6,600 £4,307

A Lesghi rug, the sable field with three medallions, enclosed by a main ivory serrated leaf and calyx border, 1.52m. x 99cm. (Phillips) $1,704 £1,200

A Kashan carpet, the ivory ground covered by three concentric medallions, 12ft.2in. x 8ft.8in. (Christie's) $9,350 £6,102

A Bidjar rug, the red field with indigo radiating medallion and design of arabesque scrolling stems, 2.08 x 1.08m. (Phillips) $1,349 £950

Late 19th century Gendje rug, the ivory, blue and gold diagonal stripes of botehs and palmettes, 5ft.9in. x 4ft.4in. (Robt. W. Skinner Inc.) $2,400 £1,666

Kazak prayer rug, dated 1311 (1894), ivory mihrab bordered in blue-green, 4ft.5in. x 3ft.7in. (Robt. W. Skinner Inc.) $800 £555

A 17th century Ushak rug, W. Anatolia, 5ft. x 3ft.3in. (Robt. W. Skinner Inc.) $27,000 £18,750

Mid 19th century Bergama rug, W. Anatolia. (Robt. W. Skinner Inc.) $2,000 £1,388

A Kirman carpet of compart-
mental design, 4.45 x 2.66m.
(Phillips) $3,976 £2,800

A late 19th century Seraph
carpet, 14ft.1in. x 10ft.
(Christie's) $11,000 £7,179

A Chi-Chi rug, the indigo field
with rows of stepped and
hooked medallions, 1.65 x
1.05m. (Phillips) $1,136 £800

Late 19th century Kazak
prayer rug, Southwest
Caucasus, 5ft.10in. x 3ft.
4in. (Robt. W. Skinner Inc.)
$1,300 £902

A 19th century Bidjar
carpet, Gerus Workshop,
7ft.8in. x 11ft.1in. (Robt.
W. Skinner Inc.)
$9,500 £6,597

Late 19th century Kuba rug,
the ivory and red Afsham
design on a blue field within
a diamond main border, 4ft.
9in. x 3ft.5in. (Robt. W.
Skinner Inc.) $1,600 £1,111

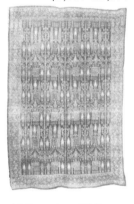

Late 19th century Baluch
prayer rug, the white mihrab
with blue, pink and mauve
spidery flowerheads, 2ft.8in.
x 4ft.1in. (Robt. W. Skinner
Inc.) $2,800 £1,944

Late 19th century Bidjar carpet
with all-over stylised tree
pattern on a dark blue ground
within a red turtle border, 7ft.
6in. x 11ft.4in. (Robt. W.
Skinner Inc.) $3,800 £2,533

A 19th century Konya-area
Kelim, the central panel composed of a grid of five hexagons
on an abrashed violet field, 4ft.
7in. x 5ft.7in. (Robt. W.
Skinner Inc.) $1,600 £1,111

A silk Tabriz prayer rug with copper-red field, 5ft.4in. x 4ft.1in. (Christie's) $4,342 £3,080

A silk Kashan rug, the ivory field with powder blue pendant medallion, 2.07 x 1.28m. (Phillips) $6,248 £4,400

Late 19th century Karagashli rug, the deep red square field with flowerheads on a midnight blue field, 4ft. x 2ft.9in. (Robt. W. Skinner Inc.) $4,200 £2,916

Early 19th century Konya prayer rug, Central Anatolia, 6ft.5in. x 3ft.9in. (Robt. W. Skinner Inc.) $1,800 £1,250

Late 19th century Ladik Yastik, a square grid of rust, blue and violet flowerheads, 3ft.4in. x 2ft. (Robt. W. Skinner Inc.) $1,900 £1,319

Mid 19th century S. Caucasian rug, the narrow field composed of five square, three filled with Memling guls, 6ft.3in. x 3ft.2in. (Robt. W. Skinner Inc.) $625 £434

Late 19th century Karadja carpet, N.W. Persia, 10ft. 8in. x 17ft.3in. (Robt. W. Skinner Inc.) $14,000 £9,722

Late 19th/early 20th century Serapi carpet, the rust-red field with blue and ivory lobed medallions, 11ft.4in. x 14ft.7in. (Robt. W. Skinner Inc.) $2,800 £1,944

Late 19th century Shirvan prayer rug, the yellow gold field woven in a flower filled trellis, 3ft.8in. x 4ft.10in. (Robt. W. Skinner Inc.) $3,900 £2,708

An Uzbek Bochara suzani, the linen ground embroidered in coloured silks, 2.46 x 1.46m. (Phillips) $755 £500

A Qum rug, the ivory field with an overall pattern of cusped flowerheads, boteh and medallions, 6ft.9in. x 4ft.4in. (Christie's) $1,435 £990

A Sarouk rug, the ivory field with rows of boteh enclosed by a main sable stylised flowerhead border, 1.95 x 1.19m. (Phillips) $1,368 £950

A Kashan silk rug of prayer design, 2.10 x 1.25m. (Phillips) $4,032 £2,800

A Tabriz silk prayer rug, the pistachio mihrab with a hanging bowl of flowers. (Phillips) $2,304 £1,600

One of two India Drugget scatter rugs, designed by Gustav Stickley, circa 1910, 38in. wide. (Robt. W. Skinner Inc.) $650 £455

A hand-knotted woollen rug, the design possibly by A. Knox, with Celtic motif in pink and blue on a white ground, 153.5 x 86cm. (Christie's) $527 £345

A 19th century Aubusson tapestry rug with plum field, 1.84 x 1.87m. (Phillips) $5,472 £3,800

Late 19th/early 20th century Kuba rug, Eastern Caucasus, 4ft.7in. x 3ft.3in. (Robt. W. Skinner Inc.) $2,400 £1,600

A mid 19th century Rescht cover, the red ground with yellow, green and blue insertions with ivory silk embroidery, 2.20 x 1.44m. (Phillips) $634 £420

Late 19th century Baluch rug, (sides and ends rebound), 3ft.10in. x 7ft. (Robt. W. Skinner Inc.) $625 £416

A 19th century Spanish Aubusson part metal thread Entre Fenetre, 3.26 x 1.88m. (Phillips) $3,600 £2,500

A 'Savonnene' carpet, the ivory trellis field enclosed by a grey foliate meander border, 4.50 x 3.20m. (Phillips) $5,760 £4,000

A Ziegler carpet, the mustard field with a central lozenge-shaped terracotta pendant medallion, 3.42 x 3.36m. (Phillips) $7,800 £5,200

An Isfahan carpet, the ivory field with scrolling palmettes and flowering vine, 10ft.2in. x 6ft.8in. (Christie's) $3,987 £2,750

India Drugget area carpet, Nile pattern, circa 1910, 9ft.10in. x 7ft.8½in. (Robt. W. Skinner Inc.) $475 £332

An Agra carpet, the wine field with an all over design, 4.5 x 3.6m. (Phillips) $6,048 £4,200

Late 19th/early 20th century Sennah mat, 3ft.7in. x 1ft. 9in. (Robt. W. Skinner Inc.) $200 £133

Early 20th century Chinese
rug, 3ft.1in. x 4ft.10in.
(Robt. W. Skinner Inc.)
$1,100 £763

Late 19th/early 20th
century Kazak rug, the red
field with central blue stepped hexagon, 5ft.3in. x 6ft.
5in. (Robt. W. Skinner Inc.)
$3,100 £2,152

Late 19th/early 20th cen-
tury Feraghan rug, C.Persia,
7ft.3in. x 4ft.8in. (Robt.
W. Skinner Inc.)
$4,200 £2,916

Late 19th century Shirvan
rug with an ivory 'wine cup'
main border, 5ft.8in. x 3ft.
8in. (Robt. W. Skinner Inc.)
$3,400 £2,361

Early 20th century Heriz
carpet, the brick-red field
with dark blue and blue-
green central medallion,
8ft.9in. x 11ft. (Robt. W.
Skinner Inc.)
$2,000 £1,398

Late 19th century Serapi
carpet, the rust-red field
with dark blue lobed
medallions, 8ft.2in. x 12ft.
6in. (Robt. W. Skinner Inc.)
$7,500 £5,208

Late 19th century Kuba rug,
the electric blue field with
all-over geometric floral grid,
5ft.3in. x 4ft. (Robt. W.
Skinner Inc.) $4,500 £3,125

Early 19th century 'pin-wheel'
Kazak rug, 5ft.8in. x 7ft.5in.
(Robt. W. Skinner Inc.)
$4,300 £2,986

Mid 19th century Kazak
rug, the abrashed yellow green
to blue green field with four
hooked hexagons, 4ft.9in. x
6ft.8in. (Robt. W. Skinner
Inc.) $6,500 £4,513

Late 19th/early 20th century
Kazak rug, 8ft.2in. x 5ft.9in.
(Robt. W. Skinner Inc.)
$4,000 £2,777

Mid 19th century Bordjalou
Kazak rug, 5ft. x 6ft.7in.
(Robt. W. Skinner Inc.)
$5,100 £3,541

Late 19th/early 20th century
Kazak rug, 4ft.7in. x 6ft.5in.
(Robt. W. Skinner Inc.)
$3,100 £2,152

Late 19th century Kazak
rug, 4ft.8in. x 7ft.10in.
(Robt. W. Skinner Inc.)
$1,800 £1,250

Late 19th century Konagend
rug, E. Caucasus, the lattice
of ivory stylised floral designs
on a dark blue field, 4ft.5in.
x 3ft.8in. (Robt. W. Skinner
Inc.) $2,700 £1,875

Early 19th century Ghiordes
prayer rug, 4ft. x 5ft.6in.
(Robt. W. Skinner Inc.)
$3,900 £2,708

Mid 19th century Kuba rug,
E. Caucasus, the red field
woven in a trellis of red, blue,
black and ivory diamonds,
3ft.7in. x 4ft.6in. (Robt. W.
Skinner Inc.) $900 £625

Early 20th century Kashan carpet
with an all-over trellis of flower
filled cartouches, 10ft.2in. x 15ft.
8in. (Robt. W. Skinner Inc.)
$8,000 £5,555

A Chi-Chi rug, the indigo
field with stepped hooked
medallions, 1.85 x 1.29m.
(Phillips) $2,272 £1,600

677

Late 19th century Kazak rug, the red field with three blue and green medallions, 4ft.4in. x 3ft.5in. (Robt. W. Skinner Inc.)
$1,100 £763

Mid 19th century Kazak rug, S.W. Caucasus, 3ft.11in. x 5ft.8in. (Robt. W. Skinner Inc.) $3,600 £2,500

An Indian Dhurry, the ivory field with lozenge design and stylised flowering plants, 2.08 x 1.18m. (Phillips)
$2,448 £1,600

Late 19th/early 20th century cloud-band Kazak long rug, 8ft.8in. x 4ft.1in. (Robt. W. Skinner Inc.)
$1,800 £1,250

A 19th century E. Turkestan Kashgar silk mat, 3ft.1in. x 3ft.2in. (Robt. W. Skinner Inc.) $2,900 £2,013

Late 19th century Ersari Chuval with all-over mina khani pattern, 5ft.3in. x 3ft. (Robt. W. Skinner Inc.)
$350 £225

Late 19th century Chi-Chi rug, the blue field with all-over pattern of geometrical shapes, 3ft.10in. x 5ft.4in. (Robt. W. Skinner Inc.)
$300 £193

Late 19th century Lesghi star E. Caucasian rug, 2ft.8in. x 3ft.7in. (Robt. W. Skinner Inc.) $700 £451

Late 19th century Afshar rug, S.W. Persia, the yellow green field with all-over grid of small red flowerheads and blue boteh motifs, 4ft.2in. x 5ft.2in. (Robt. W. Skinner Inc.)
$4,500 £3,125

A 19th century E. Caucasian long rug, 4ft.5in. x 8ft.6in. (Robt. W. Skinner Inc.) $2,400 £1,666

Cotton Disney characters scatter rug, 1950's, 45 x 59in. (Robt. W. Skinner Inc.) $35 £24

Mid 19th century Kuba rug, the abrashed blue field filled with ivory and abrashed green shield-like palmettes, 3ft.7in. x 6ft. (Robt. W. Skinner Inc.) $3,800 £2,638

A 19th century Chinese carpet, embossed phoenix figures on an ivory-taupe field, 8ft.9in. x 11ft.5in. (Robt. W. Skinner Inc.) $3,100 £2,122

A Kashan silk rug, the ivory field with a crimson cartouche pendant medallion, 2.06 x 1.24m. (Phillips) $1,872 £1,300

An Afshar rug, the field with yellow, indigo and plum-red columns of stylised plants, 4ft.9in. x 3ft.8in. (Christie's) $2,481 £1,760

A shield Kazak rug with tomato-red field, 7ft.9in. x 5ft.11in. (Christie's) $3,190 £2,200

Late 19th century Malayer rug, the ivory field woven in a design of offset palmettes on leafy vines, 4ft.4in. x 6ft. 4in. (Robt. W. Skinner Inc.) $2,400 £1,666

Late 19th century East Caucasian rug, the dark blue field with two saw-tooth edged medallions, 4ft. x 5ft. 8in. (Robt. W. Skinner Inc.) $950 £612

Needlework sampler, silk yarns worked on ivory linen ground fabric, by 'Harriatt Shoveller, 1799', England, 12½ x 17in. (Robt. W. Skinner Inc.) $1,600 £1,118

Framed needlework pictorial sampler, inscribed 'Harroit Hoyle, Aged 21, 1834', 24 x 24in. (Robt. W. Skinner Inc.) $2,200 £1,538

Needlework spot sampler, Germany, 1759, vivid polychrome silk yarns on natural linen fabric, 12 x 21½in. (Robt. W. Skinner Inc.) $2,500 £1,748

Needlework sampler, 'Sally Butman her work in the 11th year of her age, 1801', Marblehead, Mass., 10.3/8 x 12½in. (Robt. W. Skinner Inc.) $15,000 £10,489

Needlework sampler, England, dated 1826, silk yarns in a variety of stitches on natural linen ground, 13 x 15½in. (Robt. W. Skinner Inc.) $700 £489

A needlework picture, by Mary Fentun, dated 1789, 21¼ x 16½in. (Christie's) $2,860 £2,001

An early 19th century needlework sampler by S. Parker, aged 14 years 1817, 37 x 32cm. (Phillips) $862 £560

An early 19th century needlework sampler, by Elizabeth Campling, aged 12 years, the linen ground embroidered in silks, 31.5 x 34.5cm. (Phillips) $338 £220

A nicely worked needlework sampler, by Sarah Iesson, the linen ground embroidered in silks, 33 x 21cm. (Phillips) $708 £460

Late 18th century needlework sampler, worked in silk yarns of gold, light blue, red, brown, ivory and black on natural linen, 7 x 10½in. (Robt. W. Skinner Inc.) $3,300 £2,307

A needlework sampler worked in silk yarns on natural coloured linen, 'Susanah Cadmore, 1805', 12½ x 13¼in. (Robt. W. Skinner Inc.) $500 £349

An early 19th century needlework sampler, inscribed 'Rachel Fowler's work finished May 29, 1837', 40 x 32cm. (Phillips) $739 £480

Late 18th century Spanish needlework sampler with silk embroidered stylised floral and geometric designs, 15½ x 18½in. (Robt. W. Skinner Inc.) $300 £209

A needlework family record, silk yarns in shades of blue, green, pale peach, ivory and black on natural linen ground fabric, 18¼ x 14½in. (Robt. W. Skinner Inc.) $900 £629

A needlwork sampler, by 'Sarah Pell, Feberery 21, 1830', wool yarns on white wool fabric, 12½ x 16in. (Robt. W. Skinner Inc.) $850 £594

An early 19th century needlework sampler by Elizabeth Bushby, March 6, aged 10 years, 1822, 45 x 42cm. (Phillips) $523 £340

Framed needlework pictorial verse sampler, by Eliza. A. Machett, New York, March 22, 1828, 16½ x 16in. (Robt. W. Skinner Inc.) $500 £333

Needlework sampler, by 'Elizabeth Tonnecliff, her work done in 1791', silk yarns, 16 x 20¼in. (Robt. W. Skinner Inc.) $8,700 £6,083

A mid 17th century needlework sampler in drawnthread, cutwork and needlepoint stitches, 75 x 22.5cm. (Phillips) $1,155 £750

An 18th century silk embroidered sampler, Europe, 20 x 35in. (Robt. W. Skinner Inc.) $7,500 £5,244

A 17th century needlework sampler, probably by Mary Tratt of Boston, 7½ x 22¾in. (Robt. W. Skinner Inc.) $2,500 £1,748

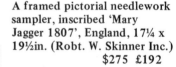

A framed pictorial needlework sampler, inscribed 'Celia(?) Procter Montrose 1833', England, 16 x 20in. (Robt. W. Skinner Inc.) $425 £297

A late 17th century needlework sampler, embroidered in silks, 36 x 14cm. (Phillips) $446 £290

A framed pictorial needlework sampler, inscribed 'Mary Jagger 1807', England, 17¼ x 19½in. (Robt. W. Skinner Inc.) $275 £192

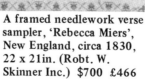

Late 19th century Bidjar sampler, N.W. Persia, 3ft. 10in. x 4ft.11in. (Robt. W. Skinner Inc.) $4,500 £3,125

A framed needlework verse sampler, 'Rebecca Miers', New England, circa 1830, 22 x 21in. (Robt. W. Skinner Inc.) $700 £466

Needlework sampler, England, 'Margaret Smith, aged 12 AD 1848', worked in heavy wool yarns, 17 x 18in. (Robt. W. Skinner Inc.) $600 £419

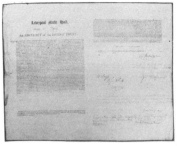

Liverpool Music Hall 1798. Share No. 261, on vellum. (Phillips) $522 £360

Canterbury Navigation and Sandwich Harbour 1826, one £20 share, tear top right. (Phillips) $181 £125

Keller-Dorian Colorfilm Corpn. $20 share certificates 1932, 4 examples, also Fox Film Corpn. 1931-3 warrants, 4 examples. (Phillips) $188 £130

Poyais: Pouaisian 3% Consolidated Stock 1827, £250 Bond, hand signed by Gregor MacGregor. (Phillips) $362 £250

South Africa: The Great Kruger Gold Mining Co. Ltd. 1889, 100 x £1 shares. (Phillips) $406 £280

Republic of China (Pacific Loan) 1937, U.S. $1,000 bond. (Phillips) $435 £300

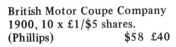

The Company of Proprietors of the Herefordshire and Gloucester Canal Navigation 1793, £100 share certificate, on vellum. (Phillips) $377 £260

British Motor Coupe Company 1900, 10 x £1/$5 shares. (Phillips) $58 £40

Australia: Western Australian Co. Settlement of Australind 1841, with 'Duplicate Original', Town Order certificate for ¼ acre. (Phillips) $493 £340

BASKETS

A George III Irish oval bread basket on rim foot, by Joseph Jackson, Dublin, 1786, 14¾in. long, 26oz. (Christie's) $2,988 £2,090

An Unger Brothers basket, 24cm. across, stamped with monogram and Sterling 925 Fine, numbered 02616. (Phillips) $460 £320

A shaped oval swing-handled cake basket with applied foliate border, Sheffield, 1914, 12in., 23oz. (Christie's) $438 £264

A George III shaped oval bread basket, by Sarah Buttall, 1770, 14in. long, 37oz. (Christie's) $4,604 £2,860

A George III small sugar basket, by Charles Hougham, 1790, 8cm. high, 4oz. (Phillips) $459 £300

A George II Irish shaped oval bread basket, by Geo. Hill, Dublin, 1760, 15in. long, 72oz. (Christie's) $23,595 £16,500

A George I circular bread basket, by Thomas Farren, 1725, date letter struck twice, 12¾in. diam., 94oz. (Christie's) $111,540 £66,000

A George II oval cake basket, by John Jacob, 1742, 36cm. wide, 63oz. (Phillips) $18,960 £12,000

A Victorian silver gilt basket, by Barnard & Co., 1846, 6¼in. diam., 13oz.3dwt. (Christie's) $1,301 £770

BEAKERS

A Latvian tapering cylindrical beaker and cover, by C. Dey, Riga, circa 1740, 10½in. high, 23oz. (Christie's)
$2,478 £1,620

A late 17th century Continental covered beaker, maker's mark EA conjoined, perhaps for Everhard Alffen of Cologne, circa 1680, 14.5cm. high, 8oz. (Phillips) $1,215 £850

A Hungarian parcel gilt slightly tapering cylindrical beaker, by Johannes (Hans) Retsch, Brasso, circa 1630, 5¼in. high, 3oz.12dwt. (Christie's)
$5,348 £3,740

A German parcel gilt beaker on three ball feet, by Gerdt Eimbke (Eimeke) III, circa 1690, 5in. high, 8oz. (Christie's) $2,809 £1,836

A small beaker designed by Jean Puiforcat, 4.8cm. high, silver coloured metal. (Phillips) $259 £180

A William and Mary plain beaker, pricked with initials AL.IM, by James Daniel, Norwich, 1689, 3½in. high, 3oz.3dwt. (Christie's)
$3,146 £2,200

One of two George III interlocking beakers, each pair forming a barrel, by C. Aldridge and H. Green, 1778, overall height of a barrel 5¼in., 16oz.18dwt. (Christie's)
$3,304 £2,160

One of a pair of silver beakers, by John Taylor and H. Hinsdale, N.Y., 1804-30, 3½in. high, 9oz. (Christie's) $770 £538

A Swedish parcel gilt trumpet shaped beaker, by P. Eneroth, Stockholm, 1776, 8¾in. high, 14oz.5dwt. (Christie's)
$1,156 £756

A Connell two-handled bowl, designed by Kate Harris, with bottle-green glass liner, London hallmarks for 1904, 39.1cm. diam., 22oz.15dwt. without liner. (Christie's) $1,425 £990

A presentation punch bowl, by Tiffany & Co., N.Y., 1890-91, 9in. high, 15¾in. diam., 101oz. (Christie's) $24,200 £16,935

A 17th century Dutch oval brandy bowl, by Hindrick Muntinck, Groningen, 1661, 6.5oz. (Phillips) $1,029 £720

A covered silver sugar bowl, by Edmund Milne, Phila., circa 1785, 7¼in. high, 11oz. (Christie's) $3,850 £2,694

An Omar Ramsden silver punch bowl with everted rim, London hallmarks for 1931, 23.6cm. wide, 65oz.14dwt. (Christie's) $6,732 £4,400

A George III Scottish swing-handled, boat-shaped sugar bowl, by John Leslie, Aberdeen, circa 1785, 9.5cm. high, 10.5oz. (Phillips) $750 £500

A sugar bowl, the cover with a green stone finial, by Tiffany & Co., N.Y., 1877-91, 3¼in. high, gross weight 13oz. (Christie's) $10,450 £6,894

A Scottish silver bowl, designed by D. Carleton Smythe, 48.5cm. across, bearing Glasgow hallmarks for 1905. (Phillips) $547 £380

A George II circular punch bowl on moulded foot, Dublin, probably 1754, town mark and Hibernia only, 9¼in. diam., 34oz. (Christie's) $3,146 £2,200

BOWLS

An Art Nouveau Continental white metal bowl in the style of J. Hofman, 14in. across. (Christie's) $716 £462

William III style Victorian punch bowl, by Walker & Hall, Sheffield, 1898. (Reeds Rains)
$1,108 £770

An Omar Ramsden silver gilt bowl, London hallmarks for 1935, 46.2cm. wide. (Christie's) $13,370 £9,350

A George II Channel Islands circular sugar bowl and cover, by G. Henry, Guernsey, circa 1740, 4in. diam., 6oz.10dwt. (Christie's) $7,436 £4,400

An Unger Brothers silver bowl of flower form, 15.4cm. diam., stamped maker's monogram, Sterling 925 Fine, 0850 (3oz.). (Phillips)
$145 £100

A late Victorian spiral fluted bowl, by James Dixon & Sons, Sheffield, 1893, 9¼in., 22.75oz. (Christie's)
$589 £385

A centrepiece bowl with a scalloped rim, the sides fluted, by Simeon Coley, N.Y., circa 1768, 8.7/8in. diam., 21oz. 10dwt. (Christie's)
$28,600 £18,870

A Victorian boat-shaped sugar bowl, makers Messrs. Barnard, London, 1883, 5in. high, 8oz., and a matching sugar spoon, London, 1882. (Hobbs & Chambers)
$228 £160

A German shaped circular bowl, the ground decorated with a pastoral scene, 9in. diam. (Christie's) $440 £264

SILVER

A Dutch plain shaped
octagonal casket, by J.
Logerat, The Hague, 1728,
5¼in. long, 14oz.16dwt.
(Christie's) $8,592 £5,616

A smoker's set, comprising
a two-handled tray, a cigar
box, four ashtrays and a
matchbox holder, by Asprey
& Co. Ltd., 1937, 1938 and
1943, tray 17¼in. long, wt.
excluding cigar box 103oz.
(Christie's) $6,606 £4,620

A Swiss silver gilt and enamel
singing bird box, the movement stamped C. Bruguier a
Geneve, 9.5cm. wide.
(Phillips) $7,250 £5,000

A George II square sugar
box, together with two tea
caddies, by Thos. Heming,
1747, 60oz. (Christie's)
$11,566 £7,560

A Charles II oval silver
gilt tobacco box with
detachable cover, maker's
mark W H only, circa
1675, 4in. long, 5oz.10dwt.
(Christie's) $1,573 £1,100

A Guild of Handicraft
silver and enamel box and
cover, London hallmarks for
1901, 10cm. diam., 6oz.5dwt.
gross weight. (Christie's)
$665 £462

A 19th century Swiss
oblong silver gilt and
enamel singing bird box,
by Chas. Bruguier,
3.7/8in. long. (Christie's)
$4,957 £3,240

A Victorian biscuit box, in
the form of a book, 21cm.
long, circa 1870. (Phillips)
$429 £300

A George II silver gilt shaped
oblong toilet box, by Ayme
Videau, 1755, the cover, unmarked, 6¾in. long, 36oz.
(Christie's) $4,131 £2,700

CANDELABRA

One of a pair of French six-light candelabra, by J. Chaumet, Paris, 1918, 24½in. high, 471oz. (Christie's)
$22,000 £15,496

Pair of Louis XVI four-light candelabra, by Antoine Boullier, Paris, 1787, with the charge of Henri Clavel and export discharge mark, 26in. high, 269oz. (Christie's) $99,000 £69,735

One of a set of four Italian six-light candelabra, Rome, mid 19th century, maker's mark CV in oval, 19¼in. high, 526oz. (Christie's)
$57,200 £40,291

One of a pair of silver gilt two-light candelabra, the branches bearing marks for Wm. Elliot, London, 1812, bases unmarked, 16¼in. high, 179oz. (Christie's)
$33,000 £23,245

A two-branch candelabrum, designed by Soren Georg Jensen, 17.7cm. high, 26oz.10dwt. (Christie's) $2,044 £1,430

A Russian Hanukah lamp, 1879, assaymaster OC, possibly Minsk, struck with the name L. Zammer and town mark a crescent between mullets, 21¼in. high, weight of branches 30oz. (Christie's)
$3,146 £2,200

Pair of Spanish four-light candelabra, by Juan de San Fauri, Madrid, 1762, with the warden's mark of Melun, 19¾in. high, 180oz. (Christie's) $88,000 £61,987

A Victorian three-light candelabrum/centrepiece, by W. & G. Sissons, Sheffield, 1865, 24¾in. high, 165oz. (Christie's)
$4,719 £3,300

Pair of French four-light candelabra, by Puiforcat, Paris, circa 1900, 17¼in. high, 210oz. (Christie's) $8,250 £5,811

CANDLESTICKS

One of a pair of Continental candlesticks, probably German, maker's mark possibly FO, 10in. high, 24oz. (Christie's) $2,809 £1,836

Pair of George III cast candlesticks, by Ebenezer Coker, 1768, 25.5cm. high, 34oz. (Phillips) $1,950 £1,300

One of a pair of German silver gilt candlesticks, by F. Proll, Cassel, circa 1840, 10in. high, 36oz. (Christie's) $6,600 £4,649

One of a set of four Dutch silver candlesticks, by P. Kersbergen, The Hague, 1772, 10in. high, 95oz. (Christie's) $34,606 £24,200

A pair of plated candlesticks of circular baluster form, 13in. high. (Parsons, Welch & Cowell) $154 £100

One of a pair of German candlesticks, Allenstein, circa 1750, maker's mark I.C. over S, 7¼in. high. (Christie's) $3,304 £2,160

One of a set of four German cast candlesticks, probably by J. W. Voigt, Osnabruck, circa 1740, 8½in. high, 69oz. (Christie's) $33,048 £21,600

A pair of Louis XV candlesticks, by Etienne Pollet, Paris, 1743, 10.1/8in. high, 52oz. (Christie's) $5,500 £3,874

One of a pair of George III Corinthian candlesticks, by Ebenezer Coker, 1762, 35cm. high. (Phillips) $2,850 £1,900

CANDLESTICKS

One of a pair of William IV
cast silver gilt candlesticks,
by Paul Storr, 1835, 23cm.
high, 31.5oz. (Phillips)
$18,000 £12,000

An Art Nouveau silver 'counter-
balanced' candlestick, 16.5cm.
high, marked KK, London,
1905. (Phillips) $288 £200

One of a pair of William and
Mary candlesticks, 1693,
maker's mark B in script,
crown above, 7½in. high,
38oz. (Christie's)
$18,176   £11,880

One of four Louis XV/XVI
candlesticks, by Joseph-
Theodore Vancombert, Paris,
two 1771, and two 1775,
10.5/8in. high, 81oz.
(Christie's) $13,200 £9,298

A pair of stylised silver and green
onyx candlesticks, probably made
by Dixon & Sons for Hyams,
22cm. high, London marks for
1907. (Phillips) $892 £620

One of a pair of 18th century
German candlesticks, by
Johann Balthasar Heggenauer,
Augsburg, 1783/85, 23.5cm.
high, 28oz. (Phillips)
$1,650 £1,100

One of a pair of German
table candlesticks, by C.
Lieberkuhn II, Berlin,
circa 1735, 8in. high, 31oz.
(Christie's) $11,011 £7,700

Pair of silver gilt candlesticks,
French or English, circa 1680,
8in. high, 37oz. (Christie's)
$52,800 £37,192

One of a pair of George III
candlesticks, by Wm. Holmes,
1780, 11½in. high, 43oz.
(Christie's) $3,932 £2,750

Pair of WMF Art Nouveau
silver coloured metal candlesticks, 11in. high. (Reeds Rains)
$465 £300

One of a pair of Georg Jensen
candlesticks, designed by
S. Bernadotte, 6cm. high,
8oz.16dwt. (Christie's)
$871 £605

Pair of late 18th century
Corinthian column Paktong
candlesticks, 11in. high.
(Woolley & Wallis) $906 £600

A pair of neo-Gothic candlesticks with cluster columns,
circa 1770, 30cm. high.
(Phillips) $285 £190

One of a pair of George II
candlesticks, by Wm. Cafe,
London, 1759, 11¾in. high,
57oz.10dwt. (Christie's)
$7,700 £5,025

A pair of candlesticks, American,
each with a removable bobeche
above a vasiform candlecup,
circa 1841, 7¾in. high, 19oz.
(Christie's) $1,210 £846

Pair of George II plain candlesticks,
with spool-shaped sockets and
detachable nozzles, by J. Cafe,
1742, 8in. high, 33oz. (Christie's)
$3,775 £2,640

One of a pair of Louis XVI
silver gilt candlesticks, by
E. Moreau, Paris, 1776,
10.5/8in. high, 38oz.10dwt.
(Christie's) $6,600 £4,649

Pair of early George III Doric
column candlesticks, by E.
Coker, London, 1764, 12in.
high. (Woolley & Wallis)
$1,221 £820

CASTERS

A caster, the domed pierced cover with pinecone finial, by Zachariah Brigden, Boston, 1770-85, 5¼in. high, 3oz. (Christie's) $2,200 £1,451

Three George I plain pear-shaped casters, by Samuel Welder 1716 and 1717, 6¼in. and 7¼in. high, 18oz.5dwt. (Christie's)
$4,427 £2,750

One of a pair of German silver gilt casters, by B. F. Behrens, Hanover, date letter I, circa 1755, 8¾in. high, 29oz. (Christie's)
$22,000 £14,496

A caster of baluster form, by John Edwards, Boston, circa 1745, 5½in. high., 3oz. (Christie's) $3,520 £2,159

A set of three late 17th century West Country casters, by Gabriel Felling of Bruton Co., Somerset, circa 1690, 28oz. (Phillips)
$45,760 £32,000

A Belgian octagonal pear-shaped caster, Brussels, 1730-33, maker's mark AL, 7½in. high, 9oz.18dwt.(Christie's)
$3,445 £2,640

A Belgian caster, by Peter Alio, Jnr., Brussels, 1737-40, 7¼in. high, 7oz.10dwt. (Christie's)
$4,180 £2,944

A set of three Queen Anne silver gilt casters, by Charles Adam, 1703, 8in. and 6½in. high, 22oz. (Christie's) $18,590 £11,000

A George II large plain vase-shaped caster, by Samuel Wood, 1753, 8¾in. high, 21oz. (Christie's)
$2,359 £1,650

CENTREPIECES

An Art Nouveau centrepiece
of open boat shape, 57.5cm.
long, silver coloured metal,
possibly Austrian or German.
(Phillips) $2,304 £1,600

A George III Irish epergne,
by Thomas Jones, Dublin,
1789, 17½in. high, 180oz.
(Christie's) $28,314 £19,800

A George II epergne, by Paul
de Lamerie, the waiters 1736,
the centrepiece 1737, 14¼in.
high, 301oz. (Christie's)
          $1,101,100 £770,000

Early 20th century French
silver gilt centrepiece, Paris,
maker's mark AD, bird
between, 10¾in. high, 134oz.
(Christie's) $6,600 £4,649

A Victorian centrepiece, by
Messrs. Barnard, 1844, 64cm.
high, weight excluding glass
bowl 327oz. (Phillips)
          $12,000 £8,000

A William IV six-branch
centrepiece, by Benjamin
Smith, 1836, 25¼in. high,
421oz. (Christie's)
          $10,626 £6,600

A George III openwork epergne,
by Francis Butty and Nicholas
Dumee, 1769, 19in. high, 117oz.
(Christie's) $8,651 £6,050

Late 19th century Viennese
silver gilt and enamel centrepiece, in glazed showcase,
25½in. high overall.
(Christie's)
          $69,400 £45,360

A George III epergne, by Thos.
Pitts, 1770, 51cm. high,
156oz. (Phillips)
          $12,155 £8,500

CHAMBERSTICKS

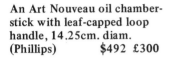

An Art Nouveau oil chamberstick with leaf-capped loop
handle, 14.25cm. diam.
(Phillips) $492 £300

One of a pair of Victorian
fluted shaped circular chamber
candlesticks, by Robinson,
Edkins & Aston, Birmingham,
1840, 6¼in. high, 24.25oz.
(Christie's) $1,280 £800

A Victorian silver gilt small
chamber candlestick in the
manner of Paul de Lamerie,
by S.W., London, 1841, 11cm.
diam. (Christie's) $400 £250

A George IV chamberstick
with conical snuffer, T.B.,
London, 1822, and a matching chamberstick, London,
1832, each 5½in. diam.,
total weight 22oz. (Christie's)
          $1,496 £935

Pair of George III circular
chamber candlesticks, by
T. Hannam and J. Crouch,
London, 1801, 20oz.
(Heathcote Ball & Co.)
          $4,401 £2,700

A George III chamber candlestick with detachable nozzle
and conical snuffer, by E.
Coker, London, 1771, 5¾in.
high, 7.75oz. (Christie's)
          $760 £528

An early Victorian chamber
candlestick, by Joseph and
John Angell, London, 1837,
6½in. high, 8.75oz.
(Christie's) $506 £352

Small Georgian silver chamber
candlestick with snuffer,
Sheffield, 1809. (Lawrence
Butler & Co.) $290 £190

A Victorian gadrooned
circular chamber candlestick
in the 18th century taste,
R.S., London, 1870, 7¾in.
high, 7.75oz. (Christie's)
          $352 £220

CHOCOLATE POTS

A Queen Anne plain tapering cylindrical chocolate pot, by Gabriel Sleath, 1711, 9¾in. high, gross 27oz. (Christie's)
$6,292 £4,400

Late 18th century French silver chocolate pot, 8in. high, 23 troy oz. including wooden handle. (Robt. W. Skinner Inc.)
$2,400 £1,500

An early George III pear-shaped chocolate pot with hinged cover, maker's mark W.C., London, 1763, 9¾in. high, 18oz. all in. (Lalonde Fine Art) $768 £480

An early 18th century silver chocolate pot, by Wm. Fawdery, London, 12oz. (Robt. W. Skinner Inc.)
$500 £312

Georgian silver chocolate pot with ebony handle, London, 1816. (Lawrence Butler & Co.)
$382 £250

A Queen Anne plain tapering cylindrical chocolate pot, by Edmund Pearce, 1705, 10½in. high, gross 22oz. (Christie's)
$5,662 £3,960

A Queen Anne plain tapering cylindrical chocolate pot, by Jonah Clifton, 1710, 9¾in. high, gross 20oz. (Christie's)
$7,078 £4,950

A silver baluster shaped chocolate pot, by Samuel Kirk & Son Co., Baltimore, 1903-07, 10¼in. high, gross wt. 25oz. (Christie's)
$1,430 £1,000

A Queen Anne plain tapering cylindrical chocolate pot, by William Pearson, 1711, 24cm. high, 25oz. (Phillips)
$9,840 £6,000

CIGARETTE BOXES

A Georg Jensen white metal cigarette box, stamped GJ 925S and inscription 6 Oktober 1933, 10¾in. wide. (Christie's) $1,718 £1,210

A Continental oblong wood lined cigarette box decorated in the Art Deco style, 6¼in. long, engraved dated 1938. (Christie's) $652 £450

A rectangular cigarette box, designed by Jorgen Jensen, Dessin JJ, Georg Jensen 857 A, 16cm. wide, 13oz.15dwt. (Christie's) $943 £660

CIGARETTE CASES

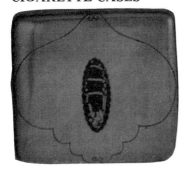

A Wiener Werkstatte cigarette case, the design attributed to Carl Otto Czeschka, 8.5cm. wide, silver coloured metal. (Phillips) $936 £650

An Edwardian gilt lined rounded oblong quadruple cheroot case, J. G., Birmingham, 1905, 5in. high. (Christie's) $170 £110

A Continental cigarette case, cover enamelled with a nude lying on the edge of the shore, with English import marks for 1906. (Phillips)
$528 £350

A Portuguese enamel cigarette case, the cover depicting a bare-breasted Classical girl, circa 1900. (Phillips) $573 £380

A Victorian cheroot case, by Yapp & Woodward, Birmingham, 1854, 12.7cm. high, 4.75oz. (Phillips) $271 £180

Late 19th century Austrian enamel cigarette case, the cover enamelled with an Ancient Egyptian scene, circa 1895. (Phillips)
$906 £600

CLARET JUGS

A Victorian slender vase-shaped claret jug, by Elkington & Co., 12¾in. high. (Christie's)
$221 £143

A Hukin & Heath silver mounted claret jug with ebony handle, designed by Christopher Dresser, London hallmarks for 1880, 22.5cm. high. (Christie's)
$1,504   £1,045

A Victorian pear-shaped claret jug, W.H., London, 1868, 13in. high, 23.25oz. (Christie's) $988 £638

A Victorian silver gilt mounted glass claret jug, by E. J. and W. Barnard, 1872, 12¼in. high. (Christie's)
$2,516 £1,760

A Victorian parcel gilt claret jug formed as a bird, by George Fox, 1877, (patched), 8¼in. high, 22oz. (Christie's) $3,470 £2,268

A William IV and Victorian silver mounted ruby glass claret jug, by C. Reily and G. Storer, 1836, 12in. high. (Christie's) $8,855 £5,500

A Victorian silver mounted glass claret jug, by Elkington & Co., Birmingham, 1878, 10½in. high. (Reeds Rains)
$1,512 £1,050

A French silver gilt mounted tapering cylindrical clear glass claret jug, by Charles-Nicholas Odiot, Paris, circa 1860, 11in. high. (Christie's)
$3,470 £2,268

A Victorian silver mounted clear glass claret jug, by Wm. Hutton & Sons Ltd., 1894, 13¾in. high. (Christie's)
$2,044 £1,430

COASTERS

One of a pair of William IV circular decanter stands, makers Howard, Battie & Hawkesworth, Sheffield, 1832, 10oz. (Woolley & Wallis) $1,639 £1,100

A set of six Wiener Werkstatte circular wine glass coasters, designed by J. Hoffman and K. Moser, 5.5cm. diam., silver coloured metal. (Phillips) $1,296 £900

One of a pair of George III circular decanter stands, by John Roberts & Co., Sheffield, 1806/10. (Woolley & Wallis) $1,152 £720

A Hutton & Sons silver wine bottle coaster, 16.80cm. high, total weight 19oz., maker's marks for Sheffield, 1905. (Phillips) $374 £260

A wine coaster, stamped marks 925.S Georg Jensen & Wendel A/S 289A, 9.5cm. high, 14oz.10dwt. (Christie's) $1,415 £990

Georgian mahogany and brass bound bottle coaster. (Lots Road Galleries) $214 £150

One of a pair of George III wine coasters, London, 1795, maker Michael Plummer, 4¾in. diam. (Hobbs & Chambers) $1,644 £1,150

Pair of Regency moulded circular wine coasters, by S. C. Younge & Co., Sheffield, 1820, 6¼in. diam. (Christie's) $1,500 £968

A Liberty & Co. silver and enamel wine coaster, Birmingham hallmarks for 1905, 9.5cm. diam., 2oz.14dwt. gross wt. (Christie's) $706 £462

COFFEE POTS

A Queen Anne plain tapering cylindrical coffee pot, by Richard Raine, 1712, 9.5/8in. high, gross 24oz. (Christie's) $5,820 £4,070

A Victorian silver coffee pot, London, 1898, 27¼oz. (Parsons, Welch & Cowell) $392 £260

A William III plain tapering cylindrical coffee pot, by John Martin Stockar, 1701, 8.7/8in. high, gross 17oz. 12dwt. (Christie's) $2,516   £1,760

A Queen Anne plain tapering cylindrical coffee pot, by Anthony Nelme, 1713, 8¾in. high, gross 22oz. (Christie's) $4,089 £2,860

A George III silver coffee pot, London 1817, makers S. Royes and J. E. Dix, 9in. high, 28oz. (Parsons, Welch & Cowell) $508 £330

A George I cylindrical coffee pot engraved with a coat-of-arms, by John Edwards II, 1726, 9in. high, gross 25oz. (Christie's) $2,988 £2,090

A George III plain pear-shaped coffee pot, by Robt. Peat, Newcastle, 1778, 11in. high, 30oz. gross. (Christie's) $2,831 £1,980

A George IV coffee pot on circular foot, 8in. high, London, 1824, 26oz. (Hobbs & Chambers) $572 £400

A Liberty silver coffee pot, designed by A. Knox, Birmingham, hallmarks for 1906, 21.6cm. high. (Christie's) $673 £440

SILVER

COFFEE POTS

A Belgian coffee pot, Tournai, 1771, maker's mark NH below a sunburst, 15½in. high, gross weight 36oz. (Christie's) $8,250 £5,811

A William IV fluted pear-shaped coffee pot, by Paul Storr, 1836, the finial by J. S. Hunt, 8¼in. high, 26oz. (Christie's) $2,123 £1,485

A George II pear-shaped coffee pot, by Isaac Cookson, Newcastle, 1737, 10in. high, gross 30oz. (Christie's) $2,359 £1,650

A George II pear-shaped coffee pot, by Samuel Courtauld, 1753, 10½in. high, 40oz. (Christie's) $33,033 £23,100

A Victorian silver coffee pot with ivory finial, Sheffield 1874, maker's mark J.H., 20oz. (Parsons, Welch & Cowell) $477 £310

Early 20th century repousse decorated sterling silver coffee pot, Gorham Mfg. Co., 12.7/8in. high, approx. 26 troy oz. (Robt. W. Skinner Inc.) $1,100 £718

A George III plain pear-shaped coffee pot, by Hester Bateman, 1781, 32cm. high, 27.5oz. (Phillips) $5,056 £3,200

A Victorian silver coffee pot, London, 1897, 25¼oz. (Parsons, Welch & Cowell) $422 £280

A Queen Anne plain tapering cylindrical coffee pot, by John Rand, 1707, 9½in. high, gross 18oz.18dwt. (Christie's) $4,404 £3,080

CREAM JUGS

A cream pitcher, by Albert Coles, N.Y., circa 1869, 6¼in. high, 6oz. (Christie's) $330 £202

A Victorian cream jug, by Messrs. Garrard, London, 1884. (Reeds Rains) $244 £170

A cream pitcher, marked 'ID', probably Phila., 1790-1810, 6¾in. high, 5oz. (Christie's) $1,045 £689

A cream pitcher, helmet-shaped, by Henry J. Pepper, Delaware, 1813-26, 5¾in. high, 7oz. (Christie's) $605 £423

A cream pitcher with a scalloped rim and scroll handle, by Z. Brigden, Boston, 1770-85, 4.7/8in. high, 3oz. (Christie's) $2,200 £1,451

A Continental fluted pear-shape milk jug with an elaborate scroll handle, 6½in. high. (Christie's) $136 £82

A cream pitcher, pyriform, by Philip Syng, Jnr., Phila., 1750-80, 4in. high, 3oz. (Christie's) $6,600 £4,354

A George III inverted pear-shaped cream jug, probably by R. and D. Hennell, London, 1766, 4¼in. high. (Christie's) $168 £110

A silver pyriform cream pitcher, by Samuel Minott, Boston, circa 1750-60, 4¼in. high, 3oz. (Christie's) $1,980 £1,385

A Victorian egg cruet, the basket 23cm. wide, with six egg cups, 7cm. high, by Robt. Hennell, 1851, and six spoons, by F. Higgins, 35oz. (Phillips) $1,501 £1,050

A George III two-handled boat-shaped cruet stand, by Robert Hennell, 1781, the bottle mounts by Wm. Abdy II, 1798, 13in. long, 14oz.11dwt. (Christie's) $1,730 £1,210

A Victorian six-cup egg cruet, by Henry Wilkinson & Co., Sheffield, 1846, 6in. high, 20.75oz. (Christie's)
$356 £230

A Hukin & Heath electro-plated cruet set, attributed to Dr. C. Dresser, 4¾in. high. (Christie's) $67 £45

A George III Irish Warwick cruet, the base engraved 'In all 49oz.9 pwts', 9½in. high, 48oz. (Christie's)
$4,089 £2,420

An early George III cinque-foil Warwick cruet on shell and scroll feet, by J. Delmester, London, 1763, 9¾in. high, 23.5oz. (Christie's) $657 £440

A Hukin & Heath silver condi-ment set designed by Dr. C. Dresser, London hallmarks for 1881, 14.2cm. high. (Christie's)
$1,598 £1,045

A China Trade egg cruet on four ball feet, by Khecheong, probably Canton, circa 1860, 10½in. high, 39oz. (Christie's)
$1,101 £770

Victorian cruet, oblong with central scrolled handle, London, 1852, 18½oz. (Hobbs & Chambers)
$524 £330

CUPS

A French silver gilt and enamel vase-shaped cup and cover, circa 1830, both cover and body with guarantee mark 1819-38, 9¾in. high, gross 24oz. (Christie's) $1,415 £990

A handled cup, with an S-scroll handle, by Thos. Coverly, Rhode Island, 1730-60, 2½in. high, 2oz. (Christie's) $2,860 £1,887

A Victorian silver gilt two-handled vase-shaped cup and cover, by John S. Hunt, 1949, 28¾in. high, 88oz. (Christie's) $3,775 £2,640

Judaica: An 18th century German silver gilt Kiddush cup, Augsburg, 1763/5, 13cm. high, 3.75oz. (Phillips) $4,131 £2,700

One of a pair of George III Irish two-handled cups, maker's mark WH, Dublin, circa 1760, 29oz. (Phillips) $1,401 £980

An Austro-Hungarian stirrup cup modelled as a kitten's head, circa 1870, 7.4cm. high, 4.25oz. (Phillips) $906 £600

A German parcel gilt cup and associated cover, Nuremberg, circa 1620, maker's mark IF, 9¼in. high, 6oz.3dwt. (Christie's) $1,415 £990

A William IV two-handled cup, by Paul Storr, 1835, the foot stamped Storr & Mortimer, 10½in. high, 109oz. (Christie's) $14,943 £10,450

A late Victorian neo-classical style two-handled trophy cup, by Charles S. Harris, London, 1899, 15in. high, 81oz. (Woolley & Wallis) $789 £530

CUPS

A 19th century French racing trophy cup, the lower part of the foot electroplate, circa 1870, 38cm. high, weighable silver 115oz. (Phillips) $2,574 £1,800

A George III Scottish gilt lined cup, W. & P. Cunningham, Edinburgh, 1791, 9¼in. high, 21.75oz. (Christie's) $290 £190

A George III silver gilt two-handled cup and cover, by Philip Rundell, 1818, the cover 1819, 13in. high, 94oz. (Christie's) $3,460 £2,420

A silver gilt two-handled 'Trafalgar Vase', by B. Smith, 1807, the finial by C. Gordon, circa 1835, 15¾in. high, 104oz. (Christie's) $4,719 £3,300

A spout cup, by Edward Winslow, Boston, circa 1710-20, 3¼in. high, 4oz. (Christie's) $19,800 £13,064

An Indian Colonial two-handled campana-shaped cup and cover, by Pittar & Co., Calcutta, circa 1838, 10½in. high, 45oz. (Christie's) $1,101 £770

A replica of the Broderers Cup, circa 1830, maker's mark only JB perhaps for John Beauchamp, cf. Grimwade No. 1785, 16in. high, 61oz. (Christie's) $3,146 £2,200

A Regency silver gilt two-handled campana shaped cup, by W. & P. Cunningham, Edin., 1818, 10¼in. high. (Reeds Rains) $504 £350

A Victorian campana shaped cup on a floral foot, maker's initials probably I.S., London, 1864, 7in. high, 10oz. (Christie's) $330 £198

One of a pair of second-course dishes, bearing probably spurious marks, D crowned possibly from Riom, 1781-85, maker's mark SWB, 13½in. diam., 68oz. (Christie's) $1,320 £929

A George III shaped oblong entree dish, cover and handle, by Paul Storr, 1809, 16½in. wide overall, 68oz. (Christie's) $4,957 £3,240

A Louis XVI second-course dish, by Jacques-Charles Mongenot, Paris, 1788, with the charge and discharge of Henri Clavel, 15in. diam., 44oz. (Christie's) $3,300 £2,324

One of a pair of George III silver gilt kidney shaped vegetable dishes, by B. Smith, 1807, 11¾in. long, 66oz. (Christie's) $15,697 £10,260

One of ten Louis XV dinner plates, by various makers, 10.1/8in. diam., 184oz. (Christie's) $4,400 £3,099

One of a pair of German meat dishes, by Johann C. Otersen, 1784-91, 18in. long, 119oz. (Christie's) $11,000 £7,748

One of a pair of French second-course dishes, by J. Chaumet, Paris, circa 1918, 14in. diam., 136oz. (Christie's) $8,800 £6,198

A set of four German second-course dishes, by Franz A. H. Nubell, circa 1820, 12¼in. diam., 154oz. (Christie's) $26,400 £18,596

One of a pair of shaped circular silver gilt dishes, circa 1700, maker's mark only WH between rosettes and pellets, 15in. diam., 65oz. (Christie's) $5,948 £3,888

DISHES

One of a set of six Queen Anne soup plates, by Philip Rollos I, London, 1706, 9.7/8in. diam., 108oz. (Christie's)
$55,000 £38,742

One of four George III shaped oblong entree dishes and covers, by Paul Storr, 1814, each on hot-water stands by Matthew Boulton, 11in. long, 281oz. (Christie's)
$28,314 £19,800

A Louis XV second-course dish, Paris, 1771, 12¾in. diam., 34oz. (Christie's)
$1,760 £1,239

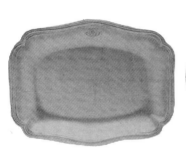

One of a pair of Louis XV entree dishes, Paris, 1773, maker's mark apparently that of Jean-Francois Genu, 11in. long, 41oz. (Christie's)
$5,500 £3,874

An Arts & Crafts fluted circular cake stand on a rising foot, J.S.B., London, 1915, 12¼in. high, 26.75oz. (Christie's) $506 £352

A 17th century German silver gilt shaped oval dish, by Hans Mehrer, Augsburg, circa 1660, 46.5cm. long, 31.5oz. (Phillips) $6,000 £4,000

A Louis XVI dish, by Jacques Debrie, Paris, 1777, decagonal, 11.3/8in. diam., 22oz. (Christie's) $4,400 £3,099

A set of twelve Spanish dinner plates, by Larranaga, San Sebastian, mid 18th century, 9½in. diam., 185oz. (Christie's) $13,200 £9,298

A George II circular strawberry dish, by Paul Crespin, 1735, 9½in. diam., 19oz. 5dwt. (Christie's)
$4,296 £2,808

One of a pair of George III shaped circular vegetable dishes, by J. Parker and E. Wakelin, 1768, 11in. diam., 43oz. (Christie's)
$5,948 £3,888

A Louis XVI large second-course dish, by Jacques-Charles Mongenot, Paris, 1788, with the charge of Henri Clavel, 18in. diam., 101oz. (Christie's)
$9,350 £6,586

One of a set of six Austrian dinner plates, by Ferdinand Ebenwimer, 1776, 9.7/8in. diam., 98oz. (Christie's)
$5,500 £3,874

A Louis XV second-course dish, by A. Pinel, Rodez, circa 1750, 14¼in. diam., 51oz. (Christie's)
$6,600 £4,649

One of a pair of German silver gilt second-course dishes, by G. Menzel, 1717-18, 12¾in. diam., the covers by C. Winter, 1729-30, 11.3/8in. diam., 163oz. (Christie's)
$192,500 £135,597

One of a pair of George II fluted dishes, by B. Godfrey, London, 1735, 8.3/8in. diam., 25oz. (Christie's)
$15,400 £10,847

Eighteen German dinner plates, by Joachim C. Neuss, seven 1801 and eleven 1804, 10in. diam., 345oz. (Christie's) $26,400 £18,596

One of a pair of silver covered vegetable dishes, by Tiffany & Co., N.Y., 1947-55, 5in. high, 11in. wide, 92oz.10dwt. (Christie's) $2,860 £2,001

A set of twelve George III silver gilt dinner plates, by John Wakelin and Wm. Taylor, London, six 1787 and six 1788, 9¼in. diam., 181oz. (Christie's)
$26,400 £18,596

DISHES

A Louis XV basin, by Gilles
Degage, Nantes, 1766, 12in.
diam., 30oz. (Christie's)
$1,760 £1,239

A Louis XVI second-course
dish, Paris, 1782, maker's
mark illegible, 13in. diam.,
27oz. (Christie's)
$880 £619

One of three George IV
second-course dishes, by
Philip Rundell, London,
1822, 11.7/8in. diam., 87oz.
(Christie's) $8,250 £5,811

One of a set of four George II
fluted dishes, by B. Godfrey,
London, 1732, 8.3/8in. diam.,
52oz. (Christie's)
$39,600 £27,894

One of a set of four Russian
silver gilt second-course
dishes and covers, the covers
by J. W. Feurbach, 1766,
12.5/8in. diam. of dishes,
391oz. (Christie's)
$41,800 £29,443

One of a pair of Louis XV
silver gilt dinner plates, by
Nicolas Outrebon, Paris,
1738, 10in. diam., 50oz.
10dwt. (Christie's)
$4,400 £3,099

Part of a set of thirty-six
German silver gilt dinner
plates, by Johann H. Fromm,
1821-41, 9in. diam., 375oz.
(Christie's) $30,800 £21,695

One of a set of four George
III entree dishes, covers and
handles, by Paul Storr, 1812,
12in. long, 236oz. (Christie's)
$15,697 £10,260

Twelve Austrian dinner plates,
seven 1761, and five 1763,
maker's mark IS, 9¾in. diam.,
203oz. (Christie's)
$9,900 £6,973

A shaped oval French meat dish, by Jacques-Gabriel-Andre Bompart, Paris, 1798-1809, 23in. long, 83oz.10dwt. (Christie's) $2,860   £2,014

A George II small shaped circular dish, by Paul de Lamerie, 1738, 6.1/8in. diam., 9oz.8dwt. (Christie's) $9,123 £6,380

A German meat dish, by Johann C. Otersen, 1784-91, 22in. long, 49oz. (Christie's) $5,280 £3,719

One of a pair of German silver gilt second-course dishes, by G. Menzel, Augsburg, 1717-18, 15.7/8in. diam., 113oz. (Christie's) $99,000 £69,735

One of a pair of Dutch meat dishes, The Hague, 1756, maker's mark a head in a shield with coronet above, 22in. long, 199oz. (Christie's) $9,350 £6,586

One of a set of four French silver gilt cake plates, by J. Chaumet, Paris, circa 1918, 10½in. square, 104oz. (Christie's) $7,150 £5,036

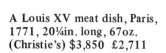

A Louis XV meat dish, Paris, 1771, 20¼in. long, 67oz. (Christie's) $3,850 £2,711

A Charles I shaped circular two-handled sweetmeat dish, 1634, maker's mark IP a bell between, 8½in. diam., 5oz. 10dwt. (Christie's) $4,089 £2,860

A Belgian meat dish, by Henricus de Potter Sr., Brussels, 1757, 13in. long, 28oz. (Christie's) $2,640 £1,859

A German deep dish, by J. J. Biller II, Augsburg, 1773-75, 17¼in. long, 24oz. (Christie's) $3,850 £2,711

A Russian silver gilt souffle dish, by Carl Tegelsten, St. Petersburg, 1850, 10in. diam., 32oz. (Christie's) $7,700 £5,423

One of a pair of German meat dishes, by Franz A. H. Nubell, circa 1820, 18¼in. long, 123oz. (Christie's) $24,200 £17,046

One of a set of twelve plates, by Gorham Manuf. Co., 1907, 10¼in. diam., 204oz. (Christie's) $4,400 £2,903

One of a pair of Louis XV meat dishes, by Barthelemy Samson II, Toulouse, 1768, 13½in. long, 51oz. (Christie's) $4,180 £2,944

One of a pair of Louis XVI entree dishes, by F. Corbie, Paris, 1783, 9½in. square, 40oz. (Christie's) $4,950 £3,486

An oval meat dish and cover, designed by H. Nielsen, stamped marks Dessin HN Georg Jensen 600S, 46.7cm. wide, 129oz. (Christie's) $11,011 £7,700

One of a set of four George III silver gilt dessert dishes, by John Wakelin and R. Garrard I, London, 1799, 9in. long, 73oz. (Christie's) $55,000 £38,742

One of a pair of William IV Irish shaped oblong entree dishes and covers, by James Fray, Dublin, 1834, 11¾in. long, 168oz. (Christie's) $4,719 £3,300

One of a pair of George III oval two-handled entree dishes and covers, by A. Fogelberg, 1772, 11in. long, gross 55oz. (Christie's) $2,988 £2,090

One of four George III cushion shaped entree dishes, covers and handles, by J. Angell, 1818, one handle by R. Gainsford, 1820, 12in. long, 272oz. (Christie's) $6,279 £4,104

One of a pair of Georgian entree dishes and covers, one London, 1767, maker's mark IW, the other by J. Bridge, 1825, 14.1/8in. long, 101oz. (Christie's) $6,050 £4,261

One of twelve George III shaped circular dinner plates, by George Methuen, 1752, 9½in. diam., 174oz. (Christie's) $6,940 £4,536

A pair of Victorian oval plated entree dishes, 12in. long. (Parsons, Welch & Cowell) $246 £160

One of three George II second-course dishes, by P. Archambo I and Peter Meure, London, 1753, 11.7/8in. diam., 79oz. (Christie's) $8,250 £5,811

One of six German dinner plates, 1784-91, five with maker's mark IFF, and one by J. P. Crutzenberg, 9½in. diam., 76oz. (Christie's) $7,700 £5,423

One of a pair of French fish platters, by J. Chaumet, Paris, circa 1918, 27½in. long, 255oz. (Christie's) $18,700 £13,172

One of six German dinner plates, four by the widow of J. C. Lieberkuhn, circa 1740, and two by A. Fickert, late 19th century, 9.5/8in. diam., 107oz. (Christie's) $6,050 £4,261

EWERS

An Austro-Hungarian wine
ewer, 1821, 41in. high.
(Christie's) $1,496 £935

A Victorian baluster wine
ewer, by Elkington & Co.,
Ltd., Birmingham, 1893,
12¼in. high, 54oz.
(Christie's) $2,602 £1,540

An American ovoid wine
ewer, by Samuel Kirk,
Baltimore, circa 1830,
16¼in. high, 48oz.
(Christie's) $3,160 £1,870

A presentation ewer, by
Baldwin Gardiner, N.Y., circa
1835, 13½in. high, 45oz.
10dwt. (Christie's)
$1,100 £674

A ewer, by John Kitts, Louis-
ville, 1838-76, 12¼in. high,
17oz. (Christie's)
$2,640 £1,619

A George II helmet shaped
ewer, by David Willaume II,
1742, 10½in. high, 53oz.
(Christie's)
$69,400 £45,360

A vase-shaped silver ewer, by
Thos. Fletcher, Phila., circa
1838, 13¼in. high, 39oz.
(Christie's) $1,320 £923

A large covered ewer, bearing
spurious marks for Charles-
Cesar Haudry, Paris, 1745,
11in. high, 55oz. (Christie's)
$13,200 £9,298

A pitcher, by Adolf Himmel,
New Orleans, circa 1854-61,
11in. high, 25oz. (Christie's)
$1,650 £1,012

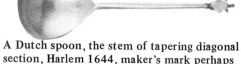

A James I apostle spoon surmounted by the gilt figure of St. Paul, 1604, maker's mark a crescent enclosing a W, probably for Wm. Cawdell. (Christie's) $1,288 £842

A Dutch spoon, the stem of tapering diagonal section, Harlem 1644, maker's mark perhaps that of Dirck Dircksz. (Christie's)
$1,321 £864

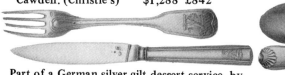

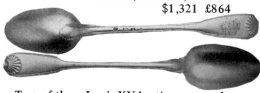

Part of a German silver gilt dessert service, by Abraham Warnberger IV, Augsburg, 1781-89, eleven pieces by C.-H. Constant, Berlin, 1788-1802, 36 pieces, 29oz.10dwt. (Christie's)
$3,300 £2,324

Two of three Louis XV basting spoons, by Nicolas Collier, Paris, 1768, with the charge and discharge of Julien Alaterre, 12½in. long, 17oz.10dwt. (Christie's) $3,080 £2,169

Part of a Louis XV silver gilt dessert service, by the Widow of Jean-Frederic Fritz, Strasbourg, 1773, one spoon and two knives Vienna, 1790, 150oz., 54 pieces. (Christie's) $8,250 £5,811

Part of a set of eighteen Louis XV silver gilt dessert spoons and eighteen dessert forks, by Johann Heinrich Oertel, Strasbourg, circa 1773, 75oz. (Christie's) $9,900 £6,973

Part of a set of twelve George II fiddle and shell pattern dessert forks and six matching dessert spoons, by Paul de Lamierie, circa 1740, 27oz. (Christie's) $20,449 £14,300

Part of a Louis XVI silver gilt dessert service, by Jean-Louis Kirstein, Strasbourg, 1778, 98oz., 54 pieces. (Christie's)
$15,400 £10,847

FLATWARE

A 16th century French spoon, the stem of tapering diamond section, with cone finial, marked with a crowned date letter? said by Emery to be circa 1450. (Christie's)
$826 £540

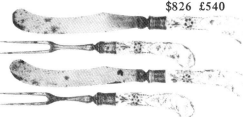

Part of a set of six Bow polychrome knives and forks, the pistol-grip handles enamelled in Chinese style, circa 1750, the handles 7.5 and 7cm. (Phillips) $1,047 £680

Four of twelve Dutch silver gilt table knives and twelve dessert knives, Amsterdam, circa 1750, maker's mark I.B. (Christie's) $2,860 £2,014

Part of a Mappin & Webb silver table service, 'Rosalind', designed by Eric Clements, London, hallmarks for 1963, in teak canteen, 153oz. 8dwt. gross weight. (Christie's) $7,435 £4,860

Part of a Louis XV silver gilt dessert service by the workshop of Jean-Louis Imlin III, Stras., the knives 1770, the forks and spoons 1769, 69oz., 36 pieces. (Christie's) $7,700 £5,423

Part of a Louis XVI silver gilt dessert service, the twelve dessert spoons and twelve dessert forks by J.-E. Langlois, Paris, 1782, the twelve dessert knives, Paris, 1779, 36 pieces. (Christie's) $17,600 £12,397

Part of a set of twelve Louis XVI table spoons and ten table forks, by N. Collier, Paris, 1776, together with two other table forks, 71oz., 24 pieces. (Christie's) $3,300 £2,324

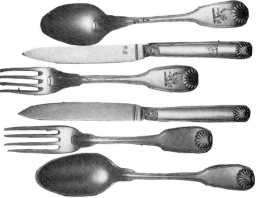

Part of a Louis XVI silver gilt dessert service, by Johann-Heinrich Oertel, Strasbourg, 1778, 1779, etc., fiddle, thread and shell pattern, 119oz., 54 pieces. (Christie's)
$13,200 £9,298

Part of a Georg Jensen 75-piece 'Pyramid' pattern table service, designed by Harald Nielsen, 1926, stamped marks, 132oz.6dwt. gross weight. (Christie's) $8,712 £6,060

Part of a German silver gilt dessert service, by Phillip Jacob Jager I, Augsburg, 1732-33, 146oz., 66 pieces. (Christie's) $19,800 £13,947

Two of twenty-one Dutch table knives and twelve dessert knives, nine Maastricht, circa 1760, maker's mark on some FH crowned, the rest Amsterdam, maker's mark on some IB. (Christie's) $1,320 £929

Part of a set of French porcelain-handled table silver, by Puiforcat, Paris, circa 1900, the handles Chantilly, 18th century, 54 pieces. (Christie's) $3,080 £2,169

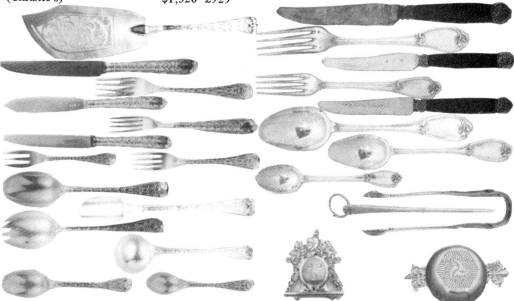

Part of a 138-piece Elizabethan pattern composite table service, 1846, 1864, 1883 etc., some modern, weight without table and cheese knives 250oz. (Christie's) $8,651 £6,050

A 19th century canteen dinner service, flatware by Henin et Vivier, dishes by Puiforcat, Paris, circa 1870, weighable silver 341.5oz., 156 pieces. (Phillips) $6,864 £4,800

FLATWARE

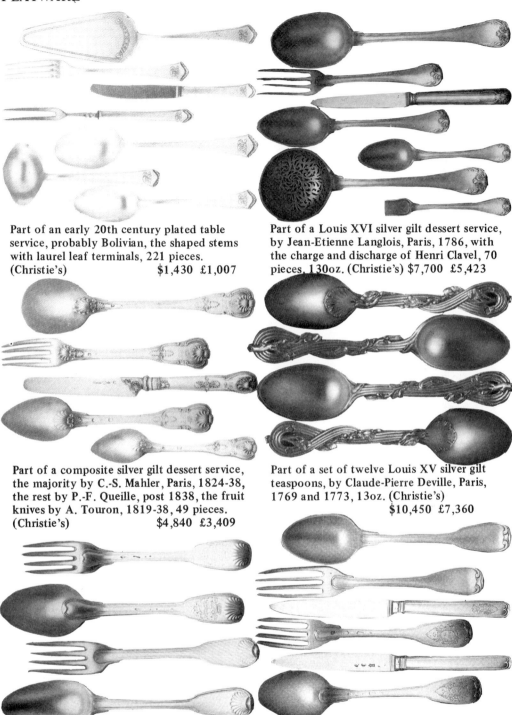

Part of an early 20th century plated table service, probably Bolivian, the shaped stems with laurel leaf terminals, 221 pieces. (Christie's) $1,430 £1,007

Part of a Louis XVI silver gilt dessert service, by Jean-Etienne Langlois, Paris, 1786, with the charge and discharge of Henri Clavel, 70 pieces, 130oz. (Christie's) $7,700 £5,423

Part of a composite silver gilt dessert service, the majority by C.-S. Mahler, Paris, 1824-38, the rest by P.-F. Queille, post 1838, the fruit knives by A. Touron, 1819-38, 49 pieces. (Christie's) $4,840 £3,409

Part of a set of twelve Louis XV silver gilt teaspoons, by Claude-Pierre Deville, Paris, 1769 and 1773, 13oz. (Christie's) $10,450 £7,360

Part of a set of twenty-seven Louis XV table-spoons and twenty-seven table forks, by Nicolas Collier, Paris, 1768, fiddle, thread and shell pattern, 156oz. (Christie's) $7,700 £5,423

Part of a Louis XV silver gilt dessert service, by Edme-Pierre Balzac, Paris, 1768/69, the reeded fiddle pattern, together with a silver table fork, circa 1777, 69oz., 37 pieces. (Christie's) $11,000 £7,748

FLATWARE

A soup ladle, Persian pattern, by Tiffany & Co., N.Y., 1872–circa 1875, 12¾in. long, overall, 7oz.10dwt. (Christie's) $385 £269

A soup ladle, wave edge pattern, with a spirally-fluted oval bowl, by Tiffany & Co., N.Y., 1884-91, 10¾in. long, 5oz.10dwt. (Christie's) $418 £292

A pair of late 18th century tongs, marked 'IE', English or American, 5½in. long, 1oz. (Christie's) $550 £384

Stilton scoop with ivory handle and silver mount, marked Sheffield 1935. (Peter Wilson) $84 £60

Part of a French silver gilt dessert service, by Francois-Daniel Imlin, Strasbourg, Warden's mark a five, for 1785 or 1796, fiddle and thread pattern, 37 pieces, 115oz. (Christie's) $9,900 £6,973

Part of a set of twelve Louis XV/Louis XVI tablespoons and twelve table forks, by Antoine Chaye, Paris, 1752, fiddle and thread pattern, 68oz. (Christie's) $1,760 £1,239

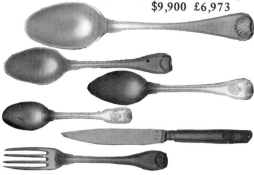

Part of a Louis XV silver gilt dessert service, Strasbourg, 1770 and 1771, thread and shell pattern, 78oz., 52 pieces. (Christie's) $18,700 £13,172

Part of a Louis XV silver gilt dessert service, fiddle, thread and shell pattern, 70oz., 36 pieces. (Christie's) $7,700 £5,423

Two of twelve Louis XV dessert knives and six cheese knives, by Jean-Pierre Chezelle, Paris, 1766, weight of dessert knives 30oz. (Christie's) $8,800 £6,198

Three of thirty-six, possibly late 18th century, Dutch table knives, eighteen cheese knives and twelve fruit knives, 66 pieces. (Christie's) $9,900 £6,973

FLATWARE

A French 'Puritan' spoon, with notched top to the stem, engraved with initials FH, Paris 1621, maker's mark perhaps HR. (Christie's)
$1,404 £918

A Dutch spoon with curved stem of diamond section and hoof finial, by E. Loesinck, Groningen 1656, together with another. (Christie's) $1,404 £918

A soup ladle with a circular bowl, by James Kendall, Delaware, 1795-1808, 11¾in. long, 5oz.10dwt. (Christie's) $825 £577

Early 17th century French three-pronged table fork with lobed top, by C. Ferrand, maker's mark perhaps CP for Chas. Payen. (Christie's)
$3,139 £2,052

Part of a Louis XV agate-handled dessert service, by Eloy Guerin, Paris, 1740, 24 pieces. (Christie's) $15,400 £10,847

Five of twelve George III stag-hunt pattern table forks, by Paul Storr, 1816, 43oz. (Christie's) $1,487 £972

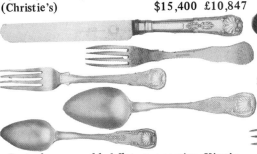

Part of an assembled flatware service, King's pattern, by R. & W. Wilson, Philadelphia, 1825-46, 175oz. excluding knives. (Christie's)
$3,080 £2,155

Part of a service of fruiting vine design, also a pair of pierced and engraved fish carvers with bone handles, 1906, weighable silver 22oz., 68 pieces. (Phillips) $1,573 £1,100

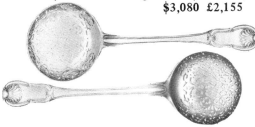

A Louis XV sugar sifter, Paris, 1744-50 and a silver gilt example, Paris, 1738-44, 8¼in. and 8.5/8in. long, 7oz. (Christie's) $935 £658

Part of a set of seventeen silver gilt dessert-spoons and seventeen dessert forks, all with Belgian surcharge mark of 1814-1832, 61oz. (Christie's) $2,750 £1,937

An Art Nouveau silver picture frame, 35cm. high, marked WN and for Chester 1903.
(Phillips) $518 £360

A Wm. Hutton & Sons Arts & Crafts silver picture frame, London hallmarks for 1903, 20cm. high. (Christie's)
      $2,272 £1,485

A Wm. Hutton & Sons Arts & Crafts silver picture frame, London hallmarks for 1903, 20cm. high. (Christie's)
      $2,187 £1,430

An Edwardian Art Nouveau silver and enamel photograph frame, Wm. Hutton & Sons Ltd., London, 1904, 10.25in. high, also an Elkington & Co. vase, Birmingham, 1906.
(Reeds Rains) $1,162 £750

A Liberty & Co. silver and enamelled picture frame, 19 x 14.50cm., with Art Nouveau hinged support, hallmarked L. & Co., Birmingham, 1899.
(Phillips) $2,664 £1,850

An Art Nouveau photograph frame, maker's marks W.N. and Chester hallmarks for 1903, 31cm. high. (Christie's)
      $3,048 £1,870

A late Victorian oblong photograph frame, Birmingham, 1895, 8½in. high. (Christie's)
      $273 £190

An Art Nouveau silver picture frame, 28cm. high, marked SB, Birmingham, 1903.
(Phillips) $374 £260

A late Victorian oblong photograph frame, by Wm. Comyns, London, 1904, 6¾in. high. (Christie's)
      $230 £160

GOBLETS

One of two Edwardian silver gilt goblets, by Edward Barnard & Sons Ltd., 1902 and 1903, 10¼in. high, 46oz. (Christie's)
$1,415 £990

One of a pair of George III gilt lined goblets, London, 1770. (Christie's) $880 £550

A German silver gilt goblet, by Johann Cristoph Treffler, Augsburg, early 18th century, 4½in. high, 3oz.5dwt. (Christie's) $7,064 £4,180

Early 19th century Spanish Colonial silver gilt chalice, 8½in. high, 12oz. (Christie's)
$1,870 £1,317

One of a pair of George III plain goblets, by John Wakelin and Wm. Taylor, 1779, 6in. high, 15oz. (Christie's) $2,359 £1,650

Late 18th century goblet on trumpet foot, circa 1790. (Phillips)
$150 £95

A China Trade goblet, by Leeching, probably Hong Kong, circa 1870, 7½in. high, 8oz.14dwt. (Christie's) $707 £495

An Omar Ramsden beaten silver goblet, the foot with inscription MCMXXI, 5in. high, London hallmarks for 1920. (Christie's)
$271 £180

An early 19th century Mexican silver gilt chalice, maker's mark possibly that of Jose M. Martinez, 9¼in. high, 22oz. (Christie's) $2,200 £1,549

SILVER

A George III inkstand, by Samuel and George Whitford, London, 1804, 9in. long, 17.75oz. free. (Christie's) $960 £600

A late Victorian oblong inkstand, by Wm. Comyns, London, 1895, 12¼in. long, 16oz. (Christie's) $950 £638

An early Victorian shaped oblong inkstand, by R.F.A., Birmingham, 1838, 11½in. long, 20.75oz. (Christie's) $2,288 £1,430

A Victorian shell-shaped inkstand, by Elkington & Co., 1851, 9¾in. long. (Christie's) $1,022 £605

A rectangular inkstand, fitted with a candleholder, by John and Thomas Settle, Sheffield, 1817, 15oz. (Christie's) $3,300 £2,024

A Victorian rococo silver gilt shaped oval inkstand on bun feet, by G. Fox, London, 1875, 10in. long, 9.25oz. free. (Christie's) $1,108 £770

A George III inkstand, by Samuel and George Whitford, London, 1804, 10in. long, 29oz. weighable silver. (Christie's) $2,420 £1,579

An Australian plate mounted emu egg inkstand, 11in. wide, circa 1870. (Abridge Auctions) $680 £425

A George III silver gilt shaped circular inkpot and cover, by B. Smith II and B. Smith, Jnr., 1817, 6in. high, 32oz. (Christie's) $4,647 £2,750

A George II oblong inkstand, by Edward Wakelin, 1751, 13½in. long, 59oz. (Christie's) $11,511 £7,150

A late Victorian circular tortoise-shell inkstand with plated rococo scroll mounts, on bun feet, London, 1899, 5¼in. (Christie's) $385 £249

An oblong gallery inkstand on bracket feet, 8in. long, 13.25oz. free. (Christie's) $401 £242

722

INKSTANDS

A William IV inkstand on shell and foliate feet, by Joseph and John Angell, London, 1836, 8in. long, 10oz. (Christie's)
$924 £550

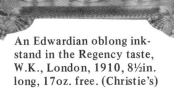

An Edwardian oblong inkstand in the Regency taste, W.K., London, 1910, 8½in. long, 17oz. free. (Christie's)
$1,095 £660

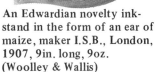

An Edwardian novelty inkstand in the form of an ear of maize, maker I.S.B., London, 1907, 9in. long, 9oz. (Woolley & Wallis)
$1,280 £800

A George II shaped rectangular inkstand, by John Jacob, 1752, 11in. long, 43oz. (Christie's)
$13,013 £7,700

An 18th century style beaded oblong inkstand on ball feet, 8in. long. (Christie's)
$144 £90

A Dutch 19th century beaded oblong gallery inkstand on bracket feet, 6in. long, 13oz. (Christie's)
$320 £200

Victorian gilt metal inkwell modelled as a parakeet on a branch, the head hinged to reveal a space for the well. (Lots Road Galleries)
$214 £150

A Victorian Scottish inkwell, by Aitchison of Edinburgh, 1885, inkwell 15cm. high. (Phillips) $1,296 £900

Plated inkwell in the form of a Zulu warrior, 10in. high. (Worsfolds) $217 £150

An Edward VII inkstand, by J. B. Carrington, 1903, 29cm. wide, weighable silver 40oz. (Phillips) $2,054 £1,300

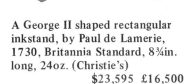

A George II shaped rectangular inkstand, by Paul de Lamerie, 1730, Britannia Standard, 8¾in. long, 24oz. (Christie's)
$23,595 £16,500

A Victorian inkstand, by Chas. Thomas and G. Fox, 24cm. diam., 1852, 27oz. (Phillips)
$1,716 £1,200

A George III beaded vase-shaped hot water jug by J. B. Stephenson, London, circa 1775, 11¼in. high, 23oz. gross. (Christie's) $618 £418

A pitcher of baluster form, with a curved spout and S-scroll handle, by Jones, Ball & Poor, Boston, circa 1852, 11¼in. high, 29oz.(Christie's) $1,100 £725

An urn-shaped pitcher, by Charters, Cann & Dunn, N.Y., circa 1850, 8½in. high, 12oz. (Christie's) $264 £184

A silver gilt mounted tiger-ware jug with mermaid thumbpiece, 7½in. high. (Christie's) $4,250 £2,640

A vase-shaped pitcher, American, with unidentified eagle touch mark, circa 1825-35, 12in. high, 35oz. (Christie's) $1,430 £1,000

A 19th century American 'ivy chased' jug, by Tiffany & Co., circa 1870, 23cm. high, 27.5oz. (Phillips) $3,003 £2,100

A silver vase-shaped pitcher, with double scroll handle, by Samuel Kirk & Son, 1846-61, or 1880-90, 10in. high, 25oz. (Christie's) $1,100 £769

A Louis XVI hot milk jug, by Nicolas Canet, Paris, 1785, 6¼in. high, 9oz.10dwt. (Christie's) $1,760 £1,239

A George I covered jug, maker Paul de Lamerie, Britannia Standard, London, 1724, 7in. high, 16oz. (Hobbs & Chambers) $600 £420

JUGS

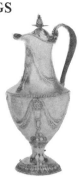

A George III vase-shaped hot water jug, by Emick Romer, 1776, 12in. high, gross 30oz. (Christie's) $5,205 £3,080

A Louis XVI hot milk jug, Paris, 1780, maker's mark indistinct, 5¼in. high, gross weight 6oz. (Christie's) $1,650 £1,162

A Louis XVI hot water jug, by Louis Clery, Paris, 1789, with the charge and discharge of Jean-Francois Kalandrin, 9¾in. high, gross weight 20oz. (Christie's) $1,320 £929

A vase-shaped ewer, by Wm. Forbes for Ball, Black & Co., N.Y., 1851-circa 1860, 16½in. high, 46oz. (Christie's) $1,100 £725

A pitcher of baluster form with an open handle, by Gorham Manuf. Co., 1897, 8¾in. high, gross weight 31oz. (Christie's) $1,980 £1,306

A small pitcher, designed by J. Rohde, stamped marks JR Georg Jensen GJ 295 432A, circa 1928, 22.7cm. high, 17oz. (Christie's) $1,494 £1,045

An Elkington & Co. electroplated jug designed by Dr. C. Dresser, 19.3cm. high. (Christie's) $1,982 £1,296.

One of a matched pair of plain vase-shaped hot water jugs, 9in. high, 20.75oz. gross. (Christie's) $390 £264

A milk pot on three scroll legs with pad feet, by T. Stoutenburgh, N.Y., circa 1735, 4¾in. high, 7oz.10dwt. (Christie's) $4,400 £2,903

Mid 19th century Australian silver mounted emu's egg table ornament on a wood plinth, by Wm. Edwards, 11½in. high. (Christie's)
$5,977 £4,180

A Charles Boynton silver toast-rack of oval, almost boat shape, 9.5cm. high, 5.5oz., marked CB for London 1936. (Phillips) $504 £350

Mid 17th century German silver gilt mounted canister, unmarked, 6½in. high. (Christie's)
$4,719 £3,300

A parcel gilt toothpick-holder formed as the figure of Neptune standing before a shell, Oporto, circa 1850, 7in. high, 10oz. 6dwt. (Christie's)
$943 £660

A set of three Tiffany & Co. spirit flasks, the flattened rectangular bodies with screwed hinged covers, 20.6cm. high. (Christie's)
$2,059 £1,430

A George III argyll, by H. Bateman, 1775, 18cm. high, 10oz. (Phillips)
$3,003 £2,100

A silver mounted coconut cup, by Peter and Anne Bateman, 1792, 4¾in. high. (Christie's)
$786 £550

A Victorian cylindrical commemorative urn, formed as the Choragic monument of Lysicrates in Athens, 1888, 8in. high, 50oz. (Christie's)
$1,101 £770

Late 19th century silver mounted cut glass beehive honeypot, unmarked, 8¾in. high. (Christie's)
$8,262 £5,400

MISCELLANEOUS

A silver menu holder, with a caption 'Give me a Bite', 10cm. wide, 1.25oz., marked H. & A, Birmingham, 1901. (Phillips) $136 £95

A Continental model knight in Gothic style armour, import marks, 13¼in. long. (Christie's) $3,146 £2,200

A small silver mounted prayer-book, the interior printed in German and with date 1652, 3in. long. (Christie's) $1,337 £935

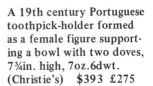

A Dunhill architect's lighter, silver metal formed as a 12in. box ruler surmounted by a lighter with wheel and flint mechanism. (Christie's) $871 £605

A Charles II shaving jug, dish and soap box, the jug circa 1677, the dish 1682, the soap box circa 1680, 52oz. (Christie's) $38,005 £24,840

A 19th century Portuguese toothpick-holder formed as a female figure supporting a bowl with two doves, 7¾in. high, 7oz.6dwt. (Christie's) $393 £275

A toastrack, the base in the form of 'The Man in the Moon', the handle as a cast owl, 17cm. wide, 5cm. high, circa 1900. (Phillips) $371 £260

A Victorian plated spoon warmer, in the form of a ship's buoy, 21cm. long, circa 1870. (Phillips) $200 £140

A Dutch silver plated jardiniere with rope twist rim, on paw feet, 20½in. wide. (Christie's) $4,404 £3,080

'Zeppelin' a white metal cigarette and match holder, 22.8cm. long. (Christie's) $267 £187

Late 19th century Viennese silver gilt and enamel coach and horses, maker's initials F.W., 10½in. long. (Christie's) $1,817 £1,188

MG Magic Midget George Eyston's Record Breaking Car, modelled as a silver petrol lighter, Birmingham, 1931, 7½in. long. (Onslow's) $1,573 £1,100

An ivory and silver cigar holder on six flattened ball feet, by Tiffany & Co., N.Y., 1881, 6½in. high. (Christie's) $5,280 £3,694

A George III honey skep and stand, by Paul Storr, 1799, with clear glass liner, 4¼in. high, 10oz.11dwt. (Christie's) $12,641 £7,480

A George IV fireman's arm badge, by R. Emes and E. Barnard, 1823, 6in. high, 9oz.5dwt. (Christie's) $2,479 £1,540

A George III plain vase-shaped argyll, by Wm. Elliott, 1818, 8½in. high, gross 25oz. (Christie's) $3,718 £2,200

A WMF plated corkholder, each cork surmounted by a sculptural figure, 15.5cm. high. (Christie's) $896 £550

A late 19th century Russian vodka set, maker's mark IIN (Cyrillics), St. Petersburg, circa 1890, 7oz. (Phillips) $1,072 £750

MUGS

A gilt lined christening mug with loop handle, 3¾in. high, and another 3¾in. high. (Christie's) $158 £105

A 19th century Indian Colonial gilt lined baluster mug, Hamilton & Co., Calcutta, 6¼in. high, 13oz. (Christie's) $403 £264

A Victorian beaded tapering christening mug, London, 1865, 4in. high. (Christie's) $330 £198

An early George III baluster mug, by T. Whipham and C. Wright, London, 1760, 8.5oz. (Woolley & Wallis) $752 £470

A small mug, barrel-shaped, with a reeded rim and foot-rim, by Thadeus Keeler, N.Y., circa 1805-13, 2oz. (Christie's) $440 £290

A George I mug with scroll handle, by George Wickes, London, 1726, 8.9oz. (Woolley & Wallis) $662 £460

A silver applied enamelled copper mug, by Gorham Manuf. Co., Providence, 1881, 6½in. high. (Christie's) $1,650 £1,154

An 18th century Channel Islands mug on collet foot, 8.75cm. high, by Philippe Le Vavasseur dit Durell, circa 1745, 5oz. (Phillips) $514 £360

A Victorian christening mug with loop handle, W. E., London, 1878, 4½in. high. (Christie's) $248 £160

MUSTARDS

A Victorian melon fluted pear-shaped mustard pot, by Joseph Angell, London, 1859, 4¼in. high. (Christie's) $118 £82

A Regency cauldron mustard pot on floral and scrolling foliate feet, London, 1816, 5in. high, 9oz. free. (Christie's) $285 £198

A George IV gilt lined mustard pot, by Pearce & Burrows, London, 1825, 4½in. high. (Christie's) $174 £121

A 17th century Continental silver gilt mustard pot of inverted bell shape, circa 1680, 16cm. high, 7.5oz. (Phillips) $800 £560

A Liberty & Co. three-piece silver condiment set, Birmingham hallmarks for 1899, pepper-pot 5.5cm. high. (Christie's) $589 £385

A Victorian mustard pot, by W. H., London, 1841. (Christie's) $422 £264

A Victorian circular mustard pot, with blue glass liner, by G. R., London, 1855. (Christie's) $440 £275

A Victorian medieval-style baluster mustard pot and matching castor, by John Hardman & Co., Birmingham, 1869, 13.75oz. (Christie's) $918 £638

A Victorian hexagonal mustard pot, with blue glass liner, London, 1843. (Christie's) $387 £242

PORRINGERS

A Commonwealth two-handled porringer, by Gilbert Shepherd, 1658, 2½in. high, 4oz.14dwt. (Christie's)
$2,516 £1,760

A silver Guild of Handicrafts single handled porringer with attributed design to C. R. Ashbee, 7in. long, London hallmarks for 1903. (Christie's) $785 £520

A Charles II two-handled porringer, 1679, maker's mark IR, between rosettes, probably for John Ruslen, 3¼in. high, 4oz.17dwt. (Christie's) $2,202 £1,540

A circular silver porringer, by Daniel Russell, Rhode Island, circa 1740-71, 7¾in. long, overall, 8oz. (Christie's) $1,870 £1,308

A William and Mary two-handled porringer and cover, by J. Jackson, 1690, 7¾in. high, 28oz. (Christie's) $4,957 £3,240

A porringer with a pierced keyhole handle, marked 'Davis', early 19th century, 5½in. diam., 8oz. (Christie's) $1,540 £945

A Charles II two-handled porringer and cover, 1663, maker's mark AC or CA in monogram, 7¼in. high, 32oz. (Christie's) $10,224 £7,150

An early 18th century porringer, possibly by Wm. Gibson, London, circa 1705, 7¾in., 13.25oz. (Christie's) $673 £440

A Charles II two-handled porringer, engraved 'Little Canfield Church', 1675, 2¾in. high, 4oz.2dwt. (Christie's) $1,179 £825

One of a pair of German silver gilt trencher salts, by Paul Solanier, Augsburg, apparently 1710-12, 1¾in. long, 8oz.10dwt. (Christie's) $2,860 £2,014

A condiment set comprising two salt cellars, two mustard pots, two pepperettes and two spoons, in a fitted case. (Christie's) $387 £250

One of a pair of oval salts, by Bigelow Bros. & Kennard, Boston, circa 1860, 2¾in. high, 4½in. long, 7oz. (Christie's) $385 £254

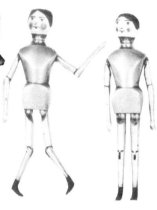

Two of a set of four 18th century Americal oval salts on pedestal bases, by Lewis Fueter, N.Y., circa 1785, 13.75oz. (Phillips) $2,700 £1,800

A set of four George II salt cellars, by Paul de Lamerie, London, 1733, scratch weight 32oz.19dwt. (Heathcote Ball & Co.) $4,890 £3,000

A pair of Edwardian novelty peppers, the articulated bodies with porcelain heads, 13.5cm. long, 1905. (Phillips) $1,859 £1,300

One of four George II silver gilt salt cellars, two by Anne Tanqueray, London, 1732, and two by D. Willaume II, 1753, 3½in. diam., 20oz. (Christie's) $3,850 £2,711

Two of a set of four Victorian cast salts, fashioned as shells supported by stylised dolphins, 8cm. wide, circa 1860. (Phillips) $829 £580

A Louis XV covered double salt cellar and two single examples, by J. T. Van Cauwenbergh, Paris, 1771 and 1773, the double 6in. long. (Christie's) $3,080 £2,169

SALTS & PEPPERS

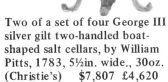

A Victorian novelty cruet in the form of three acorns, C. F., Sheffield, 1876, 4in. high. (Christie's) $131 £85

Two of a set of four George III silver gilt two-handled boat-shaped salt cellars, by William Pitts, 1783, 5½in. wide., 30oz. (Christie's) $7,807 £4,620

One of three William and Mary circular trencher salts, 1814, maker's mark IL.WA, 12oz.18dwt. (Christie's) $2,044 £1,430

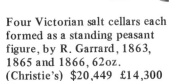

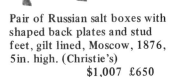

A pair of Regency gadrooned and gilt lined cauldron salt cellars, by R. Garrard, London, 1808, 4in., 24.25oz. (Christie's) $1,937 £1,250

Four Victorian salt cellars each formed as a standing peasant figure, by R. Garrard, 1863, 1865 and 1866, 62oz. (Christie's) $20,449 £14,300

Pair of Russian salt boxes with shaped back plates and stud feet, gilt lined, Moscow, 1876, 5in. high. (Christie's) $1,007 £650

One of a set of four George III silver gilt octagonal salt cellar stands, by Robert and Samuel Hennell, 1805, 5¼in. long, 28oz. (Christie's) $4,626 £3,024

A set of four George II silver gilt salt cellars, by George Wickes, London, 1754, 3.1/8in. diam., 31oz. (Christie's) $14,300 £10,072

One of a pair of George II/III salts, by David Hennell I, 1760, 7cm. diam., and J. Pasley, Dublin, 1770, and a pair of Russian salt spoons, 1861, 10oz. (Phillips) $379 £240

SAUCEBOATS

One of a pair of George III
two-handled double-lipped
sauceboats, by Thos.
Heming, 1761, 38oz.
(Christie's) $5,783 £3,780

A sauceboat, oval, with a
scalloped rim and double
scroll handle, by John Coburn,
Boston, circa 1750, 8½in. long,
14oz. (Christie's)
$18,700 £12,338

One of a pair of George III
sauceboats, by Thos. Heming,
1760, 21cm. long, 32oz.
(Phillips) $3,318 £2,100

One of a matching pair of
George III sauceboats, by
D. Smith and R. Sharp,
1760/62, 22cm. long, 27oz.
(Phillips) $2,054 £1,300

One of a pair of 19th century
French hallmarked silver
rococo serving boats, 10½in.
long, approx. 54 troy oz.
(Robt. W. Skinner Inc.)
$2,700 £1,764

One of a pair of Belgian
double-lipped sauceboats,
Mons, 1778, maker's mark
CL crowned, 7¼in. long,
19oz.10dwt. (Christie's)
$5,500 £3,874

One of a pair of late Victorian
cast shell-shape sauceboats,
by Charles S. Harris, London,
1897. (Woolley & Wallis)
$685 £460

One of a pair of silver gilt sauceboats and stands in the style of
D. Willaume II, 1965, together
with a pair of ladles, 66oz.
(Christie's) $2,478 £1,620

One of a pair of George III
plain oval sauceboats, by
Wm. Skeen, 1763, 5¾in. high,
35oz. (Christie's)
$4,275 £2,530

One of a pair of George II
sauceboats, by Edward
Wakelin, 1749, 9¼in. long,
38oz. (Christie's)
$2,974 £1,944

An Austro-Hungarian 19th
century gilt lined double-
lipped sauceboat on an oval
stand, 9¾in. wide, 23.25oz.
(Christie's) $404 £242

One of a pair of George II
Irish shaped oval sauceboats,
by J. Hamilton, Dublin, circa
1745, 33oz. (Christie's)
$3,304 £2,160

SNUFF BOXES

A George IV oblong snuff box, the cover engraved with the Nassau Balloon rising over Norwich, by T. Shaw, Birmingham, 1824, 7.9cm. long. (Phillips) $724 £480

An engraved snuff box, oval, with channel-moulded and rope-moulded sides, by B. Schaats, N.Y., circa 1720, 2.1/16in. wide, 2oz. (Christie's) $17,600 £12,316

A George III oblong engine turned gold snuff box, by A.J. Strachan, London, 1815, 18ct., 3½in. long. (Christie's) $4,404 £3,080

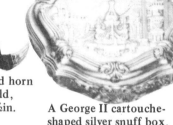

An early 19th century oval French snuff box, Paris, 8.9cm. long. (Phillips) $428 £280

An English hallmarked silver and horn presentation snuff mull, Sheffield, 1901-02, by Walker & Hall, 20½in. wide. (Robt. W. Skinner Inc.) $1,300 £812

A George II cartouche-shaped silver snuff box, circa 1740, unmarked, 3in. long. (Christie's) $1,156 £756

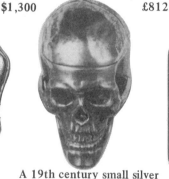

A Louis XV cartouche-shaped silver gilt snuff box, Paris, with the decharge of Julien Berthe (1750-56), 3in. long. (Christie's) $1,505 £935

A 19th century small silver snuff box modelled as a skull with articulated jaw, 1.5/8in. long. (Christie's) $755 £528

A George IV silver gilt oblong table snuff box with double hinged cover, by Thos. Edwards, 1820, 3¾in. long, 9oz.4dwt. (Christie's) $1,258 £880

A Victorian oblong engine-turned snuff box, inscribed 'Coronation 1841 the Derby Winner', by F. Clarke, Birmingham, 1841, 8.3cm. long. (Phillips) $459 £300

An 18th century Scottish silver mounted mother-of-pearl and lignum vitae oval snuff mull, 2¼in. high. (Christie's) $1,144 £715

A William IV oblong table snuff box with hinged cover, by Chas. Reily and George Storer, 1835, 4in. long, 10oz.12dwt. (Christie's) $943 £660

A Charles II lidded tankard,
by Dorothy Grant, London,
1681, 20oz. (Woolley & Wallis)
$6,400 £4,000

A 19th century German
silver mounted ivory tankard
of a battle, the lid, handle
and base silver, 30cm. high.
(Christie's) $3,509 £2,420

A George II plain baluster
pint tankard, by Fuller
White, London, 1748, 5in.
high, 12oz. (Christie's)
$434 £280

A New York Yacht Club
Trophy flagon, by Whiting
Manuf. Co., circa 1892,
10in. high, 35oz.10dwt.
(Christie's) $880 £580

A William III plain cylindrical
tankard and cover, by Thos.
Brydon, 1695, 6½in. high,
24oz. (Christie's)
$6,729 £4,180

A George II baluster tankard,
by Thomas Mason, 1743, 8in.
high, 30oz. (Christie's)
$5,505 £3,850

A Charles II plain tankard,
circa 1670, letter G a coronet
above and three fleur-de-lys
below, 8in. high, 37oz.
(Christie's) $7,865 £5,500

A Charles II large cylindrical
tankard, 1679, maker's mark
IC a mullet below, 7.5/8in.
high, 41oz. (Christie's)
$9,914 £6,480

A James II slightly tapering
cylindrical tankard, 1686,
maker's mark SD, pellet
below, possibly for Samuel
Dell, 7in. high, 24oz.17dwt.
(Christie's) $33,048 £21,600

TANKARDS

A Continental lidded tankard on leaf-capped berry feet, with presentation inscription and date 1771, 6¼in. high, 20.25oz. (Christie's)
$2,304 £1,600

A tankard, the domed lid with a pineapple finial, by Wm. Hollingshead, Phila., 1760-85, 10½in. high. (Christie's) $3,080 £2,032

A silver cylindrical tankard, by John Brevoort, N.Y., circa 1740, 6¾in. high, 26oz.10dwt. (Christie's)
$2,860 £2,000

A Chinese tankard with bamboo-style scroll handle, 5½in. high. (Christie's)
$341 £220

A Queen Anne Irish tankard, by Philip Tough, Dublin, 1708, 23cm. high, 44.75oz. (Phillips) $4,290 £3,000

A George III tapering cylindrical tankard, by Robert Sharp, 1791, 6¾in. high, 30oz. (Christie's)
$4,604 £2,860

A Charles II cylindrical tankard, 1677, maker's mark IA in dotted oval, 7.3/7in. high, 32oz. (Christie's) $4,626 £3,024

An early George III baluster pint tankard, by S. Courtald, London, 1764. (Woolley & Wallis) $864 £540

A William III provincial plain tapering cylindrical tankard, Norwich 1701, maker's mark HA, 6½in. high, 21oz.12dwt. (Christie's) $33,462 £19,800

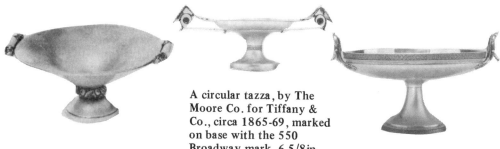

A circular tazza, by The
Moore Co. for Tiffany &
Co., circa 1865-69, marked
on base with the 550
Broadway mark, 6.5/8in.
high, 17½in. wide, overall,
41oz. (Christie's)
$3,850 £2,694

A Charles Boynton silver
stemmed bowl, 12.5cm. diam.,
5.75oz., maker's mark for
London 1937. (Phillips)
$273 £190

A tazza with two scrolling
strapwork handles, by
Tiffany & Co., 1870-75,
6½in. high, 12.5/8in. wide,
overall, 23oz.10dwt.
(Christie's) $1,320 £923

A Georg Jensen white metal
tazza, the bowl cast on the
underside with trailing vines
laden with fruit, 19cm. high,
17oz.15dwt. (Christie's)
$2,217 £1,540

Pair of Victorian shaped
circular comports on rising
circular bases, by R. Garrard,
London, 1880, 9in. diam.,
42.25oz. (Christie's)
$2,112 £1,265

A Continental 19th century
parcel gilt tazza with three
applied caryatid handles,
8¾in. high. (Christie's)
$480 £300

A Georg Jensen miniature
tazza, designed by J. Rohde,
4.8cm. high, together with
a similar tazza. (Christie's)
$502 £308

A pair of pierced and engraved
circular tazzas with applied
stylised foliate rims, 8½in.
diam., 19.75oz. (Christie's)
$240 £150

A pair of Victorian silver gilt
comport dishes, by Robert
Garrard, 1857, 25cm. diam.,
14.5cm. high, 73oz. (Phillips)
$2,016 £1,400

TEA & COFFEE SETS

A four-piece tea service, by John B. Jones Co., Boston, circa 1838, each piece globular with applied relief foliate decoration on the body, teapot 9¼in. high, gross weight 84oz.10dwt. (Christie's) $1,430 £1,000

A six-piece tea service and tray, by Gorham Manufacturing Co., comprising a kettle on stand, a coffee pot, a teapot, a covered sugar bowl, a cream pitcher, a waste bowl and a large two-handled tray, kettle 13in. high, tray 31¼in. long, gross weight 374oz. (Christie's) $16,500 £11,546

A Tetard Freres combined tea and coffee set, the teapot, 18.5cm. high, the coffee pot and cover, 22.5cm. high, wooden tray, 67.2cm. long, stamped on tray Prodbon E., Paris. (Phillips) $1,440 £1,000

TEA & COFFEE SETS

An 'Aesthetic Movement' style teaset, in the manner of C. Dresser, total weight 14oz., Birmingham, 1907. (Phillips) $576 £400

A Victorian four-piece coffee and teaset of Gothic style, the arched panels with classical figures, by Hayne & Cater, 1847, 68oz. (Phillips) $2,700 £1,800

A Victorian four-piece matching coffee and tea service of pear shape and with basket-weave bodies, by Robert Hennell, coffee pot, teapot and milk jug 1859, sugar bowl 1857, 79.5oz. (Phillips) $3,861 £2,700

A Hukin & Heath plated teaset, designed by C. Dresser, teapot 11.5cm. high, with design lozenge for October 1872, numbered 2109. (Phillips) $216 £150

A three-piece tea service, by Colin and J. W. Forbes, N.Y., 1810-20, gross weight 51oz. 10dwt. (Christie's) $1,100 £769

Three-piece teaset with fluted decoration, approx. weight 16oz., Sheffield 1906 and 1912. (Peter Wilson) $239 £170

TEA & COFFEE SETS

Part of a five-piece tea and coffee service, by Tiffany & Co., N.Y., 1907-47, coffee pot 9¼in. high, gross weight 125oz. (Christie's) $2,420 £1,693

A Victorian four-piece tea and coffee set, makers E. & J. Barnard, London, 1852, coffee pot en suite, maker D. & C. Hands, London, 1845, 69oz. all in. (Woolley & Wallis) $1,937 £1,300

A three-piece tea service, by Tiffany & Co., N.Y., teapot 9in. high, gross weight 71oz. (Christie's) $1,760 £1,231

A three-piece tea service, by John Targee, N.Y., circa 1810-14, teapot 9in. high, gross weight 61oz. (Christie's) $2,420 £1,596

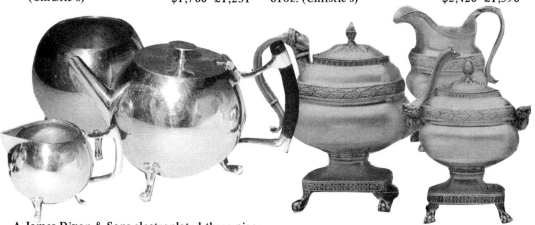

A James Dixon & Sons electroplated three-piece teaset, designed by Dr. C. Dresser, registration mark for 25 April 1880, teapot, 10.4cm. high. (Christie's) $6,336 £4,400

A three-piece tea service, by Fletcher & Gardiner, Phila., 1813-25, teapot 9in. high, gross weight 87oz. (Christie's) $6,600 £4,618

TEA & COFFEE SETS

A George III matching four-piece coffee and tea service, the baluster bodies highly embossed in the revised rocaille manner, bearing the mark of John Wakefield, coffee pot 1819, teapot, sugar and milk, 1820, 103oz. (Phillips) $2,700 £1,800

A plain octagonal pear-shaped tea and coffee service, in the Queen Anne style, by Sebastian Garrard, 1920, height of tea kettle 13¼in., gross 158oz. (Christie's)
$3,775 £2,640

A five-piece tea service, by Gorham Manufacturing Co., circa 1865, comprising two teapots, a covered sugar bowl, a cream pitcher and a waste bowl, teapot 8in. high, gross weight 110oz. (Christie's) $2,640 £1,847

TEA & COFFEE SETS

An American tea and coffee service, by Geradus Boyce, New York, circa 1825,
coffee pot 12in. high, gross 157oz. (Christie's) $1,730 £1,210

A three-piece enamelled demitasse service, by
Tiffany & Co., N.Y., bearing the touch mark of
the Pan-American Exposition in Buffalo, 1901,
coffee pot 9in. high, gross weight 37oz.10dwt.
(Christie's) $24,200 £16,935

'Como', a Christofle electroplated four-piece
modernist teaset, designed by Lino Sabattini,
circa 1955, teapot 22cm. high. (Christie's)
                    $2,674 £1,870

A Russian fluted vase-shaped tea and coffee set, each on a spreading circular foot with
scroll feet and shell and scroll border, height of coffee pot 9in., 182oz. (Christie's)
                    $5,618 £3,672

A six-piece tea and coffee service, by Bigelow, Kennard & Co., Boston, circa 1901, kettle 12in. high, gross weight 168oz. (Christie's) $4,180 £2,757

A six-piece tea and coffee service with a plated tray, by the Mulholland Bros., Evanston, Illinois, 1916-19, coffee pot 9¼in. high, tray 25¼in. long, gross weight 170oz. (Christie's) $3,850 £2,694

A Victorian four-piece plated tea and coffee set in fitted mahogany case. (Parsons, Welch & Cowell) $468 £310

TEA CADDIES

A George III octagonal tea caddy, by Henry Chawner, 1791, 13oz. 8dwt. (Christie's)
$2,516 £1,760

A Liberty & Co. silver and enamel tea caddy of oval section, Birmingham hall-marks for 1907, 9.3cm. high, 5oz.2dwt. gross weight. (Christie's)
$316 £220

A Victorian silver mounted glass tea caddy, Chester, 1900. (Reeds Rains)
$316 £220

A George III shaped oval tea caddy, by Robt. Hennell, London, 1782, 4.75in. high, 14oz. (Woolley & Wallis)
$4,000 £2,500

A Ramsden & Carr silver tea-caddy and spoon, London hallmarks for 1931, 10.9cm. high, 13oz.7dwt. gross wt. (Christie's) $2,524 £1,650

A George III shaped oval tea caddy, by Wm. Plummer, 1784, 14oz. 15dwt. (Christie's)
$2,044 £1,430

A Dutch oblong tea caddy, Sneek 1737, maker's mark illegible, probably FE for Feddeiedes Edema, 6oz. 5dwt. (Christie's)
$1,156 £756

A Victorian tea caddy, maker George Fox, London, 1874, 5in. high. (Hobbs & Chambers)
$800 £560

A Queen Anne plain oblong tea caddy, maker's mark overstruck with another, perhaps that of Thos. Farren, 10oz. (Christie's)
$2,974 £1,760

TEA KETTLES

A pyriform kettle on stand, by Grosjean & Woodward for Tiffany & Co., 1854-65, 11.5/8in. high, 30oz. (Christie's) $990 £692

A Dutch tea kettle, stand and lamp, by H. Nieuwenhuys, Amsterdam, 1751, 13½in. high, gross weight 69oz. (Christie's) $6,600 £4,649

Late 19th century rococo Revival hallmarked silver kettle on stand, by Tiffany & Co., 10¼in. high, approx. 24 troy oz. (Robt. W. Skinner Inc.) $600 £392

George II English hallmarked silver kettle on stand, by E. Wakelin, 11¾in. high. (Robt. W. Skinner Inc.) $3,400 £2,222

An F. Minsfiberg kettle-on-stand with ivory handle and ivory finial, 29.2cm. high. (Christie's) $2,689 £1,650

An Edwardian part-fluted tapering oval tea kettle with ebonised wood handle and finial, by Henry Wilkinson & Co. Ltd., London, 1908, 12in. high, 37.5oz. gross. (Christie's) $716 £462

A Victorian inverted pear-shaped tea-kettle, stand and lamp, by D. & C. Hands, 1856, 15½in. high, 72oz. (Christie's) $2,656 £1,650

A George III plain circular tea kettle, stand and lamp, by John Scofield, 1787, 12½in. high, gross 55oz. (Christie's) $2,359 £1,650

A tea kettle on stand, retailed by Starr and Marcus, N.Y., circa 1910, 14½in. high, 53oz. 10dwt. (Christie's) $1,210 £798

TEAPOTS

A George II Scottish bullet-shaped teapot, by Wm. Aytoun, Edinburgh, 1736, assaymaster Archibald Ure, gross 22oz. (Christie's) $2,831 £1,980

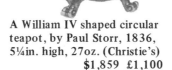

A William IV shaped circular teapot, by Paul Storr, 1836, 5¼in. high, 27oz. (Christie's) $1,859 £1,100

A rounded rectangular teapot, probably by Israel Trask, Mass., circa 1813-25, 6½in. high. (Christie's) $165 £115

A Victorian silver oval drum teapot in 18th century style, London 1858, makers Hands & Son, 19½oz. (Parsons, Welch & Cowell) $323 £210

A Victorian oval half fluted silver teapot, London 1898, makers Barnard Bros., 25¼oz. (Parsons, Welch & Cowell) $231 £150

A fluted oval teapot, marked 'Revere', 6in. high, gross weight 15oz.10dwt. (Christie's) $1,430 £943

A pyriform teapot with a domed hinged cover, by Peter Van Dyck, N.Y., circa 1720-35, 7¾in. high, 25oz. (Christie's) $93,500 £65,431

An urn-shaped teapot with a domed cover, by Bailey & Co., Phila., circa 1848-65, 10¾in. high, gross weight 37oz. (Christie's) $1,100 £725

A Dutch silver pear-shaped teapot on rim foot, Amsterdam, 1722, 5¼in. high, gross 9oz.10dwt. (Christie's) $3,460 £2,420

A George III plain oval teapot, with beaded borders, 12.5cm. high, 1782. (Phillips) $734 £480

A square teapot, the hinged cover with a green stone finial, by Tiffany & Co., N.Y., 1877-91, 5in. high, gross weight 15oz. (Christie's) $16,500 £10,886

A George III circular teapot with ivory finial and scroll handle, by Paul Storr, 1809, 6¼in. high, gross 40oz. (Christie's) $4,131 £2,700

SILVER

TRAYS & SALVERS

One of a pair of George II shaped circular salvers, by David Willaume II, 1743, 13¼in. diam., 118oz. (Christie's)
$85,924 £56,160

A silver tray, by Howard & Co., N.Y., circa 1900, 18¼in. diam., 78oz.10dwt. (Christie's)
$1,430 £1,000

A George II shaped circular salver on scroll feet, by John Swift, 1751, 22¾in. diam., 136oz. (Christie's)
$7,550 £5,280

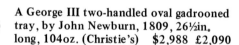

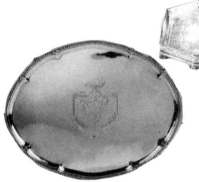

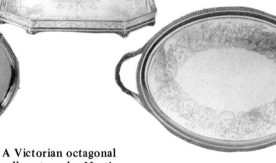

One of a pair of George III shaped oval salvers, by Thos. Hannam and John Crouch, 1776, 15¾in. long, 80oz. (Christie's) $5,287 £3,456

A Victorian octagonal gallery tray, by Martin Hall & Co. Ltd., Sheffield, 1877, 19½in. long, 84oz. (Christie's) $4,089 £2,860

A George III two-handled oval gadrooned tray, by John Newburn, 1809, 26½in. long, 104oz. (Christie's) $2,988 £2,090

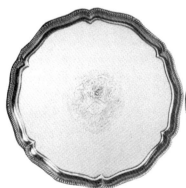

A George II shaped circular salver, by George Wickes, 1739, 13in. diam., 43oz. (Christie's) $3,635 £2,376

An oval tray on eight claw and ball feet, by Omar Ramsden, 1923, 22¾in. long, 85oz. (Christie's) $2,478 £1,620

A George II salver, by John Kincaid, London, 1744, 17in. diam., 71oz. (Christie's) $4,400 £3,099

TRAYS & SALVERS

A large silver gilt shaped circular salver, on four curved openwork vine tendril feet, by Wm. Cripps, 1750, 22½in. diam., 157oz. (Christie's) $29,743 £19,440

One of a set of five Regency Sheffield gilt salvers engraved with the Royal Arms for the period 1801-16, 26cm. diam. (Phillips) $3,744 £2,600

An early Victorian presentation circular tray, by Joseph & Albert Savory, London, 1845, 76oz., 18.5in. diam. (Woolley & Wallis) $1,192 £800

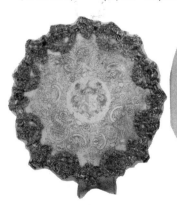

One of a pair of silver bread trays with open foliate handles, by S. Kirk & Son Co., Baltimore, 1903-07, 14¼in. long, 44oz. (Christie's) $1,430 £1,000

One of a pair of William and Mary silver gilt salvers, circa 1690, 11¼in. diam., 82oz.10dwt. (Christie's) $220,000 £154,968

A two-handled tray, chrysanthemum pattern, by Tiffany & Co., N.Y., circa 1882, 30in. long, 262oz. (Christie's) $6,600 £4,618

A George IV shaped circular salver, by William Pitts, 1822, 22½in. diam., 202oz. (Christie's) $7,865 £5,500

A small salver, square, with cusped corners and a moulded rim, by Jacob Hurd, Boston, circa 1740-50, 5¾in. square, 5oz. (Christie's) $8,800 £5,806

A set of six George III silver gilt dinner plates, by Eliz. Godfrey, London, 1761, in the George I style, 9½in. diam., 89oz. (Christie's) $7,700 £5,423

A George III two-handled
oval soup tureen and
cover, by Paul Storr, 1807,
12¾in. high, 176oz.
(Christie's)
$28,314 £19,800

A tureen designed by Henning
Koppel, the cover stamped
HK H 10 Georg Jensen 925
S 1034, 72cm. long, 105oz.
(Christie's) $31,460 £22,000

A George II two-handled
gadroon edge oval soup
tureen and cover, 40cm. long,
by Edward Wakelin, 1754,
95oz. (Phillips)
$7,007 £4,900

One of a pair of George III
sauce tureens, maker Samuel
Hennell, London, 1811, 7½in.
wide, overall, 62oz. (Hobbs &
Chambers) $2,359 £1,650

A covered soup tureen, with
domed oval lid, by Bailey &
Kitchen, Phila., 1833-46,
15½in. high, 16in. wide, 127oz.
(Christie's) $3,520 £2,322

A Victorian oval plated soup
tureen and cover, 11½in.
wide. (Parsons, Welch &
Cowell) $257 £167

An early Victorian two-
handled soup tureen and
cover, by B. Smith II,
1837, 12in. high, 197oz.
(Christie's)
$7,865 £5,500

A George II soup tureen and
cover, London, 1759, maker's
mark probably that of Wm.
Reynolds, 17in. long, 117oz.
10dwt. (Christie's)
$18,700 £12,205

One of three early 20th century French covered tureens,
by Olier et Caron, Paris, 11in.
long, 130oz. (Christie's)
$2,860 £2,014

URNS

A George III small two-handled coffee urn, by Thos. Daniell, 1785, 15in. high, gross 34oz. (Christie's) $2,974 £1,760

A Victorian plated tea urn of fluted urn shape, makers James Dixon & Son, 17in. high. (Parsons, Welch & Cowell) $154 £100

A George III two-handled vase-shaped tea urn, by Paul Storr, 1802, 20½in. high, gross 122oz. (Christie's) $10,626 £6,600

A plated coffee urn with applied lion mask ring handles, 13in. high. (Christie's) $550 £358

A William IV melon-fluted two-handled tea urn on a square base, by J. W. & E. H., Sheffield, 1837, 18in. high, 145oz. (Christie's) $3,580 £2,310

A two-compartment caviar container of urn-shaped form, by Omar Ramsden and Alwyn Carr, 1903, 25.5cm. high, 27.75oz. (Phillips) $2,145 £1,500

An Old Sheffield plate vase-shaped tea urn, 17¼in. high. (Christie's) $464 £320

A coffee urn, with a conical cover, by Samuel Kirk & Son, Baltimore, probably 1846-61, 16½in. high, 56oz.10dwt. (Christie's) $3,520 £2,322

A George III two-handled oval tea urn, by Samuel Hennell and James Taylor, 1814, 13¾in. high, gross 143oz. (Christie's) $4,247 £2,970

SILVER

A WMF Ikora patinated metal vase, shouldered ovoid shape with short cylindrical neck, 23.6cm. high. (Christie's)
$462 £302

A tall silver vase, made by H. G. Murphy and R. M. Y. Gleadowe, 25.5cm. high, 29.5oz., maker's marks for London, 1935. (Phillips) $3,024 £2,100

A vase-shaped pitcher, in the Japanese taste, by Gorham Manuf. Co., Providence, 1885, 9in. high, 40oz.10dwt. (Christie's)$6,600 £4,618

A WMF Ikora patinated metal vase, elongated ovoid shape on stepped circular foot, 31.6cm. high. (Christie's)
$462 £302

A Cartier two-handled silver vase, London import marks for 1930, on ebonised stand, 29.2cm. high, 60oz.15dwt. (Christie's) $1,584 £1,100

A silver twin-handled vase, 16.6cm. high, 12.5oz., stamped E.J.B. maker's marks, Birmingham, 1909. (Phillips)
$403 £280

A Quezal vase with silver overlay decoration, 9in. high. (Christie's)
$604 £400

A WMF Ikora patinated metal vase, ovoid shape, inlaid with a figure on horseback in silver, gilt and dark grey, 20.2cm. high. (Christie's) $593 £388

An urn-shaped vase with two cast mask handles, by Shreve, Stanwood & Co., Boston, 1860-69, 13in. high, 24oz. (Christie's)
$715 £500

VINAIGRETTES

A George III gilt lined purse vinaigrette with wrigglework decoration, by S. Pemberton, Birmingham, 1816. (Christie's) $255 £165

A William IV vinaigrette, the cover chased in relief with a ruined building, by Taylor & Perry, Birmingham, 1835. (Phillips) $800 £500

A George IV rectangular purse shaped silver vinaigrette, by Clark & Smith, Birmingham, 1824, 1.25in. long. (Woolley & Wallis) $159 £95

A William IV tartan engraved silver vinaigrette, by N. Mills, Birmingham, 1837, 1.5in. long. (Woolley & Wallis) $126 £75

A Victorian gilt lined engine-turned book vinaigrette, by Edward Smith, Birmingham, 1857, 1½in wide. (Christie's) $240 £150

A miniature Regency silver vinaigrette, maker IL, Birmingham, 1817, 0.75in. long. (Woolley & Wallis) $75 £45

A cylindrical double-ended pill box/vinaigrette, 3oz., London, 1917. (Peter Wilson) $70 £50

A Regency rectangular vinaigrette, the gilt interior with a pierced engraved grille, maker possibly Wm. Shaw, London, 1813, 1.15in. long. (Woolley & Wallis) $100 £60

A William IV 'castle-top' vinaigrette, by Nathaniel Mills, Birmingham, 1836. (Phillips) $489 £320

A Victorian 'castle-top' vinaigrette, the cover decorated with a view of Windsor Castle, by J. Tongue, Birmingham, 1844. (Phillips) $428 £280

An oblong 'castle-top' vinaigrette chased with a view of Litchfield Cathedral, by N. Mills, 1843-4. (Christie's) $1,652 £1,080

An early Victorian 'castle-top' vinaigrette, the cover chased with a view of Windsor Castle, by Francis Clarke, Birmingham, 1838. (Phillips) $459 £300

One of a set of four George III silver gilt two-handled wine coolers, collars and liners, by Paul Storr, 1813, 11in. high, 689oz. (Christie's) $371,800 £220,000

A large plated two-handled ice bucket with ornate rim, 11in. diam. (Dickinson Davy & Markham) $150 £95

One of a pair of George III two-handled vase-shaped wine coolers, by Matthew Boulton & Plate Co., circa 1825, 9½in. high. (Christie's) $6,729 £4,180

A Victorian silver gilt two-handled vase-shaped wine cooler, by A. Benson and H. H. Webb, 1893, 12½in. high, 106oz. (Christie's) $3,775 £2,640

One of a pair of Queen Anne cylindrical wine coolers, by J. Bodington, circa 1710, 9½in. high, 216oz. (Christie's) $390,390 £231,000

One of a pair of Old Sheffield tapering bucket-shaped wine coolers with applied ram's mask and ring drop handles, 7½in. high. (Christie's) $892 £572

A German two-handled wine cooler, by Hermann Julius Wilm, Berlin, circa 1855, 15¼in. high, 327oz. (Christie's) $12,397 £7,700

One of a pair of Old Sheffield two-handled campana shaped wine coolers, each with a detachable collar and inner liner, 8¼in. high. (Christie's) $1,453 £950

One of a pair of Old Sheffield plate two-handled fluted campana shaped wine coolers with detachable liners, 10½in. high. (Christie's) $1,162 £750

WINE LABELS

A George III rectangular wine label, incised 'Vidonia', by S. Meriton II, circa 1775. (Phillips) $189 £120

An early 19th century wine label of cast openwork fruiting vine design, possibly Irish, circa 1820. (Phillips) $422 £280

A George III wine label, incised 'Champagne', by Margaret Binley, circa 1765. (Phillips) $142 £90

A Victorian cast wine label, title scroll incised 'Red Constantia', by Rawlings & Sumner, 1843. (Phillips) $573 £380

A George III shaped oblong wine label, incised 'Lisbon', by B. Bickerton, circa 1765. (Phillips) $221 £140

A Victorian stamped-out hunting horn wine label, incised 'Port', by G. Unite, Birmingham, 1857. (Phillips) $474 £300

A George III crescent-shaped wine label, by Benjamin Tait, Dublin, circa 1785. (Phillips) $205 £130

A George III oval thread-edge wine label, by Phipps & Robinson, circa 1790. (Phillips) $189 £120

A George III cast scallop shield wine label, 'Sherry', by Wm. Eley, 1814. (Phillips) $458 £290

A George IV Irish wine label, incised 'St. Peray', by L. Nolan, Dublin, 1825. (Phillips) $474 £300

A George III Scottish wine label, incised 'Rum', by W. P. Cunningham, Edinburgh, circa 1795. (Phillips) $205 £130

A George III bead-edged wine label, incised 'Burgundy', by S. Barker, circa 1790. (Phillips) $347 £220

A rectangular silhouette on paper by John Buncombe, of Catherine Reynolds of Newport, circa 1785, 90 x 70mm. (Phillips) $226 £150

A rectangular conversation piece by Wm. Welling, of a husband and wife taking tea, signed and dated 1874, 280 x 380mm. (Phillips) $4,832 £3,200

A gentleman standing full-length profile, by Augustin Edouart, cut-out on card, signed and dated 1836, 10¾in. high. (Christie's) $495 £324

A full-length profile of a family group, by Augustin Edouart, signed and dated 1825, cut-outs on card, 13in. high. (Christie's) $1,573 £1,100

Pair of early 20th century silhouettes, 'The Bull Fighters', by Wilhelm Hunt Diederich, 9½ x 13in. (Robt. W. Skinner Inc.) $450 £315

An oval black silhouette by John Buncombe, of a lady, circa 1800, 95mm. high. (Phillips) $143 £95

Pair of early 19th century bronzed silhouettes by F. Frith, signed and dated 1844, 10½ x 8½in. (Parsons, Welch & Cowell) $512 £320

A gentleman profile to left, by John Miers, on plaster, oval 3½in. high. (Christie's) $131 £86

SPECTACLES

Late 19th century spectacles with papier-mache case decorated in the Chinese taste. (Christie's) $99 £65

A pair of brass framed Chinese spectacles, with folding sides and quartz lenses. (Christie's) $260 £170

One of two pairs of late 18th century burnished steel turn-pin sides spectacles. (Phillips) $496 £320

A pair of Georgian silver blue-tinted spectacles with double turn-pin sides, London, 1825, possibly by J. Hobbs. (Phillips) $496 £320

An 18th century pair of steel ring side spectacles with tinted lenses in a leather case, 5in. long. (Christie's) $229 £150

A pair of 18th century burnished steel green tinted protective folding sides spectacles with circular lenses. (Phillips) $434 £280

A pair of folding spectacles with tortoiseshell frame, by Theodore Hamblin Ltd., together with another three pairs and a quantity of gilt spectacle parts. (Christie's) $130 £85

A pair of 16th century leather nose spectacles, 9cm. wide. (Phillips) $2,480 £1,600

A pair of silver turn-pin sides 'D' cup blue smoke lenses, together with another three pairs. (Christie's) $382 £250

A pair of 19th century brass and tortoiseshell folding-sides spectacles with deep clouded brown quartz lenses, in shagreen case, 6½in. long. (Christie's) $336 £220

A pair of 19th century brass and horn folding-sides spectacles with horn ear pieces and brown quartz lenses, in brown stained sharkskin case, 17.8cm. long. (Christie's) $367 £240

A pair of Chinese brass framed turn-pin sides spectacles with brown tinted quartz lenses, in a brown stained sharkskin case, 6¾in. long. (Christie's) $183 £120

A grey stone figure of a lion, some earth encrustation, Tang Dynasty, 19cm. high. (Christie's) $1,258 £880

An 18th century soapstone seal carved with a recumbent dreaming figure, 11cm. wide. (Christie's) $2,202 £1,540

A dark stone figure of Guanyin, seated in dhyanasana, Tang Dynasty, 39.5cm. high, mounted on black marble stand. (Christie's) $14,157 £9,900

A Romano-Celtic stone shrine, carved in relief with a figure, possibly dedicated to a tree deity, 25.5 x 18.5cm. (Phillips) $1,530 £1,000

A Sumerian brick fragment impressed with four lines of cuneiform —'Ur Namma, King of Ur, who built the temple of Namma', 27 x 29cm. overall. (Phillips) $290 £190

A Polynesian sandstone head, with disc-shaped headdress. (Phillips) $428 £280

An 18th/19th century polychrome and gilt soapstone rectangular tea caddy and cover, 14.5cm. high. (Christie's) $1,101 £770

A Roman pottery oil lamp, 13cm. long, complete with original limestone mould, Christian, North African, 5th century A.D. (Phillips) $130 £85

Little Lady with Handbags, carved limestone figure, by Wm. Edmondson, Tennessee, circa 1935, 13in. high. (Christie's) $4,400 £2,903

A carved stone figure of Hercules, partly draped with lion's skin, holding golden apples of the Hesperides, 40in. high. (Robt. W. Skinner Inc.) $800 £559

A naturalistically coloured stone carving of a chimpanzee, 53.5cm. high. (Phillips) $460 £320

Early 19th century stoneware architectural bust, modelled in the form of a Naval officer, 18in. high. (Peter Wilson) $564 £400

An 18th century soapstone figure of the 145th Lehan, 12.5cm. high. (Christie's) $1,179 £825

A Buddhist stone stele, dated to the 2nd year of Zheng Guan of the N. Wei Dynasty, 36cm. high. (Christie's) $943 £660

A 19th century sandstone life-size figure of a young maiden, signed E. Morton, 66in. high, complete with a sandstone plinth, 28in. high. (Reeds Rains) $2,635 £1,700

A late 19th/early 20th century Italian alabaster group of two Bacchic putti supporting an urn, by E. Battiglia, 91cm. high. (Christie's) $3,030 £2,090

One of a pair of 5th century A.D. large stone figures of chimera, heavily carved from a matt grey material of limestone type, approx. 55.5cm. high. (Christie's) $157,300 £110,000

A sandstone head of rounded form, on a long cylindrical neck, 27cm. high, perhaps Romano-Celtic. (Phillips) $229 £150

A late 17th/early 18th century Brussels Genre tapestry depicting four children with a dog, 3.4 x 2.8m. (Phillips) $8,352 £5,800

Late 17th century Flemish tapestry woven in blues, reds, browns and green wools and silk, 8ft.11in. x 10ft.7in. (Christie's) $8,591 £6,050

Late 17th century Flemish tapestry woven in wools and silk, 100 x 142in. (Christie's) $4,373 £3,080

A 17th century Flemish tapestry woven in fresh and well-preserved colours, 11ft. x 14ft.11in. (Christie's) $7,810 £5,500

A 17th century Brussels verdure tapestry woven with Eurydice being bitten by a serpent, 11ft. x 16ft.6in. (Christie's) $12,320 £7,700

Early 18th century Brussels tapestry woven in silks and wools with fishermen and ladies in a landscape, 9ft.10in. x 9ft. (Christie's) $12,320 £7,700

A Flemish verdure tapestry woven in brown, green and blue wool, 9ft.3in. x 4ft.5in. (Christie's) $1,874 £1,320

A 17th century Spanish armorial tapestry woven in greens, blues, yellow and orange wool, 11ft.1in. x 9ft.10½in. (Christie's) $4,998 £3,520

Late 17th century Brussels tapestry woven in wools and silks, restored, 14ft. x 9ft.4in. (Christie's) $8,591 £6,050

Late 16th century Flemish tapestry woven in silks and wools, 101 x 91in. (Christie's) $6,248 £4,400

A Flemish tapestry cartoon painted on canvas, 112 x 159in. (Christie's) $5,935 £4,180

A 17th century Brussels verdure tapestry, depicting a dog and animal beside a river, framed by trees and foliage, 2.92 x 2.46m. (Phillips) $5,184 £3,600

An 18th century Aubusson pastoral tapestry, depicting a hunting party with equestrian figures, ladies, hound and falcons in a foliate landscape, 2.33 x 2.75m. (Phillips) $3,456 £2,400

A tapestry woven in fresh colours in wools and silks, 56 x 85¼in. (Christie's) $5,467 £3,850

A 17th century Brussels tapestry woven in well preserved silks and wools with Bacchus seated in a gilded chariot, 9ft.1in. x 12ft.4in. (Christie's) $28,160 £17,600

A late 19th century Japanese panel of k'o-ssu tapestry worked in pastel silks and gold thread, 0.77 x 0.22m., and companion. (Phillips) $664 £440

Late 18th century needlework pocketbook, silk yarns worked in a variant of the Queen stitch, probably New England, 4¾ x 4in. (Robt. W. Skinner Inc.) $550 £384

An 18th century crewel embroidered pocketbook, Mass.. (Robt. W. Skinner Inc.) $9,000 £6,293

A 19th century Chinese picture, the whole embroidered in coloured silks and couched gold thread with a fiery dragon, cosmic and other symbols, 69 x 97cm. (Phillips) $862 £560

A 19th century French shawl designed with curled cones, the centre with medallion, the border with niche designs, 3.40 x 1.64m. (Phillips) $323 £210

A 17th century Biblical needlework picture, England, 12 x 16in. (Robt. W. Skinner Inc.) $2,500 £1,748

A late 19th century Chinese embroidered picture, 89 x 24.5cm., and two others. (Phillips) $573 £380

A Chinese coverlet of ivory silk embroidered in coloured silks, 2.30 x 2.10m., knotted fringe. (Phillips) $554 £360

A Japanese wall hanging of deep grey silk embroidered in shades of green, pink and ivory, 1.52 x 0.93m., lined. (Phillips) $1,132 £750

A 19th century Chinese picture of a kylin, the whole embroidered in coloured silks and couched gold thread, 56 x 53cm. (Phillips) $924 £600

A coptic woven linen square in black, red and cream, 15 x 18cm., contained in a cotton bound folder, 4th-5th century A.D. (Phillips) $142 £95

A 17th century needlework cushion, silk and metallic yarns in a variety of stitches, England, 8 x 10in. (Robt. W. Skinner Inc.)
$3,000 £2,097

An 18th century style pictorial needlework wall hanging, circa 1880, 22½ x 26in. (Robt. W. Skinner Inc.) $600 £419

An embroidered wall pocket of ivory cotton and silk yarns worked in chain stitch, 4½ x 11in. (Robt. W. Skinner Inc.)
$650 £454

A silk needlework picture, by Mary Flower, Phila., 1768, 23in. wide. (Christie's)
$187,000 £123,382

A 17th century crewel embroidered panel, America or England, 20 x 37in. (Robt. W. Skinner Inc.)
$300 £209

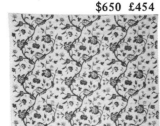

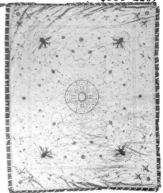

An undyed linen panel with crewel work embroidery in multi-coloured wools, 2.18 x 1.74m. (Phillips)
$634 £420

Early 20th century flatweave saddle cover, S. Caucasus, N. Persia, 4ft. x 4ft. x 7½in. (Robt. W. Skinner Inc.)
$400 £266

A late 19th century Chinese coverlet of yellow silk, embroidered in pink, blue, green and ivory silks, 2.60 x 2.14m., fringed and lined. (Phillips)
$1,201 £780

Late 19th century Soumak bag face, S. Caucasus, (minor wear), 1ft.7in. x 1ft.6in. (Robt. W. Skinner Inc.) $650 £433

One of a pair of 17th century needlework stumpwork pictures, England, 5¼ x 4¼in. (Robt. W. Skinner Inc.) $2,300 £1,608

A Chinese needlework picture, the ivory silk ground embroidered in shades of blue, brown, ochre and ivory, 36cm. square. (Phillips) $286 £190

A late 19th century Chinese k'o-ssu picture of fighting warriors on horseback and on foot, with companion, 1m. x 0.25m. (Phillips) $656 £400

Needlework picture, 'Shepherdess of the Alps', N.Y., 1800, 12½ x 15¼in. (Robt. W. Skinner Inc.) $1,800 £1,258

A late 19th century Chinese k'o-ssu cover, the centre worked in pastel silks on a gold thread ground, 1.84 x 1.44m., lined. (Phillips) $1,771 £1,150

Late 18th century silk embroidered picture, New England, 21 x 19in. (Robt. W. Skinner Inc.) $3,500 £2,447

A printed velvet curtain designed by C. A. Voysey, 262 x 239.5cm. (Christie's) $3,965 £2,592

An Arts & Crafts linen cover embroidered in red and ivory linen, 1.46 x 1.58m. (Phillips) $453 £300

French 'Bouvet a Plat' or coachbuilder's router in cormier wood by Mines de Suede. (David Stanley Auctions) $635 £410

A 13½in. panel raising plane, by I. Dogdell, with replaced sole fence and offset handle (spur chipped) round topped iron, by R. Moore. (David Stanley Auctions) $418 £270

A mahogany staircase saw with 7½in. blade. (David Stanley Auctions) $53 £38

A hand-operated diamond cutting machine with copper cutting wafers. (David Stanley Auctions) $93 £60

An early R/H side axe, 11½in. edge, with star decoration, sharply cranked handle. (David Stanley Auctions) $85 £55

A beech plough by Gabriel, with brass thumb screw at the end of the stems. (David Stanley Auctions) $1,085 £700

An ultimatum brace by Wm. Marples with boxwood infill, handle and head with ebony ring. (David Stanley Auctions) $2,402 £1,550

A 19C two-handled French floor plane. (David Stanley Auctions) $141 £100

A shipwright's large ash brace with 18in. sweep and 2in. fixed centre bit. (David Stanley Auctions) $217 £140

An early goosewing axe with 18½in. blade, two smiths marks and simple decoration. (David Stanley Auctions) $141 £100

A Swiss jewelling and wax lathe lacks tool rest. (David Stanley Auctions) $58 £38

A Stanley No. 196 circular rebate plane. (David Stanley Auctions) $775 £500

Pair of mahogany steel tipped trammels with knurled brass tightening screws, 9in. overall. (David Stanley Auctions) $178 £115

A 2½in. quirked ogee plane by Crow. (David Stanley Auctions) $88 £57

A screwstem plough with boxwood stems and nuts, by J. Miller, Clayton St. (David Stanley Auctions) $108 £70

Early 25½in. try plane with flat iron handle. (David Stanley Auctions) $558 £360

A mahogany sash fillester with boxwood fence and stem wedges. (David Stanley Auctions) $178 £115

A beech button chuck brace with rosewood head and neck, by Deanes, London Bridge. (David Stanley Auctions) $68 £44

A Stanley-Marsh No.100 miter machine, lacks saw. (David Stanley Auctions) $31 £22

A mahogany A square with lead bob. (David Stanley Auctions) $55 £36

A bookbinders plough complete with cutting press. (David Stanley Auctions) $124 £80

A 'Peter Rabbit' chickmobile, hand car, No. 1103, circa 1935. (Christie's) $605 £424

Volkswagon 'Beetle' cabriolet with fibre glass white body, 5 h.p. Briggs & Straton engine, 6ft.6in. long. (Peter Wilson) $1,339 £950

Early 20th century lithographed tin wind-up toy, Japanese 'Chick-Chick', 10in. long. (Robt. W. Skinner Inc.) $240 £150

Lead model Mickey and Minnie Mouse barrel organ group. (Hobbs & Chambers) $58 £38

Four Disney stuffed figures, comprising a velveteen Mickey Mouse and Pluto; two corduroy 'Widgets', late 1930s-40s. (Christie's) $440 £286

A printed tinplate station, by Carette, circa 1912. (Christie's) $332 £220

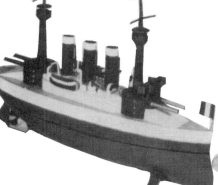

A pale golden plush covered teddy bear with embroidered snout and slight hump, 15½in. high, with Steiff button. (Christie's) $1,337 £935

A restored and repainted early Marklin three-funnel tinplate battleship, German, circa 1910, 17in. long. (Christie's) $679 £450

A gold short plush covered teddy bear, slight hump, 15½in. high, circa 1926. (Christie's) $269 £187

Painted and lithographed tin wind-up sedan, circa 1930, 11½in. long. (Robt. W. Skinner Inc.) $500 £347

A Victorian carved wooden rocking horse. (Parsons, Welch & Cowell) $755 £500

Lehmann 'Naughty Boy' tin wind-up toy, 1904-35, 4.5/8in. long. (Robt. W. Skinner Inc.) $275 £190

A late 19th century glazed and cased model of M. Osborne's — The Butcher's Shop, 46.5 x 43.5cm. (Phillips) $1,072 £750

Two early 20th century jointed teddy bears, one with blonde mohair, 19in. high, the other yellow mohair, 16½in. high. (Robt. W. Skinner Inc.) $350 £243

Spot-On — 2A Presentation Set. (Phillips) $1,072 £750

Lehmann 'Paddy and the Pig' tin wind-up toy, 1903-35, 5½in. long. (Robt. W. Skinner Inc.) $300 £208

A 19th century carved and painted wood horse pull toy, mounted on wooden base with wheels, 11in. high. (Christie's) $495 £326

A 20th century wind-up toy, French celluloid spherical artist, 4in. high, and a Japanese mohair pup in basket, 6in. high. (Robt. W. Skinner Inc.) $110 £76

Lehmann 'Zig-Zag' tin wind-up toy, 1910-45, 5in. long. (Robt. W. Skinner Inc.)
$550 £381

A 19th century carved wooden rocking horse, painted piebald with leather bridle, material covered saddle and grey horse-hair tail, 7½ hands high. (Christie's) $1,494 £1,045

Lehmann tin wind-up 'Li La', Germany, circa 1903, 5½in. high. (Robt. W. Skinner Inc.)
$500 £347

Max lithographed tin Amos and Andy, N.Y., 1930, 11½in. high. (Robt. W. Skinner Inc.) $650 £451

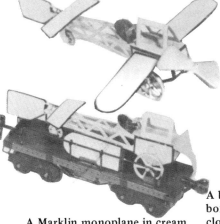

A Marklin monoplane in cream and green, fitted to a double bogie, plane 20cm. long. (Phillips) $286 £200

A bisque-headed jack-in-the-box, modelled as a smiling clown, in paper covered wooden box with pull string for lid, 4¾in. high. (Christie's) $597 £418

Late 19th century hide covered horse pull toy, Germany, horse 24in. long, height on platform 27in. (Robt. W. Skinner Inc.)
$500 £347

Spot-On — 145 L.T. Route-master Bus (transfer Radiator), (M), boxed. (Phillips)
$543 £380

Blonde mohair jointed teddy bear, 1910, 17in. high. (Robt. W. Skinner Inc.) $275 £190

Spot-On — 156 Mulliner Luxery Bus (pale blue/silver), (M), boxed. (Phillips) $600 £420

Dinky model Guy van, 'Weetabix', No. 514, boxed. (Hobbs & Chambers) $662 £460

A 'Nora Wellings' pre-war fur fabric monkey, 11½in. high. (Reeds Rains) $56 £36

Early 20th century embossed die cut Santa sleigh with reindeer, Germany, 15¾in. long. (Robt. W. Skinner Inc.) $200 £138

Spot-On — 110 2B A.E.C. Major Brick Lorry (E to M), boxed. (Phillips) $257 £180

Spot-On — 'A' Presentation Set T1, comprising Bentley Saloon, Consul Classic, Triumph TR3, Isetta, Austin A40. (Phillips) $185 £130

A Peek Freans biscuit tin 'Castle' made of four different sections, manufactured by Huntley Bourne & Stevens, 1923. (Phillips) $371 £260

A Marklin tinplate clockwork constructor racing car, 1935, red, No. 7. (Hobbs & Chambers) $446 £310

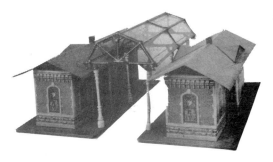

Two No. 116 Ives Union Stations, together with platform cover, circa 1928. (Christie's) $1,760 £1,233

American Flyer Manufacturing Co., Model No. 560 spring-driven monoplane, 54cm. long, span 60cm., boxed. (Phillips) $257 £180

Early 20th century Walbert lithographed tin wind-up ferry boat, 13¾in. long. (Robt. W. Skinner Inc.) $200 £138

Spot-On — Presentation Pack of four Sports Cars (E to M), boxed. (Phillips) $314 £220

Gama tinplate 300 friction Cadillac in red and black, (M), boxed, 31cm. long. (Phillips) $786 £550

Spot-On — 110/4 4000 gallon Auto Petrol Tanker (M), boxed. (Phillips) $572 £400

A German tinplate horse-drawn open carriage finished in cream and green, the felt covered tinplate horse supported on a flywheel setting the horse in motion. (Phillips) $1,430 £1,000

Fleischmann, tinplate clockwork liner No. 67, 51cm. long. (Phillips) $1,144 £800

1911 Rolls-Royce 40/50 h.p. Silver Ghost two-seat roadster, coachwork replica of H. J. Mulliner 'Balloon Car' by Wilkinson, Reg. No. R 1064, Chassis No. 1582, Engine No. 1582. (Christie's) $143,820 £94,000

1925 Talbot-Darracq 12 h.p. four-door tourer, Reg. No. HU 1651, Chassis No. DC 4803, Engine No. 48042. (Christie's)
$8,109 £5,300

1930 Chrysler 77 four-seat roadster, coachwork adapted by Rustless Iron Corp., Reg. No. JT 5518, Chassis No. R2058W, Engine No. 30332941. (Christie's) $39,150 £27,000

1934 Lagonda M45 4½ litre four-seat tourer, Chassis No. Z11165, Engine No. TB 2915. (Christie's) $29,070 £19,000

1957 BMW 503 V-8 two-door four-seat Cabriolet, Reg. No. 262 EBK, Chassis No. 69201, Engine No. 30242. (Christie's)
$32,130 £21,000

1968 Jaguar E-Type 4.2 litre two-seater fixed head coupe, Reg. No. WGK 711G, Chassis No. IE 21899, Engine No. 7E 18189-8. (Christie's) $19,125 £12,500

1955 Bentley R-Type four-door Sports saloon, Reg. No. PXU 283, Chassis No. B532X, Engine No. B262. (Christie's) $12,240 £8,000

1938 Humber Imperial drophead Coupe, coachwork by Thrupp & Maberly, Reg. No. EVH 871, Chassis No. 6001265, Engine No. 6001248. (Christie's) $9,180 £6,000

1934 MG KI Magnette Supercharged four-seater Sports tourer, coachwork by Corsica, Reg. No. JB 3717, Chassis No. KO 354, Engine No. 539 AKD. (Christie's)
$71,145 £46,500

1925 Rolls-Royce 40/50 h.p. Silver Ghost four-seater tourer, coachwork replica of Barker by E. R. Reeves, Reg. No. XY 82, Chassis No. 122AU, Engine No. TU 144. (Christie's)
$74,970 £49,000

1935 Lagonda Rapier Sports two-seater, Reg. No. BYN 857, Chassis No. D11438, Engine No. D3186. (Christie's)
$8,874 £5,800

1917 Haynes Light 12 Model 41 Type T four-seater tourer, unregistered, Chassis No. 21225, Engine No. 21225. (Christie's)
$30,600 £20,000

1935 Hillman 20/70 De Luxe four-door saloon, Reg. No. BMM 18, Chassis No. 10491, Engine No. 20/10496. (Christie's)
$3,060 £2,000

1947 Daimler DB18 four-door saloon, Reg. No. JK 9366, Chassis No. D50189, Engine No. 11057. (Christie's)
$2,295 £1,500

1933 Marendaz Special 13/70 two-seater tourer, Reg. No. JB 1477, Chassis No. 4242, Engine No. 4242. (Christie's) $9,180 £6,000

1926 Rolls-Royce Twenty foursome drophead Coupe, coachwork by Salmons, Reg. No. OX 20, Chassis No. GOK 64, Engine No. G1606. (Christie's)
$21,420 £14,000

1966 Maserati Sebring two-door GT fixed head coupe, coachwork by Vignale, Reg. No. NGP 280D, Chassis No. 101/10/091, Engine No. 101/10/091. (Christie's) $9,945 £6,500

1928 Rolls-Royce Twenty Prince of Wales Cabriolet, coachwork by Barker, Reg. No. UL 6654, Chassis No. GFN 35, Engine No. DGA. (Christie's) $36,720 £24,000

1973 Alfa Romeo Montreal two-door Sports coupe, Reg. No. WAM 142, Chassis No. AR 1426322. (Christie's) $7,344 £4,800

1959 Bentley S1 four-door Sports saloon, Reg. No. 976 HYP, Chassis No. B52 GC, Engine No. 5688 or 5G88. (Christie's) $9,945 £6,500

1971 Mercedes-Benz 280 SL roadster, Reg. No. WBH 3995, Chassis No. 11304422001195, Engine No. 1309. (Christie's) $13,005 £8,500

1965 Aston Martin DB5, fixed head Coupe, registration no. BOP1C, 'Supperlegra' 2995 cc. engine. (Peter Wilson) $14,452 £10,250

1933 Austin Seven two-door saloon, Reg. No. AMG 347, Chassis No. 176032, Engine No. M176710. (Christie's) $3,060 £2,000

1934 MG Midget PA Sports two/four-seater, Reg. No. ATU 634, Chassis No. HA 0403, Engine No. 1956A 135P. (Christie's) $13,005 £8,500

1960 Jaguar MK IX four-door Sports saloon, Reg. No. CSV 156, Chassis No. C775119 D/N, Engine No. N/C 9283/8. (Christie's) $11,475 £7,500

1928 Rolls-Royce Twenty four-door Sedanca De Ville, coachwork by Thrupp & Maberly, Reg. No. GJ 7623, Chassis No. GKM 52. (Christie's) $39,780 £26,000

1928/9 Rolls-Royce Phantom I Experimental Sports tourer, coachwork replica of Jarvis by Keith Bowley, Reg. No. XV 2332, Chassis No. 56WR. (Christie's) $68,850 £45,000

1965 Ferrari 275GTS two-seater Spyder, coachwork by Pininfarina, Reg. No. GGJ 4C, Chassis No. 07395, Engine No. 213. (Christie's) $67,320 £44,000

1929 Rolls-Royce 20/25 two-door Sportsman's coupe, coachwork by Thrupp and Maberly, Reg. No. UW 793, Chassis No. GX 012, Engine No. 55M. (Christie's) $30,600 £20,000

1927 Bentley Red Label Speed Model 3 litre four-seater tourer, coachwork by Vanden Plas, Reg. No. YE 7477, Chassis No. LM 1330, Engine No. LM 1332 55. (Christie's) $41,310 £27,000

1926 Vauxhall 14/40 four-door saloon, coachwork by Mulliner, Reg. No. YP 9827, Chassis No. LM 3885, Engine No. CH 3884. (Christie's) $9,180 £6,000

1928 Bentley 4½ litre four-seater, Sports tourer, coachwork replica of Vanden Plas, Reg. No. YX 1916, Chassis No. MF 3172, Engine No. MF 3172. (Christie's) $70,380 £46,000

1931 BSA Single-Cylinder OHV Solo motorcycle, Reg. No. RJ 3145. (Christie's)
$612 £400

1922 Ariel Sports 3½ h.p. Solo motorcycle, Reg. No. CJ 5030, Frame No. 932311690. (Christie's) $2,448 £1,600

1931 Dunelt Monarch 350 c.c. Solo motorcycle, Reg. No. VE 7835, Frame No. 8717, Engine No. 555. (Christie's) $1,071 £700

1972 BSA Gold Star Trials motorcycle, Reg. No. NUY 842K, Frame No. HE 15507, Engine No. HE 15507. (Christie's) $765 £500

1924 BSA 4¼ h.p. motorcycle combination, Reg. No. TC 8454, Frame No. 7323, Engine No. 9006. (Christie's) $3,825 £2,500

A late 19th century child's bicycle with 16in. detachable driving sheel. (Christie's)
$589 £380

1924/5 Indian Scout Vee Twin Solo motorcycle, Reg. No. XW 1903, Frame No. 55Y078, Engine No. 55Y078. (Christie's)
$3,366 £2,200

1939 Norton International Solo motorcycle, unregistered, Engine No. D1122926. (Christie's) $3,978 £2,600

1939 Brough-Superior 1150 Vee-Twin Solo motorcycle, Reg. No. FXW 184, Frame No. M 82119, Engine No. LTZ G 652105. (Christie's) $3,672 £2,400

1909 Premier Vee Twin 499 c.c. Solo motorcycle, Reg. No. 1910 DG, Frame No. 5238, Engine No. B40. (Christie's) $3,978 £2,600

1913 Rover 496 c.c. Solo motorcycle, Reg. No. FH 1332, Frame No. 31538. (Christie's) $3,978 £2,600

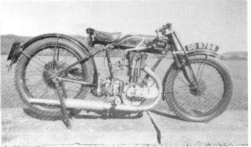

1924 AJS 350 c.c. 'Big Port' Solo motorcycle, Reg. No. DD 9758, Frame No. H80593, Engine No. 41910. (Christie's) $1,683 £1,100

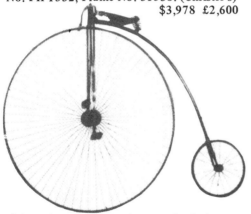

A bicycle with a 52in. driving wheel, the shaped handlebars terminating with wooden knobs. (Christie's) $852 £550

1938 Sunbeam-Talbot Ten Sports saloon, Reg. No. JC 5811, Chassis No. 40460, Engine No. N/1453. (Christie's) $3,060 £2,000

1932 BSA 350 c.c. 'Twin Port' Solo motorcycle, Reg. No. FO 2861, Frame No. Z43096, Engine No. Z53385. (Christie's) $918 £600

1919 Calthorpe 2¾ h.p. Solo motorcycle, Reg. No. OE 1152, Frame No. A301, Engine No. Y708. (Christie's) $2,295 £1,500

A moulded copper 'North Wind' weathervane, in the form of a cherub's head blowing stylised air, 23in. high, 56½in. long. (Christie's) $18,700 £11,472

Copper car weathervane, Prides Crossing, Mass., circa 1914, 3ft.8in. long. (Robt. W. Skinner Inc.) $6,250 £3,906

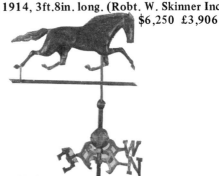

Late 19th century 'Racing Horse and Jockey' weathervane, U.S., 17in. long. (Robt. W. Skinner Inc.) $3,100 £2,167

A moulded copper weathervane in the form of a running horse, by Harris & Co., Boston, circa 1878, 20in. high, 26in. wide. (Christie's) $1,320 £870

'Mayflower' silhouette weathervane, attributed to E. G. Washburne & Co., N.Y., circa 1920, 36in. long. (Robt. W. Skinner Inc.) $1,900 £1,328

An American 19th century cast iron horse weathervane, 26in. high, 35in. wide. (Christie's) $16,500 £10,122

'Foxhound' weathervane, L. W. Cushing & Sons, Waltham, Mass., circa 1883, with traces of gold leaf and weathered verdigris surface, 27in. long. (Robt. W. Skinner Inc.) $12,500 £8,741

A hollow gilt copper and cast iron weathervane in the form of a bull, American, 1885-1890, bull 39in. long, 23in. high. (Christie's) $3,300 £2,309

A locomotive and tender copper weathervane, America, circa 1882, 61in. long. (Robt. W. Skinner Inc.) $185,000 £115,625

A gilded centaur weathervane, probably A. L. Jewell & Co., Waltham, Mass., circa 1860, 30¼in. high, 40in. long. (Robt. W. Skinner Inc.) $130,000 £81,250

Late 19th century trotting horse weathervane, made by J. Howard & Co., 40in. long. (Robt. W. Skinner Inc.) $9,250 £5,781

Early 19th century gold leaf dove figure, America, 13in. high, 23in. wide. (Robt. W. Skinner Inc.) $1,300 £866

'Flying Horse' weathervane, A. L. Jewell & Co., Waltham, Mass., circa 1870, 35½in. long. (Robt. W. Skinner Inc.) $7,000 £4,895

Cast iron and sheet iron cock weathervane, U.S., circa 1860, 22in. high. (Robt. W. Skinner Inc.) $2,100 £1,468

'Colonel Patchen' full bodied copper running horse weathervane, America, late 19th century, 40½in. long. (Robt. W. Skinner Inc.) $1,200 £750

Late 19th century ewe weathervane, moulded sheet copper body and tail with cast metal head, 29in. wide, 18in. high, America. (Robt. W. Skinner Inc.) $1,100 £733

A Maori wood feather box of elliptical form, 32cm. long. (Phillips) $900 £600

A 19th century carved wood dragon, articulated from head to tail, legs move, Japan, 27½in. long. (Robt. W. Skinner Inc.) $700 £486

A beechwood sculpture, carved as reclining woman, in the style of Hagenauer, 43.4cm. long. (Phillips) $216 £150

A large wood head of Guanyin, Ming/early Qing Dynasty, 58cm. high, wood stand. (Christie's) $2,044 £1,430

A North Italian late 18th/ early 19th century walnut panel. (Parsons, Welch & Cowell) $1,087 £720

Late 17th/early 18th century Buddhist sculpture of Amida Nyorai, 48.4cm. high. (Christie's) $1,249 £880

A carved wood figure of Guanyin seated, probably Ming Dynasty, 73cm. high. (Christie's) $4,719 £3,300

Pair of giltwood wall lights of Regency design, 37½in. high. (Christie's) $1,239 £810

One of a pair of late 17th century Italian giltwood lions, 22½in. high. (Christie's) $4,686 £3,300

Mid 19th century burl wood bowl, circular, with a moulded rim, American, 24in. diam. (Christie's) $1,980 £1,306

Five carved and painted wooden ducks, various carvers. (Christie's) $770 £502

A wooden fretwork jig-saw puzzle, in the style of Jan Toorop, 39.4cm. long. (Christie's) $712 £495

Mid 19th century painted wooden splint basket, probably Pennsylvania, 11in. wide, 7½in. high, 8in. deep. (Christie's) $825 £544

A carved walnut figure of St. Lucy, traces of original polychrome, the reverse hollowed, 44.5cm. high, probably S. German. (Phillips) $720 £500

A Regency rosewood book-rack with spindle-filled super-structure and one drawer, 16¼in. wide. (Christie's) $2,946 £2,090

Probably 19th century carved and stained maple figure of an eagle, American, 34½in. high. (Christie's) $8,250 £5,443

A group of Yoruba wood figures, comprising a soldier, a native bearer, an Oba and two Colonial officials. (Phillips) $1,759 £1,150

An Australian fruitwood vase of elongated shape, with silver shield-shaped plaque, 17¾in. high. (Christie's) $139 £99

Late 19th century carved
and painted wooden boxer
figure, America, 18in. high.
(Robt. W. Skinner Inc.)
$2,200 £1,466

An Egyptian wood building
clamp incised with hiero-
glyphs — Seti I, 19th Dynasty,
1318-1304 B.C., 26 x 12cm.
(Phillips) $690 £460

An Egyptian anthropoid
wood sarcophagus, 174cm.
high, late Dynastic-
Ptolemaic Period. (Phillips)
$4,896 £3,200

A Hagenauer carved wood
and metal bust of a woman
in profile, 12½in. high.
(Christie's) $1,344 £880

One of a pair of giltwood
wall brackets with D-
shaped tops, 13½in. high.
(Christie's) $1,487 £972

A 19th century carved and
polychromed wood head of
a young woman, Spain, 10¾in.
high. (Robt. W. Skinner Inc.)
$550 £384

A Baule wood male figure of
elongated form, standing on
a rectangular base, 48cm.
high. (Phillips) $270 £180

A mahogany latticework
waste-paper basket on bracket
feet, 14½in. wide. (Christie's)
$5,104 £3,520

A New Guinea lime spatula,
34cm. high, and a bamboo
comb, 27.8cm. high. (Phillips)
$165 £110

19th century sailor's pine art carving, 14in. high. (Robt. W. Skinner Inc.) $350 £233

Early 20th century gilt wooden trade sign in the form of a fish, American, 57¼in. long, 17in. high. (Christie's) $4,400 £3,079

A 19th century European carved and painted wood Blackamoor, painted in polychrome and gilded, 56¾in. high. (Robt. W. Skinner Inc.) $1,400 £979

A 19th century N. American carved pine wood doll torso with holes in the head for wig. (Christie's) $235 £165

A 19th century carved walnut panel with a coat-of-arms and motto Le Main Tiendrai, 46in. wide. (Christie's) $2,478 £1,620

A polychromed Yosegizukuri wood figure of Daruma, 51cm. high. (Christie's) $1,093 £770

A Senupo wood rhythm pounder carved as a female figure on a circular base, 112cm. high. (Phillips) $390 £260

Early 20th century carved wooden relief fishing scene, probably Maine, 18 x 24½in. (Robt. W. Skinner Inc.) $1,500 £1,000

An African wood staff, the finial carved as a human head with elongated ringed neck, 44cm. high, and a wooden snake, 57cm. long. (Phillips) $75 £50

A Solomon Island wood bowl
of oval section, 44cm. long.
(Phillips) $390 £260

A mid Victorian black and
gilt japanned tole hubble-
bubble, with metal label of
Lowe, London, 10½in. high.
(Christie's) $346 £242

A New Guinea lime spatula,
37.5cm. high. (Phillips)
                    $630 £420

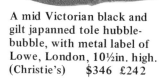

Pair of decorated border
woodcut blocks by Eric Gill,
of naked maidens among
foliage, 18.6 and 18.9cm.
high, excluding bases.
(Christie's) $2,019 £1,320

Penobscot figural polychrome
wood club, pommel in form
of wolf's head, 48in. long.
(Robt. W. Skinner Inc.)
                    $425 £297

Pair of Italian gilt and silvered
blackamoor figures. (Parsons,
Welch & Cowell) $2,160 £1,350

A Continental carved wooden
tankard with hinged cover,
8in. high. (Prudential Fine
Art) $2,184 £1,300

Northwest coast wood carving,
Nootka, of a reclining seal,
possibly a net float. (Robt. W.
Skinner Inc.) $475 £332

Pair of late 19th century
miniature clogs with leather
uppers. (Peter Wilson)
                    $55 £35

INDEX

ANTIQUES REVIEW